In the Words of Women

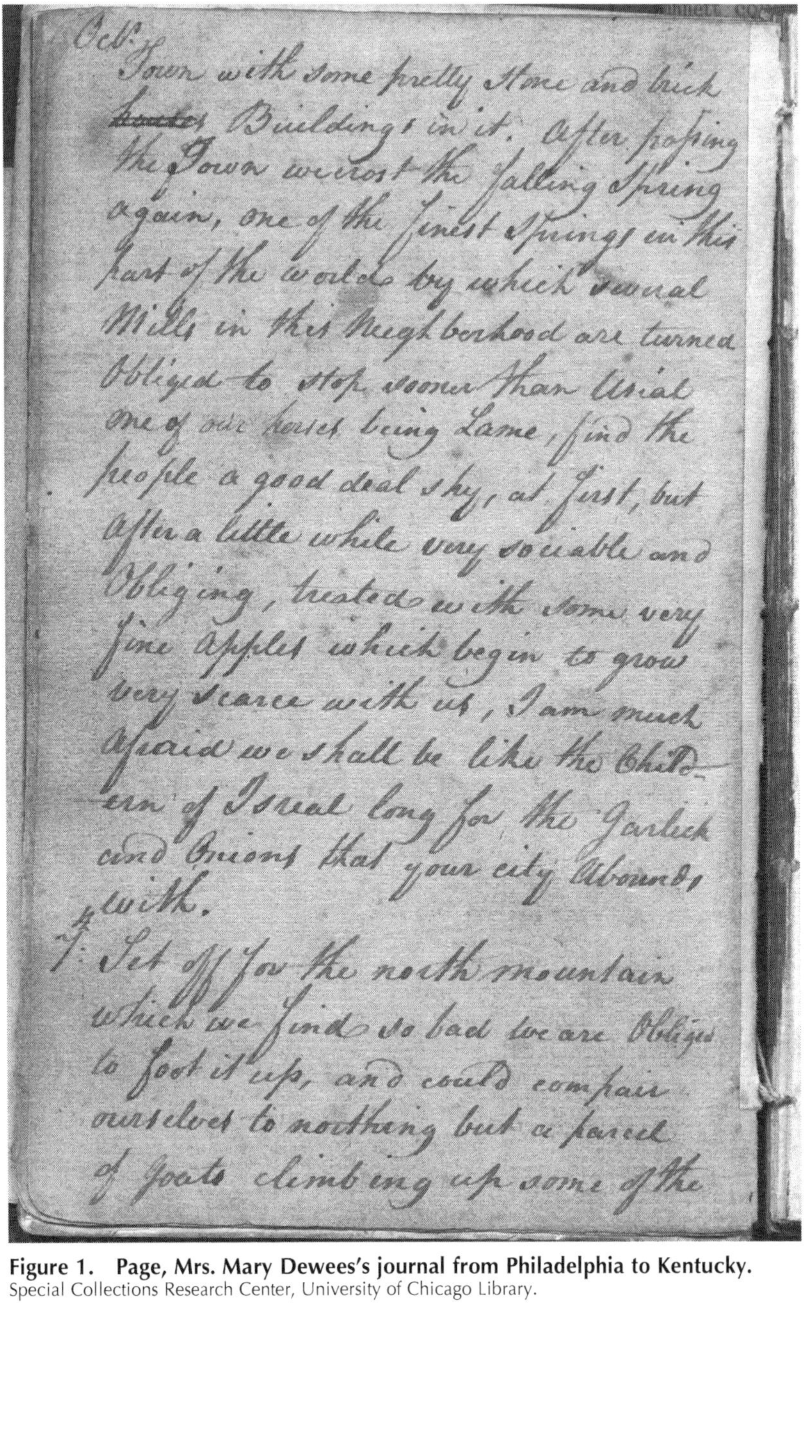

Oct.

Town with some pretty Stone and brick
~~houses~~ Buildings in it. After passing
the Town we cross the falling Spring
again, one of the finest Springs in this
part of the world by which several
Mills in this Neighborhood are turned
Obliged to stop sooner than Usial
one of our horses being Lame, find the
people a good deal shy, at first, but
After a little while very sociable and
Obliging, treated with some very
fine apples which begin to grow
very scarce with us, I am much
Afraid we shall be like the Child-
ern of Israel long for the Garlick
and Onions that your city Abounds
with.

7. Set off for the north mountain
which we find so bad we are Obliged
to foot it up, and could compair
ourselves to nothing but a parcel
of goats climbing up some of the

Figure 1. Page, Mrs. Mary Dewees's journal from Philadelphia to Kentucky.
Special Collections Research Center, University of Chicago Library.

Figure 2. *Phillis Wheatley, Negro Servant to Mr. John Wheatley, of Boston* (1773).
Library of Congress, Digital ID: ppmsca 02947.

In the Words of Women

The Revolutionary War and the Birth of the Nation, 1765–1799

Louise V. North, Janet M. Wedge, and
Landa M. Freeman

LEXINGTON BOOKS
Lanham • Boulder • New York • Toronto • Plymouth, UK

Published by Lexington Books
A wholly owned subsidiary of The Rowman & Littlefield Publishing Group, Inc.
4501 Forbes Boulevard, Suite 200, Lanham, Maryland 20706
http://www.lexingtonbooks.com

Estover Road, Plymouth PL6 7PY, United Kingdom

British Library Cataloguing in Publication Information Available

Library of Congress Cataloging-in-Publication Data

North, Louise V.
  In the words of women : the Revolutionary War and the birth of the nation, 1765-1799 /
Louise V. North, Janet M. Wedge, and Landa M. Freeman.
    p. cm.
  Includes bibliographical references and index.
  ISBN 978-0-7391-5018-4 (cloth : alk. paper)—ISBN 978-0-7391-5019-1 (paper : alk.
paper)
  1. United States—History—Revolution, 1775-1783—Women—Sources. 2. Women—
United States—History—18th century—Sources. 3. Women—United States—
Biography. 4. United States—History—Revolution, 1775-1783—Sources. 5. United
States—History—Colonial period, ca. 1600-1775—Sources. 6. United States—
History—1783-1815—Sources. I. Wedge, Janet M. II. Freeman, Landa M., 1937- III.
Title.
  E276.N67 2011
  973.3082—dc22

                                                                    2011006373

Printed in the United States of America

Contents

Foreword

Like Alice in her adventures through the looking glass, historians of women in the American Revolution have come to realize the truth of the White Knight's warning: you have to run twice as fast to stay in one place. It was not always so. In the early decades of the 19th century, women like Elizabeth Ellet could fill two volumes with accounts of female patriots and their deeds during the nation's struggle for independence. But by the end of the century, the professionalization of History, insured by the creation of PhD programs in the field, led to a gender amnesia: grand and sweeping accounts of the nation's rise to prosperity and influence, reconstructions of military campaigns and political rivalries, along with biographies of Presidents and captains of industry, left little room for the role of women in creating and sustaining the nation. Their stories found refuge in the archives of groups like the Daughters of the American Revolution, and in the pages of local studies that carried the stigma of "antiquarian" or "amateur" history. Women's letters and diaries sat unread in attics and in archives where they were catalogued as "miscellaneous documents" or, in some cases, simply identified as a famous man's "other papers." In textbooks, individual women bobbed on the ocean of male achievements and then sank below the waters. All that was left were names—Virginia Dare, Pocahontas, Abigail Adams, Elizabeth Cady Stanton, and Eleanor Roosevelt—and the vague sense that something they had done or been had briefly lifted them out of the sea of anonymous women.

But in the 1960s, as Joseph Heller might say, something happened. Graduate history programs opened their doors to a new, heterogeneous collection of future scholars: white women, African Americans, sons and daughters of immigrant groups, bright and eager talents from modest family backgrounds rather than privileged enclaves. Looking into the mirror of American history, these young men and women could not find themselves—and many of them set out to find the missing figures and the silenced voices. Among the most determined were women historians studying the 18th century.

Entering the archives with steely determination, these historians leafed through the miscellaneous files, scoured the papers of famous men to discover the papers of forgotten wives and daughters, poured over court records and wills, sermons and etiquette books, newspaper essays, military order books, applications for compensation made to the British and the American governments—and produced a revolutionary reinterpretation of the American Revolution. The cast of characters was no longer exclusively male; the landscape of protest, war, and peace had been transformed.

Yet, if women have been written into the story of our nation's founding, our task is far from done. For the voices of the women of the revolutionary generation have sometimes been lost in the rush to provide analysis and narration of their roles. The story is too often told *about* the women who protested, boycotted, fought, nursed, spied and took over the task of running farm and shop, but the voices we hear do not come from the women themselves. We know what women did, but we are not steeped in how women perceived what they had done. Without these 18th century voices, our history is incomplete. As editions of the correspondence of men like Washington, Franklin, Hamilton, Jay, and Jefferson are joined on the bookshelves by the memoirs and diaries of ordinary soldiers, planters and merchants, the voices of women grow faint, filtered—in danger of being lost.

The challenge is to bring those voices to the written page, to make us as familiar with the cadences of the housewife and the camp follower as we are with the tempo of Patrick Henry's oratory. And above all, we must hear what these women felt and observed and how they made their choices and faced the consequences of their actions in their own words.

This is the challenge that the editors of *In the Words of Women: The Revolutionary War and the Birth of the Nation, 1765-1799* have met. This collection promises to help free us from the need to run faster to stay in one place; it offers us the possibility of winning our race to produce a richer, more complex history of the era of American independence.

Carol Berkin
New York 2009

Acknowledgments

Our adventure of discovery, which began with the correspondence of Founding Father John Jay and his wife Sarah Livingston Jay, led us to continue our research in their time period but in pursuit of the writings of women. This too has been exhilarating and fascinating. Our journey would have been much more onerous had it not been for the generous encouragement of many people. We were the fortunate recipients of the enthusiasm and friendship of Carol Berkin, Presidential Professor of History at City University of New York, and of David Gellman, Professor of History at DePauw University, who gave us welcome suggestions and support. Our deep gratitude also goes to Elizabeth Nuxoll, Editor of the Jay Papers, and to William Pencak, Professor of American History at Pennsylvania State University.

Information retrieval by electronic means has expanded at an amazing rate over the six years that we have worked on this book; we have benefited from that growth, finding appropriate sources to explore in greater depth. Libraries and historical associations, however, remain the mother lode for the original writings of women. In our travels and doing the research, we are greatly indebted for the expert assistance of the staffs of:

American Antiquarian Society; American Folk Art Museum, New York City; American Jewish Archives, Cincinnati, Ohio; American Philosophical Society; Boston Public Library/Rare Books; Columbia University, Rare Book & Manuscript Library; Connecticut Historical Society; Gilder Lehrman Institute of American History, New York City; The Grolier Club, New York City; Historic Hudson Valley, Archival Collection, Tarrytown, New York; Historical Society of Pennsylvania; Honnold/Mudd Library Special Collections, Claremont, California; The Huntington Library, San Marino, California; John C. Hart Library, Shrub Oak, New York; John Jay Homestead New York State Historic Site; Knox's Headquarters New York State Historic Site; Lancaster County [Pennsylvania] Historical Society; Library of Congress; Long Island Oyster Bay [New York] Historical Society; Maine Historical Society; Massachusetts Historical Society; The Morgan Library & Museum Reading Room; Mount Vernon Estate & Gardens; Museum of the City of New York; National Archives; National Library of Scotland Manuscript Collection; New Hampshire Historical Society;

The New-York Historical Society Library Manuscript Department; New York Public Library, Manuscript and Archives Division; New York State Historical Association; New York State Library Archives; New York University, Fales Library and Special Collections; North Carolina Department of Archives and History at Raleigh; Pennsylvania County Historical Society; Pennsylvania Historical Society; Princeton University Press; Rhode Island Historical Society; Sharon [Connecticut] Historical Society; University of Missouri Press; University of South Carolina Press; University of Wisconsin Press; Wesleyan University Press; Westchester County [New York] Archives; Westchester County [New York] Historical Society; Yale University, Sterling Memorial Library.

We also thank them for permission to quote from materials we found in their collections as well as Professor Elaine F. Crane, Fordham University; John Jackson, G. S. MacManus Co., Bryn Mawr, Pennsylvania; and Ellen R. Cohn, editor of the Franklin Papers. Our heartfelt acknowledgments for their stalwart enthusiasm for our project go to Tracy Potter (Massachusetts Historical Society), Ted O'Reilly (The New-York Historical Society), Michele Lee (Mount Vernon Estate & Gardens Library), Kim Reynolds (Boston Public Library/Rare Books), Jim Shea (Longfellow National Historic Site), John L. Bell, Benjamin Bromley (Earl Gregg Swem Library, College of William and Mary), Jamie Kingman Rice (Maine Historical Society), Jude Pfister (Washington Headquarters, Morristown, New Jersey), Heather Tennies (Lancaster County Historical Society), Sheila Mackenzie (National Library of Scotland), Richard C. Malley (Connecticut Historical Society), Courtney Wagner (American Folk Art Museum), William Wedge, and Cathy W. Miranker.

Our appreciative thanks go to Andrew Bingham for his foray into the James Iredell Papers at the North Carolina Department of Archives and History at Raleigh; to Patrick Alexander, Pennsylvania State University Press, to Eleanor Phillips Brackbill, Director of Education at the Neuberger Museum, Purchase, New York, and to the late Heidi S. Terralavoro, who read sections of the manuscript and made insightful suggestions for its improvement. We are grateful for the professional guidance we received from Erin Walpole and Laura Grzybowski at Lexington Books.

A collective tip of our hats to Reinout E. Hunningher, Jefferson Freeman, James H. North, and Nicholas Wedge for their always welcome encouragement and suggestions, whether literary or technical. We dedicate this volume to them.

Fatti maschi, parole femine
Masculine deeds, feminine words

(17th century Italian saying)

Editorial Guidelines

Our adventures delving into archival treasure troves housed in historical societies and libraries began more than a decade ago while doing research on John Jay, his wife Sarah Livingston Jay, and their extended families. In reading their correspondence, these figures from history came to life, and we shared with them the good times, and the bad. Along the way, we encountered many other people who, we felt, also deserved to be heard—thus the genesis of this book. We had been fortunate that the bulk of the Jay research was accomplished at Columbia University's Rare Book & Manuscript Library, but this time we had to go far afield to find original documents (see the Acknowledgments). The books by Mrs. Elizabeth Fries Ellet as well as those by modern writers gave us names of women to consider, as did suggestions from other scholars. The Internet has burgeoned as a research tool in recent years, leading us to material we might otherwise not have found. We are certain there are other voices still waiting to be discovered.

We have selected the words of women that move the narrative along, have a strong emotional impact, and will inform and enrich the reader's knowledge of American life in the latter part of the eighteenth century. It is clear from the wealth of material uncovered that women felt a need to put their thoughts on paper, for themselves or to share with friends. As Jemima Condict, daughter of a New Jersey farmer and preacher, put it: "Sometimes after our people is gone to Bed I get my Pen for I Dont know how to Content myself without writeing Something."[1] Our goal is to allow women to express their thoughts, whether on battles, smallpox outbreaks, birth or death.

While we have made every effort to include a broad spectrum of society, living in the North and the South, the majority of women are middle to upper class, and white, as they would have received some formal education. Deborah Read Rogers Franklin's spelling may have been poorer than Sarah Livingston Jay's, but both wrote vivid letters that are engrossing to read. Women loyal to the British crown and those who sided with the "rebels" also are heard. Native Americans and African Americans have their say, although—as their cultures relied on strong oral traditions—written documents by these women are scarcer. Martha Washington's slave Oney Judge admitted that, though taught excellent sewing skills, she did not learn to read or write while in her owner's household.

It is our intention to weave an integrated, interconnected narrative across class, ethnicity, locale, and age to produce a clearer picture of an extraordinary time.

Inevitably, worthy women and interesting documents had to be rejected: perhaps the materials had been published elsewhere (such as the Petition of an African Slave Belinda of 1782) or would have required too much editorial explanation to make sense in a limited space (such as the letters of Elizabeth Gates). By the same token, how could we ignore the poetry of Phillis Wheatley or the words of Abigail Smith Adams? Their contributions add significantly to our narrative.

Primary sources need to be used with caution. Some purported women's writings did not originate in the eighteenth century, such as *Theatrum Majorum. The Cambridge of 1776 . . . with which is incorporated The Diary of Dorothy Dudley* (Cambridge, Massachusetts, 1876), created and published for the commemoration of the Cambridge Centennial or *Personal Recollections of the American Revolution A Private Journal* by "Lydia Minturn Post," editor Sidney Barclay (Port Washington, Kennicat Press, 1859). Also excluded were Helen Evertson Smith's imagined scenarios in *Colonial Days and Ways—as Gathered from Family Papers* (1900) and the plagiarized *Letters of an American Woman Sailing for England in 1784 Quaint Message from Love Lawrence, Daughter of an American Clergyman, Who Left her Country to Marry a Loyalist whose Political Principles Were Opposed to the New Republic An Interesting Glimpse of Life* by Edith Willis Linn (*The Journal of American History*. New Haven, Connecticut, 1909, Third Number, Third Volume) which quotes, nearly word for word, Abigail Smith Adams's account of her own voyage to England in 1784![2]

Many documents by women have been destroyed. No letters of Catherine van Rensselaer Schuyler, wife of General Philip Schuyler, exist, or of Dorothy Quincy Hancock, wife of the first signer of the Declaration of Independence. From the lively Catherine Littlefield Greene, wife of General Nathaniel Greene, only one letter remains. What happened to the letters she—and many other women—wrote? Were they lost during the war or over time? Were they perhaps thought inconsequential? Did men with an eye on the future destroy letters that might have reflected poorly on their families or honor? John Jay destroyed many of his family papers before his death, and his sons culled the voluminous correspondence even further in subsequent years. Only two letters between Martha and George Washington have survived—surely there were more. It seems she destroyed them.

These losses leave a gap, not unlike a missing piece in a puzzle. We attempt to fill it by listening to the voices of other women to gain insight into that era. Each writer, when first introduced in this volume, is placed in the context of the narrative, although some biographical information may be found in the Dramatis Personae. We have tried to retain the authenticity of each woman's spirit by using as much of a document as possible but have done judicious editing when necessary. Since part of the attraction of the manuscripts—letters, diaries, contemporary newspaper submissions—lies in their tone and style, most of the prevailing conventions have been retained, including abbreviations and contractions although without superscript. When the meaning is not clear, the word has been supplied. For example, because wh may mean with or which, we provide the appropriate word.

That punctuation during this period was minimal will soon become evident to readers. Periods have been added where thoughts clearly end, or to break up run-on sentences; the ubiquitous dashes have sometimes been replaced by periods or semicolons. Sentences thus created begin with capital letters. Long sections have been divided into paragraphs for ease of reading.

Spelling tended to be arbitrary, but we have transcribed the words as written, clarifying only to aid comprehension. It may sometimes be helpful to say the word aloud: "Gaus" but we added "[gauze]" after it. English spellings were still in use, such as in "neighbour" and "favour." Only for Deborah Franklin and her sister-in-law Jane Mecom have we silently modernized the spelling, believing that the reader's appreciation of their thoughts would be seriously diminished by having to decipher each word. Thus, Deborah Franklin's "All our good friends Colle on us as yousall" becomes "All our good friends call on us as usual." The use of some words may also strike the reader as odd because of changes in meaning: "condescension" in the eighteenth century meant a gracious acknowledgment of someone's opinion, while today the word has a more patronizing connotation; the word "interesting" was a synonym for "important."

We urge readers to savor the variety and richness of the voices heard in these documents, to reflect on the difficulties and complexities in the accounts that they share with us, and to marvel at their hardiness and commitment. We invite you to be a witness as the women speak for themselves.

"Hear us, therefore, for we speak of things that concern us."

Women of the Seneca Nation 1790

Figure 3. Map of the United States (ca. 1784).

Timeline

1754-1763   French and Indian War between the British and the French and their allies by which the victorious British acquire Canada and all land east of the Mississippi River (except for New Orleans). Part of a larger conflict called the Seven Years War (1756-1763).

1763   In the Proclamation of 1763, the British declare the western frontier closed to settlement.

1765   The Stamp Act imposes a direct tax on colonists to offset British war debts. Protesting "taxation without representation," colonists organize the Sons of Liberty, meet in the Stamp Act Congress, and refuse to buy British goods.

1766   Parliament repeals the Stamp Act, but reaffirms its right to legislate for and tax the colonies.

1767   The Townshend Acts levy new taxes to pay the costs of governing and protecting the colonies.

1768   Boston is occupied by the British.

1770   Parliament repeals the Townshend duties, except for the tax on tea.
The Boston Massacre occurs.

1773   The tea tax is reduced, but Britain grants a monopoly on the sale of tea to the East India Company, causing further resentment.
The Boston Tea Party.

1774   Parliament passes the Coercive Acts to punish Boston.
The First Continental Congress meets in Philadelphia.

1775   Violence erupts in Lexington and Concord between colonists and British soldiers, who try to seize rebel ammunition depots.
Boston is under siege.
The Second Continental Congress is convened; it names George Washington commander-in-chief of the Continental Army.
An American expedition to take Canada fails.
The British attack on American fortifications at Bunker's Hill and Breed's Hill succeeds but the British suffer huge losses.

1776   The British evacuate Boston.
Thomas Paine's *Common Sense* is published.
Congress approves the Declaration of Independence, which is publicly proclaimed throughout the colonies.

1776	The British attack New York. Washington retreats into New Jersey, leaving the British in control of the city.
	In a surprise attack on December 26, Washington crosses the Delaware and captures Trenton from a Hessian force.
1777	States draw up their constitutions.
	Patriots are defeated in the battle of Brandywine.
	The British occupy Philadelphia.
	American forces defeat British General Burgoyne at Saratoga.
	The patriot army winters at Valley Forge.
1778	France agrees to an alliance with the United States.
	The British abandon Philadelphia and return to New York.
	Savannah falls to the British.
1779	American General Benedict Arnold turns traitor.
1780	Charleston is taken by the British.
1781	The Articles of Confederation are adopted.
	British General Cornwallis surrenders at Yorktown.
1782	The preliminary treaty of peace is agreed to in Paris.
1783	The definitive Treaty is signed.
	The British army evacuates New York.
	Washington resigns his commission and bids farewell to his troops.
1786-1787	The United States suffers from a postwar economic depression.
	Shays's Rebellion takes place in Massachusetts.
1787	A Constitutional Convention convenes in Philadelphia.
	Delegates propose and agree to a new Constitution.
1788	New York City becomes the temporary capital of the United States.
	Nine states ratify the Constitution ensuring its adoption.
1789	A new government is elected and takes effect.
	Washington is inaugurated as president.
	The French Revolution begins.
1790	Philadelphia named temporary capital of the United States until a new capital, called Washington, is built on a site on the Potomac.
1791	American General Arthur St. Clair and his forces are defeated by Indians in Ohio.
	The first ten amendments to the Constitution, known as the Bill of Rights, are ratified.
1795	Jay's Treaty with Britain is ratified in spite of much opposition.
1797	John Adams becomes the second president.
1798	The Alien and Sedition laws are passed.
1798-1800	In spite of troubles with France, war is averted.
1799	George Washington dies at Mount Vernon.

Dramatis Personae

Adams, Abigail Smith (1744-1818) married lawyer John Adams in 1764. They had five children. A renowned letter writer, she often signed her letters with the nom-de-plume "Diana" or "Portia."

Adams, Mrs. Nathaniel Owen (fl. 1777), wife of a blacksmith in White Plains, New York. Moved to Maugerville, New Brunswick, after the War.

Akerly, Margaretta (1782- ?), daughter of Samuel Akerly, a shipbuilder, and Priscilla Titus. She married (1803) Sylvanus Miller, a judge who served in the New York legislature.

Ambler, Mary Cary (1732-1781), daughter of Wilson Cary of Virginia; married (1754) Edward Ambler. They had two children, John and Sarah.

Angell, Tryphena Martin (fl. 1775-1790), daughter of Moses Martin of Salem, New York; married Augustus Angell.

Asgill, Lady Sarah Theresa Pratviel (d. 1816), daughter of the French Huguenot merchant Daniel Pratviel; second wife of Charles Asgill (d. 1788), merchant and, at one time, Lord Mayor of London. They had a son and a daughter.

Bache, Sarah Franklin (1743-1805), daughter of Benjamin Franklin and Deborah Read, half-sister of William. Married Richard Bache in 1767; their children included Benjamin F. Bache (1769-1798), later anti-Federalist newspaper editor. Her portrait by John Hoppner is at the Metropolitan Museum of Art.

Bailey, Abigail Abbot (1746-1815), daughter of Deacon James Abbot and Sarah Bancroft of New Hampshire. Married (1767) Asa Bailey; they had seventeen children.

Bard, Sarah (1754-1837), daughter of Peter Bard and Mary De Normandie; she was the youngest of eight children. Her sister Mary (1746-1821) married a cousin, Dr. Samuel Bard, in 1770. Sarah never married; eventually moved in with her sister in Hyde Park, New York [now the Vanderbilt Estate].

Barnes, Christian Arbuthnot (d. after 1792), daughter of John Arbuthnot and Abigail Little. She married Henry Barnes in 1746, settled in Marlborough, Massachusetts, where he became a merchant and served as a magistrate. They had one daughter, Chrisy (d. June 1782). They were proscribed and banished in 1778.

Bartlett, Mary (1730-1789) married her cousin Dr. Josiah Bartlett in 1754. They settled in Kingston, New Hampshire, and had twelve children, eight of whom reached adulthood.

Beekman, Cornelia Van Cortlandt (1753-1847), daughter of Pierre Van Cortlandt and Joanna Livingston in New York; married Gerard G. Beekman in 1769. They had four children.

Bell, Cornelia (1755-1783), daughter of John Bell, married William Paterson in 1779. Died giving birth to their third child. Her loyalist brother Andrew had a distinguished career in Perth Amboy, New Jersey, after the War.

Bland, Martha Daingerfield (d. 1804), wife of Dr. Theodorick Bland of "Kippax" plantation, Virginia; wrote chatty letters to her sister-in-law, Frances Bland Randolph Tucker (1752-1788). After her husband's death in 1790, Martha married Nathan Blodget, a merchant; then Patrick Curran, a French sea captain.

Bleecker, Ann Eliza Schuyler (1752-1783), daughter of Brandt Schuyler and Margareta Van Wyck. Well educated by her mother, she married John Bleecker in 1769 and settled near Albany, New York. Her poetry and fiction were published after her death.

Brown, Sophia Waterhouse (1760-1837), daughter of Dr. John Waterhouse and Sophia Watson; married John Brown II of the Bahamas in 1780. He died before 1788; her parents-in-law supported her by sending money, food, clothing, and slaves.

Bull, Mary Lucia (1742-1814), daughter of Stephen B. Bull and Elizabeth Bryan of Beaufort County, South Carolina; she married Jacob Guerard in 1782.

Cameron, Nancy (Ann?) Jean (fl. 1785), wife of John Cameron. He had emigrated from Scotland in 1773 and died in Montreal early 1786.

Carrington, Elizabeth J. Ambler Brent (1765-1842), daughter of Jaquelin Ambler and Rebecca Lewis Burwell of Virginia. She and her sisters, Mary (Mrs. John Marshall) and Ann, were well educated by their father; later in life, Eliza began (but did not finish) a novel, *Variety or the Vicissitudes of Long Life*, using elements of her friend Rachel Warrington's life. Eliza's second marriage was to Col. Edward Carrington (1748-1810), who commanded the artillery at the battle of Yorktown.

Cary, Sarah Gray (1753-1825), only daughter of Ellis Gray of Boston. Married (1772) Samuel Cary who had business in Grenada, where they lived for many years. They had thirteen children. Friend of Mercy Otis Warren. Her miniature (ca. 1769) was painted by John S. Copley.

Chapman, Zerviah Sanger (1718-1812), of Rhode Island, married Stephen Chapman in 1734; they had at least fourteen children, among them Hannah (1737-1821), who married Simon Arnold; Lucy (1739-?), who married Reuben Blanchard; and Nathaniel (1742-1820), who married Phebe Rhodes.

Clarke, Charity (1747-1838), daughter of Thomas Clarke and Mary Stillwell of New York. Married Rev. Benjamin Moore; their only child was Clement Clarke Moore, scholar and poet. Her cousin Joseph Jekyll (d. 1837) was a lawyer, politician, and wit.

Clinton, Cornelia (1774-1810), daughter of New York Governor George Clinton and Cornelia Tappan. Married Edmond Genêt (1763-1834) in 1794. They had six children.

"Coincoin," Marie Thérèze (1742-ca. 1817), born to enslaved Africans François and Marie Françoise in Louisiana. Manumitted by her paramour in 1778, Coincoin, by hard work and shrewd business acumen, became wealthy, owned "Melrose" plantation.

Condict, Jemima (1755-1779), daughter of Daniel Condict and Ruth Harrison of New Jersey, farmers. She married Aaron Harrison, a cousin, early in 1779, and died after giving birth to a son.

Conyngham, Ann Hockley (1757-1811), daughter of a Philadelphia merchant, married Capt. Gustavus Conyngham in 1773. They are buried at St. Peter's Episcopal Churchyard in Philadelphia, Pennsylvania.

Cooper, Mary Wright (1714-1778), wife of Joseph Cooper of Oyster Bay, Long Island. They had six children, two of whom reached adulthood though Mary outlived them. Mary Cooper was a member of the New Light Baptist Church.

Cranch, Mary Smith (1741-1811), daughter of Rev. William Smith and Elizabeth Quincy; sister of Abigail Adams. Married Richard Cranch (1727-1811). They had three children.

Custis, Eleanor "Nelly" Parke (1779-1852), daughter of John P. Custis and Eleanor Calvert. She married Lawrence Lewis in 1799; they had eight children, four lived to adulthood. She befriended Elizabeth Bordley (1777-1863) while living in Philadelphia during George Washington's presidency.

Deming, Sarah Winslow (1722-1788), wife of John Deming, sister of Joshua Winslow. She was a skillful creator of cut-paper pictures.

Dewees, Mary Coburn (fl. 1787) married Samuel Dewees, moved to Kentucky with their two children, Rachel and Sallie. Three more children were born in Kentucky.

Drinker, Elizabeth Sandwith (1735-1807), wife of Henry Drinker; they had nine children, five of whom lived to adulthood. She was an important member of Philadelphia's Quaker community.

Edenton, North Carolina, Ladies, Resolution signers 1774.

Emery, Sarah Anne (ca. 1789-after 1879), daughter of David Emery and Sarah Smith, lived on a farm near Newburyport, Massachusetts.

Eve (fl. 1776-1782), a slave belonging to the Peyton Randolph family of Williamsburgh, Virginia.

Eve, Sarah (1749/50-1774), daughter of sea captain Oswell Eve and Anne Moore, lived on a farm in Philadelphia. One of thirteen children; she died shortly before her wedding.

Farmar, Elizabeth "Eliza" Halroyd (fl. 1774-1789), third wife of Dr. Richard Farmar, "Practitioner of Physic," in Philadelphia; married in London.

Fergusson, Elizabeth Graeme (1737-1801), daughter of Dr. Thomas Graeme and Anne Diggs. Attended Anthony Benezet's school, her mother encouraging her studies and literary pursuits. Courted—and then jilted—by William Franklin, she secretly married the Scot Henry H. Fergusson in 1772.

Fisher, Elizabeth "Betsey" Munro (1759-ca. 1812), daughter of loyalist Rev. Harry Munro. In 1776, Betsey married Donald Fisher; fled to Canada during the War. They had at least five children; three survived to adulthood.

Flagg, Mary Magdalene (1773-1817), daughter of George Flagg and Mary M. Henderson of Charleston, South Carolina. In 1794, she married Ray Greene of Rhode Island, who later became a senator.

Foote, Elizabeth (1750-?, m. 1778), and *Abigail Foote* (1757-?, m. 1791), of Colchester, Connecticut, daughters of Israel Foote and Elizabeth Kimberly.

Foster, Rebecca Faulkner (1761-1834), daughter of Col. Francis Faulkner and Rebecca Keyes of Acton, Massachusetts; married Dwight Foster, lawyer and politician, in 1783. They had four children. Her miniature (ca. 1830) by Eliza Goodridge is at the American Antiquarian Society.

Franklin, Deborah Read Rogers (1708-1774), common-law wife of Benjamin Franklin, mother of Sarah (later Bache), and stepmother of William Franklin, the last royal governor of New Jersey.

Franks, Rebecca (1760-1823), daughter of loyalist David Franks and Margaret Evans. In 1782, she married British officer Henry Johnson, and moved to Bath, England.

Franks, Rebecca (fl. 1799), daughter of Abraham Franks, a Philadelphia merchant who moved to Montreal before the Revolution. Sister of patriot David S. Franks. Not to be confused with loyalist Rebecca Franks.

Freeman, Elizabeth "Mum Bett" (ca. 1744-1829), runaway slave of John Ashley of Sheffield, Massachusetts. Freed in a celebrated court case (1781). Married while enslaved and had several children.

Frost, Sarah Scofield (1754-1817), daughter of patriot Josiah Scofield of Stamford, Connecticut. Married to loyalist William Frost, she was forced to flee to Long Island, and then emigrated to New Brunswick.

Galloway, Grace Growden (1727-1782), daughter of Lawrence Growden. Married Joseph Galloway in 1753. Of four children, only their daughter Elizabeth reached adulthood.

Gill, Sarah Prince (1728-1771), daughter of Rev. Thomas Prince; first wife of merchant Moses Gill of Boston. Her portrait by John S. Copley is at the Museum of Rhode Island School of Design.

Glover, Ann (fl. 1780), of North Carolina; mother of two children, widow of Sergeant Samuel Glover.

Graham, Isabella Marshall (1742-1824), Scottish-born wife of Dr. John Graham; they had three children. After his death, Graham opened a school in New York City.

Grant, Abigail Crofoot (ca. 1750-1823), daughter of Daniel Crofoot and Margaret Hiller of Glastonbury, Connecticut. In 1770, she married Azariah Grant Jr.; they had ten children, at least five reached adulthood. The family moved to Berlin, Vermont, in the 1790s.

Griffitts, Hannah (1727-1817), daughter of Thomas Griffitts and Mary Norris, prominent Quakers of Philadelphia. A prolific writer, she frequently signed her works "Fidelia."

Gutridge, Molly (fl. 1778) of Marblehead, Massachusetts, writer of a broadside.

Hampton, Mrs. A. (fl. 1776) of New York City, whose daughter Polly lived with the loyalist Rev. Charles Inglis and his wife Margaret in New Windsor, New York.

Heaton, Hannah Cook (1721-1793), oldest of ten children of Jonathan Cook and Temperance Rogers. In 1743 married Theophilus Heaton Jr.; they had four children, two lived to adulthood.

Hill, Frances Baylor (1748-1802), daughter of Dr. Robert Baylor and Mollie Brooke of Virginia. Married a cousin, Edward Hill.

Hodgkins, Sarah Perkins (1750-1803), second wife of shoemaker Joseph Hodgkins of Ipswich, Massachusetts; they had a daughter and a son.

Holyoke, Mary Vial (1737-1802), only child of a Boston merchant. Married Dr. Edward A. Holyoke, a founder of the American Academy of Arts and Sciences in Boston; they had twelve children.

Horry, Harriott Pinckney (1748-1830), daughter of Charles Pinckney and Eliza Lucas; in 1768 married Daniel Horry (d. 1785), a widower sixteen years older than she. Forced to buy protection from the British during the War to prevent his property's destruction, Horry was able to escape confiscation of his lands by the Americans after the War thanks to the influence of his brothers-in-law, Charles C. and Thomas Pinckney.

Hulton, Anne (d. 1779), sister of the British Commissioner of Customs Henry Hulton. Returned to England August, 1775.

Ingraham, Hannah (1772-1869), daughter of loyalist Benjamin Ingraham, lived in New Concord, New York. Their property confiscated, the family emigrated to what is now Frederikton, New Brunswick. Hannah never married.

Inman, Elizabeth Murray Campbell Smith (1726-1785), born in Scotland, established herself as a businesswoman in Boston (1749), selling millinery and sewing supplies; she taught needlework, and helped other women to do likewise. She also oversaw the education of her nieces. Her portrait by John S. Copley is at the Museum of Fine Arts, Boston.

Jay, Sarah Livingston (1756-1802), daughter of William Livingston and Susannah French; married lawyer John Jay in 1774 and accompanied him on his diplomatic mission to Europe during the War. They had six children.

Jefferson, Martha Wayles Skelton (1749-1782), daughter of John Wayles. At age eighteen, she married Bathurst Skelton and bore him a son John (d. 1771). Widowed, she married Thomas Jefferson on New Year's Day 1772. They had six children; two survived to adulthood.

Jefferson, Martha "Patsy" (1772-1836), daughter of Thomas Jefferson and Martha Wayles. She married (1790) Thomas M. Randolph Jr., later governor of Virginia. They had twelve children. Patsy also served as First Lady for her father during his presidency.

Jefferson, Mary "Polly" (1778-1804), sister of Patsy Jefferson. Married a cousin John Wayles Eppes in 1797. They had three children; she died of complications after childbirth.

Jemison, Mary (1742/3-1833), daughter of Thomas Jemison and Jane Erwin, was born on board a ship sailing from Ireland. The family settled in Pennsylvania. Taken captive by Senecas, she was named "Degiwene," married twice, had eight children. After the Revolution, she settled near Castile, New York, and, in 1797, was the largest landowner in the area (now part of Letchworth State Park).

Judge, Oney (ca. 1774-1848), daughter of Andrew Judge, runaway dower slave of Martha Washington.

Kitty (fl. 1790s), young slave who belonged to Susannah Ferguson Brown of New Providence, the Bahamas, but worked for Sophia Waterhouse Brown in Perth Amboy, New Jersey.

Knox, Lucy Flucker (1756-1824), daughter of Thomas Flucker, Secretary of Massachusetts Colony, and Hannah Waldo. Married bookseller Henry Knox in 1774 against her father's wishes; they had twelve children, three of whom lived to adulthood.

La Tour du Pin Gouvernet, Henriette-Lucie Dillon, marquise de (1770-1853), daughter of Arthur Dillon and Lucie de Rothe, sought refuge in America during the Reign of Terror in France; settled (1794-1796) with her husband, a soldier and diplomat, and their two children near Albany, New York. Of six children, only the youngest survived her.

Lear, Susanna (ca. 1770-1825?) married Captain James Duncan of Philadelphia, who served in the War. He was given 500 acres in the Shenango Valley, Pennsylvania. They had three children.

Leech (Leach), Christiana Young (1737-1814), born in Germany to Wilhelm Jung and Anna Elizabetha Wagnerin, who emigrated to Philadelphia in 1744. Married (1753) John Leech (Leisch); they had seven children, including twins. Her diary was written in German.

Liston, Henrietta Marchant (1752-1828), daughter of Nathaniel Marchant. Married British diplomat Robert Liston in 1796, prior to sailing for America. Her portrait by Gilbert Stuart is at the National Gallery, Washington, D.C.

Livingston, Catharine W. (1751-1813), daughter of William Livingston and Susannah French. Well educated at home, she married widower Matthew Ridley, an associate of Robert Morris. They had two daughters. Her second marriage was to a cousin, John Livingston.

Livingston, Susan (1748-1840), eldest daughter of William Livingston and Susannah French, teacher of her nephew, Peter A. Jay, and of her niece, Susan Ridley (later Sedgwick). Married (1794) Judge John Cleves Symmes, and moved to North Bend, Ohio. There she designed her own house, but, within 10 years, left her husband and returned east.

Macaulay, Catharine Sawbridge (1731-1791), English historian and political activist. Came to the United States in 1784 and visited a.o. Mercy O. Warren and George Washington.

Manigault, Ann Ashby (1705-1782), wife of Gabriel Manigault (1704-1781), a wealthy planter and merchant in South Carolina. Her portrait by Jeremiah Theüs of 1757 is at the Metropolitan Museum of Art.

McEachron, Maria (ca. 1759-?) of Argyle, New York.

McGee, Ruth, indentured servant to Josiah Hibberd of East Whiteland, Pennsylvania, who, in 1779, owned 150 acres and some livestock.

McGinn, Sarah Kast (ca. 1717-1791), widow of Tim McGinn, a friend to the Iroquois, and a loyalist (her family's property was confiscated during the War), served as an intermediary between the British and Native Americans.

McKean, Sally (1777-1841), daughter of Thomas McKean, governor of Pennsylvania. Married (1798) Carlos Fernando Martinez, Chevalier de Yrujo. Her portrait by Gilbert Stuart is at the Metropolitan Museum.

Mecom, Jane Franklin (1712-1794), sister of Benjamin Franklin. She married a saddler, Edward Mecom, in 1727 in Boston. They had twelve children.

Metcalf, Elizabeth "Betsy" (1786-1867), daughter of Joel Metcalf and Lucy Gay of Providence, Rhode Island. She taught school before her marriage to Obed Baker, a teamster, in 1807. They had six children.

Montgomery, Janet Livingston (1743-1828), daughter of Robert Livingston and Margaret Beekman. Married Richard Montgomery in 1773. A very capable businesswoman, she operated a successful commercial nursery, "Château de Montgomery" (now "Montgomery Place," New York).

Morris, Margaret Hill (1737-1816), daughter of Dr. Richard Hill and Deborah Moore, Quakers; married merchant William Morris in 1758. They had six children. She used her knowledge of medicines to aid the sick.

Morris, Mary White (1749-1827), daughter of Thomas White and Esther Hewlings Newman. Married (1769) financier Robert Morris; they had seven children. Her husband called her "the partner of my happy moments and the sharer in my sorrowful hours," which surely she was when he landed in debtor's prison.

Morton, Eliza Susan (1773-1850), daughter of New York City merchant John Morton and Maria Sophia Kemper; fled to Basking Ridge, New Jersey, during the War. In 1797, married Josiah Quincy, Massachusetts politician, later mayor of Boston and then president of Harvard College. Part I of Eliza's *Memoir* was "written from memory" in 1821.

Murray, Judith Sargent Stevens (1751-1820), daughter of Captain Winthrop Sargent and Judith Saunders, who encouraged her studies in Latin, Greek, and the sciences. She married John Stevens (d. 1786), and subsequently John Murray, founder of the Universalist denomination.

Norris, Deborah (1761-1839), daughter of Quaker Charles Norris and Mary Parker. Educated at home and at Anthony Benezet's school in Philadelphia. In 1781, married Dr. George Logan, whose memoir she wrote. They had three sons.

Oakley, Phoebe (fl. 1777) of White Plains, New York.

Osborn, Sarah Haggar Wheaten (1714-1796), twice married, taught school; one of her pupils was Mary Fish (later Silliman). Influential religious leader in Newport, Rhode Island.

Osborn, Sarah Matthews (ca. 1756-1858), of Blooming Grove, New York, married Aaron Osborn, a blacksmith. They had two children, Phebe and Aaron Jr. After the War, she discovered that her husband was a bigamist. She later married John Benjamin, and moved to Pennsylvania.

Palmer, Mary (1775-1866), daughter of Joseph P. Palmer Jr. and Elizabeth Hunt of Massachusetts. After the War, the Palmers, to make ends meet, took in boarders, one of whom was Royall Tyler (1757-1826), lawyer and author of *The Contrast*, the first commercially successful American comedy. Tyler married Mary (apparently pregnant) in 1794. They had eleven children. Mary wrote *The Maternal Physician* (1811), giving advice on childrearing.

Payne, Dolley (1768-1849*)*, daughter of Quaker John Payne and Mary Coles. Married (1790) John Todd and had two sons. After Todd and the younger son died, Dolley was introduced to James Madison by Aaron Burr.

Phaebe, a runaway slave of Dinwiddie, Virginia, about forty years old.

Phelps, Elizabeth Porter (1747-1817), wife of Charles Phelps, Jr., a lawyer and farmer. They had two children, Charles Moses and Elizabeth, but also raised from infancy, Thankful "Mary" Richmond, as their own.

Pinckney, Eliza Lucas (1722-1793), daughter of George Lucas, a British officer posted in Antigua, where she was born. At age sixteen, she successfully managed her father's plantation near Charleston, South Carolina. Sent indigo seeds by her father, Eliza Lucas perfected a method of producing indigo cakes to make a high quality blue dye, which became a profitable industry. She also conducted experiments with hemp and flax. In 1744, she married widower Charles Pinckney (d. 1758); they had three children.

Pinckney, Mary Stead (ca. 1751-1812), daughter of wealthy merchant Benjamin Stead and Mary Johnson of Charleston, South Carolina; second wife (1786) of Charles C. Pinckney, lawyer and politician.

Powell, Anne (ca. 1760-1792), daughter of loyalist John Powell and Janet Grant, left Boston in 1775 for England. When her brother, William Dummer Powell, was appointed judge in the Western District of Canada, Anne accompanied him, his wife Anne Murray (a niece of Elizabeth Murray Inman), and six children from Montreal. She married Isaac Winslow Clarke.

Punderson, Prudence (1758-1784), eldest daughter of Ebenezer Punderson and Prudence Geer of Preston, Connecticut. Married (1783) Dr. Timothy W. Rossiter; died after giving birth to a daughter, Sophia. A gifted artist with her needle, her embroideries are at the Connecticut Historical Society.

Randolph, Ann Cary (1745-1789), first wife of Col. Thomas M. Randolph of Virginia. Children in fifteen pregnancies included Judith, Anne, and Thomas Jr., who married Martha "Patsy" Jefferson.

Rawle, Anna (1757-1828), daughter of Francis Rawle and Rebecca Warner. Married John Clifford in 1783. One daughter survived to adulthood.

Reed, Esther DeBerdt (1746-1780), daughter of Dennis DeBerdt, English-born wife of Joseph Reed (1741-1785). They had six children.

Revere, Rachel Walker (1745-1813), second wife of engraver/silversmith Paul Revere; married in 1773, four months after the death of his first wife Sarah Orne, leaving him with eight children; Paul and Rachel had eight more.

Riedesel, Baroness Frederika Charlotte Louise von, née von Massow (1746-1808), left Germany with her three young daughters in 1776 to join her husband Col. Baron Friederich Adolphus von Riedesel, who was with the British troops in Canada. The couple would have four more children.

Robbins, Jane Prince (1740-1800), daughter of Moses Prince and Jane Bethune. In 1761 married Rev. Chandler Robbins, minister of the First Congrega-

tional Church in Plymouth, Massachusetts. They had nine children, including Hannah (b. 1768), who married Benjamin I. Gilman of Marietta, Ohio,
in 1790.

Robinson, Sarah Franklin (1764-1806), daughter of Quaker Samuel Franklin
and Esther Mitchell. Married William T. Robinson in 1781 in New York
City. They had thirteen children.

Samuel, Rebecca Alexander (fl. 1790s), wife of Hyman Samuel, a watchmaker.
Immigrants from Germany, they lived in Petersburg, Virginia, before moving to Richmond by 1796.

Schaw, Janet (ca. 1734-ca. 1801), daughter of Gideon Schaw and Anne Rutherfurd of Lauriston, Scotland; sister of Robert, a South Carolina plantation
owner, and Alexander, a customs officer in the West Indies.

Schieffelin, Harriet Lawrence (1758-1838), daughter of John Lawrence, a Quaker
merchant in New York City. She wrote poetry under the name "Mathilda."
Married Jacob Schieffelin, a British officer billeted at her home.

Schuyler, Shinah Simon (1762?-1815), daughter of Joseph Simon of Lancaster,
Pennsylvania. Married Dr. Nicholas Schuyler of Troy, New York.

Sedgwick, Catharine Maria (1789-1867), daughter of Theodore Sedgwick and
Pamela Dwight. A successful author, she never married.

Seton, Elizabeth Ann Bayley (1774-1821), daughter of Dr. Richard Bayley and
Catherine Charlton. Married (1794) William Magee Seton. They had five
children. She wrote letters to Julianna Sitgreaves Scott (1765-1841). Converted to Catholicism and was beatified in 1975.

Shaw, Elizabeth Smith (1750-1815), sister of Abigail Adams and Mary Cranch.
She married Rev. John Shaw; they had three children. Her second husband
was Rev. Stephen Peabody. Her portrait by Gilbert Stuart is at Arizona
State University.

Sheftall, Frances Hart (1740-1820) moved from Charleston, South Carolina, to
Savannah, Georgia, upon her marriage in 1761 to Mordecai Sheftall, a
rancher and influential leader of the Jewish community. They had several
children, including Perla (ca. 1763) and Sheftall (ca. 1765). After the War,
they returned to Savannah.

Shippen, Alice Lee (1736-1817), sister of Richard, Francis, and Arthur Lee of
Virginia; wife of Dr. William Shippen of Philadelphia, they had eight children, two of whom reached adulthood.

Shipton, Elizabeth, born in England, married (Oct. 1780) Aquila Giles (1758-
1822). Settled in Maryland; had ten children, eight of whom survived infancy. Friend of Julianna Sitgreaves Scott.

Silliman, Mary Fish Noyes (1736-1818), daughter of Rev. Joseph Fish and Rebecca Pabodie of Connecticut. She married John Noyes in 1758; they had
five children. After his death, she married the widower Gold S. Silliman,
with whom she had two sons; the younger, Benjamin, would become a
prominent chemist, geologist, and physicist. After Silliman's death, she
married John Dickinson of Connecticut.

Smith, Sarah (fl. 1776-7), widow of a cabinetmaker in New York City.

Stockton, Annis Boudinot (1736-1801), daughter of Elias Boudinot and Catherine Williams. Married lawyer Richard Stockton in 1757/8. They had six children. Their house "Morven" in Princeton, New Jersey, was used not only by Lord Cornwallis as his headquarters during the War, but, in 1783, was also frequented by members of Congress when Princeton temporarily became the seat of government.

Thomson, Hannah Harrison (ca. 1729-1807), daughter of Richard Harrison and Hannah Norris; sister of Benjamin Harrison (a signer of the Declaration of Independence), and wife of Charles Thomson, Secretary of the Continental Congress. They had no children of their own, but did raise her two nieces and a nephew. Her portrait by Joseph Wright is at Tudor Place Historic House, Washington, D.C.

Tilghman, Mary (ca. 1762-?), daughter of loyalist James Tilghman and Anne Francis; sister of Tench Tilghman, aide-de-camp to George Washington.

Totten, Mary (fl. 1777), a widow with several children, residing on the Cortlandt Manor, New York.

Trist, Elizabeth House (ca. 1751-1828), daughter of Mary Stretch House, wife of Nicholas Trist. She had one child, Hore Browse Trist (d. 1804). A friend of Thomas Jefferson, she resided at or near Monticello the last part of her life. Her grandson Nicholas Trist married Virginia Randolph, Jefferson's granddaughter, in 1824.

V. V., Mary, (fl. 1774), unidentified author of "A Dialogue, Between a Southern Delegate, and His Spouse," a propaganda piece published in Boston.

Wadsworth, Harriet (1769-1793), daughter of Jeremiah Wadsworth, commissary general during the War, and Mehitable Russell. Her cousin, the artist John Trumbull, wished to marry her but she died of consumption.

Walton, Cornelia Beekman (1708-1786), widow of William Walton, a shipping merchant, whose wealth came from the slave trade. Their elegant house was on Pearl Street, New York City, and their portraits by John Wollaston are at The New-York Historical Society.

Ward, Phebe Fowler (fl. 1783), wife of Edmund Ward, a prominent citizen of Eastchester, New York. She managed the farm and their six children by herself during the War. They emigrated to Canada in October 1783.

Ward, Susanna Holyoke (1779-?), eleventh child of Mary and Edward Holyoke.

Warren, Mercy Otis (1728-1814), daughter of James Otis and Mary Allyne. In 1754, she married James Warren and moved to Plymouth, Massachusetts. They had five sons. A prolific writer, she wrote under various pseudonyms, a.o. "Fidelia" and "Marcia." Her portrait by John S. Copley is at the Museum of Fine Arts, Boston.

Washington, Elizabeth Foote (d.1812) married Lund Washington (1737-1796), who had managed Mount Vernon until 1785 for his cousin George.

Washington, Martha Dandridge Custis (1731-1802), daughter of John Dandridge and Frances Jones of Virginia. In 1749, she married Daniel P. Custis; they had four children, of whom only John lived to adulthood. Left a wealthy widow in 1757, Martha was courted by George Washington and married him in 1759. Although they had no children, they were the loving care-givers of Martha's grandchildren as well as other family members.

Wells, Louisa Susannah (ca. 1755-1831), daughter of loyalist Robert Wells, a publisher in Charleston, South Carolina; her brother John supported the American cause. Married Alexander Aikman (1782) in England.

Wheatley, Phillis (ca. 1753-1784), abducted from Senegal in 1761, purchased by John Wheatley, a Boston merchant. Highly intelligent and a gifted poet, first published in 1767, she was manumitted in 1773, married John Peters in 1778. Abandoned by her husband, and impoverished, she (and her third child) died of complications after childbirth.

Wilkinson, Elizabeth "Eliza" Yonge (1757-1813?), daughter of Francis Yonge and Sarah Clifford; married Joseph Wilkinson 1774. After the War, she married Peter Porcher, half-brother of her friend Mary Porcher. They had four children.

Willett, Susannah Nicoll Jauncey Vardill (ca. 1746-?), daughter of Edward Nicoll and Agnes de Meyer. Her third marriage was to the Revolutionary War hero Marinus Willett. She divorced him in 1799.

Winslow, Anna Green (1760-1779), daughter of Joshua Winslow and Anna Green of Massachusetts. Her father had been appointed commissary general of the British forces in Nova Scotia, and Anna was sent to Boston for her schooling, boarding with her aunt, Sarah Deming.

Winslow, Sarah (1745-1822), daughter of Edward Winslow Sr. and Hannah Howland Dyer of Plymouth, Massachusetts. She traveled to England to present claims for compensation for their confiscated property at the end of the War. Settled in New Brunswick; never married.

Winthrop, Hannah Fayerweather (d. 1789), wife of John Winthrop, professor of Mathematicks and Natural Philosophy at Harvard College. Close friend of Mercy Otis Warren. Her portrait by John S. Copley is at the Metropolitan Museum of Art.

Wister, Sarah "Sally" (1761-1804), oldest daughter of Quaker Daniel Wister and Lowry Jones. She attended Anthony Benezet's school for girls, was well-read, and adept with her needle. She never married, but took care of her elderly mother during the remaining years of her life. Sally Wister's sampler (1773) is at the Philadelphia Museum of Art.

Wright, Patience Lovell (1725-1786), daughter of John Lovell and Patience Townsend of Oyster Bay, Long Island. Gained renown as a sculptor: her wax portrait of William Pitt, Earl of Chatham, is in Westminster Abbey. Her sister Rachel was also a sculptor, and her son Joseph became a well-known portrait painter.

Yeates, Sarah Burd (1748/9-1829), daughter of James Burd and Sarah Shippen of Philadelphia. Married lawyer Jasper Yeates in 1767; he later was an associate justice of Pennsylvania's Supreme Court. They had nine children (including twins), four of whom lived to adulthood.

Setting the Scene

(Say,) can a woman's voice an audience gain?

Annis Boudinot Stockton

Countless volumes have been written about the American Revolution and the early Republic. The central roles that George Washington, Thomas Jefferson, Benjamin Franklin, and other giant figures played continue to have an extraordinary hold on the imagination of readers young and old. It should not be otherwise. Yet an incomplete picture of the formative years of the United States emerges, because a large segment of the population—women—have either been ignored or relegated to footnotes. Yes, acknowledgments of the importance of such women as Mercy Otis Warren and her writings, of the insightful Abigail Smith Adams's correspondence, or of Jane McCrea, whose murder was used as an effective propaganda tool against Native Americans, appear in the literature. Nonetheless, too often women were viewed as incidental to the men who dominated the course of momentous occurrences and affected their lives. Anecdotes of Elizabeth "Betsy" Ross sewing a flag or Margaret Corbin ("Molly Pitcher") manning the cannon after her husband was killed or Lydia Darragh, "a little poor insignificant old woman,"[1] alerting General Washington to an imminent British attack are stirring stories but that is all they are, stories. They tell us nothing of the women's ideas or of their reactions to the events unfolding around them. And those events were significant.

The war that pitted the colonists against the Mother Country was initially not about independence. The British landed their well-drilled army to reestablish its authority[2] after the protests and violence occasioned by the Stamp Act and the Townshend Acts and to take what the colonists viewed as punitive actions. Ordinary men rushed to Boston to defend their "liberties." There was no standing army to confront the redcoats, only ill-assorted groups of militia. Some women also responded to the call to arms: camp followers, wives who refused to be left behind, women disguised as soldiers. The British had assumed that their superior forces would quickly bring an end to the "rebel" uprising, but found they were no match for the guerilla warfare the colonists then waged—sniping from behind stone walls, attacking suddenly and quickly disappearing.[3] Nor were British soldiers prepared to fight on rough, wild terrain, territory unlike the European fronts they were accustomed to.

One must remember that the loyalties of the colonists at first were not to the greater good but rather to their own town or colony. Benjamin Franklin's famous cartoon of the colonies as separated parts of the body of a snake with the slogan "Join, or Die" was as powerful a portrayal of the sectional jealousies that existed among the thirteen colonies in 1775 as it had been when first published in 1754.[4] The dangers of war, of epidemics spread by the armies, the economic hardships, the devaluation of the currency, and the uncertainty of survival played havoc with everyone's lives, whether patriot, loyalist, or uncommitted.

This book is an exploration of the observations and experiences of women who lived during the period 1765 to 1799 as expressed *in their own words*. Using excerpts of letters, diaries, journals, pamphlets, poems, plays, depositions, newspaper articles, the authors/editors demonstrate that everyday life continued, though with more complexity, during the political and military upheavals of the era. For modern readers, it is difficult to fully comprehend the circumscribed lives women led in eighteenth-century America; rarely traveling beyond the place where they were born, their roles were established early by their parents and reinforced by local religious leaders. Patriarchal societal strictures maintained the order of their often anonymous lives. When a woman was acknowledged at all, it might be in an obituary as the "wife of" or "daughter of" a man. If particularly praiseworthy, she might be cited as "respectful and peculiarly punctual in filial duty"[5] or as having "a sweetness of disposition, and singular propriety of conduct."[6] William Livingston, the father of several daughters, described the male ideal of women: they were "strangers to dissipation; nor were they seen constantly abroad. Their own habitation was their delight; and the rearing of their offspring their greatest pleasure . . . Queens without a crown, they were 'a crown to their husbands'; And not only saved their earnings by their economy; but augmented their treasure by their industry."[7] This view would have resonated with many, at all levels of society. Obedience to a father, husband, brother, even a son, supposedly possessed of greater intelligence and worldly knowledge, was regarded as the proper behavior for women.

During the American Revolution, the day-to-day existence of many white women—cooking, churning, washing, ironing, gardening, pickling, carding, spinning, weaving, sewing, teaching, shopping, visiting, not to forget dealing with pregnancies, miscarriages, illnesses, and death—changed. For black slave women, particularly on plantations, who performed unskilled field-labor,[8] and for many Indian women, whose main tasks were agricultural, the conflict disrupted but did not essentially alter their lives. White women not only had to manage their homes or farms and safeguard their families, especially if the men went off to war, but they were also called upon to support the political actions taken by the men. For example, had women not abstained from the purchase and use of imported goods, non-importation strictures would have been far less effective. Home-manufactured products became badges of honor. The contributions of men were not negated but, as Mary Fish Silliman claimed, "I have in some measure acted the *heroine* as well as my dear Husband the Hero." Or as Abigail Smith Adams wrote her husband in Holland, "I will take praise to myself. I feel that it is my due, for having sacrificed so large a portion of my peace and happiness to promote the welfare of my country."[9] To understand why Mary Silliman thought herself a "heroine" or why Abigail Adams took "praise to herself" allows the reader to participate in their lives, to become engaged in their hopes and fears.

The diversity of women's experiences found expression in a variety of forms. Phillis Wheatley, a young African slave, wrote poetry, signing it with her slave name. Mercy Otis Warren's political plays were published anonymously; although her history of the American Revolution, written largely during the 1780s, did not appear until 1805, her interest in politics is clear from her incisive letters. She wrote to the British historian Catharine Macaulay, "But 'tho America stands Armed with resolution & Virtue, She still Recoils at the thought of Drawing the sword against the state from whence she derived her Origen,"[10] a sentiment that paralleled that of her male contemporaries. A well-written letter was a joy to receive and something to savor, as Margaret Hill Morris noted to her sister Milcah: "when there's a pleasant passage, or witty remark . . . I read it for the benefit of our little circle, and then there's a sort of exclamation—oh! children when will you be able to write such a letter."[11] Sharing ideas, concerns, and affection on paper, the writers become real to us.

Journals and diaries were other forms of communication or remembrance. Ann Ashby Manigault of Charleston, South Carolina, used her journal to record visits, marriages, and deaths but showed little emotion: "1779. May 4. Great uneasiness on account of the British troops. 9th. Great Confusion as they were very near. 10. They were in sight of CharlesTown. 11th. Much fireing, and it was expected the town would be attacked."[12] Sally Cary Fairfax of Virginia, on the other hand, only made occasional, not wholly serious notations: "on Thursday, the 2nd of Jan, 1772, Margery [a slave] went to washing, & brought all the things in ready done, on Thursday the 9th of the same month. I think she was a great while about them, a whole week if you will believe me, reader."[13] For Quaker women, keeping a journal was particularly important, not only to recount daily events but as an opportunity for reflection and spiritual growth. Moreover, their journals were meant to be shared with family or close friends; it was well-known that Philadelphia Quaker Elizabeth Sandwith Drinker kept a journal—it was even mentioned in her obituary.

Women who were illiterate are heard in their recollections as told to family members or friends. Snapshots of anonymous lives may be gleaned from newspaper advertisements or announcements. Appearing in the *Constitutional Gazette* of New York on March 7, 1776 were the following: "Wanted, a Girl about twelve years old, to do the housework of a small Family." And "Wants a Place A healthy young Woman, with a good breast of Milk. Enquire of the Printer."[14] Businesswomen placed advertisements, giving the modern reader a wonderful view of what was fashionable:

> Just imported from London and selling by the subscriber, at a low advance for ready money only, . . . For ladies, a very neat and genteel assortment of wedding, mourning and second mourning, and children's shoes of all sizes, artificial hair pins, breast flowers equal in beauty to any ever imported, and so near resembles nature, that the nicest eye can hardly distinguish the difference; colored and white silk French kid, lamb gloves and mitts for ladies, girls, and chil-

dren. . . . As the above goods are fashionable, new and good, she hopes to meet with encouragement.

(Catherine Rathell, Oct. 6, 1768 in *Virginia Gazette*)

Advertisements were used for other purposes as well. When the brother of Christiana Young Leech of Kingsessing, Pennsylvania, failed to return from a trip collecting botanical specimens in Maryland, it was she who placed an advertisement, anxiously inquiring whether anyone had seen him.[15] Slave owners frequently resorted to newspapers to trace runaways: the cruelty and inhumanity of slavery is vividly captured in such advertisements:

RUN away from the Subscriber, in King and Queen, the 5th of October 1774, a Negro Woman named HANNAH, of the Middle Stature, remarkably black, has been hurt in one Side (I think the right) which makes her limp as she walks; had on, when she went away, a Negro Cotton Jacket, and a Virginia Cloth Petticoat, striped with black Yarn. Whoever secures her so that I may get her again (if in this Colony) shall have 40 s. Reward.

JOHN CARDWELL (June 17, 1775 in *Virginia Gazette.*)

Women, in their attempts to be heard, availed themselves of petitions and depositions. These documents reveal the social and economic stresses women had to deal with just to survive. Ruth McGee, an Irish indentured servant, went to court in Pennsylvania suing her Quaker master for her promised "freedom Dues . . . A new Suit of clothes for freedoms and five Pounds in Money."[16] On the other hand, Sarah Matthews Osborn waited many years to file a pension claim for her service during the War. She recalled, while at West Point, "the uproar occasioned when word came that a British officer had been taken as a spy." She trekked, "part of the time on horseback and part of the time in a wagon" with the army to Philadelphia, and on to Yorktown, Virginia, where, after the surrender of General Cornwallis, she carried food to the soldiers "whom she was in the habit of cooking for."[17]

To retain the immediacy of the voices of the 124 women presented in this volume, their accounts have been divided into three sections: the first narrates events chronologically, from the prelude to the Revolution through its prosecution and aftermath—broadly ranging from New England to the South. The second section deals with daily life in wartime and in peace. The last section returns to a chronological progression, surveying the beginnings of the new government and how it dealt with difficult issues at home and abroad. When placed within historical contexts, readers may more readily enjoy the famous like Martha Dandridge Custis Washington and the lesser known such as Christiana Young Leech. The focus remains squarely on the women themselves, as observers and/or participants, involved or not, expressing in words their perspectives on their experiences.

Finally, readers may become their own historians by drawing inferences and conclusions for themselves; to consider, for instance, what significant changes, if any, occurred in the lives of women after the War. Although Mercy Otis Warren viewed the country, "established on the broad basis of the elective voice of the people,"[18] with justifiable pride, a sizable portion of the American population was, in fact, disenfranchised. Education for women became more accepted—but only for the elite. Black women were still enslaved or obliged to work in subservient positions. Native American women actually lost some of the stature and influence they had enjoyed within their nations. The continued denial of economic, political, and religious independence limited, once again, women's influence to the domestic realm. Elizabeth Ann Seton succinctly reflected that view: "And myself! I am jogging on old style, trying to accomplish every duty, and hoping for the reward [of heaven]." Elizabeth Murray Inman, on the other hand, had a different perspective. Although in poor health, stuck in an unhappy marriage, a loyalist living in straitened circumstances, the fifty-seven-year-old Inman would not meekly accept her brother John Murray's criticisms of her efforts to be independent and self-sufficient, not to mention encouraging those qualities in other women. She retorted, "I rejoice that the spirit of Independence caused such exertions as to place me in a situation that I am content to pass the remainder of my days in, untaught as I was I am surprised & my heart overflows with gratitude at the success I have met with."[19]

Part I
Women During the American Revolution

Figure 4. *A New Touch on the Times by a 'Daughter of Liberty'* (1779). Woodcut, detail. Courtesy of The New-York Historical Society.

Chapter 1

advancing toward a State of Independancy

The British were triumphant. The signing of the Treaty of Paris in 1763 had brought an end to the Seven Years' War, the empire-building conflict between England and France that had engulfed large portions of the globe. France had lost a continent, been driven out of Canada, and ceded Louisiana and territories west of the Mississippi River to its ally Spain, which, in turn, had yielded possession of East and West Florida to England. Though the French and Indian War, as it is called in America, was viewed as tangential to the larger conflict, the colonists who had fought for King and Country thought otherwise. Putting aside differences and pulling together, they had helped defend themselves against England's enemies and had prevailed.

As a result, the colonists gained confidence and self-assurance in their ability to manage their own affairs. While nominally under the control of the Crown, the colonies in reality had become virtually autonomous. Given their distance from England and the difficulties of communication, they were able to govern themselves for the most part and to ignore the mother country's economic strictures and duties when it served their interests. Nevertheless, the colonists insisted they possessed the rights claimed by all Englishmen since the Magna Carta. They enjoyed many privileges that their compatriots in Britain did not, including a degree of religious toleration, and considerable freedom of the press. While they were proud of being part of the great British Empire they were not willing any longer to be subordinate members politically or economically.

Because the War had seriously depleted British coffers, the government of George III sought to raise money for "defraying the expenses of defending, protecting and securing" America. One attempt was the Stamp Act of 1765, which imposed a direct tax on such items as bills of lading, playing cards, dice, and marriage licenses. Protests throughout the colonies were many and often violent: stamp agents were tarred and feathered, officials were hanged in effigy. Delegates from nine of the thirteen colonies met to discuss how to deal with the growing discontent. In addition to sending a list of their grievances to the King, they agreed to stop the importation of British goods. Groups such as the Sons of Liberty enforced the ban and encouraged the use of homespun garments. Clothing and fabric production were in the domain of women, consequently their support was essential.[1]

DEBORAH READ ROGERS FRANKLIN, the industrious and frugal helpmeet of Benjamin Franklin, had not accompanied her husband to England, where he had gone to represent Pennsylvania's interests. Also left behind were his sister, Jane Mecom; his son William, the governor of New Jersey; and his daughter Sally. In Deborah's capable hands he left the day-to-day management of their affairs and the oversight of the construction of their new house. Never complaining that she had to act as both father and mother during her husband's long absence, she described her daily life with resolution and good-humor although it became increasingly difficult. Deborah never saw him again. (As Deborah's idiosyncratic spelling is frequently difficult to decipher, only the first paragraph has been kept as written. It's best to read it out loud.)

nothing . . . but pamphlets and Scurrility

[Philadelphia] Feb the 10, [1765]

I am set down to Confab a littel with my dear child as it Semes a Sorte of a hollow day for we have an ox arosteing on the [Delaware] river and moste pepel semes plesd with the a fair but as I partake of none of the divershons I stay at home and flatter myselef that the next packit [boat] will bring me a letter from you. . . .

We have nothing stirring among us but pamphlets and Scurrility but I have never said or done anything or any of our family, you may depend on it nor shall we. All our good friends Call on us as usual and we have been asked out but I have not gone but Sally has within this month. But She was at Billeys [Governor William Franklin] almost seven weeks.

This day the man is putting up the fireplaces that Came from London; the dark one is in the parlor. I am in hopes the hearths will be laid. The weather will begin to be warmer and the Sun Stronger. The plasterer is a finishing the lathing of the stair Cases and I am a getting the lower part of the house cleaned, all ready for the laying the kitchen floor. All this about the house.

Feb. 17

On Friday I got a man to help George [a Franklin slave] to Cut and Clear away the Ice at the street door and about the pump . . . It was near three feet thick. I never knew such a winter in my time but I am in hopes the worst of the weather is over. For several days, George and myself have been at the New house a getting the rooms ready for the painter . . . I shall get the hearths Laid and, if very Cold weather is, then we Can make a fire to prevent the paint receiving any damage. I only wish I was removed, then I hope to be more relieved, but I have not one hour my own at this time as a report is got about that you are arrived in London, and our friends all Come to know for themselves.

Feb. the 21

This morning is so very Cold that I Can hardly hold a pen in my hand so shall write to you again as soon as possible. . . .

I am my Deareste Childe youre afeckshonet wife   D Franklin

disorder in this part of the world

My Dear child   September 22 1765

I have received yours by Capt. Friend and one which was to a Come by N York and by the packet and yesterday by Capt. Cotin; they all give me pleasure indeed and I love to hear from you. I am so very poor a writer that I dont undertake to say anything about the disorder in this part of the world. But to me it seems we are very wicked and so is the people in London and other places on your side the water. I pray god mend us all.

You will see by the papers what work has happened in other places and something has been said relating to raising a mob in this place. I was for 9 days kept in one Continued hurry by people to remove and Sally was persuaded to go to Burlington [New Jersey, where William Franklin resided] for safety. But on monday last we had very great rejoicing on account of the Change of Ministry* and a preparation for bonfires at night and several houses threatened to be pulled down. Cousin [Josiah] Davenport Came and told me that more than twenty people had told him it was his Duty to be with me. I said I was pleased to receive Civility from anybody, so he stayed with me some time. Towards night, I said he should fetch a gun or two as we had none. I sent to ask my Brother [John or her brother-in-law Peter Franklin] to Come and bring his gun also, so we made one room into a Magazine. I ordered some sort of defense upstairs such as I Could manage myself. I said when I was advised to remove that I was very sure you had done nothing to hurt anybody. Nor I had not given any offense to any person at all nor would I be made uneasy by any body nor would I stir or show the least uneasiness. But if anyone Came to disturb me, I would show a proper resentment and I should be very much affronted with anybody. . . .

I should not forget Mr. John Ross and Brother Swore it is Mr. Saml Smith [a Philadelphia merchant] that is a setting the people a-mading by telling them that it was you that had planned the Stamp act . . . but as I dont go much to town I maybe shall be easy for awhile after the election is over but till that I must be disturbed. . . . god bless you and keep you is the prayer of yours forever

D Franklin

*In August 1765, Prime Minister George Grenville (1712-1770), who had instituted the Stamp Act, was replaced by Charles Watson-Wentworth, 2d marquess Rockingham.

O how I despise such men

My Dear Child   [Oct. 8-13, 1765]

I have been to see Mr. Hughes [the designated stamp distributor] who I found a little better and able to stir himself which I know will give you pleasure and the more so as you will hear no doubt how he has been used and by men that better things might be expected from. First to have the bells muffled and send two Drums about the town to raise the mob, and send them under Mr. Hughes' window; then send messengers to tell him that they was a Coming and would be there in a minute and almost terrify his wife and Children to death; and after this, the man who was at the head of their affair to Complement himself with the merit of preventing the mob from falling on and destroying Mr. Hughes and his whole family. . . . O how I despise such men. . . .

Yesterday I put on board of Capt. Friend the same bail [bucket] that you
sent to us filled with Cranberries. I Could not get as many as would fill a Barrel
nor I Could not get a half Barrel . . . I hope they will keep. . . .

I thank you for the worsted, the Sugar nippers, and the muslin for my apron,
and for the Curtains. I think them very handsome. . . .

as ever yours till Death   D Franklin[2]

The Stamp Act was repealed—"the Town [Philadelphia] illuminated upon
the occasion" dryly noted Elizabeth Sandwith Drinker in her Journal (May 20,
1766)—but the colonists were not appeased; they claimed that the British Parliament was not only tyrannical in taxing those who had no representation but
was impinging on their "natural rights." Undeterred, the British imposed a new
tax (Townshend Acts 1767) on imports of glass, lead, paints, paper, and tea.
Once again, there were protests, boycotts, and violence.

HANNAH GRIFFITTS, a Quaker, was a prolific writer of letters and poetry. Involved in the religious and political concerns of her day, she did not wish to
publish her poems, usually signed with a pseudonym, but shared them with
friends and family. Her cousin, Milcah Martha Moore, copied Griffitts's poem
in her *Commonplace Book*.

The female Patriots

Address'd to the Daughters of Liberty in America, 1768

Since the Men from a Party, on fear of a Frown,
Are kept by a Sugar-Plumb, quietly down,
Supinely asleep, and depriv'd of their Sight
Are strip'd of their Freedom, and rob'd of their Right.
If the Sons (so degenerate) the Blessings despise,
Let the Daughters of Liberty, nobly arise,
And tho' we've no Voice, but a negative here,
The use of the Taxables, let us forbear,
(Then Merchants import till yr. Stores are all full
May the Buyers be few and yr. Traffick be dull.)
Stand firmly resolved and bid Grenville to see
That rather than Freedom, we'll part with our Tea
And well as we love the dear Draught when adry,
As American Patriots,—our Taste we deny,
Sylvania's, gay Meadows, can richly afford
To pamper our Fancy, or furnish our Board,
And Paper sufficient (at home) still we have,
To assure the Wise-acre, we will not sign Slave.
When this Homespun shall fail, to remonstrate our Grief
We can speak with the Tongue or scratch on a Leaf
Refuse all their Colours, the richest of Dye,

The juice of a Berry—our Paint can supply,
To humour our Fancy—and as for our Houses,
They'll do without painting as well as our Spouses,
While to keep out the Cold of a keen winter Morn
We can screen the Northwest, with a well polish'd Horn.
And trust Me a Woman by honest Invention,
Might give this State Doctor a Dose of Prevention.
Join mutual in this, and but small as it seems
We may jostle a Grenville and puzzle his Schemes
But a motive more worthy our patriot Pen,
Thus acting—we point out their Duty to Men,
And should the bound Pensioners, tell us to hush
We can throw back the Satire by biding them blush.[3]

CHARITY CLARKE, at nineteen years of age, had visited relatives in England, returning to her home in Chelsea, New York City, during the summer of 1767. The daughter of a retired British Army captain, and thus a potential loyalist, she was, in fact, not afraid to speak her mind in support of the American cause, urging that "the honesty of her heart & sincerity of her professions" merited the esteem of her younger cousin, Joseph Jekyll of Lincoln's Inn, London. Her letters, containing lively commentary on the political situation, ended abruptly in 1774 prior to her marriage to the Reverend Benjamin Moore, an America-born Tory and rector of Trinity Church.

we will found a new arcadia

[Claremont, New York June 16th, 1768]

You see my dear Joe I loose no opertunity of writing to you & like the woman in the Gospel, am determined to be importunate till you grant my request of leting me hear from you oftner, it is I know not how many months since I have received one line; and have been expecting to hear I know not how many fine things of the King of Denmarks masqiurade; I will own I wished myself at that entertainment & work Just wishing I were preparing to go Rhenelaugh* to night; don't think for all this that I prefer England to America; I would not quit my woods & rivers, for all the gay amusements you abound with, you need not talk of the old story of sower [sour] grapes; I assure you the way of life that would be to me the most agreable is downright Indian; and if you English folks won't give us the liberty we ask . . . I will try to gather a number of Ladies armed with spining wheels, & attended by dying swains, who shall all learn to weave, & keep sheep and will retire beyond the reach of arbitrary power; cloathed with the work of our hands & feeding on what the country affords, without any of the cares Luxuries, or oppression of an long inhabited country, in short we will found a new arcadia; you Imagine we cannot live without your assistance, but I know we can; banish every thing but the necessaries of life; & we will want nothing but what our country will afford. We shall then be happy; no more Slaves to fashion, & ceremony; *freedom* can content & peace shall be our constant companions. Each Father shall be king of his family & no other power shall be admitted; the first who shews any marks of ambition shall with the joint consent of the community be sent back to dwell with those who prefer slavery and Luxury, to Liberty & a sufficiency.

I left home a few days ago in order to spend a month with a young lady near an hundred miles from N York and came by water when I had the pleasure of sailing up such a river [the Hudson] as England can not boast of, it is true we did not see a country so well cultivated as it might have been had it run through any part of England; but it is the most romantick prospect you ever saw, nor does it want any variety that rocks which seem made almost for the foundation of a world, woods & mountains can give it. Nor is it entirely uncultivated we saw feilds of Grain & vilages & frequently houses, the winding of the river & the number of sloops that were going & coming made it a delightful scene; you may boast the work of art, and beauties the consequence of countries long settled & filled with inhabitants. Nature has given us the advantage & when this country is as much improved as yours, we will exceed you as much in the beauty &c of that, as we do now in virtue, excel the inhabitants of Great Britain.

You may think I puff, I will appeal to Capt. Jekyll; he knows wither I do or no. . . .   your affectionate Cousin & Sincere friend Chay. Clarke

*Rhenelaugh is Ranelagh Garden, a tavern and pleasure garden used for concerts, fireworks, and entertainments in London. There was also one on Broadway in New York.

I am kniting stockins

[Harlem Nov. 6, 1768]

My dear Cousins letters, together with the Bundle I have received & am vastly pleased with, my gown was beyond my expectations, and everything else in good order. . . . so you will not commend (or indeed believe there is any thing in our) Patriotism, as for being complimented on the occasion we americans despise Compliments of any kind, but shew you we are not tired of our spining wheels, & that the love of novelty (as you are pleased to call it) has been of some use to us. Mrs Watkins has had spun in her house, a suit of Cloth for Mr. Watkins, as handsome as he wishes to wear, I am kniting stockins for my father of yarn spun at Mr W which he declares will be the best he was ever master of. As to your republican systems we never thought of them happy under the Constitution of G.B. provided that was not exceeded, but when there is the least shew of opression or invading of Libertys, you may depend on our exerting ourselves to the utmost of our power, & though the Heroines may not distinguish themselves at the head of an army, yet that Hero who stands forth for the Liberty of his country & shews he has it at heart shall be the greatest favorite of the ladies.

What a pretty figure your expedition to Boston will make in History . . . shall not we have the English news papers filled with the belicous [bellicose] Conquest of Boston, how prudent a Comander, whose wisdom should so fright a people as to disperse them (when never gathered together) without the loss of a man and restore quiet to a City (that was at peace before) without the least blood shed. Governor [Sir Francis] Bernard is . . . thought the cause of the present disturbance by misrepresenting the people of Boston at home, of every thing that passes tho you I suppose will have a full account in the papers. General Gage is gone to see what can be done with this troublesome people who contrary to every other people don't like to entertain a parcel of men in thier own houses when there is Barracks ready for thier reception.

The American politicians think you are a set of very wise men in England; they admire your proceedings vastly, your resenting our refusal of paying taxes, you have no right to lay on us, & Grumble at paying yourselves, we think very generous,—as to Insurrection we know of none, & unruly mobs we leave to England, they don't govern America—and it is very remarkable that during the time of the stamp act when there were such numbers of people gathered together there was no blood shed . . . wig & Tory still appear in our papers though they are seldom read & news from Boston is all that commands attention at present . . . don't you wish my Epistle was at an end? You shall have your wish Imediately.

The King I hope is inclined to do us good

My dear Cousin   [Chelsea Decr 8 1768]

When I spoke of my Arcadian scheme did not I mention something of spinning Wheels & weavers? I think I did, at least I meant it, don't you think a country may be fine by nature without the assistance of the Husbandman? I boast a variety in America, a large extent of country should not I think be all improved to make it pleasing especially where nature does so much as in this country she has done, let each country be left to the enjoyment of its inhabitants . . . The King I hope is inclined to do us good, the ministers I wish may shew themselves prudent, Americans will shew they are only obstinate in the right & that reason has ever guided their actions. I wish you near enough to mend my pen, its badness hurries me to conclude.

the attention of every American is fixed on England

My dear Joe   [March 31, 1769]

The attention of every american is fixed on England: the last accounts from thence are very displeasing to those who wish a good understanding between Britain & her Colonies; the Americans are firm in their resolution of no importations from England. The want of money is so great among us, that Land sells for less than half price: the merchants have no cash to buy bills of exchange which are now very low it is feared be fore next year the town will be filled with Bancrupts; this is want of paper currency; the papers have abounded with complaints from Boston of the military & of thier Governor.

where Virtue reigns

                                                 [New York Oct. 28, 1771]

You smile at our Routs & talk of Strange matamorpheses, but they are only supposed ones, yes the Rigid Beauties of N York frequent assemblies, where inocent amusement promotes good humour, where modesty may appear without a Blush, where Inocence has no foe, & where Virtue reigns; are the assemblies of Great Britain such? If they are, unjustly do we condemn them, as Fashion is an Usurper submitted to in most part of the Globe. America is not free from her

Governmint, but then it is only the Habit she takes directions of; our manners are Governed by Reason, and Religion forms our principles—

That Spirit which led Americans to their distress, & made them clad themselves in Homespun, is not fled, & when cause is given will exert itself with double vigor, while we can with Honor wear the soft & ornamental Garbs which Britain furnishes us with, we will repay her for them,—But no sooner do they appear the Badges of disgrace & the marks of true submission to unjustifiable exertions of power than with disdain we will cast them from us, & shew you we *can* do without them.

When americans marry, affection founded on esteem unites them, Truth & Virtue their choice—Love & Constancy their reward; they marry not Gold nor form Alliances with Titles—so need not fear divorce. Coteries we know not the meaning of—affective patriotism & True Virtue will I trust distinguish America in every Age; and among every nation. —So my Dear Coz you see your fears are growndless, America still practices the long (though unboasted) list of Virtues which the Generality of English men have scarce an Idea of. . . .

> your affectionate Cousin & friend   Cha Clarke[4]

ANNE HULTON, late in 1767, accompanied her brother Henry Hulton, his wife Elizabeth and their year-old son, from England to Boston where he had been named Commissioner of Customs by King George III. Almost from the very moment they set foot on American soil, their lives were in danger. Anne Hulton's letters to her friend Mrs. Adam Lightbody in Garston (near Liverpool), England, dramatically describe the upheavals experienced by the colonists, loyalist and patriot alike.

it is quite a State of Anarchy

Dr Madam   Castle William Boston Harbor June 30, 1768
I presume it will be agreeable to you to hear that my Brors Family had a good Voyage of 5 Weeks & arrived all well at Boston the 5th Inst. You will be surprized to hear how we were obliged to fly from the Place in six Days after & take Refuge on board the *Romney* Man of War lying in Boston Harbour. Mrs. Burch at whose house I was, had frequently been alarmd with the Sons of Liberty surroundg her house with most hideous howlings as the Indians, when they attack an Enemy. To many insults & outrages She had been exposed since her arrival, & threatened with greater voilences. She had had removed her most valuable Effects & held herself in readiness to depart at an hours notice. The Occasion soon happend, when my Sister [in-law] & I accompanyd her at 10 oClock at night to a Neighbours house, not apprehendg much danger, but we soon found that the Mobs here are very different from those in Old England where a few lights put into the Windows will pacify, or the interposition of a Magistrate restrain them. But here they act from principle & under Countenance, no person daring or willing to suppress their Outrages, or to punish the most notorious Offenders for any Crimes whatever. These Sons of Voilence after attacking Houses, breakg Windows, beating, Stoning & bruizing several Gentlemen belonging to the Customs, the Collector mortally, & burning his boat. They

consultd what was to be done next, & it was agreed to retire for the night. All was ended wth a Speech from one of the Leaders, concludg thus, "We will defend our Liberties & property, by the Strength of our Arm & the help of our God, to your Tents O Israel." This is a Specimen of the Sons of Liberty, of whom no doubt you have heard, & will hear more.

The next Day the Commissrs had sufficient notice of their danger & the Plots against them. All their friends Advised em to retire to a more secure place, The Governor particularly telling em it was not in his power to protect em.

That Eveng Saturdy We set off in a Barge under a Convoy of Man of Wars Boats, wth Mariners, their bayonets fixed, to the *Romney*, a fifty Gun Ship of War, lying ready in the Harbour. About fifty of us Refugees, were well accommodated, & very genteelly entertaind there for nine Days, The Captns Lady being on board. On the 21st Inst We removed to this Castle, by the Governors permission. This was a Scene you will beleive quite new to me, & indeed the series of events since leaving Old England appears romantic. . . .

From the inherent Republican, & leveling principles, heres no subordination in the Society. Government is extirpated, & it is quite a State of Anarchy. There are some sensible & good people that are greatly alarmed at their impendg fate,—The infant Colonies have been advancing toward a State of Independancy. Many things have concurrd to bring on the Crisis sooner than expected. The Sedition has been falsely representd at home as a dying Faction—but the defection is too general. Most of the other Provinces are only waiting to see the event of this effort in Boston. The poison of disaffection has been infused & spread by inflamatory writers over the Continent.

[The unrest subsided, and the Hulton family was able to leave Castle William Island by November. Henry Hulton bought a house in Brookline, which they very much enjoyed; even there, however, they came under attack and were forced to return to the fort. Anne Hulton took up her pen to chronicle the situation.]

a Plot artfully contrived

Castle Island Near Boston, July 25. 1770

It's true we have long been in a dangerous situation, from the State of Government. The want of protection, the perversion of the Laws, & the spirit of the People, inflamed by designing men. Yet our house in the Country has been a place of retreat for many, from the disturbances of the Town, & tho' they were become very alarming, yet we did not apprehend an immediate attack on our House, or that a Mob out of Boston sho'd come so far, before we had notice of it, & were fully perswd. there are Persons more obnoxious than my Bror, that he had no personal Enemy, & confident of the good will of our Neighbours (in the Township we live in) towds. him so that we had no suspicion of what happened the night of June the 19th—we have reason to believe it was not the sudden outrage of a frantic Mob, but a Plot artfully contrived to decoy My Bror into the hands of assassins, at Midnight when the Family was asleep. Had not a merciful Providence preventd their designs, we had been a distressd Family indeed.

Between 12 & 1 o'Clock he was wake'd by a knocking at the Door, he got up, enquired the person's name and business, who said he had a letter to deliver to him, wch came Express from New York. My Bror puts on his Cloaths, takes his drawn Sword in one hand, & open'd the Parlor window wth the other. The Man ask'd for a Lodging—said he, I'll not open my door, but give me the letter. The man then put his hand, attempting to push up the window, upon wch my Bror hastily clap'd it down, instantly wth a bludgeon several violent blows were struck wch broke the Sash, Glass & frame to pieces. The first blow aimed at my Bror Head, he Providentialy escaped, by its resting on the middle frame, being double. At same time (tho' before then, no noise or appearance of more Persons than one) the lower windows, all round the House (excepting two) were broke in like manner. My Bror stood in amazement for a Mint. or 2, & having no doubt that a number of Men had broke in on several sides of the House, he retired Upstairs.

You will believe the whole Family was soon alarm'd, but the horrible Noises from without, & the terrible shrieks within the House from Mrs. H: & Servants wch struck my Ears on awaking, I can't describe, & shall never forget.

I cou'd imagine nothing less than that the House was beating down, after many violent blows on the Walls & windows, most hideous Shouting, dreadful imprecations, & threats ensued. Struck with terror & astonishment, what to do I knew not, but got on some Cloaths, & went to Mrs. H: room, where I found the Family collected; a Stone thrown in at her window narrowly missd her head. When the Ruffians were retreating with loud huzza's & one cry'd he will fire,— no says another, he darn't fire, we will come again says a third—Mr and Mrs H: left their House immediately & have not lodged a night since in it.

The next day we were looking up all the Pockit pistols in the house some of wch were put by, that nobody coud find 'em & ignorant of any being charged, Kitty was very near shooting her Mistress, inadvertently lets it off. The bullets miss'd her within an inch & fixd in a Chest of Drawers. Here was another miraculous escape, so that we have reason to be thankful, we are all safe & well, tho' truly Prisoners in a Castle, the old place of refuge.

But there is no security from the virulence of Lying Tongues, can you believe it, that a person shall suffer abuse, an attack upon his House, & attempt on his Life, & afterwds the reproach of having done it himself. . . .

If G: Britain leaves Boston to itself, tho' its own honour will not be maintaind thereby, it will certainly be the greatest punishment that can be inflicted on the place and people, but a cruelty to some individuals, who have shewn themselves fr[ien]ds. to Governmt. The Town is now in the greatest confusion, the People quarreling violently about Importation, & Exportation.

The New Yorkers having broke thro' their nonimportation agreemt, is a heavy Stroke, & tho' 90 out a 100 of the Mercts. & traders here, want to do the same, yet they are terrified to submit to [the] Tyranny of that Power they at first set up, & are going to reship their British Goods, tho' its expected there will be some broken Noses first, & that these combinations cannot hold long. However the Trade of the Town is ruin'd & the principal Branch that of Ship Building, wch supported some hundred of Families, is removed by the Glassgow Mercts. to other places, because their Goods were not allowd to be [disposed] of here.

[Several months later, back in the house in Brookline, Anne Hulton portrayed their lives as farmers to her friend on March 20, 1771.]

I am Director General of the Vegatible Tribe

I fancy the Spring is opening upon you in O: England whilst we are surrounded with a deep Snow & freezing with severe cold, a long & sharp winter we shall have, & perhaps, towards May or June suddenly emmerge from the depth of it, into the height of Summer, without the pleasure of a Spring, or but a short one. Yet here are pleasures which even this frozen state, & sequesterd Situation affords, for there are few days but what we might make excursions in Sleighs (carriages without wheels that travel extreamly quick 10 or 12 Miles an hour,) while Nature Smiles in a bright Sky, & a white world around us. We don't in the least envy the inhabitants of the Town, finding here no want of society as you may think, when Mrs H: had near 50 Ladies from Boston &c to visit her in her Lying in.

We are Farmers without expecting to reap any profit, besides that of health & pleasure. I believe it's very conducive to my Brors Health being obliged to ride to Town frequently, & the relaxation & amusement wch his little Farm affords. He has made great improvements, & built Barns, Stables, and many conveniences, amongst the rest a Green house, in order to preserve Vegetables in the Winter, & raise early plants so that we may be supplied all the year round. Tho' this appears quite a necessary, & is generaly approved as a great convenience, yet it's what has not been done before in this Province. I have studied Gardening here, & by my observation, & experience, have acquired a little Skill, so that I am Director General of the Vegatible Tribe. Tho' our Farmer is a good common Gardener, yet many things we require, wch are not used to be raised here. We put in the Green house last fall 500 heads of the finest Celery that ever was seen here. I have never seen a Artichoke or Broccoli in this Country, but shall attempt to raise these now. . . . I have been told that it's only of late years that Greens or Cabbages have been raised in this Country at all or in any plenty. All Greens or roots are calld by the name of Sause here. As to fruits, Apricots & Necterans are rarieties indeed, but Peaches, Strawberries, & Gooseberries grow wild, yet these, compared with those cultivated in Gardens in Old Engld are in Size as crabs to Apples, & of little value, we have these in Garden cultivated besides currance & rasberries but all scarse wth us, the Birds devouring 'em when ripe.

My Bror has planted some hundreds of Fruit Trees of all sorts . . . There's a great enemy to the Fruit, a kind of Worm that rises out of the Ground into the Trees, as soon as the Frost breaks, destroys the Apples ere they Bud, & all the Leaves, so that all the Trees round us, appears with a most dreary aspect in the Summer. There's only one remedy to prevent this Evil, found out, that is, Taring all the Trees for about 3 months every Evening after sunsett. This is a great piece of work for our Farmer, for if one evening be miss'd it renders all ineffectual, & even this practice destroys the Trees in time, to guard against wch, a girdle of Cloth is bound round each Tree, by this means my Bror has preserved his Fruit, whilst many of our Neighbors who wod not be at the trouble & expense, have all been destroyd, . . .

It's not so very cheap Living in this Country as some imagine, tho' provisions are plenty, yet they grow dearer I believe all over the world, as its what the Inhabitants here complain of. Some think the Navy & Army has helpd to raise the prices of things, however I believe the People are so civil to us Strangers, or new comers, to make us pay more handsomely for everything, than they do their own people. Fish is the cheapest thing for wch we must Send to Boston. Butchers meat passes our Door; we pay for mutton & veal 3d & 3½d Sterling a pound. Beef something Less, Pork more. Fresh butter is not to be procured in Winter, but we get fine Tub Butter at 6½d Sterlg a pound.

Our wild fowl are cheifly Quails, Partridges, Pigeons, & Robins—woodcocks & Snipes are great variety. . . . we have rabbits & Hares but very different from what they are in England. What they call Hares are more like Rabbits, small & white as Snow, & unsavory meat . . . Squrrils are eat here. . . . We in this retreat are never better satisfied [than] wth plain Roast. . . .

Dear Madm your Affectionate   A Hulton[5]

Not only British officials were under attack, so too were ordinary people: businessmen and women, who continued to trade with Great Britain, and who saw their livelihoods endangered.

CHRISTIAN ARBUTHNOT BARNES, the wife of Henry Barnes, a businessman in Marlborough, Massachusetts, kept her friend, Elizabeth Murray Campbell Smith, who was in Scotland, informed of the situation. Smith, a successful Boston business woman who sold women's hats and dry goods as well as teaching sewing, assisted other women to become self-sufficient. Two orphaned Bostonian sisters, Ame and Elizabeth "Betsy" Cuming, benefited from Smith's help in setting up a small shop, giving sewing lessons and importing dry goods from England. The sisters were outraged by the accusations against them of not adhering to the non-importation agreements: "to try to inger two industrious Girls who were Striving in an honest way to Get there Bread." Though listed as "Enimys to their Country," as Mrs. Barnes related, the shop prospered.

Polliticks is a Puddle I never chose to dabble in

Marlborough, November 20, 1769

Last thrusday, which was Thanksgiving Day a Ball was given by Mrs. [James] Murray at Brush Hill [in Milton, Massachusetts] to a number of Gentlemen and Ladys from Boston. Miss E. Cumings was one of the Party. Their goods and ours are arrived in very good order, which has caused a Commity [Committee] from the Well disposed [the patriots] to wait upon them and write to Mr. Barnes with a desire that the Goods may be stored till further orders. And so they are to better purpose I hope then they design'd them for; they are well

Charg'd and I dare say will have a quick Sail [sale]. In short those dareing Sons of Libberty are now at the tip top of their Power and . . . even to Speak disrespectfully of the well disposed is a Crime equal to high Treason . . . When the deluded multitude finds they have been led astray by false maxims they may Possibly turn upon them with their own Weapons, what they are many innocent Sufferers have fatally expearanced. This is my Private opinion, but how I came to give it is a mistry for Polliticks is a Puddle I never chose to dabble in.

Enimys to their Country

Dec 23, 1769

Oh how I long to have one political Laugh with you would you not be deverted to see Squire Barnes and the Two little Miss Cumingses Posted together in a News Paper as Enimys to their Country; do Bless you, send us a little Dash of Politicks from tother side the Water that we may see something that has the appearance of Truth, for our well disposed support such a vast quantity of lies with their other articles that they begin to find a Difficulty in vending them. . . . and now Madm I have only to wish you a Merry Christmas and take my leave of you. . . .Your affectionate Friend,   C. Barnes

I want to vent myself

June 28–July 6, 1770

Dear Mad'm,—It is long since I have dabled in Politicks, and sorry I am to resume the subject. . . . nor would I now trouble you with it but that I want to vent myself, and . . . "To whom shall I complain if not to you?"

The Spirit of discord and confusion which has prevail'd with so much violence in Boston has now begun to spread it self into the country. These Poor deluded People with whom we have lived so long in Peice & harmony have been influenced by the Sons of Rapin to take every method to distress us, at their March meeting they enter'd into resolves Simuler to those you have often seen in the Boston news Papers. At their next meeting they Chose four inspectors, (Men of the most virulent disposition of any in the Town,) to Watch those who should purchas goods at the Store with intent that their names should be recorded as enimies to their Country. This did not deter those from coming who had not voted to the resolves. . . .

While all this was in agitation their was great outrages committed & insults offer'd to the Importers in Boston, so that some of them have been compell'd to quit the Town as not only their Property but their lives were in Danger. Nor are we wholly free from apprehentions of the like treetment, for they have already begun to commit outrages. The first thing that fell a Sacrifice to their mallace and reveng was the Coach, which caused so much decention between us. This they took the cushings out of and put them in the Brook, and the next night Cut the Carraig to peices. Not long after they Broke the Windows at the Pearl Ash Works. . . .

The greatest loss we have as yet met with was by a mob in Boston, who, a few Nights ago, atacked a wagon Load of goods which belong'd to us. They abused the Driver, and cut a Bag of Pepper, which contain'd three hundred pd, leting it all into the street; then gather'd it up in their Hand[kerchie]fs & Hatts, and carried it off. The rest of the load they order'd back into the Publick Store, of which the well disposed Commity keeps the Key. . . .

[The 11th of June] an Effigy was Hung upon a Hill in Sight of the House, with a paper Pin'd to the Breast, whereon was wrote Henry Barnes an Infamous importer. This Hung up all Day, and at night they Burnt it, a few nights after they Stole the covering from the wagon (which was tar'd to secure the goods from the Weather) and the same night Stole a man's Horse from a neighbouring Stable. They Dres'd an Image in this wagon covering, tar'd the Horse Saddle & Bridle, Placed the Image upon his back, and set him loose about the Town, with an infamous Paper Pin'd to the Breast, which was sum'd up with wishing of us all in Hell. But still finding that their malace had no effect, that their Proceedings did not deter the other Towns from coming more then ever to the Shop and that we appear'd unmoved at all that Pas'd, they made a Bold Push and drop'd an incendiry Letter. . . .

It is not possible for me to express what I suffer'd upon the perusal of this Letter. I could not recolect any one Person that we had ever injured or even wish'd ill to, nor could I imagin'd such Villiny ever enterd into the Heart of man. . . . [I received word] that one of the McMasters had been carted out of Town at Noon Day in a most ignominious manner, and that the other two Brothers had fled for their Lives. That the news arrived by Hall had revived the Spirit of the other Party to such a degree that they had every thing to fear, and that it was every Body's opinion poor Preston would be Hanged, (this is the officer who is in jail for the unhappy affair on the fifth of March)*. A Gentleman arrived from Boston in the evening and confirm'd all these accounts and likewise told us that Mr. Hultons windows had been Broke and the family had fled to the Castle for protection. You may Judge what sleep I had that night, and, indeed, we have ever since slept in such a manner that it can hardly be called rest. It is the business of the Evening to see the fire Armes Loaded, and lights Properly Placed in the Store and House; and this precaution we have taken ever since we received the Letter which is now 5 Days in which time we have remain'd unmolested. . . . this is our present sittuation and if we do not soon have good news from England I am afraid it will still be worse.[6]

*The Boston Massacre

SARAH PRINCE GILL, the wife of another merchant, viewed the political situation very differently. Using the pseudonym "Sophronia," she wrote to the renowned English historian, Catharine Sawbridge Macaulay, urging her to write a history of America and offering to put her in touch with American intellectuals. Viewed as "very learned" and with "a Genius uncommonly strong and penetrating" by her contemporaries, Sarah Gill was a member of the intellectual set of Boston society, a fact clearly reflected in the correspondence she had with Macaulay.

Love of Liberty . . . beats in every Pulse

Madam
                                                                    Boston April 25, 1769
The Noble Zeal you have exerted in the Sacred Cause of Liberty & the Rights of Mankind demand the Tribute of Gratitude from every Mind capable of those glorious Sentiments, and every heart that glows with this generous Ardor.

Permit the Innocent Boldness of the meanest of your readers who admires the Patriotic Spirit of Mrs. Macaulay, and venerates her as One raised up, accomplished, and inclined by Heav'n to transfuse the benign emanations to various Realms.

New England, the Land of my Nativity (A Priviledge I glory in!) was First settled on the plan of Civil & Religious Freedom. Worthy Men, and Patriots all were those who Formed this Civil Community. Their lives were spent, their talents employed, their estates consumed, they suffered hunger and thirst, and cold and weariness, and Labour and Toil,—They Jeoparded their lives amidst numerous tribes of savage Barbarians; and all this, that they and their Posterity might enjoy the right of thinking, of Judging, and Acting for themselves; and have no arbitrary Power to molest their humble repose. . . .

It is with Pleasure Madam, I hear of your design to treat of the settlement of these Northern Collonies. I hope you will have the aid of the most accurate Peices that give Light on the Subject—Not One of all the Historians who have attempted this have done Justice to the Theme. . . .

When I reflected on the Quallities you are endowed with for Works of this Nature, I feel regret that you are not on the Field where the history was Acted; for give me leave to say, no Person can form a full Idea of the American Spirit & Love of Liberty, but those who dwell in or visit the Clime; it is inwrought in their Frame; transpires in every breath; and beats in every Pulse; but of those ignoble Souls (and such exist in ev'ry Country) whose private interest, and sordid Avarice, wou'd sacrifice the Wellfare of Kingdoms and Countries to their Lust of Domination and Wealth! The Disgrace of Humane Nature, and the Plague of Society these!

If Madam, you are in want of Intelligence on any Subject of Former or Later American Affairs, & will please to signify the Articles; the Assistance of our Ablest Patriots in Boston (with whom I have the honour of a Personal Acquaintance) will not be wanting when ever you make the Requisition.—In this Case a Line Directed to me Under Cover to Mr. Moses Gill, Merchant in Boston, will come safe to me.

a Generous Madness

Hannover Street Boston Dec: 8. 1769

My design was, in part, to pave the way for a more Superior hand than mine to transmit you such Authentic Accounts of this Country as wou'd render your History more Compleat;—That design Madam was accomplished when you wrote Mr. *Otis* on this head. As that Valluable Gentleman (the *Cato* of America, as Mr. Dickenson is its Cicero) has wrote you very Largely on American Affairs I am happily excused.

I would not, I hope I do not, carry my notion of Patriotism beyond the Standard of Truth, yea, of Truth confirmed by Fact. Souls there have been, Souls there are, who have Sacrificed darling Interests for their Countries Good. Even in this Age of Corruption Venality and Dissipation I am frequently the Wittness of Such a Conduct. I Glory in my Country, I Glory in Boston my native Town on this Account.—And tho the Pathetic Writings and warm Addresses of Some have been termed Enthusiastic Raphsody, high Flights of a raised Imagination &c., and the Spirited United Conduct of Others deem'd Madness and Faction, yet in my humble Opinion these are the Genuine results of a Rational Enthusiasm, a Generous Madness, and a truly Loyall Faction. What more Generous than the Merchant who depends on Commerce, stopping the resource of his own gain to procure the Liberty of his Country? What more Loyall than to prefer the good of the Empire to that of a Few mercenary Place-Men* Pensioners &c? What more Rational than to employ the Powers of Genius, and of Eloquence, in stating and defending the rights of Humanity?—Yes, My Dear Madam, there are among Us of Men very many, of Women not a Few animated with this Philosophy.

You Lament the want of such a spirit in *"Our Sex."* I have Observed and Mourned it Also, but I find this is chiefly among our City Ladies: that it takes rise from that Levity of Manners, that dissipation of Thought, that Low Ambition of Title and Show which Characterises our Modern Women; Amusements and Pageantry have absorbed their every Care and destroyed the Noblest Feelings of the Humane Heart! When sick of Contemplating this, and Conversing with these, I turn me to those who think and Act more becoming Rationals. And many do I know who are warm Assertors and steady Friends of Liberty; Especially is this evident among the most serious religious Women of New England. . . . Our Ancestors wisely took care to instill the principles of Liberty into the minds of their Children, to this provident care it is owing that America hath made such a Noble stand against the inroads of Despotism, and produced such Able Defenders of her Rights.

I know not any Tracts that set our Controversy with the Parent Country in so Just & Clear a Light as Mr. Dickensons Letters†, Mr. [James] Otis's Rights of the Collonies, & that Collection of Peices entitled *the Sentiments of America.* All which I conclude you have. If any thing shou'd transpire I will not fail to transmit them. Happy shou'd I think myself if in any instance I cou'd serve the Cause, tho' as the smallest spring in the Grand Machine.

*place-man: one appointed by the sovereign to a remunerative public office as a reward for service or loyalty, usually a derogatory term.

†John Dickinson (1732-1808), American patriot, author of *Letters from a Farmer in Pennsylvania,* published in 1767 and 1768.

A Gentleman of Clear Sense

Madam   Hannover Street Boston March 24 [1770]

If Madam you will excuse a Liberty prompted by zeal for the Common Cause, I wou'd just hint that the Author of the "Dissertations on the Cannon & Feudal Laws," is Worthy your *correspondence* If you chuse to maintain *one* in Boston. . . . I conclude you have heard the real Author is John Adams Esq; Barrister at Law in Boston; A Gentleman of Clear Sense, Precision of Sentiment and Expression, and thoroughly Awake in the Cause of Liberty. With the warmest wishes for the Continuance of your valluable Life & Opportunities for Public Service, I am with the truest respect Madam

your very obedient humble Sert   Sophronia[7]

PHILLIS WHEATLEY, a young black slave bought in 1761 by John and Susanna Wheatley, was educated by her mistress. Within sixteen months, she had not only attained incredible mastery of the English language but could read the "most difficult Parts of the Sacred Writings." Her own "Curiosity led her" to write poetry. So amazing were her skills that Wheatley had to undergo rigorous questioning by Governor Thomas Hutchinson of Massachusetts, the Reverend Samuel Cooper, James Bowdoin, and John Hancock to prove that the poems were her original work. In this poem, written in 1772 and published the following year, the poet apparently hoped that William Legge, Earl of Dartmouth, newly appointed Secretary of State for the American Department, would be sympathetic to America's grievances.

my love of freedom

To the Right Honourable William, Earl of Dartmouth

Hail, happy day, when, smiling like the morn,
Fair *Freedom* rose *New-England* to adorn:
The northern clime beneath her genial ray,
Dartmouth, congratulates thy blissful sway:
Elate with hope her race no longer mourns,
Each soul expands, each grateful bosom burns,
While in thine hand with pleasure we behold
The silken reins, and *Freedom's* charms unfold.

. . . .

No more, *America*, in mournful strain
Of wrongs, and grievance unredress'd complain,
No longer shall thou dread the iron chain,
Which wanton *Tyranny* with lawless hand
Had made, and with it meant t'enslave the land.
Should you, my lord, while you peruse my song,
Wonder from whence my love of *Freedom* sprung,
Whence flow these wishes for the common good,
By feeling hearts alone best understood,
I, young in life, by seeming cruel fate
Was snatch'd from *Afric's* fancy'd happy seat:
What pangs excruciating must molest,
What sorrows labour in my parent's breast?
Steel'd was that soul and by no misery mov'd
That from a father seiz'd his babe belov'd:
Such, such my case. And can I then but pray
Others may never feel tyrannic sway?

For favours past, great Sir, our thanks are due,
And thee we ask thy favours to renew,
Since in thy pow'r, as in thy will before,
To sooth the griefs, which thou did'st once deplore.[8]

ANNA GREEN WINSLOW, sent to Boston in 1770 to board with her aunt, Sarah Winslow Deming, and to attend school, wrote a journal for her mother and father Joshua Winslow, commissary general of the British forces in Cumberland, Nova Scotia. For two years (1771-1773), undeterred by the political turmoil around her, this cheerful young girl, "a whimsical child," as her aunt called her, reported on ordinary life: sermons she heard, people she visited, her studies, fashions, and the weather.

As I am (as we say) a daughter of liberty

November the 29th [1771].—My aunt Deming gives her love to you and says it is this morning 12 years since she had the pleasure of congratulating papa and you on the birth of your scribling daughter. She hopes if I live 12 years longer that I shall write and do everything better than can be expected in the *past* 12. I should be obliged to you, you will dismiss me for company.

30th Nov.—My company yesterday were Miss Polly Deming, Miss Polly Glover, Miss Peggy Draper, Miss Bessy Winslow, Miss Nancy Glover, Miss Sally Winslow, Miss Polly Atwood, Miss Hanh Soley. Miss Attwood as well as Miss Winslow are of this family. And Miss N. Glover did me honor by her presence, for she is older than cousin Sally and of her acquaintance. We made four couple at country dansing; danceing I mean. In the evening Mr. [Josiah Jr.] Waters hearing of my assembly, put his flute in his pocket and played several minuets and other tunes, to which we danced mighty cleverly. But Lucinda* was our principal piper. . . .

*Lucinda, born in Africa, had been purchased by Mrs. Deming when about seven years old. Upon her owner's death, she was given her freedom, but resided in the family of Gen. John Winslow; she was still living in 1795.

Dec. 14th.—The weather and walking have been very winter like . . . I went to Mrs. Whitwell's last wednessday—you taught me to spell the 4 day of the week, but my aunt says that it should be spelt wednesday. My aunt also says, that till I come out of an egregious fit of laughterre that is apt to sieze me & the violence of which I am at this present under, neither English sense, nor anything rational may be expected of me. . . .

1st Jany 1772. I wish my Papa, Mama, brother John Henry, & cousin Avery & all the rest of my acquaintance at Cumberland, Fortlaurence, Barronsfield, Greenland, Amherst &c. a Happy New Year. I have bestow'd no new year's gift, as yet. But have received one very handsome one, viz. the History of Joseph Andrews abbreviated. In nice Guilt and flowers covers. . . .

Jany 17th. [I have been to] a very genteel well regulated assembly which we had at Mr. Soley's last evening . . . There was a large company assembled in a handsome, large, upper room in the new end of the house. We had two fiddles, & I had the honor to open the diversion of the evening in a minuet with miss Soley. . . . our treat was nuts, rasins, Cakes, Wine, punch, hot & cold, all in great plenty. We had a very agreeable evening from 5 to 10 o'clock. For variety we woo'd a widow, hunted the whistle, threaded the needle, & while the company was collecting, we diverted ourselves with playing of pawns, no rudeness Mamma I assure you. Aunt Deming desires you would *perticulary observe*, that the elderly part of the company were *spectators only*, they mix'd not in either of the above describ'd scenes. . . .

Feb. 9th.—My honored Mamma will be so good as to excuse my useing the pen of my old friend just here, because I am disabled by a whitloe on my fourth finger & something like one on my middle finger, from using my own pen; but altho' my right hand is in bondage, my left is free; & my aunt says, it will be a nice oppertunity if I do but improve it, to perfect myself in learning to spin flax. I am pleased with the proposal & am at this present, exerting myself for this purpose. I hope, when two, or at most three months are past, to give you occular demonstration of my proficiency in *this art*, as well as several others. My fingers are not the only part of me that has suffer'd with sores within this fortnight, for I have had an ugly great boil upon my right hip & about a dozen small ones—I am at present swath'd hip & thigh, as Samson smote the Philistines, but my soreness is near over. My aunt thought it highly proper to give me some cooling physick, so last tuesday I took 1-2 oz Globe Salt (a disagreeable potion) & kept chamber. Since which, there has been no new eruption, & a great alteration for the better in those I had before.

I have read my bible to my aunt this morning (as is the daily custom) & sometimes I read other books to her. So you may perceive, I *have the use of my tongue* & I tell her it is a good thing to have the use of my tongue. . . . I tell my Aunt I feel a disposition to be a good girl, & she pleases herself that she shall have much comfort of me today. . . .

Feb. 21 Thursday. . . . I purchas'd with my aunt Deming's leave, a very beautiful white feather hat, that is, the out side, which is a bit of white hollond with the feathers sew'd on in a most curious manner white & unsullied as the falling snow, this hat I have long been saving my money to procure for which I have let your kind allowance, Papa, lay in my aunt's hands till this hat which I spoke for was brought home. As I am (as we say) a daughter of liberty I chuse to wear as much of our own manufactory as pocible. . . .

Feb. 22d.—Since about the middle of December, ult[imo, the previous month]. we have had till this week, a series of cold and stormy weather—every snow storm (of which we have had abundance) except the first, ended with rain, by which means the snow was so hardened that strong gales at N W soon turned it, & all above round to ice, which this sevennight was from one to three, four & they say, in some places, five feet thick, in the streets of this town . . . I have spun 30 knots of linning yarn, and (partly) new footed a pair of stockings for Lucinda, read a part of the pilgrim's progress, coppied part of my text journal (that if I live a few years longer, I may be able to understand it, for aunt sais, that to her, the contents as I first mark'd them, were an impenetrable secret) play'd some, tuck'd [ate heartily] a great deal (Aunt Deming says it is very true) laugh'd enough, & I tell aunt it is all human *nature*, if not human reason. And now, I wish my honored mamma a very good night.

Monday noon Feb. 25th. I have been to writing school this morning and Sewing. The day being very pleasant, very little wind stirring. . . . Dear mamma, I suppose that you would be glad to hear that Betty Smith who has given you so much trouble, is well & behaves herself well & I should be glad if I could write you so. But the truth is, no sooner was the 29th Regiment encamp'd upon the common but miss Betty took herself among them (as the Irish say) & there she stay'd with Bill Pinchion & awhile. The next news of her was, that she was got into gaol for stealing: from whence she was taken to the publick whipping post. The next adventure was to the Castle, after the soldier's were remov'd there, for the murder of the 5th March last. [1770: after the Boston Massacre it was demanded that the troops no longer be quartered in Boston.] When they turn'd her away from there, she came up to town again, and soon got into the workhouse for new misdemeanours. She soon ran away from there and sit up her old trade of pilfering again, for which she was put a second time into gaol, there she still remains. About two months agone (as well as I can remember) she & a number of her wretched companions set the gaol on fire, in order to get out, but the fire was timely discovered & extinguished, & there, as I said she still remains till this day, in order to be tried for her crimes. I heard somebody say that as she has some connections with the army no doubt but she would be cleared, and perhaps, have a pension into the bargain. . . .

March 9th.—After being confined a week, I rode yesterday afternoon to & from meeting in Mr. Soley's chaise. I got no cold and am pretty well today. This has been a very snowy day today. Any body that sees this may see that I have wrote nonsense but Aunt says, I have been a very good girl to day about my work however—I think this day's work may be called a piece meal for in the first place I sew'd on the bosom of unkle's shirt, mended two pair of gloves, mended for the wash two handkerchiefs, (one cambrick) sewed on half a border of a lawn apron of aunts, read part of the xxist chapter of Exodous, & a story in the Mother's gift. Now, Hond. Mamma, I must tell you of something that happened to me to-day, that has not happen'd before this great while, viz My Unkle [John Deming] & Aunt both told me, I was a very good girl. . . . I have been writing all the above gibberish while aunt has been looking after her family—now she is out of the room—now she is in— & takes up my pen in *my* absence to observe, I am a little simpleton for informing my mamma, that it is *a great while* since I was prais'd because she will conclude that it is *a great while* since I deserv'd to be prais'd. I will henceforth try to observe their praise & yours too. I mean deserve. It's now tea time—as soon as that is over, I shall spend the rest of the evening in reading to my aunt. It is near candle lighting. . . .

May 16.—Last Wednesday Bet Smith was set upon the gallows. She behav'd with great impudence. Thursday I danc'd a minuet & country dances at school, after which I drank tea with aunt [Elizabeth Green] Storer. To day I am somewhat out of sorts, a little sick at my stomach.[9]

The colonists continued to protest indirect taxes imposed by the Townshend Acts of 1767. John Dickinson in his *Letters from a Pennsylvania Farmer* argued that the taxes were levied to raise revenue for the Crown, and urged the boycott of English goods in retaliation. Massachusetts quickly agreed. As the protests grew more violent, British troops were sent to enforce compliance and Boston, in es-sence, became an occupied city. Emotions ran high, mobs prowled the streets, soldiers and friends of the government were under attack. On March 5, 1770, a mob menaced seven British soldiers under Captain Thomas Preston, who were guarding the Customs House. The ensuing melee left five of the mob dead, including Crispus Attucks, a black man. This tragic event (the Boston Massacre) was immediately engraved by Paul Revere and effectively used as propaganda. In the subsequent trial on charges of manslaughter, Preston and six of his men were acquitted: their lawyers were the patriots John Adams and Josiah Quincy.

Two months later, news arrived from England that the Townshend duties had been repealed, except for the three-pence on tea. The tea tax had been retained for the benefit of the nearly bankrupt East India Company, which had a monopoly on importing tea to the colonies. When the ships carrying the tea arrived in Boston, bands of radicals (including Samuel Adams and Paul Revere), disguised as Indians, dumped the cargo into the harbor (December 16, 1773). A week later, in Charleston, South Carolina, more than 22,000 chests of tea were impounded and stored in a warehouse. In Philadelphia, friendly persuasion did the trick: the captain of the ship *Polly*, which was laden with tea, was taken home for dinner by a leading Quaker merchant, given provisions for his ship, and sent on his voyage home to England, cargo intact.

For Boston, punishment was swift and harsh: the port was closed; the royal governor, Thomas Hutchinson, was replaced by General Thomas Gage, commander-in-chief of the British forces in America; those responsible for the violence were to be tried, not by American jurors who might be sympathetic, but in England; and the residents were to provide housing for the British troops occupying the city. These new edicts, known in America as the Intolerable Acts, clearly signaled to all the colonies that the Mother Country meant business.

Still, there was ambivalence and hope that somehow the colonies and Great Britain might reconcile. When General Gage arrived in Boston, he was offered a welcoming banquet by prominent citizens, "the appearance of politeness and good humor was kept up through the *etiquette* of the day."[10] Before long, however, people would be under pressure to take sides—loyalist or patriot. To be neutral would be difficult if not impossible.

JEMIMA CONDICT in her Journal:

it is tea that caused it

[New Jersey] Saturday October 1, 1774

It seams we have troublesome times a Coming for there is great Disturbance a Broad in the earth & they say it is tea that caused it. So then if they will Quarel about such a trifling thing as that What must we expect But war & I think or at least fear it will be so.[11]

HANNAH GRIFFITTS's poem, included in the *Commonplace Book* of Milcah Martha Moore, clearly reflects her familiarity with the works of John Milton, even spoofing the older poet's cadence to humorous effect.

> *The Ladies Lamentation over an empty Cannister*
>
> Whence all this hideous wild uproar,
> I ne'er shall love the Congress more
> 'Twas they devis'd the evil Deed,
> To kill this prescious Indian Weed,
> Come just Resentment guide my Pen,
> And mark our mad Committee Men,
> Pray what is Freedom, Right or Laws,
> To such a vast important Cause?
> Why all their Malice shewn to Tea
> So near, so dear—belov'd by me,
> Reviving Draught, when I am dry—
> Tea I must have, or I shall dye,
> Not all the Herbs our Gardens yield
> Not all the Produce of the Field,
> Can please my Palate or atone,
> For this one wicked Act alone.
> But King, nor Parlaiment, nor North,*
> (That publick Object of our Wrath,)
> Nor Congress, nor Committee Muster,
> With all their Malice, noise & Bluster,
> Sure will not dare—to hinder me,
> From getting fresh Recruits of Tea.
>   [signed] Europa[12]

*North: Frederick, Lord North, British prime minister 1770-1782.

FIFTY-ONE LADIES OF EDENTON, NORTH CAROLINA, met together and resolved to abstain from drinking tea as well as from purchasing English goods, thereby supporting the resistance to the taxes throughout the colonies. A print by Philip Dawes published in London shortly after this resolve portrayed this patriotic deed in less than complimentary terms, caricaturing the ladies as inebriated or flirtatious, neglectful of the child under the table. Most humiliating, a dog urinates on the gown of one of the signers.

Resolution of October 25, 1774

We the Ladys of Edenton do hereby Solemnly Engage
not to Conform to the Pernicious Custom of Drinking Tea,
or that we the aforesaid Ladys will not promote ye wear
of any Manufacture from England untill such time
that all Acts which tend to Enslave this our Native Country
shall be Repealed.[13]

During the previous years, committees of correspondence had sprung up throughout the country, keeping various groups in touch with each other. Thus Boston's punishment by the British was quickly met with sympathetic support from the other colonies. More important, the committees paved the way for the First Continental Congress. Twelve of the thirteen colonies sent delegates—only Georgia was missing—who met on September 5, 1774 in Philadelphia. They discussed many topics: the removal of the standing army, the unconstitutionality of the Intolerable Acts, the "extravagance" of horse-racing, cock-fighting, and attending plays. Their deliberations produced a Declaration of Rights and Resolutions and a ban on the importation of British goods. Still hoping to find a peaceful resolution, they not only drafted a petition to King George III and an address to the people of Great Britain, but also agreed to reconvene in May 1775.

Though there was some conciliatory movement in Parliament to come to terms with the patriots—Prime Minister Frederick, Lord North was even in secret negotiations with Benjamin Franklin in London—it all came to naught. War instructions were on their way to General Gage.

CHARITY CLARKE to her cousin Joseph Jekyll:

what care we for your fleets & armies

Greenwitch [New York City] Septr 10th 1774

It is my turn to blush at a long silence. I confess my Cousin the needle & not the pen has given me employ for some time past, & that not from choice but necessity. In Feby last my Father lost his house with every thing that was in the upper storry by fire, by which means the number of my Garments were reduced to only what I had on, so when you reflect on the adage: womens work is never done you may imagine it required a little more than common industry to repair the work of years. . . .

Let me know the success of your application to parliament, though when you remember they will not let us keep what we have got, they will hardly give you what you want. . . .

Splenetic Ideas are not the growth of our climate, murmurs & Rebellion are the produce of Europe. Americans disclaim them; in what instance pray are the Americans called Rebels? What have they done to deserve the name? They have asserted their rights, and are determined to maintain them, for daring to do which Englishmen (who have boasted the love of Liberty more than any people on earth) have blocked up the port of Boston & encamped near the Town to distress their trade & insult the inhabitants. . . . She thinks they have done wrong & to convince them of it sends fleets, armies & acts of Parliament . . . what care we for your fleets & armies, we are not going to fight with them unless drove to it by the last necessity, or the highest provocation. . . .

Luxurious Sons of Albion! whilst rolling in wealth, enjoying all your lavish thoughts can imagine, having your very wishes prevented, commanding all that Earth, Sea, or Air can give you, could you behold your brethren of America, descended from the same stock, the richest among them enjoying no more than what you would esteem the comforts of life, the poorest filling forests you would deem impenetrable, ploughing mountains your feeble limbs could not ascend, you could not avoid crying out, let them enjoy the fruit of their Labour, it is by the sweat of their brow they earn their bread, nor have they a portion to spare. And the poorest Kind among them might answer, Heaven alone shall prevent òur enjoyment of it, you cannot deprive us. The Arms that support my family shall defend it, though this body is not clad with silken Garments, these Limbs are armed with strength, the Soul is fortified by Virtue, and the love of Liberty is cherished within this bosom—England was once the protector of Freemen, states struggling for Liberty sought her assistance. . . .

England in her conduct to America has done an act she cannot answer to Justice, and in all probability an act that in a few years may make the title of North as odious to Englishmen as it is to Americans, and that proud mistaken minister may be convinced that even should he bring America to sue for pardon at his feet, his country would loose more by the Loss of their affections than could be gained by her submission . . . that America might have cause to revere her as a parent assist her commerce & continue to flourish under her protection, but alas! her wise men are not listened to. The Curse of Empires a proud ambitious minister governs in Britain, by his sophistry makes the King deaf to the remonstrances of his subjects, by his bribery obtains the majority of Parliament, & by his power would spread Tyrany to the western continent but its inhabitants are not sank in Luxury nor are they dazled by pomp, their eyes watch over their Liberty observe every encroachment and oppose it, and is this their crime in your eyes my Cousin? Do you condemn them for not being polite enough to give away the property of their posterity? surely you ought not too quickly condemn America.[14]

MERCY OTIS WARREN, born into a wealthy family, received her education at home, being allowed to listen in on the lessons of her brother James. She married James Warren, who encouraged her intellectual pursuits. As "Fidelia," she wrote poetry and dramas with distinct political overtones and, during the 1780s, began her *History of the Rise, Progress, and Termination of the American Revolution*, arguably the first overview of the conflict between England and America, although not published until 1805. It was to Abigail Adams in Braintree that she confessed how worried she was about the safety of her husband and five sons.

my fears . . . fill my heart with anxious Concern

Plimouth August 9th 1774
Shall I own to you that the Woman & the Mother daily arouse my fears & fill my Heart with anxious Concern for the decission of the Mighty Controversy between Great Britain & the Colonies. For if the sword must finally terminate the dispute besides the feelings of Humanity for the Complicated distress of the Community; no one has at stake a Larger share of Domestic Felicity than myself, for not to mention my fears for him with whom I am most tenderly Connected: Methinks I see no Less than five sons who must Buckle on the Harness And perhaps fall a sacrifice to the Manes* of Liberty Ere she again revives &

spreads her Chearful Banner over this part of the Globe, but I quit the painful Revire [reverie] and desire to Leave all my Cares in his Hand who wills the universal Happiness of his Creatures.[15]

*Manes: in ancient Rome, the deified souls of ancestors to whom homage was paid.

JANE FRANKLIN MECOM, a younger sister of Benjamin Franklin, "my peculiar favorite" as he dubbed her, was married to Edward Mecom, a small tradesman and saddler, in 1727 in Boston. Over the next twenty-two years, they had twelve children. Moreover, Jane looked after her parents, took in boarders, and ran a small shop to make ends meet. Her life was not an easy or happy one: her husband apparently sick, her sons unable to make their way in life, several of her daughters dying after giving birth. Although "Sorrows roll upon me like the waves of the sea," she delighted in her correspondence with her brother. He was her mainstay, and she was extremely proud of him. Franklin, in turn, was very supportive of Jane and her family. Her description of the situation in Boston must have given him no little concern.

we have already had miracles wrought in our favour

My Ever Dear Brother   Boston Novr 3 1774

I have Just recd yrs of August 18; wonder to see you complain of not receiving leters from Boston . . . it is like they have been Intercepted . . . I think it is not Profanity to compare you to our Blessed Saviour who Employed much of His time while here on Earth in doing Good to the body as well as souls of men, & I am sure I think the comparison Just, often when I hear the calumny Invented & thrown out against you while you are Improving all your Powers for the Salvation of them very Persons . . . I am as Happy as the Present state of affairs will Permit owing to your Bounty without which I must have been distressed as much as many others; Docter Chauncy says we have already had miracles wrought in our favour, one of which is the Uniting of the Colonies in such a manner, another the Extraordinary fruitful seasons & Bounty of our friends & looks on it as a token of Gods Design to deliver us out of all our troubles, but at Present we have a meloncholy Prospect for this winter at Least.

The towns being so full of Profligate soldiers & many such Officers, there is hardly four & twenty hours Passes without some fray amongst them & one can walk but a little way in the street without hearing their Profane language. We were much surprised the other day upon hearing a Tumult in the street & looking out saw a soldier all Bloody damning His Eyes but He would kill Every Inhabitant He met, & Pressing into a shop opposite us with His Bayonet drawn, bursting through the Glass Door, & the man of the house pushing Him out & he to do what mischief He could, Dashing the china & Earthenware which stood on the window, through the sashes with the most terrible Imprecations. The case it seems was He Perceived they sold liquor & went into the House Demanding some. But being refused, He went into the closet & took out a gun & said His commanding officer told Him he might take any thing out of any house He had a mind to, upon which the battle Ensued, & the man & His servant were both very much wounded. . . .

I think our Congress Address to the People of England is a Grand Performance & does them Honour & shows there was Really the wisdom among them
that the Colonies Endeavored to collect, which Joined with yours . . . will, I
hope, work some Glorious Effect. . . .

I have had no letter from Philadelphia a long time though I have written
several times. The last I wrote, I heard my sister [Deborah Franklin*] Put under
her cushion, I suppose in order to Read at more Leisure & Perhaps never
thought of it more & one of the children got it & tore it up, as we know my sister
is very forgetful. . . . yr Ever Affectionat & obliged Sister   Jane Mecom[16]
*Deborah Franklin died in December, 1774.

MARY V. V., whose true name has not been discovered, is most likely the author
of this satirical piece in which a pro-Tory wife castigates her husband for being
a delegate to the First Continental Congress. The play not only mocks the (to
her) ridiculous flailing of discontented citizens against the superior power of
Great Britain but also lauds the greater wisdom of women. It was widely distributed, prompting a friend of James Madison to call it "grossly scurrilous" (January 4, 1775).

A Fragment, Inscribed To the Married Ladies of America,
By their most sincere, And Affectionate Friend, And Servant, Mary V.V.
Printed in the Year M,DCC,LXXIV [1774]

· ·

Husband: You mistook me, my Dear, I did not pretend,
             Every Measure of Congress, right or wrong to defend;
             Many Things they've left undone, they shou'd surely have done,
             Many Things they have done, they shou'd have sure let alone . . .
             I bear, for all that, with your Caprice, and your Tricks,
             But, prithee Dear, dabble not in our Politics.

Wife: Prithee! ha, ha, ha, Prithee! my Senator grave!
             Sir! I'll make you repent of that Speech, to your Grave;
             Why had'st not said, KNOW THEN, like the mighty Congress,
             I presume you'd a Hand in that "civil Address":
             Indeed, my sweet Sir, when you treat with your Betters,
             You should mind how you speak, and how you write Letters.

Husband: That Horse-laugh is all feign'd, with much better Grace,
             You know, Ma'm, you cou'd hit me a Slap in the Face:
             Consider, my Dear, you're a Woman of Fashion,
             'Tis really indecent to be in such Passion;
             Mind thy Household-Affairs, teach thy Children to read,
             And never, Dear, with Politics, trouble thy Head.

Wife: ·
             Wou'd! instead of Delegates, they'd sent Delegates Wives;
             Heavens! we cou'dn't have bungled it so for our Lives!

· ·

Let Fools, Pedants, and Husbands, continue to hate
The Advice of us Women, and call it all Prate:
Whilst you are in Danger, by your good Leave, my Dear,
Both by Night and by Day, I will ring in your Ear—
Make your Peace:—Fear the King:—The Parliament fear:
Oh! my Country! remember, that a Woman unknown,
Cry'd aloud,—like *Cassandra*, in Oracular Tone,
Repent! or you are forever, forever undone.[17]

The presence in Boston of General Gage and his troops—some 4,000 men—did nothing to lessen the tensions. Local militias began stockpiling gunpowder and collecting arms. Gage hoped to subdue the smoldering rebellion by capturing two of the rebel leaders, Samuel Adams and John Hancock, and to destroy the supplies known to be at Concord. Paul Revere and William Dawes Jr. were able to warn the two men, who were staying in Lexington.

Ferrying seven hundred troops from the Boston Common across the Charles River in the middle of the night (April 18-19, 1775) took several hours, and the British troops arrived in Lexington around 5 A.M. Gunfire broke out—who fired first is unclear. The skirmish left eight militiamen dead. The British sent to Boston for reinforcements, but continued on to Concord. There they destroyed what ammunition they could find, and began the trek back to the city.

News of the fighting spread like wildfire; men and boys converged on the area, and, hiding behind trees and stonewalls, they sniped at the Redcoats. At Menotomy (now called Arlington), the retreating army, bolstered by reinforcements, had its bloodiest encounter. Once safe in Boston, the British assessed their losses: nearly 300 dead or wounded; the rebels had fewer than one hundred.

JEMIMA CONDICT noted in her Journal a few days after the battle:

every Day Brings New Troubels

[Pleasantdale, New Jersey] April 23, 1775
As every Day Brings New Troubels So this Day Brings News that yesterday very early in the morning They Began to fight at Boston. The regulors We hear Shot first there; they killd 30 of our men A hundred & 50 of the Regulors.[18]

HANNAH FAYERWEATHER WINTHROP lived at 93 Mount Auburn Street, Cambridge, with her second husband, astronomer John Winthrop, Hollis Professor of Mathematicks and Natural Philosophy at Harvard College. Cambridge was a small village, its residents farmers, trades people, or teachers. Writing her friend Mercy Otis Warren in Plymouth, Hannah Winthrop minced no words in describing the horrors of the war as it engulfed their peaceful lives.

beat of drum & ringing of Bell

[April 1775]

Nor can I yet forget, nor will old Time ever erase the horrors of that midnight Cry, preceeding the Bloody Massacre at Lexington, when we were rousd from the benign Slumbers of the season, by beat of drum & ringing of Bell, with the dire alarm, That a thousand of the Troops of George the third were gone forth to murder the peacefull inhabitants of the Surrounding Villages. A few hours with the dawning day convinced us the Bloody purpose was executing, The platoon firing assuring us, the rising sun must witness the Bloody Carnage. Not knowing what the Event would be at Cambridge at the return of these Bloody ruffians, and seeing another Brigade dispatchd to the assistance of the former, Looking with the ferocity of Barbarians, It seemd necessary to retire to some place of Safty till the Calamity was passd. My partner [part cut out] had been a fortnight Confind by illness. After dinner we set out not knowing whither we went. We were directed to a place calld fresh pond a bout a mile from the town, but what a distressd house did we find there filld with women whose husbands were gone forth to meet the Assailiants, 70 or 80 of these with numbers of infant children, crying and agonizing for the Fate of their husbands.

In addition to this scene of distress we were for Some time in Sight of the Battle, the glistening instruments of death proclaiming by an incessant fire, that much blood must be shed, that many widows & orphand ones be left as monuments of that persecuting Barbarity of British Tyranny. Another uncomfortable night we passd, some nodding in their chairs, others resting their weary limbs on the floor. The welcome harbingers of day gave notice of its dawning light but brings no news. It is unsafe to return to Cambridge as the enemy were advancing up the river & firing on the town. To stay in this place was impracticable. Methinks in that hour I felt the force of my mother Eves Soliloquy on being driven out of Paradise, comparing small things with great

> O unexpected Stroke, worse than of death!
> Must I thus leave thee, Paradise, thus Leave
> Thee, native soil. . . .

Thus with precipatancy were we driven to the town of Andover, following Some of our acquaintance, five of us to be conveyd with one poor tired horse, & chaise. Thus we began our pilgrimage alternately walking & riding, the roads filled with frighted women & Children Some in Carts with their tattered furniture, others on foot fleeing in to the woods.

But what added greatly to the horror of the Scene was our passing thro the Bloody field at Menotomy which was strewd with the mangled Bodies, we met one Affectionate Father with a Cart looking for his murderd Son & picking up his Neighbors who had fallen in Battle, in order for their Burial.

I should not have chose this town for an Asylum being but 20 miles from sea ports where men of war & their Pirates are stationed. . . .

I subscribe Yours unalterably   [no signature][19]

SARAH WINSLOW DEMING, the aunt of Anna Green Winslow, was also forced to flee, as she recounted in a letter written two months later to her niece Sarah

"Sally" Winslow. With her were her husband's niece Sally, and her slave Lucinda. Her husband John apparently returned to Boston. Even eight weeks after the events she describes, Deming was still so upset that she had to pause in the midst of her writing.

the *crisis* the *very crisis*

My Dear Niece   [Providence, Rhode Island, ca. June 18, 1775]
 I was very unquiet from the moment I was informed that *more troops* were coming to Boston. 'Tis true that those who had wintered there, had not given us *much molestation*, but an *additional strength* I dreaded and determined if possible to get out of their reach, and to take with me as much of my little interest as I could. Your uncle Deming was very far from being of my mind from which has proceeded those difficulties which peculiarly related to myself—but I now say not a word of this to him; we are joint sufferers and no doubt it is God's will that it should be so. . . .
 April 17, I was told that all the boats belonging to the men of war were launched on Saterday night while the town inhabitants were sleeping except some faithful watchmen who gave the intelligence. . . .
 On Tuesday evening 18 April we were informed that the companies above mentioned were in motion, that the men of war boats were rowed round to Charlestown ferry, Barton's point and bottom of ye common, that the soldiers were run thro the streets on tip toe (the moon not having risen) in the dark of ye evening, that there were a number of handcuffs in one of the boats, which were taken at the long wharf, & that two days provision had been cooked for 'em on board of one of the transport ships lying in ye harbor. That whatever other business they might have, the main was to take possession of the bodies of Mess. [Samuel] Adams & [John] Hancock whom they & we knew where they were lodged. We had no doubt of the truth of all this, and that expresses were sent forth both over the neck & Charlestown ferry to give our friends timely notice that they might escape. N. B. I did not git to bed this night till after 12 oclock, nor to sleep till long after that. . . .
 Early on Wednesday the fatal 19th April before I had quited my chamber one after another came running to tell me that the kings troops had fired upon and killed 8 of our neighbors at Lexington in their way to Concord.
 All the intelligence of this day was dreadful. Almost every countenance expressing anxiety and distress: but description fails here. . . . Towards morning I fell into a profound sleep, from which I was waked by Mr. Deming between 6 and 7 o. c. informing me that I was Gen. Gage's prisoner, all egress & regress being cut off between the town and the country. Here again description fails. No words can paint my distress—I feel it this instant (just eight weeks after) so sensibly that I must pause before I proceed.
 This was Thursday 20th. April. About 9 o. c. a. m. I was told that the way over the neck was opened for foot passengers but no carriage was permitted to cross the lines. I then determined to try if *my feet* would support me thro, tho I trembled at such a degree that I could scarce keep my feet in my own chamber, had taken no sustenance for the day & very sick at my stomach. I tyed up a few

things in my handkerchief, put on my cloak, & was just setting out upon my march with Sally & Lucinda when I was told that carriages were allowed to pass. By this time I was so faint that I was obliged to sit down. . . . I therefore besought Mr. Deming to get a carriage for me. . . . He went forth and over awhile & returned and told me there was not a carriage or another to be got for love or money: ah can any one that has not felt it know my sensation. Surely no.

Mr. D. threw himself into the easy chair & said he had not strength enough to move another step. I expected to see Sally fall into hysterick fitts every minute. Lucinda holding herself up by anything she could grasp, I bid her however git us some elixer drops & when we had taken it in a little wine mixed with water which happened to be boiling I prayed Mr. D. once more to let us try to get off on foot. He said he would presently, & see me out but positively would come back again. . . . *This moment* I thot the *crisis* the *very crisis*—I had not walked out at the top of the Court since last October—I went down and out to the edge of the street where I saw and spoke with several friends near as unhappy as myself, in a few moments the light of a chaise, which I engaged to take me off when it returned from Roxbury . . . Before this chaise returned Mr Deming engaged another & while we were waiting I might have packed up many necessaries but nobody had any business that day—there was a constant coming and going; each hindered the other: some new piece of soldier barbarity that had been perpetrated the day before, was in quick succession brought in—I was very ill—but to cut short about 3 o'clock p. m. the chaises returned . . . We set off immediately Mr D & I in one; Sally, Lucinda with Jemmy Church to drive the other. We were stopped and inquired of whether we had any arms &c by the first and second sentinels, but they treated us civilly and did not search us. The third & last sentinels did not chalenge us, so we got safe thro ye lines. We had not resolved to go. In *that* respect we resembled Abraham & I ardently wished for a portion of his faith.[20]

ANNE HULTON also depicted the horrific situation, writing to Mrs. Lightbody in Liverpool.

Stone Walls Served as a cover to the Rebels

[Late April 1775]

On the 18th instt. at 11 at Night, about 800 Grenadiers & light Infantry were ferry'd across the Bay to Cambridge, from whence they marchd to Concord, about 20 Miles. . . .

The People in the Country (who are all furnished with Arms & have what they call Minute Companys in every Town ready to march on any alarm), had a signal it's supposed by a light from one of the Steeples in Town, Upon the Troops Embarkg. The alarm spread thro' the Country, so that before daybreak the people in general were in Arms & on their March to Concord. About Daybreak a number of the People appeard before the Troops near Lexington. They were called to, to disperse, when they fired on the Troops & ran off, Upon which the Light Infantry pursued them & brought down about fifteen of them. The Troops went on to Concord & executed the business they were sent on, & on their return found two or three of their people Lying in the Agonies of Death, scalp'd & their Noses & ears cut off & Eyes bored out—Which exasperated the Soldiers exceedingly—a prodigious number of People now occupying the Hills, woods, & Stone Walls along the road. The Light Troops drove some parties from the hills, but all the road being inclosed with Stone Walls Served as a cover to the Rebels, from whence they fired on the Troops still running off whenever they had fired. . . .

The Troops returned to Charlestown about Sunset after having some of 'em marched near fifty miles . . . The next day the Country pourd down its Thousands, and at this time from the entrance of Boston Neck at Roxbury round by Cambridge to Charlestown is surrounded by at least 20,000 Men, who are raising batteries on three or four different Hills. We are now cut off from all communication with the Country & many people must soon perish with famine in this place. . . .

at present a Solemn dead silence reigns in the Streets, numbers have packed up their effects, & quited the Town, but the General [Gage] has put a Stop to any more removing, & here remains in Town about 9000 Souls (besides the Servants of the Crown).[21]

JANE MECOM with her neighbors fled Boston, "to seek my fourtune with hundred others not knowing whither." She was grateful to find refuge with friends in Warwick, Rhode Island, where she remained for the next six years. She wrote her brother who had returned to Philadelphia:

an Agitation of mind

My Ever Dear & Much Hond Brother   Warwick 14 May 1775

God be Praised for bring you safe back to America & supporting you through such fatigues as I know you have suffered while the ministry have been distressing Poor New England in such a cruel manner. . . . The commotion the Town was in after the battle ceased by the Parties coming in bringing in there wounded men causd such an Agitation of mind I believe none had much sleep, since which we could have no quiet, as we under stood our Brethern without were determined to Disposes [Dispossess] the Town of the Regulars, & the General shuting up the town not Leting any Pass out but through such Great Dificulties as were allmost insupportable.[22]

RACHEL WALKER REVERE, hearing that her husband had been captured at Concord by the British and anxious for his safety, sent him a letter enclosing 125 pounds by Dr. Benjamin Church, a member of the Massachusetts Provincial Congress. Paul Revere never received the letter. Unbeknownst to the rebels, Church was a spy for the British and delivered the letter to General Gage instead. What became of the money is unknown.

Keep up your spirits

[April/May 1775]

my Dear by Doctr Church I send a hundred & twenty five pounds and beg you will take the best care of your Self and not attempt coming in to this town again and if I have an opportunity of comeing or sending out any thing or any of the Children I Shall do it. Pray Keep up your spirits and trust your self and us in the hands of a good God who will take care of us. Tis all my Dependance for vain is the help of man.

Aduie my Love from your affectionate   RRevere[23]

The call to arms raised regiments from all over the colonies, and they converged on the Boston area. The militiamen began digging trenches and redoubts around Boston, blocking all avenues of escape. General Gage, joined by Generals John Burgoyne, Henry Clinton, and William Howe, decided to occupy Bunker Hill but found the rebels already entrenched there. As the British advanced up Bunker Hill and Breed's Hill, the rebels opened fire and, as General Burgoyne commented, it was "one of the greatest scenes of war that can be conceived . . . a large and noble town [Charlestown] in one great blaze. The hills around covered with spectators." The British won the day but at a huge cost.

ABIGAIL CROFOOT GRANT lived in Glastonbury, Connecticut, with her husband Azariah Grant Jr. Married in 1770, they already had two children when Azariah joined a local regiment on May 9, 1775, marched towards Boston, and encamped near Roxbury. This letter was copied by a member of Grant's regiment and sent to an acquaintance, with the comment that Grant himself "makes a Jest of it as much as any of his Mates do. Tho he Owns & Swears it is Certainly his Wifes hand, She Certainly wrote it &c &c."

exert myself bravely in so good a Cause

August the 19th A.D. 1775

Loving Husband after Love to you I would inform you that we are well through Gods mercy upon us, and through the Same Mercy I hope these Lines will find you well also. I keep writing to you again & again & never can have only one Letter from you, tho I hear by Captn Wm Riley news that makes me very Sorry, for he Says you proved a Grand Coward when the fight was at Bunkers hill & in your Surprise he reports that you threw away your Cartridges So as to escape going into the Battle. I am loath to believe it but yet I must unless you will write to me & inform me how it is. And if you are afraid pray own the truth & come home & take care of our Children & I will be Glad to Come & take your place, & never will be Called a Coward, neither will I throw away one Cartridge but exert myself bravely in so good a Cause. So hopeing you will let me know how it is, & how you do, So bidding you farewell, wishing you the best of heavens Blessings & a Safe & manlike return, subscribing myself

your Loveing wife untill Death   Abigail Grant[24]

ABIGAIL SMITH ADAMS, the daughter of the Reverend William Smith and Elizabeth Quincy, had been educated at home, acquiring a pious upbringing from her parents, and a keen interest in politics from her grandfather Josiah Quincy. She kept her husband in Philadelphia informed.

My bursting Heart must find vent at my pen

Dearest Friend   [Boston] Sunday June 18 1775

The Day, perhaps the decisive Day is come on which the fate of America depends. My bursting Heart must find vent at my pen. I have just heard that our dear Friend Dr. [Joseph] Warren is no more but fell gloriously fighting for his Country—saying better to die honourably in the field than ignominiously hang upon the Gallows. Great is our Loss. . . . The Battle began upon our intrenchments upon Bunkers Hill, a Saturday morning about 3 o clock and has not ceased yet & tis now 3 o'clock Sabbeth afternoon.

Tis expected they will come out over the Neck to night, & a dreadful Battle must ensue. Almighty God cover the heads of our Country men, & be a shield to our Dear Friends. How many have fallen we know not—the constant roar of the cannon is so distressing that we can not Eat, Drink or Sleep . . . I shall Tarry here till tis thought unsafe by my Friends, & then I have secured myself a retreat at your brothers [Elihu] who has kindly offerd me part of his house [in Randolph, Massachusetts]. I cannot compose myself to write any further at present.

Tuesday afternoon

I am not able to give you any authentick account of last Saturday, but you will not be destitute of inteligence. . . . I ardently pray that you may be supported thro the arduous task you have before you. . . . The Spirits of the people are very good. The loss of Charlstown affects them no more than a Drop in the Bucket.

June 25 1775 Braintree

When we consider all the circumstances attending this action we stand astonished that our people were not all cut off. They had but one hundred feet intrenched, the number who were engaged, did not exceed 800, & they had not half amunition enough. The reinforcements not able to get to them seasonably the tide was up & high, so that their floating batteries came upon each side of the causway & the row gallies keeping a continual fire. Added to this the fire from fort hill & from the Ship, the Town in flames all round them & the heat from the flames so intence as scarcely to be borne; the day one of the hottest we have had this Season & the wind blowing the smoke in their faces—only figure to yourself all these circumstances, and then consider that we do not count 60 Men lost. My Heart overflows at the recollection. . . .

Your Brother is very desirous of being in the army, but your good Mother is really voilent against it. I cannot persuaid nor reason her into a consent. Neither he nor I dare let her know that he is trying for a place. My Brother has a Captains commission, and is stationd in Cambridge. I thought you had the best of inteligence or I should have taken pains to have been more perticuliar. As to Boston, there are many persons yet there who would be glad to get out if they could. Mr. [Thomas] Boylstone & Mr. [Moses] Gill the printer with his family are held upon the black list tis said. 'Tis certain they watch them so narrowly that they cannot escape. . . .

Nabby Johny Charly Tommy all send duty. Tom says I wish I could see *par*. You would laugh to see them all run upon the Sight of a Letter—like chickens for a crum, when the Hen clucks. Charls says *mar* What is it? Any good news? & who is for us & who against us, is the continual inquiry. . . .

Yours ever more,

the most abject slaves

Braintre July 5 1775

The present state of the inhabitants of Boston is that of the most abject slaves under the most cruel & despotick of Tyrants. Among many instances I could mention let me relate one. Upon the 17 of june printed hand Bills were pasted up at the corner of streets & upon houses forbideing any inhabitant to go upon their houses or upon any eminence upon pain of death. The inhabitants dared not to look out of their houses nor bee heard or seen to ask a Question. Our prisoners were brought over to the long wharff and there laid all night without any care of their wounds or any resting place but the pavements till the next day, when they exchanged it for the jail, since which we hear they are civily treated. Their living cannot be good, as they can have no fresh provisions. Their Beaf we hear is all gone, and their own wounded men die very fast, so that they have raisd a report that the Bullets were poisond. Fish they cannot have—they have renderd it so difficult to procure it, and the Admiral is such a villan as to oblige every fishing schooner to pay a Dollor every time they go out. The money that has been paid for passes is incredible. Some have given ten twenty 30 and forty Dollors to get out with a small proportion of their things. . . .

You Scarcely make mention of Dr. Franklin. Surely he must be a valuable member [of the Congress]. . . .

We have had some fine rains, since I wrote you last. I hope we shall not now have famine added to war. Grain Grain is what we want here—meat we have enough & to spair. Pray don't let Bass [a servant] forget my pins. . . . We shall very soon have no coffee nor sugar nor pepper here—but huckle berrys and milk we are not obliged to commerce for. . . .

Good Night with thoughts of thee do I close my Eyes; Angels gaurd and protect thee, and may a safe return ere long bless thy   Portia[25]

[John was full of admiration for his wife's fortitude: "You are really brave, my dear, you are an Heroine."]

HANNAH WINTHROP to Mercy Otis Warren:

my Blood boils with resentment

Dear Mrs. Warren, the Friend and Sister of my heart,   [late June 1775?]

What a great Consolation is it, That tho the restless ambition & unbounded avarice & wicked machinations of some original Characters have deprivd us of many of the pleasures of life, yet are they not able to take from us the heartfelt Satisfaction of mutual affection, of Friendly Converse? Your Favor [letter] Truly Delineates human nature in a disagreable light, The Contrast is very striking. What have we to expect from Such Vitiated Persons as you present to View of the British Generals, I hope their wicked inclinations will be restraind. I am

Charmed with the Portrait you give of General Washington! Must not we expect Success under the direction of So much goodness?

But my heart Bleeds for the people of Boston my Blood boils with resentment at the Treatment they have met with from Gage! Can any thing equal his Barbarity, Turning the poor out of Town without any Support? Those persons who were bereft of any means of Support Stoppd & Searchd, not sufferd to Carry any thing with them! Can any thing equal the distress of parents seperated from their Children, The tender husband detain in Cruel Captivity from the Wife of his Bosom, She torn with anxiety in fearful looking for & expectation of Vengance from the obdurate heart of a Tyrant, Supported by wicked advisers? Can a mercifull Heaven look on these things & not interpose? Is there not a day of retribution at hand? Should these things Continue what a horrid Prospect would a severe Winter afford? How many must fall a Sacrifice to the unrelenting rigours of Cold & want,— be ye cloathd & be ye warmd will be of little efficacy to the trembling naked limbs or the hungry Soul of many a one who once lived in affluence. I believe human nature never produced but one Parallel Tyrant, Cesar Borgia, the Series of whose Cruelties will at any time make human nature shudder. . . .

Where is the Historic page that can furnish us with such Villainy. The laying a whole town in ashes, after repeated promises that if they would protect their troops in their return from Concord, it should be the last place that should suffer harm. How did they give shelter to the wounded expiring Soldiers & their spouses, their beds were prepard to receive them, the women readily engaged in pouring balm in to their wounds, making broths & Cordials to Support their exhausted spirits, for at that time the Softer Sex had not been innured to trickling blood & gaping wounds. Some of the unhappy Victims died, they gave up the ghost Blessing the hands that gave relief, and now in return for this kindness, they take the first opportunity to make 500 householders miserable, involving many a poor widow & orphan in one common ruin. Be astonished O heavens at this & let the inhabitants of america tremble to fall into the hands of such a merciless foe![26]

ELIZABETH MURRAY CAMPBELL SMITH INMAN, the friend of Christian Barnes, did not flee. She had returned to her house in Cambridge from Scotland in the summer of 1771, and married Ralph Inman, a wealthy merchant, soon thereafter. On April 19, 1775, Inman was stranded in Boston, his wife at the Cambridge farm. She wrote:

we are thought wonders

Cambridge 22nd April, 1775

You know how fond I am of grandeur . . . but never imagined I should arrive at the muckle [great] honor of being a General; that is now the case. I have a guard [American] at the bottom of the Garden, a number of men to patrol to the Marsh, and round the farm, with a body guard that now covers our kitchen parlor, and now at twelve o'clock they are in a sweet sleep, while Miss Denforth and I are in the middle parlor with a board nailed across the door to protect them from harm. The kitchen doors are also nailed. They have the closet for their guns. . . . The women and children have all left Cambridge, so we are thought wonders. . . . There is not one servant will stay if I go. Poor Creatures, they depend on me for protection, and I do not chuse to disappoint them: as far as it is in my power I will protect them.

This day we had a visit of an officer from our headquarters with written orders to our guards to attend in a very particular manner to our directions. He said we were the happiest folks he had seen. To convince you of that I'll tell you how we are employed. Jack [a slave] is in the garden, the others are planting potatoes. We intend to make fence and plant Corn next week. To show you the goodness of the people, they say we may have what provisions we want.

[During the next weeks, the Inmans exchanged letters as to what to do. Elizabeth Inman, ever practical, first proposed moving to St. John, New Brunswick, lock, stock, and barrel but went to her brother's farm instead. As the summer progressed, she realized she could make a profit on harvesting the summer crop, and she was loathe to leave the farm. When she learned that her husband was actually planning to flee to England, leaving her behind, and that he accused her of aiding the rebels, she made her displeasure clear.]

what else am I accused of

Dear Sir   Brush-Hill, July 30th, 1775
In my last I told you I was planning night and day. These plans were well meant and not selfish. However, as they do not suit you, I rest satisfied. If you had given Mrs. Hooper the letter and told her you would be glad if she would stay in town till I could come in, she would certainly have done it, and according to my desire she might have sent for fresh meat. I am sure it would have been granted, as G. Washington says he will do every thing in his Power to serve her.

Words cannot describe my astonishment when I received your message . . . that you would go to London . . . If this is a return for the many anxious and fatigueing days I have had, I leave it to your better Judgement, and will endeavor to submit. To save you from every anxiety that is in my power to prevent, I enclose your order on Clark & Nightengale. . . . Now, Sir, you have received this valuable treasure (an order for one hundred pound sterling), I beg you'll cast off your cares. Anxiety is very bad for the health, which you'll require a great share of, as well as money and good spirits, in seeing and being seen in England.

You have sent a List of debts with directions to get Intrest but not principle. I hate to be insulted, therefore cannot make any demand at present, nor at any other time, without a power [of attorney] from you; no doubt you'll leave one with some friend before you sail. Believe me, Mr. Inman, I am not anxious about a mentinence. Experience has taught me, water-gruel and salt for supper and breakfast, with a bit of meat, a few greens or roots, are enough for me. No doubt you blame me to your numerous acquaintance for not coming to Town. I think they ought to hear my reasons before they condemn me. In the first of the bussle you wrote to me that I was better in the Country than in town, after that you wrote to me you could not command but seventy pound sterling a year, and provisions were very dear and scarce. A few weeks after that, you invited me and your large family into town, which family, I mean those you had before I lived at Cambridge, spent three hundred and twenty pound sterling a year, and the produce of the farm. This invitation I thought very seriously of, and would have accepted it with pleasure on my own account, but was and am certain it would have been cruel on theirs. Therefore I wrote to you that sum would not buy them the worst of provisions in the cheapest times, and proposed my staying to assist them in protecting and taking care of the crop that could be saved, in order to maintain them, till they could raise another in some quiet part of the country. The hay we were obliged to move; there was twenty-five Ton of it. I paid three pound ten shilling O. T. [Old Tenor, colonial paper currency] a load for bringing it here. At that time your carts and Brush-hill ones were employed in bringing furniture &c. The rye turns out very well, they are now thrashing it. There is but little hay any where, the drought has been very severe. . . .

As to the aspersion of this being G[eneral Charles]. Lee's headquarters, I cannot imagine how it arose. I never saw him till Saturday at the Lines. None of the gentlemen have been here but Mr. Sargent once to wait on his lady. As to having letters directed to my care, I could not deny that privilege to those that asked me. They knew Mr. Sargent lived in your house, who went to head quarters every day, and had an opportunity to take them up and send them here. I beg to know what else I am accused of. Be assured, Dear Sir, I will with pleasure account for every action that I remember since the year seventeen hundred and twenty-six (the year of my birth).

I have not had the manners to return one of the visits the Ladies paid me on my arrival here.   Adieu Dear Sir.[27]

ELIZABETH FOOTE and ABIGAIL FOOTE of Colchester, Connecticut, were engaged in their busy, daily routines when the news of the momentous events in Boston arrived. It seemed to have little effect on their lives. Elizabeth Foote wrote in her Journal:

to fight the regulars

[Thursday April 13, 1775]—I made a gown for Mrs. [Amos] Wells and about noon went to Mr. Jones, from thence to Mr. Otis's and Hannah came home with me to work and we fixed our wheels to spin linen and Mrs. Wells owed me 7s 6d for my work being 7 per day.

Tuesday 18—I rose before the sun and made apple pies and dumplins for breakfast and Lura Jones and Sally Otis came back with us last night we meeting of them and so stay'd to breakfast, but they said they would not if it had not rained. I did housework and spool'd a little. . . .

Thursday 20—I did housework and made gowns for Lieut. Wells's wife. At night it rained and they stayed all night. In the morning they paid me the money and so went home.

Friday 21—In the morning we heard they had begun to fight at Boston. About noon there came an Indian and his wife (he said it was) here and I bought a snuff bottle of 'em with bread and cheese and cider. I did housework and quilled [quilted] for Ellen as I have done all this week.

Saturday 22—I just got the work done up and the quilts filled when Jonah came and told me to go making biscuit for to carry to fight the regulars which I did and baked a pudding and you may guess at the rest. . . .

Tuesday 25—Morning milked the cows and went to Capt. Caverly's but came right back to get some bacon and beef tongues for Mr. Wilde on the town's cost, which weighed 8 lb 12 oz and Jonas Cleavland had 13 lb pork and 7 lb 8 oz of cheese on the town cost last Saturday.

[Abigail Foote also kept a journal.]

begun to spool a piece. . . made cheese

[June 1775] Thursday 29—I begun to spool a piece for Israels [their brother] shirts and a little before night went down to Mr. Caverlys old house to pick some cherries.

July [1775] Sunday 9—I stayed at home in the forenoon and made cheese. In the afternoon I rid Israels mare to Antioch.

Wednesday 12—I went to Mr. Otis's and spooled some of Mrs. Wright's yarn and come home about noon and sot my piece to work and Eliza Wells was here and I helped Israel pole hay a little.

Monday 17—Israel killed a calf and I dressed the feet and went and carried some veal to Noah Foots and there was a thunder shower [in the] afternoon.

[Elizabeth Foote sometimes found it difficult to keep her journal up to date.]

Procrastination is surely the thief of time

[October Wednesday 18 1775]—I forgot what I did.

Tuesday 24—I lay a bed till sun an hour high. I got up and carded a little while and then writ journal for 2 weeks back and Alice went home sick after she had spun 4 knots. Procrastination is surely the thief of time.[28]

From Philadelphia, George Washington wrote to his wife Martha at Mount Vernon: "My Dearest . . . It has been determined in Congress that the whole Army raised for the defence of the American Cause shall be put under my care." (June 18, 1775). Though loathe to accept the assignment, he viewed it as "a kind of destiny." Instructed to go to Boston immediately, he arrived in early July and found an army with fewer men than he had hoped, no discipline, little equipment or gunpowder. By winter, many of the men had gone home, their enlistment terms having expired; General Gage was recalled to England; and Washington bided his time.

MARTHA DANDRIDGE CUSTIS WASHINGTON was the eldest daughter of the planter Col. John D. Dandridge of Tidewater Virginia. She had little formal education but acquired all the requisite social graces and housekeeping skills thought necessary for a woman. In her youth she was an excellent horsewoman.

A wealthy widow when she married George Washington in 1758, their life together at Mount Vernon was a contented one. When Congress ordered General Washington to Boston, Martha Washington too prepared for war, instructing her slaves in spinning, knitting, smoking meats, making jams; she actively participated in these activities. She was also determined not to be left behind. On November 16, with her son Jack and daughter-in-law, Elizabeth "Nelly" Calvert Custis, she began her trek north, traveling via Philadelphia, and arrived in Cambridge a month later. She described what she found in a letter to a young friend, Elizabeth Ramsay, in Alexandria, Virginia.

I shuder every time I hear the sound of a gun

Dear miss   Cambridge December the 30th 1775

I now set down to tell you that I arrived hear safe, and our party all well—we were fortunate in our time of setting out as the weather proved fine all the time we were on the road—I did not reach Philad till the tuesday after I left home, we were so attended and the gentlemen so kind, that I am lade under obligations to them that I shall not for get soon. I don't doubt but you have seen the Figuer our arrival made in the Philadelphia paper—and I left it in as great pomp as if I had been a very great some body.

I have waited some days to collect some thing to tell, but allas there is nothing but what you will find in the papers—every person seems to be cheerfull and happy hear,—some days we have a number of cannon and shells from Boston and Bunkers Hill, but it does not seem to surprise any one but me; I confess I shuder every time I hear the sound of a gun—I have been to dinner with two of the Generals, [Charles] Lee & [Israel] Putnam and I just took a look at pore Boston & Charls town—from prospect Hill Charlestown has only a few chimneys standing in it, thare seems to be a number of very fine Buildings in Boston but god knows how long they will stand; they are pulling up all the warfs for fire wood—to me that never see any thing of war, the preperations, are very terable indeed, but I endevor to keep my fears to my self as well as I can. . . .

This is a beautyfull Country, and we had a very plasent journey through new england, and had the plasure to find the General very well we came within the month from home to Camp.

I am Dear miss your most affectionate Friend . . .   Martha Washington[29]

[A month later, she continued to her sister Anna Maria Dandridge Bassett at Eltham, Virginia.]

I suppose thare will be a change soon

My dear Sister   Cambridge January the 31, 1776

I have wrote to you several times, in hopes it would put you in mind of me, but I find it has not had its intended affect. I am really very uneasy at not hearing from you and have made all the excuses for you that I can think of but it will not doe much longer. If I doe not get a letter by this nights post I shall think myself quite forgot by all my Freinds. The distance is long yet the post comes in regularly every week—

The General, myself, and Jack are very well. Nelly Custis is I hope getting well again, and I beleive is with child. I hope noe accident will happen to her in going back [to Virginia]. I have not thought much about it yet god know whare we shall be; I suppose thare will be a change soon but how I cannot pretend to say—A few days agoe Gen [Henry] Clinton, with several companyes Sailed out of Boston Harbor to what place distant for, we cannot find out. Some think it is to Virginia he is gon, others to New York—they have been keept in Boston so long that I suppose they will be glad to seek for a place where they may have more room as they cannot get out anywhere here but by water—our navey has been very successful in taking thair vessels; two was taken last week loded with coles and potatoes wines & several other articles for the use of the troops—If General Clinton is gon to New York,—General Lee is there before him and I hope will give him a very warm reception,—he was sent thare some time a goe to have matters put in proper order in case any disturbances should happen, as thare are many Tories in that part of the world, or at least many are susspected thare to be unfreindly to our cause at this time—winter hear has been so remarkable mild the Rivers has never been frozen hard enough to walk upon the Ice since I came heer. My Dear sister be so good as to remember me to all enquireing friends. . . .

I am my Dear Nancy your ever effectionate sister   Martha Washington[30]

ABIGAIL ADAMS to John Adams in Philadelphia:

A fine, quiet night no allarms no Cannon

Sunday Noon [Braintree 17 March 1776]
Being quite Sick with a voilent cold I have tarried at Home to day; I find the fireing was occasiond by our peoples taking possession of Nook Hill, which they kept in spite of the Cannonade, & which has really obliged our Enemy to decamp this morning on board the Transports; as I hear by a mesenger just come from Head Quarters. Some of the Select Men have been to the lines & inform that they have carried off [every] thing they could possibly take, & what they could not they have [missing] . . . many articles of good Household furniture having in the course of the week come on shore at Great Hill [Hough's Neck], both upon this & Weymouth Side, Lids of Desks, mahogona chairs, tables &c. Our People I hear will have Liberty to enter Boston, those who have had the Small pox. The Enemy have not yet come under Sail, I cannot help suspecting some design which we do not yet comprehend; to what quarter of the World they are bound is wholy unknown, but tis generally Thought to New york. Many people are Elated with their quitting Boston, I confess I do not feel so, tis only lifting the burden from one shoulder to the other which perhaps is less able or less willing to support it. To what a contemptable situation are the Troops of Britain reduced! I feel glad however that Boston is not distroyed. I hope it will be so secured & guarded as to baffel all future attemps against it—I hear that General Howe said upon going upon some Eminence in Town to view our Troops who had taken Dorchester Hill unperceived by them till Sun rise, "My God these fellows have done more work in one Night than I could make my Army do in three months" & he might well say so for in one Night two forts & long Breast Works were sprung up besides several Barracks.

300 & 70 teems were imployed most of which went 3 load in the Night, beside 4000 men who worked with good Hearts.

Monday morning

A fine quiet night no allarms no Cannon. The more I think of our Enemies quitting Boston, the more amaz'd I am, that they should leave such a harbour, such fortifications, such intrenchments, and that we should be in peaceable possession of a Town which we expected would cost us a river of Blood without any Drop shed. Shurely it is the Lords doings & it is Marvelous in our Eyes. Every foot of Ground which they obtain now they must fight for.[31]

Although Boston was now freed from the enemy, the War had just begun. Turmoil and destruction spread to other areas. Canada, New York City, and Charleston, South Carolina, were early targets.

The Second Continental Congress, when it assembled on May 10, 1775 in Philadelphia, faced a myriad of problems; still, all the members agreed—as the United Colonies of America—to resist what were viewed as the unconstitutional acts of the British Parliament. Few thought of independence. News that the Olive Branch Petition (signed by most of the Congressional delegates) had been rejected; that all trade with the colonies was forbidden; and that any American vessel was considered fair game for capture, the crew to be impressed into the Royal Navy; pushed the Congress into reconsidering its position. Moreover, the continued skirmishes between the British and the patriots as well as the disastrous American defeat at Quebec forced those who had been neutral to take a stand either for or against going to war.

Very influential in this regard was the publication in January 1776 of a pamphlet, *Common Sense,* by an Englishman, a recent arrival in America. Arguing that the only guarantee for American liberty was independence, Thomas Paine's work was widely read and discussed. By May 1776, Virginia appointed a committee headed by George Mason to devise a declaration of rights and a plan for governing an independent state. While men debated, women, left tending farms and raising children, took steps to implement their own ideas.

Although women were not able to vote, serve on juries, or participate in the political process, they found other methods to articulate their concerns and demands. Some, such as Abigail Adams, wrote their absent husbands. Some, as food costs spiraled out of control, wrote broadsides or took to the streets, confronting merchants who they believed were hoarding or overcharging. In August 1776 in Kingston, New York, a crowd of women surrounded the chamber where the Committee for Detecting and Defeating Conspiracies was meeting to demand tea; in May 1777, twenty-two women and three Continental soldiers in Poughkeepsie, New York, seized tea from the wife of merchant Peter Messier, not just once but on three different occasions.

ABIGAIL ADAMS, writing to John Adams in Philadelphia, reported

a great Scarcity of Sugar and Coffe

[Boston July 31, 1777]

You must know that there is a great Scarcity of Sugar & Coffe, articles which the Female part of the State are very loth to give up, especially whilst they consider the Scarcity occasiond by the merchants having Secreted a large Quantity. There had been much rout & Noise in the Town for several weeks. Some Stores had been opend by a Number of people & the Coffe & Sugar carried into the market & dealt out by pounds. . . . A Number of Females, some say a hundred, some say more, assembled with a cart & trucks, marchd down to the ware House [of merchant Thomas Boylston] & demanded the keys, which he refused to deliver. Upon which one of them Seazd him by his Neck & tossd him into the cart, upon his finding no Quarter, he deliverd the keys, when they tipd up the cart & dischargd him; then opend the warehouse, Hoisted out the Coffe themselves, put it into the trucks & drove off. . . . A large concourse of Men Stood amazd, Silent Spectators of the whole transaction.[32]

MOLLY GUTRIDGE signed this "composition," adding "Be sure it is no imposition."

A New Touch on the Times Well adapted to the distressing
Situation of every Sea-port Town
By a Daughter of Liberty, living in Marblehead

Our best beloved they are gone,
We cannot tell they'll e'er return,
For they are gone the ocean wide,
Which for us now they must provide.
　　For they go on the roaring seas,
For which we can't get any ease,
For they are gone to work for us,
And that it is to fill our purse.
　　And to fill our houses too,
What more could we then have them do?
They now do more than we deserve,
Wan't it for them we now should starve,
Starve then we should and perish too,
And without them what could we do?
　　We must do as well as we can,
What could women do without man,
They could not do by night and day,
Go round the world, and that they'll say,
　　They could not do by day or night,
I think that man's a woman's delight,
It's hard and cruel times, to live,
Takes thirty dollars to buy a sieve.
　　To buy sieves and other things too,

To go thro' the world how can we do,
For times they grow worse and worse,
I'm sure it sinks our scanty purse.
Had we a purse to reach the sky,
It would be all just vanity,
If we had that and ten times more,
'Twould be like sand upon the shore.
For money is not worth a pin,
Had we but salt we've any thing,
For salt is all the Farmer's cry,
If we've no salt we sure must die.
We can't get fire nor yet food,
Takes 20 weight of sugar for two foot of wood,
We cannot get bread nor yet meat,
We see the world is nought but cheat.
We cannot now get meat nor bread
By means of which we shake [our head]
All we can get it is but rice
And that is of a wretched price
And as we go up and down,
We see the doings of this town,
Some say they an't victuals nor drink,
Others say they are ready to sink.
Our lives they all are tired here,
We see all things so cruel dear,
Nothing now-a-days to be got,
To put in kettle or in pot.
These times will learn us to be wise,
We now do eat what we despis'd
I now have something more to say,
We must go up and down the Bay
To get a fish a-days to fry,
We can't get fat were we to die,
Were we to try all thro' the town,
The world is now turn'd up-side down.
. . . .
I now have ended this my song.[33]

Women viewed their actions as "patriotic" just as their insistence on the use of homespun garments was. It was a limited way to be heard. Of course, there were some encouraging signs: the constitution of New Jersey, adopted in 1776, defined a voter as an adult inhabitant, who owned property worth fifty pounds and who had been a resident for at least one year. Nowhere did it state that the voter had to be a white male. As married women, by and large, were limited in the property they could own themselves, this left the vote to single women. And, until 1807, when the New Jersey State legislature redefined the voter as a white, tax-paying, male adult, vote they did. Free blacks were also not disenfranchised at first, though few would have qualified given the property requirement.

Some women were beginning to test the waters. Mrs. Inman had a business that was able to flourish even in a male-dominated society. There were others as well: female publishers Hannah Watson of *The Connecticut Courant*; Clementina Rind of the *Virginia Gazette*, whose motto was "Open to ALL PARTIES but influenced by NONE"; Sarah Goddard of *The Providence Gazette*, and her daughter Mary Katherine Goddard, who published *The Maryland Journal* in Baltimore. Mary Katherine Goddard was able to continue printing the paper (one of the most circulated papers in the Colonies) throughout the War only by stocking dry goods and stationary, and offering bookbinding to make ends meet. As prices soared and subscribers were unable to pay, Goddard took payment in kind, which she would then sell: butter, beef, beeswax, feathers, cotton rags. Then, in August 1775, she was appointed Postmistress of Baltimore, a post she held until late 1789. Most important for her was the authorization by Congress, on January 18, 1777, to print the first official issue of the Declaration of Independence.

ABIGAIL ADAMS had some questions for her husband in Philadelphia.

Who shall frame these Laws?

November 27 1775

Tis a fortnight to Night since I wrote you a line during which, I have been confined with the Jaundice, Rhumatism and a most voilent cold; I yesterday took a puke which has releived me and I feel much better to day. . . .

I was pleasing myself with the thoughts that you would soon be upon your return. Tis in vain to repine. I hope the publick will reap what I sacrifice.

I wish I knew what mighty things were fabricating. If a form of Goverment is to be Established here what one will be assumed? Will it be left to our assemblies to chuse one? and will not many men have many minds? and shall we not run into Dissentions among ourselves?

I am more & more convinced that Man is a dangerous creature, & that power whether vested in many or a few is ever grasping, & like the grave cries give, give. The great fish swallow up the small, and he who is most strenuous for the Rights of the people, when vested with power, is as eager after the perogatives of Goverment. You tell me of degrees of perfection to which Humane Nature is capable of arriving, & I believe it, but at the same time lament that our admiration should arise from the scarcity of the instances.

The Building up a Great Empire, which was only hinted at by my correspondent may now I suppose be realized even by the unbelievers. Yet will not ten thousand Difficulties arise in the formation of it? The Reigns of Goverment have been so long slakned, that I fear the people will not quietly submit to those restraints which are necessary for the peace, & security, of the community; if we seperate from Brittain, what Code of Laws will be established. How shall we be governd so as to retain our Liberties? Can any government be free which is not adminstred by general stated Laws? Who shall frame these Laws? Who will give them force & energy? Tis true your Resolutions as a Body have heithertoo had the force of Laws. But will they continue to have?

When I consider these things and the prejudices of people in favour of Ancient customs & Regulations, I feel anxious for the fate of our Monarchy or Democracy or what ever is to take place. I soon get lost in a Labyrinth of perplexities, but whatever occurs, may justice & righteousness be the Stability of our times, and order arise out of confusion. Great difficulties may be surmounted by patience & perseverance.

I believe I have tired you with politicks. . . . All Letters I believe have come safe to hand. I have Sixteen from you, & wish I had as many more.

Adieu. Yours.

make use of that power only for our happiness

Braintree March 31 1776

I feel a gaieti de Coer to which before I was a stranger. I think the Sun looks brighter, the Birds sing more melodiously, & Nature puts on a more chearfull countanance. We feel a temporary peace, & the poor fugitives are returning to their deserted habitations.

Tho we felicitate ourselves, we sympathize with those who are trembling least the Lot of Boston should be theirs. But they cannot be in similar circumstances unless pusilanimity & cowardise should take possession of them. They have time & warning given them to see the Evil & shun it.—I long to hear that you have declared an independancy—and by the way in the new Code of Laws which I suppose it will be necessary for you to make I desire you would Remember the Ladies, & be more generous & favourable to them than your ancestors. Do not put such unlimited power into the hands of the Husbands. Remember all Men would be tyrants if they could. If perticuliar care & attention is not paid to the Laidies we are determined to foment a Rebelion, and will not hold ourselves bound by any Laws in which we have no voice, or Representation.

That your Sex are Naturally Tyrannical is a Truth so thoroughly established as to admit of no dispute, but such of you as wish to be happy willingly give up the harsh title of Master for the more tender & endearing one of Friend. Why then, not put it out of the power of the vicious & the Lawless to use us with cruelty & indignity with impunity. Men of Sense in all Ages abhor those customs which treat us only as the vassals of your Sex. Regard us then as Beings placed by providence under your protection & in immitation of the Supreem Being make use of that power only for our happiness. . . . I need not say how much I am Your ever faithfull Friend.

[Abigail Adams shared her husband's reactions with Mercy Otis Warren in Plymouth.]

he cannot but Laugh at My Extrodonary Code of Law

Braintree April 27 1776

[His] Letters to me have been generally short, but he pleads in Excuse the critical State of affairs & the Multiplicity of avocations and says further that he has been very Busy, & writ near ten Sheets of paper, about Some affairs which he does not chuse to Mention for fear of accident.

He is very Sausy to me in return for a List of Female Grievances which I transmitted to him, I think I will get you to join me in a petition to Congress, I thought it was very probable our wise Statesmen would Erect a New Government & form a new code of Laws, I ventured to Speak a word in behalf of our Sex, who are rather hardly dealt with by the Laws of England which gives such unlimitted power to the Husband to use his wife Ill. . . .

In return he tells me he cannot but Laugh at My Extrodonary Code of Law: that he had heard their Struggle had loosned the bands of Government; that children & apprentices were dissabedient, that Schools & Colledges were grown turbulant, that Indians Slighted their Guardians, and Negroes grew insolent to their Masters. But my Letter was the first intimation that another Tribe more Numerous & powerfull than all the rest were grown discontented. This is rather too coarse a complement, he adds, but that I am so sausy he wont blot it out.

So I have help'd the Sex abundantly, but I will tell him I have only been making trial of the Disintresstedness of his virtue, & when weigh'd in the balance have found it wanting.

It would be bad policy to grant us greater power say they Since under all the disadvantages we Labour we have the assendancy over their Hearts

And charm by accepting, by submitting sway.

I wonder Apollo & the Muses could not have indulged me with a poetical Genious. I have always been a votary to her charms but never could assend Parnassus myself. . . . Good Night my Friend.   Portia

[Abigail Adams to John Adams:]

I have not felt in a humour to entertain you

B[raintre]e May 7-9 1776

I believe tis near ten days since I wrote you a line. I have not felt in a humour to entertain you. If I had taken up my pen perhaps some unbecomeing invective might have fallen from it; the Eyes of our Rulers have been closed & a Lethargy has Seazd almost every Member. I fear a fatal Security has taken possession of them. Whilst the Building is on flame they tremble at the expence of water to quench it. In short two months has Elapsed since the evacuation of Boston, & very little has been done in that time to secure it, or the Harbour from future invasion till the people are all in a flame; and no one among us that I have heard of even mentions expence, they think universally that there has been an amaizing neglect some where. . . . "Tis a Maxim of state That power & Liberty are like Heat & moisture; where they are well mixt every thing prospers, where they are single, they are destructive."

A Government of more Stability is much wanted in this colony, and they are ready to receive it from the Hands of the Congress, and since I have begun with Maxims of State I will add an other viz. that a people may let a king fall, yet still remain a people, but if a king let his people slip from him, he is no longer a king. And as this is most certainly our case, why not proclaim to the World in decisive terms your own importance?

Shall we not be dispiced by foreign powers for hesitateing so long at a word?

I can not say I think you very generous to the Ladies, for whilst you are proclaiming peace & good will to Men, Emancipating all Nations, you insist upon retaining an absolute power over wives. But you must remember that Arbitary power is like most other things which are very hard, very liable to be broken—and notwithstanding all your wise Laws & Maxims we have it in our power not only to free ourselves but to Subdue our Masters, and without voilence throw both your natural & legal authority at our feet

"Charm by accepting, by submitting sway
Yet have our Humour most when we obey."

. . . . Our Little ones whom you so often recommend to my care and instruction shall not be deficient in virtue or probity if the precepts of a Mother have their desired Effect, but they would be doubly inforced could they be indulged with the example of a Father constantly before them. . . . Johnny & Charls have the Mumps, a bad disorder, but they are not very bad. Pray be kind enough to remember me at all times & write as often as you possibly can to your   Portia

I make out better than I did

[Braintree] May 27 [1776]

My Heart is as light as a feather and my Spirits are dancing. I received this afternoon a fine parcel of Letters & papers . . . it was a feast to me. . . . I would not have you anxious about me. I make out better than I did. I have hired a Negro fellow for 6 months, am to give him ten pounds which is much lower than I had any prospect of getting help, & Belcher is exceedingly assiduous & I believe faithfull in what he undertakes. If he should purloin a little I must bear that; he is very diligent, and being chief engineer is ambitious. If you could find a few moments leisure just to write him a few lines & let him know that I had wrote you that he had the care of the place, and that you should be glad of his best Services upon it, of his constant care & attention, I believe it would go a good way towards insureing it.[34]

MARY BARTLETT, raised in Newton, New Hampshire, married her cousin Josiah Bartlett in 1754. A doctor, he augmented his income through transactions in land and lumber. The couple had twelve children, eight of whom survived to adulthood. Bartlett served in the Second Continental Congress and was a signer of the Declaration of Independence. He served on various committees and was present after the battle of Bennington in August 1777 to attend the wounded. Like so many other women, Mary Bartlett, left in charge of the farm and the education of the children, had to make the decisions for their welfare without her husband.

Being busy, she may have dictated the letters to her eldest daughters and then signed them.

this year will Decide the fate of America

My Dear   Kingstown [New Hampshire] June 30th 1776
   This morning I Recd your Seventh Letter and am thankfull to hear you are in good health. I wish you Peace and Prosperity in all your lawfull undertakeing. . . .
   As for farming business I Beleive Biley and Peter [servants] maniges Pretty well. . . . As for hay I belive it will be near or quite as Scarce with us as it was last year. . . . Inglish Corn Looks very well. If we have Rains I Hope it will turn out well. We had a fine Shower Last Sunday Evening. Indian Corn Some Backward But it Grows fast now; the weather very hot and Dry; the worms has eat Considerably of our Corn in the new ground; and Some other People Complain of the worms among their flax and Corn. Apples very Scarce I belive there will not be much Cyder made this year. However I hope and trust we Shall be Provided for as we have Been in times Past Caried throw many trials and Difficulties Beyond Expectation.

                                         July 13, 1776
   The times Looks Dark and Gloomy upon the account of the wars. I belive this year will Decide the fate of America which way it will turn God only knows, we must look to him for Direction & Protection.

                                 Kingstown July 20th 1776
   The men among us are very backward about going into the war they are not Contented with the Province bounty. Our men have had a town meeting & have voted to raise their bounty to fifty Dollars a man beside their wages. They are to begin their march to Day & meet at Esqr. Webster's at Chester. . . .
   We hear of wars and tumults from one end of the Continent to the other; I Should be glad to Know if Your courage holds out yet about keeping & Defending america. I Remain Yours &c.

                                 Kingstown Septembr 9th 1776
   Pray Do come home before Cold weather as you Know my Circumstances* will be Difficult in the winter If I am alive. In hast from yours &c

                                            Mary Bartlett[35]

*Mary was pregnant.

Chapter 2

Things indeed look dark

On March 17, 1776, General William Howe evacuated Boston and sailed for Halifax, Nova Scotia, taking with him soldiers, loyalist supporters, women, children, and servants. There he waited for reinforcements before moving to New York City. General Henry Clinton had left a month earlier, his object to meet with Admiral Sir Peter Parker off the Carolinas and to secure Charleston for the British. However, the patriot forces prevailed there, and Clinton returned to New York.

Having sent troops on ahead to begin building fortifications, General Washington and his forces, 18,000 strong, also progressed toward New York City. Both sides were anxious to take control of this major port on the Eastern seaboard: the British as a way to isolate troublesome New England from the other colonies and thus crush the rebellion, the Americans to thwart them and gain the upper hand. Militias were recruited to support the Continental Army; leaving their families, farms, and businesses to be managed by the women, the men streamed toward New York City.

AN UNKNOWN LADY, whose letter was printed in the *American Remembrancer* on April 11, 1776, calmly assessed the situation for a friend in England.

you must be solicitous to hear from us

If you have any idea of our situation you must be solicitous to hear from us. When you are informed that New York is deserted by its old inhabitants and filled with soldiers from New England, Philadelphia, Jersey, etc. you will naturally conclude the environs of it are not very safe for so undisciplined a multitude as our Provincials are represented to be; but I do believe there are few instances of so great a number of men together with so little mischief done by them. . . . they have been employed in creating fortifications in every part of town; it would make you sorry to see the place so changed. . . . You may recollect a sweet situation at Horne's Nook [East 89th Street], that Jacob Walton purchased, built an elegant house . . . he was obliged to quit the place; the troops took possession and fortified there. When Mrs. Walton received the order to go out of her house she burst into tears, for she was fixed to her heart's desire.[1]

Newly wed Gold Selleck Silliman, a lawyer and a major in Connecticut's militia Fourth Regiment, received orders from Governor Jonathan Trumbull to "march forthwith to New York with a part of his regiment, there to wait the arrival of General Washington" (March 19, 1776). Silliman, accompanied by his son Billy, arrived in New York on March 29, quickly found comfortable lodgings with some other officers, toured the fortifications, and voiced confidence in the ability of the Americans to withstand a British attack. "I . . . have taken a Veiw of the greater Part of the Fortifications in this City, and am of Opinion that it would be extreamly difficult for an Army to force its Way into this Town from the Water." His young stepson James Noyes came to visit him for two days in mid-April and reported to his grandmother Rebecca Pabodie Fish:

> I see four large Ships there; one a seventy Gun Ship; and I saw the kings Statue, and he set on a great Horse, both coverd over with leaf Gold; and the King had one bullet hole through his cheek and another through his neck, and they talk of running his Majesty up into Bullets, for he and his horse are made of lead. The houses most all join together; and I never see such a fine place in my life.

By early summer, the city was not so "fine" anymore: many inhabitants had fled to the country for safety. A plot against General Washington's life had been discovered and one suspect executed. There were dysentery and smallpox outbreaks due to the unsanitary living conditions. The scarcity of troops and weapons and skirmishes with Tories as well as the uncertainty of the whereabouts of the British heightened tensions for the Americans. On July 2, 1776, General William Howe landed his troops on Staten Island without opposition; ten days later, two British ships, the *Phoenix* and the *Rose*, sailed up the Hudson River past the blazing guns of the American artillery, and Admiral Richard Howe's ships of war arrived in New York harbor.

MRS. A. HAMPTON, whose sympathies clearly were with the British, vividly described the frightening confusion and dangers of that day to her daughter Polly at Col. Thomas Ellison's house in New Windsor, New York.

this deplorable Cyte

My dear Child   3 miles from new York August 4th 1776
    Oh polly you Cannot be Suficinlly thankful that you are out of this deplorable Cyte [City], where Every thing that once was delightful now only Serves to make one wretched. For my part I cannot Spend one day in it for there is Scarcely one in that I know, all friend gone, gone and god only knows when we Shall return perhaps never.
    I have been as far as haverstraw Since you left this but Could not Content my Self So far from my mother So nancy and I returnd that Same day about 4 hours be fore the Ships went up the river. I never underwent Such a fright in all

my life, Cannons roring, drums Beating to arms, all things in Confusion, my mother out of town, not a friend to go to. Poor nancy and I we had no other refuge but to run for our Lives and indeed we was in great Danger but I was insenceable of it for the Bullets flew thick over our heads as we went up the Bowrey. But thank god we Escaped. What we are reservd for heaven only knows.

I hope you Spend your time more agreable then we do here for there is nothing to be heard but rumour upon rumour. So that I think our time ought to be Spent in Suplicating god, that he would be gratious and gather us from all places whence we are Scattered, and Bring us to our native place and that he would Establish us upon Such foundations of rightiousness and peace that It may nevermore be in the power of our restless adversaries to disturb us. Dear polly I have a good deal to Say more—but Shall Conclude at present with my Earnest wish for your welfare from your Affectionate Mother   A. Hampton

PS . . . I Send you a Lock of my hair[2]

MARY FISH NOYES, a widow, lived in New Haven, Connecticut, with her three sons, Joseph, John, and James. To make ends meet, she took in boarders— students and professors at Yale College as well as members of Connecticut's General Assembly. Besides economic worries, Mary also suffered from a "spiritual deadness" and depression, the result of having lost not only her husband but also two young daughters, and her mother-in-law. However, Mary became increasingly confident in managing the affairs of her family and, thanks to her boarders, became interested in political developments: "hearing so many worthy People of sense converse on affairs so interesting." Into her life came Gold Selleck Silliman, "one whose person and address are exactly agreeable to my taste." They were married on May 24, 1775. While the British and American forces assessed the situation in New York and waited for reinforcements, Mary was able to exchange letters with her husband, and family members visited him. Silliman sent his dirty laundry home.

embark'd in the glorious Cause

My dearest Beloved,   Fairfield July 30, 1776
By the first water conveyance will send you what is left of another old Cheese, and one of the oldest of my new ones. I wonder if a Ham or Bacon would not be acceptable, pray let me know of any thing that may contribute to your comfort you shall have any thing in my house you send for even tho it is for your *Wife* . . . I keep a particular account of our expenses at home; not that I expect to be call'd to account, but for my own satisfaction. . . .
Yours in everything else, your wife (or would be)   Mary Silliman

Fairfield Augt. 7, 1776
What is the reason my dearest says he would not have any Sheep or fowls sent till he writes for them. I'll tell him what I flatter my self is the reason. Don't he hope he may have leave to run home a little while by and by? Yes that he would do with all his heart if the times will allow of it and whether they will is in the womb of providence and I desire to wait on that. . . . I do view you safer where you are embark'd in the glorious Cause than I should any where else . . .

What is the reason that the fleet lies so long inactive? Are they hesitating whether to strike the final blow, or are they recruiting that they may come on us with the greater violence? I desire to leave it with God who sets at helm. . . .

[Augt. 9]—8 oClock how do you do this morning my dearest? . . . I send Jobe [a slave] with this and . . . with some Balm Mother sends you for your own use or to give away to the sick. Bille writes me that yesterday those Row gallys were to make another attack on those Ships up the river, long to know the event of their expeditions, as well as what aspect the enemys present conduct wears in your sight. . . .

I lately hear that the hot ashes of white Oak wood quensh'd in spring water is an excellent thing for the Dysentary.[3]

By mid August, the British army—reinforced by nearly 9,000 Hessian mercenaries, 1,000 British Guards, and fugitive black slaves—totaled 32,000 strong, a formidable force facing the ill-prepared and ill-equipped Americans. On August 22, the British landed troops on Long Island and the Battle of Brooklyn began. Five days later, the British had outmaneuvered and out-fought their opponents—Washington lost more than 1,000 men (900 of whom were taken prisoner) and was barely able to evacuate his troops, some artillery, and provisions across the East River to safety.

Gold Silliman wrote Mary on August 25 that their moves from "Place to Place are so quick & sudden that we have no Opportunity nor Means to convey Beds &c but go only with the Cloaths on our Backs, & our Blankets and a little ready cooked Victuals." In the aftermath of the defeat, soldiers, including members of Silliman's militia, deserted in droves or pretended to be ill so they might be discharged. As the Americans retreated north, and the British prepared to cross into Manhattan, Silliman wrote on September 11:

> we were left to guard the city untill all the rest of the troops were drawn off, and about half an Hour or an Hour after all the other Troops were gone I was ordered with my Brigade to march out of the city and man the Lines on the East River opposite to Bayard's Hill Fort [Grand and Mulberry Streets], where I marched & saw the Regular Army land above me and spread across the Island from one river to the other untill my retreat seemed to be entirely cut off, and soon after received an Order to retreat if I could.

Silliman and the remaining troops did pull back in the nick of time to Harlem Heights (west side of Manhattan, north of 125th Street).

The flow of letters continued between Mary and her husband:

at leasure to converse with the Beloved of my Soul

Dearest Sir,   Fairfield Aut 1776 10 o.Ck PM [Aug. 24-26]
I will for your sake take care of your wife as good care as I can, but she is a little unruly, sometime and get out in the garden to work and gets cold—and I wish her heart was as clear of ill weeds as her garden, but she is as carefull of

worrying her self as she can on all accounts, but she has a great deal on her hands and mind, tho has no reason to complain of any one branch of her family . . . I hear a havy fire was heard from 4 o Clock yesterday P.M. till 3 this morning. If so there has been a dreadfull Battle and, my dearest without doubt was in it. And have you surviv'd it my dear? . . . don't be concerned about my lowness of flesh my dearest, I am very well . . . I don't expect to grow fat till I have the pleasure of seeing you.—*If I do* then.

wont you be willing to take company with you Love?

My dearest beloved, Fairfield Septr. 1, 1776 9 o clock P.M.

And you don't know but that if you live to come home you must sometimes take your Blanket and go out and lie in the woods. And wont you be willing to take company with you Love? . . . I thank my dearest that he left his company and shut himself in a chamber to converse with her whose heart he has, and who is not conscious, that he is ever out of her mind in her waking hours and now and then she has a sweet interview with him in her Sleep. Not withstanding the enemys formidable appearance in preparation, will they not withhold hostilities untill General Sullivan returns? The prisoners here vaunt over us, saying the day is their own, and if it had not been for them D---d contrary winds they would have been in possession of New York before now. . . . I thank you my dearest for seting so much by my Letters. It seems it is not with these as with other commodities; when very plenty, they grow cheap. No we are two misers, the more we have the more we want and like them we love to keep them to look on; and are not willing they should be so much as handled by any other than our selves. Well, we'll keep them, they wont rust by lying, and like virtue they'll shine tho' worn by the fond readers eye. What reason have we to be thankfull (to use your expression in a former Letter) that we can teach paper to articulate. . . . It is late you'd better go to bed. Well I promis'd to be obedient and will go. Good night my dearest Beloved. Heaven protect you.

Septr. 1 10 o clock P.M. When a child I never was more rejoiced when I had done my work and might go to play, than I am now when all are abed, and my domestick care laid by, and I at leasure to converse with the Beloved of my Soul; for I have no interruption; all nature is still calm and serene. And such is the state of my mind this evening with respect to you, myself, and own. . . . O what reason have I to bless God who has sent me good news from you again, as he does by another dear Letter. . . . What woman is there that is blessed as I am in so often receiving tokens of her husbands remembrance. . . . your absence is rendered more tolerable, as each dear favour is a rich *Cordial* to the tender heart of your loving wife. Let those who are strangers to the godlike passion with which our hearts always glow, ask the question you suppose asked (what can he have to say more to what he wrote yesterday) the sweet reflection that our subject is such a copious one that we trust life tho long will not be enough to exhaust it, but that it will still be our theme (tho greatly refined) throughout the endless ages of eternity when God will be all in all, for love never faileth, And God is love. . . . Your very affectionate and dutifull wife

I am sorry our Milisha behave so odly

Fairfield Septr 8 9 o clock P.M.

I want to know how you live, and whether I can send any thing to you that will be comfortable. I send Bottle of Mintwater, and some Ink, which I forgot to apologize for my not sending in two or three of my last till seald. We have been put to it to get ink powder, but at last Billy found some of it at N Haven. . . . I am sorry our Milisha [Militia] behave so odly, and ungratefully defect their Posts. Things indeed look dark, but let us remember that it is frequently darkest just before day. Their deserting you does not weaken the almighty arm, which I hope will ere long be strecht out for our deliverance. A heavy fireing has been heard this day, long to hear the cease, and especially whether my dear Husband is safe. . . .

Septr 9—9 o clock A.M. . . . How are you this morning? what has been the fireing heard ever since it was light till little while ago?

do bid me hold my tongue

Dearest Sir   Fairfield Septr 10 1776

A heavy cannonading was heard here yesterday. Our Milisha flock in numbers home, What is the matter? They say they were discharged, some own they ran away. . . .

Septr 12. . . . Your wife is so in debt [in writing letters to him] . . . she is a bankrupt for she never expects to pay all, so my Creditors must compound, and be content with but small acknowledgements. But how I chatter away, do bid me hold my tongue; no don't neither because that would not be good manners.

Last night Mr. Sturgis paid off his bill £ fifteen. 4 sh. 5/ took for court fees or something so now I can help you if you want. Prue and Sarah finish spinning here tomorrow, must pay them off. I have had the good luck to buy 30 Bushels of ----- [torn] wheat at 4/5 a Bushel.

I think their cause is not good

My dearest Beloved   Fairfield Septr 15 1776 9 o clock P.M.

[Jose] and Billy both have the vapours about you this day, on hearing a heavy fireing of Cannon this morning I am oblig'd to exjert my self to comfort them, and tell them now our faith is put to the tryal, and we ought to pray that our faiths fail not. But they say Dadda is as likely to be killed as any other. I tell them, no, he put his trust in God, and then read them a part of your last dear letter wherein you say you doubt not but when God's wise purposes are answered you shall be returned safe &c—which seemed to quiet them—Johnne is as stidy [steady] as an old philosopher, doing his duty in every particular. Jimme says Mamma don't the Regulars trust in God too? I tell him I don't know what they do, but I think their cause is not good. By this scetch you may see how the dear Creatures hang upon me. O that I might have stidiness and wisdom to set them an example worthy of imitation.

My Beloved,   Fairfield Septr 19 1776 9oClock P.M.

We met with Mr. Peck, who told me he saw you well siting on a rock, eating a peice of Beef roasted on the end of a stick by the fire . . . I congratulate you and the army that your out of that dirty City. . . . Let the regulars take your leavings.

My Beloved   Fairfield Septr 21 1776 9 oClock PM

A great light was seen last night and this morning till a greater in the heavens appeared, towards New York. Some suppose the Regulars burnt that place, and are going off to some other, how is it my dearest? . . .   Mary Silliman

---

The *New York Gazette and Weekly Mercury* of September 30, 1776 reported that

> we had a terrible fire in this city, which consumed about one thousand houses, or nearly a fourth of the whole city. . . . Because the rebels had removed all the bells of the city, the alarm could not be speedily communicated. . . . our friends were the perpetrators of this atrocious deed . . . whilst . . . our enemies were the people who gallantly stept forth, at the risk of their lives, to snatch us from destruction.

Due to strong winds, the fire spread quickly; the British and the Americans pointed accusing fingers at each other as the perpetrators of the conflagration. There was even a rumor that a woman had started it. Silliman wrote his wife from camp in Harlem Heights (September 22):

> A most extraordinary Manaeuvre of the Enemy has taken Place; The Night before last about Midnight a most tremendous Fire was seen from our Lines to the Southward which continued the whole Night . . . it must be the Regulars, and what they shd do it for I cant conceive unless they are going to some other Place which I see no Signs of.

Three days later, however, he was of the opinion that it had been "our own People in the City that set it on Fire, which I believe is true for they executed several of our Friends there for it, the next Day." Mary's concern was for her husband: she sent him provisions, his repaired clothing, family news, and her stalwart encouragement and love.

I wish you had your Bed again

My Beloved   Fairfield Sept. 26 1776 10 o.Clock P.M.

Why wont you send home all your things as they want washing? It gives your fond wife pleasure even to see, and have the handling of things that you wear, tho a *little soiled.* . . . I . . . send you two Gall. Rum, (we have about seven left of our old store) and we don't use much now, and a Box of Sugar, and a little Butter. . . .Through mercy I am quite well of my Cholick, have yet a cold, but it is wareing away. These cold nights make me shudder for you (*to say no more*) I wish you had your Bed again—O George what hardships dos thy tyranny put thy late Subjects to! God only knows if it will not be returned on thine own head—But may he rather open thine eyes and chang thine heart.

[Silliman was anxious to return home, but duty and honor kept him at his post. He often dined with General Washington and did not want to lose his good opinion by asking for leave. As the British moved inland, he urged his wife and family to find safer quarters. Mary wrote her husband (now near Mamaroneck, New York):]

My dearest Beloved   Fairfield Octr 24-1776
    O my Love how tenderly am I touch'd when I view your present situation, it is as a *Partridge* in the Wilderness to day in one place, eating your food out of a wooden Box with no *Saus* (except I hope a good Stomach) at night oblig'd to travel through unknown fatigues, before you reach the destin'd place . . . Your little Billet wrote in the woods, has so far awaken'd us, as that we thought most prudent to look out for a house to repair to if need be. Billy has this day ingag'd one at North Stratford and he thought with his Grand parents most prudent to carry some of our "most" valuable things there, and go our selves as we see approaching danger . . . But why should I trouble you with these matters? My only appology is, it is *natural* for a *woman* that loves her *Husband* to fly to him for advice, as it is to breathe and I should make no apology were You not exersisd with greater concerns. Thank you my dearest for every line in your dear letters, but especially for every tender affectionate expression, which always meets an equal return in the heart of her Beloveds most affectionate dutifull Wife
                                                    Mary Silliman

    [After the Battle of White Plains, Silliman, quoting "the Prints," described the situation of the armies to his wife, "we set exactly like two Cats in a Garret growling at One another and watching the fitest Season for flying at Each Other; how it will End God only knows." (October 31, 1776). Mary Silliman ventured to claim that]

                I have in some measure acted the heroine
My Best Beloved   Fairfield Novr 10 1776
    O this long tedious absence! But it draws neigher to a close I trust and hope, and I will endeavour to hold out to the end; for I have the vanity to think I have in some measure acted the *heroine* as well as my dear Husband the Hero.[4]

SARAH PERKINS HODGKINS, wife of Joseph Hodgkins, a shoemaker of Ipswich, Massachusetts, had a stepdaughter and two young children. When her husband marched off to war as a lieutenant with the Ipswich Minute Men in April 1775, she, like so many other women, was left to provide for the children as well as for her elderly father-in-law, and to grieve alone when their one-year old son died. Despite her protestations, Joseph kept reenlisting although he came home from time to time: he saw action at Bunker Hill, Long Island, the Hudson Highlands, and Valley Forge. Sarah wrote to her husband in camp Prospect Hill (Boston):

to converse together

Ipswich Jan ye 8 1776

Loving Husband these Lines come with my kind regards to you hopeing they will find you in as good health as they leave me and the rest of the family at this time. I received two Letters from you since left home & was glad to hear you were well. I want to hear again. Don't mis any oppertunity you may have of writing to me Sence that is all the way we have to converse together. It is much to my greif that it is so. I am a good deal concerned about you on account of the army being so thin for fear the enemy should take the advantage. I hear you have lost one of your company & hope it will be sanctified to you all . . . I conclude by Subscribing my Self your most afectionate companion till Death

Sarah Hodgkins

PS . . . my pens blots so that I have made a wick of my Letter but I trust you wont expose it so I wish you a good night.

[Sarah sent another letter to her husband in camp on Long Island:]

a making you a Shirte

Ipswich June ye 2 1776

Loving Husband these Lines come with my most afectionate regards to you hoping they will find you in good health as they Leave me at this time through the goodness of God . . . I am rejoiced to hear you are well. I am Sorry to hear that you are amongst a People that are So unkind as you inform me they are. Monday night—my Dear I began to write a Letter Last night but it was So Late before I begun I could not write much. I have been very busy all day to day a making you a Shirte. You Sent to me to Send you a couple & I had but one ready for the Cloth that I intended to make you Some Bodys of. I have not got it Quite done So I was abliged to take one off of the Cloth I had in the house & I have got it done & washd and Sister Perkins is now a ironing of it . . . I must Jest tell you that Sally [their daughter] meet with a mishap Last monday. She Scolt her arm prity bad but it Seems to be in a good way to be well Soon. The rest of us are in a comfortable State of health. I want to See you very much. Sometimes I am almost impatient but concidering it is Providence that has parted us I desire to Submite & be as contented as I can & be Thankfull that we can hear from one another.

[Sarah Hodgkins wrote again some months later:]

you may think I am too free in expressing my mind

Ipswich October ye 19 1776

My Dear . . . It greives me to think what you have to undergo but I hope it will be for our good. By what you write I think you are not in so Dificult a Situation as when you wrote before. I am glad to hear you are So well off as to have a log house to live in and I Should be glad if you could have more of the Comfortable nesecaries of Life than you have, but I hope you will be carried through all you are to meet with in the way of your duty & in Gods good time be returned home in Safty. I want very much to See you. I hope we Live to See this Campaign out we shall have the happiness of living together again.

I dont know what you think about Staying again but I think it cant be inconsistant with your duty to come home to your family. It will troble me very much if you Should ingage again. I dont know but you may think I am too free in expressing my mind & that it would have been time enough when I was asked but I was afraid I Should not have that oppertunity So I hope will excuse my freedom . . . It grows Late So I must conclude at this time by subscribing myself your most afectionate Companion till Death   Sarah Hodgkins[5]

MARY TOTTEN, a widow of Cortlandt Manor, New York, saw her farm and house devastated by the advancing and retreating troops of General Washington. She, with her son Joseph Totten, went to court to seek redress.

a Reasonable allowance in my Favour

To Whomsoever the Hearing and Redress of Grievances and Damages occasioned by the opperations of the Forces raised and employed in the American cause of Liberty does or must belong—

The Remonstrance and Submissive application and Request of Mary Totten of the Manor of Cortlandt in the County of West-Chester and Province of New-york (Widow) for herself and distressed fatherless Children, Sheweth that Since the arrival and Encampment of the Forces on her Farm near Croton River, She has by the Work carried on, and Devastations Made, Sustained (in and on her Farm and appurtenances beside her being obliged to abandon her House and Business) Damages insupportable and to her Business relieved by your compassionate consideration and a Reasonable allowance in my Favour being sadly unable to contribute So large a Share to the public good, wherefore, in hopes of being heard and considered, this application is Submissively Made. . . .

Manor of Cortlandt   Mary totten

December 19th: 1776

We, the Subscribers, Freeholders of the Neighbourhood with the within named Mary Totten & Joseph Totten, are well acquainted with her Farm and its Circumstances both before and Since the late encampment of the Soldiers there upon View and Deliberate consideration do Judge that the Damages are within Bounds as follows: viz

	£	S	D
In the Article of Fence on the west side of the hill . . . Burnt	8	0	0
In that of Fence on Bryan Hill . . . Eighty Rods burnt	8	0	0
In D[itt]o: . . . wheat, about forty rods burnt	8	0	0
In Do: about the house & barn & below the Loghouse	3	0	0
In Do: on each Side of the Road and elsewhere used in Picketing	16	0	0
In Damage of Wheat on the Ground thro which runs an Entrenchment about forty Rods	15	0	0
Three Loads Hay, Pd. out to the Continental Team	7	10	0
Wheat in Sheaf, Pd. out to Do:	10	0	0

Damage of Removal from Dwelling house (and Business) by order about four weeks	8	0	0
Damage done by turning Continental Team into Indian Corn . . .	12	0	0
Damage done in and upon the remarkably thrifty and flourishing grove of excellent young Timber at one of the Places of Encampment	10	0	0
besides Some other Articles of lesser consequence	£ 105	10	0

[Signed]   Joseph Cornell   Josiah Quimby   Thomas Van Tassel

[On March 11, 1777, Mary Totten signed the following statement:]

Sir, Be pleased To pay the Bearer here of Joseph Totten The above account and his Receit Shall be your Discharge. For the same From me[6]

It is unlikely that Mary Totten's petition was honored. The American forces were on the run, their supply centers in Peekskill, New York, and in Danbury, Connecticut, soon destroyed by the pursuing British. Although many women tried to maintain some semblance of order amidst the uncertainties of the troop movements and the political hostilities around them, patriot and loyalist families alike were frequently forced to move from their homes for safety. Mary Walton Morris, the wife of Lewis Morris, a signer of the Declaration of Independence, fled from their magnificent house "Morrisania," then on the outskirts of New York City, to Westchester with her family and "a great deal of Furniture and all her Linnen and wearing apparel."[7]

MRS. NATHANIEL ADAMS, wife of a blacksmith, who lived on Village Street in White Plains, testified to the burning of her house and barns, and the inhumane treatment she received from some of the retreating American troops at the court-martial of Major Jonathan Austin on November 12, 1776. She was called as the first witness.

they would blow her through

[Major Jonathan Austin of the Sixteenth Massachusetts Regiment and his men] told her to get things out of the house as quick as possible; that she attempted to take some things out of a bed room, when some of the men told her to be gone or they would blow her through; that the party would not suffer her to dress her children, but drove them out of doors naked; that she asked Major Austin why he could not save her house, and burn others, he replied, Because you are all damned Tories.

[Washington had ordered some days previously that houses and barns were not to be put to the torch without a special order from a "General Officer." Austin had had no such order; moreover, further evidence showed he had plundered items from the house for his own use. Austin was court-martialed for "singular wantonncss and cruelty" (as Washington put it) and discharged from the army.]

PHOEBE OAKLEY, fleeing her home, had stored her valuables at her brother-in-law's house for safekeeping. Unfortunately, the house was near the site where the Battle of White Plains occurred, and was plundered by American soldiers. Her complaint listed the items stolen:

a trunk filled with Linen & cloaths . . . five feather beads [beds] & bedding, one looking glass, one Copper Coffey-Kettle, with lamp and stand, two muffs in cases, a long blue cloth cloak, one pair of brass knobbed hand irons, one painted and one woolen floor-cloth, one copper Tea Kettle, two Pewter dishes & one dozen of plates, a whole set of Tea China, and a small red trunk . . . a pair of boots almost new, a pair of brass Candle-sticks and some books.[8]

[Some items were returned to her, but the rest had disappeared.]

PRUDENCE PUNDERSON, eldest daughter of Ebenezer Punderson, a wealthy merchant employed by the British Commissary General Department, sought refuge on Long Island late in 1778. The family was separated, the oldest children living at first with their father in Huntington, the youngest with their mother in East-hampton. Their daily lives were now vastly different from what they had been used to at home in Norwich, Connecticut. The twenty-year-old Prudence, a talented artist with her embroidery needle, wrote her grandmother that her sister Hannah and "myself will have some domestick work which we are not accustomed to, other ways our imployments will be much as usual." Though now impoverished, frequently moving to new lodgings and working for her board, Prudence wrote her friend Sally Rositer that dangers were ever present. Yet Prudy (as her sister called her) retained her sense of humor, and both girls displayed considerable bravery in this incident.

you are a dead man

The treasiores of Poverty, Protecks our peace

Dear Sally   March 15th A[nno] 1779

Last Evening, about 9 some Body taped at our door. Thinking no harm I open'd it, & instantly rushed in too men with blacked faces who snack'd the Candle from my hand & were well armed each a gun & pistol. Without the least stop they rushed into Papas Beadroom not with standing (Sister Hannah seeing where they were going) started before them & held the first door—We find, Dear Sally, a nesessaty of our mimic-ing the amisons [amazons], which we will according to our abilities. Papa is still senseless & wild not awake'd from his sleep, tho rased on his elbow & they enter'd the room one Cockt his Gun at Papas breast Cry'd you are a dead man. I instantly seiz'd it & forst him without the door. Sister encountered with the other one, who once pointed his gun at her, but she being not frightned from her affections stood her ground. Seeing them both without the door & finding it necessary Papa should be in a position for his own defence; I steped back got his Pistols & putting them under my apron slipt them by those fiends unperceiv'd, handed them to Papa who was but just come to himself. The one had enter'd the second time with his Gun Cockt in the former position, I grasped & wave'd it out of mischeifs way till by a sudden spring thirst [thrust] him without the door & half acrost the next room. The other now fearing to stand his ground alone, not knowing the bad State of Papas Pistols, one without primeing & the other lain loaded more then 6 Months & not knowing my want of strength, believe he feared I should disarm his mate for he followed close my elbow. Sister fasten'd the door after us while Papa escaped in his shirt. They knowing he were gone set on their business. One stood sentry while the other pillage'd us £20 worth of apparel beside many Papours of valew in three or four minutes time & quit the House—[9]

The British occupied New York City for the duration of the War, and very advantageous it was for them. They could strike into New England, up the Hudson River, or into New Jersey—all of which they did. Provisions were readily available from Long Island and Westchester County, both loyalist enclaves, as well as from the Mother Country. Their troops were regularly reinforced from abroad and supported by Britain's superior naval force. British soldiers and officers moved into the homes of those who had left the City: for example, the house of rebel leader Isaac Sears at 49 Queen Street housed Hessian officers. Some of the estimated 1,550 soldiers' wives and their children found lodging in several buildings on the same street.[10]

General Washington, on the other hand, was in a precarious position: vulnerable to enemy attack, with little support from the local farmers, and his troop numbers shrinking by desertions and soldiers, whose enlistment terms had ended, returning home. He built Fort Lee and Fort Washington on either side of the Hudson River but lost both—after the inconclusive Battle of White Plains. He retired further up the Hudson River before retreating with his 3,000 men into New Jersey, pursued by General Lord Cornwallis. Inexplicably, General Howe did not at first join in this pursuit, instead sending a large fleet up to Newport, Rhode Island, before returning to the chase.

The British advance into New Jersey did not go as planned. Cornwallis, with an army of British Regulars and Hessians, hoped to "bag the fox," but he was not able to engage and defeat Washington in a major battle. As one British officer put it: "As we go forward into the country the rebels fly before us and when we come back they always follow us. 'Tis almost impossible to catch them. . . . We seem to be playing at bo peep."[11]

Washington, hoping to keep his dispirited and exhausted army intact, marched toward Philadelphia through neutral countryside, receiving no cooperation from local militias. On December 7-8, the army crossed the Delaware River, using boats gathered over a twenty-mile radius. As winter set in, General Howe decided to suspend the campaign, trusting that Washington's army would also retire during the cold months. He housed members of his army (many of them German mercenaries) in private homes, and returned to New York City, where he could enjoy gracious living and the charms of his mistress.

Realizing that the period of enlistments of his ill-clothed and starving men would expire at the end of the year, Washington needed a victory to keep his army intact. On a bitter, snowy Christmas night, he led his men back across the Delaware River to Trenton, staging a surprise attack on the 1,500 Hessians quartered there. At a cost of only four wounded (including Lieutenant James Monroe, later president of the United States), the Americans took 900 prisoners, gaining arms, cannon, and, importantly, new enlistments! By New Year's Day, Washington had 5,000 men and was ready to march to New Brunswick. He eluded the British forces under Cornwallis but, on the road to Princeton, met another contingent of Redcoats. The battle lasted an hour, Washington personally rallying his men to victory. He then settled in Morristown for the winter, keeping up the pressure by sending out parties to capture Hackensack, Elizabethtown, and Newark.

Prisoners of War

Left behind in New York City were over 3,000 American prisoners of war. If the prisoner was an officer, either an exchange following a strict set of rules might be arranged, or he might be put on parole if he gave his word of honor to return when called. Ransom money might be demanded to free prisoners. Lucy Flucker Knox, the wife of General Henry Knox, realistically voiced her need for ready cash should her husband be captured: "I wish I had fifteen guineas to spare to spend . . . for necessarys—but I have not. The very little gold we have must be reserved for my Love in case he should be taken—for friends in such a case are not too common."[12] (August 23, 1777).

[Robert Keith, taken prisoner by the British at the fall of Fort Washington, described his good fortune in receiving aid from a generous woman:]

she espoused the same Cause

MRS. SARAH SMITH, Widow of Mr. John Smith, Cabinet maker, late of New York, being an elderly Lady, of a benevolent christian Disposition, was remarkably charitable and very serviceable to the american Prisoners in the years 1776 and -77, to my certain Knowledge. I, being one of that unfortunate Number captivated at Fort Washington, was brought with the Rest of my fellow Sufferers to New York. In our approach to the City this good Lady met us with her Bounty, and followed us to several Places of Confinement with Refreshments; which were very acceptable to us who had been three Days destitute of the necessary Supports of Life.

When the Officers had their Parole of the City, she invited those whom she met with, to come to her House, and partake of such as She could afford them; and desired them to invite their Acquaintance, also to come and partake with them. Her House was kept open, and her Table spread, almost constantly for several Weeks. She bestowed both Food and Raiment with so hearty good will, that relieving the distressed appeared to be her greatest Satisfaction. She greatly alleviated my Misfortune, by receiving me into her Family as a Boarder; where I had the best Opportunity of being acquainted with her Conduct. Her extraordinary Liberality induced me sometimes to express my Concern lest She would bring herself to Poverty and Distress—To which She replied, she espoused the same Cause in which they were suffering; therefore, while She had any thing to give, they should be welcome to share with her, and when it was out of her Power to relieve them, She was willing to suffer with them.

[The rank and file, when taken prisoners, were much less fortunate than the officers. Crowded together in disease-ridden and unsanitary conditions in churches, on ships in the harbor, in Bayard's sugar mill "The Sugar House," or in the notorious Provost prison (near present day City Hall), they received few provisions (Congress was to supply American prisoners) and had no contact with their families. Undaunted, Mrs. Smith even ventured there.]

by the Authority of the word of God

As She was comforting the disconsolate one Day, in the Provost, She bid them be of good Cheer, the Scale might turn, and the Day might come, when they would guard, in the same Provost, those who were now guarding them there. The Guard, overhearing this Address, shut her immediately in another Room, saying, that was the fittest Place for such a d----d Rebel.

After She got out of Gaol, She was likely to suffer for want of Bread, and sent to see if I could procure her some flour on Long Island, where I was then upon Parole. As I could procure but little, I wrote to Mr. Pintard, our Agent there, to Supply her out of the Flour sent by Congress for the use of the american Prisoners, which Request he was kind enough to comply with. Her personal Distresses did not yet make her forget the poor Prisoners; but for their Relief she went thro' the city, craving Alms from the well disposed People of her acquaintance. This coming to the Ears of the Mayor and Aldermen, they sent for, and examined her concerning it. She honestly confessed the Fact, and they asked by what Authority she acted. She replied, by the Authority of the word of God.[13]

[Mrs. Smith was ordered out of the city, permitted to take "only one Bed and her wearing Apparel." She disposed of her property, gave the money to prisoners, and moved to Clarkstown, New York, in late 1777.]

ANN HOCKLEY CONYNGHAM was personally unable to aid her husband as he was a prisoner on board a ship bound for England. Instead, she penned a graphic appeal to the Congress and its president at the time, John Jay.

Good God my heart Shudders at the thought

Hond Sir   Phila. July 17. 1779

I beg leave to trouble your Excellency and the Honorable Congress, with the perusal of the inclosed letter from my Husband, Capt. Gustavus Conyngham, late Commador of the Cutter *Revenge*, now a Prisoner and in Irons on board a British Packet, bound to England. . . .

I take the liberty of calling the attention of Congress to his distressed Situation and of requesting that thay would be pleased to take such Steps for his relief as have in Similar instances prevented the execution of the bloody and vindictive purposes of the enemy upon the Officers and Citizens of these States. . . .

But to hear of a Person thus dearly connected being chained to the hold of a ship in vain looking back towards the beloved Country for whom he had fought, wasting his Health and Spirits in hopeless grief and at last Compleating the measure of his Sufferings by an ignominious Death . . . Good God my heart Shudders at the thought. Forbid it Heaven. Forbid it Honble Gentlemen the Guardians of the lives and Happiness of the good People of these States that a freeman and a Soldier of America should even fear or feel a moments distress or pain from the hands of Englishmen Unrevenged.

The Delay of a single Hour may fix my Husband's fate for ever. Pardon me therefore whilst I once more intreate your immediate Attention to his case, consider Sirs the safety of your numerous Officers and Soldiers by Sea and land is connected with that of my Husband. This I presume will be sufficient motive with you to procure Justice for him and to afford some consolation to Honble Sirs and Gentleman Your most obedient and most devoted   Ann Conygham[14]

MARY SILLIMAN found that her heroic fortitude was constantly being challenged: General Gold Silliman, who had been recalled by Connecticut's governor to guard the home front, also became a prisoner of war. Not captured during battle, he was the victim of a more unusual tactic. He and his son Billy were seized by the British at home in the middle of the night on May 1, 1779 and taken to New York. Anxious weeks passed before Mary heard from her husband: Billy, being ill, was allowed to come home on parole. Silliman intended to go to Long Island to be inoculated for the smallpox, and to arrange parole or exchanges for several of his men.

Matters did not go smoothly. A month later, Silliman had moved to Gravesend but had not been inoculated. He was able to obtain parole to Long Island for Ensign Bissell, who had been incarcerated in the Sugar House for more than eight months. But "two or three Days ago he forfeited his Honour, broke his Parole & ran away. If I had had the least Doubt of his Honour I never would have opened my Mouth in his favour."

Mary received discouraging word from the governor who doubted that General Silliman would be released soon. Since he was a general in the militia (not the Continental Army), it would be difficult to find a British prisoner of war of similar rank for exchange. She worried about his smallpox inoculation, about the extended family, and "my approaching Hour of Perrel": Mary gave birth on August 8, 1779 to their second son Benjamin. It was for him that, twenty years later, she recalled the events of his father's kidnapping. Mary Silliman recorded in her Journal:

to surprize and take him at a midnight hour

In ye year 1779 He was by the Capt. general or Governor stationed to guard the coast in the visinity of Fairfield, having the care of all the outposts in that country, and his own house was allowed to be his headquarters. In this situation he continued untill the first day of May . . . When general Clinton the commanding officer at N.York sent a whale boat of Torys to surprize and take him at a midnight hour, when we were all asleep the house was attacked.

I was first awaked by his calling out who's there, and at that instant there was a banging at both doors, they intending to break them down, or burst them open, and this was done with great stones as big almost as they could lift. They left them at the door. My dear companion then sprang up caught his gun, and ran to the front of the house, and as the moon shone he saw them through the winder and attempted to fire, but his gun only flashed and missed fire. At that inst the enemy burst in a window sash and all and jumped in, seazed on him and said he was their prisoner, and he must go with them. He asked if he might not dress himself. They said yes, if he would be quick.

All this time I lay quaking, and they followed him into the bedroom, where I and my dear little boy [Sellek] lay, with their guns and Bayonets fixed and their appearance was dreadful and I feared the consequences as to my self as well as to him as it was but about three months before the birth of my last Child. And it was then that their prisoner addressed them in mild terms and begged them to leave the bedroom and told them that there being there would frighten his wife. They then withdrew for a minute or two but returned when he asked them out again. They hurrying him he went out and shut the door. After that I heard them breaking windows which they wantonly did with the britches [breeches] of there guns. They then asked him for his money, he told them he had none but some continental and that would do them no good. They then asked him for his papers; he told them his publick papers were all sent abroad, and his private ones would do them no good. . . . He told them mildly he hoped he was in the hands of gentlemen, and that it was beneath them to plunder. With this argument he quieted them so that they plundered but very little. They then told him he must go; he asked if he might go and take leave of his wife. They said go if he would make hast he then came in and dropped a bundle of his most valuable private papers under some thing on the table, took leave of me, with great seeming fortitude and composure, and went away with them.

As soon as I heard the door shut I rose and went to the bedroom of our Son Wm Silliman, and I found he was gone tho I did not hear anything of them taking him. I then went to the door and saw them leading away their prisoners. . . . They took them down about two miles to their whale boat where they had left one man [head of Black Rock harbor] and proceeded on their voyage to long Island.

This event took place the first of May 1779 and I heard nothing from them in three weeks. . . . They had a boisterous time over but that did not prevent some of the men from casting their eyes on some matters they had plundered from the house, especially a beautiful fuzee and a pr. of elegant Pistols inlade with silver, all over and an elegant sword, which one of them who had worked at our hous [making shoes] took much pleasure in flourishing about and he it was that it was we suppose, piloted them to our house.

When they had arrived at Long Island shore, they were haled by a Col. Simco* who commanded there. *Have* you *got him?* Yes. Have you lost any men? No. That's well, says Symco, your *Sillimans*, nor your *Washington* are not worth a man! He then ordered his men to the guard house with their prisoners. Says your father, am I going to the guard house? Yes. When they came there, says your father to the adjutant, it is thus you treat prisoners of my rank? He said, we don't look on you as we should on a continental Gen, but a militia General. But how will you view me when my exchange is talked of. I understand you sir, and went out, and suppose reported to his commanding officer. Soon after that your father and brother had an invitation to breakfast at a neighbouring house where they went and refreshed themselves. Soon after a horse and Carriage was sent for him and yr Br. to ride to Nyork escorted by a guard of dragoons. . . . He was ordered to flat Bush in long Island, where he remained untill he was exchanged for Judg Jones. The circumstances of whose capture, were some what singular, and very interesting to us.

By all my investigation, and that of my friends, we could not find any in the possesion of the Americans that the British would accept of for your father. I wrote to the Governor for direction and assistance in the matter. He too felt himself much interested not only from his personal friendship for the prisoner, but for the people, as he said he had not a more faithful oficer than he, but he knew of none that the enemy would accept for him. At length it was thought but to attempt a capture for that purpose.

*Captain John Graves Simcoe of the Queen's Rangers, later lieutenant governor of Upper Canada.

[The person decided upon was Thomas Jones of Tryon Hall, (Massapequa), Long Island, who was a judge of the ministerial Supreme Court of the Crown. He had been arrested earlier in the war but was home on parole. Mary wrote to her parents in Stonington about the excitement surrounding his capture.]

a very extraordinary affair

Most dear Hond. Parents   [Stratford] Janry. 9, 1780

The capture of this *Judge Jones* was a very extraordinary affair, which would never have been attempted were it not for the purpose of exchanging Mr. Silliman as we had no one in our hands, the enemy would exchange him for. Capt. [David] Hawley of this place, and one Capt. [Samuel] Lockwood of Norwalk with 24 men attempted this Hazardous enterprise and after they landed on Long Island they had to travel about sixty miles to his house, which they say is one of the most magnificent buildings on the Continent.

They march'd a night, and hid them selves a days in the woods. They arriv'd at his house 9 oClock in the evening saturday night [Nov. 6, 1779]. They rap'd at the door, but as instruments of musick was playing in the House they were not heard, so they broke in the Pannels of the door, jump'd in, met the Judge in the entry took him and march'd off 30 miles that night, lay still in the woods next day and arriv'd here monday night following, They conducted the Judge to a Tavern at Stratfield. . . . It affected me with pity for him and his Lady. Our *Sons* Billy, and Jose went immediately to wait on him with my compliments, and an invitation to breakfast with me the next morning, which he did, and behav'd in character. He is now on his parole at Middleton. . . .

Little Selleck is a sweet little prattling creature, & says the *old saucy Regulars* have got Pappa, and *he* will whip them, wants every day to send pappa an apple. *Benne* is a sweet a Babe as ever I had in my life and I think the largest of his age. He weighs 20 pounds. I get along comfortably on every account have a thousand mercies amidst my affliction. . . .

your very affectionate dutifull lonely Daughter   Mary Silliman[15]

[In her memoir, Mary provided additional details to the story.]

the Judge humed *very* loud

[Captain Hawley had] kindly *offered*, I think to undertake the enterprise . . . laid hold of the Judge who he found in the entry, and told him he was his prisoner. And as providence ordered it there was there a young gentleman on a visit whose name was Hulet [Willet]. Him they took too, and he served very well to exchang for yr Brother. They soon hurried them out of the house, and they had to pass nigh a guard. When they came there, the Judge *humed* very *loud*. Capt Hawly who had him by the hand told him he must not do so, but he repeated his hum. Hawly then told him if he humed again he would run him through. He afterwards desisted, and they went on through the night, and when morning came, they conducted the Judg to such lodging as they had, which was among the bushes, untill the next night, they went on, and reached the whale boat I think the third night. And glad were they to find it for had it been taken off in their absence they would have been in a woful evil. They then went aboard and proceeded unmolested, untill they arrived at Newfeild.

News came to me in the morning that Capt. Hawly has arrived with Judge Jones. Altho I was glad that the event had taken place; yet my heart was full of sympathy for him and his family, who I knew well how to pity as I had my self so greatly gone through the same trial and wishing to make his captivity as easy as possible, I sent yr Br to invite him to our house to break fast. He came under a guard; I was introduced to him and he to me. I observed to him that the fortunes of war had brought him here under disagreable circumstances and as I could so well sympathiz with him and his family I wished to do every thing in my power for his accomodation untill the purpose of his capture was effected, when I hoped that Mrs Jones, my self, and our partners would be made happy in seeing each other again. But to my disappointment, I found him insensible, and devoid of compliance and a sullen discontent sat on his brow. He made no reply but asked this question: *did they plunder when they took your husband?* I told him not much. He said they have plundered my house; I don't beleive they left my wife a second sheet. This I was sorry to hear and afterwards inquiring of Capt. Hawly he told me that he had held up the idia [idea] to his men that there should be no plundering. But when they landed on the other side the men said what are *we* to get by it if we take Judge Jones? We run a great risk; we don't know but we may be killed. Unless you give us leave to plunder we will go no farther. Thus he saw that the expedition would be frustrated and he was obliged to tell them that they might plunder.

But to return I got as good a dinner for my captured guest as I could, and my family paid him every attention, but he was very unsociable all the while he stayed which [was] only two or three days when he was ordered I think by the Capt general to Middletown, thinking our house an unsafe place. Mr. Hulet who was taken with him was paroled by Capt. Hawly and did not come when the

Judg did, but came on afterwards, and was exchanged for your Br. [Billy] and went home. . . .

But to return to my own situation after your Hond. Father was taken, I had a large family and the care and weight lay on me. But I was enabled to get along from day to day but lived in a constant alarm. The dreadful fright that I had, when he was taken, made me feel like the timorous roe, and I started at every noise, fearing the enemy who were often infesting our coasts, but I endeavoured to put my trust where I ought.

[Mary endured many frightening and frustrating days for it was not until April 27, 1780, that her beloved husband finally was exchanged and allowed to come home.]

the flag of truce

Judge Jones was sent for from Middletown, and a vessel hired by us to take him in, and the same to bring yr. pa if they would let him come, and we agreed that if they obtained him, two flags should be hoisted when they returned, that we might know in certain if he was coming. The vessel sailed with Judg Jones about 8 oClock in the morning, from our harbour. They had a fine wind, and I saw them go with great rapidity, and we hoped that in two or three days, we should receive him who had been so long separated from us.

But about 1 oClock we saw the same vessel returning and to our surprize, we saw two flags. This we could not understand as we knew they had not had time to go to NYork in the time they had been gone. The fact was, that the same day, we were sending the Judge off, they at NYork were sending off your father; and the vessels met. Their flag of truce hailed ours, and asked if they had Judge Jones on board. Yes. Well, we have got Gen. Silliman too was their answer, and they soon boarded each other, and as I had sent a fine fat turkey for your father's comfort on his voyage home they hastened to dress it that the Judge might dine with him before he went on which he did [the two adversaries were actually acquainted], and took leave and each vessel went its way. When ours came with in call of our fort, and battery, at Blackrock, one called to know if they had Gen. Silliman on board. He then leaped on deck and waved his hat, on which there was so loud a shout, that we heard them plain at our house, and then all the cannon was fired off and the same took place when he landed at the wharf. This was very pleasing to us at the house as well as to your father to see such testimonials of joy at his return.[16]

Chapter 3

every one . . . could shoot very well

The Hudson River was and is one of the most important waterways in America. The colonists appreciated its value, both strategic and economic. It provided access to the interior of New York and also, with a few portages to Canada, facilitating trade and making it possible to monitor the western and northern frontiers. The significance of the Hudson was not lost on the British during the Revolution. If they could gain control of the river, New England, the source of the rebellion, could be isolated from the rest of the colonies, making it much easier to bring the Americans to heel. To accomplish this, a tripartite plan was conceived whereby a substantial army, commanded by "Gentleman Johnny" Burgoyne, would push south toward Albany from Canada, by way of Lake Champlain, Lake George, and the upper Hudson. Another force led by Brigadier General Barry St. Leger would move toward that city from the west via Lake Ontario, Oswego, and the Mohawk Valley. A third contingent under General William Howe was expected to move upriver from British-held New York City, capture forts along the way, and rendezvous with Burgoyne at Albany.

In June of 1777 General Burgoyne was on the move with an artillery train and 9,500 men, including British regulars, German mercenaries, a sizeable contingent of Indians, and a few hundred Canadians and Tories. Major General William Phillips was Burgoyne's second in command, and Major General Simon Fraser led a regiment of British regulars. The Germans were led by Major General Friedrich von Riedesel.

The Northern Department of the American army was commanded by General Horatio Gates, who had replaced General Philip Schuyler. The dislike of the two generals for each other affected troop deployments, strategy, and morale. Friction also existed between members of the Continental Army and the state militias, which were considered capable but undisciplined; they tended to materialize when local areas were threatened and disappear when the danger had passed.

ABIGAIL ADAMS, in a letter to her husband from Braintree July 25, 1775, described Burgoyne, who was stationed in Boston at the time. She took a dim view of him.

the horrible wickedness of the man

General Burgoyne lives in mr. Samll. Quincys House. a Lady who lived opposite Says she Saw raw meat cut & hacked upon her Mahogona Tables, & her Superb Damask curtain & cushings exposed to the rain as if they were of no value. How much better do the Tories fare than the Whigs? . . . A Late letter from London . . . has left me no room to think that he is possessd either of Generosity virtue or Humanity. His character runs thus—as to Burgoyne I am not Master of Language Sufficient to give you a true Idea of the Horrible wickedness of the Man, His designs are dark His Dissimulation of the Deepest die, for not content with Deceiving Mankind he practices deceit on God himself, by Assuming the Appearance . . . of great attention to Religious Worship when every action of his life is totally abhorant to all Ideas of true Religion Virtue or common Honesty. An Abandoned Infamous Gambler of broken fortune . . . wholly bent on Blood tyrany and Spoil.[1]

Congress had authorized an invasion of Canada in June of 1775, hoping that its "oppressed Inhabitants" would join their southern neighbors in resisting the British and perhaps even become a fourteenth colony. The so-called "northern campaign" ended in disaster. Routed in an attack on Quebec during a blizzard in the dead of winter, the Americans fled in disarray; General Richard Montgomery was killed and Benedict Arnold wounded. With a small force of disease-ravaged Americans, woefully lacking in provisions and ammunition, Arnold maintained a presence outside Quebec throughout the winter. Unable to withstand an attack in the spring, what remained of the expeditionary force retreated and abandoned the ill-conceived Canadian campaign.

Camp followers

It was common for numbers of women—"camp followers" was the rather pejorative name given to them—to travel with armies of fighting men at this time. While some did provide sex, for the most part these women were soldiers' wives, often with children—who cooked and washed clothes for the men and nursed the ill and wounded.

Among the women who made the incredibly difficult march to Quebec with Benedict Arnold's force during the fall and winter of 1775 was Mrs. Grier, a sergeant's wife, described in the journal of John Joseph Henry as a "large, virtuous and respectable woman." Wading single file through an icy pond, Henry found Mrs. Grier in front of him. "My mind was humbled, yet astonished," he wrote, "at the exertions of this good woman. Her clothes more than waist high, she waded before me to firm ground. No one, so long as she was known to us, dared to intimate a disrespectful idea of her." Mrs. Grier came to a tragic end: "A woman belonging to the Pennsylvania troops was killed to-day by accident—a soldier carelessly snapping his musket which proved to be loaded."[2]

There were women accompanying British armies too. For those officially "attached," rations were provided in recognition of the useful services they performed. At various times there were between 1,000 and 2,000 women (and children) with Burgoyne's forces. Many were wives who came along to care for their husbands, but there were only a few whose husbands were high-ranking officers.

Mercenaries

Mercenaries were commonly used by countries in Europe short of military manpower, which was the case with Britain in 1775 at the start of the American Revolution. The small states of Germany proved to be the best source of trained soldiers. Dynastic bonds and the prospect of revenue—substantial even though the states had to equip the soldiers themselves—disposed the German princes to favor British requests. Hesse-Hanau and Brunswick provided the bulk of Burgoyne's mercenaries. The Duke of Brunswick eventually supplied more than 4,000 men. The first contingent led by Baron Friedrich von Riedesel, who became a general, sailed for Canada to join Burgoyne in April 1776.

Women also accompanied the hired troops. The Anhalt-Zerbst Regiment with 1,164 men listed thirty-four "soldiers' wives who served as washerwomen." The Brunswickers departed with seventy-seven women. The wife of General von Riedesel too chose to follow her husband.[3]

BARONESS FREDERICKA VON RIEDESEL kept a journal describing her sea voyage, her arrival in Canada, and later, her experiences on the battlefields in New York. She traveled from her home to England in 1776.

we might be eaten by the savages

I set out on my journey on the 14th of May at five o'clock in the morning from Wolfenbüttel; and notwithstanding my passionate longing to see my husband once more I still felt the greatness of my undertaking too much not to have a heavy heart, especially as my friends had not ceased to repeat to me the dangers to which I exposed myself. Gustava, my eldest daughter, was four years and nine months old; Frederica, my second, two years; and Caroline, my youngest daughter, just ten weeks old. I had, therefore, need of all my courage and all my tenderness to keep me from relinquishing my unprecedented wish to follow my husband. They represented to me not only the perils of the sea, but told me, also, that we were in danger of being eaten by the savages, and that the people in America lived upon horse-flesh and cats. Yet all this frightened me less than the thought of going into a country where I could not understand the language. . . . As soon as [Rockel, her father's forester] heard of the departure of my husband, and that I was to follow him, he left every thing . . . in order to accompany me as a footman, and during our whole journey, he has showed all of us the greatest attachment and attention, especially for the children, whom he made it his duty to carry and take care of.[4]

[The Baroness's departure from England was delayed by a number of problems, but during her enforced stay she was presented at court. She finally sailed on April 16, 1777. Her description of the sea voyage and her welcome in Canada is fascinating.]

no time to be sick. . . . the helm broke. . . .
divine services. . . . big codfish. . . . a number of whales

On the 19th we passed Plymouth under a fine breeze. Most all were well, and my children and I were pleasantly situated as if we had been at home. The weather was so beautiful that we danced upon deck. Our music consisted of a capital fifer and three drummers.

On the 20th, 21st, 22nd, and 23rd we had contrary winds, storms, very high swelling waves, and bad weather generally; and, in addition the men were all sick. I, alone, had no time to be so, for my servants were nearly the sickest of all, and I was, therefore, constantly called upon to wait on my three children. I believe there is nothing better for sea-sickness than to be right busy; for on the first day out I was as sick as the others, but when I saw my children sick and without care, I thought only of them, and found myself actually better, with a good appetite. In general, one does nothing on board a ship but eat and drink. Every day we had four, and oftentimes, five and six dishes, which were right well prepared. In the morning, when I was up, I breakfasted in our cabin, washed and dressed the children, afterwards myself, and then went up on deck. When I could, I worked; at two o'clock we ate dinner, drank tea at six o'clock; and at eight in the evening, I went downstairs and undressed the children. Then I had my supper, and at ten o'clock went to bed. . . .

On the 25th we experienced a calm, and remained nearly at the same place. The helm [rudder] broke, but the captain, who knew well what to do in such emergencies, at once replaced it. We had then made only two hundred and fifty leagues since our departure.

I know not whether it was the hope of so soon seeing my husband that gave me good spirits, but I found the sea not so dreadful as many had painted it to me, and had not the least repentance for having undertaken the journey. . . .

On the 27th we had divine worship. It was exceedingly edifying to see the entire ship's crew kneel down, and observe the fervency with which they prayed. In the evening, the wind shifted, and the ship staggered so dreadfully, that many were again attacked with fresh sea-sickness, though not as badly as at first. I often fell down; one of my daughters had a finger crushed by the swinging round of a door, and the other hurt her chin. . . .

At last, upon the 6th, toward noon, the wind changed, and during the 7th we had a very good wind, and made one hundred and thirty leagues in twenty-four hours. All were delighted, and paid visits to the different ships. The ship, *Henry,* which had on board one hundred and thirty-four of our troops, was so polite as to raise its flag and call out, "Long live the dear wife of our general and the good general himself!" I cried, in my turn, "Long live the entire ship!" and showed them my three children as the choicest treasures I possessed. Thereupon they again shouted, "Hurrah! hurrah!"... My whole heart was stirred within me....

Upon the 8th we fell in with a ship, which at first they took for an American. Although we had nothing to fear on that account, still I was a little anxious as I did not particularly long to be present at a naval combat. A cable parted on board of the man-of-war, *Blonde*, and knocked four sailors into the sea. One of them was rescued, but the other three were drowned....

On the 23rd the wind was changeable. We saw the banks, but could not yet reach them.... We had now been five weeks at sea, and had only made sixteen hundred and sixty miles. Besides, it was so misty, that the men-of-war fired a cannon every hour, to guard against the other ships losing themselves.

One of the ships, called the *Silver Eel*, lost her main-mast, and in the night, with the *Porpoise,* separated from us; a circumstance that caused me some uneasiness, as my entire baggage, and my husband's wine and regimentals were on board that ship. Neither did those ships rejoin us until the 30th....

On the 27th, 28th, and 29th, we had a good wind and beautiful weather. The ship, *Blonde,* caught one hundred fish. A large portion of them were cod fish, some of which weighed fifty pounds, and were very fine. They were hung around the ship by their mouths, their entrails taken out, and the sockets of their eyes filled with salt: in this way they were nicely preserved for a long time.

On the 30th we had the most beautiful weather in the world, but a calm. It was a magnificent sight to see some thirty ships upon the open sea, which was as clear as a mirror. By this time, we had passed the Great Bank, and had made in all, twenty-one hundred and twenty-one leagues—over two-thirds of our journey. We saw a large number of whales very close to our ship, among which were several young ones, thirty-five to forty feet in length....

On the 6th [of June] we actually saw land and mountains . . . My impatience increased with every day, and I sought to drive it away with work. I had already, during the voyage, embroidered a double night-cap for my husband, two purses, and seven caps for myself and the children, and . . . many other little things....

On the 10th at four o'clock in the morning the anchor was weighed; and we were now safely over all the dangerous places. It is a ravishing sight to behold both sides of the shore at this place—the houses, the great cataract of Montmorency, and then Quebec, which we came in sight of at ten o'clock, on the morning of the 11th. . . . The city of Quebec itself . . . is as *dirty* as possible and very incommodious, for one is obliged to ascend a great mountain in going through the streets. There are, also, few handsome houses, but the inhabitants are polite people. . . .

When it was known in Quebec that I was nearing the city, I was saluted with cannon by all the ships in the harbor; and at twelve o'clock, noon, we saw a boat approaching us, containing twelve sailors dressed in white and wearing silver helmets and green sashes. These seamen had been sent to fetch me from the ship, and brought me a letter from my husband, in which he wrote that he had been obliged to set out for the army. This news greatly grieved and frightened me, but I resolved, at the same time, to follow him, even if I should be with

him only a few days. I seated myself, with my entire family, in the boat. . . . At
the General's [Guy Carleton, the British governor of Canada], I was received by
all with friendship. Indeed they did not seem to know how they could sufficiently express their joy at my arrival.[5]

Burgoyne's campaign began well, with a victory at Fort Ticonderoga, a severe setback for the rebels and a serious blow to their morale. Reaching Skenes-
borough, the British general decided to send the bulk of his troops on an overland route rather than by water to Fort Edward. A distance of twenty-three
miles, through a rugged area of few roads, thick forests, swamps and marshes, it
took the force as many days to make the trek. Rebels added to the natural obstacles by blocking roads with felled trees, destroying bridges, and flooding fields.

Although General Burgoyne was aware of the risks of a long supply line as
the troops moved south, he expected loyalists along the way to provide manpower, horses, food, and supplies. Arriving at Fort Edward in July of 1777, he
let it be known to inhabitants of the area that they should actively help the British, or at least not interfere with them. Loyalists and neutrals were to identify
themselves by wearing white bits of paper on their hats. For those who would
take an oath of allegiance to the king, Burgoyne offered "Protection," a written
pass that would allow movement in and out of the British camp. The assumption
was that it would guarantee the safety of loyalist lives and property. This was
not always the case.

ELIZABETH MUNRO FISHER, the wife of a loyalist, recorded what happened to
her and her child.

I was willing to lay down and die

At this time Burgoyne came down with his army to Skeensborough; this put
the country all in confusion; knowing not what to do, colonel Williams, being a
head man on the side of the country, came to Mr. Fisher, and begged of him, as
he had been in the British army, to go and procure a protection for him and all
the committee in Salem. . . . Accordingly Mr. Fisher took leave of his family,
and went to see General Burgoyne; he made known his errand, and sent Baker
back with the result to Colonel Williams. I expected Mr. Fisher home every day.

A few days after Baker's return, a party of riflemen surrounded our house,
about six o'clock in the morning, and inquired for Mr. Fisher. I told them he was
not at home; they asked me where he was gone—I told them; upon which they
ordered me out of my house, with a threat that if I did not immediately comply
they would burn me in it. I took my child from the cradle and went out of the
house.—I sat down at a little distance, and observed them taking out all my furniture, and then they burnt the house. In this situation, without a home and no
one near me to whom I could appeal for advice and assistance—not knowing
where nor which way to go to find Mr. Fisher, I was at a loss what to do.—At
last, seeing a man drive a cow, I asked him which way he was going.—He answered to the camp.—I asked him if he would let me go along with him.—Yes,

said he, if you can keep up with me. I arose from the ground (for I was sitting down with my child on my lap) and followed him. I walked that day, in company with this man, twenty-two miles, and carried my child; by the middle of the day I had neither shoe nor stockings on my feet; my shoes, being made of silk, did not last long, and my stockings I took off and threw away, on account of the fatigue of carrying my child and walking so far.—I was willing to lay down and die. On the road this man would often say that he did not know but a party of Indians might be out a scouting, and if so, we should fall a sacrifice to them; at first I was alarmed, but my fatigue at length was so great that I told him I wished they might come and kill me and my child, for I was almost exhausted. I had nothing to eat or drink all that day, except the water he gave me out of the brooks with his hat. We saw several houses, but the people had fled from them. About sunset we came to a house where we found a woman and seven children. Her husband had gone—I stayed there that night; the next day the man went with his cow into the camp; this cow was all he had, and he wanted to sell her for money. I sent by him to Mr. Fisher, letting him know where I was. Mr. Fisher came to me that evening, and the next day I went into the camp. After I had been a few days in the camp, I bought every thing my child and I needed. I related to Mr. Fisher what had been done at home—he was much surprised at Williams' conduct, as he had sent him, and the men that burnt the house were under his command—my furniture was sold at his house as tory property.[6]

[Asa Fitch, a country doctor and a noted etymologist, in 1847, began to ask his elderly patients questions about their experiences during the American Revolution when they were young. He carefully recorded their answers and, although they may be the imperfect recollections of people advanced in years, they reflect the uncertainties and trials their families faced.]

TRYPHENA MARTIN ANGELL of Salem recounted her family's experience.

stolen by the Tories

In the war Father was away from home when the families evacuated the town. He was either in the army or away with a scouting party and so was not here to aid us in getting away. We lived then in a log house. . . . The town was full of exaggerated and alarming reports. . . . It was said [that Burgoyne] had a hundred thousand soldiers with him—British, Hessians, and Indians—and was coming down through this place and would kill every enemy of the King.

Daniel Livingston was living at that time in a house of Father's down near where the old bridge across the kill was. He helped us to get away. Some of our things were buried, others sunk in the well, and the rest were put into the ox-cart. . . Mother rode on the old mare and I was tied on behind her or had to hold on to her. . . .

On the road somewhere towards Hoosick was a large slough hole [swamp] or brook across which poles were laid to keep the horses, et cetera, from miring in it. The foot of the horse we rode got caught between these poles so that she fell pitching Mother and me off into the mud. We were not hurt but badly fright-

ened and sadly besmeared with muck and mud. A few days after our arrival at
Brown's my brother Moses was born. We came back before cold weather. . . .
part of our things were buried in time of the retreat before Burgoyne: pots and
kettles, a large brass kettle, pewter platters and other dishes, the iron trammel [a
chain and hook for raising and lowering a kettle] that hung in the chimney.
When we got back we found all these things had been stolen by the Tories. We
never got any trace as to who it was that had taken them.[7]

ANN ELIZA SCHUYLER BLEECKER was living in Tomhanik, north of Albany,
when the area came under threat from Burgoyne's advancing army. Not only
was she afraid of being caught in the midst of the fighting, but she also feared
raids by the Indians. In a letter to her brother Leonard, she described the situation in the area and urged him to be

a genuine Son of Liberty

Dear Lenny,   Albany Augt 5 1777
    It gives me a singular pleasure to find your March was so agreeable, and the
Country you passed through so much to your Task. I hope it will Excite you to
Exert yourself in defending so Blooming a country from the Degridations of an
Inhuman Enemy—we are all put in the greatest Confusion by the Loss of Ticonderoga, and Retreat of our Army to Stillwater, the Savages commit unheard of
Barbarities on the Frontiers, and the Distress'd Inhabitants are flying from their
Farms, (where plenty rewarded their Industry); to penury and Contempt—I
came off with the utmost Expedition with only my Plate and some wearing apparel, not venturing like Lott's wife to look back, but where we shall go farther I
know not—to what a desolate condition can this ill conduct of a few Command-
ers reduce a Country, it is true they have drawn on themselves the general
Odium of the people, but if the Scene of Horror and Bloodshed (which they
must have foreseen would attend the Evacuation of the Fort [Ticonderoga])
could not Induce them to try and preserve it—such harden'd Men I say will also
be Callous to Contempt—my pen is so bad that I can scarcely proceed. I only
wish you may prove a genuine Son of Liberty and a defender of the Rights, and
so Resemble those Ancient Worthies who were the Support of their Country and
an Honor to . . . Human Nature.[8]

> [Gathering some belongings as Burgoyne approached, Ann Bleecker
> fled with her two children (her husband was away). Her younger child,
> Abella, contracted dysentery and died. Bleecker wrote the following
> poem in October 1777, though it was not published until 1790, seven
> years after her death. She never recovered from the loss of her daughter.]

WRITTEN IN THE RETREAT FROM BURGOYNE

Rich in my children—on my arms I bore
My living treasures from the scalper's pow'r:
When I sat down to rest beneath some shade,
On the soft grass how innocent she play'd,

While her sweet sister, from the fragrant wild,
Collects the flow'rs to please my precious child;
Unconscious of her danger, laughing roves,
Nor dreads the painted savage in the groves!

. . . . But soon my loved *Abella* hung her head,
From her soft cheek the bright carnation fled;
Her smooth transparent skin too plainly shew'd
How fierce thro' every vein the fever glow'd.
—In bitter anguish o'er her limbs I hung,
I wept and sigh'd, but sorrow chain'd my tongue;
At length her languid eyes clos'd from the day,
The idol of my soul was torn away;
Her spirit fled and left me ghastly clay!

Then—then my soul rejected all relief,
Comfort I wish'd not, for I lov'd my grief:
'Hear, my *Abella*!' cried I, 'hear me mourn,
'For one short moment, oh! my child return;
'Let my complaint detain thee from the skies,
'Though troops of angels urge thee on to rise.'
All night I mourn'd—and when the rising day
Gilt her sad chest with his benignest ray,
My friends press round me with officious care,
Bid me suppress my sighs, nor drop a tear;
Of resignation talk'd—passions subdu'd,
Of souls serene and christian fortitude;
Bade me be calm, nor murmur at my loss,
But unrepining bear each heavy cross.

'Go!' cried I raging, 'stoick bosoms go!
'Whose hearts vibrate not to the sound of woe;
'Go from the sweet society of men,
'Seek some unfeeling tyger's savage den,
'There, calm—alone—of resignation preach,'

. . . . Nor shall the mollifying hand of time,
Which wipes off common sorrows, cancel mine.[9]

Burgoyne's three-part plan for capturing Albany was rapidly unraveling. Short of food and in need of horses, in mid-August he authorized a raid by Germans and Indians on Bennington, Vermont. Local militiamen converged on the town and defeated the invaders in two engagements, killing at least 1,000 and taking hundreds prisoner. This American success, after so many losses, raised morale and increased enlistments. For Burgoyne, the defeat was compounded by the failure of the British diversionary attack on Albany from the west—Brigadier General St. Leger's troops and their Indian supporters had been routed at Fort Stanwix by Benedict Arnold.

BARONESS VON RIEDESEL finally joined her husband at Fort Edward on August 14 where, after the battle of Bennington, they spent three weeks together.

I ate bear's flesh for the first time

We led . . . a very pleasant life. The surrounding country was magnificent, and we were encircled by the encampments of the English* and German troops. We lived in a building called the Red House [General Burgoyne's headquarters]. I had only one room for my husband, myself and my children, in which my husband also slept, and had besides all his writing materials. My women servants slept in a kind of hall. When it was beautiful weather we took our meals under the trees, but if not, in a barn, upon boards, which were laid upon casks and served as a table. It was at that place that I ate bear's flesh for the first time, and found it of capital flavor.[10]

*The Cockney troops pronounced Riedesel as "Red-Hazel."

With the coming of the Revolution, Indians of different nations had tried to remain neutral or, if that proved impossible, to ally themselves with the side thought most likely to win and serve their interests, chiefly to protect their ancestral lands from further encroachment. They also wished to continue to sell furs and deerskin and to buy European goods, among them guns, powder, and spirits. Renowned for their skill in traversing wilderness areas, Indians were valued as advance scouts, guides and trackers by both the patriots and the British. The Iroquois Confederacy—the largest union of Indians north of the Ohio River, known as the Six Nations—included Mohawks, Senecas, Cayugas, and Onandaguas, who sided with the British, and Oneidas and Tuscaroras who cast their lot with the Americans. The Oneidas were closer geographically to American settlements and a great many had been Christianized. Some one hundred fifty Indians, mostly Oneidas, were sent to reinforce General Gates's troops as they prepared to engage Burgoyne at Saratoga.

Indians, numbering five hundred or more, fought for Burgoyne; they were his "eyes." Nevertheless, the Canadian Indians disappointed him: "when plunder is in their way . . . it is impossible to drag them from it." He welcomed the arrival of Indians from western tribes because they "profess war, not pillage."[11]

Burgoyne, however, soon came to regret the presence of his Indian allies. While their ferocity instilled fear into the hearts of the rebels and was a potent psychological weapon—George III had insisted on their participation—Indians were difficult to control, especially when under the influence of alcohol. They were more likely to engage in rampages, scalping prisoners as well as women and children—scalps were considered legitimate trophies of war—and looting, than following orders and fighting according to accepted European rules of combat.

MARIA MCEACHRON of Argyle was eighteen years old in July of 1777. She told this story of an Indian attack to Asa Fitch.

Blood was tracked all around the floor

My father, Yerry Killmore, told my brother Adam to go and help Allen get in his wheat, but Adam felt lazy and wouldn't go, and Father used afterwards to say he could forgive Adam for all his disobedience, he was so glad he disobeyed him at this time. So he sent his Negro Tom, who was a young man grown, in Adam's place and the wench Sarah, who was about twelve years old, and my sister Catherine also went along. They went on foot early on Saturday morning and [were to] return home at night. They wrought together in the harvest field, Mistress Allen binding the sheaves, the black girl carrying them together, Allen and Tom reaping, and Catherine at the house taking care of the babe and getting their dinner . . . To make more sure of killing all, it was supposed the Indians lurking in the woods waited till they should be all in the house at dinner, for twas then that the attack was made. Catherine and the Negroes not coming home at night, on Sunday morning Father sent the boy Abram, Tom's brother, on horseback. . . .

Allen was found on the path to the barn and near to the barn. A piece behind him was Catherine; behind her and halfway from the house to the barn was Mistress Allen with her babe in her arms and placed at her breast—where it must have been put by the Indians, for to scalp it they must have had it out of its mother's arms. The two children and the Negro girl had tried to hide themselves in the bed, for they were found there, the bedclothes gashed and bloody from the tomahawks. Blood was tracked all around the floor. Bullet holes were perforated through the door, and there was one bullet through the cupboard door in the northeast corner of the house.[12]

Jane McCrea was another woman whose murder by Indians horrified both the British and the Americans. Jane, a beautiful woman in her twenties, was living in the Fort Edward area with her brother, a colonel in the New York militia. Having fallen in love with a local Tory serving in Burgoyne's army, and expecting to be married, she remained behind when her brother evacuated his family as the British neared. Late in July, a party of Indians broke into the log cabin where Jane was staying; they killed and scalped her, later sporting their prize, so the story goes, before the intended bridegroom. The murder so outraged Americans that it was used as an effective propaganda tool to raise enlistments.[13] Burgoyne tried but was unsuccessful in disciplining the Indians.

As fall approached, it became clear that a major battle between American and British forces was in the offing. Still determined to reach Albany, Burgoyne crossed to the Hudson's west bank at Saratoga where he received word that General William Howe had decided to move on Philadelphia rather than come up the Hudson to support him. General Henry Clinton, who remained in New York City, did attack forts in the Hudson Highlands, but returned to his base instead of continuing on to Albany. Sensing an opportunity for a decisive action, George Washington sent reinforcements to General Gates; numbers of eager militiamen also materialized. Consequently, by mid-September 1777, a rebel force of some 7,000 men occupied a well-fortified position at Bemis Heights.

Most of Burgoyne's Indian allies, smarting under his reprimands and fearing possible defeat, deserted him. Nevertheless, on the morning of September 19, Burgoyne moved forward to confront the American forces in a clearing called Freeman's Farm. The fighting was furious. When night fell, even though the Americans had withdrawn to Bemis Heights, it was clear that they had fought the British to a standstill.

Reeling from staggering losses, Burgoyne realized he was on his own: food was in short supply and morale was poor, with desertions on the rise. His position was made even more desperate by news that his escape route back to Canada was virtually blocked. Refusing advice to attempt a withdrawal, Burgoyne launched another attack. The Americans carried the day.

BARONESS VON RIEDESEL was in the middle of it all.

every one . . . could shoot very well

As we were to march farther, I had a large calash made for me, in which I, my children, and both my women servants had seats; and in this manner I followed the army . . . We passed through boundless forests and magnificent tracts of country, which . . . were abandoned by all the inhabitants, who fled before us, and reinforced the army of the American general Gates. . . . This cost us dearly, for every one of them was a soldier by nature, and could shoot very well; besides, the thought of fighting for their fatherland and their freedom inspired them with still greater courage. . . .

I was more dead than alive

Suddenly . . . on the 7th of October, my husband, with the whole general staff, decamped. Our misfortune may be said to date from this moment. I had just sat down with my husband at his quarters to breakfast. General Fraser, and, I believe, Generals Burgoyne and Phillips, also, were to have dined with me on that same day. I observed considerable movement among the troops. My husband thereupon informed me, that there was to be a reconnoisance, which, however, did not surprise me, as this often happened. On my way homeward, I met many savages in their war-dress, armed with guns. To my question where they were going, they cried out to me, "War! War!" which meant they were going to fight. This completely overwhelmed me, and I had scarcely got back to my quarters [Smith house], when I heard skirmishing, and firing, which by degrees, became constantly heavier, until, finally, the noises became frightful. It was a terrible cannonade, and I was more dead than alive.

About three o'clock in the afternoon, in place of the guests who were to have dined with me, they brought in to me, upon a litter, poor General Fraser (one of my expected guests), mortally wounded. Our dining table, which was already spread, was taken away, and in its place they fixed up a bed for the general. I sat in a corner of the room trembling and quaking. The noises grew continually louder. The thought that they might bring in my husband in the same manner was to me dreadful, and tormented me incessantly. The general said to the surgeon, "Do not conceal any thing from me. Must I die?" The ball had gone through his bowels . . . Unfortunately, however, the general had eaten a hearty breakfast, by reason of which the intestines were distended, and the ball, so the surgeon said, had not gone . . . between the intestines, but through them. I heard him often, amidst his groans, exclaim, "O, fatal ambition! Poor General Burgoyne! My poor wife!" Prayers were read to him. He then sent a message to General Burgoyne, begging that he would have him buried the following day at six o'clock in the evening, on the top of a hill, which was a sort of redoubt. I knew no longer which way to turn. The whole entry and the other rooms were filled with the sick, who were suffering with the camp-sickness, a kind of dysentery. Finally, toward evening, I saw my husband coming . . . . he drew me one side and told me that every thing might go very badly, and that I must keep myself in constant readiness for departure, but by no means to give any one the least inkling of what I was doing. . . .

My lady [Harriet] Ackland occupied a tent not far from our house. In this she slept, but during the day was in the camp. Suddenly one came to tell her that her husband was mortally wounded, and had been taken prisoner. At this she became very wretched. We comforted her by saying that it was only a slight wound, but as no one could nurse him as well as herself, we counseled her to go at once to him, to do which she could certainly obtain permissions. She loved him very much, although he was a plain, rough man, and was almost daily intoxicated; with this exception, however, he was an excellent officer. She was the loveliest of women. I spent the night in this manner—at one time comforting her, and at another looking after my children, whom I put to bed. As for myself, I could not go to sleep, as I had General Fraser and all the other gentlemen in my room, was constantly afraid that my children would wake up and cry, and thus disturb the poor dying man, who often sent to beg my pardon for making me so much trouble. About three o'clock in the morning, they told me that he could not last much longer. I had desired to be apprised of the approach of this moment. I, accordingly, wrapped up the children in the bed coverings, and went with them into the entry.

Early in the morning, at eight o'clock, he expired. After they had washed the corpse, they wrapped it in a sheet, and laid it on a bedstead. We then again came into the room, and had this sad sight before us the whole day. At every instant, also, wounded officers of my acquaintance arrived, and the cannonade again began. A retreat was spoken of, but there was not the least movement made toward it. . . . We learned that General Burgoyne intended to fulfill the last wish of General Fraser, and to have him buried at six o'clock, in the place designated by him. . . . Precisely at six o'clock the corpse was brought out, and we saw the entire body of generals with their retinues on the hill assisting at the obsequies. The English chaplain, Mr. Brudenel, performed the funeral services. The cannonballs flew continually around and over the party. The American general, Gates, afterwards said, that if he had known that it was a burial he would not have allowed any firing in that direction. . . . The order had gone forth that the army should break up after the burial, and the horses were already harnessed to our calashes. . . . we drove off at eight o'clock in the evening. . . .

On the 9th, we spent the whole day in a pouring rain, ready to march at a moment's warning. The savages had lost their courage, and they were seen in all directions going home. . . . Toward evening we came at last to Saratoga, which was only half an hour's march from the place where we had spent the whole day. I was wet through and through by the frequent rains, and was obliged to remain in this condition the entire night, as I had no place whatever where I could change my linen. I, therefore, seated myself before a good fire, and undressed my children; after which, we laid ourselves down together upon some straw. I asked General Phillips, who came up to where we were, why we did not continue our retreat while there was yet time, as my husband had pledged himself to cover it, and bring the army through? "Poor woman," answered he, "I am amazed at you! completely wet through, have you still the courage to wish to go further in this weather! Would that you were only our commanding general! He halts because he is tired, and intends to spend the night here and give us a supper." In this latter achievement, especially, General Burgoyne was very fond of indulging. He spent half the nights in singing and drinking, and amusing himself with the wife of a commissary, who was his mistress, and who, as well as he, loved champagne.

On the 10th . . . General Burgoyne, in order to cover our retreat, caused the beautiful houses and mill at Saratoga belonging to General Schuyler, to be burned. . . . About two o'clock in the afternoon, the firing of cannon and small arms was again heard, and all was alarm and confusion. My husband sent me a message telling me to betake myself forthwith into a house which was not far from there. . . . it harbored none but wounded soldiers, or women! We were finally obliged to take refuge in the cellar . . . My children laid down on the earth with their heads upon my lap, and in this manner we passed the entire night. A horrible stench, the cries of the children, and yet more than all this, my own anguish prevented me from closing my eyes.

On the following morning the cannonade again began. . . . I advised all to go out of the cellar for a little while, during which time I would have it cleaned, otherwise we would all be sick. They followed my suggestion, and I at once set many hands to work, which was in the highest degree necessary; for the women and children being afraid to venture forth had soiled the whole cellar. After they had all gone out and left me alone, I for the first time surveyed our place of refuge. It consisted of three beautiful cellars, splendidly arched. I proposed that the most dangerously wounded of the officers should be brought into one of them; that the women should remain in another; and that all the rest should stay in the third, which was nearest the entrance. I had just given the cellars a good sweeping, and had them fumigated by sprinkling vinegar on burning coals, and each one found his place prepared for him—when a fresh and terrible cannonade threw us all once more into alarm. Many persons, who had no right to come in, threw themselves against the door. My children were already under the cellar steps, and we would all have been crushed, if God had not given me strength to place myself before the door, and with extended arms prevented all from coming in; otherwise every one would have been severely injured. Eleven cannon balls went through the house, and we could plainly hear them rolling over our heads. One poor soldier, whose leg they were about to amputate, having been laid upon a table for this purpose, had the other leg taken off by another cannon ball, in the middle of the operation. His comrades all ran off, and when they again came back they found him in a corner of the room, where he had rolled in his anguish, scarcely breathing. I was more dead than alive, though not so much on account of our own danger, as for that which enveloped my husband, who, however, frequently sent to see how I was getting along, and to tell me that he was still safe. . . . We spent the remainder of this night in the same way as the former ones. . . .

On the following morning, however, we got things better regulated. . . . I preferred to remain near the door, so that in case of fire I could rush out from the room. I had some straw brought in and laid my bed [clothes] upon it, where I slept with my children—my maids sleeping not far from us. . . . Often my husband wished to withdraw me from danger by sending me to the Americans; but I remonstrated with him on the grounds, that to be with people whom I would be obliged to treat with courtesy, while, perhaps, my husband was being killed by them, would be even yet more painful than all I was now forced to suffer. He promised me, therefore, that I should henceforward follow the army. . . . I endeavored to divert my mind from my troubles, by constantly busying myself with the wounded. I made them tea and coffee. . . . Often, also, I shared my noonday meal with them. . . . One of our greatness annoyances was the stench of the wounds when they began to suppurate. . . . Not all . . . who were with us deserved our compassion. There were, also, poltroons [cowards] in our little company, who ought not to have remained in the cellar.[14]

Burgoyne began seriously to consider surrender. After consulting with his officers, he decided to ask General Gates for terms. Arrogant, even in defeat, he sent his own list of conditions to the American commander, who, surprisingly, agreed to them. The Saratoga "Convention" called for British and German forces to lay down their arms and march to Boston where they would be sent back to England with the stipulation that they would never again fight in America.

ELIZABETH FISHER gave a vivid account of events leading to Burgoyne's defeat.

they . . . saluted us with a cannonball

We . . . concluded to remain in the British army; we stayed in the camp till Burgoyne capitulated. In October . . . I was eye witness to the death of General Frazer—I was in the same house with him—I saw his death and burial. After we were defeated we saw hard times; provisions were scarce, and not to be had for money.

I must now give you some account of what passed from the time of our retreat till the capitulation took place. We retreated after the last battle to Saratoga, where we encamped a small distance from the river, to prevent their cannon having any command over us . . . waiting General Burgoyne's orders. We were deprived of all comforts of life, and did not dare to kindle fire for fear we should be observed from the other side of the river, and they might fire on us, which they did several times. Being about the middle of October, we suffered cold and hunger; many a day I had nothing but a piece of raw salt pork, a biscuit, and a drink of water—poor living for a nurse. At this time I had my child at my breast, being eleven months old. One day, wearied of living in this manner, I told some of the soldiers' wives if they would join me, I would find out a way to get some provisions cooked—seven of them joined me. I spoke to some of the soldiers that were invalid, and told them if they would make up a fire back in the wood, and get a large kettle hung on, we would fill it with provision, and cook it, which would last us some time. They consented to do it for a guinea; they went to work and built up a fire, hung on the kettle, and put water in it, then we women put in what we pleased; we soon filled it with a variety; it began to boil; we all kept a distance from the fire for fear of the cannon that were placed on the other side of the river on a high hill; they soon discovered our fire, and saluted us with a cannon ball; it struck and broke our kettle to pieces, and sent the provision in the air. We met with no hurt only losing our intended feast. . . .

A few days after the capitulation took place [October 17], when I saw the troops lay down their arms, I was glad, for I was wishing to get out of the camp. Mr. Fisher said he should go to Canada. I refused going with him, and went back to Hebron.[15]

SARAH KAST MCGINN, a loyalist woman of Tryon County, New York, was much valued by both the rebels and the British for her ability to communicate with the Indians. She threw in her lot with the British army, and, after the flight of their Indian allies and the defeat at Fort Stanwix, she was sent to Indian country to try to soothe the ruffled feelings of those who had fought with the British and lost men. In her petition to the Crown in 1787 (in the third person) for compensation for losses she suffered, McGinn cited in particular a service she performed after Burgoyne's defeat at Saratoga.

to carry an Account . . . favourable to Government

October 1777

The Rebels have destroyed, plundered and taken almost all her Property, because they alledged and not without reason that she was tampering with the Indians in favour of Government. . . .

She made her escape to [the British army before the battle of Fort Stanwix] with her Family except a Son [William] who she was obliged to leave to their Mercy, who was out of his Sences and bound in Chains, as he had been for several Years, and sometime afterwards was burn't alive in said Situation. . . .

That if your Petitioner had not got away, the Rebels would certainly have obliged her to act for them with the Indians. The Rebels by way of inducement to come over to their Side offered her 12/ York Currency per day and a Guard of 30 Men to protect her against any harm from the King's troops, which offer she refused with Contempt.

That after our Forces returned from Fort Stanwix to Oswego your Petitioner was sent . . . to Quayonga [Cayuga] Castle to be of every Service in her Power to Government among the Indians during her stay there. It happen'd that an Indian was going with a Belt of Wampam to the different Indians from General

Schuyler acquainting the Six Nations that all the King's Troops had been defeated and taken Prisoners at Saratoga by the American Army, and if the Six Nations would not come immediately and make their Peace with the Congress they would find means to compell them; which Belt your Petitioner stopt and prevailed upon the Indian to carry an Account of a different Nature favourable to Government and encouraged the Six Nations, who soon after went to War against the Rebels on the Frontiers.[16]

BARONESS VON RIEDESEL described how she was treated by Americans after Burgoyne's surrender and commented on the curiosity of spectators on the journey from Albany to Boston.

no one cast at us scornful glances

At last, my husband sent to me a groom with a message that I should come to him with our children. . . I, therefore, again seated myself in my dear calash, and, in the passage through the American camp, I observed, with great satisfaction, that no one cast at us scornful glances. On the contrary, they all greeted me, even showing compassion on their countenances at seeing a mother with her little children in such a situation. I confess that I feared to come into the enemy's camp, as the thing was so entirely new to me. . . .

As it was already late in the season, and the weather was raw, I had my calash covered with coarse linen, which in turn was varnished over with oil; and in this manner we set out on our journey to Boston, which was very tedious, besides being attended with considerable hardships.

I know not whether it was my carriage that attracted the curiosity of the people to it—for it certainly had the appearance of a wagon in which they carry around rare animals—but often I was obliged to halt, because the people insisted upon seeing the wife of the German general with her children. For fear that they would tear off the linen covering from the wagon in their eagerness to see me, I very often alighted, and by this means got away more quickly. However, I must say that the people were very friendly, and were particularly delighted at my being able to speak English, which was the language of their country.[17]

HANNAH WINTHROP, in a letter to Mercy Otis Warren, provided a description of the arrival of the Convention Army in Boston and complained of the burden their upkeep would be to the townspeople.

a sordid set of creatures

Cambridge, November 11, 1777

Last thursday, which was a very stormy day, a large number of British Troops came softly thro the Town via Watertown to Prospect hill, on Friday we heard the Hessians were to make a Procession in the same rout; we thot we should have nothing to do with them, but View them as they Passt. To be sure, the sight was truly astonishing, I never had the least Idea that the Creation produced such a sordid set of creatures in human Figure—poor, dirty, emaciated men, great numbers of women, who seemd to be the beasts of burthen, having a bushel basket on their back, by which they were bent double, the contents seemd to be Pots & kettles, various sorts of Furniture, children peeping thro the gridirons & other utensils, Some very young Infants who were born on the road; the women with bare feet, cloathd in dirty raggs such Effluvia filld the air while they were passing, had they not been smoaking all the time, I should have been apprehensive of being contaminated by them.

After a noble Looking advanced Guard Genl. J—y Bn [Johnny Burgoyne] headed this terrible group on horseback, The other General also Cloathed in Blue Cloaks. Hessians Waldecker Anspachers Brunswickers &c &c &c followed on. The Hessian Generals gave us a Polite Bow as they Passd—not so the British their Baggage waggons drawn by poor half starvd horses. But to bring up the rear, another fine noble looking Guard of American Brawny Victorious Yeomanry, who assisted in bringing these Sons of Slavery to terms. Some of our Waggons drawn by fat oxen, driven by joyous looking Yankies closd the cavalcade.

The Generals & other officers went to Bradishs, where they Quarter at present. The Privates trudgd thro thick & thin to the hills, where we thot they were to be confind, but what was our Surprise when in the morning we beheld an inundation of those disagreable objects filling our streets? How mortifying is it? they in a manner demanding our Houses & Colleges for their genteel accomodation. Did the brave G- Gates ever mean this? Did our Legislature ever intend the military should prevail above the Civil? is there not a degree of unkindness in loading poor Cambridge, almost ruined before this great army seem to be let loose upon us & what will be the consequence time will discover. . . .

It is said we shall have not Less than seven thousand persons to feed in Cambridge & its environs, more than its inhabitants. Two hundred & fifty cord of wood will not serve them a week, think then how we must be distressd, wood is risen to £5.10 per Cord & but little to be purchased. I never thought I could lie down to sleep Surrounded by these enemies, but we strangly become enured to most things which appear difficult when distant. . . .

PS. Gl Bn has repeatedly said he was convinced it was impossible Great Britain should ever subdue America he therefore wishd a union might take place that would never be broken, & that he might get home Soon to prevent any more attempts that way. . . .We hear no Parole signd yet.[18]

SUSAN LIVINGSTON, on November 1, 1777, wrote to her sister, Sarah Livingston Jay, from New Jersey:

two Generals wished to avoid fighting

The Articles of Capitulation that appeared in Loudons last Paper are not relished this way, neither by Whigs, nor Tories, the latter say if Mr. Burgoyne was in a Situation to obtain such Terms he ought to have fought, the Former say if Burgoyne was obliged to surrender at all, Gates might have brought him to what Terms he pleased, so that it looks as if the two Generals wished to avoid fighting. The Troops will go home & Garrison the Forts abroad, & let those Garrisons come to America—so it will be only an exchange of Men.[19]

Most Americans agreed with Susan Livingston. Congress shortly repudiated Gates's agreement with Burgoyne, and the British and German troops remained prisoners. Early in 1778 they were marched to Virginia where their upkeep was less costly.

The battle of Saratoga was one of the most important of the Revolution, indeed a decisive one. The defeat and surrender of General Burgoyne and an army of more than five thousand men on October 17, 1777, marked a turning point in the war. It prevented the British from dividing the colonies by taking control of the Hudson River. It raised the morale of the forces after the stunning loss of New York City in 1776 and largely indecisive engagements in New Jersey. And perhaps most important of all, the American victory at Saratoga convinced France not only to recognize the rebellious states as an independent nation but also to enter into an alliance with them against her traditional enemy. Without France's money, supplies, arms and ammunition, as well as naval support, it is unlikely that the patriots would have been able to continue the war, let alone win it.

Chapter 4

branded by the names of rebellion and treason

Pennsylvania, the result of William Penn's efforts to establish a colony free of religious persecution, had its foundations firmly rooted in the Religious Society of Friends, or Quakers. Penn's "holy experiment" flourished: Philadelphia, the fertile ground where Quakers, Baptists, Catholics, Episcopalians, Jews, Lutherans, Methodists, and Presbyterians might share buildings for worship until each could build its own sanctuary. By the 1760s, it had grown into the largest and most sophisticated city in North America. Over four hundred ships a year docked in its port, unloading manufactured goods, rum, molasses, indentured servants, and African slaves. New ships were being constructed in its shipyards. Merchants, artisans, mechanics, shopkeepers, and printers readily found jobs and wealth in this diverse community. Its central location in the colonies was also advantageous; it is not surprising that, when the delegates to the First Continental Congress decided to meet to "determine upon wise and proper measures" in dealing with Great Britain, they chose Philadelphia and the newly constructed Carpenters' Hall for their deliberations.

The delegates came to a colony whose political system was in flux. Quakers, in control of Pennsylvania's legislature, felt increasingly threatened by more recent settlers—often Presbyterians and their anti-Quaker allies—who were agitating for changes to the government's traditional, conservative policies of nonconfrontation and loyalty to the Crown. The Society's opposition to violence and its belief that refusing to pay taxes amounted to "defrauding the King of his dues" were being challenged.

Whereas severe reactions to the Stamp Act broke out in the other colonies, they were muted in Pennsylvania. Though many Quakers signed the nonimportation agreement of 1765, others refused to do so.[1] By 1774, Friends were being advised not to take part in any public meetings or actions. No longer politically powerful, they were viewed by the patriots at best with suspicion and at worst as loyalists.

The Religious Society also experienced divisions among its members: some pressing for stricter adherence to their religious principles, others eager to participate in the public debate on liberty. Pressure was brought to bear on members who did not abide by the strictures of the Society. If a non-complying member could not be persuaded to change his mind, he was disowned; unacceptable actions included bearing arms, paying for a replacement for military service, making war supplies, and providing food or care of soldiers. One group, viewing their rights of conscience abridged by the Society, organized the 'Free Quakers,' wishing "only to be freed from every species of ecclesiastical tyranny . . . and to secure equal liberty to all."[2]

Women had been important members in the Society from its inception. They had contributed to Quaker doctrine, stimulated its charitable efforts, and promoted its ideals through education and ministry. Many women not only spoke during worship but also traveled as ministers or "as companions in service" with men. Women were viewed as equal to men, managed their own meetings for Quaker business, and were heard with respect. The cohesiveness of the Quaker community as a religious and economic unit made it into a powerful political force but it was its mutual accountability that exercised the strong control over what members said, how they acted, what they wore. By the mid-1770s, the Society, promoting strict observance of its tenets, retreated into exclusivity, resulting in a decline in membership.

The merchant Henry Drinker and his wife Elizabeth were among the conservative Quakers. Henry Drinker had been one of the signers of the non-importation agreement in Philadelphia and was reluctantly involved with the refusal of Philadelphia radicals to land the shipment of tea. He wrote on November 19, 1773: "we are in the way of trouble & no doubt but that class of Men among us called the Sons of Liberty will treat us as very bad Men for acting a part we conceive becomes every good & honest Man circumstanced as we are, & truly desirous of preserving the peace & good order of the City."[3] His firm, James & Drinker, acquiesced to pressure and did not unload the tea.

ELIZABETH SANDWITH DRINKER began her journal approximately two years before her marriage in 1761, and continued it for almost fifty years. Her entries detail the events of her life, ranging from the births, illnesses, and deaths of family members to the viewing of an elephant—"The innocent, good natured ugly Beast"—weather, books she read, and the yellow fever epidemic of 1798. That she kept a journal was even mentioned in her obituary, in which she was characterized as an "affectionate wife and tender mother." Many Quaker women wrote journals not only to record daily events but also to nurture their spiritual lives, their thoughts often shared with others. Elizabeth Drinker refers to herself, family members, and close friends by initials. The days of the week are denoted as First Day, meaning Sunday, Second Day, Monday, and so forth.

the Tea Ship, was at Chester

1773 April the 11 First Day—After Dinner—H[enry] D[rinker] Josey James, and myself, cross'd Delaware, the wind pretty high at NW, did not sail—

E[lizabeth] D[rinker] road on the Old Mare as far as Moores-Town, had not been on Horse back for 15 years past . . .

Decr. 2, 1773. A[bel]J[ames] and HD sent a paper to the Coffee-House this Evening conserning the Tea. . . .

Decr. 23 began to Snow last night, and continued most of this morning, the first Snow we have had this Winter; we have been favourd with a remarkable fine Fall.

Decr. 24. an account from Boston, of 342 Chests of Tea, being Thrown into the Sea.

Decr. 25. John Parrock [Quaker loyalist] call'd this Evining to inform that the Tea Ship, was at Chester.

Decr. 27. began to Snow about noon, continued 24 hours, tis' now (the 28) near 2 feet deep . . . The Tea Ship, and Cargo, sent off this Morning.[4]

PATIENCE LOVELL WRIGHT, a Quaker widow, had become famous for her life-like sculptures made of wax. In 1772, she traveled to England, where her first sitter was her compatriot Benjamin Franklin. Other "eminent Personages" had their portrait busts made: the historian Catharine Macaulay, King George III, and Queen Charlotte. Moving in London's high society, Patience Wright thought herself in a unique position to gather information for the Americans, as she wrote her friend John Dickinson:

Women are always usful in grand Events

Sir   Pallmall april 6th 1775
   · The Ld Chamberlin and Comon Counsil have a desire to asist the Congress and wish you god Speed, a Blessing to the world, and to Keep america as an asalum for all lovers of Liberty and Publick vertue to flye unto from tyrony and opresion. The fleat is any moment to sail and a new Constructed Cannon, lite, Portable on horse Back, 32 Inches Long, wide muzzel to fire at the Inhabitants and kill many at a shot. Meny thousand fire arms sent out of the tower and shipt on bord the transports at dedford. Meny hundred Cags [kegs] of flints marked BOSTON on Each Cagg with all Implements of WARR. But this is all well known to you in america. I much wish to asist you in giving you the Early Intelegenc and a few Hints may be usful. . . .
   Howe is to land at new york. The Delancy Breed is married in England and, by that means the names of the inhabitan in new york are Known to the ministry and they Expect to bribe them with Contacts and Places and ther port left open to devide the Coloneys and to deceve the peopl, But I depend on the Vertue of the Peopel. Pray take cear [care] of Jo galoway, dr Smith, Jo Read, delancy* &c. Ther letters are seen in [Lord] Dartmouth offic—depend on my Information is a undeniable fact. . . .
   I am hapy to live in the days when I see with my own Eyes, I here with my own Ears, and Know the wicked Counsel that is against you, as also to be so Hapy to Know meny of the gentlemen in the Congress and am not a silent spec-tatr on the grand works of provedenc. . . . By good authority I write you this. Women are always usful in grand Events. . . .

Take this Hint from your old friend and devotd humbl srvt   Patience Wright[5]

*Joseph Galloway and Joseph Reed of Philadelphia, the DeLancey family and Chief Justice William Smith of New York.

ELIZA HALROYD FARMAR, the English wife of Dr. Richard Farmar, who came to Philadelphia ca. 1767, was equally dismayed by the actions of the British ministry, as this letter to her nephew Jack Halroyd, a clerk at the East India Company in London shows.

if your devilish Minestry and parliment don't make some concesions

My Dear Jack—   June 28th, 1775
    We have nothing going on now but preparations for war . . . there is hardly a man that is not old but is leaving, except the Quakers; and there is two Companys of them, all in a Pretty Uniform of Sky blue turn'd up with white. There is Six or Seven different sorts of Uniforms beside a Company of light Horse and one Rangers and another of Indians: these are all of Philadelphia; besides all the Provinces arming and Training in the same Manner for they are all determined to die or be Free. It is not the low Idle Fellow that fight only for pay, but Men of great property are Common Soldiers who say they are fighting for themselves and Posterity. There is accounts come that they are now fighting at Boston and that the Army set Charles Town on fire in order to land the Troops under cover of the Smoak. . . .
    The People are getting into Manufacture of different Sorts particularly Salt Peter and Gunpowder; the Smiths are almost all turned Gunsmiths and cannot work fast enough. God knows how it will end but I fear it will be very bad on both sides; and if your devilish Minestry and parliment don't make some concesions and repeal the Acts, England will lose America for, as I said before, they are determined to be free.[6]

ESTHER DEBERDT met her future husband Joseph Reed in 1764 when he came to London to study law in the Temple. When Reed returned to Philadelphia to take care of family matters, his father having declared bankruptcy, the young lovers maintained an affectionate correspondence ("Do you want to hear that I still love?" Esther to Joseph.) Married in London, Esther arrived in Philadelphia with her husband and her mother in October 1770; her brother Dennis DeBerdt remained in England. By October 1772, there were two children ("wish I could stop with that number, but I don't expect that," she commented wryly), and by mid-1774, there were three: Martha, Joseph, and Hetty. From a loyal British citizen, anxious to return to her native land (1771), Esther Reed would become a committed supporter of the patriot cause (1775)—even more so at first than her American husband. Her clear-headed intelligence shines through the letters she wrote to her brother about the increasing tensions between England and her colonies.

my hands are pretty full of business

Nov. 2d 1774

when I tell you I have another daughter, you will not wonder that I have this time been a little negligent in answering letters. I assure you my hands are pretty full of business. Three children seem to take up all my time and attention. . . .

Many people here are very sanguine in their expectations that the Acts will be repealed immediately. . . . The People of New England . . . are prepared for the worst event, and they have such ideas of their injured Liberty, and so much enthusiasm in the cause, that I do not think that any power on earth could take it from them but with their lives. The proceedings of the Congress will show you how united the whole continent is in the cause, and from them you may judge of the sense of the people. . . .

what is to be the fate of this once rising country?

Feb. 13, 1775

[Mr. Reed's] business requires so much head work. . . . This with his late attention to politics has engrossed him more than common. . . . Of politics, I suppose you will expect me to say something, though everything now must come from you, and we are anxious to know what is to be the fate of this once rising country. It now seems standing on the brink of ruin. But the public papers will tell you everything, and Mr. Reed will also write you on the subject, so that little will be left for me to say, only that the people are in general united. The Quakers are endeavouring to steer a middle course, and make perhaps a merit of it to Government at home. How far their conduct will answer, I don't know, but it is despised here. One great comfort I have is, that if these great affairs must be brought to a crisis and decided, it had better be in our time than our childrens. . . .

I love to think of England and of old times, perhaps I may see it again. It is surely a noble country, but such wishes and hopes I must keep concealed: perhaps they had better not rise at all. . . . adieu. Believe me, ever most assuredly and affectionately,   Yours, E. Reed[7]

[In July 1775, increasing danger as well as the poor health of her daughter Martha forced Esther Reed to move in with her friend Esther Bowes Cox at Green Bank (Burlington), New Jersey, and from there to Perth Amboy. After George Washington asked her husband, now a lieutenant colonel with the Pennsylvania troops, to be his military secretary, he was absent from home a great deal of the time. Esther Reed graphically described her situation to her brother.]

Where sleeps the Virtue & Justice of the English Nation?

Amboy Septr 8th 1775

You will see by the date of this my dear Dennis that I am from home; the health of my dear Girl which always suffers in the Summer Months was the Chief reason of my coming here. I find it very beneficial to her & pleasant for myself—I received yours of the 20 & 21st of June. The News they contained tho' not very material I sent to my dr Mr. R at the Camp. He is yet there amidst all the confusion & horrors of War, before this time you knew our dreadful situation, here indeed & every Southern Province. We only here the Sound, but it is such a one, as sometimes shakes my firmness & resolution, but I find the human Mind can be habituated to all most anything, even the most distressing Scenes, after a while become familiar.

I am happy that Mr. R's situation at the Camp is the most eligable he coud have been placed in, his accomodations, with the General, in his Confidence, & his Duty in the Councils, rather than the Field. While his person is safe from danger I chearfully give up his profitts in Business (which were not trifling) & I acquics without repining at his being so long absent from me. I think the Cause in which he is engaged so just, so Glorious & I hope will be so victorious that private interest & pleasure may & ought to be given up without a murmur.

But where sleeps all our Friends in England? Where sleeps the Virtue & Justice of the English Nation? will nothing rouse them? or are they so few in Number & small in Consequence that tho' awake, their voice cannot be heard for the multitude of our Enemies—how strange woud this Situation of things have appeared even in Prospect a few years ago? coud we have forseen it when we parted in England it would probably have prevented that Seperation. We might often, if we coud forsee Events provide against approaching evils, but I believe it is right we shoud not, for tho our private happiness might have been promoted, yet our Country woud not been benefited, for at this time she requires all her friends & has a right to expert services from such heads & hearts as can most conduce to her Safety. We impatiently wait to hear what effect the Battle of Bunker Hill has both on our friends & Enemies. A few weeks I suppose will let us know. . . .

I take it for granted that I am writing to some curious person in office & that my Letter, insignificant as it is, will be open'd before you get it. One from Mr. Lane Secry of the Jersey Society to Mr. R came here with the seal quite broke as if it was done on purpose to shew they dare & woud do it.

I hope it is no Treason to say I wish well to the cause of America tho' guess Treason is not now tho't much of—however I am safe in telling you how much my love is kept alive tho' at this distance & with what undiminished Affectn I am Ever truly Yours,   No Reason sign name now[8]

[On October 28, 1775, back in Philadelphia, Esther Reed expanded on the mood of the times.]

we are struggling for our liberties

It is with particular pleasure I now sit down to write to my dear Dennis, as I am free from the fear of any prying intruder; the thought that my late letters have been subjected to such curiosity has been a painful restraint upon me, and perhaps I have not been cautious enough in what I have written, but so it is, and if I have committed treason, it must remain. . . . [Mr. Reed's] service has proved of so much consequence in the councils of the Camp, that he has devoted himself to the service of the public, and I doubt not it will give him as much pleasure in the recollection as any occurrence in his life; —indeed, my dear Dennis, the cause in which he is engaged is the cause of Liberty and virtue, how much soever it may be branded by the names of rebellion and treason. But I need not vindicate or explain the motives of our conduct to you. . . . It seems now to depend on the reception of our last Petition from the Congress to the King, if that should be so considered as to lay a foundation for negotiation, we may be again reconciled,—if not, I imagine WE SHALL DECLARE FOR INDEPENDENCE, and exert our utmost to defend ourselves. This proposition would have alarmed almost every person on the continent a twelvemonth ago, but now the general voice is, if the Ministry and Nation *will* drive us to it, we must do it, rather than submit, after so many public resolutions to the contrary. In this case . . . no trade can be carried on between the two countries. . . .

My dear little girl . . . has again recovered her usual health, but she is of so delicate a constitution, that she often droops and alarms me. My son Joseph and daughter Hetty are both well. Mama keeps her health and spirits amazingly. Mr. Reed has recovered his by his journey to the Camp. Everybody tells me he is grown so fat I should hardly know him on his return, which I expect will be one day this week. He has been gone from home above four months; his business has suffered not a little, but in such times like these every person must sacrifice something. . . . Adieu, my dear Dennis,—think of us often; remember we are struggling for our liberties and everything that is dear to us in life.

I am ever, most affectionately,   Yours, E. Reed[9]

[Despite the threatening situation, Esther Reed could still find some humor in it.]

pardons are to be distributed

Phila. Feb. 25, 1776

We understand pardons are to be distributed to the Rebels, & smile at the thot of a neighboring Gov. [William Franklin of New Jersey] giving them to his father and other relations. I suppose they must be humbly asked. If these are the only terms that are offered, I fear they will not be accepted; instead of receiving pardons, they merit applause of every Friend of Liberty & Mankind, thus principled it is hard they shoud be stigmatized with the names of Rebels & leaders of Factions &c, & drove to the hard necessity of defending themselves at the hazard of their Lives—& even supposing their Liberties not in the danger they imagind yet surely they have had some reason to be alarmed & to be watchful & attentive to so great an object is virtuous & to defend it when they think it attackd is brave—but I dismiss a Subject on which I am much inclined to write, as it engrosses every heart & every Tongue . . . .   Your most Affecte[10]

MARGARET HILL MORRIS, the eighth daughter of Dr. Richard and Deborah Moore Hill of Maryland, was raised by her older sister Hannah in Philadelphia. At twenty-one, she married William Morris Jr., a dry-goods merchant, who died in 1765, leaving her with three small children and expecting another. After struggling for some years to provide for her family, Margaret decided to move in with her sister Sarah Moore Dillwyn, wife of the Quaker preacher George Dillwyn, who lived in Green Bank, New Jersey. The house overlooked the Delaware River. Another sister Milcah Martha Hill Moore and family lived nearby. Burlington, like Philadelphia, had a strong Quaker base; in 1776, well over 100 members worshipped in its hexagonal meeting house.

As warring factions approached Philadelphia, people fled their homes seeking safety. When Milcah Martha Moore moved her family north of Philadelphia, Margaret began her Journal "for the amusement of a sister," reporting on the events in their lives. Filled with facts and rumors, she comments—often with a twinkle in her pen—on the dangerous events unfolding around her. From these pages emerges the portrait of a courageous, compassionate, even wise woman, treading—not always successfully—the fine line of being neither patriot nor loyalist. The Journal begins in early December 1776, as General Cornwallis and his army marched through New Jersey, the British fleet blockaded the Delaware River, and General Washington and his troops fled into Pennsylvania. On the river near Margaret Morris's house were "galleys" or "gondolas" of the Pennsylvania Navy that were to prevent the crossing of British troops.

my heart almost died within me

December 6th, 1776

Being on a visit to my friend M S. at Haddonfield. I was preparing to return to my Family, when a Person from Philada told us the people there were in great Commotion, that the English fleet was in the River & hourly expected to sail up to the City; that the inhabitants were removing into the Country, & that several persons of considerable repute had been discoverd to have formd a design of setting fire to the City, & were Summoned before the Congress and strictly injoind to drop the horrid purpose—when I heard the above report my heart almost died within me, & I cried surely the Lord will not punish the innocent with the guilty, & I wishd there might be found some interceeding Lotts & Abrahams amongst our People. . . . I thought of my S D. [Sarah Dillwyn] the beloved Companion of my Widowd State—her Husband at the distance of some hundred miles from her—I thought of my own lonely situation, no Husband to cheer, with the voice of love, my Sinking spirits. My little flock too, without a Father to direct them how to Steer,—all these things crouded into my mind at once, & I felt like one forsaken—a flood of friendly tears came to my relief—& I felt an humble Confidence, that he, who had been with me in six troubles would not forsake me now—While I cherishd this hope my tranquility was restord, & I felt no Sensations but of humble Acquiescense to the Divine Will—& was favord to find my Family in health, on my Arrival, & my Dear Companion not greatly discomposd, for which favor I desire to be made truly thankful—

12th—The people of the gallies, Suspecting that some troops were yet either conceald in Town or in the Neighborhood of it, have been very Jealous of the inhabitants, who have been often alarmd with reports, that the City [Philadelphia] woud be Set on fire, Many have gone in haste & great distress into the Country, but we still hope, no Mischief is Seriously intended—A Number of Men landed on our Bank this Morning, & told us it was thier settled purpose to set fire to the Town—I begd them not to set my house afire—they askd which was my House, I showd it to them, & they said they knew not what hinderd them from fireing on it last Night, for seeing a light in the Chambers, they thought there were Hessians in it, & that they pointed the Guns at it Several times, I told them my Children were Sick, which obligd me to burn alight all Night—Tho they did not know what hinderd them from fireing on us, I did, it was the Guardian of the Widow & the Orphan, who took us into his Safe keeping, & preservd us from danger, oh—that I may keep humble, & be thankful for this, as well as other favors Vouch safed to my little flock—

13th—This day we began to look a little like ourselves again. The troops were removd some miles from Town as we heard. . . . but the Suspicions of the Gondola Men still continued, & search was made in & about the Town for Men distinguishd by the Name of Tories. . . . There was no appearance of the formidable Hessians. . . . some of the Gentlemen who entertaind the foreigners were pointed out to the Gondola Men—2 Worthy inhabtants were seizd upon & dragd on board—from the 13th to 16th we had various reports of the advancing & retireing of the Enemy—Parties of Armd Men rudely enterd the Houses in Town, & diligent search made for Tories, the 2 last taken releasd & sent on Shore.

bless me, I hope you are not the Hessians

About noon this day, (the 16) a very terrible account of thousands coming into Town—& now actually to be seen on Gallows Hill—My incautious Son [John] catchd up the Spy Glass, & was running to the Mill to look at them. I told him it wd be liable to misconstruction, but he prevaild on me to let him gratify his curiosity, & he went, but returnd much dissatisfyd, for no troops coud he see. As he came back poor Dick took the glass & resting it against a tree, took a view of the fleet—both of these was observd by the people on board, who suspected it was an Enemy that was watching thier Motions—They Mannd a boat & sent her on Shore—aloud knocking at my door brought me to it—I was a little flutterd & kept locking and unlocking that I might get my ruffled face, a little composd. At last I opend it, & half a dozen Men all Armd, demanded the keys of the empty House—I asked what they wanted there they said to Search for a D----d tory who had been spying at them from the Mill—the Name of a Tory so near my own door seriously alarmd me—for a poor refugee [Dr. Jonathan Odell] dignifyd by that Name, had claimd the shelter of my Roof & was at that very time conceald, like a thief in an Auger hole*—

I rung the bell violently, the Signal agreed on, if they came to Search—& when I thought he had crept into the hole—I put on a very simple look & cryd out, bless me I hope you are not Hessians—say, good Men are you the Hessians? do we look like Hessians? askd one of them rudely—indeed I dont know; Did you never see a Hessian? no never in my life but they are Men, & you are Men & may be Hessians for any thing I know—but Ill go with you into Col Co [Colonel John Cox†] house, tho indeed it was my Son at the Mill, he is but a Boy & meant no harm, he wanted to see the Troops—so I marchd at the head of them, opend the door, & searchd every place but we coud not find the tory— strange where he coud be—we returnd; they greatly disapointed, I pleasd, to think my house was not Suspected—the Capt smart little fellow Named Shippen [William Shippin] said he wishd he coud see the Spy glass—S D [Sarah Dillwyn] produced it—& very civilly desird his acceptance of it, which I was sorry for—as I often amusd myself in looking thro it—they left us, & Searchd J Vs [James Verree] & the 2 next houses—but no tory coud they find.

*a secret, windowless room entered through the back of a closet; a warning bell, activated by a knob near the front door, hung nearby.

†John Cox, a Philadelphia businessman, owner of Batsto (site of an iron furnace), which supplied the Continental Army with cannon shot and bomb shells, kettles, etc. He and his wife Esther Bowes Cox were also friends of Esther DeBerdt Reed.

[Margaret Morris experienced another scare some days later when she feared her young son had been taken prisoner.]

a Mothers pangs for her Son

17th . . . early this Morning J V [James Verree], sent in beg I wd let my Son go a few miles out of Town on some business for him—I consented, not knowing of the formidable doings up Town—when I heard it, I felt a Mothers pangs for her Son—all the day, but when night came, & he did not appear, I made no doubt of his being taken by the Hessians—a friend made my mind easy by telling me he had himself passt thro the Town where the dreadful Hessians were said to be playing the very mischief (JV, again) it is certain there were Numbers of them at Mount Holly—but behavd very civilly to the People, excepting only a few persons who were in actual rebellion as they termd it—whose goods &c they injured—this Evening every Gondola Man sent on board, with strict orders not to set a foot on the Jersey Shore again—so far so good.

Don Quixote, Junr mounted his horse

18th—this Morning gives us hope of a quiet day—but my mind still anxious for my Son not yet returnd—our Refugee [Jonathan Odell] gone off today out of the reach of Gondolas, and tory hunters. . . . My Son returnd at Night, & to his Mortification saw not one Hessian, light horse, or any thing else worth seeing, but had the Consolation of a little adventure at York bridge, being made to give an account of himself as he went out yesterday, his Horse detaind, & he orderd to Walk back to Town & get a pass from Gen: [Joseph Reed] Read, this he readily agreed to, but instead of a pass, Col Cox accompanyd him back to the Bridge, & Don Quixote, Junr mounted his horse & rode thro their ranks in triumph.

Scare us out of our Witts

20th . . . a friend from Town calld in about 4 oClock—& told us they were all acoming, we askd if he had seen them; no—but he heard they were Just here. We askd him how we, at this distance from Town shd know of thier coming, they might popp upon us here, & Scare us out of our Witts, as we had no Man in the house—he said, oh—you will know it fast enough I warrant, why the Noise of the Waggons, & rattling of the Cannon will be heard at a great distance—& I advise you to make good use of your time till they do come, & put all things of gold & Silver out of thier way—& all linen too, or youll lose it—I said they pillaged none but Rebels—& we were not such, we had taken no part against them, &c—but that Signified nothing, we shoud loose all &c—after he was gone, my S D, & myself askd each other why it was that all these Stories did not put us into a fright, we were not even discomposed—Surely it is a favour never to be forgotten—We conclude to sit up a little later than usual to Night, but no Rattling coud we hear.

teach the Children to pronounce "Vicates"

21st—more snow last Night. . . . get quite in the fidgets for News, send Dick to Town to collect some, he returns quite Newsless, good mind to send him back again—W D [William Dillwyn] —comes at last, tells us all we expected to hear, pleases us by saying we shall have timely notice of thier coming, gives a hint that the feeble & defenceless will find safety & protection, rank ourselves amongst the Number having no Man with us in the house—Determine not to be unprovided again, let them come, or not, as the Weather is now so cold, provisions will keep good several days—We pity the poor fellows who were obligd to be out last Night in the Snow. Repeat our Wishes that this may be a Neutral Island—quite sleepy—go to Bed, & burn a lamp all Night—talk as loud as usual & dont regard the creeking of the door—no Gondola Men listening about the Bank—before we retired to bed this Evening, an attempt was made to teach the Children to pronounce "Vicates" [Wie geht's? or Hello] like a Dutch [Deutsch or German] Man—Our good Neighbor a little concernd to think there is not one in Neighborhood that will be able to interpret for us when the Hessians are quarterd on us—at last by meer dint of Conjuration, I discover that his Maid is a Dutch Woman, & we resolve, Nemi. Con: [nemine contradicente: no one speaking in opposition] that she shall be the interpreter of the bank—& her Master thinks it will be a great thing to have one that can speak for us.

they Never fought with Naked Men

22d . . . We heard yesterday that Gen: [Charles] Lee was taken Prisoner by a Party of light horse who surrounded him & took him to New York (hope privately, that he will not escape)—to day (the 22d) we hear Gen: Howe is at trenton, & it is thought there will be an engagement soon. . . . We hear this afternoon that our Officers are afraid thier Men will not fight & wish they may all run home again. A peaceable Man ventured to Prophesy to day, that if the War is continued thro the Winter, the British troops will be scard at the sight of our Men, for as they Never fought with Naked Men, the Novelty of it, will terrify them & make them retreat, faster than they advanced to meet them, for he says, from the present appearance of our ragged troops, he thinks it probable, they will not have Cloaths to cover them a Month or 2 hence. . . .

26th—the Weather very stormy. . . . a great Number of flat Bottom Boats gone up the River, we cant learn where they are going to.

[As the year came to a close, Margaret Morris confessed to fluctuating emotions: pity for the soldiers and gratitude that her family had a roof over its head.]

there is a God of Battle, as well as a God of peace

27th—a letter from Gen [Joseph] Read to his Br[other: Bowes Reed]—informing him that Washington had had an engagement with the Regulars on the 25th early in the Morning, taking them by surprize, killd fifty, & took 900 prisoners. The loss on our side not known, or if known, not sufferd to be publick.—It seems this heavy loss to the Regulars was oweing to the prevailing custom among the Hessians of getting drunk on the eve of that great day which brought peace on Earth & good Will to Men—but oh, how unlike Christians is the Manner in which they Celebrate it, can we call ourselves Christians, while we act so Contrary to our Masters rules—he set the example which we profess to follow, & here is a recent instance that we only profess it; instead of good will, envy & hatred seem to be the ruling passions in the breasts of thousands. This evening the 27th about 3000 of the Pensylvania Militia, & other Troops landed in the Neck, & marchd into Town with Artillery, Baggage &c, & were quarterd on the inhabitants, one Company were lodged at J Vs & a guard placed between his house & ours, We were so favord as not to have any sent to our House. An Officer spent the Evening with us, & appeard to be in high spirits, & talkd of engaging the English as a very triffling affair, Nothing so easy as to drive them over the North River &c—not considering there is a God of Battle, as well as a God of peace, who may have given them the late advantage, in order to draw them out to meet the Chastisement that is reservd for them.

a sorrowful Year

January the first, 1777—This New Years day has not been usherd in with the usual Cerimonies of rejoiceing &c, & indeed I believe it will be the beginning of a sorrowful Year to very many People—Yet the flatterer hope, bids me look forward with Confidence & trust in him who can bring order out of this great Confusion—I do not hear that any Messengers have been in Town from the Camp.

Suspect they have run away

3d—This Morning between 8 & 9 oClock we heard very distinctly, a heavy fireing of Cannon, the sound came from towards Trenton, about noon a Number of Soldiers, upwards of a thousand came into Town in great Confusion, with Baggage & some Cannon—From these Soldiers we learn there was a smart engagement Yesterday at Trenton, & that they left them engaged near Trenton Mill, but were not able to say which side was Victorious. They were again quarterd on the inhabitants, & we again exempt from the Cumber of having them lodged in our house—Several of those who lodged in Col Co [Colonel Cox] house last Week, returnd to Night, & askd for the key—which I gave them, About bed time I went in the next house to see if the fires were safe, & my heart was melted with Compassion to see such a number of my fellow Creatures lying like Swine on the floor fast aSleep, & many of them without even a Blanket to cover them. It seems very strange to me that such a Number shoud be allowd to come from the Camp at the very time of the engagement, & I shrewdly Suspect they have run away for they can give no account why they came, nor where they are to March next.

6th [actually the 4th]—the accounts hourly coming in are so Contradictory & various, that we know not wch to give credit to. We have heard our people have gaind another Victory, that the English are fleeing before them, some at Brunswick—some at Prince Town. . . . a Number of Sick & wounded brought into Town, calls upon us to extend a hand of Charity towards them—Several of my Soldiers left the next house, & returnd to the place from whence they came, upon my questioning them pritty close, I brought several to confess they had ran away, being scared at the heavy fireing on the 3d—There were several pritty innocent looking lads among them, & I simpathized with thier Mothers when I saw them preparing to return to the Army.

What sad Havock

5th—I heard to day that Captain [William] Shippen who threatend to shoot my Son for spying at the Gondolas, is killd. I forgave him long ago, for the fright he Occasiond me, & felt sorry when I heard he was Dead—We are told to day that Gen. [Hugh] Mercer is killd, & Mifflin wounded—What sad Havock will this dreadful War make in our Land. . .

9th. . . . We hear Washington has sent to buy up a Number of Stoves, from whence it is Conjectured he is going into Winter Quarters—The Weather very cold, more snow falling has almost filld the River with Ice & we expect it will be strong enough to Walk over in a day or two. . .

11th—the Weather very cold—& the River quite shut—I pity the poor Soldiers now on thier March, many of whom will probably lay out in the fields this cold Night—What cause have I for gratitude that I & my household are Shelterd from the Storm.[11]

MARY WHITE MORRIS, wife of the Philadelphia merchant and financier, Robert Morris, was among those fleeing Philadelphia at the approach of the troops; she sought refuge with her stepsister Sophia Hall near Aberdeen, Maryland. Her distress was heightened by the medical needs of her son Thomas. Members of the Continental Congress moved their deliberations to Baltimore but left Robert Morris to oversee affairs in Philadelphia.

I Thought I was Prepared for every Misfortune

Dear Mr. Morris   December the 20 [1776]

    I long to give You an Account, of the many Difficulties, and uneasyiness we have Experienced in this journey. Indeed my Spirits, were very Unable to the task, after that greatest Conflict, Flying from Home, the Sufferings of our poor little Tom, distress'd us all, and without the Affectionate assistance of Mr. [Aquila] Hall, and the Skillfulness of Doctor Cole, whose Services I shall never forget, I don't know what might have been the Consequence, as it was a boil of an uncommon Nature, and Required the Surgeons Hand; we had reason to Apprehend too, we should lose our goods, the many Circumstances, of this Affair, I must leave till I see you, as neither my Patience, nor Paper will hold out. . . .

Joseph [a servant] has returnd to Town for His Cloaths, I lent him our White Horse, he will wait on you for my nedles that are in a White nedle book in our tea table Draw[er] in the back Parlor, if they are not there, Hero must apply to Anna for She must find them, Excuse me for troubleing you for what youll call trifling but indeed they are very necessary to me.

I Thought I was Prepared for every Misfortune, for as you Observe, of late we have little Else, yet when Lee[12] is taken Prisoner, who is Proof Against those feelings, His loss must Occation, and add to that the Triumph of our Enemys, and the mortification his Sensibility must Suffer. . . . I was Upstairs with my Children, when my mother Deliverd me your first Letter, you never Saw greater joy Sparkell in the Eye, then did Bobs, when he found it was from his Pappa, Read it out loud, mamma, will you, do mamma, till he was observed, which put a Stop to his Pleaseing Curiosity, your Darling Daughter is very Hearty and Saucier than ever, Bil is as stout as Ussiall [usual], but Tom looks very thin, and will while his Sore Discharges as it does at Present, do give me the Pleasure of Hearing from you by every Opportunity   your Affectionate M. Morris

[Ten days later she commented on the Battle of Trenton.]

I hope indeed the Tide is turning

Dear Mr. Morris   December the 30 [1776]

We had been for many Days Impatiently wishing for a Letter from you, as the News we hear from any Other Quarter is not to be Depended on, but when the Welcomed one arrived, which brought those glad Tidings, it more than Compensated, for what our late Unfortunate Curcumstances, Prepared our Minds to Expect, which was Nothing more, then our Armys being on the Defencive, and fearing least their Numbers were not even Equal to that, but Retreat as Usiall, but I hope indeed the Tide is turning, and that our Great Washington will have the Success His Virtues Deserve, and Rout that Impious Army, who from no Other Principle but that of enslaveing this Once Happy Country, have Prosecuted this Cruell War. . . . and I was the Happy means of making many joyfull Hearts, as we had many Guests added to our large Family to Celebrate Christmas. . . .

Anna was right about my Shifts, but my needles I left in the tea Tabel drawer, put them there Myself, intending to put them in my Pocket the last thing, so She must know were they are, Bil and Hetty are well and so is
                                    your Affectionate Mary Morris

[As soon as she was able, Mary returned to Philadelphia to be with her husband. Her reactions to being home once more are touching; she clearly relished relating the latest rumors of the movements of the troops to her mother, Esther Hewlings White.]

I must not look upon my Self as at home

My dear Mamma   March the 25 1777

Last Wensday noon I had the pleasure to arrive safely in Dear Philadelphia after a much pleasanter Journey than I expected from our Seting off, it made me very Happy to find my Self at home, after so long an Absence, with the terrible

Apprehensions we fled with of never seeing it again, it looks more like it Used to do a great deal, than what I expected to see it, from the Accounts we had, in Short I have seen so many more of my Acquaintances then I expected, and with such Chearfull Happy Countenances as made me forget for a Day or two, that I must not look upon my Self as at home, but prepare my mind for alarms, which its expected we shall have; as soon as the Roads will Admit of the Enemys moving theres Varyous Opinions, where they mean to open this Summers Campane. General [Horatio] Gates, who is jest gone from here, thinks they Intend to the North [Hudson] River, to join Carltons Army, and compleat there First Plan, others think Philad. is still their Object, while some beleive it will be on the Eastern Shore in Maryland. However a very little time will Determine, and we Shall want to know before we move to our Farms. . . .

Everybody Exclaim at my Thinness,* Several of my Acquaintances did not know me, till they had time to recollect, and then declared there was very little traces of my former Self, I attribute it to want of Exercise, as I enjoyd such good health. . . .

I remain with the Utmost Affection   your Dutifull Daughter M. Morris

*Mary is pregnant.

[Mary Morris had more information to impart a few days later:]

don't you feel quite important, I assure you I do

My Dear Mamma   April the first [1777]

A little time Unmolest'd holding our Selfs in Readiness to fly again, if the enemy moved this way, they are not yet in motion in the Jerseys, but have sent some Ships up the north River, and Destroyd one of our magazines, many think, as I told you in my last, that their Arms will be turnd to that quarter this Spring, the Congress has appointed General Gates Commander of our northern Army, he fully expects to be visitd by them, but the Discovery of a plot last week, makes me Affraid he is mistaken, and that this is still their object. Theres a fellow [James Molesworth] who is Commissioned by Lord Howe, been tampering with our Pilots, makeing them great Offers, and promises of makeing their Fortunes, if they would go with him to New York. The Honest fellows, took 50 pounds as an Earnest of their promise, but with the good intention of proveing the fact, went Immediately to the Generals and lodged their Information, Accordingly he was produced and Confessd the Charge. He is an Englishman, has Served Cucessively the late mayors of this City as a Clark, went to new York, was Introduced to Lord Howe, by your Freind Joseph Galloway for those purposes which Commission, has Ended this day with his Life. There is three women Concernd, and Mr. David Franks Suspected, from His Connection with one of those Women, as he Interests Him Self a good deal about her, but I fancy its from no worse a motive than a tender Attachment. . . .

Mr. [John] Hancock intends Resigning his Seat in Congress and going home, it is Imagined he will be appointd Governor of Boston. They meant to have Complimentd Mr. Morris with the Presidentship [of Congress] but he told the Gentlemen who informed Him of it, he could not Serve, as it would Interfere intirely with his private Business, so begd it might be drop'd. Any peice of Intelligence I give you that only Concern our Selfs and freinds, I hope will be confined to Mr. Halls Family. . . .

By a Vessel that's arrived at Connectigut with a very Valuable Cargo of Arms, Ammunition, Woolens, and a variety of other articles, the Congress have still a more Valuable one, Dispatches from Doctor Franklin. The French have lent us a Hundred Thousand Pounds Sterling without Interest, payable when the United States, have Established Independance and peace. He is received as our Embassador, and says we have every thing to expect, from the favorable Disposition of the French.

don't you feel quite important, I assure you I do, and begin to be Reconsiled to Independence. . . .

your very affectionate Daughter   Mary Morris

poor Tom has been under Doctor Shippens Hands ever since we got home it was a great misfortune he had not the attendance of a good Surgeon before, as it would have saved him a good deal of Pain.

[On April 8th, Mary Morris, buoyed by the promise of French help, took up her pen again, urging her mother to come back to Philadelphia.]

see how Confident every one now seems of Success

It is well worth the Ride to see how Confident every one now seems of Success, *Except the Torys*. Theres no Other news from the Camp, than that Deserters are comeing in Constantly, who all agree, that the Enemy are very Sickly, and a general Defection between the Hessian and British Soldiery. These accounts joind to the Curcumstances of their not moveing yet, all this fine weather, Joind the good News from France, has given Life and Spirit to every body who wishes us Success. . . . we have reason to think, there will be a Bank Established in France, for the Support of our Continentall money. . . .

Please to make my Compliments to Mrs. West tell her I cant meet with a Silver thimble nor the buying in this City nor a white metal one—but I can purchase her a pinch backd one with a Steel top if that will do.

[Confidence melted away as rumors fueled fears that the British troops were indeed on their way to Philadelphia.]

we now begin to be Alarmd for Our City

My Dear Mamma   April the 14 1777

There is orders from the Governor, to Innoculate all the Troops that are quarterd there [in New Town] Immediately. . . . There are now three men of War in our Bay, which look as if they intend this way; Mr. Morris has met with a great loss, as well as the Continent, by them, the ship *Morris* with a most Valuable Cargo of Arms, Ammunition, and dry goods. She had provided Her self with guns, to keep off any common Attack, but was most Unfortunately beset by three, the *Roe buck* one of them, at our Capes, She defended her Self bravely as long as it was possible, and then the Captain run her on Shore, and very bravely blew her up, and poor fellow, perished HimSelf, in his Anxiety to do it Effectively. We are prepareing for another flight in packing up our furniture, and Removeing them to a new purchase Mr. Morris has made 10 miles from Lancaster, no Other than the famous House that belongd to Stedman and Steagle at the Iron Works, where you know I Spent 6 Weeks, so am perfectly well acquainted with the goodness of the House and Situation. The Reason Mr. Morris made this purchase, he looks upon the other not Secure if they come by water. I think Myself very luckly in haveing this Assylum, it being but 8 miles fine road from Lancaster where I expect Mr. Morris will be if he quits this, besides many of my freinds and Acquaintances. So I now Solicite the pleasure of your Company, at this ones [once] famous place. . . .

We now begin to be Alarmd for Our City, theres 8 Sail of Men of War, at our Capes, and its thought are only waiting for their Transports to make an attempt. . . . I hope youll let me know if there is any thing in your House, you wish me to pack up and take care of for you. . . .

This Alarm is not like the first, every body as yet, seems quite Composed.

[Two weeks later Mary Morris, still in Philadelphia, grumbled:]

Theres no doubt, if General Washington had a Tolerable Army, he might with Ease, take every Man of them in Brunswick, but we cant deserve so fortunate an Event, Else our Contrimen wou'd have Spirit Enough to Undertake it.[13]

CORNELIA BELL who resided in Bridgewater, New Jersey, experienced very different emotions. Her much beloved brother Andrew, a lawyer, supported the British cause and was in New York City, serving as secretary to Sir Henry Clinton. Although Cornelia sided with the Americans, and married an outspoken supporter of independence, William Paterson, in 1779, the close ties between brother and sister were not broken. She astutely commented upon the impact of plundering armies.

But such are the effects of War

"Bellfield" Jan'y 30th, 1777

I am much oblig'd to you for the anxiety you express on my account concerning the British Troops penetrating this part of the country. Thank Heaven I have seen none of them yet and hope I never shall, though we have been in daily expectation of them for some time past; but from the character we have of them they will not be very desirable visitors, as they mark their own way with ruin and devastation. 'Tis impossible to picture the distress they have brought upon innocent families who have lain in their route, by plundering them of their property, not leaving them the necessaries of life; even Protections are no security, as they have been known to plunder those who have taken them and remain'd peaceably at their habitations. I think their proceedings in that way all very impolitic, as they make themselves many enemies who would otherwise have been their friends.

But such are the effects of War, and those who are so unfortunate as to live within their reach must submit. Gracious Heaven! avert those evils that are impending over our devoted heads and grant us Peace. I am not yet without my fears of their coming up this way, tho this neighborhood is swarming with troops from Crooks to Boundbrook, which I hope will keep them from disturbing our quiet. We are so fortunate as to have General [Philemon] Dickinson at our house. . . . General Dickinson is really an acquisition, for the little inconveniences we must unavoidably suffer are greatly compensated for by his easy, genteel behaviour and the pleasure his conversation affords. . . .

Your sincere, affect. Friend and Sister, Cornelia Bell

I enclose you General Washington's Proclamation, which, perhaps, will be new to you and the American Crisis, a mere piece of scurrility.*

*General Washington had urged those supporting the American cause to sign an oath of allegiance and those "who prefer the interest and protection of Great Britain" to "withdraw themselves and families within the enemy's lines." Thomas Paine's *The Crisis Number One* with its famous opening line, "These are the times that try men's souls," was published on January 19, 1777.[14]

[On March 4, 1777, apparently chastised for her political views, Cornelia Bell wrote in a conciliatory tone:]

every one cannot be of the same opinion

I'll not trouble you with any more of my politics; they are so disagreeable to you. Every rationale creature, you know, has a right to think, and every one cannot be of the same opinion. I am not a politician. I detest it in a female character as much as you, but we must say something, even if it is nonsense. . . .

Adieu, my best beloved Brother; believe me with truest affection

Your sincere friend and Sister, Cornelia Bell[15]

Despite the unspoken military code that avoided military action in wintertime, General Washington, in his headquarters at Morristown, New Jersey, sent troops out on raids to capture Hackensack, Elizabethtown, and Newark. As Captain Nathan Peters wrote his wife Lois in Preston, Connecticut, on January 8, 1777: "Our late Sucksess has Given Our Troops Great Sparits and seam Determined To Endure Every Hardship like Good soldiers. The Genl Requested the Continental Troops to Tarry six weaks After the First day of Janr . . . My Company Agread to Tarry to A Man."[16] The soldiers had indeed endured every hardship; they also needed rest. General Washington waited and watched. In which direction would the British army—encamped near New Brunswick—move? Would it be toward Philadelphia or northward into the Hudson River Valley? Although his troop strength had grown, it was not sufficient to defend both locations simultaneously.

MARTHA DAINGERFIELD BLAND, wife of Theodorick Bland, a member of General Washington's staff, was able to join her husband during the lull in fighting. Delighted to be at Morristown, she depicted a merry scene for her sister-in-law, Frances Bland Randolph, in Virginia.

now let me speak of our *Noble and Agreable Commander*

May 12, 1777

It was my dear Fanny, with great pleasure that I read your agreeable letter & heard of all your healths, but it is so long since the date that you may be all married or dead by this time. Four months may bring many unforseen things to light. . . . I left Philadelphia last month (the first day) & came to Morristown where Genl Washington keeps Headquarters. Mrs. Washington had arrived three weeks before me, so that I could with a good face make a visit to Camp. I had been from Jany to Aprl from your Brother & you may suppose we were very glad to meet. I had many Qualms of consiance about visiting a camp. . . . I found Morris a very clever little village, situated in a most beautiful valley at the foot of 5 mountains. It has three houses with steeples which give it a consequential look . . . it has two familys—refugees from New York in it otherwise it is inhabited by the errentest rusticks you ever beheld—you cannot travil three miles without passing through one of these villages all of them having meeting houses and court houses &c &c, decorated with steeples which gives them a pretty Airy look & the farmes between the mountains are the most rural sweet spots in nature, their medows of a fine luxuriant grass which looks like a bed of velvet interspersed with yellow blue and white flowers. They represent us with just such scenes as the poets paint Arcadia: purling rills, mossy beds &c but not crying swains & lovely nymphs tho there are some exceeding pretty girls. . . . realy I never met with such pleasant looking creatures, & the most inhospitable mortals breathing; you can get nothing from them but "dreadful good water" as they term everything that is good. Desperate and dreadfull are their favorite words, you'd laugh to hear them talk. . . .

Assending from small to great things—now let me speak of *our* Noble and Agreable Commander (for he commands both Sexes) one by his Excellent Skill in Military Matters, the other by his ability politeness and attention. We visit them twice or three times a week by particular invitation—Ev'ry day frequently from Inclination—he is generally busy in the forenoon—but from dinner till night he is free for all company. His Worthy Lady seems to be in perfect felicity while she is by the side of her *Old Man* as she calls him, we often make partys on Horse Back the Genl his lady Miss [Susan] Livingstone & his Aid de Camps who are Colo Fitz Gerald . . . Colo Johnson . . . Colo Hamilton a sensible Genteel polite young fellow a West Indian—Colo Meade—Colo Tillman . . . Colo Harrison . . . Capt Gibbs. . . . These are the Genls family all polite sociable gentlemen who make the day pass with a great deal of satisfaction to the Visitors—but I had forgot my subject almost, this is our riding party Generly—at which time General Washington throws off the Hero—and takes on the chatty agreeable companion—he can be down right impudent sometimes—such impudence, Fanny, as you and I like. . . .

God Bless you, adieu   M. Bland[17]

LUCY FLUCKER KNOX, wife of General Henry Knox and the daughter of loyalists who had fled to England, was much less fortunate than Martha Bland. She had not seen her husband in nearly six months despite many pleas to be allowed to join him. She—like all soldiers' wives— supplied her husband with necessaries whenever possible.

all my hopes are that it will not, cannot last

Boston May [1777]

As I can think of no address which would convey an idea, of my Affection, and esteem, I will omit it intirely, rather than do injustice to my heart, a heart wholly absorbed in love and anxiety for you—I cannot at this time tell where you are, nor form any judgment where you are going—we hear both Armys are in motion, but what thier rout is, we cannot hear . . . nor have we yet, been able to conjecture—what a situation, for us who are at such a distance—how much more we suffer for you than you for yourselves, all my hopes are that it will not, cannot last. . . .

This will be handed you by Capt Seargent who will also deliver you your box of pickles—I have got seven yards of linnen for breeches for you, am afraid to have it made up here, for fear it should be spoiled as it cost twenty shillings pr yard—sure there must be a tailor in Morristown—if there is not don't scold at me—seven pound lawful for two pair of breeches is a great deal of money—too much not to have them made neat—the pretty waistcoat I wrote you of upon examining I found to be painted—that the first washing would have spoiled—but I will be upon the look out for you. . . . the price of every things is so exorbitant indeed it is difficult—to get the necessarys of life here, at any price—the evil increases daily—beef is at eaight pence a pound—if you will take half an ox neck, shins, and all you may get it for seven pence—for butter we give ten shillings a pound—for eggs two pence a peice, and for very ordinary Lisbon wine, twenty Shillings a gallon—as for flour it is not to be had at any price, nor cider; nor Spirit—a pretty box we are in.

This and the behaviour of our town meeting has almost made me a tory— will you believe me when I tell you that old Mr [John] Erving is among the numbers who they have passed a vote to confine in close jail, until they can determine what farther is to be done with them—this upon the suspicion of thier being torys—I do not mean to blame them for ridding themselves of those persons—who in case of an attack, would like take a part against them—but there meddling with that old gentleman who has been superanuated this ten years can be from no other motive, but to share his estate—the Colonels [Thomas] Crafts, [Paul] Revere, [Isaac] Sears are the three leading men of the place—the first of these mentioned to dissolve the meeting—and lett the people revenge there own cause—quite milatary was it not—in short the mob have so much the upper hand at present. . . . I believe my nerves are much weakened by the mercury I have taken, in the true meaning of the word *Adieu.*   your own Lucy Knox

our lovely baby sends her pap—par (as she calls him) a kiss—

[When General Knox asked his wife how she was bearing up, she responded, allowing a little jealousy to spice the letter:]

there is such a thing as equal command

My Dearest Friend   Boston August 23rd 1777

How shall I describe my feelings to find myself entirely alone, to reflect that the only friend I have in the world is at such an immense distance from me, to think that he may be sick and I cannot assist him; ah poor me my heart is ready to burst, you who know what a trifle would make me unhappy, can conceive what I suffer now—When I seriously reflect, that I have lost my father mother Brother and sisters, entirely lost them, I am half distracted. True I chearfully renounced them for one far dearer to me than all of them—but I am totally deprived of him—I have not seen him for almost six months, and he writes me without pointing out any method by which I may ever expect to see him again—tis hard my Harry indeed it is. I love you with the tenderest the purest affection. I would undergo any hardships to be near you and you will not lett me—suppose this campaign should be like the last carried into winter—do you intend not to see me in all that time—tell me dear what your plan is. . . .

I am more distressed from the hott weather than any other fears. You grant you may not go farther southard—if you should I positively will come too. I believe Genl Howe is a paltry fellow but happy for us that he is so. . . . What has become of Mrs. [Nathanael] Greene, do you all live together—or how do you manage. . . . Oh that you had less of the military man about you—you might then after the war have lived at ease all the days of your life. But now I don't know what you will do—your being long accustomed to command will make you too haughty for mercantile matters—tho I hope you will not consider yourself as commander in chief of your own house—but be convinced . . . that there is such a thing as equal command. . . .   Adieu my love. LK[18]

In late July 1777, General William Howe made his move; transporting 18,000 troops by sea to Head of Elk in Chesapeake Bay, he planned to march the fifty miles to capture Philadelphia and bring the war to an end. General Washington, with 12,000 ill-equipped troops, could only hope to slow Howe's march. The two sides clashed at Brandywine Creek near Wilmington on September 11, 1777. Howe's superior forces and tactics dealt Washington's soldiers a major blow. The *Pennsylvania Ledger* reported: "The rout of the [Americans] . . . became general. They were pursued as long as daylight and the fatigued condition of the [British] troops would permit. . . . It was difficult to ascertain the number of the enemy killed, as they were scattered over a great extent of ground."[19] Then General Howe marched into Philadelphia.

Less than a month later, Washington attacked Howe's encampment at Germantown—but it turned into another rout. Joseph Plumb Martin remembered: "After the army had collected again and recovered from their panic, we were kept marching and countermarching, starving and freezing, nothing else happening, although that was enough." Albigence Waldo, a surgeon from Connecticut, also complained: "Dec. 14th Poor food—hard lodging—cold weather—fatigue—nasty clothes—nasty cookery. . . . Dec 15th . . . What have you for dinner boys? 'Nothing but fire cake & water, Sir'. . . . What have you got for breakfast, lads? 'Fire cake and Water, Sir.'"[20]

Before Christmas, a bedraggled, sorry looking army of Americans took up winter quarters at Valley Forge. Martin recalled:

> But we were now absolutely in danger of perishing . . . Had there fallen deep snows (and it was the time of year to expect them) or even heavy and long rain-storms, the whole army must inevitably have perished. Or had the enemy, strong and well provided as he then was, thought fit to pursue us, our poor emaciated carcasses must have "strewed the plain."[21]

But General Howe and his army did not pursue; they were happily en-sconced in Philadelphia.

CATHARINE W. LIVINGSTON, daughter of Governor William and Susannah French Livingston, resided in that part of New Jersey where much of the military action had been taking place. As a result she was able to send the latest news to her sister and brother-in-law, Sarah ("Sally") and John Jay, in Fishkill, New York. An intelligent and courageous young woman, Kitty was a trusted confidante of many important patriots, and had access to a wealth of information.

what the Canker worm dont eat the Locusts destroy

My Dear Sister & Brother   Persippiney, Novr. 21st 1777

This Evening we received a Letter from Pappa, informing us that we have lost Fort Mifflin, with about thirty men killed, before our Troops evacuated the Garrison, & seventy wounded. The wounded with the rest of the Troops made their escape before the Enemy took possession; Our men were so galled by the grape shot of a large India Man* who came within one hundred yards of the Fort, that it was impossible to stand it; they removed, all the Stores & fired the Barracks, when they found the place no longer tenable.

Gen: Washington is reinforced with two Thousand Troops from the South-ward, Five from the Northward, & some hundreds from this State, of the Militia, of the Pensylvania Militia only twelve hundred have lent him their assistance. The Philadelphians have lent Gen: Howe twenty thousand pound sterling & He has given the Old money of Pensylvania, New Jersey, & New York a Curency. The Quakers mount guard & do all Military duty that is required of them. . . . They write from our Camp that the Philadelphians come out in shoals, that some of them had not bread for several days before they left the City. Gen: [Sir Henry] Clinton did not Sail with the fleet, he has been seen very lately at New York, & on Staten Island. . . . I hope our successes to the Southward will be more favorable than those to the Northward, but I fear something serious will happen before the close of the Campaign tho it is late in the Season. . . .

Yesterday I returned from Elizabeth. Gen. [Philemon] Dickenson is at that Post with between eight hundred & a Thousand Troops. My Fathers House for six weeks was made a Guard House, for a Bullock Guard, the first instance I beleive of a Governors House being so degraded. I do not exaggerate In telling you the Guards have done ten times the Mischief to the House that the Hessians did; they have left only two locks in the House, taken off many pains of glass, left about a third of the paper hanging, burnt up some mahogany banisters, a Quantity of timber, strip'd the roof of all the lead, one of the men was heard to boast that he had at one heat taken 30 pd. of Lead off. The furniture that Mamma left there when Sally & myself was last down is stolen except a few things of which there is only some fragments. It is as in the time of Pharoah what the Canker worm dont eat the Locusts destroy. . . . I have imperceptibly got to the last side of my paper, you can't complain of postage for blank paper, perhaps more would be agreeable—the least intimation of which will be carefully observed by your truly Affectionate Sister.[22]

*an armed merchant ship normally engaged in trade with Asia, though often adapted for naval use in wartime.

ELIZABETH DRINKER had been having a difficult time: the constant alarms and the poor health of her young son caused her grief. Even worse was the aggressive identification of Quakers as Tories, which intensified when the Continental Congress ordered that those who were "disaffected" be disarmed or arrested. More than twenty Friends, including Henry Drinker, were summarily jailed after refusing to sign an oath of allegiance and sent into exile in Winchester, Virginia. Appeals to Pennsylvania's Executive Council (whose president was a cousin of one of the prisoners) proved useless.

offering a Parole for him to sign

1777 Sepr the 2 third Day—HD. having been, and continuing to be unwell . . . went towards Noon into the front Parlor to copy the Monthly meeting minuits . . . when Wm. Bradford; one [Bluser] and Ervin, entred, offering a Parole for him to sign—which was refus'd. . . . they. . . . called the 4th, in the morning and took my Henry to the [Masonic] Lodge—in an illegeal, unpredesented manner—where are several, other Friends with some of other proswasions, made prisoners. . . .

11. . . . Some time after dinner Harry came in a hurry for his Master Horse for a Servent to ride, informing me that the waggons were waiting at the Lodge to take our dear Friends away. I quickly went there; and as quickly came away finding great a number of People there but few women, bid my dearest Husband farewell, and went in great distress . . . the waggons drove off about 6 o'clock. . . .

12 . . . this has been a day of Great Confusion to many in this City; which I have in great measure been kept out of by my constant attension on my sick Child. Part of Washingtons Army has been routed, and have been seen coming into Town in Great Numbers; the perticulars of the Battle, I have not attended to, the slain is said to be very numerous,—hundreds of their muskets laying in the road, which those that made off have thrown away. . . .

25 . . . most of our warm people are gone off, tho there are many continue here that I should not have expected. Things seems very quiate and still, and if we come off so, we shall have great cause of thankfullness. . . .

here are the English in earnest

26. Well, here are the English in earnest, about 2 or 3000, came in, through second street, without oppossition or interruption, no plundering on the one side or the other, what a satisfaction would it be to our dear Absent Friends, could they but be inform'd of it. . . .

[Oct.] 6 . . . The heaviest fireing that I think I ever heard, was this Evening, for upwards of two hours, thought to be the English troops, engag'd with the Mud-Island Battry,—an Officer call'd this Afternoon to ask if we could take in a Sick or Wounded Captain; I put him off by saying that as my Husband was from me, I should be pleas'd if he could provide some other convenient place, he hop'd no offence, and departed. . . .

16 . . . 5 Weeks this day since my dearest Henry left us, the thoughts of the approaching cold season, and the uncertainty when we shall meet again, is at times hard to bare. . . .

18th . . . The Troops at Germington are coming within 2 or 3 miles of this City to encamp—provisions are so scarce with us now, that Jenney gave 2/6 p. lb. for mutton this Morning—The people round the Country dose not come near us with any thing, what little butter is brought at 7/6. . . .

[Dec.] 18th . . . An Officer who calls himself Major Carmon or Carmant [Major John Crammond], call'd this Afternoon, to look for Quarters for some Oiffecer of distinction, I plead off, he would have preswaded me that it was a necessary protiction at these times to have one in the House; said I must consider of it, that he would call in a day or two, I desir'd to be excus'd, and after some more talk we parted, he behaved with politeness, which has not been the case at many other places; they have been very rude and impudent at some houses,—I wish I may come off so; but at same time fear we must have some with us, as many Friends have them, and it seems likely to be a general thing. This has been a trying day to my Spirits. . . . I have just finish'd a Letter to my dearest tis now past 12 o'clock, and Watch has put me in a flutter, by his violent barking, as if some one was in the Alley, which I believe was the case—hail since Night.

31st. J. Cramond who is now become one of our Family, appears to be a thoughtful sober young man, his Servant also sober and orderly; which is a great favour to us. . . .

1778. [Jan.] 19 This Morning our officer mov'd his lodgings from the bleu Chamber to the little front parlor, so that he has the two front Parlors, a Chamber up two pair of stairs for his bagage, and the Stable wholly to himself, besides the use of the Kitchen, his Camp Bed is put up.

offred them their Liberty on taken a Test, which is all sham

[Feb.] 3 . . . mett Sucky Jones . . . who told me her mammy wanted to speak with me; she intends to go before long to G. Washington, on account of her Son; she hinted as if she would like me to go with her,—which I think will not suit me; tho' my Heart is full of some such thing, but I dont see the way clear yet. . . .

5 . . . our dear Friends are to be continu'd at Winchester 'till further orders, and that the Congress has again offred them their Liberty on taken a Test, which is all sham, as they know they will not do it. . . .

7 . . . I have been much distress'd at times, when I have thought of my being still here, when prehaps it might be in my power to do something for my dear Husband.

[After much discussion lasting many weeks, the women decided to draw up a paper requesting the release of the prisoners to present to Congress at Lancaster; Elizabeth Drinker was one of four women appointed to deliver it. They made a visit to Valley Forge hoping to enlist the aid of General Washington.]

GW. came and discoars'd with us freely

[April] 5 . . . I left home after dinner went to Mary Pleasants where were a great Number of Friends mett to take leave of us, We took Coach at about 2 o'clock, Susannah Jones, Phebe Pemberton, M. Pleasants and Myself—with 4 Horses, and two Negros who rode Postilion. . . .

6 . . . proceeded on to the American Picket guard, who upon hearing that we were going to head-quarters, sent 2 or 3 to guard us further on to another guard where Coll. Smith gave us a pass for Head Quartrs, where we arriv'd at about ½ past one; requested an audience with the General—set with his wife, (a sociable pretty kind of woman) untill he came in . . . it was not long before GW. came and discoars'd with us freely, but not so long as we could have wish'd, as dinner was serv'd in, to which he had invited us, there was 15 of the Officers besides the Gl. and his Wife, Gen. Green, and G. Lee. We had an eligant dinner, which was soon over; when we went out with the Genl. Wife up to her Chamber, and saw no more of him,—he told us, he could do nothing in our busyness further than granting us a pass to Lancaster, which he did. . . .

10 we arose by times this Morning dress'd ourselves, and after Breakfast, went to Lancaster. . . . we were this day waited upon by T[imothy]. Matlack, who undertook to advise us, and prehaps with sincerety—we paid a visit to 3 of the Councilors . . . after the [State Executive] council had set some time, T.M. came for our address, which was sign'd by all the Women concern'd, he say'd he would come for us, when it was proper, but after above an hour waiting, he inform'd us, that our presence was not necessary, and put us off in that way. . . .

14 went to Town before Breakfast, to look for Joseph Reed, who we mett with at one Attleys, with Thos. McClane, and 2 others . . . we discourc'd with 'em for some time, they appeard kind, but I fear tis from teeth outwards . . . in our journey to day we found the roads so bad, that we walk'd part of the way, and clim'd 3 fences, to get clear of the mud. . . .

[The Council refused to give the women a hearing. Realizing that the charges against the Quakers were unfounded, and that their continuance in exile might prove troublesome in the future, the Council ordered the remaining prisoners—two having died—brought to Lancaster from their eight-month-long stay in Virginia. The Quakers never received an apology for their treatment.]

were wellcom'd by many

25 . . . about one o'clock my Henry arrived at J Webbs, just time enough to dine with us; all the rest of our Friends came this day to Lancaster; HD. much hartier than I expected, he look fat and well.

27 . . . our Friends apply'd to Counsil this Morning for a proper discharge, which was not comply'd with, but a permission to pass to Potts-Grove, in the County of Philada. was all they would grant. . . .

30 . . . we set off after 8 o'clock, and traveled on without interuption, were well-com'd by many before, and on our entrence into the City—where we arrived about 11 o'clock, and found our dear Families all well, for which favour and Blessing and the restoration of my dear Husband, may I ever be thankful.[23]

SARAH "SALLY" WISTER and her siblings had been taken for safety to a relative in North Wales, Pennsylvania, by her parents. The well-educated sixteen-year-old was delighted when General William Smallwood of Maryland asked to use the house as his headquarters. Unable to post letters to her best friend Deborah Norris in Philadelphia, the flirtatious Sally chronicled her excitement in her journal.

dress and lips were put in order for conquest

To Deborah Norris.

Tho' I have not the least shadow of an opportunity to send a letter, if I do write, I will keep a sort of journal of the time that may expire before I see thee, the perusal of it may some time hence give pleasure in a solitary hour. . . .

5th day septm 26th [actually 25th] . . . our cousin Jesse [Foulke] heard that Gen Howe's Army had move down towards Philadelphia, Then my dear our hopes & fears were engage'd for you however my advice is summon up all your resolution, call Fortitude to your aid, dont suffer your spirits to sink, my dear; theres nothing like courage, tis what I stand in need of myself but unfortunately have little of it in my composition. . . .

Oct the 19th 1777 [20th] seconday. . . . [in] the afternoon Cousin Prissa [Priscilla Foulke] and myself were sitting at thee door I in a green skirt dark short gown, &c. Two genteel men of the military order rode up to the door. Your servant ladies, &c ask'd if they cou'd have quarters for Genl Smallwood. Aunt [Hannah] Foulke thought she cou'd accommodate them . . . one of the officers dismounted and wrote Smallwoods quarters over the door which secur'd us from straggling soldiers. After this he mounted his steed and rode away. When we were alone [our] dress and lips were put in order for conquest and the hopes of adventures gave brightness to each before passive countenance. . . . I feel in good spirits tho surrounded by an Army, the house full of officers, yard alive with soldiers, very peaceable sort of men tho', they eat like other folks, talk like them, and behave themselves with elegance, so I will not be afraid of them. That

I wont. Adieu I am going to my chamber to dream, I suppose, of bayonets and swords, sashes, guns, and epaulets. . . .

Secondday 26th oct. [27th] . . . the General and officers drank tea with us, and stay'd part of the evening . . . so lidy [Lydia Foulke] and me seated ourselves at the table in order to read a verse book. The Maj [William Stoddard] was holding a candle for the Genl who was reading a newspaper. He look'd at us turn'd away his eyes, look'd again, put the candle stick down, up he jump'd out of the door he went. Well said I to Lydy he will join us when he comes in. Presently he re-turn'd and seated himself on the table. Pray ladies is there any songs in that book, yes many, cant you favr me with a sight of it? no major tis a borrow'd book. Miss Sally cant you sing? No. Thee may be sure I told the truth there. Liddy saucy girl told him I cou'd he beg'd and I deny'd, for my voice is not much better than the voice of a raven. We talk'd and laugh'd for an hour. He is very clever amiable and polite. He has the softest voice, never pronounces the R at all. . . . Oh Debby I have a thousand things to tell thee. . . .

Third day [Oct. 28]. . . . when will sallys admirers appear? ah that indeed. Why Sally has not charms sufficient to pierce the heart of a soldier, but I won't dis-pair. Who knows what mischief I yet may do. . . .

Decemb. 5th sixthday oh gracious Debby I am all alive with fear. The English have come out to attack . . . our army. They are on Chestnut Hill our army three mile this side, what will become of us, only six mile distant, we in hourly expec-tation of an engagement. I fear we shall be in the midst [of] it. Heaven defend us from so dreadful a sight. The battle of Germantown and the horrors of that day are recent in my mind. It will be sufficiently dreadful if we are only in hearing of the firing to think how many of our fellow creatures are plung'd into the boundless ocean of eternity few of them prepar'd to meet thier fate. . . .

Fifthday Decemr 11th. our Army mov'd as we thought to go into winter quar-ters, but we hear there is a party of the enemy gone over Schuykill so our army went to look at them I observ'd to Stodard so you are going to leave us to the English. Yes hahaha leave you for the E. He has a certain indifference about him somtimes that to strangers is not very pleasing. He somtimes is silent for min-utes. One of these silent fits was interrupted the other day by his clasping his hands and exclaiming aloud oh My God I wish this war was at an end. . . .

Seventhday Decembr 20th, General Washingtons army have gone into Winter quarters at valley forge. We shall not see many of the military now. We shall be very intimate with solitude I am afraid stupidity will be a frequent guest. After so much company I cant relish the idea of sequestration.

[Sally later summed up how boring life was after the military departed.]

a sigh from the inmost recesses of my heart

My residence at Northwales, was at times almost insupportable, especially when we, were without company and a succession of rainy disagreeable weather—I saunter'd thro' the house, upstairs then down again, out of one chamber into the other, snatch up a book, find it old, throw it peevishly down—

take my [needle] work, this employs me a few minutes toss it away—a sigh
from the inmost recesses of my heart, oh dear oh dear, go to the door—a long
lane very muddy, the Barn—fences and trees, as common as my finger's a
strange comparison—turn from the tiresome view in a pet. . . . jump up—in a
stupid mood—hie to my glass, spend more time there than is ever necessary, for
want of better employment—put on my cap sometimes strait and tolerable, frequently crooked and intolerable—adjust my dress toss up the window hearing a
noise and fancying it some smart Military or other swain—disappointed nothing
but J McGlathary, driving a stray horse home—or the Pigs running to the daily
supply'd trough   slam down the sash, in anger, provoking Pigs or horses—walk
very leisurely—or else as fast as I can, down stairs and into the parlour, Mama
and Betsy [her sister] at work—silence reigns throughout the room, 'till broke
by inquiring of Sally where her work is—I do not know, perhaps lost, throw
myself in an arm chair.[24]

ALICE LEE SHIPPEN, a member of the distinguished Lee family and wife of Dr.
William Shippen, director of the Continental Army hospitals, was separated not
only from her husband, who was in the field, but also from her children, Anne
and Thomas, who were at boarding school. The fourteen-year-old Anne, known
as Nancy, attended Mrs. Rogers' School in Trenton, New Jersey, which seemed
a safe haven from the battling armies. Alice, who had to flee her elegant home in
Philadelphia, had one overriding concern: the proper education of her daughter.

you have been taught your duty

My dear Nancy   Reding 22 Sept. 1777
    I was extremely surprized when the waggon return'd the other evening
without one line from you after I had been at the trouble & expence of sending
for you as soon as I was inform'd 4000 troops were landed in Elizabeth-Town.
Surely you should not omit any opportunity of writing to me, but to neglect such
a one was inexcusable, but I shall say the less to you now, because you have
been taught your duty & I take it for granted Mrs. Rogers has already reproved
you for so great an omission, but do remember my dear how much of the beauty
& usefulness of life depends on a proper conduct in the several relations in life,
& the sweet peace that flows from the consideration of doing our duty to all with
whom we are conected. I am sorry it is not in my power to get you the things I
promised. It was late before I got to Philadelphia the afternoon I left you & the
shops were shut the next day. I have looked all over this place but no muslin,
satin or dimity can be got. . . .
    Your Pappa thinks you had better work a pr. of ruffles for General Wash-
ington if you can get proper muslin. . . . Tell me how you improve in your work.
Needle work is a most important branch of a female education, & tell me how
you have improved in holding your head & sholders, in making a curtsy, in going out or coming into a room, in giving & receiving, holding your knife & fork,
walking & seting. These things contribute so much to a good appearance they
are of great consequence. Perhaps you will be at a loss how to judge wether you
improve or not, take this rule therefore for your assistance. You may be sure you

improve in proportion to the degree of ease with which you do any thing as you have been taught to do it . . . ask Mrs. Rogers opinion as a friend who now acts for you in my place . . . Give my compliments to her & tell her I thank her for the care she takes of you. . . . Dont offend Miss Jones by speaking against the Quakers. . . . There is an alarm here the enemy are said to be coming this way, tis lucky you are not with me. . . . I believe I will write to you as soon as I get settled [in Maryland]. Farewell my dear. Be good & you will surely be happy which will contribute very much to the happiness of

Your Affect. Mother   A. Shippen.

[Alice Shippen was less sanguine some months later. Safe at the Lee home in Virginia, she was overcome by fears for the wellbeing of her son in Maryland, and her husband in Bethlehem, Pennsylvania.]

my fears render me so miserable

My dear Mr. Shippen,   Stratford 17 Janry. 1778

What is become of you & my dear Tommy—it is almost 3 months since I left my dear Mr. Shippen & I have received but one short letter with my gown & apron but you are harried with business, your good for nothing Doctors & commisarys give you all the Trouble. O! when shall I have you all to myself? & it is now two months since I parted with our dear our only son, the pledge of our love & have not heard once from him—surely if he was well he wou'd contrive a letter to me, he is certainly ill or dead of that vile feaver Crags son had, my fears render me so miserable it is impossible for me to stay here where I find I cannot hear from those I love most. I shall return to Frederick-Town where you must my dear Mr. Shippen get a lodging for me. . . . If I cou'd correspond with you at this distance it would be some thing, but when I set down to write I feel myself tied up [with] the uncertainty of what I write getting to you only, I cou'd now fill a volume but no matter you shall know all when we meet. Perhaps it will be in the world of spirits & then we can convey our Ideas with delightful ease & certainty.

Are you sorry for the Ladies of Philadelphia? Had they taken my advice they wou'd now have breathed in free air as I do. O! how good it is to do right, My dear Mr Shippen tho' we are loosing thousands having loved (our) country and its interests invariably more than supports me under every difficulty. I feel I love in my very heart the true liberty of America the liberty of saying & doing everey thing that is beautiful & proper.

Adieu my dear faithful husband, direct for me at the Post Office at Leedstown & believe for it is really true that I am intirely & unalterably Yours[25]

REBECCA FRANKS, daughter of the well-to-do Jewish merchant David Franks and Margaret Evans, an Episcopalian, was not in need of Alice Shippen's pity. She was delighted by the presence of British officers, who were often entertained at her family home in Philadelphia. She was invited to General Howe's elaborate dinners, and attended balls, concerts, and plays (including one written by the British playwright Susanna Centilivre). Though Rebecca Franks had strong Tory inclinations, she maintained her friendship with at least one patriot friend, Anne Harrison Paca, the wife of Maryland Congressman William Paca.

I can scarce have a moment to myself

Dear Nancy,   Thursday Feby. 26, '78

You can have no idea of the life of continued amusement I live in. I can scarce have a moment to myself. I have stole this while everybody is retired to dress for dinner. I am but just come from under Mr. J. Black's hands and most elegantly am I dressed for a ball this evening at Smith's where we have one every Thursday. You would not Know the room 'tis so much improv'd.

I wish to Heaven you were going with us this evening to judge for yourself. I spent Tuesday evening at Sir Wm. Howes where we had a concert and Dance. I asked his leave to send you a Handkerchief to show the fashions. He very politely gave me permission to send anything you wanted, tho' I told him you were a Delegate's Lady. I want to get a pair of Buckles for your Brother Joe.

If I can't, tell him to be in the fashion he must get a pair of Harness ones. The Dress is more ridiculous and pretty than anything that ever I saw—great quantity of different coloured feathers on the head at a time besides a thousand other things. The Hair dress'd very high. . . . I assure you I go less in the fashion than most of the Ladies—no being dress'd without a hoop. . . .

No loss for partners, even I am engaged to seven different gentlemen for you must know 'tis a fix'd rule never to dance but two dances at a time with the same person. Oh how I wish Mr. P[aca] wou'd let you come in for a week or two—tell him I'll answer for your being let to return. I know you are as fond of a gay life as myself—you'd have an opportunity of rakeing as much as you choose either at Plays, Balls Concerts or Assemblys. I've been but 3 evenings alone since we mov'd to town. I begin now to be almost tired. Tell Mrs. Harrison that she has got a gentleman in her house, who promised me not to let a single thing in it be hurt and I'm sure he'll keep his word. . . . The clock is now striking four, and Moses [her brother] is just going out to dinner—quite the Congress hours. . . . All your Philadelphia friends well and desire their loves—Mine to all in Maryland. . . . I must go finish dressing as I'm engaged out to Tea.

God bless you,
Becky. F.

I send some of the most fashionable Ribbon and Gauze have tried to get Joe's buckles in all the best shops, but in vain.[26]

This description of gaiety notwithstanding, Philadelphia was an occupied city. Members of the British army and wealthy loyalists were able to obtain supplies, but others, particularly the poor, suffered greatly. Prices soared, and even Elizabeth Drinker, burdened with housing a British officer and his staff, complained on March 25, 1778: "our Hay is out, and I believe I must sell our poor Cow." Looting and pillaging for valuables and for wood to burn were daily occurrences. Prisoners of war were dying of the cold, starvation, and disease.

At Valley Forge, General Washington's army was not faring much better. It is estimated that nearly 2,500 men died during that winter. Deserters, possibly fifty a day, further depleted the troops. The Continental Army was totally disorganized, the weapons old, few horses left to move the artillery, the men demoralized. Of the 7,556 ready and able to fight, a great many lacked clothing.[27]

General Washington was confronted with other troubles: dissatisfaction with his war strategy voiced by several members of Congress, and the mutinous actions of some of his own officers. Thanks to his coolheaded response to these ambitious ploys for power, he prevailed and retained his command.

During this winter of problems, Washington was greatly helped by the arrival of the Prussian "Baron" Friedrich Wilhelm von Steuben in late February 1778. Horrified at the army's condition, von Steuben (whose English was almost nonexistent) proceeded to write a manual in French with instructions on marching and maneuvers on the battlefield. Translated and copied in long hand, the chapters were handed to the various companies as they came from von Steuben's desk. To demonstrate his instructions, he created a model company to show what he expected. As von Steuben wrote a friend:

> Believe me . . . the task I had to perform was not an easy one. My good republicans wanted everything in the English style . . . when I presented a plate of *sauer kraut* dressed in the Prussian style, they all wanted to throw it out of the window. Nevertheless, by the force of proving by *Goddams* that my cookery was the best, I overcame their prejudices.[28]

Joseph Martin noted unhappily: "I was kept constantly . . . engaged in learning the Baron de Steuben's new Prussian exercise. It was a continual drill."[29]

Early spring found the British on the move once again. An American encampment near the Crooked Billet Tavern (Hatboro, Pennsylvania) was surrounded and attacked on May 1, with grievous losses. But General Washington also received some good news that day: King Louis XVI of France had agreed to "acknowledge our independence, and make a treaty with us of amity and commerce." Several days later this alliance was "splendidly celebrated" with speeches by the chaplains, battalions marching in precise formation before General Washington and his staff, the discharging of cannon and musketry in a *feu de joie*, followed by a feast for the officers. As the *New-York Journal* reported on June 15, 1778: "Mrs. Washington, the Countess of Stirling [Sarah Livingston Alexander], Lady Kitty her daughter, Mrs. Greene, and a number of other ladies, favored the feast with their company, amongst whom good humour and the graces were contending for the pre-eminence."[30]

MARTHA WASHINGTON had joined her husband at Valley Forge; in a letter to Mercy Otis Warren, she described their accommodations in the best possible terms and seemed to hint politely that the increasing hostility between her husband and General Horatio Gates extended to their wives.

I found the General very well

Dear madam   Valley forge March the 7th 1778

I hope, and trust, that all the states will make a vigorous push early in this spring, if every thing can be prepard for it, and thereby putting a stop to British cruelties—and afford us that peace liberty and happyness which we have so long contended for. . . .

I came to this place about the first of February whare I found the General very well. . . . The Genral is in camped in what is called the Great Valley on the Banks of the Schuykill; officers and men are cheifly in Hutts, which they say is tolarable comfortable; the army are as healthy as can well be expected in general—the Generals appartment is very small he has had a log cabben built to dine in which has made our quarter much more tolarable than they were at first.

It would give me pleasure to deliver your compliments to Mrs. [Elizabeth] Gates, but she lives at so great a distance from me that I have not seen her since we parted at Newport two years agoe. . . .

I am Dr Madam with esteem your affectionate Friend and very Hble servt

Martha Washington[31]

France, still smarting from its losses at the end of the Seven Years' War, had entered into an alliance with the Americans to retaliate against its old enemy, forcing the British to reassess their military strategies. Howe's hope that his occupation of Philadelphia would end the conflict with the colonists proved futile; he was relieved of his command. A farewell extravaganza financed by some of his officers and designed by Captain John André was prepared. Calling it *The Meschianza* (derived from the Italian meaning "medley"), André created and arranged for triumphal arches, costumes, a medieval tournament, a gambling casino, a ball, fireworks, and a banquet with tables groaning under the weight of delicacies, desserts, and wines. Rebecca Franks, costumed as the Queen of the Burning Mountain, was present. So too, at André's behest, was Peggy Shippen, Alice Shippen's niece.[32]

Howe's successor, Sir Henry Clinton, had been ordered to evacuate Philadelphia. The British army, accompanied by many loyalists who feared reprisals from the Americans, retreated through New Jersey toward New York. General Washington followed but on a parallel line. On a blistering hot June 28, 1778, near Monmouth County Court House, the two armies engaged. In the midst of battle, General Charles Lee, disobeying orders, retreated. Disaster for the Americans was averted only by the appearance of the main body of the Continental Army led by Washington. Then, under cover of night, the British managed to slip away to safety into New York. Washington moved northward, half encircling the city.

Philadelphia was once again under American control. Sally Wister noted in her journal on June 20, 1778: "I understand that Genl Arnold who bears a good character has the command of the city and that the soldiers conducted with great decorum."[33]

ELIZABETH DRINKER was less complimentary of the Americans' conduct. Even she, however, was unprepared for the terrible punishment exacted from two of her neighbors, Abraham Carlisle and John Roberts, accused of aiding the British during their occupation of the city.

Gallop'd about the Streets in a great hurry

[May] 30 . . . tis reported that the British Army are giving the remainder of their Stores of Wood and Hay, to the poor, which seems to prove they intend 'eer long to leave us. . . .

[June] 9—The Major left us at a little past one, this Morning . . . Sister and self stay'd at the door untill the two Regiments, (which quarter'd up Town) had past—J[ohn]. C[rammond]. bid us adieu as they went by—and we saw no more of them, a fine moon-light Morning. . . .

18—last night it was said there was 9000 of the British Troops left in Town 11,000 in the Jersyes; this Morning when we arose, there was not one Red-Coat to be seen in Town; and the encampment, in the Jersys vanish'd—Colll. Gordon and some others, had not been gone a quarter of an hour before the American Light-Horse enter'd the City, not many of them, they were in and out all day. . . . the few that came in today, had drawn Swords in their Hands, Gallop'd about the Streets in a great hurry, many were much frightn'd at their appearance. . . .

30 . . . it is said that there has been a great Battle on First day last [June 28], that great numbers of the British Troops were slain and taken, a young Solider that is disorderd in his senses, went up our Stairs this Afternoon, we had no man, in the House, Isaac Catheral came in and went up after him, found him in the entry up two pair Stairs, saying his prayers—he readly came down with him. . . .

[July] 2—The Congress came in to day: fireing of Cannon on the Occasion—rain and thunder this Afternoon. I hope it will be Cooler. . . .

4 . . . A great fuss this evening it being the Annaversary of Independance, fireing of Guns, Sky Rockets &c—Candles were too scarce and dear, for Alluminations, which prehaps sav'd some of our Windows. . . .

Augt. the 1st. The weather very warm,—our Neighbor Abraham Carlisle was yesterday taken up, and put into Jail. . . .

20th. Grace Galloway turn'd out of her House this forenoon, and Spanish officers put in—this is the first day we have had without rain for 8 or 10 days past . . .

[Sept.] 25—Abraham Carliles tryal came on to day and is not yet concluded, are at a loss to judge how it will go with him. . . .

26 . . . I went in this Afternoon to visit our depress'd Neighbor Carlile, whose Husband they have brought in gilty of High treason, tho' it is hop'd by many that he will not suffer what some others fear he will. . . . a year this day since the British Troops entrd.

[Oct.] 2 . . . John Roberts is brought in gilty at which some are surpis'd as they did not expect it, who had attended the court—there is some demur in his case, as I understand this evening—very fine weather. . . .

Novr. 3 . . . I was inform'd that preparations were making this evening for the Execution of our poor Friends tomorrow Morning—Notwithstanding the many pertitions that have been sent in, and the Personal appearance of the Destress'd wives and Children; before the Council . . . I am still of the mind, that they will not be permitted, to carry this matter to the last extremity. . . .

Novr. 4. they have actually put to Death; Hang'd on the Commons, John Robarts and Am. Carlisle this morning or about noon—an awful Solemn day it has been—I went this evening with my HD. to Neigr. Carliles, the Body is brought home, and laid out—looks placid & Serene—no marks of agony or distortion, the poor afflicted widdows, are wonderfully upheld and suported, under their very great tryal—they have many simpathizing Friends.[34]

GRACE GROWDEN GALLOWAY, daughter of a wealthy Quaker businessman, was another victim of Philadelphia's shifting political scene. Her husband, Joseph, had been deeply involved in Pennsylvania politics, and, in 1774, had been appointed to the Continental Congress, where he attempted to maintain a conciliatory tone toward the British. Two years later, despite Benjamin Franklin's urging him to join the patriots, Galloway became instead an advisor to General Howe's forces. When the British marched into Philadelphia, Galloway was named the city's civil administrator. Grace Galloway, unhappy in her marriage, her sizeable inheritance under the control of her husband, found solace in her only surviving child, Elizabeth. Even she was taken from her when the British evacuated the city, her husband and daughter fleeing with them. Grace, desperate to retain her inherited property, remained behind in the vain hope that her presence would prevent it from being confiscated. She had not reckoned on the vindictiveness of Commissioner of Forfeited Estates, Charles Willson Peale. His duties included arresting accused traitors and seizing their properties, the sale of which would yield him a five percent commission. No wonder he and his cohorts appeared at Grace Galloway's door the day after the British left, as she recounted in her diary.

pray take Notice I do not leave my house of My own accord

Wednesday . . . [June 17, 1778] this evening parted with my dear Husband & child. . . .

This day Thursday the 18th the American Troops came into Town.

Friday the 19th was warn'd by peal that he must take possession of my house for the state. . . .

[July] Tusday the 21st . . . about 2 o'clock they came—one smith a hatter & Col Will & one Shriner & a Dutch Man I know not his Name—they took an inventory of everything even to broken China & empty bottles. . . . they told Me they must advertise the house I told them they must do as they pleased but till it was decided by a Court I wou'd not go out Unless by the force of a bayonet but when I knew who had a right to it I should know how to act. . . .

Wenesday the 22 . . . Sent for Mr. [John] Dickison last Night & he told Me he wou'd look over the law to see if I cou'd recover My own estate & this evening he came & told Me I cou'd Not recover dower & he fear'd my income in My estate was forfeited likewise & that no tryal wou'd be of service: but advised Me to draw up a peti'on to the Chief Justice Mccean [Thomas McKean] for the recovery of my estate & refused a fee in the Politest Manner, but begg'd I wou'd look on him as My sincere friend . . . so I find I am a beggar indeed. I expect every hour to be turn'd out of doors & where to go I know not no one will take me in & all the Men keeps from Me. . . .

[August] Saturday the 8th . . . Peal & Will came to let Me know that I must go out a Monday Morn: for they wou'd give the spaniard [Don Juan de Miralles] Possession. . . .

Thursday the 20th [Her lawyer William] Lewise sent me word that I must shut my doors & windows & if they wou'd come to let them Make a forcible Entry. Accordingly I did so & a little after 10 oclock they Knocked Violently at the door three times; the Third time I sent Nurse & call'd out myself to tell them I was in possession of my own House & wou'd keep so & they shou'd gain No admittance. Hereupon which they went round in the yard & Try'd every door but cou'd None Open, then they went to the Kitchen door & with a scrubbing brush which they broke to pieces, they forced that open—we Women standing in the Entry in the Dark they made repeated strokes at the door & I think was 8 or 10 Minuets before they got it open. When they came in, I had the windows open'd; they look'd very Mad. Their was peel, smith, the Hatter & a Col Will a pewterer in second street. I spoke first & told them I was Used ill: & show'd them the Opinion of the Lawyers. Peel read it: but they all despised it & peel said he had studied the Law & knew they did right. I told them Nothing but force shou'd get me out of My house. Smith said they knew how to Manage that & that they wou'd throw my cloaths in the street. . . .

Peel & Will went over the House to see Nothing was Embassell'd [embezzled] & Locking Up the things at last Smith went away. . . . after every Mortifying treatment I was tiard [tired] & wanted to be turn'd out. Peel went upstairs & brought down My Work bag & 2 bonnets & put them on the side table; at last we went in the Entry to sit. . . . two of the Men went out & after staying some time return'd & said they had been with the council & that they had done right & must proceed. I did not hear this myself but the rest of the Women did. Mrs [Molly] Craig asked for My Bed but they wou'd let Me Have Nothing & as I told them acted entirely from Malice: after we had been in the Entry some time Smith & Will went away & Peel said the Chariot was ready but he would not hasten me. I told him I was at home & in My own House & nothing but force shou'd drive me out of it. He said it was not the first time he had taken a Lady by the Hand, an insolent wretch . . . as the Chariot drew up Peel fetched My Bonnets & gave one to me the other to Mrs Craig: then with greatest air said come Mrs Galloway give me your hand. I answer'd indeed I will not nor will I go out of my house but by force. He then took hold of my arm & I rose & he took me to the door. I then Took hold on one side & Looked round & said pray take Notice I do not leave my house of My own accord or with my own inclination but by force & Nothing but force shou'd have Made Me give up possession. Peel said with a sneer very well Madam & when he led me down the step I said now Mr Peel let go My Arm I want not your Assistance. He said he cou'd help me to the Carriage. I told him I cou'd go without & you Mr Peel are the last Man on earth I wou'd wish to be Obliged to. Mrs Craig then step'd into the Carriage & we drove to her house where we din'd.[35]

[Under English law, when a woman married, any property she brought to the union belonged to the husband, unless a premarital agreement had been drawn up. After the birth of a child, the husband had total control of his wife's finances. In return, this law of *coverture* afforded a wife the legal right to the financial support and protection of her husband, in life as well as death; if she survived him, she had a right to a dower: one-third of the existing property at the time of his death.[36] The same court that denied Grace Galloway her inheritance (being the wife of a loyalist), awarded her widowed stepmother an annuity—at the expense of her stepdaughter.

Other women, living in households with divided loyalties, faced similar predicaments but were rescued by influential friends: Cornelia Bell by her husband-to-be, William Paterson; Theodosia Prevost, the wife of a British officer stationed in Jamaica, by Governor William Livingston and Aaron Burr.

Grace Galloway, though aided by Quakers, was not so fortunate: she did not regain her inheritance. Frustrated at every turn in her appeals, her furniture sold at auction, she was, by turns, defiant and despondent. She lived, until her death three years later, impoverished, bitter, and lonely.]

Laughed at the whole wig party

[April 1779] Tusday the 20th [While visiting a neighbor, I] got My spirits at command & Laughed at the whole wig party. I told them I was the happyest woman in twown for I had been striped & Turn'd out of Doors yet I was still the same & must be Joseph Galloways Wife & Lawrence Growdons daughter & that it was Not in their power to humble Me for I shou'd be Grace Growdon Galloway to the last & as I had now suffer'd all that they can inflict Upon Me I shou'd now act as on a rock to look on the wrack of others & see them tost by the Tempestuous billows while I was safe ashore; that if My little fortune wou'd be of service to them, they May keep it for I had exchanged it for content: that a Wooden waiter was as Useful tho not so sightly as a silver one; & that wou'd Never let these people pull Me down for, While I had the splindid shilling left, I wou'd be happy in spight of them; I cou'd Not do as Diogenes (Drink out of the first brook therefore threw his cup away as Useless) but I wou'd keep My Wooden cup if I cou'd get No other; & be happy to the last if I cou'd not get a silk gown I cou'd get a Linsay one & so it kept Me warm I owed Not. My borrowed bed I told them was down & I cou'd Lay Me down & sleep composely on it without feeling one thorn which was More than the Creatures cou'd Do who had rob'd Me: but all that vext Me was that I shou'd be so far humbled as to be ranked as a fellow creature with such brutes for I cou'd not think they cou'd be call'd Men, so I ran on & was happy. . . . am not sorry at anything I said for I now defye the Villans.

a man who wou'd Grasp at all I have

[Friday August 1779] the 27th—More resign'd today but think all lost; had the Deed for the 24th share of Durham [Iron Works, in which she had inherited an interest] & find it made in J G's Name only. Oh how has this Unhappy man injured me & my Child for this deed Cuts off all the water from my estate yet he was so base as to take it out of My family. . . . the Unfair conduct of this man has quite [distressed] my temper as his ill conduct has ruin'd me & as I cannot tell the world, I abuse the English Army for their base & treacherous conduct. Jesey Jones here in the evening. I talked to her very freely & said we ware all sold & that we ware brought to beggary. . . . said I now hated both sides & said we ware all betray'd—everbody is Now Near giving Up. . . . I was so low I cou'd not help sheding tears. My ever Dearest Child, what can I do for thee, as to J G tho I have some affection for him yet I dispise & Abhor his vanity & baseness & am Now truly set against him yet I do not tell anyone—this makes it worse to bear but all his Unkindness is in my mind & all within Distress & Confusion; I seem quite an Out Cast of Mankind & my soul struck with a Thousand Daggers to find how this man has imposed Upon me as well as treated Me Unkindly. Was it not for my dearest Child I wou'd embrace poverty much sooner than live with a man who wou'd Grasp at all I have yet treat me worse than a slave. . . . everybody else does something for the suport of their familys. . . . I will never live with him more.[37]

ELIZABETH GRAEME, the youngest child of Dr Thomas Graeme and Anne Diggs Graeme, received an excellent education, her interest in learning encouraged by her mother. She wrote poetry, made translations from French literature, and created her own metrical version of the Book of Psalms. After a trip to England where she had enjoyed the fashionable salons, Elizabeth Graeme invited friends to gatherings—"Attic Evenings"—for literary and political discussions at her home, Graeme Park (Horsham, Pennsylvania). Among the frequent guests were the artist Benjamin West, the poet Annis Boudinot Stockton, and Dr. Benjamin Rush. At age thirty-four, Elizabeth Graeme married the Scot, Henry Fergusson, a man eleven years her junior, and, upon the death of her father that same year, she inherited Graeme Park.

During the War, her ill-advised attempt to negotiate a reconciliation between the Americans and the British made Elizabeth Fergusson's patriotic sentiments suspect. The fact that her husband had been appointed commissary of American prisoners during Howe's occupation of Philadelphia also damaged her credibility. Pennsylvania's Council confiscated her home, and her possessions were sold at auction. She, like Grace Galloway, petitioned the state's Supreme Court and its Assembly. She pointed out that she had always supported the patriots, and that her property had been unfairly taken because of her husband's political involvement; she could list "Gentlemen in, and of Britain, that now hold landed Property here, which have never been Seizd, some of whom are at this time acting in the Military Line." Elizabeth Fergusson also hoped for help from her influential friends, in particular John Dickinson, whose own house "Fair-Hill" had been plundered by the British.

I was ever on the Side of my Country

Sir
                                                    Graeme park Sept 10 1779

A painful period in some Respects to both of us has Rolld round Since I had the honor to adress you, either in Person or by Letter. The last time I saw you was in the beginning of December 76 in your own house; at *Fair-Hill*; Poor Fair Hill! there it stands as a Monument of low Motives of British Soldiers; But if I begin thus; I shall never come to the Point which leads me at this time to Trouble you. Without trying you Sir with a long preamble, it is finaly to beg your Interest with the Members of the House, provided you think there is any thing in My Situation, that places me in a diferent Line from the Bulk of the Wives of unfortunate proscribd. . . .

May I be allowd to touch on my own Conduct since this unhappy Contest, I have for my own part Constantly remaind on the Premises; earnestly praying for Peace But if the Sword must decide our Fates, Sincerly wishing it might be on the Side of *America*; which in my short View of things I lookd on to be the Injurd Party.

I never went into the City while the British were There without a Pass, I had no Acquaintance with the Military Gentlemen, and my stay but very short; I returnd And Spent my days with one Female friend In Silence and Solitude.

At the time Mr Fergusson took the Department of Commissary of Prisoners, I wrote to Him . . . to endeavor to diswade him from Acting in any Shape under *General Howe*, These Letters could be producd did the Showing them answer any Valuable Purpose. The Seizing the Personal Estate and the Rise of all the Articles of Life have renderd my affairs so Embarassd that if I am not Speedily Redressd, Want and Distress must compose the Remaining part of the Days of your Petioner dear sir   E. Fr.

. . . . I enter most Confidentialy into what I say to you, I know your honor, and your goodness. If Mr Fergusson is really within the Letter of the Law; I make no doubt but I shall suffer the Full Penalties in my fortune.

The Jewish Proverb is here fully verified "The Parents have Eaten sour Grapes And the Childrens Teeth are set on Edge." Believe me Sir, I would not Deceive you, I was ever on the Side of my Country, The Dislike I mention now to Mr Fergussons taking a part under Gen Howe is not an Ostensible Character, held out to answer certain Purposes. The Winter the British passed in Philadelphia was the most Completely miserable I ever passd in my Life, I should prefer Annihiliation to a Repetition of it. . . .

If you think it worth while Sir to Exert your Influence in my behalf, It is necessary to give you a hint that I already stand well with the City Members; It is the Back County Members whose Votes I am not Certain of obtaining; and things are in this Delicate Situation, that any point made by a Certain Set, would tho good in its Self meet with opposition, such as the Effect of Parties, and Cabals; But all these things you know far better than I can Suggest them. . . .

I remain Sir with all possible Respect your most Obedient humble Servant
                                                    Elizabeth Fergusson

[John Dickinson answered the letter but claimed that, as Elizabeth Fergusson noted, "he had no Influence, which I look on as a genteel way of declining the affair." Thanks to others, however, Graeme Park was eventually restored to her. There she lived quietly, writing poetry and corresponding with friends. Unfortunately, her ill health and straitened circumstances forced the sale of the property to a niece's husband in 1790. Elizabeth Fergusson never saw her own husband again. Years later she recalled him as "the man that has proved the Source of so much Sorrow to me. . . . yet a man one once loved and expected to have passed ones Life with, to such a temper as mine cannot be the object of Indiference, tho he may be of extreme Resentment."[38]]

SARAH FRANKLIN BACHE, daughter of Benjamin Franklin, had fled Philadelphia four days after giving birth on September 10, 1777. Upon returning the following summer, her husband Richard found his father-in-law's house in better shape than he had expected, though the British had "carried off with them some of your musical Instruments, viz: a Welch harp, bell harp, the set of tuned bells which were in a box, Viol de Gambo, all the spare Armonica Glasses and one or two of the spare cases. Your armonica is safe." Sarah Bache was aghast at the high prices of things in town when she wrote her father.

I can scarcely beleive I am in Philadelphia

Dear and Honoured Sir   Philadelphia, October. 22d. 1778

This is the first opportunity I have had since my return home of writing to you. We found the House and Furniture in much better order than we could expect, which was owing to the care the Miss Cliftons took of all we left behind. My being removed four days after my little Girl [Elizabeth] was born made it impossible for me to remove half the things we did in our former flight. I have much to tell you but my little Girl has the small Pox just coming out and a good deal restless tho in a fine way, she takes up most of my time as I have none but a very young Girl to attend her. She is a fine Brown lass, but her sparkling black eyes make up for her skin, and when in health she has a good colour. I would give a good deal you could see her, you cant think how fond of kissing she is, and gives such old fashioned smacks. General Arnold says he would give a good deal to have her for a school Misstress to teach the young Ladies how to kiss. . . .

I chose to stay in the Country on the Childrens account till the summer was over, and if it had suited Mr. Baches business it would have been better to have stay'd there altogether. Their is hardly such a thing as living in town every thing is so high the money is old tenner [tenor: colonial paper currency] to all intents and purposes. If I was to mention the prices of Common necessaries of life it would astonish you. I have been all amaizment since my return such an odds has two years made, that I can scarcely beleive I am in Philadelphia. This time twelve month when I was in town I never went out nor bought any thing leaving it till I got up again, expecting we should stay, so that we ran away quite unprovided. I had two peices of linnen at the weavers it has been there these eighteen months, and if it had not been for my Friends must have suffered as it could not be bought w[h]ere we were. I should tell you that I had seven table Cloths of my own spinning cheifly wove before we left Chester county. It was what we were spinning when you went. I find them very usefull and they look very well, but they now ask four times as much for weaving as they used to ask for the linnen, and Flax not to be got without hard money. . . . The Children as well as myself want linnens and common cloaths. Buying them here is out of the Question. They realy ask me six dollars for a pair of Gloves, and I have been obliged to pay fifteen pound fifteen shillings for a common Gallomanco [Calamanco] peticoat without quilting, that I once could have got for fifteen shillings. I buy nothing but what I realy want, and wore out my silk ones before I got this, I do not mention these things by way of complaint, I have much less reason to complain than most folks I know, besides I find I can go without many things I once thought absolutely necessary. . . .

The Chest of papers you left with Mr. Galloway Mr. B[ache] went up about. Bob [a Franklin slave] brought them to town. The lid was broke open and some few taken off the top, Mr. B collected those about the flour [floor] had it naild up and they are all safe here. Mr. Galloway took not the least care of them, and used you as he did every body else very ill. . . . Your Dutiful Daughter S Bache[39]

MARY MORRIS had also come home. As her family duties and social obligations once more took up her time, she had some gossip about General Benedict Arnold, the governor of the city, to transmit to her mother, who had remained with the Hall family.

such Strange Conduct

November the 10 1778

I know of no News, Unless to tell you that we are very gay. As such, we have a great many Balls and Entertainments and Soon, the Assembly will begin, tell Mr. Hall Even our military Gentlemen here, are too Liberal to make any Distinction between Wig and Tory Ladyes. If they make any, Its in favor of the latter, such, Strange as it may seem, is the way those things are Conducted at present in this City. It Originates at Headquarters, and that I may make some Apology for such Strange Conduct, I must tell you that Cupit has given our little General a more Mortal wound, than all the Host of Britons cou'd, unless His present Conduct can Expiate, for His past,—Miss Peggy Shippen is the fair One. [40]

[Such levity only briefly obscured the fact that the war was not over. Dangers were ever present, concern for friends and family constant. Mary Morris conveyed her worries about their situations in a letter to her friend Catharine Livingston in Elizabethtown, New Jersey.]

destress . . . as would melt your Simpathetick Heart

June 10th. [1780]

Thrice welcome my dear is your last letter, I find Myself much releived from my Apprehensions about you being informed where you are, that you are well, & as yet safe from the insults of your Victoryous foe. . . .

I write this in the green House, which room far exceeds our expectations in beauty, & Conveniance, The stilness, coolness, Shade & harmony which the little Songsters afford that inhabit the grove that runs to the back of it, all of these as it shoud seem, should dispose my mind to tranquility, & fill my Imagination with a variety of such pleaseing Subjects as would afford you an amusing Epistle; but quite otherways is my Situation, this delightfull retreat cannot prevent my feelings being wounded for the suffereings of a Number of my Sex in this State, who are compeld to leave it, by that Cruell Edict of our Counsels, a resolve which oblidges all the women whose Husbands are with the enemy, & Children whose parents are there, to repair to *them* Immediately; a determination like this which admits of no Exceptions, is unjust & cruell, they are bound by law to Contribute toward the support of those Women & there is many whose conduct has not Merited it, tho there is Others that have, Yet why not discriminate between the Innocent & guilty. The destress of many of those poor Sufferers are such & their Relations, as would melt your Simpathetick Heart; Mrs. Furgerson is determind not to go, She says they may take her life, but shall never banish her from Her Country, This Ladys uncommon good Sense, and great virtues, has allways distinguished her as the first with us. . . .

I dare say you have heard of the Ladys plan for raiseing a Subscription for the Army. I will enclose you one of them but there is an Alterration taken place instead of waiting for the Donations being sent the ladys of each Ward go from dore to dore & collect them. I am one of those, Honourd with this business. Yesterday we began our tour of duty & had the Satisfaction of being very Successful. There were two ladys that were very liberal One 8000 dollars & 10000. . . .

Adieu. . . .   MM[41]

ESTHER REED had suggested the idea of a subscription to raise money for the relief of the Continental soldiers and orchestrated a network of women to solicit sufficient funds to relieve. Furthermore, to forestall any possible criticism of this undertaking, Esther Reed published "The Sentiments of an American Woman" in which she reviewed the brave deeds of women throughout history and extolled the courage and self-sacrifice of the men in the Continental Army.

our love for the public good

On the commencement of actual war, the Women of America manifested a firm resolution to contribute as much as could depend on them, to the deliverance of their country. Animated by the purist patriotism, they are sensible of sorrow at this day, in not offering more than barren wishes for the success of so glorious a Revolution. They aspire to render themselves more really useful; and this sentiment is universal from the north to the south of the Thirteen United States. Our ambition is kindled by the fame of those heroines of antiquity, who have rendered their sex illustrious, and have proved to the universe, that, if the weakness of our Constitution, if opinion and manners did not forbid us to march to glory by the same paths as the Men, we should at least equal, and sometimes surpass them in our love for the public good. . . .

Who knows if persons disposed to censure, and sometimes too severely with regard to us, may not disapprove our appearing acquainted even with the actions of which our sex boasts? We are at least certain, that he cannot be a good citizen who will not applaud our efforts for the relief of the armies which defend our lives, our possessions, our liberty? The situation of our soldiery has been represented to me; the evils inseperable from war, and the firm and generous spirit which has enabled them to support these. But it has been said, that they may apprehend, that, in the course of a long war, the view of their distresses may be lost, and their services be forgotten. Forgotten! never; I can answer in the name of all my sex. Brave Americans, your disinterestedness, your courage, and your constancy will always be dear to America, as long as she shall preserve her virtue.

We know that, at a distance from the theatre of war, if we enjoy any tranquility, it is the fruit of your watchings, your labours, your dangers. If I live happily in the midst of my family, if my husband cultivates his field, and reaps his harvest in peace; if, surrounded with my children, I myself nourish the youngest, and press it to my bosom, without being affraid of seeing myself seperated from it, by a ferocious enemy; if the house in which we dwell; if our barns, our orchards are safe at the present time from the hands of those incendiaries, it is to you that we owe it. And shall we hesitate to evidence to you our gratitude? Shall we hesitate to wear a cloathing more simple; hair dressed less elegant, while at the price of this small privation, we shall deserve your benedictions. Who, amongst us, will not renounce with the highest pleasure, those vain ornaments, when she shall consider that the valiant defenders of America will be able to draw some advantage from the money which she may have laid out in these; that they will be better defended from the rigours of the seasons, that after their painful toils, they will receive some extraordinary and unexpected relief; that these presents will perhaps be valued by them at a greater price, when they will have it in their power to say: *This is the offering of the Ladies. . . .*

by An AMERICAN WOMAN[42]

[By July 4, 1780, Esther Reed was pleased to write General Washington that the ladies had raised "200,580 dollars, and £625 6s. 8d. in specie, which makes in the whole in paper money 300,634 dollars." She was also proud of the fact that the contributors were from all levels of society: from a black woman, Phillis, to Adrienne de Noailles, Marquise de Lafayette. In his acknowledgement, Washington requested that, rather than giving cash, the "fair associates" use the funds to buy linen to make shirts instead. Esther Reed, though uncertain whether shirts were needed, agreed.]

an idea prevails among the ladies

Sir,   Banks of the Schuykill, July 31st, 1780
Ever since I received your Excellency's favour of the 20th of this month, I have been endeavouring to procure the linen for the use of the soldiers . . . I have been informed of some circumstances, which I beg leave to mention, and from which perhaps the necessity for shirts may have ceased; one is the supply of

2000 sent from this State to their line, and the other, that a considerable number is arrived in the French fleet, for the use of the army in general. Together with these, an idea prevails among the ladies, that the soldiers will not be so much gratified, by bestowing an article to which they are entitled from the public, as in some other method which will convey more fully the idea of a reward for past services, and an incitement to future duty. Those who are of this opinion propose the whole of the money to be changed into hard dollars, and giving each soldier two, to be entirely at his own disposal. This method I hint only, but would not, by any means wish to adopt it or any other, without your full approbation. If it should meet with your concurrence, the State of Pennsylvania will take the linen I have purchased, and, as far as respects their own line, will make up any deficiency of shirts to them, which they suppose will not be many after the fresh supplies are received. If, after all, the necessity for shirts, which, though it may cease, as to the Pennsylvania Troops, may still continue to other parts of the army, the ladies will immediately make up the linen we have, which I think can soon be effected, and forward them to camp. . . .

I have the honour to be, dear Sir, With the highest esteem,

Your obedient servant, E. Reed[43]

The theater of war had now shifted away from Philadelphia, to the north as well as to the south, the armies at a stalemate. General Washington, unable to budge the British from New York City, waited for the promised French fleet. The British used terror tactics—raiding and burning villages—hoping for surrender. Instead, the Americans retaliated with incursions of their own. In the south, Georgia once more flew the British colors and installed a royal governor. The Americans sent reinforcements to bolster the defenses of Charleston, South Carolina. The long-awaited French fleet came and eventually engaged the British in a battle near Savannah. The French incurred heavy losses and returned to France. Victory for the Americans remained elusive.

Chapter 5

the heavy Cloud that hangs over us

The colonial war had become a world war. By mid 1778, Great Britain, unable to subdue her rebellious colonies, was confronted first by the belligerent actions of France, and subsequently those of Spain and Holland. Other European nations, organized as the Armed Neutrality, assumed a state of passive resistance toward England. Europe, South America, the Caribbean, and even Asia were pulled into the hostilities.

The immediate hope for the colonies was that France's naval force would break the British blockade of America's coastal waters. Throughout the War, the British had been able to sail between Halifax and Florida, moving troops and goods, with little damage inflicted by the fledgling Continental navy or by privateers. Yet, several years passed before the French would provide the help General Washington sought.

For the time being, British forces still controlled New York City and Newport, Rhode Island. They now devised a new plan to re-establish a strong military presence in the South, which was viewed as a loyalist enclave. A large troop contingent was accordingly shifted from New York to Georgia; it routed the Continentals at Savannah, and marched toward Augusta. With the British colors flying once more over Georgia, the Regulars then attempted to capture Charleston, South Carolina as well, but the American forces held on for another year.

Though the English hoped for loyalist assistance, neither they nor the Americans had taken sufficient notice of the dissatisfaction and turmoil that existed among people in the Backcountry; Native Americans, who saw their ancestral lands invaded with impunity by land speculators: settlers whose lives were threatened by Indians, local ruffians, and corrupt government officials; and homesteaders who were barely able to eke out an existence in the wilderness. Some joined the British in the hope of securing their own survival, but the loyalists were not well enough organized to give the needed support. The British attempted to recruit slaves by promising freedom to those who would leave their masters and join their army. All too frequently, for those who took the bait, the result was death or re-enslavement.

JANET SCHAW, a "lady of quality," of a certain age, stepped on board ship in Edinburgh, Scotland traveling to North Carolina via the West Indies. Surviving debilitating storms and threats of capture by Algerine pirates, she reached Cape Fear on February 14, 1775, and journeyed on to "Schawfield," the plantation of her older brother, Robert. Janet Schaw chronicled her travels in exquisite detail, describing whom she met, and what she experienced. During her eight-month stay, she was clearly not afraid to express her opinion on political developments and what she saw as the country's ruin.

a daring Villain

We got to Schawfield to dinner, which is indeed a fine plantation, and in the course of a few years will turn out such an estate, as will enable its master to visit his native land, if his wife [Anne] who is an American will permit him, which I doubt. This plantation is prettily situated on the northwest branch of the river Cape Fear. Every thing is on a large Scale, and these two great branches of water come down northeast and northwest, and join at Wilmington. . . . We have an invitation to a ball in Wilmington, and will go down to it some day soon. This is the last that is to be given, as the congress has forbid every kind of diversion, even card-playing. . . .

We had yesterday a curious tho' a frightful diversion. On a visit down the river, an Alligator was observed asleep on the bank. Mrs. Schaw was the first who saw it, and as she is a notable house-wife was fired with revenge at the loss of many a good goose they had stolen from her. We crept up as softly as possible hardly allowing the oars to touch the water, and were so successful as to land part of the Negroes before it waked, which it did not do till all was ready for the attack. Two of the Negroes armed with strong oars stood ready, while a third hit him a violent blow on the eye, with which he awaked and extended such a pair of jaws as might have admitted if not a Highland cow, as least a Lowland calf. The negroes who are very dextrous at this work, presently pushed the oars down his throat, by which means he was secured, [but not] till he received thousands of blows which did him no harm, as he is covered with a coat of Mail, so strong and compact, that he is vulnerable no where but in the eye, and a very small opening under the throat and belly. His tail is long and flexible, and so are his huge arms. With these he endeavoured to catch at his assassins, but the superior arts of man are more than a match for his amazing strength. Was superior reason never used to a more unworthy purpose it were well; for he is a daring Villain, an insolent robber, who makes war on the whole animal creation, but does not man do the same? Even worse, for this monster does not devour his fellow-monsters. . . .

He is indeed a frightful animal of which a lizard is the miniature, and if you can raise a Lizard in your imagination fifteen foot in length with arms at least six feet and these armed at the end with hands and claws resembling the talons of the eagle and clothe all with a flexible coat of mail, such as is worn on the back of a Sturgeon; if you have strength of imagination for this, you have our Alligator, which was at last overcome by pushing out his eyes and thrusting a long knife into his throat. After all I could not see this without horror and even something that at least resembled compassion. The sight joined to the strong smell of musk that came from him made me sick, and I was very glad when they left him and pushed the boat from the shore.

[Though Janet Schaw may have admired the brute strength of the alligator, she had only disdain for the human inhabitants of the area.]

a most disgusting equality

I think I have read all the descriptions that have been published of America, yet meet every moment with something I never read or heard of. I must particularly observe that the trees every where are covered over with a black veil of a most uncommon substance, which I am however at a loss to describe. It is more like sea weed than any vegetable I ever saw, but is quite black and is a continued web from top to bottom of the tallest trees and would be down to the ground, were it not eat up by the cattle. But as it is full of juice and very sweet, they exert their whole strength to obtain it, in which they receive no assistance from their Masters, tho' they own it is excellent feeding, but they are too indolent to take any trouble, and the cattle must provide for themselves or starve. . . .

Nature holds out to [people] every thing that can contribute to conveniency, or tempt to luxury, yet the inhabitants resist both, and if they can raise as much corn and pork, as to subsist them in the most slovenly manner, they ask no more; and as a very small proportion of their time serves for that purpose, the rest is spent in sauntering thro' the woods with a gun or sitting under a rustick shade, drinking New England rum made into grog, the most shocking liquor you can imagine. By this manner of living, their blood is spoil'd and rendered thin beyond all proportion, so that it is constantly on the fret like bad small beer, and hence the constant slow fevers that wear down their constitutions, relax their nerves and infeeble the whole frame. Their appearance is in every respect the reverse of that which gives the idea of strength and vigor, and for which the British peasantry are so remarkable. They are tall and lean, with short waists and long limbs, sallow complexions and languid eyes, when not inflamed by spirits. Their feet are flat, their joints loose and their walk uneven. These I speak of are only the peasantry of this country, as hitherto I have seen nothing else, but I make no doubt when I come to see the better sort, they will be far from this description. For tho' there is a most disgusting equality, yet I hope to find an American Gentleman a very different creature from an American clown. Heaven forefend else.

[In Wilmington to attend the ball, Janet Schaw's sense of the ridiculous spared no one, not even herself.]

dressed out in all my British airs

The ball I mentioned was intended as a civility, therefore I will not criticize it . . . [it] would at best resemble a Dutch picture, where the injudicious choice of the subject destroys the merit of the painting. Let it suffice to say that a ball we had, where were dresses, dancing and ceremonies laughable enough, but there was no object on which my own ridicule fixed equal to myself and the figure I made, dressed out in all my British airs with a high head and a hoop and trudging thro' the unpaved streets in embroidered shoes by the light of a lanthorn carried by a black wench half naked. No chair, no carriage—good leather shoes need none. The ridicule was the silk shoes in such a place. I have however gained some most amiable and agreeable acquaintances amongst the Ladies. . . .

I am sorry to say, however, that I have met with few of the men who are natives of the country, who rise much above my former description, and as their natural ferocity is now inflamed by the fury of an ignorant zeal, they are of that sort of figure, that I cannot look at them without connecting the idea of tar and feather. Tho' they have fine women and such as might inspire any man with sentiments that do honour to humanity, yet they know no such nice distinctions, and in this at least are real patriots. As the population of the country is all the view they have in what they call love, and tho' they often honour their black wenches with their attention, I sincerely believe they are excited to that crime by no other desire or motive but that of adding to the number of their slaves.

[Janet Schaw visited her young relative Fanny Rutherfurd at "Point Pleasant" plantation outside of Wilmington and, while there, attended a funeral.]

flock down like crows to a carrion

Every body of fashion both from the town and round the country were invited, but the Solemnity was greatly hurt by a set of Volunteers, who, I thought, must have fallen from the moon; above a hundred of whom (of both sexes) arrived in canoes, just as the clergyman was going to begin the service, and made such a noise, it was hardly to be heard. A hogshead of rum and broth and vast quantities of pork, beef and corn-bread were set forth for the entertainment of these gentry. But as they observed the tables already covered for the guests, after the funeral, they took care to be first back from it, and before any one got to the hall, were placed at the tables, and those that had not room to sit carried off the dishes to another room, so that an elegant entertainment that had been provided went for nothing. At last they got into their canoes, and I saw them row thro' the creeks, and suppose they have little spots of ground up in the woods, which afford them corn and pork, and that on such occasions they flock down like crows to a carrion.

They were no sooner gone than the Negroes assembled to perform their part of the funeral rites, which they did by running, jumping, crying and various exercises. They are a noble troop, the best in all the country.

[As the weather grew warmer, Janet Schaw continued to describe and wonder at the bounties that Nature provided and express her disgust at the "indolence" of the white inhabitants who failed to take advantage of them. She grudgingly acknowledged, however, that slaves did so, supplementing their meager food allowances with food found in the wild.]

this profusion is in general neglected

The congress has forbid killing Mutton, veal or lamb, so that little variety is to be had from the domestick animals; but indulgent nature makes up for every want, by the vast quantities of wild birds, both of land and water. The wild Turkeys, the wild pigeon, a bird which they call a partridge, but above all the rice-bird, which is the Ortalon in its highest perfection, and from the water the finest ducks that possibly can be met with, and so plenty that when on wing sixteen or eighteen are killed at a shot. The beauty of the Summer-duck makes its death almost a murder. The deer now is large, but not so fat as it will be some time hence; it is however in great plenty, and makes good soup. The rivers are full of fine fish, and luxury itself cannot ask a boon that is not granted. Do not however suppose by this that you meet elegant tables, far from it; this profusion is in general neglected. The gentlemen indeed out of idleness shoot deer, but nothing under a wild turkey is worth a shot. As they are now on the eve of a War, or something else I dare not name, perhaps they save their powder for good reasons. . . .

They have the true vulture here, with the bald head, which they call Turkey buzard, as he is a little less than a turkey. The bears are exceeding troublesome and often carry off the hogs. I have got a whelp, which was only a day old when its dam was killed. Miss Rutherfurd is fond of it, but tho' only a fortnight old, it is too much for her already. We have also a fawn, which is much more beautiful than any I ever saw at home and tame as a dog. The Negroes are the only people that seem to pay any attention to the various uses that the wild vegetables may be put to. For example, I have sent you a paper of their vegetable pins made from the prickly pear, also molds for buttons made from the calabash, which likewise serves to hold their victuals. The allowance for a Negro is a quart of Indian corn pr day (an infant has the same allowance with its parents as soon as born), and a little piece of land which they cultivate much better than their Master. There they rear hogs and poultry, sow calabashes, &c and are better provided for in every thing than the poorer white people with us. They steal whatever they can come at, and even intercept the cows and milk them. They are indeed the constant plague of their tyrants, whose severity or mildness is equally regarded by them in these Matters.

[Early in June 1775, the tensions between rebels and loyalists escalating, Janet Schaw was in Wilmington and witnessed the drill exercises of the militia under the leadership of Robert Howe. Local residents, moreover, were pressured into signing oaths of allegiance to the state.]

a cry of tar and feather

We came down in the morning in time for the review, which the heat made as terrible to the spectators as to the soldiers, or what you please to call them. They had certainly fainted under it, had not the constant draughts of grog supported them. Their exercise was that of bush-fighting, but it appeared so confused and so perfectly different from any thing I ever saw, I cannot say whether they performed it well or not; but this I know that they were heated with rum till capable of committing the most shocking outrages. . . . They at last however assembled on the plain field, and I must really laugh while I recollect their figures: 2000 men in their shirts and trousers, preceded by a very ill beat-drum and a fiddler, who was also in his shirt with a long sword and a cue at his hair, who played with all his might. They made indeed a most unmartial appearance. But the worst figure there can shoot from behind a bush and kill even a General Wolfe.

Before the review was over, I heard a cry of tar and feather, I was ready to faint at the idea of this dreadful operation. I . . . was so much afraid the Victim was one of my friends . . . and he indeed proved to be one, tho' in a humble station. For it was Mr Neilson's poor English groom. You can hardly conceive what I felt when I saw him dragged forward, poor devil, frightened out of his wits. However . . . his punishment was changed into that of mounting on a table and begging pardon for having smiled at the regiment. He was then drummed and fiddled out of the town, with a strict prohibition of ever being seen in it again.

One might have expected, that tho' I had been imprudent all my life, the present occasion might have inspired me with some degree of caution, and yet I can tell you I had almost incurred the poor groom's fate from my own folly. Several of the officers came up to dine, amongst others Coll: Howe, who with less ceremony than might have been expected from his general politeness stept into an apartment adjoining the hall, and took up a book I had been reading, which he brought open in his hand into the company. I was piqued at his freedom, and reproved him with a half compliment to his general good breeding. He owned his fault and with much gallantry promised to submit to whatever punishment I would inflict. You shall only, said I, read aloud a few pages which I will point out, and I am sure you will do Shakespear justice. He bowed and took the book, but no sooner observed that I had turned up for him, that part of Henry the fourth, where Falstaff describes his company, than he coloured like Scarlet. I saw he made the application instantly; however, he read it thro', tho' not with the vivacity he generally speaks; however he recovered himself and coming close to me, whispered, you will certainly get yourself tarred and feathered; shall I apply to be executioner? I am going to seal this up. Adieu.

> [Despite her considerable courage and composure in times of crisis, Janet Schaw, her maid, and the Rutherfurd children were forced to take refuge on board an English ship in the early fall. As she reviewed her stay in North Carolina and the increasing political turmoil that necessitated her flight, she was firm in her conviction that the Americans had brought disaster upon themselves.]

I have fled from the tar-pot

Rejoice with me, my friends, to find me safe this length. You suppose I have fled from the tar-pot. In truth I am not sure what might have happened, had I stayed much longer, for the ill humour was come to a very great height.

Our coming here [on board a frigate of war], for we are all here, is the most extraordinary thing that has yet happened, and was so sudden and surprising, that I am not yet sure, if I am awake or in a dream. . . .

Farewell unhappy land, for which my heart bleeds in pity. Little does it signify to you, who are the conquered or who the victorious; you are devoted to ruin, whoever succeeds. Many years will not make up [for] these few last months of depredation, and yet no enemy has landed on their coast. Themselves have ruined themselves; but let me not indulge this melancholy.[1]

HARRIOTT PINCKNEY HORRY, the daughter of Charles Pinckney and Eliza Lucas, and wife of Daniel Huger Horry, prepared to flee her native city of Charleston, South Carolina. She communicated her feelings of unease and anxiety to a cousin in Georgetown, some fifty miles to the north.

calls for all our Fortitude to meet the Awful Event

28th Novr. 1775

At about this Season of the year I used to flatter myself with the pleasure of seeing my dear Cousin, and enjoying that free & unreserved conversation so pleasing to the social mind. . . . But alas! how uncertain is the prospect of this felicity now! how uncertain 'tis when we shall meet again! My Mother, Daniel [her young son] and myself intend to go to a little Plantation House at Ashepoo in search of safety, when we can stay no longer here; but think with what reluctance I must leave the place of my nativity, this poor unhappy Town, devoted to the Flames, when I leave in it my Husband, Brothers, and every known male relation I have, (infants excepted,) exposed to every danger that can befall it. . . . an universal dejection appears at present, the heavy Cloud that hangs over us ready to burst upon our heads calls for all our Fortitude to meet the Awful Event with that decency and resignation becoming Xtians [Christians]; the Scandalous conduct of many among us, leaves us not much to hope, a most humiliating Circumstance to all true lovers of their Country. Almost all the Women, and many hundred *Men* have left Town. . . . My Brother [Charles C. Pinckney] is at the Fort. Tom [Thomas Pinckney] is at present recruiting. . . .

Adieu my dear Cousin,   be assured of the most sincere attachment &c.[2]

Harriott Horry's fears were allayed—at least for the moment. Still, marauding by armed factions, looting, and wanton destruction were everyday occurrences, anxiety and uncertainty the ruling emotions.

Fifty-two-year-old Flora McDonald, as with so many other Scots seeking better lives, had come to North Carolina with her husband and family. Confronted by political mayhem and forced to take sides, Allan McDonald joined a loyalist brigade of fellow Scotsmen. Attired in kilts, brandishing broadswords, they advanced to the sound of bagpipes on Moore's Creek Bridge [Currie, North Carolina], where patriots awaiting them scored a decisive victory on February 26, 1776. McDonald was taken prisoner and, as Flora wrote, was "dragged from gaol to gaol for 700 miles till lodged in Philadelphia Gaol, remaining in [patriot] hands for 18 months before exchanged." She herself, sick at home, was "dayly oppressed with straggling partys of plunderers from their Army, and night robbers who more than once threatened her life, wanting a confession where her husband's money was. Her servants deserted her, and such as stayed grew so very insolent that they were of no service to her." Later she complained, "I may fairly say we both have suffered in our person, family and interest, as much as if not more than any two going under the name of Refugees or Loyalists, without the Smallest recompence."[3]

Because Rebecca Brewton Motte, a widow, had her home outside of Charleston commandeered by the British, she moved to a small farmhouse nearby. In early May 1781, Generals Francis "Swamp Fox" Marion and Henry "Light-Horse Harry" Lee came to visit and explained the necessity of destroying her house so they might dislodge the enemy. "With a smile of complacency this exemplary lady listened . . . declaring that she was gratified with the opportunity of contributing to the good of her country." Moreover, it was she, who suggested the use of a bow and arrows she owned to set the roof of the house on fire: "the first arrow struck and communicated its fire. A second was shot at another quarter of the roof, and a third at a third quarter." The British soon hung out a white flag, "not a drop of blood was shed. . . . [the British] accompanied their captors to Mrs. Motte's and partook with them of a sumptuous dinner, soothing in the sweets of social intercourse the ire which the preceding conflict had engendered. The deportment and demeanor of Mrs. Motte gave a zest to the pleasures of the table."[4]

General Benjamin Lincoln commanded some 3,000 men at Charleston. The British troops, under Sir George Prevost, augmented by loyalist militia and Cherokee Indians, advanced from East Florida, intent on taking the city. Lincoln's defense, with the aid of General William Moultrie and the timely arrival of Count Casimir Pulaski's cavalry unit, forced Prevost to retire to Savannah.

ANN ASHBY MANIGAULT lived with her merchant husband in Charleston. In her journal, she noted those things that were important to her: the weather, her health, the marriages and deaths of people in the community.

Great Confusion

May 4 [1779]. Great uneasiness on account of the British troops.

9th. Great Confusion as they were very near.

10. They were in sight of CharlesTown.

11th. Much fireing, and it was expected the town would be attacked—Benj: Huger killed by our own people by mistake—

12th Many Flags sent into town. They marched off in the night—

13th Pretty quiet, but they are very troublesome in the country—

15th We hear nothing of them—

16th We are still very uneasy, they are ravaging the country—

17th to 21st The same, and Genl. Lincoln cannot prevent it.—

22d Some of our people went to Johnson's Fort, were fired upon, and a good many wounded—

23d Count Pulawsky had a skirmish with them. . . .

Sept. 6. Count D'Estaign arrived from Georgia.

7. My leg broke out. . . .

20th Had the Gout in both feet.[5]

MARY LUCIA BULL, at Ashley Hall plantation, northwest of Charleston, was directly in the path of Prevost's army as it approached Charleston. She described her situation in May 1779 to her friend Susanna Stoll.

I expected nothing but death

Many thanks my Dr. Sukey, for your kind inquiry's about me & still more thanks for acquainting me of your situation. We left Prince Williams the day after you parted with us. My Brother attempted bringing his Negroes with him, but we were obliged to leave them in Pon pon [Edisto] River, from whence they returned home; thear was a few put on board Mr. River's Schooner—which arrived safe in Charles-Town; Nancy & self have six among them, they went about the Town for their victuals. We have our two maids with us; Mariah is with the rest of our negroes at Oakatees, (I believe), under the care of Mr. Flower & Mr. M. Garvey. It is impossible for me to describe to you what I felt, while the British Army was on this side Ashley-Ferry, we never went in to our beds at night, had Candles constantly burning & were alarmed at every noise that we heard. Mrs. Bull was plundered of some of her clothes, my Aunt Bellinger's Chamber door was burst open & a great many of her things taken, in short everybody in the House lost something except Nancy & myself. As soon as we saw them taking things about the House we went into our Chamber, had the window shut & stood against the door, (for it could not lock.) One Man came & turned the Brass but did not push against it hard enough to find out it was not lock'd.

But, good heavens, my Sukey, think what we must have suffered when a parcel of Indians came bolting into the House, as for my part, I expected nothing but death, & indeed, at that moment it was indifferent to me whether I lived or died, yet I could not bear the thought of being murder'd by the Savages. One of the British Colonels came to the House, we told him we were very uneasy about the Indians & common Soldiers, he was sorry they disturbed us, (he said), but we had better fee [pay] him to stay with us, for he had good spirits, cou'd sing a good Song & had a deal of chitty-chatty, Whether he said that to divert us, (for we were very dull) or whether he felt a little for our distress as he appeared to do, I will not undertake to say. You ask me what we intend doing—that is a question that I know not how to answer. I am as yet quite undetermined what to do. . . .

And now, my Sukey, I must beg that you will not be uneasy about me, I am as happy as your absence and the times will permit me to be. . . . I remain your unchangeable Friend,   Mary Lucia Bull[6]

ELIZA LUCAS PINCKNEY and her family suffered greater losses. Her son Thomas reported that the British had burned his plantation on the Ashepoo River to the ground, had "destroyed all the furniture, china, etc, killed the sheep and poultry and drank the liquors." They also had taken with them his nineteen slaves, but left the sick women and young children.

I feel not for myself

Hampton, Santee, May [17], 1779

My dear Tomm,—I have just received your letter with the account of my losses, and your almost ruined fortunes by the enemy. A severe blow! but I feel not for myself, but for you; 'tis for your losses my greatly beloved child that I grieve; the loss of fortune could affect me little, but that it will deprive my dear Children of my assistance when they may stand most in need of it. . . . Your Brother's timely generous offer, to divide what little remains to him among us, is worthy of him. I am greatly affected, but not surprised at his Liberality.

I know his disinterestedness, his sensibility and affection. You say, I must be sensible you can't agree to this offer; indeed my dear Tomm I am very sensible of it, nor can I take a penny from his young helpless family. Independence is all I want and a little will make us that. Don't grieve for me my child as I asure you I do not for myself. While I have such children dare I think my lot hard? God forbid! I pray the Almighty disposer of events to preserve them and my grandchildren to me, and for all the rest I hope I shall be able to say not only contentedly but cheerfully, God's Sacred will be done![7]

[Eliza Pinckney had taken refuge at her daughter's plantation "Hampton," where she was joined by many friends also seeking safety. Among her worries was how to prevent the British from taking their slaves: Daniel Horry her son-in-law owned well over 300.]

unless they choose to go to them

Backlow [the overseer] wrote me he would keep the boat to bring the women and children from Ashepoo as soon as there was any danger. . . .

I sent Prince the taylour to order the Belmont people to cross Scott's Ferry and come to me at Santee . . . but they are not come. The enemy was at Belmont and distroyed every thing in the house, but took none of the negroes. Those at Beech Hill were thought safe and ordered to stay where they were. . . . I wish you or your Brother were near enough to direct what should be done, but I dispair of yr being able to do any thing, and as the Enemy are retreating to Ashley River, I think they are out of the way of being taken at present unless they choose to go to them, and in that case I fear we should not be able to prevent it.[8]

ELIZABETH "ELIZA" YONGE WILKINSON, a young widow, who lost her husband and son within the first year of marriage, had returned to her father's home on Yonge's Island, south of Charleston. For her friend Mary Porcher, Eliza Wilkinson recalled her change of heart toward the British, and the treatment she endured at their hands and those of ruffians. Eliza and her relatives moved several times out of danger's way.

we commenced perfect statesmen

You know we had always heard most terrible accounts of the actions of the British troops at the northward; but, (fool that I was), I thought they must be exaggerated, for I could not believe that a nation so famed for humanity, and many other virtues, should, in so short a time, divest themselves of even the least trace of what they once were. . . . Once we heard that the enemy had surrounded the town [Charleston] . . . however, it seemed that they had cut off all means of provision getting to town, and that our troops there were in a starving condition.

Such reports as these were constantly circulated about, and half distracted the people. Some believed, others disbelieved. I was one of the unbelievers. However, it was the constant topic of conversation. Some said one thing, some another; and depend upon it, never were greater politicians than the several knots of ladies, who met together. All trifling discourse of fashions, and such low little chat was thrown by, and we commenced perfect statesmen. Indeed, I don't know but if we had taken a little pains, we should not have been qualified for prime ministers, so well could we discuss several important matters in hand.

"Shares there, I say; shares."

We saw not any of our [American] friends for a great while; they had taken a different route to Willtown, Pon Pon, and other places; where they heard the negroes were very unruly, and doing great mischief; so they rode about from plantation to plantation, in order to quell them in time. We grew melancholy and unhappy . . . and hourly expected unwelcome visitors; but seeing nor hearing nothing of them, only that they were erecting forts at the Ferry, I began to be in hopes they would not be so free in obtruding their company on us, as they had done elsewhere; but at length the time arrived. The 2d of June [1779], two men rode up to the house; one had a green leaf, the other a red string in his hat; this made us suspect them as spies (for we hear M'Girth's men wore such things in their hats.) They were very particular in their inquiries "if there were any men in the house?" (Foolish fellows! if there were, they would not have had time to have asked us that question.)—"If any had been there?" "No." "Did any go from here this morning?" Impertinents, thought I; do you think that we are bound to answer to all your interrogations! but I must not say so. "Well," says one, "do you know Col. M'Girth will be along here presently with two hundred men? You may expect him in an hour or two." Ah! thought I—I'd far rather (if I must see one) see old Beelzebub; but here are some of his imps—the forerunners of his approach. "Why," (said my friend, Miss Samuells,) "if Col. M'Girth should come, I hope he wont act ungenteelly, as he'll find none but helpless women here, who never injured him!" "O!" says one, "he'll only take your clothes and negroes from you." After a little farther chat, they rode off, leaving us in a most cruel situation, starting at every noise we heard, and dreading the enemy's approach. . . .

Well, now comes the day of terror—the 3d of June. (I shall never love the anniversary of that day.) . . . I heard the horses of the inhuman Britons coming in such a furious manner, that they seemed to tear up the earth, and the riders at the same time bellowing out the most horrid curses imaginable; oaths and imprecations, which chilled my whole frame. Surely, thought I, such horrid language denotes nothing less than death; but I'd no time for thought—they were up to the house—entered with drawn swords and pistols in their hands; indeed, they rushed in, in the most furious manner, crying out, "Where're these women rebels?" (pretty language to ladies from the *once famed Britons!*) That was the first salutation! The moment they espied us, off went our caps, (I always heard say none but women pulled caps!) And for what, think you? why, only to get a paltry stone and wax pin, which kept them on our heads; at the same time uttering the most abusive language imaginable, and making as if they'd hew us to pieces with their swords. But it's not in my power to describe the scene: it was terrible to the last degree; and, what augmented it, they had several armed negroes with them, who threatened and abused us greatly. They then began to plunder the house of every thing they thought valuable or worth taking; our trunks were split to pieces, and each mean, pitiful wretch crammed his bosom with the contents, which were our apparel, &c. &c. &c.

I ventured to speak to the inhuman monster who had my clothes. I represented to him the times were such we could not replace what they'd taken from us, and begged him to spare me only a suit or two; but I got nothing but a hearty curse for my pains; nay, so far was his callous heart from relenting, that, casting his eyes towards my shoes, "I want them buckles," said he, and immediately knelt at my feet to take them out, which, while he was busy about, a brother villain, whose enormous mouth extended from ear to ear, bawled out "Shares there, I say; shares." So they divided my buckles between them. The other wretches were employed in the same manner. . . . They took care to tell us, when they were going away, that they had favored us a great deal—that we might thank our stars it was no worse.

> [Some time later, Eliza Wilkinson was able to join her parents and was delighted by a surprise visit.]

something in his countenance that commands respect

A company of horsemen rode up to the house we were in, and told us the General was coming along, and would be there presently; they had scarcely spoken, when three or four officers appeared in view. They rode up . . . he introduced one of the officers to Father. "General Lincoln, Sir!" Mother was at the door. She turned to us, "O girls, Gen. Lincoln!"—We flew to the door, joy in our countenances! for we had heard such a character of the General, that we wanted to see him much. When he quitted his horse, and I saw him limp along, I can't describe my feelings. The thought that his limping was occasioned by defending his country from the invasion of a cruel and unjust enemy, created in me the utmost veneration and tender concern for him. You never saw Gen. Lincoln, Mary?—I think he has something exceedingly grave, and even solemn, in his aspect; not *forbiddingly* so neither, but a something in his countenance that commands respect, and strikes *assurance* dumb. He did not stay above an hour or two with us, and then proceeded on to camp.[9]

The winter of 1779-80 was an especially severe one: "Our Winter set in earlier & with more severity than is remembered by the Oldest liver among us. . . . the Chesapeak at twenty Miles below Anopolis a firm bridge . . . In Virginia it has impeded all Trade, several of there Vessels have been cut to peices & sunk by the ice. . . . To the Eastward the Snow impeded all traveling in the State of New York—it cut off Communication from Neighbour to Neighbour," reported Catharine Livingston from Philadelphia.[10]

For the soldiers of the Continental Army, the weather was only one of many problems: they had no ammunition, no clothing, and few provisions. Worst of all, many had not been paid their wages for many months. As the money was often sent home to support family members, it was not just the soldiers who lived on the edge of starvation. The hardships of war exacted many victims.

ANN GLOVER had stayed at home when her husband Samuel enlisted in 1775 with the 2nd North Carolina Continental Line. He served his country bravely, and attained the rank of sergeant. Ordered to begin the march south to defend Charleston, Glover and his men, unpaid, malnourished, and ill-equipped, protested—with awful consequences.

willing to endure all the dangers and Hardships of war

PETITION TO THE GENERAL ASSEMBLY OF NORTH CAROLINA, 1780
The Humble Memorial of Ann Glover, widow of Samuel Glover . . . Humbly Sheweth, That your Peitioner's late Husband well and faithfully discharged his Duty as a Soldier and Friend to the Cause of American freedom and Independence, & marched to the Northward under the Command of Col. Robert Howe . . . [and] was deemed by him and every other officer in that Battalion a good soldier, and never was accused of being intentionally Guilty of a breach of the Laws, Martial or Civil . . . [When ordered] to the Southward, at which time he had above twelve month's pay due for his services as a soldier, and which he ought to have received, and would have applyed for the sole support of himself, his wife, your Petitioner, and two helpless orphan Children. That many of the poor soldiers then on their March . . . possessed of the same attachment & affection to their Families as those in Command, but willing to endure all the dangers and Hardships of war, began their March for the Defence of the State of South Carolina, could they have obtained their promised but small allowance dearly earned for the support of their distressed families in their absence . . . a General Clamor arose among the common soldiery, and they called for their stipend allowed by Congress, but it was not given them, altho' their just due. Give your poor Petitioner leave to apologize for her unhappy Husband's conduct . . . and ask you what must the Feelings of the Man be who fought at Brandywine, at Germantown, & at Stony Point & did his duty, and when on another March in defence of his Country, with Poverty staring him full in the face, he was denied

his Pay? His Brother soldiers, incensed by the same Injuries and had gone through the same services . . . looked up to him as an older Soldier, who then was a Sergeant, raised by his merit from the common rank, and stood forth in his own and their behalf, & unhappily for him demanded their pay, and refused to obey the Command of his superior Officer, and would not march till they had justice done them. The honest Labourer is worthy of his hire. Allegiance to our Country and obedience to those in authority, but the spirit of a man will shrink from his Duty when his Services are not paid and Injustice oppresses him and his Family. For this he fell an unhappy victim to the hard but perhaps necessary Law of his Country. The letter penned by himself the day before he was shot doth not breathe forth a word of complaint against his cruel Sentence, Altho' he had not received any pay for upwards of fifteen months. . . . Your humble Petitioner, distressed with the recollection of the fatal catastrophe . . . request[s] that you will extend your usual Benevolence & Charity to her & her two children . . . I am, &c   Ann Glover[11]

[Sergeant Glover was executed on February 23, 1780, as an example to the other soldiers, his widow granted charity the following year.]

By March 1780, General Lord Cornwallis and Sir Henry Clinton, in hopes of subduing South Carolina, had assembled a formidable force to mount an amphibious attack on Charleston. The American troops occupying the city, aided by the small Continental navy, prepared for a frontal onslaught from the sea but neglected to defend the land approaches from the south. The British surrounded the city, and General Lincoln was forced to surrender unconditionally on May 12, 1780. Cornwallis quickly established control over most of the state; South Carolina and Georgia, once more, belonged to the British Empire.

"We have been humbled to the dust, again plundered, worse than ever plundered!" Eliza Wilkinson wrote. "Ah! my foreboding soul! what I feared has indeed taken place. S. Carolina growns under the British yoke; her sons and daughters are exiled, driven from their native land; and their pleasant habitations seized by the insulting victors."[12] The British exiled many Americans or forced them to buy "protection" to safeguard their families and property. Others seeking safety from lawless bands of marauders moved into the occupied town. People from all walks of life faced not only the deprivations of war but also the threat of epidemics.

FRANCES HART SHEFTALL had returned to her native city from Savannah, Georgia, after her husband Mordecai, Commissary General of Purchases for Georgia's militia, and their fifteen-year-old son Sheftall were taken prisoner by the British in December 1778. They endured harsh treatment at the hands of the British Army and loyalist militia and were eventually transported to Antigua. Despite the horrendous chaos, Frances was able to get a letter to her husband.

The balls flew like haile during the cannonading

My dear Sheftall,   Charls Town, July 20th, 1780

I make not the least doubt, but ere thise comes to hand that you have herd that thise place was given over to the British troops on May 12th by a caputalation after three longe months sige. During that time I retier'd into the country with my family, and a great many of our people ware at the same place. During the sige thare was scarce a woman to be seen in the streets. The balls flew like haile during the cannonading.

After the town was given over, I returned to town and have hierd a house in St. Michael's Alley belonging to Mrs. Stephens at the rate of fifty pounds sterlinge a year. And whear the money is to come from God only knows, for their is nothing but hard money goes here, and that, I can assure you, is hard enough to be got.

I am obliged to take in needle worke to make a living for my family, so I leave you to judge what a livinge that must be.

Our Negroes have every one been at the point of death, so that they have been of no use to me for thise six weeks past. But, thankes be to God, they are all getting the better of it except poor little Billey, he died with the yellow fever on the 3 of July.

The children have all got safe over the small pox. They had it so favourable that Perla had the most and had but thirty. How I shall be able to pay the doctor's bill and house rent, God only knowes. But I still trust to Providence knowing that the Almighty never sends trouble but he sends some relife. . . .

I wrote to you about three weeks agoe by way of St. Austatia [Eustatius] to Antigua, whare I mention every particular to you, but must now refer it untill it shall pleas God that we see you again. Your brother Levy went out of town during the sige toward the northward and has not returned as yet. Thise day his youngest baby, Isaac, was buried. The poor baby was sicke for about three weeks and then died. We have had no less than six Jew children buried since the sige, and poor Mrs. Cardosar [Cardozo], Miss Leah Toras that was, died last week with the small pox. Mr. DeLyon has lost his two grand children. Mrs. Mordecai has lost her child. Mrs. Myers Moses had the misfortune to have her youngest daughter, Miss Rachel, killed with the nurse by a cannon ball during the sige. . . .

Havinge so favourable an oppertunity as the flag I was willing to let you no [know] some little of our family affairs. I have nothing more at present but wish to hear from you by the first oppertunity. The children joine me in love to you and their brother, and I remain   your loving wife, Frances Sheftall[13]

[Eventually, Frances Sheftall and her young children were able to reach Philadelphia, and the family was reunited.]

MARY WHITE MORRIS described to her friend Sarah Jay in Madrid, Spain, her horrified reaction to the treatment of the inhabitants:

those dominereing Britons

My dear Mrs. Jay   Springestbury [near Philadelphia] July 29 [1781]
    Three flags have just arrived from Charles Town, south Carolina, sent by
the british for the purposes of Conveying hither the first Family's of that Place,
that they may get rid of persons they have so inhumanely plunder'd of their Estates & thereby be excused from allowing them the small pittance they proposed
for their Subsistance; there is no instance of greater tyranny than has been Exercised to these People, very unlike a generous foe; who wou'd admire the Laudable Pride that kept them from asking favors or Associateing with the enemys of
their Country; the effects were very different on those dominereing Britons, for
they very soon declared their intention of subdueing the haughty spirit of the
Carolinians; for that they ask'd favors more like the Conquerors than the Conquer'd; they put them on board small vessels, & so crowded that had their bad
fortune still pursued them in a long passage Infectious disorders were very much
to be Apprehended in the Month of July, & their poor imaciated bodys must
soon have Submited to such a foe;
    I was very much Surprized to find them in such good spirits, observeing it
they declared they experienced a degree of Happiness beyond what they thought
their Situation admited off, that breathing free Air, meeting with a Hospitable
reception from their Contrymen, & Comeing to a Land of Plenty, had given
them joyous hearts, tho they had not a farthing to purchase the fine Beef & Mutton which they eagerly hastend to market to see, soon after their Arrival. . . .
                                                          Yours Mary Morris[14]

ELIZA PINCKNEY, whose business exporting indigo cakes for dye had been very
lucrative before the War, had seen her income dissipate. Like so many other
women, she was hard pressed to meet her obligations. Despite owning considerable property in land as well as slaves, she complained to a creditor in England
that the war had made her destitute.

a single woman, accused of no crime

                                                                    [May 1782]
    I am sorry I am under a necessity to send this unaccompanied with the
amount of my account due to you. It may seem strange that a single woman,
accused of no crime, who had a fortune to live Genteelly in any part of the
world, that fortune too in different kinds of property, and in four or five different
parts of the country, should in so short a time be so entirely deprived of it as not
to be able to pay a debt under sixty pounds sterling, but such is my singular case.
After the many losses I have met with, for the last three or four desolating years
from fire and plunder, both in Country and Town, I still had something to subsist
upon, but alas the hand of power has deprived me of the greatest part of that, and
accident of the rest. Permit me to particularize in part, or you may possibly think
me mistaken in what I have now asserted, as a strange concurrence of circumstances must happen before a person situated as I was, should become thus destitute of the means of paying a small debt.

The labor of the slaves I had working at my son Charles' sequestrated Estate . . . has not produced one farthing since the fall of Charles Town. Between thirty and forty head of tame cattle, which I had on the same plantation . . . was taken last November by Major Yarborough and his party for the use of the army, for which I received nothing.

My house in Ellory Street, which Capt McMahon put me in possession of soon after I came to Town, and which I immediately rented at one hundred per annum sterling, was in a short time after filled with Hessians, to the great detriment of the house and annoyance of the tenant, who would pay me no more for the time he was in it, than twelve guineas. I applied to a Board of Field Officers which was appointed to regulate those matters, they gave it as their opinion that I ought to be paid for the time it had been, and the time it should be, in the Service of Government, which it is to this day. I applied as directed for payment, but received nothing. Even a little hovel, which I built to please one of my negroes and which in the late great demand for houses would have been of service to me, was taken from me, and all my endeavours to get it again proved fruitless.

My plantation up the path . . . which I hired to Mr. Simpson for fifty guineas the last year, and had agreed with him for eighty guineas for the present year, was taken out of his possession and I am told Major Fraiser now has it for the use of the Cavalry, and Mr Simpson does not seem inclined to pay me for the last half year of the year 1781. To my regret and to the great prejudice of the place, the wood has also been all cut down for the use of the Garrison, for which I have not got a penny. The negroes I had in town are sometimes impressed on the public works and make the fear of being so a pretence for doing nothing. Two men and two women bring me small wages but part of that I was robbed of before it reached me.[15]

Among General Lincoln's forces who had surrendered on May 12, 1780, were, according to deputy adjutant general John André (a member of Clinton's staff): major generals, colonels, "18 surgeons, 322 serjeants, 137 drummers, 4710 rank and file."[16] Though high-ranking officers might apply for parole or exchange, ordinary soldiers were confined to over-crowded prison ships, half starved, and exposed to disease with no medical aid available. The best the prisoners could hope for was a speedy death.

When Dr. Peter Fayssoux, the chief physician to the American hospitals in the South, complained of the ill-treatment to his British counterpart, Dr. John McNamara Hays, he received the reply: "Confinement of prisoners in prison-ships was the great eyesore, and there was no help for that, it must be done." Soldiers who were detained in barracks outside of Charleston were harangued to join the British troops, and, if they refused, were threatened "that the rations hitherto allowed for the support of their wives and children, from that day should be withheld; the consequence of which would be, they just starve in the streets." Fayssoux continued, "Several of the ladies of Charleston, laying aside the distinction of whig and tory, were instrumental and assiduous in procuring and preparing every necessary of clothing and proper nourishment for our poor, worn-out and desponding soldiers."[17]

The fall of Charleston was only the first of several disasters that confounded the Americans. On August 16-17, 1780, during a fierce battle at Camden, South Carolina, poorly trained militias panicked at the British charge and abandoned the field. General Cornwallis's superior troops scored a decisive victory.

A month later came the stunning news that Benedict Arnold, the Continental Army's brave hero, had been in negotiations with Sir Henry Clinton to deliver the plans of the Hudson River's crucial fort, West Point—for a price. Their go-between, John André had, by a fluke, been apprehended with the plans in his boot. Considered a spy, he was tried by a military tribunal and condemned to death by hanging.

General Washington wrote General John Cadwalader on October 5, 1780, from Tappan, New York: "We have been half of our time without provisions, and are likely to continue so. We have no magazines, nor money to form them; and in a little time we shall have no men, if we had money to pay them. . . . In a word, the history of the war is a history of false hopes and temporary devices, instead of system and economy."[18]

At last, the tide turned. Ships of the French navy under the command of Rear Admiral Comte de Grasse sailed in March 1781, via the West Indies, to Chesapeake Bay where Lord Cornwallis had, in the meantime, established his military and naval base. General Washington and Jean, Comte de Rochambeau (who had been in Rhode Island since the summer of 1780) planned their strategy. Leaving 4,000 men in White Plains, New York to deceive Sir Henry Clinton into thinking that an attack on New York City was imminent, the American and French allies marched towards Yorktown, Virginia.

SUSAN LIVINGSTON, usually a reliable source of information, conveyed the most recent news to her sister Sarah Jay in Spain, undeterred by the possibility that the letter might fall into enemy hands.

we shall hear the french & american cannon roaring

Elizabeth Town [New Jersey] July 18th 1781

General Washington is making rapid approaches to N Y. in order to beseige that fortress which has hitherto been deemed impregnable; the french fleet is daily expected, when it arrives I suppose we shall hear the french & american cannon roaring before that City. All that we have further to do is to implore the divine blessing to attend our just & virtuous endeavours. . . .

I have just been perusing a monody in the New-York paper, upon Major Andre, by a Lady. It is very long. I think the poetry pretty, & such as would do honour to the author, if she had not represented Genl Washington as a Coward & Murderer; such coarse & unmerited reflections are unwarrantable, & detract from the merit of the performance. . . .

Col. Temple arrived . . . directly from our Army in Virginia. He says the Marquis La Fayette having collected an army superior to Lord Cornwallis's has driven him into Williamsburgh, where he is now cooped up, so that after all his boasting how he would conquer the whole dominion of Virginia, he is at last inclosed within a few acres of it. . . . they had received intelligence . . . that Genl [Nathaniel] Green had taken Ninety six in South Carolina, & Augusta in Georgia, with a very large quantity of valuable stores in each place; therefore the enemy possess nothing but Charles Town, and Savanna, in all that Quarter. . . . Adieu to News. It is not often I write any, for the news of one day is generally contradicted the next. . . .   Adieu & beleive me ever Your Affecte Sister S. L.[19]

SARAH MATTHEWS OSBORN, wife of Aaron, a blacksmith, whom she had married "during the hard winter of 1780" in Albany, New York, accompanied her husband when he re-enlisted as a commissary guard on condition that she would be permitted to ride in a wagon or on horseback. That first winter, they resided at West Point. Sarah Osborn's deposition applying for her husband's pension (in 1837) gives a vivid picture of life with the Continental Army.

"Row on, boys"

While at West Point, deponent lived at Lieutenant Foot's, who kept a boarding house. Deponent was employed in washing and sewing for the soldiers. Her said husband was employed about the camp. She well recollects the uproar occasioned when word came that a British officer had been taken as a spy. She understood at the time that Major André was brought up on the opposite side of the river and kept there till he was executed. On the return of the bargemen who assisted Arnold to escape, deponent recollects seeing two of them, one by the name of Montecu, the other by the name of Clark. That they said Arnold told them to hang up their dinners, for he had to be at Stony Point in so many minutes, and when he got there he hoisted his pocket handkerchief and his sword and said, "Row on boys," and that they soon arrived in Haverstraw Bay and found the British ship. That Arnold jumped on board, and they were all invited, and they went aboard and had their choice to go or stay. And some chose to stay and some to go and did accordingly.

When the army were about to leave West Point and go south, they crossed over the [Hudson] river to Robinson's Farms and remained their for a length of time to induce the belief . . . that they were going to take up quarters there, whereas they recrossed the river in the nighttime into the Jerseys and traveled all night in a direct course for Philadelphia. . . . In their march for Philadelphia, they were under command of Generals Washington and [James] Clinton.

Deponent took her stand

She embarked at Baltimore and . . . General Clinton was in the same vessel with her. Some of the troops went down by land. They continued sail until they had got up the St. James River as far as the tide would carry them, about twelve miles from the mouth, and then landed, and the tide being spent, they had a fine time catching sea lobsters, which they ate.

They, however, marched immediately for a place called Williamsburg, as she thinks, deponent alternately on horseback and on foot. There arrived, they remained two days till the army all came in by land and then marched for Yorktown, or Little York as it was then called. The York troops were posted at the right, the Connecticut troops next, and the French to the left. In about one day or less than a day, they reached the place of encampment about one mile from Yorktown. Deponent was on foot . . . [her] attention was arrested by the appearance of a large plain between them and Yorktown and an entrenchment thrown up. She also saw a number of dead Negroes lying around their encampment, whom she understood the British had driven out of the town and left to starve, or were first starved and then thrown out. Deponent took her stand just back of the American tents, say about a mile from the town, and busied herself washing, mending, and cooking for the soldiers, in which she was assisted by the other females; some men washed their own clothing. She heard the roar of the artillery for a number of days, and the last night the Americans threw up entrenchments, it was a misty, foggy night, rather wet but not rainy. . . . Deponent's said husband was there throwing up entrenchments, and deponent cooked and carried in beef, and bread, and coffee (in a gallon pot) to the soldiers in the entrenchment.

On one occasion when deponent was thus employed carrying in provisions, she met General Washington, who asked her if she "was not afraid of the canonnonballs?"

She replied, "No, the bullets would not cheat the gallows," that "It would not do for the men to fight and starve too."

Are not you soldier enough

They dug entrenchments nearer and nearer to Yorktown every night or two till the last. While digging, the enemy fired very heavy till about nine o'clock next morning, then stopped, and the drums from the enemy beat excessively. . . .

The drums continued beating, and all at once the officers hurrahed and swung their hats, and deponent asked them, "What is the matter now?"

One of them replied, "Are not you soldier enough to know what it means?"

Deponent replied, "No."

They then replied, "The British have surrendered."

Deponent, having provisions ready, carried the same down to the entrenchments that morning, and four of the soldiers whom she was in the habit of cooking for ate their breakfasts.

Deponent stood on one side of the road and the American officers upon the other side when the British officers came out of the town and rode up to the American officers . . . rode on before the army, who marched out beating and playing a melancholy tune, their drums covered with black handkerchiefs and their fifes with black ribbands tied around them, into an old field and there grounded their arms and then returned into town again to await their destiny. Deponent recollects seeing a great many American officers, some on horseback and some on foot, but cannot call them all by name. Washington, Lafayette, and Clinton were among the number. The British general at the head of the army was a large, portly man, full face, and the tears rolled down his cheeks as he passed along. She does not recollect his name, but it was not Cornwallis. She saw the latter afterwards and noticed his being a man of diminutive appearance and having cross eyes.[20]

General Washington noted in his Journal: "October 17th [1781]—About ten o'clock the enemy beat a parley, and Lord Cornwallis proposed a cessation of Hostilities for 24 hours, that Commissioners might meet at the house of a Mr. Moore (in the rear of our first parallel) to settle terms for the Surrender of the Posts of York and Gloucester."[21]

Brigadier Charles O'Hara substituted for Cornwallis (who pleaded ill health), and formally surrendered to General Lincoln. Delight was expressed by many at this victory, which some, like Catharine Livingston, viewed as the likely end of the war: "an event that in all human probability must soon crown! with success that Allied arms."[22] Others heard of Cornwallis's surrender with consternation.

ANNA RAWLE described for her mother in New York City how Philadelphia had reacted to the news.

It is too true that Cornwallis is taken.

Oct. 22, 1781—Second day. The first thing I heard this morning was that Lord Cornwallis had surrendered to the French and Americans—intelligence as surprizing as vexatious. People who are so stupidly regardless of their own interests are undeserving of compassion, but one cannot help lamenting that the fate of so many worthy persons should be connected with the failure or success of the British army. . . .

October 24—Fourth day. I feel in a most unsettled humour. I can neither read, work or give my attention one moment to anything. It is too true that Cornwallis is taken. [Col. Tench] Tilghman is just arrived with dispatches from Washington which confirm it. . . .

October 25—Fifth day. I suppose, dear Mammy, thee would not have imagined this house to be illuminated last night, but it was. A mob surrounded it, broke the shutters and the glass of the windows, and were coming in, none but forlorn women here. We for a time listened for their attacks in fear and trembling till, finding them grow more loud and violent, not knowing what to do, we ran into the yard. Warm Whigs of one side, and [merchant James] Hartley's of the other (who were treated even worse than we), rendered it impossible for us to escape that way. We had not been there many minutes before we were drove back by the sight of two men climbing the fence. We thought the mob were coming in thro' there, but it proved to be Coburn and Bob. Shewell, who called to us not to be frightened, and fixed lights up at the windows, which pacified the mob, and after three huzzas they moved off. . . . Coburn and Shewell were really very kind; had it not been for them I really believe the house would have been pulled down.[23]

When the news of Cornwallis's surrender reached London, Prime Minister Frederick Lord North is said to have exclaimed, "Oh God! It's all over!" He was mistaken: King George III vehemently resisted North's plea to open peace negotiations with the Americans. The fighting continued, especially in the west and the south. Georgia "had been entirely laid waste by the desolations of war: the rage between Whig and Tory ran so high, that what was called a Georgia parole, and to be shot down, were synonymous."[24] In the west, the British and their Indian allies mounted raids into Pennsylvania, West Virginia, and Kentucky. In a retaliatory strike on November 10, 1782, George Rogers Clark led a force of mounted riflemen against the Shawnee Nation, burning their villages at Chillicothe, Ohio. It was the last land battle of the War.

As General Washington and Comte de Rochambeau trekked northward once more toward New York, rebels and loyalists hurled accusations of brutal atrocities at each other. None was more horrifying than an eye-for-an-eye incident in Tom's River, New Jersey. Early in 1782, a band of loyalists reduced the town to ruins, and, in the melee, had captured a captain of the local militia, Joshua Huddy, who was placed aboard a prison ship for safe-keeping. Shortly thereafter, however, he was illegally removed, without Sir Henry Clinton's knowledge, and executed in revenge for the murder of a Tory. In an effort to stem this spiral of violence, General Washington requested that Clinton turn over Huddy's murderer; Clinton refused. Washington, with the approval of Congress, then ordered that a British prisoner of war—"an officer who had surrendered without any special arrangement having been made as to how he would be treated"—be chosen by lot and executed instead. Thirteen officers, all of whom had served at Yorktown, and had been brought to Lancaster, Pennsylvania, picked a paper out of a hat; Captain Charles Asgill, nineteen years old, drew the one marked "Unfortunate."[25]

SARAH BURD YEATES had lived most of her life in Lancaster, Pennsylvania. The recent birth of her sixth child, a son, may have intensified her sympathy for Asgill and his family, as she wrote her husband, Jasper, a delegate to the Convention of Pennsylvania at York.

that poor unfortunate Young Creature

Dear Mr Yeates   Lancaster May 27th. 1782
    I long to see you & present my bargin to you. I thought Peggy [her two-year-old daughter] would be jealous but she is delighted with Him. . . . This day that poor unfortunate Young Creature whose lot it fell upon to suffer instead of Capt. Huddy is to set off for Head Quarters. Altho' it may be just or right to retaliate it seems very hard to think what a Parent must feel for an only Son 17 Years of Age whose behavior & Conduct in Life Promissed them much Pleasure to have him brought to such a death and at the same time Innocent of any Crime worthy of it seems Terible.
    All your Family are well, I am your Affectionate & dutiful   Sarah Yeates[26]

[Objections that the prisoners taken at Yorktown were protected from exemplary punishment by the Articles of Capitulation were of no use. As the summer wore on, and as the need to save face hardened positions on all sides, it was a plea to the French foreign minister that broke the deadlock.]

LADY SARAH THERESA PRATVIEL ASGILL had to cope with the news of her son's fate alone: her husband Charles gravely ill, her daughter felled by depression. Though she appealed to the King and Parliament for assistance, she received none. Desperate, she turned to Charles Gravier, Comte de Vergennes in Paris.

My son, my only son

London. July 18, 1782

Sir—If the politeness of the French court will permit a stranger to address it, it cannot be doubted but that she who unites in herself, all the more delicate sensations with which an individual can be penetrated, will be received favorably by a nobleman, who reflects honor not only on his nation, but on human nature. The object on which I implore your assistance is too heart rending to be dwelt upon; most probably the public report of it has already reached you; this relieves me from the burden of so mournful a duty. My son, my only son, dear to me as he is brave, amiable as he is beloved, only nineteen years of age, a prisoner of war, in consequence of the capitulation of York Town, is at present confined in America as an object of reprisal. Shall the innocent suffer the fate of the guilty? Figure to yourself, sir, the situation of a family in these circumstances, Surrounded, as I am, with objects of distress, bowed down by fear and grief, words are wanting to express what I feel, and to paint such a scene of misery; my husband, given over by his physicians some hours before the arrival of this news, not in a situation to be informed of it; my daughter, attacked by a fever accompanied by delirium, speaking of her Brother in tones of distress, and without an interval of reason unless it be to listen to some circumstance which may console her heart.

Let your sensibility, sir, paint to you my profound, my inexpressible misery, and plead in my favor; a word from you, like a voice from heaven, would liberate us from desolation, from the last degree of misfortune. I know how far gen. Washington reveres your character. Tell him only that you wish my son restored to liberty, and he will restore him to happiness. The virtue and courage of my son will justify this act of clemency. His honor, sir, led him to America; he was born to abundance, to independence, and to the happiest prospects. Permit me once more to intreat the interference of your high influence in favor of innocence, and in the cause of justice and humanity. . . .   Theresa Asgill[27]

[Vergennes did indeed write General Washington, informing him that since Captain Asgill was as much a prisoner of the French as of the Americans, it was the pleasure of the King and Queen of France that he should live. Washington and Congress, happy to be relieved from an untenable position by this *deus ex machina*, released the young man who returned to England as quickly as he could.]

France had expended men and money to assist the Americans, not to promote the principle of independence but as a way to disrupt the British Empire. With peace negotiations beginning, Vergennes, an astute politician, suggested to Congress that the French should guide the talks, and that no agreements be made without his consent. Benjamin Franklin, already living in Paris, began talks with the British envoy Richard Oswald in April 1782. He soon summoned John Jay, who was then in Spain attempting to obtain monetary assistance for the financially distressed Americans. By late October, a draft of a treaty had been painstakingly constructed by the two men—often avoiding Vergennes—when John Adams arrived from the Netherlands. Issues of fishing rights and the treatment of loyalists were among the stumbling blocks resolved thereafter. Henry Laurens of South Carolina, the last member of the team to arrive, insisted on adding a ban on the removal of "Negroes or other American property" by British troops, to which the other commissioners consented.[28]

For many who had stood by the Crown, the peace was not a happy one. They were hounded out of town, or banished, and forcibly removed from their properties, though some fortunate ones managed to retain their livelihoods and eventually were accepted once more into society.

Native Americans who had served as British allies were driven off their lands by speculators and settlers. Neither the British nor the American governments gave the support so crucial to the Indian Nations; instead they actually abetted their forced relocation.

For African Americans, the future was similarly bleak. Promised liberty if they joined the King's forces, an estimated 14,000 were evacuated by the British by the end of the War. However, many blacks were re-enslaved or died of disease and starvation. The Continental Army had also enlisted African Americans though fewer in number: there were two all-black regiments. New York made a special effort to enlist slaves by emancipating them after three years of service and compensating their former owners. The actions of African Americans (whether they "fought for Congress or king") were motivated by the promise of freedom, immediately or thereafter.

Even slaves and their families who had been freed by their owners were in constant danger of re-enslavement. Margareta Powell of Patuxent, Anne Arundel County, Maryland, petitioned Governor Thomas Johnson in 1779 for assistance after one of her children who had "taken the oath of fidelity and . . . entered into the service of their country," while on a furlough to see her, "they who have disinherited me have taken and sold him for life time . . . and threaten to do the same to [her other son]—and all the rest of my children and grandchildren throughout the neighborhood. They have stripped me of everything I had and burned me out of my house. . . . The man who claims this right from me and my children is one John Ashton, a Priest." It is doubtful that Powell received reparations for her losses.[29]

In New York City, Sir Guy Carleton, who had replaced Sir Henry Clinton as governor, sought to ensure an orderly withdrawal of British troops and adherents to the Crown. He also felt bound to honor the promise of freedom to slaves and would not force them to return to their masters. The name, age, health, and origin of each of the 3,000 African Americans who fled to Canada were meticulously noted by Carleton's staff; even the brief notations tell poignant stories of separation and loss. Among those aboard the ship *Aurora* bound for St. John, New Brunswick, were:

Rose Richard, 20, healthy young woman, (Thomas Richard). Property of Thomas Richard, a refugee from Philadelphia.

Daniel Barber, 70 worn out, (James Moore). Says he was made free by Mr. Austin Moore of little York nigh 20 years ago.

Sarah Farmer, 23, healthy young woman, (Mrs. Sharp). Free Negress indented to Mrs. Sharp for one year.

Barbarry Allen, 22, healthy stout wench, (Humphrey Winters). Property of Humphrey Winters of New York from Virginia.

Elizabeth Black, 24, mulatto from Madagascar, (Mr. Buskirk). Free, indentured when nine years of age to Mrs. Courtland.

Bob Stafford, 20, stout healthy Negro, (Mr. Sharp). Taken from Mr. Wilkinson in Virginia by a party from the Royal Navy about four years ago.

Joyce, 12, healthy Negress, (James Moore). Lived with James Moore for 6 years, her father died in the King's service.[30]

Many never received the acreage for farms that had been promised them. Far from home and family, they faced almost insurmountable hurdles: prejudice from whites, harsh winters, and famine. In desperation, many blacks were forced to sell themselves into indentures, freedom once more denied them.

On November 25, 1783, the British evacuation completed, General George Washington entered New York City with what remained of the Continental Army. He did not stay long. Anxious to return to private life, he bade an emotional farewell to his officers, resigned his commission to Congress sitting at Annapolis, and rode home to Mount Vernon.

Part II
Women Living Their Lives

Figure 5. *Field of Onions at Wethersfield*. Woodcut. Courtesy of the
Wethersfield [Connecticut] Historical Society.

Chapter 6

This week . . . my Family are all sick

The field of health in the eighteenth century remained much as it had been during the preceding several hundred years. Sickness, disease, and untimely death were as accepted a part of life in America as they had been in England and Europe. Cuts, bruises, colds, fevers, and the multitude of ailments that afflicted the typical family were dealt with by the woman of the house. The first line of medical defense, she was accustomed to attending to everyone's complaints. She diagnosed ailments, dispensed remedies, and "watched" family members who were ill and abed, sitting with them day and night, taking note of any change in their condition. In short, she treated every domestic medical condition, whether serious or perfunctory.

Some women practiced medicine outside of the home, becoming midwives or nurses who worked in hospitals. In a few cases, they had acquired their expertise from their fathers who were doctors. In others, they had studied folk and herbal remedies on their own. By the time she began her diary in 1785 Martha Ballard, a midwife from Hallowell, Maine, knew how to bind wounds, dress burns, and treat dysentery, sore throat, frostbite, whooping cough, and "the itch," as well as deliver babies. While her skills are impressive, she is only one of many eighteenth century women who were adept at preserving health and treating illness.[1]

ABIGAIL SMITH ADAMS, as wife of the Vice President, was clearly responsible for the well being of her household. While living in New York, her family was beset with health problems, as she wrote her sister, Mary Smith Cranch.

I have had a succession of sickness in my Family

August 9th, 1789

This week I shall not be able to see any company unless it is to Tea, for my Family are all sick, Mrs. Smiths [her daughter, Nabby] two Children with the Hooping Cough, Charles with the dysentery, Louissa & Polly with a complaint similar. To Charles I gave a puke last night & his complaints have abated.

Louissa & Polly are to take one to night. If we had not been so fortunate in our situation I do not know how we could have lived. It is very sickly in the City.

[Abigail Adams took up her pen again nine months later to let her sister know of more illness, including that of President Washington. Abigail feared that, should he die, the fragile new government could not survive.]

Not a Creature has escaped in our Family except its Head

N[ew] York, May 30 1790

I was allarmed at not hearing from you, & feard that you were all sick. The disorder termd the Influenza has prevaild with much voilence, & in many places been very mortal, particularly upon Long Island. Not a Creature has escaped in our Family except its Head, and I compounded to have a double share myself rather than he should have it at all. Heitherto he has escaped, not so the President. He has been in a most dangerous state, and for two or three days I assure you I was most unhappy. I dreaded his death from a cause that few persons, and only those who know me best, would believe. It appears to me that the union of the States, and concequently the permanancy of the Government depend under Providence upon his Life. At this early day when neither our Finances are arranged nor our Government sufficiently cemented to promise duration, His death would I fear have had most disastrous concequences. I feard a thousand things which I pray I never may be calld to experience. Most assuredly I do not wish for the highest Post. I never before realizd what I might be calld to, and the apprehension of it only for a few days greatly distresst me, but thanks to Providence he is again restored.[2]

MARTHA JEFFERSON RANDOLPH described widespread illness at her plantation, Bellmont, in a letter to her father, Thomas Jefferson.

more sickness than I ever saw in a family in my life

January 22nd, 1798

It was with infinite pleasure that we learned you had got the better of your cold and were at least comfortably if not agreeably fixed for the winter. It is much more than we can boast of, for the extreme dampness of the situation and an absolute want of offices of every kind to shelter the servants whilst in the performance of their duties, have occasioned more sickness than I ever saw in a family in my life. Pleurisies, rhumatism and every disorder proceeding from cold have been so frequent that we have scarcely had [anyone] at any one time *well* enough to attend the sick.[3]

Concocting medicines was another skill that some women acquired, in addition to diagnosing illness and nursing the sick. The ingredients they used were frequently those that grew in a kitchen garden: rosemary, mint, marigolds, roses, and tansy, among them. These plants along with others, often boiled in water, were taken orally or mixed with butter, oil, or lard to make ointments and salves.

A few women became so expert at diagnosing and treating ailments that they set themselves up in business, becoming what we might call today nurse practitioners. With Dr. William Buchan's popular *Domestic Medicine* in hand, they dispensed advice as well as medication.[4]

SARAH ANNE EMERY recalled how her injured little brother was successfully treated by a remedy suggested by a neighbor.

a recipe for a burn

My little brother, like other baby boys, toddling into mischief, contrived, during the momentary absence of mother, to pull over the teakettle, which was standing in the chimney corner, scalding his right arm and hand badly. . . . Poor little Jim's arm grew worse, Mother and Aunt Sarah became anxious, when one of the neighbors brought in Mrs. Salter's recipe for a burn. . . . It was concluded to try the prescription. A linen glove and sleeve were fitted over the burn, these were kept saturated with a mixture of olive oil and snow water, beat to a froth. In less than a week the sore was healed and a new skin formed.[5]

MARGARET HILL MORRIS, a Quaker widow from Philadelphia with four children under the age of seven, was an accomplished healer who had learned her medical skills from her father, a physician, as well as from Dr. Buchan's encyclopedia. She nursed soldiers, both British and American, during the Revolution, and assisted neighbors in need, as this letter to her sister Hannah Hill Moore attests.

it was received as gospel

March 23 79

I was calld in after meeting to day to look at a young Womans eye, who has a film growing over it. I directed Molasses to be dropt in at Night, & to take a Dose of Rhubarb once a Week to help the Molasses. It was recd as Gospel & the sale of the Rhubarb may pay for heel taps. When a patient comes for advice, if I'm at a loss, I open the book Case wch is my Apothecary shop & fumble about the bottles, & turn over Buchan, till I meet with something like the case, & then with a grave face prescribe.[6]

[Some time later Margaret Morris informed her sister Milcah Martha Moore that she had bought some medicines and planned to sell them at a moderate price in a shop she had opened.]

There is not a dose of physic to be got in this town without coming to me for it, and I have long supplied many gratuitously. I feel quite alert at the thoughts of doing something that may set me a little step above absolute dependence; the Doctor in our town will not sell any medicines, except to his own patients, so that I've no doubt of having custom enough, and all my friends here approve of my making the trial; if it succeeds, I shall add to my shop, by a little at a time, till I get a good assortment.[7]

[Exhibiting modesty as well as generosity, Margaret Morris treated all comers without necessarily expecting to be paid for her services. In her *Journal* she described her surprise at the form compensation in one instance took.]

Thier wives being Sick & no Doctor in Town

[Burlington, New Jersey] June 14, 1777

Some of the Gondola Men & thier Wives being Sick, & no Doctor in Town to apply to, they were told that Mrs M was a Skillful Woman & kept Medicines to give to the poor. . . . they Ventured to come to me & in a very humble manner begd me to come and do something for them. At first I thought they might have a design to put a trick upon me & get me aboard of thier Gondolas & then pillage my house, as they had done some others but on Asking where the Sick folks were, was told they were lodged in the Governor house so I went to see them. There was several, both men and Women, very ill with a fever, some said the Camp or putrid fever. They were broke out in blotches, & on close examination, it appeard to be the itch fever. I treated them according to art, & they all got well.

I thought I had recieved all my pay when they Thankfully acknowledged my kindness— but lo—in a Short Time afterwards, a very rough ill looking Man came to the door & askd for me. When I went to him, he drew me aside, & askd if I had any fr[ien]ds in Philada. The question alarmd me—supposing there was some mischief meditated against that poor City. However, I calmly said, I have an Antient Father; some Sisters & other near frds there. Well, said the Man, do you wish to hear from them, or to send any thing by way of refreshment to them? If you do, I will take charge of it & bring you back any thing you may send for. I was very much surprisd & thought to be sure he only wanted to get provisions to take to the Gondolas.

When he told me, his Wife was one of those I had given Medicines to & this was the only Thing he coud do to pay me for my kindness, My heart leapd with Joy, & I set about preparing something for my dear absent frds: a Quarter of Beef, some Veal, fowls, & flour were soon put up; & about Midnight the Man calld & took them aboard of his boat. He left them at R[ober]t Hopkins at the point, from whence my beloved frds took them to town; & 2 nights after, a loud knocking at our front door, greatly alarmd us. Opening the Chamber Window, we heard a Mans voice, saying, come down softly, & open the door, but bring no light. There was something Mysterious in such a call, & we concluded to go down & set the Candle in the kitchen.

When we got to the front door, we askd who are you? The Man replyd a friend, open quickly. So the door was opend & who shoud it be but our honest Gondola Man with a letter, a bushel of Salt, a Jug of Molasses, a bag of Rice, some tea Coffee & Sugar, & some Cloth for a Coat for my poor boys, all sent by my kind Sisters. How did our hearts & eyes overflow with love to them & thanks to our heavenly Father for such seasonable Supplys—

May we never forget it—being now so rich, we thought it our duty to hand out a little to the poor around us, who were mourning for want of Salt. So we divided the bushel & gave a pint to every poor person that came for it, & had great plenty for our own use.[8]

[Margaret Morris uses medical terms that may be confusing to the modern reader. The disease called "camp" or "putrid" fever could have been typhus, carried by lice and caused by a lack of sanitation. On the other hand, camp fever might have been dysentery, sometimes called the "bloody flux." "The itch" was usually scabies, a highly contagious disease similar to mange, caused by the scabies mite. It too was the result of a lack of proper sanitation and was epidemic during wartime. Its symptoms could be alleviated with sulphur ointment.[9]]

Approximately 20,000 women served at one time or another as "Women of the Army" during the seven years of the War. While the majority served as cooks, laundresses, and seamstresses, women were recruited by officers and surgeons, at the behest of George Washington, to work as nurses, these to be paid "the usual Price."[10] The General himself described their duties:

administer the medicine and diet prescribed for the sick according to order; be attentive to the cleanliness of the wards and patients, but to keep themselves clean they are never to be disguised with liquor; they are to see that the close-stool or pots are to be emptied as soon as possible after they are used . . . they are to see that every patient, upon his admission into the Hospital is immediately washed with warm water, and that his face and hands are washed and head combed every morning. . . . that their wards are swept over every morning or oftener if necessary and sprinkled with vinegar three or four times a day; nor are they ever to be absent without leave.[11]

ALICE REDMAN, a nurse during the War, whose pay was meager at best, petitioned the Governor and Council of the State of Maryland for expenses she had incurred while performing her services.

she your petitioner humbly beg

[ca. 1780]

To the honourable the Governor and council, The Humble Petition of Alice Redman one of the nurses at the hospital Humbly Sheweth that your petitioner has been a nurse at the hospital for about a year she has been deligent and carefull in her office, which she your petitioner humbly beg for an augmentation to her pay as she only is allowed two dollars a month she has at present time sixteen men for to cook and take care of she your petitioner has since she has been a nurse had a great deal of trouble she is oblige to be up day and night with some of the patients and never has been allowed so much as a little Tea, or Coffee which she your petitioner hopes your honors will take this petition into consideration and your petitioner in duty Bound will Ever Pray.

Alice Redman

P.S. She your petitioner out of that two dollars pr. month is oblige to buy brooms and the soap we wash with if your honors will please to relieve your petitioner your petitioner will ever be bound to pray.[12]

Medical men supplemented the work of housewives, either as physicians or surgeons. Physicians were sometimes graduates of a medical school, but the majority of doctors in colonial America did not have medical degrees. Those men who did might have attended the University of Edinburgh, or, after 1765, the medical college in Philadelphia, later known as the University of Pennsylvania. Surgeons, on the other hand, were considered on a par with barbers. They trained for their profession by serving as apprentices, learning how to set bones, perform amputations, and treat wounds and boils. Without anesthesia and proper sanitation, the mortality rate of their patients was about fifty percent. Medical treatments employed by doctors included bleeding, induced vomiting, blistering, and purging. The drugs they used were mercury, calomel, opium, laudanum, ipecac, rattlesnake root, and bark, all administered in unspecified quantities.[13]

JANE PRINCE ROBBINS from Plymouth, Massachusetts, writing to her daughter in Ohio about her medical problems, had consulted friends and relations, as well as doctors, in order to obtain the latest medical advice for her.

Have you any pain abt the region of the Kidneys?

December 19, 1791

The affair of your growing Disorder, is really serious & affecting. . . . I have made a business of making every possible enquiry (without particularizing too much as it respects you) respecting such kind of complaints & cant but have some reason to fear, your apprehensions are not without foundation, & your not voiding any gravelly substance or sediment leaves some grounds to fear it may be the beginning of the formation of a Stone in the bladder. I have consulted Doctr Thacher, who is really skilful, in theory & practice. And he wished me to ask you the following questns "Have you any pain abt the region of the Kidneys? & does it extend to the bladder? "Are the fits of pain attended with a Nausea or vomiting? "After the paroxysms of pain are over is your Urine turbid, or do you observe a mucous Sediment in it? "Is the Urine ever tinged with Blood especially after Exercise? & does exercise bring on pain near the neck of the bladder? "Have you pain in, before & after discharging urine. "Is a free discharge of urine sometimes suddenly interrupted so that you are obliged to void it in Drops? "Finally, Do you ever feel a numbness down the Thigh & Leg? In your next youll please to reply.

I have met with 2 Recipes, since receiving your last, (In my other letter of the 17 Oct. I wrote you 2 or 3 others, particularly the very simple one of "rubbing all the parts thoroly & freqtly with Hogsfat or Lard" which has actually done wonders in gravelly complaints & those like yours). The new ones are "Wild Carrots" a Decoction. The other, Genl Warren gave me, whose Lady has had much of yr complaints in years past. "A large handful of the fibres or roots of garden Leeks, simmered gently in 2 Qts soft water, till reduced to one." A pint taken abt 3 times morning noon & night, a proper dose for an adult pr day. In the instance given, the patient persevered five weeks & then was compleatly relieved.

If after all, my dear Child, you shld find the disorder continues & increases, & there shld be reason to fear there is a Stone, Don't delay too long I intreat you looking out for speedy, & the best advice & assistance. And I am particularly glad to be able to inform you & also requested by others to inform you, that there is a Gentleman now residing in this State, at Jamaica plains, in Roxb[ur]y, Doctor LePrilette by name, who has the highest Reputation of any man in America as a Surgeon & particularly for disorders of the kind you complain of. And when cases have come to require the Operation of the knife, he has performed it in the most incomparable & successful manner to the admiration of some of the greatest men of the faculty in this part of the world. Those of 'em in Boston, have so great an Opinion of him, that (rare as it is) they, tis s[ai]d, actually solicited him to move to Roxby to be near them, & have made him a Member of their Medical Society. I exceedingly wish you co'd see & advise with him, if yr complaints continue.[14]

ISABELLA MARSHALL GRAHAM, married to British Army surgeon, Dr. John Graham, serving in western New York State, described an unusual patient to her mother.

having a daughter not well

Niagara, February 3, 1771

We have lately had several visits from a great family. The chief of the Seneca nation having a daughter not well, he brought her to the Doctor to see what could be done for her: he, his squaw or lady, and daughters, breakfasted with us several times. I was as kind, and made all the court to them I could, though we could not converse but by an interpreter. I made the daughters some little presents, and the Doctor would not be fee'd. You will say this was foolish; but it is not with them as with us, their greatest men are always the poorest. Who knows but these little services may one day save our scalps.[15]

ELIZABETH ANN BAYLEY SETON, whose father was a doctor, relayed his advice to her friend Julianna Sitgreaves Scott.

there is no cure for the whooping cough

Dear Julia   August 31, 1798

My Father particularly directs me to tell you that there is no cure for the whooping cough; nature must have its course. But if they have pain in the breast and oppressed breathing you must have recourse to blistering, as in any other complaint of the breast. He would have written this direction himself but he has scarcely time to breathe, and never pretends to sit down except at meals. I tell you as he bid me, word for word.[16]

PRUDENCE PUNDERSON, at age twenty-two, described a serious medical problem to her sister Hannah.

my breast has been launced twice

Dec: Saturday 30th A[nno] 1780

Next monday it will be 5 weeks since I was taken with a severe fever, which ocation'd much pain in my right arm during the whole Night & in 2 or 3 days I perceived a sweeling just above my right Breast, Doctr: Mitchel endeavoured to scatter it but to no purpose; in the 2d week of my sickness for a while I was in great agony with the Cholick, but applycation of medicine soon gave me releif, my fever which has occasioned the Doctr: to look upon me dangerously Ill; has been broke for several days & the Gathering on my breast has been launced twice, the Cavity of matter lay so deep in my stomack that he was obliged to cut 3 times down with his launcet before he could reach it, he has thought that also rendered my recovery unsertain, but now is much better & gitting well, tho Doctr: Mitchel & Doctr: Mott both of them says the Bone is defected & by what I can gather of their judgments must Content my self to be as long disabled for the use of my Nedle as I have allready been, & now trespass in the limits allowd me by the Doctrs: in using my arm so much as to write you this letter about my Illness. Since my fever has been broke I have gather'd strength & health beyond expression.[17]

Diphtheria and scarlet fever, together known as throat distemper, were diseases that colonial families dealt with, in addition to throat ail, canker ail, and putrid, malignant or pestilential sore throat. Because the symptoms are similar, doctors of the time did not know that they are two separate diseases: diphtheria is caused by a bacillus, scarlet fever by a streptococcus infection. Symptoms of both include swelling, redness, and then grayish-white patches of the throat, followed by a membrane that thickens and spreads down the larynx and trachea. Breathing becomes difficult; in some cases death by suffocation is the result.[18]

MARY BARTLETT, whose husband Josiah was a doctor as well as a delegate to the Continental Congress, wrote to him from Kingstown, New Hampshire, describing a town beset by illness.

Sick with the Canker

May 17th, 1776

Leiut [John] Pearson is Better of all his Disorder's, hiccup's left him Last thursday morning; he is very weak tho' he is able to walk the house with a Staff. . . . Their has been near 30 Person's Sick with the Canker & all like to Recover. Sally Hook has been very bad with the Canker (the Doctor almost Gave her over) But now in a fare way of Recovery. I think it a Great favour of Divine Providence that we are in health when So many are Sick among us.[19]

SOPHIA WATERHOUSE BROWN of Perth Amboy, New Jersey, informed her mother-in-law in the Bahamas of sickness in her family. Isaac, the son of Kitty, a slave, contracted the malignant sore throat, which, complicated by measles, resulted in his death.

everything was done to save him

Perth Amboy April 21st 1796

The last four or five months have been the most melancholy I have spent for some time. We have never had a well family since last November. Peggy a little mulatto who lives with us was first taken ill with the malignant sore throat, then Kitty & Amelia [slaves] & a few days after myself. Poor little Isaac was the last taken ill but seized so violently both with the sore throat & measles that he died on the third day after he was taken. He was a very fine child; every thing was done to save him, but in vain. Poor Kitty was almost inconsolable.

I was never taken with any illness more suddenly than with the sore throat. When I rose in the morning I felt pretty well & the family being all sick I went about the house more than usual. I had violent shivrings several times during the day. Towards evening I felt a kind of pricking pain in one side of my throat. Just at dark I was obliged to go to bed & a most distressed night I had. The next morning I was not able to swallow a teaspoonful of any thing without the greatest pain & continued very ill for seven or eight days. However, thank God, at the end of three weeks I was once more able to get down stairs tho very weak. . . .

Was it not a great blessing my dear Mama that my Mother's health was preserved at the time the servents & myself were ill! Would to God I could say that her good health still continued but alas! I cannot. She was served a fortnight ago with what the Doctors called Irysipelas that kind of it which is generally known by the name of the Shingles. It is a most painful complaint.[20]

JANE FRANKLIN MECOM, sister of Benjamin Franklin, experienced the deaths of all of her children but one. Writing from Boston to her niece Sarah Franklin Bache in Philadelphia, she seems to have come to terms with her lot in life, considering the tragedies she had experienced.

she is all I have left

18th May, 1783

You kindly inquire after my daughter [Jane] Collas. I suppose you know she is all I have left of my twelve children; and she is not healthy; and her husband ill; sickness keeps her low, the body and mind are so connected, that if one suffers the other will suffer with it. . . . but [I] shall go to Rhode Island state in about a week, to spend the summer, where I have spent some happy years; but the scene is much altered by the death of a most desirable grand-daughter, who left three sweet children to my care. Her husband is a very good man, but nothing can repair my loss.[21]

"The diseases peculiar to women," according to Dr. William Buchan, "arise chiefly from their monthly evacuations, pregnancy, and child-birth." Most women referred to childbirth as an "illness." Unfortunately, the illness frequently resulted in the death of both mother and child. In fact the loss of a newborn was so prevalent that a burial gown or shroud was sometimes included as part of a bride's trousseau.[22]

Women often assisted other women during labor and delivery. Known as midwives, they were relied upon as a source of comfort as well as personal knowledge about the birth process. As one eighteenth-century midwifery manual expressed it, "There is a tender regard one woman bears to another, and a natural sympathy in those that have gone thro' the Pangs of Childbearing; which, doubtless, occasion a compassion for those that labour under these circumstances, which no man can be a judge of."[23]

However, in cases of emergency, particularly later in the eighteenth century, a doctor might be called in for consultation. Doctors at this time were just beginning to consider midwifery a legitimate medical specialty.

CHRISTIAN ARBUTHNOT BARNES passed along news to a friend, Elizabeth Murray Smith, regarding her pregnant slave Lady Juliet, for whom she provided the best care.

I chose to have a more experienced person

[Marlborough, Massachusetts] February 16-20, 1771

I know you will be anxious to hear how forward Lady Juliet is in her Pregnency so I must inform you that the Nurse and midwife are bespoke. Our Doct. gave a hint that he would be glad to officiate but I chose to have a more experienced Person. However I told him he might be Present if he Pleased which he says will be agreeable to him as he intends to Practice in that way himself. . . . I give you Joy my Dear last night Lady Juliet was Safly deliver'd of a Daughter.[24]

ABIGAIL ADAMS, pregnant with her last child, described to her husband in Philadelphia the unsettling premonition that she had lost her baby.

very apprehensive that a life was lost

July 9, 1777

I Sit down to write you this post, and from my present feelings tis the last I shall be able to write for some time if I should do well. I have been very unwell for this week past, with Some complaints that have been new to me, tho I hope not dangerous.

I was last night taken with a shaking fit, and am very apprehensive that a life was lost, as I have no reason to day to think otherways; what may be the consequences to me, Heaven only knows. I know not of any injury to my-self, nor any thing which could occasion what I fear.

I would not Have you too much allarmd, I keep up Some Spirits yet, tho I would have you prepaird for any Event that may happen.

I can add no more than that I am in every Situation

                    unfeignedly Yours, Yours.

[Abigail wrote another letter to John the following day.]

I must lay my pen down this moment, to bear what I cannot fly from

Tis now 48 Hours since I can say I really enjoyed any Ease, nor am I ill enough to summons any attendance unless my sisters. Slow, lingering & troublesome is the present situation. The Dr. encourages me to Hope that my apprehensions are groundless respecting what I wrote you yesterday, tho I cannot say I had any reason to allter my mind—my spirits However are better than they were yesterday, and I almost wish I had not let that Letter go. If there should be agreeable News to tell you, you shall know it as soon as the post can convey it, I pray Heaven that it may be soon or it seems to me I shall be worn out. I must lay my pen down this moment, to bear what I cannot fly from—and now I have endured it I reassume my pen and will lay by all my own feelings and thank you for your obligeing Letters.

> [In a subsequent letter to her husband, Abigail wrote that she had delivered a still-born child, a much-hoped-for daughter: "a life I know you value, has been spaired . . . altho the dear Infant is Numbered with its ancestors." She noted that "no one was so much affected with the loss of it as its Sister who mournd in tears for Hours."[25]]

MARY FISH SILLIMAN, whose husband was a prisoner of war, confided her thoughts about her impending delivery to her mother at Stonington.

this is a trying situation to be in

                    North Stratford, Connecticut July 26, 1779

I expect to be ill the first week of next month. Have no expectation of going over the second, am determined by the advice of my friends to tarry here. They tell me thers a very skillfull woman here. Sister Silliman who is my next neighbour always us'd to have Mrs. Barley, but has had this woman twice (since she liv'd here), gives this woman the preference. She lives about ¾ of a mile from this house, but she is as blind as a stone, which is a disagreable circumstance, but a skillfull meek religious woman.

I have had thoughts, and don't know but I shall wait till my time is almost, or quite out, and send for Mrs. Barley to come and stay with me till I want her. I hope I shall be directed to what is for the best.

O my dear Mother this is a trying situation to be in. Such an hour approaching, and little or no expectation of having the company, and the immediate simpathy of the two of the dearest relatives, viz. the tenderest of Husbands and the most tender and indulgent of Mothers.

[Mary Silliman continued to her father:]

awoke a little after day break; found myself ill

Fairfield September 23, 1779

Johnne wrote you the agreeable tidings of my safe delivery of a fine Son [Benjamin] (who was born the 8th day of Augt. about 6 Clock in the morning). . . . I had a fine nights rest the night before; awoke a little after day break; found myself ill; call'd Mrs. Bush, who sent for help as soon as possible, the Midwife living but about a mile (I think) off, who got to me soon with other women, and as above I was safely put to bed about 6 oClock.

I never met the trying hour with such fortitude before, nor did my trust fail till my heart and mouth was fill'd with praise, for such a signal mercy. . . . I never had so good a time before.[26]

ELIZABETH ANN SETON wrote her friend Julianna Scott of the unusual circumstances following the birth of her son.

My father. . . forcibly blew into its lungs

August 20, 1798

If wishes and thoughts could form letters . . . you would have received at least some thousands from me within these last six weeks. But from a variety of troubles, such as my nurse leaving me before the time expected, Mammy Huler's sickness during which time I had the care of my three, and little Will and Anna both ill . . . with at least a half dozen other reasons, the worst of them the loss of my fine eyes for some weeks from excessive pain occasioned by the severity of my pains in the birth of my son. . . .

I was so terribly ill in my hours of sorrow, that my poor Father could scarcely perform his office, though every exertion was necessary to save me. The dear little son was for some hours thought past hope, and the Mother within one more pain of that rest she has so often longed for, but which Heaven, I hope, for good purposes has again denied. My Father may truly be said to have given the breath of life to my child, for when it neither breathed nor moved he went on his knees and placing his mouth to its lips breathed, or I may say, forcibly blew into its lungs. And now the little soul is the most lovely, healthy being you ever saw.[27]

ELIZABETH SANDWITH DRINKER of Philadelphia described in her *Journal* the ordeal suffered by her daughter.

the Child must be brought forward

October 23, 1799

My poor dear Sally was taken unwell last night, Dan came for us early this morning. . . . [I] found Dr. Shippen half asleep in the back parlor by himself—I question'd him relative to Sallys situation, he said she was in the old way, and he think she dont require bleeding by her pulse. . . . This day is 38 years since I was in agonies bringing her into this world of trouble; she told me in tears that this was her birth day, I endeavour'd to talk her into better Spirits, told her that . . . this might possibly be the last trial of this sort, if she could suckle her baby for 2 years to come, as she had several times done heretofore &c. . . . between two and 3 o'clock in the morning Dr. Shippen desired Jacob to call up a John Perry, who lives near them, to open a vain, 'tho it is a opperation she very much dreads, she gave up to it without saying a word: he perform'd with great care and dexterity as I thought, he took twelve or 14 ounces. . . . she has taken 80 or 90 drops liquid laudanum during the day and night, but has not had many minuits of sleep for 48 hours—the Doctor says the child is wedg'd on or near the shear bone and he cannot get at it, to alter the position of its head. . . .

24th after breakfast . . . I went again to Sally, the Doctor had given her an Opium pill three grains he said, in order to ease her pain, or to bring it on more violently: neither appear'd to happen—in the Afternoon the Doctor said, the Child must be brought forward—he went out, which he had not done before. That he was going for instruments occur'd to me but I was afraid to ask him, least he should answer in the affirmative—towards evening I came home as usual . . . when Dan told us, that his mistress had a fine boy and was as well as could be expected . . . I was thankful, that I happened to be absent at the time, tho' I intended otherwise . . . The child, said he [Dr. Shippen], is a very large one for Sally—It is a very fine lusty fatt boy. . . . The Doctor was very kind and attentive during the whole afflecting scene, was there two nights and 2 days and sleep't very little—[28]

"Instruments" were beginning to come into use by midwives and doctors. Dr. William Smellie, the author of *An Abridgement of the Practice of Midwifery*, reprinted in Boston in 1786, is credited with the introduction and popularization of forceps. Following is his recommendation:

> The handles and the lowest part of the Blades . . . may be covered with any durable Leather, but the Blades ought to be wrapped round with something of a thinner kind, which may be easily renewed when there is the least suspicion of venereal Infection in a former Case; by being thus covered, the Forceps have a better hold, and mark less the Head of the Child. For their easier Introduction, the Blades ought likewise to be greased with Hog's-lard.[29]

FRANCES BAYLOR HILL of Hillsborough, King and Queen County, Virginia, provided in her diary a record of the agony and eventual death after childbirth suffered by her sister-in-law, Polly Hill. Even with the assistance of two doctors, she could not be saved.

Oh how great the loss

Fryday [September] the 8 [1797]. Sister Hill had just had a little one and was very sick . . . her baby is a fine girl tho' not so handsome as Thomas.

(Saturday) Sister Polly still continu'd to be very sick had a high fever all day. . . .

Monday. Sister Polly rather better in the morning . . . Aunt Hill sent for Mr. Hill & Doctor Williamson, they did not come till the evening & found her a great deal worse than they expect'd . . . she grew so much worse that they sent for Doctor Roberts. . . . They set up with her all night & gave her bark [quinine]. . . .

(Tuesday) she was sometimes better & then worse, the whole day kept changing . . . The Docts gave her bark & Laudanum which confus'd her head very
much. . .

(Wednesday) Sister Polly was very ill all day. . . .

(Thursday) a little better in the morning, but Oh how soon the pleasing hope
vanish'd into dispair of her ever geting well, she continu'd extreemly ill all day;
toward the evening she seemed to be a little better, but in the night she grew
worse again and Poor Dear creature kept growing worse & worse untill about 5
oclock, which was the hour of her departure. No mortal can describe the distressing scean that follow'd after every thing being done by two very eminent
Doctors & haveing had the best of nursing, to see her expire! Oh how great the
loss to her Dear & Affectionate Husband, as well as her tender relations.[30]

SARAH LIVINGSTON JAY, wife of John Jay, minister plenipotentiary to Spain,
wrote poignantly to her mother, Susannah Livingston, from Madrid about the
birth and death of her baby, Susan.

excuse my tears

August 28, 1780

On monday the 22d day after the birth of my little Innocent, we perceived
that she had a fever, but were not apprehensive of danger until the next day
when it was attended with a fit. On wednesday the convulsions increas'd, and on
thursday she was the whole day in one continued fit; nor could she close her
little eye-lids till fryday morng the 4th of Augst. at 4 o'Clock, when wearied
with pain, the little sufferer found rest in [heaven]. Excuse my tears—you too
mamma have wept on similar occasions, maternal tenderness causes them to
flow, & reason, tho' it moderates distress, cannot intirely restrain our grief.[31]

Epidemics were regarded with apprehension and terror. Unlike the childhood diseases of mumps, measles, and whooping cough, which were serious but
commonplace, epidemics, occurring at random, were much more alarming. In
fact, there is speculation that, during the American Revolution, ten to twenty
times more soldiers died from epidemics than from wounds suffered in battle.
Epidemic diseases considered dangerous at this time were smallpox, yellow fever, malaria, diphtheria, and dysentery. Even with the isolation of individuals
and the quarantine of ships, smallpox flared up every few years, especially in
urban areas. Native Americans, unlike Europeans, had never been exposed to the
disease and therefore were particularly vulnerable; they sometimes lost more
than fifty percent of their number during an outbreak.[32]

ELIZA YONGE WILKINSON of Mount Royal, Yonge's Island, South Carolina, was
thankful that she was not too badly scarred by smallpox.

My face is finely ornamented

May 19, 1781

I have just got the better of the small-pox, thanks be to God for the same. My face is finely ornamented, and my nose *honored with thirteen spots*. I must add, that I am pleased they will not pit, for as much as I revere the number, I would not choose to have so conspicuous a mark. I intend, in a few days, to introduce my spotted face in Charlestown.[33]

JANE PRINCE ROBBINS reported to her daughter, Hannah Robbins Gilman, what she had heard of an outbreak of smallpox on board a ship and the fear it inspired.

order'd her thrown overboard

October 5, 1792

I read a letter to day that come from Hannah LeBaron. she is in the West Indies, went there with a Capt De Wolf that married a daughter of Gov Bradford. He has accumulated a fortune, in the African trade, the last voyage he made, one of the poor negros broke out with the small Pox a day or 2 after he saild. upon which he inhumanly order'd her thrown over board; when he got home, search was made for him, upon which he was obliged to fly the country.[34]

Inoculation against smallpox had begun earlier in the eighteenth century. Doctors found that by introducing live smallpox pus into an incision, a healthy person would develop a light case of the pox and, as a result, acquire immunity to the disease. Although inoculation was often feared by the general public— indeed, sometimes proscribed—it was relatively safe with a mortality rate of less than one percent. Nevertheless debilitating symptoms did occur. Christiana Leech noted in her diary on April 16, 1771:

> All our children were vaccinated by Dr. Pascal; Billy, John, Max, Henry and Joseph got over it very well, but Betsy had a sore eye, and Katy got the inflammation in her mouth, and an abcess eat away her chin and lips, and all her teeth fell out, and while she got well, she is disfigured.[35]

Eyes were often affected, and general weakness could persist for months, even years. Abigail Adams explained her lapse in correspondence to her friend Mercy Otis Warren in early 1777: "My eyes ever since the smallpox have been great sufferers. Writing puts them to great pain." Mercy replied in March that she too suffered symptoms from inoculation: "weakness . . . feebleness of my limbs, and pains . . . sufficient to damp the vigor of thought and check . . . literary employments." Mercy's eyes troubled her throughout her life.[36]

LUCY FLUCKER KNOX, wife of General Henry Knox, decided to be inoculated for the smallpox, along with their daughter Lucy. From Boston, she complained to her husband.

for three days I suffered exceedingly

April 13, 1777

I wrote you last Thursday—that I hoped to be innoculated that day for the small pox but a rash breaking out in my arm induced the doctor to wait a little and dose me farther with the mercury but he has just now assured me he will finish it tomorrow morning.

[From Brookline, she continued on April 31st:]

Join with me my love in humble gratitude to him who hath preserved your Lucy and her sweet baby; and thus far carried them thro the small pox—no persons was ever more highly favored than I have been since it came out—but before for three days I suffered exceedingly—I have more than two hundred of them twenty in my face which is four times as many as you bid me have but believe some of them will leave a mark—Lucy has but one—and has not had an ill hour with it—both hers and mine have turned and are drying away. . . .

I have no glass but from the feel of my face I am almost glad you do not see it. I don't believe I should yet get one kiss and yet the Dr. tells me it is very becoming.[37]

MARY CARY AMBLER of Jamestown, Virginia, concerned about the health of her children, described (in the third person) their inoculation in her diary.

Jack was so scared

September 1770

[She] happened to meet with Mrs. Douglas returning from Baltimore in Maryland where She had been with her three children to be Inoculated for the Small Pox. . . . M Ambler inquired how far it was to Baltimore Town . . . she almost determined to carry her Chil[dre]n to that place to be Inoculated by Dr. Stephenson who she was told had Inoc[ulate]d 7000 People with the greatest Success imaginable. . . .

Monday [Sept. 8] This Morng Mrs. Brook, Mr. Lawson, M. Ambler & children went to Balte Town . . . The Dr. came & inoc. M. Ambler & Sally immediat[el]y but Jack was so scared it could not be done effect[ivel]y. . . .

Wednesday [10th] This day Dr. Stephenson came to Examine our arms & found Jacks so little affectd that he Inoculd him again & he manfully bore it. We all still find ourselves very well. . . .

Thursday [11th] This day M Ambler & Sally took Purges which made them very Sick but Jack was at liberty to run about as he took no Pill the preceding night nor any Physick this day. . . .

Sunday [14th] M. Ambler took a purge very sick with it . . . Dear Jack held out his arm for the 3d. Inoculon & never winched. . . .

Wednesday . . . The children very well still & very cheerful. This aftern The Dr. sent his Mr. Hazzlet to inocl us all again. . . .

Monday [Oct 6th]. . . . Jackey had a very high Fever all Night which continues very Smart tho he goes out of one Room into another. . . .

Tuesday [7th] A good day Jackey's Fever very High . . . his Mother watched him all night. God be thanked several Pocks appears this morning the Fever still High but the greatest Struggle thought to be over. . . .

Saturday [11th] M. Amblers Fever exceedg smart all night but has begun to decline this day a good many Pock out, the pain in the Head has now abated. . . .

Monday [13th] M. Ambler recovers fast has about 25 pock Sally has about 10 & Jack about 17 or 18. Sally and he quite happy & lively.[38]

MARY BARTLETT reported to her husband that hospitals were being set up in New Hampshire for the purpose of inoculating people against smallpox.

I fear the Small Pox will spread

Kingstown July 13th 1776

P. S. I fear the Small Pox will Spread universilly as boston is Shut up with it & People flocking in for innoculation; the Select men of portsmouth have Petitiond to the Committy of Safty now Setting in Exeter; for leave to fix an innoculating hospital in their metropolis for the Small Pox and liberty is accordingly granted and the inhabitance of Exeter intend to Petition for the Same libirty.[39]

Some communities passed laws prohibiting inoculation because many people were suspicious and fearful of it. Although George Washington had initially opposed inoculation for his army, when he discovered how susceptible his troops were, due to little contact with the disease, he subsequently recommended it for all. That decision may have been one of his most important of the war.[40]

MARY SILLIMAN described to her parents how her husband dealt with people intent upon preventing inoculation.

he should do something

[Fairfield, Connecticut] April 11, 1777

You know Mr. [Gold Selleck] Silliman is state attorney . . . he has frequently pressing desires sent him from the neighbouring Towns that he should do something about stoping Inoculation. Then he has to send Guards to collect the infected to one place and order to let none come in or go out with out liberty. But at Stratford they have been so unruly and dispers'd the Guard, he has been oblig'd at the desire of about 80 respectable inhabitants to issue out positive orders to desist and as the civil law could have no affect they should be punnish'd by Martial. This has had its desired effect. None that we know of has transgress'd since.[41]

The infectious disease yellow fever was as devastating as smallpox, its mortality rate high. People realized that yellow fever was endemic to the tropics year round and to temperate zones in the summer months but did not know the reason. The cause, the mosquito *stegomyia fasciata*, was not discovered until the end of the nineteenth century. A particularly bad outbreak of the disease occurred in Philadelphia in 1793. It has been called "the most appalling collective disaster" to strike an American city.[42]

CHRISTIANA YOUNG LEECH of Kingsessing, Pennsylvania, noted in her diary:

over 300 children lost father and mother

1793. September 9th. My eldest son, William Leech, died at 7 o'clock in the morning, of yellow fever, at the age of 37 years and two months, after a sickness of five days. Many people in the town died of this disease. . . .

There died in the town of Philadelphia, between the 1st of August, and November 9, 4031 people of yellow fever or pestilential fever; it bears a great resemblance to that dreadful disease, the plague. 17,000 inhabitants moved out of the City, and at Bush Hill was the Hospital; over 300 children lost father and mother, and were placed in one house to be cared for.[43]

ISABELLA GRAHAM, writing from New York in 1793, gave a heartrending account of the epidemic in Philadelphia to a friend.

whole families dying, and no one to nurse the last

America may boast of her government—it is good. Of her privileges—they are great—Of her prosperity—that too has been beyond all computation; yet the Lord has expressed, in awful form, his controversy with her also. A pestilential fever made its appearance in Philadelphia about two months ago. Between the 19th of August and the 5th of October, four thousand and sixty-four of its citizens died, besides many who quitted the city with infection on them, and died elsewhere. By yesterday's accounts matters are no better: several of the physicians have been carried off by it, and some of them have fled. Doctor [Benjamin] Rush's praise is in every mouth; he is still in the city, exerting himself to the utmost, and his prescriptions are universally followed. No neighbouring town will suffer any person to enter their gates till they have been fourteen days out of the city. The stages have been stopped, and even the horses shot, in some cases, where they have been bribed to force their way through. The most dismal stories have been related of whole families dying, and no one to nurse the last. It is not uncommon for people to be well, and in their graves in twelve hours. No friends attend the funerals; most of them are buried in the night, and every precaution taken to conceal the real amount of evil.[44]

With health care improving and the need for sanitation becoming apparent, people began to understand how to combat disease, how to inoculate against epidemics, how to bind wounds, how to keep a family healthy on a daily basis. Eighteenth-century women continued to attend to everyone. The ailing needed advice and/or treatment, all hoped for the best outcome. As midwife Martha Ballard wrote: "But we are yet alive & well for which we ought to be thankful."[45]

Chapter 7

safely arrived at the Haven of Matrimony

E LIZABETH SMITH SHAW, upon hearing of the marriage of her niece Abigail
"Nabby" Adams in England, sent off a congratulatory letter, reflecting on
the duties of the bride's new state.

several incumbent Duties

Haverhill [Massachusetts] November 27th. 1786

As you my Neice have given me a new Nephew, permit me to congratulate
you both upon the Celebration of your Nuptials. . . . You my Neice who have so
happily escaped the dangers, the whirlpools, and the quicksands of the single
Life, and have safely arrived at the Haven of Matrimony, will find a new *Scene*
open to your view. And that there are two very principal Characters in which
you must become the *Actress*—that of Wife and Mistress—and before a much
more *interested* Audience than you·have yet ever beheld in a publick Theatre, I
need not tell you, I mean your Husband, and your Family,—and perhaps e'er
long, you may be called to act in a third, not less important, arduous and tender.
That each have their several incumbent Duties, and that there are certain Traits
requisite, without which a Lady of your Judgment, well knows a female Character must be exceedingly imperfect. A proper reverence of yourself—a dignity of
Manners—joined with Meekness, and Condescention—gentleness, and sweetness of Temper—have most attractive Charms, and are the richest, and most
valuable Ornaments, you can adorn yourself with. They [will] render you lovely
in Youth, and (I may venture to say,) forever ensure you the attention, the Love,
and the best Affections of that Man, who is truly worthy of *you*.[1]

From birth, a girl was indoctrinated with the views held by a patriarchal society, her role to take "care of her children . . . promoting her husband's happiness and making a well-ordered home his Chief delight." In a middle-class or
lower-class milieu, her productive labors were an additional requirement. Little
is known about marriages of slaves other than tangentially through records written by whites, but it is clear that slavery was an extra burden on African-

American marriages. Throughout society, a girl learned the domestic skills necessary to run a household, was taught some basics of education, not for her own
sake, but as an aid to her husband. Marriage and procreation were her expectations in the hope of personifying the biblical admonition: "A virtuous woman is
a crown to her husband; But she that maketh ashamed is as rottenness in his
bones" (Proverbs, 12:4). The French lawyer and politician Médèric Moreau de
St. Méry, who resided for some years in Philadelphia in the 1790s, pointed out
that a married woman "lives only for her husband, and to devote herself without
surcease to the care of her household and her home. In short, she is no more than
a housekeeper."[2]

Viewed as a member of the weaker sex, both physically and mentally, she
was dependent on the care and support of a father, an older brother, a male
guardian, or a husband. Once married, a woman was considered a *feme covert*,
losing any financial independence she might have had, and, after a child was
born to the union, any property she had brought to the marriage was under her
husband's control. In return, a wife was assured by law of his financial succor. If
widowed, she was entitled to a dower: at least a one-third share of his estate.[3]

With this financial underpinning to marriage and its consequent reproductive
demands, it is perhaps not surprising to find young women less interested in "romantic" marriages than in suitable ones, in terms of background, of class, of future
prospects. The search for an appropriate partner was conducted within a girl's
social sphere. Elizabeth Brooke Carroll of Annapolis, Maryland, wrote her twenty-
three-year-old son Charles studying in Paris (September 10, 1760): "when you
return to Maryland . . . [I am not] afraid of yr being puzzled to get a wife, if you
have a mind for one the only difficulty will be to get a good one, one of a good
mind & temper & every other way agreable to make you intirely happy." The
process of courtship was one of negotiation. To Mary Cooper's grief, her change
from single maiden to married housewife had not been an improvement (July 13,
1769): "in every respect the state of my affairs is more than forty times worse."
Beautiful eighteen-year-old Anne "Nancy" Shippen abandoned her devoted ad-
mirer, Louis Guillaume Otto, a French consular officer, to marry the much older
Henry Beekman Livingston, having been persuaded by her parents of the advantages of Livingston's wealth and social position (March 1781).[4]

ANN CAREY RANDOLPH certainly had her daughter Judith's best interests at
heart when she attempted to check suitor (and first cousin) Richard Randolph's
ardor. Judith was only fifteen, Richard nineteen, as she carefully explained to St.
George Tucker, Richard's stepfather; they were just too young to be able to
make a reasonable decision.

a similarity of temper and good qualities

Dear Sir   Richmond, September 23, 1788
I was not surprised at the information your very friendly and polite letter
contained, having, like you, suspected it some time ago. It has ever been my
wish to keep my Daughters single till they were old enough to form a proper

judgment of Mankind, well knowing that a Woman's happiness depends entirely on the Husband she is united to; it is a step that requires more deliberation than girls generally take, or *even* Mothers seem to think necessary; the risk *tho* always great, is doubled when they marry very young; it is impossible for them to know each others disposition; for at sixteen and nineteen we think everybody perfect that we take a fancy to; the Lady expects nothing but condescension, and the Gentleman thinks his Mistress an Angel. As young people cannot have a sufficient knowledge of the world to teach them the necessity of making a proper allowance for the foibles to say no worse, of Humanity, they are apt to be sour when the delirium of love is over and Reason is allowed to reascend her Throne; and if they are not so happy as to find in each other a similarity of temper and good qualities enough to excite esteem and Friendship, they must be wretched, without a remedy. If the young People who have been the cause of my giving you my sentiments thus freely should ever be united I hope they will never repent of the choice they have made.

I have given Judy Richard's letters; but have desired her not to answer them before she has her Father's leave.[5]

Visiting family or friends and attending balls or assemblies gave excellent opportunities for innocent flirtations or for finding a beau.

MARY "MOLLY" TILGHMAN was preempted by her brother William from being the first to share the latest gossip of Philadelphia with her cousin, Mary "Polly" Pearce in Poplar Neck; instead she amusingly speculated on who his Lady Love might be.

the state of his Heart

Chester Town [Maryland], February 18, 1787

It was unlucky for me that Billy called at Poplar Neck as he return'd from Philada. The news of that place wou'd have afforded ample subjects for a long Letter . . . in describing the sentimental parties, the brilliant Circles, and the social petit soupérs that engag'd his Evenings, without even mentioning the morning visits, Dinners &c which completely filled up his Days. On one subject, I fancy he did not say much to you, for he has not to me. All my questions have been in vain to discover the state of his Heart, tho' he has given me a general history of the various dangers it has encounter'd. Miss Ann Hamilton's Madona softness, Sophia Francis's bewitching sprightliness, Nancy [Anne] Allen's all powerful smile, and Peggy [Margaret] Chew's Je ne scai quoi. From which of these he has suffer'd most, he will determine on reflexion, for in Philadelphia he had not time to settle the point.[6]

The bonds of friendship between young women proved fertile ground for sharing sentiments on courtship, marriage, and spinsterhood. The stalwart actions of many women during the War had lessened to a degree the disapproval of being single—that "single blessedness" as Shakespeare put it. Nonetheless, the perception that a woman would not be able to support herself and consequently become a public burden continued to fuel the paternal pressure to marry.

DEBORAH NORRIS of Philadelphia participated in a lively correspondence with two particular friends and clearly took pleasure in the intimacy of sharing ideas with them. She wrote to Sally Fisher in Duck Creek, ca. 1780:

agree upon living Old Maids

I had dressed myself for the afternoon and was seated at work, When lifting up my eyes they were Unexpectedly caught by the beauty of a small opening thro the trees, which conveyed a thousand fair ideas to my mind in a moment; the idea of my dear Sally presented itself, and the sweet delicacy of our attachment struck forcibly on my heart.

[Continuing on the topic of being single, she opined (May 6, 1780):]

—indeed my dear it seems to me that we shall neither of us marry, but for reasons rather different, thee from not having any offer thee approves, I, from having no offers to disapprove, so I think we may as well be fore hand with our destiny and agree upon living Old Maids, by the way, I think it is a situation that may be supported with great dignity, And I always thought it a striking impropriety for any person, especially one of our own Sex, to speak in that Contemptuous way of Old Maids which is sometimes common, And which too many practice.[7]

DOLLEY PAYNE, a Quaker, appreciated her circle of female friends, even as she approached her wedding day to lawyer John Todd Jr. Her heartfelt sentiments are contained in a letter to Elizabeth Brooke of Maryland.

Love is no respecter of persons

Philadelphia [December 1788]

How much am I indebted to thee dearest Eliza for throwing off that formality so stifling to the growth of friendship! and addressing first her who feels herself attached to thee by every sentement of her heart. . . . Let this [letter] . . . my Dr Betsy obliterate the idea of my neglect occasion'd by my prospects of happiness for be assur'd that no sublunary bliss whatever should have a tendency to make me forgetful of friends I so highly value.

This place is almost void of anything novell. . . . Sally Pleasants and Sam Fox according to the common saying are made one. Their wedding was small on account of the death of a cousin, Mary Rhoads. The Bride is now seting up . . . for company. I have not been to visit her but was informed by Joshua Gilpin that he met 40 [people] their paying their respects, &c. &c.

A general exclamation among the old Friends against such Parade. . . . A charming little girl of my acquaintance & a Quaker too ran off & was married to a Roman Catholic the other evening—thee may have seen her, Sally Bartram was her name. [Sarah Bartram married Claude Antoine Bertier Nov. 29, 1788.]

Betsy Wister & Kitty Morris too plain girls have eloped to effect a union with the choice of their hearts so thee sees Love is no respecter of persons.[8]

REBECCA FRANKS was alone in Philadelphia, out of touch with her brothers: Moses in the West Indies, John, a merchant like their father Abraham, in Montreal. Another brother, patriot David Salisbury Franks, had died in the yellow fever epidemic of 1793. She was a spinster, dependent on her family.

I feel friendless and desert'd

My Dear Brother   Philadelphia, February 5th 1799

    I realy am at a loss to find words to express my joy in addressing my lost Brother. . . . Oh! Brother, it is many Years since we have been with each other. I suppose you have no recollection of me and I am sure I have none of you. I have gone through many scenes since I was in Canady; I was a very young adventurer, as I may say am still, but I trust in God . . . that I shall shortly be settled with or near you, for at present I feel friendless and desert'd without parents, without connection, for my Brother Moses is never with me. If he was, my situation would be far more agreeable, but he is sometimes gone for 2 years. . . .

    My sole dependence is on his bounty. I have been under the disagreeable necessity of applying to a friend of his for Money to pay my board and get necessaries for I am oblig'd to appear genteel. . . . thank God I have never done any thing to occasion a blush in either of my Brother's faces. It would be a very great happiness to me was I capable of doing something for my self but I am not, therefore I must be content.

    I pay at the rate of five dollars per Week for my board, and is as cheap as I can get it. I am with a very worthy couple who are advanced in life without Children. They do all they can to make me comfortable, but you know that is not like being with or near our own relatives. Their is but three of us left, and I think it a very great pity that we could not all be to gather, but instead of that you are in Canada, my Brother Moses in the West Indies, and poor me in Philadelphia.

                                        [your] Affectionate Sister[9]

ELEANOR "NELLY" PARKE CUSTIS had been adopted by her grandmother and grandfather, Martha and George Washington. "She has been ever more than a Mother to me, and the President the most affectionate of Fathers. I love them more than any one." Nelly lived with them in New York and in Philadelphia, but also spent time with her natural mother and her second husband. Once her two older sisters were married, Nelly wrote her friend Elizabeth Bordley, her status would change as it was customary for the oldest unmarried girl in a family to be addressed as "Miss": "I shall be—Miss Custis— . . . *Strange most passing strange*—quite unaccountable (you will cry!) 'tis strange my Dear but nevertheless quite true beleive me—E. Custis & E. Bordley Spinsters . . . What say you to this—agreed?" When George Washington returned to Mount Vernon at the end of his second term, Nelly went too. Still, she was dismayed to learn that her name yet circulated in the gossip mills of Philadelphia.

those meddling *reporters*

Mount Vernon, August 20 [1797]

I am astonished my Dear at the report you mention . . . I wish the world would not be so extremely busy, & impertinent. E P Custis desires not its notice, & would thank those *meddling* reporters never to mention her name. I wish they would also allow her to *marry who* she *pleases* without perpetually *engaging her to those whom she never had a chance of marrying, & never wished* to be united to. The opinion of the wise (that *friendship alone* cannot exist between two young persons of different sexes) is *very erroneous & ridiculous*. I know it by *experience*, which is by far a better teacher than any of those, who pretend to know so much. I shall ever feel an interest & sincere regard for my *young adopted Brother* [George Washington de Lafayette]—but as to being *in love with him* it is entirely out of the question. Therefore *I shall certainly never be engaged or married to him*—as *whoever* is my *Husband* I must *first* love him *with all my Heart*—that is *not romantically*, but *esteem & prefer him before all others, that Man* I am *not yet* acquainted with—perhaps *never* may be, if so— then I remain *E P Custis Spinster for life*.

I am a good deal surprised at the *matrimonial news* but Wonders never will cease. *You* are right not to think of making your choice this year as you have had so many bad precedents. The people of this earth how sadly have they degenerated—the next generation I think, & hope will be better (*because they can hardly be worse than the present*). . . .   E P Custis

[A year and a half later, Eleanor had to admit to her friend that "*truth* will come to light:" she was to be married.]

that old fashioned thing called a Wife

My dearest Eliza,   Mount Vernon February 3rd 1799

Cupid, a small mischeivous Urchin, who has been trying sometime to humble my pride, took me by surprise, when I thought of nothing *less* than him, & in the *very moment* that I had (after mature consideration) made the *sage* and prudent resolve of passing through life, as a *prim starched Spinster*, to the great edification of my Friends [her grandparents] in particular, & the public in general—when I had abused & defied him, & thought my Heart impenetrable he slyly called in Lawrence Lewis to his aid, & transfixed me with a Dart, before I knew where I was. It was sometime I assure you before I could reconcile myself to giving up my favourite scheme, but resistance was vain, I had to contend with perseverance & at last was obliged to submit & bind myself to become that old fashioned thing called a *Wife & now, strange* as it may seem—I am perfectly reconciled & neither think "the day *evil*, or the Hour *unlucky*," that witnessed my solemn promise to become *Mrs. Lewis*, & take said *Lawrence* for better or worse.

That promise will soon be ratifyed—the 22nd of this month is the day which will fix my future destiny. My present prospects are the most pleasing. The Man I have chosen to watch over my future happiness, is in every respect calculated to ensure it.[10]

[Lawrence Lewis, a nephew of George Washington, had joined the family in 1798 to help deal with the constant flow of visitors; he was thus in a good position to court the lovely Eleanor. Married on Washington's birthday, Eleanor gave birth to a daughter in November, shortly before the president's death.]

ELIZABETH SHIPTON lived with her uncle and aunt William and Margaret De-Peyster Axtell, fierce loyalists, in New York City when she met Major Aquila Giles, a patriot prisoner who had been paroled to the city. Elizabeth's letters to Giles reveal humor as well as a great passion, one that needed to be kept secret from her uncle.

who is that genteel handsome young Man?

Monday Morning [ca. 1779]

But now let me tell you, you had the honor to engage the attention of my friend Mrs. Sutherland as we pass'd thro' the Village [Flatbush, New York, where her uncle had a country house] yesterday—she rides up, with, pray Miss Shipton who is that genteel handsome young Man seting there?—that ma'am is Major Giles—is it indeed? (with an arch smile) it is a great pity my dear girl he is not on our side the question—Indeed (I reply) I am quite of your openion, if *that were the case* I would not answer for the consequences—No (she returned) neither will *I* answer for the consequences as it is—Why, I hope you do not suspect my loyalty?—indeed I do not, but—but what?—Rebellion is not to last forever—true—but I am a little of openion it will outlast my youth—there the dialogue was interupted . . . and the conversation became general.

Friday morning [ca. 1779-80]

I wish with all my Heart my G[iles] your Eliza could send you an invitation to her lonely quarters . . . I really feel melancholy, nothing to interupt my cogitations except now and then the foot of my little faithfull Ranger gently laid on my Arm, as if acquainted with the feelings of his Mistress' Heart, and wish'd to tell her he would go and fetch the lovely youth who posseses so large a part of it; indeed, I *believe* I may say the whole, of this I am *Sure*, that *I* have lost it and I know no bosom so likely for it to [have] taken refuge in as yours—search—and if you find yourself really in possession of the Poor Little Fugitive use it tenderly, hide it, oh hide it from the rancourous Eye of Envy, nor expose it to the malignant snear of Malice, remember it is a sacred deposit, and you must be responsible for its safty.

inclination to know who I am scribbling to

You will think I have a vast temerity when I tell you that I am writeing at the same Table with my Uncle. . . . The old Gentleman begins to look as if he had an inclination to know who I am scribbling to, so I think I had best fold up as fast as I can.

[In another letter to Giles, she shared a nightmare occasioned possibly by the stress of having to keep her love a secret:]

the Idea hangs about me still

Monday morning [1779-80?]

How are you my G—? safe and well? you may think it an odd question—but about seven o'clock this morning I see you assassinated by one of our own servants, I was flying to the place where I see you fall, but was restrain'd by my Uncle, who told me if I proceeded I might meet with the same fate; I replied all fates were alike indifferent to me now—and broke from him, and falling on your expireing bosom the shock was so great it awak'd me—I bless'd heaven it was only a Dream—It may betray a weakness of Mind, but the Idea hangs about me still. I cannot forget it.[11]

[Released from parole at the end of April 1780, Aquila Giles assured his lady love (June 21, 1780): "I most solemnly declare to you, I truly love you & you alone . . . consider *me* my dearest Eliza, as the man you are to bless with your hand, he who will never deceive, never desert you." They were married in October 1780, most likely without her uncle's approval.]

CORNELIA CLINTON was determined never to marry without the consent of her father, Governor George Clinton. Her year-long romance with the French diplomat Edmond Genêt (known as Citizen Genêt) had very definite political overtones. During their courtship, she thanked him for a gift he had sent: "the Parrot is beautiful and as a gift of yours will claim a share in my affections . . . I shall take great pleasure in hearing it say I love you Genet."

did they know my heart

New York Government House Decr 18 1793

Let my Prompt answer to your letter express to you the pleasure the reciept of it gave me, tho I assure you I did not want that to recall you to my memory—you have never since your departure been absent from my thoughts—I sincerely wish your pressing business in Philadelphia was at an end for untill then I cannot hope to see you. . . . I hope all those who are in opposition to you may like [John] Jay & [Rufus] King be confounded—if I have Ambition (which some say I have) it is for your prosperity—As for Madam [Anne] Bingham or for what any other Madam or Miss may please to tell I care not their Ignorance is to be pitied, did they know my heart they would find that those Democratic principles serve but to endear you to me, for notwithstanding your worth I do not think I could have been attached to you had you been any thing but a Republican—support that Character to the end as you have begun, and let what may happen you, *your friends in New York will never forsake you.*

My Father does not forget you for we drink to your health every Day. . . . I regard your happiness too much to wish to see you at the risk of your honor or that of your Country, but at the same time I will promise you a kind reception from your Cornelia when you do come . . . my Brother [George Washington Clinton] is your Friend and wishes success to your Country, he Declares if

France should not be succesfull he will go crazy—his heart is rapt up in the cause of Liberty.   Cornelia[12]

[Genêt's meddling in American politics prompted President Washington to demand his recall, but a change of government in France prevented his return. Cornelia married him on November 6, 1794, and received the parental blessing as well as £2,000.]

SHINAH SIMON SCHUYLER had not only wed without her father's permission but converted from Judaism to Christianity to marry the man of her choice, Dr. Nicholas Schuyler of Troy, New York. Rejected by some of her family, Shinah maintained an affectionate bond with her sister Miriam Simon Gratz and her daughters, Frances "Fanny" and Richea in Lancaster, Pennsylvania.

advise you not to be too precipitate

December 17th, 1791

I received my dear Richea's two aggreeable letters with inexperssable pleasure. . . .

And when, pray, do you enter the list of matrimony? Seriously, my love, I must be your confident; however, my dear Fanny must enter her claim first [being the older.] You have my most cordial prayers for both your happiness whenever that happy period arrives. I would advise you not to be too precipitate, unless an extraordinary and worthy man solicits that honor, and your heart can accompany the gift. Never, my lovely girls (for I address you both), alter your situation but by uniting your selves to a worthy man and one you can love and esteem. Should even adversity be your lot, their will be a consolation experienced which your marrying for wealth will never yeild you, and compleat your misery with an undeserving man. Let esteem for virtuous principles be the first basis of love, and then your happiness will be perminant. That both of you, my dear girls, may marry agreeable to your parents, and each have a worthy husband, I sincerely wish, tho' I would still advise you to continue single. Your both young, and two or three years more will be sufficient for to think of altering your situation.

I am in exceeding good health and spirits; indeed, few have less reason to complain. I have a very dear, good husband. I think few, very few, can say they live happier, and, thank God, he's exceedingly hearty and has constant employ in either writing or visiting his patience [patients] and chatting to his little wife, for, you know, I will have some attention paid to me.[13]

SARAH GRAY CARY in Chelsea, Massachusetts, writing at about the same time, held a different opinion. She reflected on the courtship of a family friend in a letter to her son Samuel in Grenada.

We old folks . . . think her a f- - -

My Dear Boy,   Chelsea, November 11, 1791

Harriet [Horsford] has made a conquest of Mr. [George] Rose, but *under the rose* [sub rosa, i.e., in confidence]; therefore take no notice of it. The gentleman is fond of her to distraction, as the term is; but she, not fancying his person, will, I suspect, reject him, for which we old folks, papa in particular, think her a f - - - -. My dear Marget [her sixteen-year-old daughter Margaret], on her part, declares openly in favor of the sentiments of her dear Harriet, and thinks a young lady should not dispose of her person without her affections, and, on the whole, prefers love in a cottage with a man of her choice, to the wealth of the Indies with one she could never love. I confess these were also my sentiments once when a girl, but as we grow into years and learn to deliberate, we think differently. If Miss H. does not absolutely dislike, and has no partiality for any one else, we may reasonably conclude she will be tolerably happy with Mr. R. How many anxieties will she escape by uniting herself to a man who loves her, and whose love perhaps may increase by that steady serenity she will always possess, whether she gives pain or pleasure! Those wives who love least, and at the same time conduct prudently, I have always thought, possessed more abundantly their husbands' esteem; while other poor, simple souls, whose every motive is to give pleasure to the object on whom they dote, are often refused with coldness. In short, you men are better con- trolled by women whom *you love* than by those who love you.[14]

DOLLEY PAYNE TODD had lost her husband John, her young son William, and her father-in-law in the yellow fever epidemic that struck Philadelphia in 1793. Left with her son John Payne Todd, she was courted by James Madison who, she was assured by her aunt Catharine T. Coles,

> thinks so much of you in the day that he has Lost his Tongue, at Night he Dreames of you & Starts in his Sleep a Calling on you to relieve his Flame for he Burns to such an excess that he will be shortly consumed . . . he has Con- sented to every thing that I have wrote about him with Sparkling Eyes.

On September 16, 1794, Dolley took some private moments to tell her friend Elizabeth Collins Lee in Virginia of her impending marriage.

I give my Hand

As a proof my dearest Eliza of that confidence & friendship which has never been interrupted between us I have stolen from the family to commune with you—to tell you in short, that in the cource of this day I give my Hand to the Man who of all other's I most admire—You will not be at a loss to know who this is as I have been long ago gratify'd In haveing your approbation—In this Union I have everything that is soothing and greatful in prospect—& my little Payne will have a generous & tender protector.

A Settlement of all my real property with a considerable Adition of Money is made upon him with Mr. M—'s approbation. . . .

But how shall I express the anxiety I feel to see you? That friend whose goodness, at many interresting periods I have greatfully experienced would now rejoice us by the sight of her. . . .

Adeiu! Adeiu.

Dolley Payne Todd

Evening.
Dolley Madisson! Alass![15]

CHARITY CLARKE, that lively young woman, married Benjamin Moore, the Tory rector of Trinity Church in New York City in 1778. The *New York Gazette* announced the occasion in verse (May 2, 1778):

> The good Parson deserved a good Clarke,
> Such happiness fate had in store.
> 'Twas Charity blew up the spark
> And fixed the bright flame in one Moore.[16]

MARY VIAL HOLYOKE and her husband Dr. Edward Augustus Holyoke lived in Salem, Massachusetts, where Dr. Holyoke practiced medicine for fifty years. They had twelve children but only three reached adulthood. In her diary, Mary recorded her daughter's marriage and the congratulatory visits she received.

Visiting Week

Aug. 1 [1799] Our Daugr Susannah married to Mr. Joshua Ward Jr. His father, mother & Sister, Mr. Turner, Maria Pearson & Mr. Jackson here.

2. They all Dind here.

3. I went to See Mr. Wards house. . . .

5. Visiting Week. . . .

6. 16 Ladys & Gentlemen

7. 18 D[itt]o

8. 19 Ladys & Gentlem

12. Mr & Mrs. Ward Set out on a journey. . . .

20. Mr & Mrs Ward Returned Safe from their Journey.

SUSANNA HOLYOKE WARD, following her mother's example, reported on her wedding journey in her diary.

stopt at a Tavern

Aug. 12, 1799—Mr Ward & I sat out on a journey, Monday, dined at Mr Turner's, Boston, stopt at Watertown, slept at Flagg's Tavern in Weston, breakfasted at Cutlers in West Sudbury, dined at Pease's in Shrewsbury, call'd at Mrs Sumners, stopt at a Tavern in Worcester, slept at Spencer at Jenks' Tavern, stopt at a Tavern in East Brookfield, dined at Western at Cooks, went in Turn Pike road, stopt at a Tavern in Palmer, stopt at a Tavern at the entrance into Springfield, lodged & breakfasted at Williams' Tavern in Springfield, went to see the old Brick House 166 years old, call'd at Mrs Pynchons, dined at Williams Tav[ern], crossed the Connecticut river, supped & lodged at Sikes's Inn in Suffield, breakfasted there, crossed the river again, stopt at Williams' Tavern. . . . returned to Salem in the evening 19th.

29. Went to housekeeping.

May 2, 1800. Mary Holyoke born at six o'clock at night.[17]

The importance of being prudent during the rites of courtship and of making an intelligent choice for a spouse were oft-repeated parental admonitions. Novels emphasized these strictures as well: Susanna H. Rowson's *Charlotte Temple: A Tale of Truth* and Frances Brooke's *Lady Julia Mandeville* were avidly read cautionary tales. When Rachel Worrington in Yorktown, Virginia, was seduced by a French officer and bore a son out of wedlock in 1782, her friends Eliza Ambler and Mildred Smith blamed the lack of a proper education for Rachel's downfall. Sympathizing that "any girl of 16 would be enchanted" by the French officers stationed in the town, the friends felt that "had she but kept in View the dignity of her Sex" Rachel would have been able to avoid her predicament. When her seducer, a son of General Rochambeau, decamped for France, Rachel's chances for marriage—and those of her sister Camilla—were seriously compromised. Yet marry she did four years later; her son had a distinguished naval career.[18]

MARY SMITH CRANCH had a more unusual story to relate to her sister Abigail Adams in London. The young lawyer Royall Tyler, rejected as a suitor by "Nabby" Adams, had moved his lodgings from the Cranch household to that of Joseph and Elizabeth Hunt Palmer in Braintree, Massachusetts. Mary Cranch was not a little surprised at the consequence of that move.

the product of a year, or twenty weeks

Sept. 24th, 1786

We live in an age of discovery. One of our acquaintance has discover'd that a full grown, fine child may be produc'd in less than five months as well as in nine, provided the mother should meet with a small fright a few hours before its Birth. You may laugh but it is true. The Ladys Husband is so well satisfied of it that he does not seem to have the least suspicion of its being otherways, but how can it be? for he left this part of the country the beginning of september last, and did not return till the Sixth of April, and his wife brought him this fine Girl the first day of the present Month. Now the only difficulty Seems to be, whether it is the product of a year, or twenty weeks. She affirms it is the Latter, but the learned in the obstretick Art Say that it is not possible. The child is perfectly large and Strong. I have seen it my sister: it was better than a week old tis true, but a finer Baby I never Saw. It was the largest she ever had her Mother says. I thought So myself, but I could not say it. It was a matter of So much Speculatin that I was determin'd to see it. I went with trembling Steps, and could not tell whether I should have courage enough to see it till I had Knock'd at the Door. I was ask'd to walk up, by, and was follow'd by her Husband. The Lady was seting by the side of the Bed suckling her Infant and not far from her—with one sliper off, and one foot just step'd into the other. I had not seen him since last May. He look'd, I cannot tell you how. He did not rise from his seat, perhaps he could not. I spoke to him and he answer'd me, but hobble'd off as quick as he could without saying any more to me. There appear'd the most perfect harmony between all three. She was making a cap and observ'd that She had nothing ready to put her child in as she did not expect to want them so Soon. I made no reply—I could not. I make no remarks. Your own mind will furnish you with sufficient matter for Sorrow and joy, and any other sensations, or I am mistaken.

Adieu yours affectionately

ABIGAIL ADAMS, no doubt saddened by Tyler's behavior (for she had liked him) as well as relieved that her own daughter had escaped his clutches, placed the blame squarely on the woman.

her Honour her tranquility & her virtue

London, Janry 20th 1787

In this case it may be difficult to determine which was the Seducer, and I feel more inclined to fix it upon the female than the paramour, at any rate She is more Guilty, in proportion as her obligations to her Husband her children her family & the Religion of which she is a professer are all Scandalized by her and she has sacrificed her Honour her tranquility & her virtue.[19]

SALLY MCKEAN had a bit of gossip featuring a more enraged husband and a member of the Spanish delegation to America to tell her friend Dolley Madison in Virginia.

he caught the old goat

[Philadelphia] 4th August -97

I cannot seal this without giving you a little anecdote of [José Ignacio de] Viar, which I have just heard . . . he has been making love to the wife of a servant . . . a remarkable pretty woman, but no great things in point of character, the husband lives at service. He came home a few days ago to see her—it was twelve o'clock at noon—and behold—verily, he caught the old goat, with his wife, and in not the most decent situation—so the fellow very politely took him by the nose and saluted him with kiks till the corner of the next Street. He is going to make him pay a devilish large sum of money, or else he says he will prosecute him, it has made a confounded noise . . . in fact all the town knows it.[20]

Women had few options if their husbands were incompatible or strayed from the matrimonial bonds; Hannah Iredell in Edenton, North Carolina, upon discovering that her lawyer husband James had had an affair, kept her dignity and him at arm's length. He wrote her abjectly (December 2, 1779):

> The injustice and folly of my conduct appear in too glaring colours. I deserve not either your compassion or forgiveness yet what I now feel, the genuine effect of the most sincere and contrite repentance, is, I assure you, no ordinary punishment. . . . My dearest Hannah, let me move you to forgive, to believe, to confide in me. I wish, indeed I wish [to] deserve it. For God's sake banish me not for ever from your confidence and regard. That would be the greatest misery I could sustain on Earth.[21]

It would take some time before the couple was reconciled.

Obtaining a divorce was almost impossible, as the laws invested men with authority over wives. When Abigail Adams urged her husband to "Remember the Ladies," it was a plea to allow women to have more control over their own lives. Women in bad marriages, in most cases, were not in financial positions to live apart from their husbands unless they had sympathetic relatives to support them. Nancy Shippen Livingston was able to flee her jealous and overbearing husband because she had (temporarily at least) a safe haven to go to with her baby daughter; however, her husband's legal status and wealth prevailed in the end, to Nancy's detriment. Legal dependence on a husband made many women hesitate before taking steps toward separation or divorce.

HANNAH COOK HEATON of North Haven, Connecticut, endured verbal abuse and accusations from her husband Theophilus. An extremely devout wife and mother, she sometimes found solace in her faith, despite the fact that her prayers and church attendance only increased his rage against her.

i felt in some measure at his feet

October 26 1769—i met with much sorrow from one that should be my best friend. O the sin which i continually hear, i see great sins indulged, great duties neglected. It makes my heart ake and my joints week. In the evening i went out a few rods from the house and tryed to pray but how shut up i felt. . . . Now when i come in my husband was very angry because i stayed so long and he laid cruel things to my charge and said he believed it. I believe the devil stired up his mind by a story wee had just heard of a man in this place that cetched his wife away alone with another man. Now my husband spoke such dreadful words i don't love to write them and that night i might not sleep with him. The next morning he began to rage at me again. Then i up & told him that i was praying for him & for us all that as i spoke a shower of prayer come upon me. I fell to praying loud before him with a flood of tears for some time and that spirit in him was stild and i felt in some measure at his feet. I felt little then i asked him what that ment except you come as a little child you can not enter into the kingdom of heaven. He said nothing but lookt smiling & pleasent and never said anymore about this matter. Ah my poor family are trying continually to beat me off from all my religion and to get me into hell tho they don't know it.[22]

ABIGAIL ABBOT BAILEY suffered many more bitter trials than Heaton. Described as tall and slender, with dark eyes and "comely but grave features," she was married at twenty-two to Asa Bailey; they lived first in Haverhill and then Landaff, small communities in northwestern New Hampshire. All too soon it became apparent to the young wife that married life would be difficult. Raised to be subservient to man, and to do his bidding, Abigail prayed that her husband would see the error of his ways and, for years, refused to acknowledge his predatory and abusive behavior. Being married to him, she blamed herself for his sinfulness: she was to be the virtuous wife, the protectress of the family honor, and would bear her burdens as Job had done. Moreover, to whom could

Abigail turn for help? Asa Bailey had become a prominent, well-to-do citizen, and had been elected Town Selectman. Who would believe a wife's complaints?

I kept my thoughts to myself

I now left my dear parents, hoping to find in my husband a true hearted and constant friend. . . . But I met with some disappointment—I soon found that my new friend was naturally of a hard, uneven, rash temper, and was capable of being very unreasonable . . . But before one month, from my marriage day, had passed, I learned that I must expect hard and cruel treatment in my new habitation, and from my new friend. . . .

After about three years—alas what shall I say? . . . I learned . . . the *inconstancy* of a husband! In September 1770, we hired a young woman to live with us. She had been a stranger to me, I found her rude, and full of vanity. Her ways were to me disagreeable. But to my grief I saw they were pleasing to Mr. B. Their whole attention seemed to be toward each other . . . there was very improper conduct between them. . . . I kept my thoughts to myself as much as I could. . . . In my distress, my only refuge was in God.

[Later, another hired woman, having less at stake perhaps, filed a complaint against Asa Bailey for attempted rape; he was acquitted. In the meantime, the family grew. Abigail bore seventeen children in twenty-five years of marriage. Asa's behavior continued volatile and frequently irrational. One day, in 1789, he revealed a plan to sell the farm and move to Ohio: "we all consented, at last, to follow our head and guide, wherever he should think best; for our family had ever been in the habit of obedience." To Abigail's increasing despair, and once again pregnant, Asa Bailey was plotting to commit incest with their daughter Phebe.]

I felt terrified at my own thoughts

A great part of the time he now spent in the room where she was spinning, and seemed shy of me, and of the rest of the family. He seemed to have forgotten his age, his honor, and all decency, as well as all virtue. He would spend his time with this daughter, in telling idle stories, and foolish riddles, and singing songs to her and sometimes before the small children, when they were in the room. . . . this one daughter engrossed all his attention.

Though all the conduct of Mr. B. from day to day, seemed to demonstrate to my apprehension, that he was determined, and was continually plotting, to ruin this poor young daughter, yet it was so intolerably crossing to every feeling of my soul to admit such a thought, that I strove with all my might to banish it from my mind, and to disbelieve the possibility of such a thing. I felt terrified at my own thoughts upon the subject; and shocked that such a thing should enter my mind. But the more I labored to banish those things from my mind, the more I found it impossible to annihilate evident facts. Now my grief was dreadful. No words can express the agitations of my soul: From day to day they tortured me, and seemed to roll on with a resistless power. I was constrained to expect that he would accomplish his wickedness: And such were my infirmities, weakness and fears, (my circumstances being very difficult) that I did not dare to hint any thing of my fears to him, or to any creature. This may to some appear strange; but with me it was then a reality. I labored to divert his mind from his follies, and to turn his attention to things of the greatest importance. But I had the mortification to find that my endeavors were unsuccessful.

[Abigail was unable to protect or even talk to her daughter Phebe who, as soon as she turned eighteen, legally free from her father, "left us, and returned no more." Abigail, still hoping to keep the scandalous actions of her husband private, told him she would live with him no longer, and wished for a separation. He was to move far away. Asa plotted and schemed to retain control over her and his property. Incredibly, he was able to lure her alone to New York.]

govern such women as you

Mr. B. threw off the mask at once, and kept me no longer in the dark, at least relative to what was *not* the object of his journey, that it was not what he had ever said. He told me, we are now in the State of New York, and now you must be governed by the laws of this State, which are far more suitable to govern such women as you than are the laws of New Hampshire.

[Abandoned near Utica, Abigail was able to make the 250-mile journey home by herself, in time to prevent her husband's kidnapping their children. Finally incarcerated, Asa Bailey was released only after a division of property, though he insisted on taking his three oldest sons with him. Abigail who realized that he "had forfeited all legal and just right and authority over me" petitioned and was granted a divorce in 1792. "I had no expectations, or wish ever to see him again in this life."[23]]

ELIZABETH "BETSEY" MUNRO was six years old when her father, Reverend Harry Munro, married his third wife, Eve Jay. Within the year, the couple had a son Peter, and, in 1770, the family settled in Albany, New York. Having served as chaplain to Montgomery's Highlanders (77th Regiment) of the British army, Munro had been granted a patent of 2,000 acres, which he wished to have settled. As a preacher, he was frequently away from home; Betsy's relationship with her stepmother deteriorated quickly in his absence.

Her ill treatment of me was incessant

[After Peter's birth] . . . it became my business to rock the cradle; he being very cross, I was frequently whipt because I could not quiet him. Her ill treatment of me was incessant, for I never was without marks of her cruelty; she would pinch me till my flesh turned black, and then lock me up in the cellar till I almost perished for want of food. I am confident that if the servants had been as destitute of feelings as she was, I must have died. My father and she soon began to live unhappy, he finding himself disappointed in getting a fortune by her; and what contributed to increase it, she was neither handsome nor agreeable in any respect whatever—of a most desperate temper, she possessed no qualification of a lady; the longer they lived together, the more unhappy they seemed to be. . . .

The cruelty of my stepmother still continued, until, at length, the neighbours informed my father of her conduct towards me. He forbid her correcting me, and told her, that if I needed correction, he would do it. . . . at last, as nothing else would do, my father boarded me out, and sent me to school.

[Betsey, now fifteen, was very happy to be out of the reach of her stepmother but was dismayed to discover what her egotistical father had in store for her: he had consented to her courtship by one of his acquaintances. However, unlike Heaton or Bailey, the feisty Betsey decided to take matters into her own hands.]

some one to take care of me

When Mr. [Alexander] Campbell paid his visit [November 1775] I was surprised that my father could consent to his coming to see me. He was about six feet high, and forty-five years of age—no teeth, and grey hairs; of course, I could not like him. After a few visits he asked me to marry him. My answer was no. What does he do but go to Albany to see my father, in order to ask permission to make me his wife! . . . [When Campbell returned with Munro's permission] my answer to him was this—"Sir, as you have courted my father, you may marry him, for I will never marry you. . . ."

I had no relations—I had to seek my living among strangers. In the month of Janury, 1776, Mr. [Donald] Fisher became acquainted with me. . . . After he had been introduced by Mrs. Reid [her landlady], she said that she and her husband had been acquainted with Mr. Fisher many years, that he was a good man, and a man of property, and would make a better husband to me than the man my father wished me to have. Being young and unexperienced in life, I soon was made to believe that I should do well by marrying Mr. Fisher; I must confess I had no affection for him. The thoughts I had upon the subject were these: I shall have some one to take care of me—I shall have a home—I shall never be a trouble to my father, for surely he wants to be quit of me, or he would not have been so angry with me for refusing Mr. Campbell, and another thing which had great weight on my mind, was, that I should be out of my stepmother's power.

[A month after they met, and without her father's consent, Betsey married Donald Fisher on the condition that he convey all his property to her. In the ensuing years—in their flight to Saratoga and then to Canada, where the loyalist Fishers had a mercantile business "to great advantage," and to their separate return to New York State—Betsey's overriding goal was to settle on the land that her father had promised her on his patent. The self-serving Reverend had made her many promises, even given her deeds to the property before he fled to Scotland in 1778, but they were all broken.

In October 1800, two years after the death of her husband, Betsey and a young farmer, John N. Smith, were arrested for forgery on a complaint of her half-brother, who had also received the titles to the land Betsey occupied from their father, and wished to sell. She was charged with "making forging and counterfeiting a certain paper writing sealed, purporting to be a deed of conveyance for certain lands therein mentioned, and to be signed and seal and delivered by one Harry Munro to the said Elizabeth Fisher" dated February 12, 1778. Stating that she was "not guilty," Betsey had no witnesses in her defense at the trial by jury; the dark-eyed, 5'3" widow, now forty-one-years old, was sentenced on March 10, 1801 to "Life at hard Labor" (the sentence for forgery) in the state prison in New York City. Pardoned by the governor five years later, she never forgave her father and brother for their cruelty or her sons for abandoning her.[24]]

There were, of course, many instances of happy or contented marriages. Mary Jemison's husband Hiokatoo, in fifty years of marriage, treated her "with tenderness, and never offered an insult." Susannah French Livingston wrote her husband of thirty-nine-years, apologizing for only writing once "Since our Seperation, which however has only been in person, not in heart & Spirit, which brings you present every day if I did not write you in a month I Love you as much as you love me." Robert Morris, on a business trip, wrote his wife Mary: "You frequently are the Subject of my meditations whether I am in or out of company. I will not make Love to you at this time of day but I shall never fail to feel more Esteem and affection than I can express which is due to a Wife of your real merits. I am my dear Molly ever yours." They had been married eighteen years. Theodosia Bartow Prevost Burr, after only five years of married life, asked her husband (November 1787):

> Tell me, Aaron, why do I grow every day more tenacious of thy regard? Is it possible my affection can increase? Is it because each revolving day proves thee more deserving? Surely, thy Theo. needed no proof of thy goodness. Heaven preserve the patron of my flock; preserve the husband of my heart; teach me to cherish his love, and to deserve the boon.[25]

ELIZABETH "BETSY" FOOTE WASHINGTON accepted her cousin Lund Washington's proposal of marriage with some trepidation, but hoped that, with God's help, they would be happy.

never to hold disputes with my husband

[Summer of 1784]

I have now been married better than four years and I think have had the satisfaction of conducting myself to the approbation of my husband . . . I can truly say I have never had cause to repent of my marriage—so far from it, that I do think there is not one other man scarce to be found that would have suited me so well as my dear Mr. Washington and I have reason to think that he is perfectly satisfied with the choice he has made.

[Summer 1789]

One of my first resolutions I made after marriage was never to hold disputes with my husband—never to contend with him in my opinion of things—but if ever we differed in opinions not to insist on mine being right, and his wrong—which is too much the custom of my sex—they cannot bear to be thought in the wrong—which is the cause why there is so much contention in the married state—and the Lordly Sex they can never be in the wrong in their own opinion—and cannot give up to a woman but I blame my sex most. It is their business to give up to their husbands—our mother [Eve] even when she transgressed was told her husband [Adam] should rule over her—how dare any of her daughters to dispute the point. . . . I think a woman may keep up the dignity of a wife and mistress of a family without ever disputing with her husband.[26]

LUCY FLUCKER KNOX, who had left her loyalist family to marry the bookseller Henry Knox in 1774, was frequently separated from him during the War, much against her own desires. He was concerned for her safety, and assured her he had "no other Earthly love but you." It is interesting to note that many wives addressed their husbands with the honorific "Mr." or terms such as "My dearest best of Friends," while husbands used a familiar name. Lucy Knox and Theodosia Burr were exceptions in using their husbands' first names.

I wish my Harry knew how dear he is to me

My dear dear Harry   [Boston] April 16, 1777

I had like to have wrote husband and how you would have laughed—but laugh or not, be assured it is my greatest pleasure and my greatest pride to call you by that endearing name—and I think upon the hour that made you such as that when heaven bestowed upon me the greatest earthly blessing—I am sensible that I have not been duly grateful to the author of all good and perhaps that is the reason why you are so cruelly torn from me—I wish my Harry knew how dear he is to me; but it is a subject that I cannot write upon—my heart over flows at my eyes.[27]

ANNIS BOUDINOT STOCKTON had been married twenty-two years when her husband developed a malignant cancer of the lip, which spread to the throat. A talented poet, she shared her anguish with their friend Elizabeth Graeme Fergusson.

I am now all together discourag'd

[Morven, November 24, 1780]

If you could for a moment wittness my situation, you would not wonder at my silence, totaly confin'd to the chamber of a dear and dying husband, whose nerves have become so Iritable as not to be able, to bear the Scraping of a pen, on paper in his room, or Even the folding up of a letter, which deprives me of one of the greatest releifs I could have, in my present sittuation for alass I have *Leisure*, painful *Leisure* enough, thro all the tedious length of November nights . . . Indeed my dear friend, I am now all together discourag'd, I have kept up my courage by constantly flattering my self, that the ulcer would heal, but it proves so obstinate that his constitution is sinking very fast under it, and I have been very apprehensive for a week past, that he could not survive long, but he is now a little better—he desired me when I wrote, to give his most affectionate regards to you, and tell you that he never should see you more, in this world, but that he Should die as he had lived, for a great many years, your tender and sympathizing freind. . . .

yours in the Bonds of Amity, A. Stockton

[One night, Annis Stockton was able to write in the sick chamber:]

A sudden production of Mrs. Stockton's in one of those many anxious nights in which she watched with Mr. Stockton in his last illness. [1781]

I.

Sleep, balmy sleep, has clos'd the eyes of all
But me! ah me! no respite can I gain;
Tho' darkness reigns o'er the terrestrial ball,
Not one soft slumber cheats this vital pain.

. . . .

III.

While through the silence of this gloomy night,
My aching heart reverb'rates every groan;
And watching by that glimmering taper's light,
I make each sigh, each mortal pang my own.

IV.

But why should I implore sleep's friendly aid?
O'er me her poppies shed no ease impart;
But dreams of dear *departing joys* invade,
And rack with fears my sad prophetick heart.

V.

But vain is prophesy when death's approach,
Thro' years of pain, has sap'd a *dearer* life,
And makes me, coward like, myself reproach,
That e'er I knew the tender name of wife.

VI.

Oh! could I take the fate to him assign'd!
And leave the helpless family their head!
How pleas'd, how peaceful, to my lot resign'd,
I'd quit the nurse's station for the bed.

. . . .[28]

JANET LIVINGSTON MONTGOMERY was the widow of General Richard Montgomery, the Irish-born hero killed during the ill-fated American assault of Quebec on December 31, 1775. Her feelings of loss were bitterly expressed years after the event in a condolence letter to Martha Washington.

I alone stood formost in woe

Madam [March 10th 1800 Rhinbeck House Dutchess County]
Will you accept (for it is all I have to offer) the tears of a fellow suffer; and a fellow Mourner; I will make no attempts to comfort you? I well know how vain the project: twenty-four *years* are gon away since I lost my husband—And still my tears flow and my heart sighs, and my tongue repeats his name, in anguish.

Need I remind you my dear Madam of my falling tears on that day of general festivity at West Point—when you, with all the Ladies present had their Husbands at their sides—these had all, weathered the storms of War, and I alone stood formost in woe? And the woe of a widow? This you now know but to know it in its fullest extent you must have suffered as long as I have done—In any distress we are apt to look at the darkest side—it is they say from contrast that comfort is taken—how much may you derive in a comparison with me whilst the hope of this—leads me to open wounds very imperfectly closed—all the time I have Mourn'd for my lost soldier you held yours in your arms—Then what a consolation were you allowed! how favor'd to be allowed to offer every support to him—to kneel at his bedside to clasp his hand to catch his last words—to close his eyes—to gaze at a loved face to you so dear and last of all to watch over his hearse and see him confined to the grave of his fathers Whilst she who write to give you comfort Who shall console? for a Husband bleeding dieing, on the inclement field of Abraham [the Plains of Abraham at Quebec] far from help? far from friends.

Dear Madam forgive the rest as wild immagination permits me to persist no further. My Mother . . . says we are all going on towards our journeys end—and immagins we shall know and meet in happier worlds where we shall part no more.

MARTHA WASHINGTON, less than a month later, replied with great sensitivity:

the memory of the partners of our hearts

My Dear madam, mount vernon April 5th 1800
I have received with deep sensability your sympathizing letter . . . To those only who have experienced losses like ours can our distresses be known—words are in adequate to convey an idea of them—and the silent sympathy of Friends who have felt the like dispensation speaks a language better known to the heart than the most expressive eloquance can communicate—your affliction I have often marked and as often have keenly felt for you but my own experience has taught me that griefs like these can not be removed by the condolence of friends however sincear—If the mingling tears of numerus friends—if the sympathy of a nation and every testimoney of respect and veneration paid to the memory of the partners of our hearts could afford consolation you and myself would experience it in the highest degree but we know that there is but one source from whence comfort can be derived under afflictions like ours—To this we must look with pious resignation.[29]

Chapter 8

in her own sphere

Management of a household was a woman's domain. From early childhood, she had been trained and educated to perform countless domestic tasks with diligence and care, without complaint. Cooking, cleaning, making soap, washing, spinning, weaving, sewing, baking, supervising servants or laborers if she had any, taking care of the vegetable garden and the farm animals, not to mention rearing the children to follow in her virtuous footsteps: these were only some of the activities that filled a woman's day.

A woman's industry was thought to be its own reward and a "treasure" (as William Livingston put it) to the male head of the family. To be sure, the daily tasks were not identical for all women; in native or enslaved cultures, women routinely participated in agricultural labors, which was not the case for women living in urban communities. Upper-class women might keep the accounts, oversee servants and the preparation of meals, sew, pay visits, and monitor the education of the children. Pierre van Cortlandt, a wealthy New Yorker, remarked in 1789 that his wife was a "slave to Slaves." Whether a woman was poor or wealthy, her exertions, often cyclical as well as tediously routine, were absolutely indispensable to the household. There were few idle moments. Ruth Belknap, a parson's wife in New Hampshire, wittily rhymed:

> But, Oh! it makes my heart to ake,
> I have no bread till I can bake,
> And then, alas! it makes me sputter,
> For I must churn or have no butter.[1]

MARTHA WAYLES SKELTON JEFFERSON, a delicate woman with hazel eyes, and an accomplished musician, began her account book shortly after her marriage. She kept the notes in an old record book of her husband's: he was a compulsive record keeper, she was not. Politics were not within her sphere, although she did join in the effort to raise money to provide shirts for soldiers of the Continental Army in 1780. To assist her in performing her duties at Monticello, (a more modest version of its present splendor), Martha Jefferson had slaves, among them her father's concubine, Elizabeth Hemings and their children.[2]

made 46£ of soft soap

Feb 10 [1772] opened a barrel of col: harrisons floweer

13   a mutton killed

17   two pullets killed

22   a turkey killed

27   a mutton killed
            a cask of small beer brewed 15 gallon cask

28   a list of the house linen
            6 diaper table cloths [fabric woven with a small and simple pattern]
            10 ditto damask
            12 diaper napkins marked T I* 71
            12 ditto towels T I 71
            6 pr of Sheets 5 pillow-cases T I 71

Mar 1   opened a cask of butter weight 20£

10   a turkey killed
            a [mu]skrat killed

14   a cask of small beer brewed

20   a mutton killed

26   made 46£ of soft soap

27   a turkey killed

29   two pullets killed
            made 12£ of hard Soap

July 1   bought of garth 4 lb. of butter [Thomas Garth, the plantation overseer]

3   ditto 4 lb
            brewed a cask of beer

4   bought of garth lb of butter[3]

*The letter 'I' was also used for 'J.'

ZERVIAH SANGER CHAPMAN, the fifty-seven-year-old widow of Stephen Chapman of Warwick, Rhode Island, relied on the help of her extended family to get the tasks done, briefly noting in her diary the day's weather, visits, and any accomplishments, such as making a pocket: a small pouch worn under, though not part of, a skirt.

we washed, I made pocket

[June 1775]

[Sun] 18 day B—Showery. Han[na]h [her daughter] made cheese, I cut out my Shifts. Bettsey & Phebe went to Batteys

19 d 2—fair morn. Showers about noon. we washed, I made pocket

20 d 3—hanh. churned, made cheese, Brewed, Ironed. we had green pease I Spun 2 Scanes

21 d 4—cloudy. I went to Reuben [Blanchard, son-in-law]. Hanh Baked & Irond

23 d 6—I was at James Rhodes in the forenoon, after at Stepn Linittas with luci [her daughter] . . . & went to Nathl: [her son] at night & tarried

24 d 7—cloudy & Drizly 1 Shower. I finished my Shift. Nath killed pig

[Sun] 25 d B—fair. Phebe [Nathaniel's wife] Dressed pig. . . .

26 d 2—I came home. . . .

27 d 3—I washed Linn. went to town, Dinah warped

28 d 4—I Spun, doubled & twisted 9 leas [a measure of yarn] & half thred & Irond Hanh baked & Irond it raind afternoon. . . .

1 d 7 the 7th Day of the week the 1st Day of July 1775 . . . hanh Baked & Spun Some thred & helped about house[4]

MARY WRIGHT COOPER was married at fourteen to Joseph Cooper, bore him six children, and was constantly overworked as their residence, located near Oyster Bay (Long Island) harbor, seems to have served as an inn or boarding house for travelers from time to time. Despite her hard work, Mary Cooper had trouble paying her bills.

O Lord support this famaly in this sene of darkness

[1769] August the 1. New moon this morning. Tuesday. A fine clear morning. I feele much distrest, fearing I shall here from some of my credtors. Afternoon, I have done my worke and feele somthing more comfortabl. . . . Ben Hildrith is come here in littel boate with two men with him. I am up late and much freted them and thier two dogs which they keep att tabel and in the bedroom with them.

2 Wednsday. The first I herde this morning was Ben's dogs barking and yeling in the bed room. They did nothing but drink them selves drunk all the day long and sent for more rum. . . .

3 Thursday. . . . Ben behaved like a blackgarde scoundrel and as if he had been hurred by the devel.

4 Friday. They set sail to go home to my great joy, and I desier I may never se them here again. I greately dread the cleaning of hous after this detested gang. . . .

23 Wednsday. A fine clear morning with a cold north wind. My hearte is burnt with anger and discontent, want of every nessesary thing in life and in constant feare of gapeing credtors comsums my strenth and wasts my days. The horrer of these things with the continuel cross of my famaly, like to so many horse leeches, prays upon my vitals, and if the Lord does not prevent will bring me to the house appointed for all liveing. . . .

[March 25, 1771] Thirsday. Cold wind and cloudy. . . . Justice Townsend is here, writen advertisemants to make a vandue [vendue: public auction]. O Lord, support this famaly in this sene of darkness. O thou didst multiply the widdo's oyl that she might pay her debts. . . .

[May 16, 1771] Thirsday. About 8 or nine a'clock this morning Tom Smith come here and brought a morgage deed and relees, which he with an unhearde impudence rerequired me to sign all. . . .

[December 1772] 21. Moonday. . . . I am up all this night trying fat.

22 Tuesday. . . . I am greately hurred and up all this night boileing souse.

23 Wednsday. . . . I am up all this night makeing candels.

24 Thirsday. . . . I am up all this night cooking and boileing meat for myns pys.

25 Christmas, December the 25 day, Friday. Warme, the sun shine bright and warme. I and Salle [her granddaughter] hurred away to meeten and staide to the night meeten. A very greate white frost and very cold coming home.[5]

CORNELIA BEEKMAN WALTON, widow of merchant William Walton, also had monetary problems. At the beginning of the War, she and her slaves fled her home in New York City ahead of the British, and found refuge in New Jersey. Her husband's loyalist nephews, William and Jacob, remained behind, and were able to deal comfortably with the occupying forces. William moved into her house, though he was to pay her rent as well as the annuity due her. Neither was forthcoming. After waiting patiently many years, and after soliciting legal advice, Cornelia Walton coolly but firmly wrote to demand payment, not only what was owed to her, but also to her emancipated slave Mando and her children.

had the Case been reversed

Dr Nephews   Morris County April 8th 1782
    It is long since I have had an Opportunity of either Seeing or Speaking to you tho I think I have wrote twice to you on the Subject of the Annuity coming to me. And as you cannot but be sensible that after so long an Absence in the Country, continually laying out what I brought with me, I must undoubtedly be compell'd to trouble you with this Line requesting you would be pleased to send me out as much of what (you know) is my just Due, as you at present conveniently can, tho' I cannot but observe that you ought certainly to have anticipated this Request long e'er now, by sending me out such frequent Supplies [of cash], as they became due & as your Circumstances would permit. For you must allow justly that I have been exceedingly easy & silent on this Business for these several Years past, & by no means as pressing as probably you would have been, had the Case been reversed. . . .
    In Expectation of this most reasonable request being Speedily complied with, I remain with Respect to your Families Dr Nephews
                                              Your affectionate Aunt
P.S. Please to send the Cash to the Care of the Honble. Andw. Elliott Esqr now at Elizth Town who will forward the Same to me . . . my annuity has been paid me to the time I left the City, Since which it has been detained.

[On August 28, 1783, she sent William an account of the annuities that Mando and her daughters Suchy, Penny, and Nanny were to receive by the terms of her husband's will. "And as Mando & all her children are shortly going to the Island of Jamaica to live there, I should therefore be well pleased if it would suit you to pay . . . the Annuity now due to them."

Both Jacob and William maintained that it had not been "in our power, since 1776, to fulfill the intention of our Decd. Uncle in his Bequest to you." and, by July 11, 1783, Cornelia Walton was owed £6344.10 in annuities and rent. The nephews prevaricated though a polite communication was maintained between the two sides. When New York's governor, George Clinton, indicated interest in renting her house, Cornelia Walton saw her chance to dislodge William.]

the duty I owe to myself

Dear Nephew   Hanover Morris County November 12 [1783]

I have to inform you, that an Agent of his Excellency Governor Clinton has apply'd to me for the hire of my House, now in your Tenure, to enter immediately on the evacuation of the City by the British Army, & will give a good Rent—Now as you have not paid me any Rent these Eight years last past, tho' you had it at the moderate rate of £120 per year, and by what you wrote me, it appears that you will not be able to pay me any Rent for some time to come, I think it inconsistent with reason that you should have it any longer on such terms, Especially as I can now obtain three or four Hundred Pounds pr Annum for it—Therefore I must insist on your writing to Governor Clinton immediately, in my behalf that he may have said House—on Sir Guy Carlton's departure, and ask such Rent of him as you Judge it now to be worth, or I will submit it to be rated by two or three indifferent Gentleman—

As I am in great want of mony, the duty I owe to myself permits me to insist on your complying with this my just and necessary demand. . . . best Salutations to you and yours . . .   Your affectionate Aunt[6]

MARY JEMISON lived on a farm near Gettysburg, Pennsylvania with her parents and siblings when a raiding party of six Indians and four Frenchmen took them captive on April 5, 1758. Though her two elder brothers were able to escape, her parents and the other children were killed; twelve-year-old Mary was carried off down the Ohio River to a Seneca Indian town. Indians usually took prisoners for a purpose: to use for ransom, to frighten encroaching settlers, or to take the place of a slain relative.

we planted, tended, and harvested our corn

It was my happy lot to be accepted for adoption. At the time of the ceremony I was received by the two squaws to supply the place of their brother in the family; and I was ever considered and treated by them as a real sister, the same as though I had been born of their mother. . . . I was employed in nursing the children, and doing light work about the house. Occasionally, I was sent out with the Indian hunters, when they went but a short distance, to help them carry their game. My situation was easy; I had no particular hardship to endure. . . .

My sisters were diligent in teaching me their language, and to their great satisfaction, I soon learned so that I could understand it readily, and speak it fluently. I was very fortunate in falling into their hands; for they were kind good natured women; peaceable and mild in their dispositions; temperate and decent in their habits, and very tender and gentle toward me. . . .

The town where they lived was pleasantly situated on the Ohio, at the mouth of the Shenanjee. The land produced good corn, the woods furnished a plenty of game, and the waters abounded with fish. . . . We spent the summer at that place, where we planted, hoed, and harvested a large crop of corn, of an excellent quality. . . .

The corn being harvested, the Indians took it on horses and in canoes, and proceeded down the Ohio, occasionally stopping to hunt a few days, till we arrived at the mouth of the Sciota river; where they established their winter quarters, and continued hunting till the ensuing spring, in the adjacent wilderness. . . .

I had . . . been with the Indians four summers and four winters, and had become so far accustomed to their mode of living, habits and disposition, that my anxiety to get away, to be set at liberty, and leave them, had almost subsided. With them was my home; my family was there, and there I had many friends to whom I was warmly attached in consideration of the favors, affection and friendship with which they had uniformly treated me, from the time of my adoption. Our labor was not severe; and that of one year was exactly similar, in almost every respect, to that of the others, without that endless variety that is to be observed in the common labor of the white people. Notwithstanding the Indian women have all the fuel and bread to procure, and the cooking to perform, their task is probably not harder than that of white women, who have those articles provided for them; and their cares certainly are not half as numerous, nor as great. In the summer season, we planted, tended and harvested our corn, and generally had all our children with us; but had no master to oversee or drive us, so that we could work as leisurely as we pleased. We had no plows on the Ohio; but performed the whole process of planting and hoeing with a small tool that resembled, in some respects, a hoe with a very short handle. . . .

Our cooking consisted in pounding our corn into samp or hominy, boiling the hominy, making now and then a cake and baking it in the ashes, and in boiling or roasting our venison. As our cooking and eating utensils consisted of a hominy block and pestle, a small kettle, a knife or two, and a few vessels of bark or wood, it required but little time to keep them in order for use.

Spinning, weaving, sewing, stocking knitting, and the like, are arts which have never been practised in the Indian tribes generally. . . . In the season of hunting, it was our business, in addition to cooking, to bring home the game that was taken by the Indians, dress it, and carefully preserve the eatable meat, and prepare or dress the skins. Our clothing was fastened together with strings of deer skin, and tied on with the same. . . .

One thing only marred my happiness, while I lived with them on the Ohio, and that was the recollection that I had once had tender parents, and a home that

I loved. . . . Notwithstanding all that has been said against the Indians, in consequence of their cruelties to the enemies—cruelties that I have witnessed, and had abundant proof of—it is a fact that they are naturally kind, tender and peaceable towards their friends, and strictly honest; and that those cruelties have been practised only upon their enemies, according to their idea of justice.

[Mary Jemison was married to a Delaware Indian; in 1762, then a widow with a young son, she moved to a town on the Genesee River in New York. She remarried and bore her Seneca husband several children. Forced to flee after the Cherry Valley Massacre and the retaliatory "burn and destroy" tactics used by the Continental Army in the fall of 1779, Mary and her family found themselves without a home or food.]

fearing that I should get taken . . . by the Indians

I immediately resolved to take my children, and look out for myself, without delay. With this intention I took two of my little ones on my back, bade the other three follow, and traveled up the river to the Gardeau Flats [near Castile, New York] where I arrived that night.

At that time, two negroes, who had run away from their masters sometime before, were the only inhabitants of those flats. They lived in a small cabin, and had planted and raised a large field of corn, which they had not yet harvested. As they were in want of help to secure their crop, I hired to them to husk corn till the whole was harvested.

I have laughed a thousand times to myself when I have thought of the good old negro, who hired me, who fearing that I should get taken or injured by the Indians, stood by me constantly when I was husking, with a loaded gun in his hand, in order to keep off the enemy; and thereby lost as much labor of his own as he received from me, by paying good wages. I, however, was not displeased with his attention; for I knew that I should need all the corn that I could earn, even if I should husk the whole. I husked enough for them, to gain for myself, at every tenth string, one hundred strings of ears, which were equal to twenty-five bushels of shelled corn. This seasonable supply made my family comfortable for samp and cakes through the succeeding winter, which was the most severe that I have witnessed.[7]

Indentured Servants

In most families, children became part of the work force as soon as they were able: older daughters would help care for younger ones, boys were sent out to the fields or to learn a trade. Parents, to make ends meet, would often apprentice a child to acquire a marketable skill. Elizabeth Mannin, aged seven, was apprenticed to John Hilson of Philadelphia on July 21, 1772. The indenture stated that she would be "taught housewifery and mantua maker's trade, and make bonnets and cloaks, have one year schooling. To be found all necessaries and at the expiration have freedom dues."[8] Children were also hired to work without indentures, their pay being their room and board.

MARY PALMER, born into a genteel family fallen on hard times, was about fourteen years old when she was hired for a year, in 1789, by Elbridge Gerry and his
wife Ann to assist in tending their four-month-old baby. Gerry had been elected
to the newly formed Congress, and Mary was to travel with the family from
Boston to New York City, the nation's capital.

I was considered a servant

Now you must bear in mind that this was the darkest time in my father's
life. . . . He . . . was clerk in a store with a very small salary; my mother had an
infant in her arms not a year old . . . and five other children besides myself and
Joe, who was gone to sea. You will understand the idea of my going where I
should be appreciated and introduced to some of the first people . . . we were all
persuaded to think it was a fine thing. . . .

Aunt Kate came at the appointed time and took me and my little trunk to
Cambridge, and left me. Mr. Gerry . . . received me with his wonted suavity and
preceded me into a room and presented me to a handsome lady saying, 'Here,
wife, Miss Hunt has brought your little girl.' She turned to me and said, 'How do
you do?' with a pleasant smile, but coldly; turning to a young woman who seemed
to be assisting her packing for the journey asked her to show me up to the nursery,
and where to put my things. All this was so entirely different from what I expected
that my heart sank within me. I saw I was considered a servant. . . . I had long
known, that my father and Mr. Gerry had been intimate friends in the days of our
prosperity, and foolishly expected to be received and treated like the child of an
old friend in adversity. . . . I went with a heavy heart to the nursery, where was a
woman with the baby in her lap, and a little four-year-old girl playing about the
room with her doll. The woman spoke kindly to me . . . and soon asked me to take
the baby, as she had a great deal to do, as the family went on Monday. This was
Saturday. I could tend the baby; that was what I had done ever since I could remember anything, and took it. I could scarcely restrain my tears, I could not speak,
but walked the room with my little charge, till Mrs. Gerry came and told me to go,
with the young woman who entered with her, to the hall where their tea was ready
and she would nurse the babe the while; I suspected this was the servants' hall,
and would not go, saying I did not wish for any tea. They urged me, but I persisted, and went supperless to bed that night. Oh, what would I not have given to
be at home where I had always been loved and petted more than I deserved and
here everyone looked cold and strange towards me; no doubt I behaved very badly
and no one could like me. . . .

The next morning I felt calmer, but dreadful homesick! Again I was told to go
to the hall for breakfast. I went, and was surprised to see a large room with a long
table set, surrounded by domestics of every age and appearance, only they were all
white people. . . . The woman who had the baby, when I first went to the nursery,
sat at the head of the table and presided over the coffee and tea, and a middle-aged
man sat at the foot; these . . . were the housekeeper and steward, who were to take
care of all things till master came back, and appeared decent people, but the rest

were the most vulgar rude set I ever had seen, both in manners and language. I took a little breakfast, and left the table more heartsick than ever.[9]

> [Indentured servants—many of whom emigrated from Ireland— often found it difficult to collect the "freedom dues" they were entitled to at the end of their terms of servitude.]

RUTH MCGEE went to court seeking redress.

should not be detained from her . . . freedom Dues

The Humble Petition of Ruth McGee Humbly sheweth that your petitoner is poor and not Sufficient to Earn her living by reason of a child she hath to maintain, your Petitioners Master Josiah Hibberd refuseing to Let your Petitioner have her freedom Dues Which is mentioned in a pair of Indentures (Viz) A new Suit of Clothes for freedoms and five Pounds in Money and Eight months schooling of which schooling I received but four months and twenty two Days. Likewise your Petitioners Said Master Josiah Hibbard detains your Petitioners cloths that she had whilst she your Petitioner Lived with Said Master that is to say one quilted peticoat Short Gown and Apron. Likewise your Petitioner had seven years and six weeks to serve and your Petitioner had but two months to serve her Said Master Josiah Hibbard When your Petitioner was Sent to the Gaol of this county; furthermore your petitioner having Suffered the rigour of the Law your Petitioner apprehends that she should not be detained from her said freedom Dues but that your Petitioner should [have them] for her Support in this your Petitioner's Poor condition So your Petitioner Layeth this her Humble Petition before your worships for redress of said Grievances and your Petitioner in Duty bound Shall Ever Pray

May the 21st Anno Domini 1774

> [It is unlikely that Ruth McGee prevailed. She admitted to having a child out of wedlock (a crime in Pennsylvania), and had been jailed, probably whipped, as punishment. Quaker Josiah Hibberd was no doubt relieved to be rid of such a troublesome servant.[10]]

ELIZABETH SANDWITH DRINKER and her husband Henry, twenty years later, had to deal with similar behavior by their young black servant, Sally Brant, whose mother had arranged the indenture with the Drinkers.

one of the most handy and best servants we have ever had

[August 8, 1794] . . . I have been for a week past under great anxiety of mind on account of our poor little and I fear miserable S[ally] B[rant]—'tis *possible* I may be mistaken, 'tho I greatly fear the reverse.

11. . . . it was late when I retir'd to my Chamber, and later when I went to sleep—the thoughts of the unhappy Child that lay on a matrass at the foot of my bed, who does not appear to feel half so much for herself, as I do for her, keep't me wakeing. . . . H[enry]. and E[lizabeth] D[rinker]. had a trying Conversation,

if a conversation it could be call'd, with SB—poor poor Girl, who could have thought it? . . .

[October 31, 1794] . . . Sally Johnson and her daughter Franks came here before dinner, on a visit to her daughter SB. they stay'd an hour or two, eat dinner . . . she left herbs to make tea for SB. said it was good to procure an easy [labor]. . . .

[Nov.] 7 . . . I settled matters with Mary [Courtney at 'Clearfield', the Drinker farm 5 or 6 miles outside Philadelphia], concerning our poor Sall, who I intend leaving with her, 'till her grevious business is settld, I look on Mary as a well minded and well disposed woman, and who, with our help, will take the proper care of her. . . .

Decr. 2 . . . S.B. was this morning about 6 o'clock deliver'd of a daughter, the mother and Child both well. . . .

6 . . . Sister [Mary Sandwith] and William went this fore noon . . . found S.B. and her bantling well, Sally weep'd when she saw MS—and cover'd her head with the bed-cloaths—The Child is very Yellow for one so young. . . .

23 Decr. . . . S.B. is very well, and in rather too good spirits, everything considered, she had nam'd the Jaune pettet, [the little yellow one] Hannah G—bs [Gibbs], I disaprovd it, and chang'd it to Catharine Clearfield, with which she appear'd displeas'd. . . .

March 4 [1795] . . . About a mile on this side Clearfield my husband and Sister mett Joe [Gibbs], he had the impudence, as M Courtney told M[ary] S[andwith] to come up into her room, she ask'd him what he wanted, he reply'd, to see something you have got here, and then look'd into the Cradle— she ask'd him if he own'd it, he say'd No, and further this deponent sayeth not. If he had not seen the Child, he had all reason to belive it was his, but the colour was convincing, he had frequently boasted of it, but was fearful of the expences that might accrue. . . .

[April] 19 . . . Sally Johnson here this Afternoon, ask'd if SB could spend a day with her this week, to which I consented, told her of her daughters late conduct wish'd she would take her and Child off our hands, that she had a year to serve from this month, which would have been of more worth to us, had she been a virtuous girl, than any other two years of her time, a girl in her place would cost us 8 or 9/P week, that she is as capable, or perhaps more so, than any one we could hire; I was afraid of her bad example to our other little girl [Sally Dawson] &c—she appeard more angry than griv'd, said she should not care if the childs brains were beat out &c—she would never have anything to do with it—I told her we would make no account of the expences we had already been at of Sallys laying in and board, the childs nursing since &c. She said she would take her daughter provided they, nither of 'em, should ever have any thing to do with the Child—she went away rather out of humor—

When HD. come home we related the above to him, concluded were we to turn her off, upon her mothers terms, she would be in the high road to further ruin—he call'd her into the parlor this evening and talk'd closely to her, told her he had a right to send her to the work house and sell her for a servent, that it was in pity to her, and in hopes of her reformation that he did not send Joe to prision,

she had always had a good example in our house, if she did not mend her conduct she should not stay much longer in it &c. she cry'd but said nothing—How
it will end, or what we shall do with her, I know not, set aside this vile propen-
sity, she is one of the most handy and best servants we have ever had—and a
girl of very pritty manners.

[By the middle of the following month, the "poor little yellow one"
was boarded with a "Negro woman in the Neighborhood 'till we can
otherwise dispose of it." On July 2, 1795, Elizabeth Drinker was informed "that poor little Caty was dead—Jacob Morris, a black boy,
whose Mother had her to nurse brought the note, and came for a Shroud
to bury her in." Sally Brant, when told, "shed a few tears, but all, appeard to be got over in a little time after."]

[April 12, 1796] . . . Sally Johnson came to day, she very willingly agree'd to
Sallys staying with us two months longer as we shall be cleaning house &c—she
is, I expect, sensible, that we might, if inclined so to do, oblidge her to serve us
near a year longer for the expences we have been at on her and Childs account,
instead of giving her freedom Cloaths &c—I wish the poor girl may do well
when she leaves us. She has behaved herself better for a month or two past than
for a long time before. Whether it is to get the more from us, or whether she is
actualy better I know not, but must hope for the best.

[Sally Brant did leave the Drinker family but stayed in touch with
one of the other young servants—"S. Brant took tea with our Sally
Dawson" noted Elizabeth Drinker tersely on May 17, 1803.[11]]

MARY WHITE MORRIS felt some sympathy upon hearing of the extreme measures some immigrant servants willingly endured—for the benefit of the wealthy,
but to their own detriment—just to be able to purchase the bare essentials of life.

afforded the Lady's opportunityes of Supplying Themselves

[Philadelphia] novr 29 [1784]
The fashion most in vogue here at present is having teeth Transplanted,
Mrs. [Margaret Cadwalader] Merideth I saw Yesterday on Her back; She had
gone through the operation two days before of haveing two put in, & intends
having a Third, The number of Irish servants that have arrive'd this fall have
from their necessityes afforded the Lady's opportunityes of Supplying Themselves. I hope that there is no american whose necessityes are so Desperate as to
be induced by 6 Guineas to part with what is so valuable.[12]

[Most terrible was the fate of Hannah Ocuish, a twelve-year-old
Pequot Indian, who, removed from her parents' care at an early age,
was an indentured servant to Widow Rogers near New London, Connecticut. In a dispute over "some patchwork" with six-year-old Eunice
Bolles, Hannah beat the younger girl to death on July 21, 1786; she was
hanged six months later.[13]]

Slaves

Not only indentured servants but also slaves could augment a family's work force. The prevalence of slavery caused Patrick M'Robert, a well-educated Scot visiting New York mid-1774 to comment, "It rather hurts an European eye to see so many negro slaves upon the streets . . . there are computed between twenty-six and thirty thousand inhabitants in the city . . . include[ing] the slaves, who make at least a fifth part of the number."[14] His comment might equally have applied to Rhode Island, where blacks constituted six percent of the population, Newport being a major slave port, or Connecticut with three percent. The numbers were lower in the rest of New England.[15]

CHRISTIAN ARBUTHNOT BARNES, who taught select young ladies the art of fine needlework and millinery, had at least two female slaves, Juliet and Daphne. Mrs. Barnes seems to have treated them with consideration. It was, however, Daphne's son Prince who, though owned by a different family, piqued her interest, as she recounted with some pride to her widowed friend Elizabeth Murray Smith. Or was it envy—for Mrs. Smith, a wealthy business woman, had just had her portrait painted by the preeminent artist of the time, John Singleton Copley.

nothing but a Daub

My Dear Friend   Marlborough [Massachusetts], Nov. 20, 1769
   Daphneys Son Prince is here and I am siting to him for my Picture. He has taken a Coppy of my Brothers extremely well and if mine has the least resemblance I shall have a strong inclination to send it to you purely for the curiosity, tho it is nothing but a Daub for he has not proper materials to work with. If I had your fortune I would send it to you done by the Best hand.

   [On December 23, 1769, she continued to her friend, who had gone
   to Scotland to visit family:]

so much for my Domesticks of the lower order

   Mr. Barnes has lately made a purchas of Prince not solely with a Veiw of Drawing my Picture but I beleive he has some design of improving his Genus in painting, and as soon as he has procured material you shall have a sample of his performance.
   Daphney apears to be much better reconciled to a State of Slavery Since her Sons arrival. Upon the whole I believe there is not a Happier Set of Negros in any Kitchen in the Provence and so much for my Domesticks of the lower order.

   [Mrs. Barnes, though unwilling "to be at any expence on his account till I find other Peoples Judgment concur with mine," did seek ways to further the young man's talent, and considered sending him to Copley for lessons.]

the force of natural Genius

Marlborough, March 13, 1770

My little Girl [Chrisy] has been confined all Winter with a fever ocation'd as we suppose by Worms and I my self have been greatly afflicted with an Aigue in my face . . . My Hospital is a long warm Chamber where I am Seated before a good fire with Caty [Goldthwaite, Mr. Barnes's niece] on one side of me dealing out her Sentimentals, Chrisy on the other entertaining me with her inocent pratle, Prince is fix'd in one corner of the room improving himself in the Art of Painting. . . .

Were I only to descant on the Qualifications of my Limner it would be a Subject for several Sheets. He is a most surprising instance of the force of natural Genius for without the least instruction or improvment he has taken several Faces which are thought to be very well done. He has taken a Coppy of my Picture which I think has more of my resemblance than Coplings [Copley]. He is now taking his own face which I will certainly send you as it must be valued as a curiosity by any Friend you shall please to bestow it upon. We are at great loss for proper materials, at Present he has workd only with Crayons [pastels] and them very bad ones, and we are so ignorant as not to know what they are to be laid on. He has hetherto used Blue Paper but I think something better may be found out. If you should meet in your Travils with any one who is a Proficient in the art I wish you would make some inquerys into these perticulas, for people in general think Mr. Copling will not be willing to give him any instruction, and you know there is nobody else in Boston that does any thing at the Business— you could imploy some Friend who is a Judge of these things to purchas a Small assortment of Crayons with other materials proper for the Business that he may be kept imploy'd in this way till he has made some further improvement, and then I intend to Exhibit him to the Publick and don't doubt he will do Honour to the profession.

You Laugh now and think this is one of Mr. Barnes Scheems, but you are quite mistaken it is intirely my own, and as it is the only one I ever ingag'd in I shall be greatly disapointed if it does not succeed. I cannot dismis this Subject without acquainting you that this surprising Genious has every qualification to render him a good Servent, Sober deligent and Faithfull, and I believe as he was Born in our family he is of Tory Principles, but of that I am not quite so certain as he had not yet declar'd himself.

[Soon after, politics and escalating tensions between Whigs and Tories distracted Christian Barnes. Her enthusiastic support of her talented slave came to an end when the family left for Bristol, England, in March 1776, never to return. Daphney and Prince remained behind in Marlborough with Catherine Goldthwait, who hoped by her presence to save her uncle's estate. A portrait of Chrisy drawn by Prince was left with Daphney, apparently still alive in 1784. And what became of the young artist? Mrs. Barnes, in muted tones, reported on June 16, 1783, that Prince "I hear is provided for and so we shall all be in time." How he died is unknown, his portraits lost.[16]]

Life for most slaves was hard—Prince's treatment an exception. Viewed as property by their owners, slaves were poorly clothed and fed, separated from their kin, often ill treated, and forced to labor long hours. It is not surprising that many made repeated attempts to run away. Though men were more likely to try to escape, sixty-four out of 250 runaways during the War in New York and New Jersey were women.[17]

In the South, slaves and their progeny lived in perpetual bondage under brutal conditions, laboring on rice and tobacco plantations. The following advertisement is typical of the many that appeared in newspapers during the second half of the eighteenth century, and clearly reflects the desperation of enslaved people, who, in spite of overwhelming odds, persisted in their attempts to escape.

> Fifteen Pounds Reward, RAN away from the subscriber in Dinwiddie, at the time of Arnold's invasion, and supposed to have joined the British at Portsmouth, a large black fellow named NED, about 35 years of age, 6 feet high, well made, and is a fiddler. Also a mulatto wench named Phaebe, about 40 years of age, slender made, her skin covered with large spots of a dark color, resembling morphew [leprous, scaly eruptions of the skin], branded many years ago, with the letters MI on her cheeks, but now hardly discernable; she is very talkative, and pretends to know everything. She has attempted to pass for a free woman formerly, and took the name of Sukey Valentine, which name she will probably assume again. I will give Ten Pounds reward for the fellow, and Five Pounds for the wench, upon delivery. . .   JAMES GREENWAY[18]

EVE was one of twenty-seven slaves owned by the widow Elizabeth Harrison Randolph of Williamsburg, Virginia, and deemed one of the most valuable, indicating that she was a skillful young woman. She also had children. Apparently heeding Lord Dunmore's offer of "freedom to any slaves who desert rebellious masters," Eve and seven other slaves fled to the British before January 5, 1776. She was either caught or returned voluntarily—perhaps to be with her family—for in her owner's will (October 1780), there, among the "new Tea spoons four Silver Saucers all my wearing Cloths," is listed "a Negro woman named Eve and her son George" to be given to a niece. In a codicil to the will (July 20, 1782), Elizabeth Randolph added: "Whereas Eve's bad behaviour laid me under the necessity of selling her, I order and direct the money she sold for may be laid out in purchasing . . . a Boy & Girl, the Girl I give to my niece . . . in lieu of Eve." One of the witnesses to the codicil was James Madison.[19]

CORNELIA VAN CORTLANDT BEEKMAN, watching over her family's property in Peekskill, New York, after her father Pierre had fled to Rhinebeck for safety during the early years of the War, informed him how she had discovered a plan by their slaves to run away to the British at the next opportunity. What the consequences were for Jin, Libe, Margery, Brigit, and Sair is not known.

thay where all to go off

My Dear Papa   April Monday 12th 1777
    Yesterday went to Croten, the first person I saw there was Jin I askd her where she came from, She told me from Singsing. I taxd [scolded] her very

Strickt about her going to town. She sais She Never went farther than the Dock at Grahams, her heart failed to go alone with Edward Terhune, by Crying and beging he sat her a Shore. She went up the river till above our mill there fordd the river then went to our house again, and was Conseald by brigit for four weeks in the kitchen Garrit. . . . Margery was up hear in that time and I told her I had heard that Jin had been conceald at our house . . . Margery went home and told Jin that I had heard of her and that She should Stay no longer their . . . She Stayd in the woods and fed on what she got at the Stoore house untill fryday and in that Storm of rain She came to our house . . . I askd her what was the meaning of her being Conceald So long. She Said that when the row Gally Came up thay where all to go off with it and She had heard that the row Gally men weare to set our hous a fire. . . . She also Said that if Sair was not willing to go with them, and brigit Maid it her buisiness to Come up hear and tell Sair and Dine (a negro girl I have hird) that if I retreat again that they should not go with me but come to her as soon as they heard that the regulars where come again, Dine was the person that made the first discovery to me of the intention of our people to go off so soon for thay wantd her to go too, She told brother Phill [Philip Van Cortlandt] word for word as She told me when he Examind her about it, but we booth promistd her that She Shall not be hurt for bringing the plot out of their wickd intentions, thus far their Skeames have provd abortive, and I trust the Lord will pertect us farther and not Suffer our Enemey with their wicked plots to over Come us.[20]

KITTY belonged to Susannah Ferguson Brown of New Providence, the Bahamas, but had been sent to live with Susannah's widowed daughter-in-law, Sophia Waterhouse Brown, in Perth Amboy, New Jersey. Separated from her parents and a daughter Cicily, Kitty asked Sophia to send a message home.

she is very serviceable

August 1st, 1791

Kitty says I must tell you she has been very sick, five weeks no clean the house [nor] the clothes, no eat the victuals no do nothing, she say I must tell you she wants to see you very much & her Daddy Essex her Mamme & all the rest she now seems recovered & I hope will have no relaps & I am sure I have great reason to be thankful, she is very serviceable.[21]

ONEY JUDGE, a slave in the household of George and Martha Washington, was the daughter of a dower slave Betty and a white indentured servant Andrew Judge. She probably was taught needlework by her seamstress mother, her handiwork highly regarded. By the time the fifteen-year-old Oney and six other slaves accompanied President Washington and his family to New York, she was Martha Washington's personal maid.

When the capital of the new nation moved to Philadelphia, the First Family rented a large house with rooms on the second floor "sufficient for the accomodations of Mrs. Washington & the children & their maids" including Oney. Account books make mention of some of the expenses for the slaves: in February

1791, Martha Washington gave "Austin, Hercules [the cook], Moll & Oney 1 doll[ar] each & Chris. ½ doll. to buy things to send home" and, on June 6, 1792, gave money to "Austin, Hercules & Oney to go to the Play." Going to the theater was a pastime the Washingtons greatly enjoyed.[22]

Though treated relatively well, Washington's slaves were not free, their lives otherwise constrained. To circumvent Pennsylvania's 1780 law, which provided for the emancipation of slaves of citizens after a six-month residency, George Washington routinely sent the male slaves back home to Virginia. He was not willing to risk the loss of his wife's dower slaves, particularly as he would have had to reimburse her estate for them. Oney and Moll, however, were trusted, and seem to have had some freedom of movement in the city. Oney met and befriended free blacks who hid her when, faced with returning to Mount Vernon in 1796, she made her escape from the President's house. In an interview fifty years later, she gave her reasons:

did not want to be a slave always

[She said] that she was a chamber maid for Mrs. Washington, that she was a large girl at the time of the revolutionary war, that when Washington was elected President, she was taken to Philadelphia, and that, although well enough used as to work and living, she did not want to be a slave always, and she supposed if she went back to Virginia, she would never have a chance to escape.

[Oney Judge was able to secure passage on a ship bound for Portsmouth, New Hampshire. Did the captain know he had a fugitive slave aboard? Abetting a fleeing slave was considered a crime. Attempts were made to find her, Martha Washington even urging her husband to offer a reward for the runaway's return, which he refused to do. When Oney was seen by a family friend in Portsmouth, Washington renewed his efforts to capture his wife's slave.

Living with a free black family, Oney had begun a new life, working as a seamstress. In early 1797, she married Jack Staines. Oney recollected the frightening attempts to return her to the life she had fled.]

with orders to take her by force

After she was married, and had one child, while her husband was gone to sea, Gen. Washington sent on a man by the name of Bassett [Burwell Bassett Jr., Washington's nephew], *to prevail on her to go back.* He saw her, and used all the persuasion he could, but she utterly refused to go with him. He returned, and then came again, *with orders to take her by force,* and carry her back. He put up with the late Gov. [John] Langdon, and made known his business, and the Governor gave her notice that she must leave Portsmouth that night, or she would be carried back. She went to a stable, and hired a boy, with a horse and carriage, to carry her to Mr. [John] Jack's, at Greenland, where she now resides, a distance of eight miles, and remained there until her husband returned from sea, and Bassett did not find her.

She says that she never received the least mental or moral instruction of any kind while she remained in Washington's family. But, after she came to Portsmouth, she learned to read. . . . She says that the stories told of Washington's piety and prayers, so far as she ever saw or heard while she was his slave, *have no foundation*. Card-playing and wine-drinking were the business at his parties, and he had more of such company Sundays than on any other day.[23]

[Although Oney Judge Staines eluded capture, her life proved more difficult than the one she had left. She outlived her husband and three children by many years, and died a pauper in 1848. Did she regret her decision to run away? "No, I am free, and have, I trust, been made a child of God by the means."[24]]

ELIZABETH, or MUM BETT, also ran away, though she did not run far. Born in Claverack, New York, she was sold at an early age to Colonel John Ashley, a judge and prominent citizen of Sheffield, Massachusetts, and served in that family for many years. Illiterate, she listened and took an interest in the discussions that she overheard in the house: on the right to personal liberty, that all persons were "born free and equal," crucial ideas that would be included in the new constitution of Massachusetts of 1780. Mum Bett would remember them. By 1781, she was a widow with a young daughter and still enslaved, when an incident occurred that changed her life forever. Mum Bett and her younger sister were working when their mistress, Hannah Hogeboom Ashley,

in a fit of passion . . . struck at the weak and timid girl with a heated kitchen shovel; Mum Bett interposed her arm, and received the blow; and she bore the honorable scar it left to the day of her death. The spirit of Mum Bett had not been broken by ill usage—she resented the insult and outrage as a white person would have done. She left the house, and neither commands nor entreaties could induce her to return. Her master, Col. Ashley, resorted to the law to regain possession of his slave.[25]

When Bett fled the house, she went to the nearby law office of Theodore Sedgwick, and persuaded him to represent her and a fellow slave, Brom. In *Brom & Bett v. J. Ashley, Esq.*, Sedgwick and Tapping Reeve of Litchfield, Connecticut, argued in the county court that the bill of rights in the Massachusetts constitution applied to the defendants and made them free (May 1781). The jury agreed and ordered Ashley to pay thirty shillings in damages to Mum Bett, who took the last name of Freeman. She became a valued member of the Sedgwick household. Catherine, one of the children, described what Mum Bett was like.

Truth was her nature—the offspring of courage and loyalty

Mumbet had a clear and nice perception of justice, and a stern love of it, an uncompromising honesty in word and deed, and conduct of high intelligence, that made her the unconscious moral teacher of the children she tenderly nursed. . . . Truth was her nature—the offspring of courage and loyalty. In my childhood I clung to her with instinctive love and faith, and the more I know and observe of human nature, the higher does she rise above others, whatever may have been their instruction or accomplishment. . . .

Her expressions of feeling were simple and comprehensive. When she suddenly lost a beloved grandchild, the only descendant of whom she had much hope—she was a young mother, and died without an instant's warning—I remember Mumbet walking up and down the room with her hands knit together and great tears rolling down her cheeks, repeating, as if to send back into her soul its swelling sorrow, "Don't say a word; it's God's will!" And when I was sobbing over my dead mother, she said, "We must be quiet. Don't you think I am grieved? Our hair has grown white together."[26]

[On October 18, 1829, Elizabeth Freeman made her mark on her will, leaving her possessions, including a gown she had received from her African father, to her daughter Elizabeth, her granddaughter Marianne Dean, and great-grandchildren. She was buried in what is called the Sedgwick Pie in the Stockbridge, Massachusetts cemetery, memorialized by the family who loved her.]

ELIZABETH FREEMAN
known by the name of
MUMBET
died Dec. 28 1829.
Her supposed age
was 85 Years.
She was born a slave and
remained a slave for nearly
thirty years. She could neither read nor write yet in
her own sphere she had no
superior nor equal. She neither wasted time nor property.
She never violated a trust, nor
failed to perform a duty.
In every situation of domestic trial, she was the most effi
cient helper, and the tenderest
friend. Good mother Fare well.[27]

COINCOIN, the name given to Marie Thérèze when she was born in 1742, achieved her freedom in a different manner. Her African parents, slaves belonging to Louis Juchereau de St. Denis of Natchitoches, Louisiana, taught their daughter the use of medicinal herbs and roots, and possibly their native African dialect in addition to French and Spanish.

At age seventeen, Coincoin was inherited by a St. Denis family member, and bore her first child; three more followed in rapid succession, father unknown. Eight years later, she was rented to Claude Thomas Metoyer, a trader originally from La Rochelle, France. She served him "well and faithfully," bearing him ten children between 1768 and 1784. Legally, they were the property of Coincoin's owner, but Metoyer was able to purchase some of them. The "Code Noir," the law against miscegenation, caused the couple much trouble, still their cohabitation continued.

Although manumitted in 1778, it was not until 1786 that Coincoin's true independence began. That year, Metoyer married a white woman, but gave Coincoin a parcel of land and an annuity for support. Coincoin, helped by her children, became a prosperous plantation owner, sending tobacco, hides, and jars of bear-grease to the markets of New Orleans. During the ensuing years, she acquired more land, paid taxes, supported her church, and owned slaves. Most important, she was able to purchase the freedom of her own enslaved children with her hard-earned wealth.[28]

Leisure

Few housewives, even those with servants, had much leisure time. Overseeing the daily activities, working in the house or fields, often pregnant and surrounded by children, women needed to wait until all were asleep for any quiet time—to read or to write a letter. In communicating with their husbands in New York and Philadelphia respectively, Mary Fish Silliman in Connecticut found time after ten in the evening or before six in the morning, while Mary Bartlett in New Hampshire relied on her daughters to write down her dictation.

When possible, part of the daily routine was making visits, either as a social activity or to accomplish a task with other women, assisting at a child's birth, for example. This social network allowed women to get work done, yet establish supportive relationships with others. Fifteen-year-old Elizabeth Foote of Colchester, Connecticut, was employed by neighbors to weave or spin, but friends might come to help her out: (April 13, 1775) "Thursday 13 I made a gown for Mrs. Wells and about noon went to Mr. Jones, from thence to Mr. Otis's and Hannah came home with me to work and we fixed our wheels to spin linen and Mrs. Wells owed me 7s 6d for my work being 7 per day."[29]

Church attendance was another opportunity to break the tedium of a day, to exchange news, to provide information, to empathize with each other. Visiting undoubtedly strengthened the bonds of female kinship.

JANE FRANKLIN MECOM, seventy-four-years old, and living in somewhat straitened circumstances, described her day to her brother Benjamin in Philadelphia.

a Friend sitts and chats a litle

My dear Brother   Boston Janr 8–1788

I have a good clean House to Live in, my Granddaughter constantly to atend me to do whatever I desier in my own way & in my own time, I go to bed Early, lye warm & comfortable, Rise Early to a good Fire, have my Brakfast directly and Eate it with a good Apetite and then Read or work or what Els I Pleas, we live frugaly, Bake all our own Bread, brew small bear, lay in a litle cyder, Pork,

Buter, &c. & suply our selves with Plenty of other nesesary Provision Dayly at
the Dore. We make no Entertainments, but some Times an Intimate Acquaintance will come in and Pertake with us the Diner we have Provided for our selves
& a Dish of Tea in the After Noon, & if a Friend sitts and chats a litle in the
Evening we Eate our Hasty Puding (our comon super) after they are gone.[30]

ELIZABETH PORTER PHELPS of Hadley, Massachusetts, was married in 1770 to
Charles Phelps, a farmer and lawyer. In a weekly journal, she noted the sermons
she heard, the visits she made and received, and the events that occurred in the
town where she lived her whole life. She owned two slaves as well as bond servants to help her with her household tasks.

I into town of arrands

[1782] March 10. Sun. Mr. Hop[kins] pr[eached] Job 4 and 21. Doth not their
excellency which is in them go away and they Die even without hope. Monday
Lodemi Ingraham a visit here. Tuesday our Shoe-makers Left us. I a visit at
Brother Warners. Fryday Mr. Yeomans here to fix the Clock. . . . Satterday I
into town of arrands. . . .

March 31. Sun. Mr. Hop. pr. Acts 2 and 40. Save your selves from this untoward
generation—I tarried at home in the fore-noon and my Husband went up to Northampton. . . . drank tea at Cousin Cooks—on my way home met Mr. Hibbard
going for Mrs. Montague his wife in travel [travail/labor], I came home, Mrs.
Alixander had come here for a good visit. She and I rode up—found Mrs. Hibbard poorly—a Little before 12 had a son born—all comfortable after day we
got home. . . .

May 26. Sun. Mr. Lyman pr[eached] Psalm 84 and 4. pr. much about attendance
at public worship . . . Monday we had a great number of men here to raise a new
Barn, move an old one and a House—all done and safely thro the mercy of God.
Sister Warner here all the woman that came.[31]

SARAH EVE of Philadelphia poked fun in her journal at some of the rituals required by society. The daughter of Oswell Eve, a sea captain who was away for
long periods of time, the red-headed Sarah was always fashionably dressed.

One hates to be always kissed

[1773] February 26th—As fine a day as in April. In the morning Dr. [William]
Shippen came to see us. What a pity it is that the Doctor is so fond of kissing; he
really would be much more agreeable if he were less fond. One hates to be always kissed, especially as it is attended with so many inconveniences; it decom-
poses the economy of one's *hankerchief* [fabric worn to fill in the neckline], it
disorders one's *high Roll* [hair dress], and it ruffles the serenity of one's countenance; in short the Doctor's, or a sociable kiss is many times worse than a formal salute with bowing and curtseying, to "this is Mr. Such-an-one, and this
Miss What-do-you-call her." 'Tis true this confuses one no little, but one gets
the better of that sooner than to readjust one's dress. . . .

March 27th—A fine day, but still windy . . . In the afternoon Mr & Mrs Garriguse, Hannah Mitchell, Mr. Roberts, Mr. Rush (bless me, what a girl, Mr. Rush should have been set down first, I am sure, but now it is too late), and Mr. J. Giles drank Tea with us.[32]

> [Sarah's giddy comment refers to Dr. Benjamin Rush, who had begun courting her. They were to have been married at the end of 1774, but she died three weeks before their wedding. Rush, in his autobiography, does not mention her.]

SARAH BARD accompanied her aunt Sarah DeNormandie Barton and her husband Reverend Thomas Barton to Lancaster, Pennsylvania, when he was given a pulpit there. Paying visits was part of the ritual of welcome.

its Customary here to send cards

Lancaster 17th January 1776

[After a difficult journey] Wednesday which was the day we were expected many of the Gentlemen came out to meet us, but it was Thursday evening before we got there . . . In the night we were waked with a most delightful Serenade under the window consisting of two Violins, one flute, and a hautboy played extreamly well, a Compliment to Mr. and Mrs. Barton. Saturday Mr. Barton was visited by all the Gentlemen of the place; its Customary here to send cards to all those you would wish to come and have an elegant Collation served up at twelve Clock with wine punch, &c—Yesterday Aunt made her appearance and today she receives company.

Would you believe that our Church music at Lancaster exceeds any thing you ever heard, It is entirely Vocal and performed by Soldiers [British] who have been used to sing in Cathedrals. Their voices are really heavenly, so much melody I never heard before; when they begin to sing the whole congregation rise. Uncle Barton has raised a subscription for them and they are to sing every Sunday.[33]

> [Not only were visits in elite circles carefully arranged according to etiquette—much attention was given to who visited whom first—but one's dress also had to conform to the reigning fashion.]

HARRIET WADSWORTH, the sixteen-year-old daughter of Jeremiah Wadsworth and Mehitable Russell of Hartford, Connecticut, wrote her mother a careful description of the fashions. One feature paid homage to the successful flights of a new invention, the Montgolfier hot-air balloon.

the most fashionable head Dress is a Balloon hat

[New York City] March 17, 1785

I will now write a little about the Fashions which are very numerous. The young Ladies of my age wear larg Queens Caps, in the morning at home. If they go out to pay morning visits they ware Some kind of Silk gown larg white Sattin Bonnets and long Cardnals—mine is white Sattin trimmed with white furr—at home when they receive Company they Ither ware half-Dress Caps—or pin

Gaus [gauze] on their heads but most Commonly the former. Hoops at all times, but Small ones in the morning—at the Assembleys they ware full Dress Corsser [corsage] flowers, Gaus and feathers As their fancy directs. When they pay afternoon visits, the most fashionable head Dress is a Balloon hat or Levena Bonnet—Some wear half Dress Caps, the Levene Bonnet I think very becoming.[34]

[Dances, concerts, and the theater were also sources of entertainment, though the last, in particular, was frowned upon by many. Games, such as cards or chess, enjoyed great popularity.]

MARY WHITE MORRIS regaled her friend Catharine Livingston with a description of the latest musical event in Philadelphia.

the best I ever heard

April 3rd 1781

We had a concert on Tuesday last, & by much the best I ever heard, it Consisted of 12 Musicianers. We have had here all the winter a very capitol Performer on the flute, far superior to any we have ever heard before & equal's any in Europe.[35]

MARTHA DAINGERFIELD BLAND of Virginia was also in Philadelphia, as her husband was a member of Congress. She kept her sister-in-law Frances Bland Randolph Tucker informed of the "Gay Scenes" of that city.

high life below stairs!

Fairy Hill March 30th, 1781

You would wonder, who used to call me domestic, to see me so deeply enter into the dissipation of the place and yet I am but moderate in Comparison.... oh my dear such a swarm of french beaux, Counts, Viscounts, Barons & Chevaliers, among the latter—the Chevalier de la Luzern the Minister of france is my great favorite: he is one of the most amiable, the politest, easiest behav'd Men I ever knew. . . .

Yesterday we left the Noise & Smoak of the city and took possession of a Country Seat—the Seat of the fairies . . . it is 4 miles from the city on the bank of the Schulekill delightfully situated, amidst scenes for every disposition here is art abundantly display'd, & Nature in her rudest shape. . . . 'tis called Fairy Hill, & a very applicable name. I shall expect to see them dance in the garden by moonlight. . . .

We had an oratorio at the Minister's last Tuesday, it was very clever—he gives a Ball one week, a concert the next—the characters in the oratorio were Minerva, the Genius of france, of America, and the high Priest of Minerva by Miss Bond, a little snub nosed Girl about four feet high sings very smartly for a Philadelphian— & with Great Boldness—the Genius of france [by] a Mr. Brown who sings delightfully; the genius of America by Mr. Dick Peters of the board of War; the high Priest [by] a Mr. Bache son-in-law to Dr. Franklin . . . the Minister sacrifices his time to the policy of the french Court—he dislikes Music, never dances, and is a domestick Man yet he has a Ball or a Concert every week and his house full to dinner every day.

We had a Play performed by the Students in the College a few weeks ago, when there was the greatest crowd I ever saw. I went accompany'd by Mr. Marboys & Mr. Otto, the two *petit ministers* of france, Don Francisco, the Spanish Minister, and Miss [Nancy] Shippen. We went at 5 o'clock but found several hundred people in the Yard waiting for the opening of the dores. . . . [Later] when we returned, we found the dores open'd and the people climbing up the Walls to get in. Some mounted upon the heads of others and in short, such a mob that it is impossible to describe; if [British actor David] Garrick had been to perform it could not have been greater—Mr. Marboy took hold of one of my arms, don francisco of the other, Miss Shippin of his and Mr. Otto of hers— in this manner we attempted to get through the crowd—They forced us about half way the passage but I was all most suffocated and declared I would not go up the Stairs. A large woman broke our chain by forcing Mr. Marboy's hand from mine—our little party retired to a room in the College untill the Hurly Burly was over, and then went up into the Gallery.

We took possession of a Seat where we could neither hear or see anything upon the Stage and were unenvied, but I was more entertained at the Nature of Man & Woman than I could have been at the finest performed play in Europe: Governor's Ladys, presidents ladys, tallow chandlers and Cake women, shoe maker's wives & members of Congress—all setting Caps for the best places and pushing each other down for a little Air, it unluckily was the warmest night we have had—one lady loss'd her Cap, another her drop curls, another her shoes, another her Hat, in short such a scene I believe was never exhibited in America—a [Pennsylvania] Chief Justices Lady seized a Gentleman who was in her way, by the que [queue] of his hair, and broke her fan over his head—a presidents Lady fainted three times—and lossd her Cap—at last was pulled through a little trap door about as large as a chariot window . . . oh Fanny! what woud I give to have you in a corner at Some of those scenes of *high life below stairs!* . . .

Well now my dear, am I not very good to send you such a long letter, or rather you will be very good to have patience to read it.[36]

SUSANNAH JAUNCEY VARDILL WILLETT was apparently a good chess player. Though politely denying any talent, she flirtatiously accepted General Tadeusz Kościuszko's challenge to a game.

my fame *as a Chess player*

[September 1797]

It is suffitient to Conquer! generous minds never exult. The victory over General Gates & [von] Stuben, was not superior Play, but their politeness that gave me the superiority at Chess.

To receive a lesson from General Kusciusko, will be doing me a great favor and I am willing to sacrifice my *fame* as a Chess player if it can possibly contribute to his amusement one half hour—but I must pray his indulgence as I have not been in the habit of playing for many Months.

Shou'd our intentions not be prevented we intend drinking Tea with Mrs. [Mary] Gates this afternoon—You know, General I must say a civil word to *Mary*—or at some lone hour when *Spectre's Walk*, the men may *haunt* me for my attachment to you.   S.W.[37]

HANNAH HARRISON THOMSON, related to prominent Quaker families in Philadelphia, had married Charles Thomson, secretary to the Continental Congress (1774-1789), when she was forty-five. Hannah joined her husband when Congress met in New York in 1785 and lived there until his retirement in 1789. She, of course, paid the required visits and sent amusing stories or gossip about the city to a young cousin, John Mifflin, in exchange for his about her hometown.

I wish . . . you would come & eat yr Christmas dinner here

Dec. 12—[17]86

I have recd friend Johns letter after a very long silence. Am glad to hear of his Corpulancy. Fleshy Folks are apt to grow Indolent which I hope my Correspondent will guard against, and instead of the flesh Brush [brush intended for the body, for ailments like dropsy] which Physicians advise in that case, take up the Pen and exert the Imagination and rather than miss a Post, miss a Dinner. . . .

I am now at this Present writing a prisoner. Piles of Snow on each side of all our street only a narrow passage beaten in most all the streets. They visit, Jaunt, & go to Church in Sleighs. . . . I am afraid of meeting those flying machines in some of those narrow places. To keep out of danger, I stay at home. A few days ago, two Gentlemen were driving thro one of those narrow places with high banks of Snow on each side, they saw a Sleigh coming full tilt, the Horses had taken fright and disputed the way with all they met. The Gentlemen thought it the wisest way to save themselves to jump out of their Sleigh & leave their Horses to contend with each other, which they did, one droped down dead, and the other 3 almost dead. And so ended their frolick.

I wish cousin Isaac and you would come & eat yr Christmas dinner here. I will give you as good mince pies & as fat a turkey as you can procure either from Molly Newport on Market Street [Philadelphia]. You wd be delighted with the Visiting parties a wishing a happy New Year to each other and eating of *Cukies*, a little cake made for the occasion.

[Disappointed that they did not accept her invitation, Hannah continued on December 28:]

do give us a Slaying

I suppose Aunt Norris for your entertainment, on Christmas Day, told you of the Slaying [sleighing] match that Mr. Houston in Second Street gave his Daughters. Dear Papa dear Papa do give us a Slaying—at last he consented, told them to get ready and dress themselves warm, Which they accordingly did and came running. We are ready papa; he ordered the Servants to have some burnt Wine against they came back. He desired them to step up stairs with him before they went; as soon as they got into an Attick Chamber, he threw up all the windows, and seated them in two old Arm Chairs and begun to Whip & Chirrup with all the Spirit of a slaying party. And after he had kept them long enough to be sufficiently Cold, he took them down & cald for the Mulled Wine, and were all very glad to sit close to the fire and leave Slaying to those that were too Warm.

Compliments of the Season to Cousin Isaac & yourself, and send you each a Cookey as you wont come here to eat them.[38]

SARAH LIVINGSTON JAY, upon her return from Europe, found little leisure time, especially as her husband John had been elected by the Continental Congress to the post of secretary for foreign affairs. She aided him in his diplomatic duties by inviting the foremost politicians and influential people to dinner. During the years 1787 and 1788, Sarah kept a small sheaf of papers on which she wrote the names of their guests in her fine handwriting. While it is unknown what dishes were served, one guest, Abigail Adams Smith, wrote her mother that "dinner was *à la Française*, and exhibited more of European taste than I expected to find"—meaning that the dishes were placed on the table and passed around. These were exciting years politically and, no doubt, the Jays asked people of different points of view to talk with one another over a good dinner, an eighteenth-century version of networking.

Invited for the 12th Feb. [Tues.1788]

The President of Congress	Sir John Temple
Count de Moustier	Lady Do
marchioness	Mr. Van Berkel
mr. de la Foresst	Miss Do
mrs. D[itt]o	Chancellors
mr. Otto	Col. Wadsworth
mr. Gardoqui	Chaumont
mr. St. John	DuPont
miss Do	Captn. Frigate.[39]

HARRIOTT PINCKNEY HORRY of South Carolina did not have a guest list but did have a "receipt" or recipe book, begun in 1770, two years after her marriage. The book included recipes she transcribed from her mother Eliza Pinckney as well as those she gathered from other sources, changed or improved over the years. Besides a keen interest in her vegetable garden, "the management of a Dairy is an amusement she has been always fond of, and 'tis a very useful one . . . hers is perfectly neat" her mother noted with pride. Only the well-to-do would have been able to afford the luxury of a dairy; the Horrys owned many cows, and her recipes often call for milk and butter.

Preserving food was a constant concern; the book contains recipes for keeping such foods as fish, quinces, even cream. There are recipes for making soap, "cheap paint," and washing silk stockings. Although the cooking preparations would have been done by slaves, Harriott Horry seems to have been an active participant in the process.

To Pott Beef like Venison [ca. 1770]
with Eliza Pinckney's notation "Extreamly good. (My own way)"

Cut Eight Pound of Lean Beef out of the Buttock or any other lean peice into Pound Peices, take six Ozs. salt Peter, half a pint of Peter Salt and as much Common salt and rub the meat well with it and let it lie three or four days, then put it into a stone jarr and cover it with some of its own Brine and Pump Water and bake it, then Pick all the fatt and Skins from it and pound it very fine in a Marble Mortar; as you pound it pour in melted Butter enough to make it very moist, like paste. Add peper and salt to Your tast, and season it high with Spices. Then press it down in your Pot, and cover it with Clarified Butter or Mutton Suet.

To make Spruce Beer [ca.1770]

Take about half a pound of Spruce or Common Pine Tops, half a pound of China root, half a pound of Sassafrass and one quart of Indian Corn. Put all these ingredients into Seven Gallons of Water and let it boil away to five Gallons or till the Corn begins to Crack open. Take it off the fire and let it stand till 'tis cold, then put it into a Cask with about a pint of Yeast or grounds of Beer and three pints of Molasses, and when it begins to work bottle it. NB: The bottles must be well cork'd.[40]

Education

In a woman's day—though filled with a myriad of household demands, community interactions, and social obligations—there was no more vital task to accomplish than the education of the children. Before the Revolution, formal schooling was generally of short duration, especially for rural families. Mothers instructed their daughters in such skills as spinning and sewing, fathers the sons in farming or the trades. In well-to-do families, reading was taught at an early age, for it was viewed as essential to understanding the Word of God, and to becoming a responsible Christian member of society. Emphasis was on raising "virtuous" and "dutiful" children. Writing would come later.

Boys had the opportunity to attend college, entering at about fourteen years of age, girls did not. Still, many—for example, Hannah Harrison, Elizabeth Graeme, Eliza Lucas, Theodosia S. Bartow, Mary Fish, Sarah Livingston, Phillis Wheatley—were often encouraged in their pursuit of literacy and knowledge by other women, be it mother, older female sibling, or female head of household. Reading books would have been the essential part of their education: novels by Cervantes, Henry Fielding or Tobias Smollett, histories of ancient Greece and Rome, travel accounts, and moral tales as well as religious writings—in short, a humanist tutorial. Missing from this home schooling for most girls would have been any in-depth study of the sciences. Basic arithmetic or "cyphering," as it was called, and later geography were deemed sufficient for girls. Mercy Otis was fortunate in being allowed to sit in on her brother's lessons, and Harriot Pinckney was able to borrow her younger brother's books on geometry and Latin.

Before the Revolutionary War, attempts were made to establish schools for girls, the best known being the one in Philadelphia founded in 1754 by the

Quaker Anthony Benezet. Several missionaries began schools in the south for enslaved girls, but met with opposition. Despite the parental unwillingness that girls be educated on a level equal to boys, women did learn. Deborah Read Franklin's orthography may have been highly idiosyncratic but she oversaw her husband's affairs with acumen. Susannah French Livingston may have been uncomfortable writing letters but she monitored the education of her children and a grandson with expertise. Although great strides on behalf of female education were made after the War, the paternalistic view of what a woman's role in life should be remained what it had been since the Renaissance: she was to be, as John Jay wrote to his daughter Maria in 1794, "prudent, amiable and accomplished, and ever mindful of your Creator."[41]

SARAH HAGGAR WHEATEN OSBORN, an immigrant from England, ran a school in Newport, Rhode Island, to support herself and family. She also began a female prayer group to which young people, including slaves, came. Some of the local townspeople at first protested her activities but eventually she reported, "I know of no one in the town that is against me." However, her mentor, the Reverend Joseph Fish of Stonington, Connecticut, was concerned, suggesting that all her educational activities did not leave her time and energy for family and household tasks. Sarah Osborn responded politely but firmly that she was fulfilling God's will.

As to Strength Sir it is Evident I gain by Spending

Revd and Worthy Sir   March 7, 1767
. . . Permit me to set my self as a child in the Presence of her Father to Give you a Most Satisfactory account of my conduct as to religious affairs I am capable. I will begin with the Great one respecting the poor Blacks on Lords day Evenings. . . . I only read to them, talk to them, and sing a Psalm or Hymn with them, and then at Eight o clock dismiss them all by Name as upon List. They call it School and I Had rather it should be calld almost any thing that is good than Meeting. . . . the poor creatures attend with so Much decency and quietness you Might almost hear as we say the shaking of a Leaf when there is More than an Hundred under the roof at onece. . . .

In december I was affrighted at the throng and . . . I told Deacon Coggeshall . . . He Must Help me some way; he must take the overflowings I would send them down to Him. He concented and said I might send Him Some white Boys too for they pressd in Likewise.

The Next Lords day Evening I told them of it, that the Deacon was as willing to do them Good as I, and I would Have all go that could not find comfortable room here. I spoke to the Boys in particular and begd them to go once and again but they kept their places and would not stir. There was I think 38 of them. At Last I told them that If they would concent to give way to the poor Black folks *then*, as they could come no other Night, if they Had rather come and see me then go to play on Tusday Evening I would devote that to them. Then 26 of them and ten Blacks rose cheirfuly and went down to the Deacons, and His House is usualy full ever since, but I Have Seldom Less than 16 or 17 Boys. *Still* they will come and on Tusday Evenings upwards of 30 almost all weathers from Eight or nine years old to fifteen or sixteen. . . .

There is usualy 30 odd young garls every Monday Evening Except the weather is excessive bad and indeed it is surprising to see their constancy thro almost all weathers. . . . The children for cateschising on Thursday afternoon Hold on with surprising chierfulness and steadiness tho not so Numerous as before winter set in, and for that reason boys and Garls come together for the winter on one day only in the week Either Thursday or Satterday, as the weather sutes. The room is usualy full consisting of all denominations. I Have Hope that God Has awakened some few of the Little Garls to a concern about their precious Souls. . . .

But I come now to answer your tender important Enquiry . . . viz. "Have you Strength abillity and Time consistent with other Duties . . . &c."

As to Strength Sir it is Evident I gain by Spending; God will in no wise suffer me to be a Loser by His Service. . . . I have Lain by [been ill] but once this winter and comparatively know nothing about weariness to what I did when I Had so Great a School and ten or more children in family to attend. I always feel stronger when my companies break up then when they come in and blessed by God I Have a Good appetite and sleep well. . . .

As to time consistent with other duties it is Most true dear Sir that I am calld by the Providence of God as well as by His word to be a redeemer of time Precious time. And Ille tell my Worthy friend How I do My wakeing time, Except unwell or weary with Exercise Generaly prevents. The dawning of the day Mr. Osborn rises while it is yet dark, can Just see to dress &c. From which time I am alone as to any inturruption. . . . I do not Lie there but turn upon my knees my stomach soported with bolster and Pillows, and I am thus securd from the inclemency of all Seasons and from all inturruptions from family affairs. There I read and write almost Every thing of a religious Nature. Thus I redeem an Hour or two for retirement without which I must *starve* . . . I never go down till breakfast is Near ready—after Breakfast family worship; then Giving Some orders as to family affairs, I apply to my School, to which you know Sir a kind providence Has Limited my Earning time for soport of my family. And if in this time I Educate the children of poor Neighbours who Gladly pay me in washing Ironing Mending and Making, I Imagine it is the Same thing as if I did it with my own Hands. I think my family does not Suffer thro My Neglect tho doubtless if I Had a full purse and Nothing to do but Look after them some things Might be done with more Exactness then now, but Every dear friend is ready to set a stitch or Help me in any wise and all is well Here—my fragments in the intervails I pick up for keeping and drawing out accompts &c or what Ever my Hand finds to do besides refreshing the body. . . .

your sincier tho unworthy friend S. Osborn[42]

SARAH ANNE EMERY in Massachusetts was sent to school at an early age, an experience she remembered vividly ninety years later. The curriculum for girls continued to emphasize feminine skills.

twenty or thirty scholars, mostly girls

The summer I was four years old [1793-4] I began to attend school. . . . My first teacher, Master Zach. Bacon, was a native of Bradford. Female teachers would then have been deemed inadmissible in a district school. It would not have been thought possible that order could be maintained under feminine rule, where often more than half the scholars were unruly boys, many of the eldest men grown. . . . The scholars were divided into four ranks: the "Bible," "Testament," "Spelling Book," and "Primer" class. . . .

The summer I was eight years old, a Miss Ruth Emerson, from Hampstead, N.H., collected a select school. There were from twenty to thirty scholars, mostly girls; there were a few small boys. I believe the tuition was but six cents a week. This lady promoted us into "Webster's Spelling Book" and "Webster's Third Part"—books then just coming into use. Miss Emerson was a most accomplished needlewoman, inducting her pupils into the mysteries of ornamental marking and embroidery. This fancy work opened a new world of delight I became perfectly entranced over a sampler that was much admired, and a muslin handkerchief, that I wrought for mother, became the wonder of the neighborhood.[43]

CATHARINE MARIA SEDGWICK of Stockbridge, Massachusetts, a widely read author during her lifetime, recalled her "*fragmentary* childhood" in the late 1790s for her niece Alice.

no one dictated my studies

Education in the common sense I had next to none, but there was much chance seed dropped in the fresh furrow, and some of it was good seed, and some of it, I may say, fell on good ground. My father was absorbed in political life, but his affections were at home. My mother's life was eaten up with calamitous sicknesses. My sisters were just at that period when girls' eyes are dazzled with their own glowing future. I had constantly before me examples of goodness, and from all sides admonitions to virtue, but no regular instruction. I went to district schools . . . no one dictated my studies or overlooked my progress. I remember feeling an intense ambition to be at the head of my class, and generally being there. Our minds were not weakened by too much study; reading, spelling, and [Nathaniel] Dwight's Geography were the only paths of knowledge into which we were led. Yes, I did go in a slovenly way through the first four rules of arithmetic, and learned the names of the several parts of speech, and could parse glibly. . . . I enjoyed unrestrained the pleasures of a rural childhood; I went with herds of school-girls nutting, and berrying, and bathing by moonlight, and wading by daylight in the lovely Housatonic that flows through my father's meadows. . . .

Think of a girl of eight spending a whole summer working a wretched sampler which was not even a tolerable specimen of its species! But even as early as that, my father, whenever he was at home, kept me up and at his side till nine o'clock in the evening, to listen to him while he read aloud to the family [David] Hume, or Shakespeare, or Don Quixote, or [S. Butler's] Hudibras! . . .

The walking to our school-house was often bad, and I took my lunch (how well I remember the bread and butter, and "nut-cakes," and cold sausage, and nuts, and apples, that made the miscellaneous contents of that enchanting lunch basket!)[44]

MARGARETTA AKERLY attended the Moravian Female Seminary in Bethlehem, Pennsylvania, in 1794-96. The school, founded in 1742, initially enrolled only daughters of the Moravians but, as its reputation for excellence grew, after 1785, other girls were permitted to take its rigorous curriculum: reading, writing, arithmetic, German, English, history, geography, religion, music, and, of course, instruction in the feminine skills of sewing and knitting. As Margaretta explained to her widowed sister Catharine Akerly Cocks in New York City, she had much studying to do, but she was willing to undertake a needlework for her.

I have so much to learn

Wednesday. March. 23d. 1796. Bethm

About 2 hours ago I received a letter from my beloved Sister. I was sitting in Grammer school when I heard the cry of letters, letters, letters I did not at all expect one. . . . I shall not have time to write more than this letter to you and this must be shortened, for oh if you only knew what I have to do, our examination commences this day a week. And I have so much to learn I dont know what to do with myself I hardly know what I write I think of nothing only what I have to learn, this morning I was up at 4 oClock sitting by the Lamp studying & every night I have 3 or 4 books under my head. . . .

I can assure my dear Sister it will be no trouble for me to work you a screen I shall do it with the utmost pleasure, I think it will look best on white sattin . . . But I wish you to chuse a Motto. . . .   Yours sincerely M. Akerly[45]

ELIZABETH "BETSEY" METCALF of Providence, Rhode Island, had to balance school and work. When ill health forced her to drop out of school, she learned the craft of braiding straw bonnets, and created a successful business for a time until her parents decided schooling was more important.

I was fond of being first in the school

I was then old enough to write, therefore I was sent to a Mans School. But not having patience enough to be very particular about writing, I was too neglectful, and by that means never attained that art: I was always afraid of spending too much time, and would hurry my copy, in order to get time to read and study. I was particularly fond of Figures and was easy if I could get a slate and pencil. This took my attention so much from writing that I almost totally neglected it for several years. Though I do not consider that I understood ciphering, for in my opinion a person might do a thousand sums, and yet be ignorant of the first rules of Arithmetic. I however learned all the rules in the Book, which was of more use to me than the sums I did. . . .

When about 12, I engaged in a new employment which was braiding straw Bonnets . . . I began to braid in 1798. Then I was not well enough to attend school. . . . I undertook the new employment with much anxiety but. . . . I felt much pleased when I first made a bonnet. I then learned to braid all kinds of trimming by seeing the English Bonnets but it was rather difficult to find out the number of straws, but Perseverance and industry will accomplish anything. My sister then learned and we had considerable of a manufactory. . . . for 2 or 3 years it was very profitable business. I could frequently make 1 dollar a day. . . .

About 14, I went to school to Mr. J. D. a member of the Baptist Church in this town . . . He has kept the public school, in the district where I live, ever since they were opened which is between 6 & 7 years. My father (who was one of the Town Council) was always anxious to have public schools. There was great exertions made by some of the opulent citizens of the Town to prevent their being established. But they got the vote of the town, and my Father with several men of enterprising spirit was determined to carry their plan into effect. My Father was so particularly engaged, that he neglected his own business, and would not rest, until the school houses were built and repaired (which were 4 in number) and fitted for 150 scholars each. . . .

I continued going to school until 17, and probably went as much as 2 years in the time. I then began to see the value of learning and my parents were not willing I should let my work take my attention from the studies of the school. I studied Grammar, Geography and the common rudiments. Geography I found the most pleasing. Grammar I consider of use when it is perfectly understood. I was fond of being first in the school and never lost my place except by absence. . . . I can say with truth that I never felt so well pleased at any period of my life as when at school.[46]

The education for boys of well-to-do families was ongoing, whether at home or at a school, in America or abroad. Robert and Mary White Morris sent their two sons to study in Europe; John Adams took two of his sons; Benjamin Franklin his grandsons, but not his daughter Sarah, though she wished to go. A few girls did have the opportunity to go to Europe. Martha Laurens of South Carolina read at age three, and "she acquired a grammatical knowledge of the French language, a considerable eminence in reading, writing, arithmetic, English grammar, geography, the use of the globes." Although her father Henry Laurens was pleased with her eagerness to learn, he reminded her of her role in life (May 18, 1774): "When you are measuring the surface of this world, remember you are to act a part on it, and think of a plumb pudding and other domestic duties." In 1775, Martha Laurens and her younger sister Mary Eleanor traveled with their uncle and aunt to England and then to France, not for her studies but to help take care of her ailing uncle.[47]

MARTHA "PATSY" JEFFERSON was taken to Paris, after her mother died, when her father was appointed minister to France in 1785. Enrolled at the Abbaye Royale de Panthemont convent, Patsy reported on her studies in music and drawing but admitted "as for *Tite Live* [Titus Livy] I have begun it three or four times, and go on so slowly with it that I believe I never shall finish it."

MARY "POLLY" JEFFERSON, six years younger than Patsy, had been left with a relative in Virginia. When Jefferson decided to send for her, he was very specific that she travel in late spring or early summer and that she be accompanied by a responsible person. Polly protested to no avail.

I don't want to go to France

Dear Papa   [ca. 22 May 1786]
   I long to see you, and hope that you and sister Patsy are well; give my love to her and tell her that I long to see her, and hope that you and she will come very soon to see us. I hope you will send me a doll. I am very sorry that you have sent for me. I don't want to go to France, I had rather stay with Aunt [Elizabeth Wayles] Eppes. . . .
   Your most happy and dutiful daughter   Polly Jefferson

   [Tricked into going aboard a vessel to visit friends, and falling asleep, Polly awoke to find herself on the ocean, her only female companion a fourteen-year-old slave, Sally Hemings. Once in England, Polly found an advocate.]

ABIGAIL ADAMS, in diplomatic tones, made her disapproval of Jefferson's tactics clear.

She has been so often deceived

My Dear Sir   London july 6, 1787
   If I had thought you would so soon have Sent for your dear little Girl, I should have been tempted to have kept her arrival here, from you a secret. I am really loth to part with her, and she last evening upon [Adrien] Petit's arrival [who was to take her to Jefferson], was thrown into all her former distresses, and bursting into Tears, told me it would be as hard to leave me as it was her Aunt Epps. She has been so often deceived that She will not quit me a moment least She should be carried away. Nor can I scarcely prevail upon her to see Petit, tho She says she does not remember you, yet she has been taught to consider you with affection and fondness, and depended upon your comeing for her. She told me this morning, that as She had left all her Friends in virginia to come over the ocean to see you, She did think you would have taken the pains to come here for her, & not have sent a man whom She cannot understand. I express her own words. I expostulated with her upon the long journey you had been; & the difficulty you had to come and upon the care kindness & attention of Petit, whom I so well knew, but She cannot yet hear me.
   She is a child of the quickest Sensibility, and the maturest understanding, that I ever met with for her years. She has been 5 weeks at Sea, and with men only, so that on the first day of her arrival, She was as rough as a little Sailor, and then She been decoyed from the Ship, which made her very angry, and no one having any Authority over her; I was apprehensive I should meet with Some trouble, but where there are such materials to work upon as I have found in her, there is no danger. She listened to my admonitions, and attended to my advice and in two days, was restored to the amiable lovely Child which her Aunt had

formed her. In short She is the favorite of every creature in the House, and I cannot but feel Sir, how many pleasures you must lose by committing her to a convent. Yet Situated as you are, you cannot keep her with you. The Girl she has with her, wants more care than the child, and is wholy incapable of looking properly after her, without Some Superiour to direct her.

As both miss Jefferson & the maid had cloaths only proper for the Sea, I have purchased & made up for them, Such things as I should have done had they been my own; to the amount of Eleven or 12 Guineys. . . .

I have not the Heart to force her into a Carriage against her will and send her from me almost in a Frenzy; as I know will be the case, unless I can reconcile her to the thoughts of going . . . Books are her delight, and I have furnished her out a little library, and She reads to me by the hour with great distinctness, & comments on what She reads with much propriety. . . .   A. Adams

[When Polly arrived in Paris on July 15, she did not recognize her sister but, as Jefferson reported, "recollected something of me" when the three were reunited.[48] The Jefferson family returned to America in 1789.]

PATSY JEFFERSON was married in 1790 and took on the roles that had always been envisioned for her, despite her education and travel abroad: that of a prudent housewife, a devoted, if somewhat critical, sister, and a dutiful daughter.

an entire reformation on the rest of my household

Monticello January 16th 1791

I very much regret not having answered yours My Dearest Papa sooner. . . . I took an account of the plate china &c. and locked up all that was not in imediate use. . . . The spoons &c that are in use are counted and locked up night and morning so that I hope to keep them all to gather till your return. It was very troublesome in the beginning tho now I have the boys in tolerable order. Every thing goes on pretty well. I have wrought an entire reformation on the rest of my household, nothing comes in or goes out without my knowledge and I believe there is as little wasted as possible. I visit the kitchen smoke house and fowls when the weather permits and according to your desire send the meat cut out. I can give but a poor account of my reading having had so little time to my self. . . . Polly improves visibly in her spanish which she reads with much more facility than when you went away. She was surprised that I should think of making her look for *all* the words and the parts of the verb. Also when she made nonsence but finding me inexorable she is at last reconciled to her dictionary with whom she had for some time past been on very bad terms. She has been twice thru her grammar since your departure. As for the harpsichord tho I put in fine order, it has been to little purpose till very lately, I am in hope she will continue to attend to that also. She is remarkably docile where she can surmount her Laziness of which she has an astonishing degree and which makes her neglect whatever she thinks will not be imediately discovered. . . . The morning of the 13th at 10 minutes past four we had an earth quake which was severe enough to awaken us all in the house and several of the servants in the out houses. It was followed by a second shock very slight and an aurora borealis. . . .   Believe me ever your affectionate child[49]

REBECCA ALEXANDER SAMUEL, residing in burgeoning Petersburg, Virginia, had grave concerns about the education of her children, Schoene and Sammy. Orthodox Jewish immigrants from Germany, she and her husband Hyman feared that they would be absorbed by the Christian communities around them, forgetting their own traditions and beliefs. To counteract this loss, the family was planning to move to Charleston, South Carolina, where there was a larger Jewish presence. Rebecca, writing in Yiddish, vented her conflicting thoughts to her parents in Hamburg, Germany.

she has a good head to learn

[Petersburg, Virginia 1791]

Dear parents, I know quite well you will not want me to bring up my children like Gentiles. Here they cannot become anything else. Jewishness is pushed aside here. There are here ten or twelve Jews, and they are not worthy of being called Jews. We have a shohet [slaughterer of animals] here who goes to market and buys terefah [nonkosher] meat and then brings it home. On Rosh Ha-Shanah and on Yom Kippur the people worship-ed here without one sefer torah [Scroll of the Law], and not one of them wore the tallit [a prayer shawl] or the arba kanfot [small set of fringes worn on the body], except Hyman and my Sammy's godfather. The latter is an old man of sixty, a man from Holland. He has been in America for thirty years already; for twenty years he was in Charleston, and he has been living here for four years. He does not want to remain here any longer and will go with us to Charleston. In that place there is a blessed community of three hundred Jews.

You can believe me that I crave to see a synagogue to which I can go. The way we live now is no life at all. We do not know what the Sabbath and the holidays are. On the Sabbath all the Jewish shops are open, and they do business on that day as they do throughout the whole week. But ours we do not allow to open. With us there is still some Sabbath. You must believe me that in our house we all live as Jews as much as we can. . . .

For the sake of a livelihood we do not have to leave here. Nor do we have to leave because of debts. I believe ever since Hyman has grown up that he has not had it so good. You cannot know what a wonderful country this is for the common man. One can live here peacefully. Hyman made a clock that goes very accurately, just like the one in the Buchenstrasse in Hamburg. Now you can imagine what honors Hyman has been getting here. In all Virginia there is no clock [like this one], and Virginia is the greatest province in the whole of America, and America is the largest section of the world. Now you know what sort of a country this is. It is not too long since Virginia was discovered. It is a young country. And it is amazing to see the business they do in this little Petersburg. . . .

When Judah [a relative] comes here, he can become a watchmaker and a goldsmith, if he so desires. Here it is not like Germany where a watchmaker is not permitted to sell silverware. They do not know otherwise here. They expect a watchmaker to be a silversmith here. Hyman has more to do in making silverware than with watchmaking. He has a journeyman, a silversmith, a very good artisan, and he, Hyman, takes care of the watches. This work is well paid here, but in Charleston, it pays even better.

All the people who hear that we are leaving give us their blessings. They say that it is sinful that such blessed children should be brought up here in Petersburg. My children cannot learn anything here, nothing Jewish, nothing of general culture. My Schoene [her daughter], God bless her, is already three years old; I think it is time that she should learn something, and she has a good head to learn. I have taught her the bedtime prayers and grace after meals in just two lessons. I believe that no one among the Jews here can do as well as she. And my Sammy [born 1790], God bless him, is already beginning to talk.

I could write more. However, I do not have any more paper.

I remain, your devoted daughter and servant, Rebecca, the wife of Hayyim, the son of Samuel the Levite, I send my family . . . and all my friends, my regards.[50]

Before the War, educational possibilities for Native Americans were few. The Reverend Eleazar Wheelock founded an Indian charity school in Lebanon, Connecticut, in 1754, which later moved to Hanover, New Hampshire; the students were there to acquire useful knowledge but also served as a resident work force. The widow Sarah Simon sent her daughter Sarah to the school, and soon after, her son Daniel, who, in 1771, complained that he had little time for his studies because he was working so much.

> When I Came frist to this School I understood that this School was for to bring up Such Indians, as was not able to bring up themselves . . . if the doctor don't let me follow my Studys more then I have don; I must leave the School, I Cannot Speand my time here, I am old, and I must improve all the time I Can if I undertake to get learning.

The societal structure of many Indian nations was matrilineal: women had authority over the households, made the decisions on marriages, contributed to the spiritual life of the society, and took responsibility for the planting and harvesting of crops. The Seneca sisters, who adopted and educated Mary Jemison, arranged her marriage to a Delaware Indian. "Not daring to cross them, or disobey their commands," she acquiesced. Traditions were strong and maintained.

Indian women were regarded with respect. Sarah "Sally" Ainse, of the Oneida nation, became a trader after being abandoned by her husband, and eventually owned extensive property first near Detroit, then along the Thames River in Ontario, Canada. She served as an intermediary between the British and Native Americans aiding Joseph Brant, the Mohawk leader, during the War.

Nancy "Nan'Yehi" Ward of the Cherokee nation attained her powerful position by exhibiting great bravery in battle when she was eighteen, and was called "Beloved Woman" by her compatriots. Clearly a wise woman who tried to guide her people on a middle road between traditional and white man's ways, she told the commissioners of the United States (1781):

> You know that women are always looked upon as nothing; but we are your mothers; you are our sons. Our cry is all for peace; let it continue. This peace

must last forever. Let your women's sons be ours; our sons be yours. Let your women hear our words.

Mary "Molly" Brant "Koñwatsi-tsiaiéñni" could read and write the Mohawk language, which she then taught to her own children. She also sent them to English schools. At home in both Indian and white societies (she was a devout Anglican), she was an important political force in New York and Ontario in the last half of the eighteenth century. Due to her connections with her consort, Sir William Johnson, Superintendent of Indian Relations until his death in 1774, and her brother Joseph Brant, she was seen as "the wise and prudent mother in the household of the Mohawk nation."

The Revolutionary War and its aftermath deeply affected Indian nations and their traditions. Dislocation, disease, and a diminution in the influence Indian women once had, were only some of the ills that beset them. Still, Seneca matrons in 1790-1791 felt sufficiently empowered to send a message concerning their rights to a representative of President Washington:

> You ought to hear and listen to what we, women, shall speak, as well as to the sachems, for we are the owners of the land, and it is ours. It is we that plant it for our and their use. Hear us, therefore, for we speak of things that concern us while our men shall say more to you; for we have told them.[51]

ANNE POWELL, in the early summer of 1789, observed the proceedings of an assembly of 200 chiefs at Fort Erie, and was impressed at how important the opinions of the women seemed to be.

a good trait of savage understanding

They were the delegates of Six Nations; each Tribe formed a Circle under the shade of a Tree, their faces towards each other; they never changed their places, but sat or lay on the grass as they liked. The Speaker of each Tribe stood with his back against a tree. The old women walk'd one by one with great solemnity and seated themselves behind the men. . . . On seeing this respectable band of Matrons I was struck with the different opinions of mankind, in England, when a man grows infirm and his talents are obscured by age, the Wits decide upon his character by calling him "an old woman," on the banks of Lake Erie a woman becomes respectable as she grows old, and I suppose the best compliment you can pay a young Hero is saying he is *as wise as an old woman*, a good trait of savage understanding. These ladies preserve a modest silence in the debates . . . but nothing is determined without their advice and approbation.[52]

SUSANNA LEAR made a trip to New York City, Providence, Rhode Island, and Boston, Massachusetts, in the summer of 1788. In her travels, she met the young Indian Peter Otsiquette, who had been sent abroad by the Marquis Lafayette to be educated.

he is quite accomplished

Thursday [July] 31. At six o'clock the coach called to take us [from Boston] to Providence. From the appearance of things we promised ourselves a most terrible ride. There were four passengers in it when it arrived, Miss Chase, Mr. Flag, an old Quaker and an Indian Chief. At first I felt very much afraid of him, but he turned out to be the most agreeable of the company. . . . We arrived at Dedham a little after eight. . . . After breakfast the Indian Chief played several tunes on his Clarinet. He played very well. In short, he is quite accomplished. 'Tis about three years since the Marquis De la Fayette sent for him over to France and he has since been at the expense of giving him a very liberal education. He appears to have improved his time very well. His observations are just and his manners are very agreeable. He entertained us with a number of anecdotes he had picked up in France. He also gave us a very entertaining account of the manners and customs of his own Nation. At every place we stopped he serenaded us which made our journey quite agreeable. We arrived at Providence about sunset. He appeared very sorry when we got out of the coach and left him alone. About an hour after he sent a letter to us informing us he loved us very much and wished to see us again. . . . We sent an invitation to the Prince to come and dine with us. Accordingly at two o'clock he came dressed in a scarlet coat trimmed with gold lace. He really made a very good figure. After dinner at the request of Mr. Brown, I danced a cotillion with him. He dances by far the best of any person I ever saw attempt it. He also danced the War dance for us which was very terrible. In the evening we all went to a dance at Mr. Griffith's. The room was very much crowded as they had heard the Prince was to be there and everybody was anxious to see him here. He also danced the War dance at the particular request of the company.[53]

MARY MAGDALENE FLAGG and her schoolmates at the Moravian Young Ladies Seminary in Bethlehem, Pennsylvania, were intrigued and delighted when delegates from the Six Nations, on their way to Philadelphia, visited the school on March 9, 1792. It is interesting to note that one of the girls was permitted to address the visitors.

We look upon you as friends & Brethern!

On fryday towards evening we were made happy by the arrival of our Indian friends on their way to Congress. There were Fifty in Number of the Six Nations, accompanied by their Minister Mr. [Samuel] Kirkland a Presbyterian, who had lived among them about twenty Years, and a Mr. Jones their Interpreter, Mr. Allen, and several other Gentlemen.

Of the Seneca Nation there were 29, and among them the following Chiefs: Big Tree, Red-Jacket, Farmers Brother, Little Beard, Little Billy, & Captn. Shanke. Of the Oneidas were 8, all baptized; of this Nation was the venerable Father, called *good Peter*; as also the adopted son of the Marquis de la Fayette, Peter Otsiquette, who lived for 3 years at Paris, & speaks besides his own, the French and English Languages very fluently. He appears to be a very accomplished young Indian, and it appears plainly, that he has received his Education in France, & lived for a good while among White and Civilized People. There were two Cajugas. 6 Onandagoes. 3 Tuscororas. 2 Mohicanders, but of the Mohawks none.

On Saturday at half past 10 o Clock, we were permitted to go with our dear Tutoresses in the Meeting Hall, where we impatiently waited to see them. Brother Etoine welkomed them in the name of the Society of Brethren, & received from Red-Jacket a Seneca Chief many thanks for the kind reception they were favoured with in a place where they had long wished to be. . . .

Miss Eliza Fries addressed them in the name of our School in the following Speech:

> Brethren of the Six Nations! We bid you welcome in our Town! We rejoice to see you! We see you without fear & trembling! We look upon you as friends & Brethren! You are traveling a good way! You go to smoke the Calumet of Peace with our Grand Sachem George Washington & his Council! to brighten the Chain of Friendship! . . .

[On Sunday] Good Peter, and young Peter Otsiquette, accompanied by Mr. Kirkland, our dear Inspector [Jacob van Vleck] and Lady; and Mr. Hokewelder, paid us a very agreeable visit. . . . Peter Otsiquette was greatly delighted with the sound of the Forte-piano. But what we regret most, is that we are unable to set down verbally the most excellent admonitions and advice Good Peter gave to the different Classes in the School. It is however imprinted in our hearts, that we have seen and heard an Indian whose Elemant is Jesus and his Love. . . .

On Monday morning, a little past 10 they bid adieu to this Villa, and set out in a Boat on our Leheigh for the Delaware to Philadelphia. Our best wishes accompany them.[54]

Many members of the upper class would have agreed with John Jay's sentiments when he wrote to Dr. Benjamin Rush in March 1784: "I consider knowledge to be the Soul of a Republic . . . nothing shd be left undone to afford all Ranks of People the means of obtaining a proper Degree of [education] at a cheap and easy Rate."

But what would that education, especially for women, entail? Dr. Rush delivered his thoughts in an address to the Philadelphia Young Ladies Academy in 1787. The subjects he suggested included bookkeeping and writing so that women might help their husbands; history, geography, and religion so that their children might benefit; dancing and singing to promote health and "soothe the cares of a domestic life." Women, who had proven their intelligence and mettle during the War, managing without male supervision, pressed for more educational opportunities.[55]

JUDITH SARGENT STEVENS MURRAY wrote essays on manners, politics, the role women should play in society, and religion, which appeared on a regular basis in periodicals. As early as 1784, she championed a rigorous education for girls: "I think, to teach young minds to aspire, ought to be the ground work of education:

many a laudable achievement is lost, from a persuasion that our efforts are unequal to the arduous attainment." In an essay, "On the Equality of the Sexes," published in 1790, Murray argued, with some irony, that both sexes were equally capable of acquiring knowledge but that differences in their educations resulted in the inadequate instruction of women. Despite her advocacy for broader female education, Murray did not question the established view that a woman's role in life was one of domesticity.

the sister must be wholly domesticated

Will it be said that the judgment of a male of two years old, is more sage than that of a female's of the same age? I believe the reverse is generally observed to be true. But from that period what partiality! how is the one exalted, and the other depressed, by the contrary modes of education which are adopted! the one is taught to aspire, and the other is early confined and limitted. As their years increase, the sister must be wholly domesticated, while the brother is led by the hand through all the flowery paths of science. Grant that their minds are by nature equal, yet who shall wonder at the *apparent* superiority, if indeed custom becomes *second nature*; nay if it taketh place of nature, and that it doth the experience of each day will evince. At length arrived at womanhood, the uncultivated fair one feels a void, which the employments allotted her are by no means capable of filling. What can she do? to books she may not apply; or if she doth, *to those only of the novel kind*, lest she merit the appellation of a *learned lady*; and what ideas have been affixed to this term, the observation of many can testify. . . . Meantime she herself is most unhappy; she feels the want of a cultivated mind. . . .

Now, she was permitted the same instructors as her brothers, (with an eye however to their particular departments) for the employment of a rational mind an ample field would be opened. In astronomy she might catch a glimpse of the immensity of the Deity, and thence she would form amazing conceptions of the august and supreme Intelligence. In geography she would admire Jehovah in the midst of his benevolence; thus adapting this globe to the various wants and amusements of its inhabitants. In natural philosophy she would adore the infinite majesty of heaven, clothed in condescension; and as she traversed the reptile world, she would hail the goodness of a creating God. A mind, thus filled, would have little room for the trifles with which our sex are, with too much justice, accused of amusing themselves, and they would thus be rendered fit companions for those, who should one day wear them as their crown. . . .

Will it be urged that those acquirements would supersede our domestick duties. I answer that every requisite in female economy is easily attained; and, with truth I can add, that when once attained, they require no further *mental attention*. Nay, while we are pursuing the needle, or the superintendency of the family, I repeat, that our minds are at full liberty for reflection; that imagination may exert itself in full vigor; and that if a just foundation is early laid, our ideas will then be worthy of rational beings. If we were industrious we might easily find time to arrange them on paper, or should avocations press too hard for such an indulgence, the hours allotted for conversation would at least become more refined and rational. Should it still be vociferated, "Your domestick employments are sufficient"—I would calmly ask, is it reasonable, that a candidate for immortality, for the joys of heaven, an intelligent being, who is to spend an eternity in contemplating the works of Deity, should at present be so degraded, as to be allowed no other ideas, than those which are suggested by the mechanism of a pudding, or the sewing the seams of a garment? Pity that all such censurers of female improvement do not go one step further, and deny their future existence; to be consistent they surely ought.

Yes, ye lordly, ye haughty sex, our souls are by nature *equal* to yours; the same breath of God animates, enlivens, and invigorates us. . . . I dare confidently believe, that from the commencement of time to the present day, there hath been as many females, as males, who, by the *mere force of natural powers*, have merited the crown of applause; who, *thus unassisted*, have seized the wreath of fame.[56]

ANNIS BOUDINOT STOCKTON was also an author, her poetry published and, though she admitted that she ran "the risk of being sneered at by *those* who criticize female productions, of all kinds," her works were admired. She had a keen interest in education, not surprising for a mother of six children. Upon reading Mary Wollstonecraft's *A Vindication of the Rights of Women* (1792), Annis Stockton put her carefully considered reaction to the book in a letter to her oldest daughter Julia, the wife of Dr. Benjamin Rush.

there is great pains taken to improve our sex

My dear Julia,   Morven 22d of March [1793]
    I have been engaged these two days with reading the rights of women, which I never could procure before, tho it has been much longer in the neighbourhood. I have been musing upon the subject over my solitary fire till I took up the resolution to give you my sentiments upon it tho I suppose it is an old thing with you—I wonder you never Sent me your Critique—I am much pleased with her strength of reasoning, and her sentiment in general—but think that She like many other great geniuses—establish an Hypothesis and lay such a weight upon it as to cause the superstructure to destroy the foundation—and I am sorry to find a woman capable to write such strictures should Complement [Jean-Jacques] Roussaus nonesense so much as to make his Ideas of women the criterion of the rank they hold in Society. . . . I have always Contended that the education of women was not made a matter of that importance, which it ought to be—but we see that error daily Correcting—and in this Country, the Empire of reason, is not monopolized by men, there is great pains taken to improve our sex, and store their minds with that knowledge best adapted, to make them useful in the situation that their creator has placed them—and we do not often see those efforts opposed by the other sex, but rather disposed to asist them by every means in their power, and men of sense generally prefer such women, as Companions thro life. . . .
    You know that it is a favourite tenet with me, that there is no sex in Soul—I believe it as firmly as I do my existance—but at the same time I do not think that the sexes were made to be independent of each other—I believe that our

creator intended us for different walks in life—and that it takes equal powers of mind, and understanding, properly to fulfil the duties that he has marked out for us—as it does for the other sex, to gain a knowledge of the arts and Sciences, and if our education was the same, our improvement would be the same—but there is no occasion for exactly the same education. I think we may draw the Conclusion that there is no sex in Soul, from the following illustrations—that there are many men, that have been taught, and have *not* obtained any great degree of knowledge in the circle of the Sciences—and that there *have* been women who have excelled in every branch, when they have had an opportunity of instruction, and I have no doubt if those advantages were oftener to occur, we should see more instances. . . .

Yet to sum up my poor Judgement upon this wonderful book, I do really think a great deal of instruction may be gathered from it—and I am sure that no one, can read it, but they may find something or other, that will Correct their Conduct and enlarge their ideas. . . . your ever affectionate mother A Stockton[57]

[The debate on women's education and role in society continued. Demands for better instruction for women increased during the last fifteen years of the eighteenth century: new academies sprouted to accommodate them. Just as elite men were in power in government, so it was elite women who benefited from the expanded educational opportunities; yet even these were limited. Priscilla Mason, a graduate of the Young Ladies Academy in Philadelphia, delivered a "Salutory Oration" on May 15, 1793, in which she pointed out that "The Church, the Bar, and the Senate are shut against us. Who shut them? *Man*; despotic man, first made us incapable of the duty, and then forbid us the exercise."]

ABIGAIL ADAMS, uncomfortable with the subservient position of women and the negation of their ideas, always looked for ways to expand her own knowledge as well as that of members of her family. Sending her sister Elizabeth Peabody a book, she commented with some asperity:

woman is Lordess

I did not read it untill I bought it, there is no harm in it. many useful lessons, but Some which I do not assent to or approve of—I will never consent to have our Sex considered in an inferiour point of light, let each planet shine in their own orbit. God and nature designd it so—if man is lord, woman is *Lordess*— that is what I contend for and if a woman does not hold the Reigns of Government, I see no reason for her not judging how they are conducted—[58]

Chapter 9

we set out on our journey

This Breton fisherman's prayer says it all: "Oh God be good to me. Thy sea is so wide and my ship is so small." Ocean voyages during the eighteenth century were dangerous and not lightly undertaken. Transatlantic crossings were hazardous especially during the winter months, sailing vessels subject to the vagaries of the weather and dependent on navigation instruments that were rudimentary. In addition, there was the risk of being attacked by pirates or, during wartime, captured or sunk by enemy ships or privateers. Coastal travel was also perilous: there was the danger of running aground due to variations in water depth, the existence of shoals, and the lack of accurate charts. Voyages to and from Europe were long, generally taking six weeks or more. Creature comforts on board ship were minimal: quarters were tight, and privacy was limited. Meals were generally simple, based on staples that traveled well such as preserved meats, potatoes, and oatmeal, supplemented by poultry and livestock brought on board and fish caught en route. The well-to-do often provisioned themselves with wines and special foodstuffs. Passengers attempted to keep boredom at bay by reading, playing cards, engaging in conversation with compatible travelers, and playing musical instruments. Seasickness was a given.

Many loyalists fled by boat to England; diplomats and trade representatives crossed the Atlantic on government business or in the hope of economic gain. Women traveled with their husbands or relatives, rarely on their own. They often recorded their experiences and observations, both on board ship and at their destinations. Their journals and letters recount pleasures as well as trials and tribulations; many reveal a natural curiosity, an eye for telling detail, the ability to turn a phrase, and an appreciation of cultural differences.

ABIGAIL ADAMS envied her twenty-year-old cousin, Isaac Smith, Jr., for being able to travel freely abroad. She begged him for particulars of his visit to London.

almost impossible for a Single Lady to travel without injury to her character

Dear Sir. . . .   Braintree April the 20 1771

Suffer me to Snatch you a few moments from all the Hurry & tumult of London and in immagination place you by me that I may ask you ten thousand Questions, and bear with me Sir, tis the only recompence you can make for the loss of your Company.

From my Infancy I have always felt a great inclination to visit the Mother Country as tis call'd and had nature formed me of the other Sex, I should certainly have been a rover. And altho this desire has greatly diminished owing partly I believe to maturer years, but more to the unnatural treatment which this our poor America has received from her, I yet retain a curiosity to know what ever is valuable in her. . . .

Women you know Sir are considerd as Domestick Beings, and altho they inherit an Eaquel Share of curiosity with the other Sex, yet few are hardy eno' to venture abroad, and explore the amaizing variety of distant Lands. The Natural tenderness and delicacy of our constitutions, added to the many dangers we are subject too from your Sex, renders it almost imposible for a Single Lady to travel without injury to her character. And those who have a protecter in an Husband, have generally speaking obstacles sufficient to prevent their Roving, and instead of visiting other Countries, are obliged to content themselves with seeing but a very small part of their own. To your Sex we are most of us indebted for all the knowledg we acquire of Distant Lands.[1]

JANET SCHAW sailed from the Firth of Forth in Scotland on 25 October 1774, bound for North Carolina by way of the West Indies. Traveling with her on the *Jamaica Packet*, a small vessel, were her brother Alexander and three young relatives, whom she was escorting to their father, John Rutherfurd, who, like many other Scots, had settled in North Carolina. In attendance were Schaw's maid, Mrs. Mary Miller, and her brother's East Indian servant, Robert. Schaw kept a journal in which she recorded details of her sea voyage and descriptions of the geography and people of the areas she visited. She declared her plan to the friend for whom the journal was intended.

merely a Voyage

I propose writing you every day, but you must not expect a regular Journal. I will not fail to write whatever can amuse myself; and whether you find it entertaining or not, I know you will not refuse it a reading, as every subject will be guided by my own immediate feelings. My opinions and descriptions will depend on the health and the humour of the Moment, in which I write. . . . My brother has laid in store of whatever may render our Situation agreeable, and I have laid in a store of resolution to be easy, not to be sick if I can help it, and to keep good humour, whatever I lose; and this I propose to do by considering it, what it is, merely a Voyage.

[Having resolved to take what promised to be a difficult passage in stride, Janet Schaw described what their party's living quarters were like.]

hurry, bustle, noise, and confusion raged thro' our wooden kingdom

Our Bed chamber, which is dignified with the title of *State Room*, is about five foot wide and six long; on one side is a bed fitted up for Miss Rutherfurd [Fanny, in her late teens] and on the opposite side one for me. Poor Fanny's is so very narrow, that she is forced to be tied in, or as the Sea term is lashed in, to prevent her falling over. On the floor below us lies . . . Mrs Miller. As she has the breadth of both our Beds and excellent Bedding, I think she has got a most envyable berth, but this is far from her opinion, and she has done nothing but grumble about her accommodation. . . .

My brother, who was sadly fatigued, had got into his Cott, which swings from the roof of the Cabin; our two little men [the Rutherfurd boys, eleven and nine] were fast asleep in a bed just below him, when we were informed from the Deck that they were going to weigh anchor. Every body that was able, got up to see this first grand operation. My Brother descended from his Cot, the boys sprung out of bed, all hands were on Deck, hurry, bustle, noise, and confusion raged thro' our wooden kingdom, yet it was surprizing how soon every thing was reduced to order. In little more than a quarter of an hour, all was over, the watch was set, and nothing to be heard, but the sound of the man's feet moving regularly backwards and forwards at the helm, and the crowing of a Cock that the noise had waked in the Hen Coop. My Brother . . . informed us in passing our state room, that we were now underway . . . He then gave poor Fanny some Saline drops to settle her stomach, which had felt the very first motion of the ship. . . . As yet I am very well, and hope I will not be much hurt, tho' I must expect a little touch as well as others. My Brother now mounted into his Cot, the boys got to bed, we shut up our half door, and in a few moments, we were all again in the arms of Sleep.

[Some time later the Schaws were informed by the captain that "the wind had chopt about, and being now full in our Teeth," it was impossible for the vessel to proceed on its original course; instead it would have to go by the north of Scotland.]

a little good Chicken broth

It is hardly possible to imagine a more disagreeable passage at this Season of the Year than this must be. The many Islands, Shelves and Rocks, render it very dangerous, which, with the addition of a rough sea, sudden squalls, and the coldest climate in Britain, gives as uncomfortable a prospect as one wou'd wish. . . .

Quietness wou'd again have restored us to rest, had not the Cock, as harbinger of day, repeatedly told us it was now morning. Nor were we the only passengers on Board whom this information concerned, his wives and children who now heard him, made such an outcry for Breakfast, as shewed their Stomachs suffered nothing from the Sea Air.

Their demands complied with, the outcry ceased, but they kept such a Peck Pecking directly over head, that it was impossible to rest, and banished all desire to sleep. This was a Misfortune much less felt by me than my poor young friend [Fanny], who was now sick to death. I prevailed on Mrs Miller to get up and give us a dish of Tea, this she actually tried, but was not able to stand on her feet, as she was now really sick, and the motion of the Ship very violent. It was in vain for either of us to think of moving, and we were almost in despair, when fortunately I bethought me of Robert, my brother's Indian servant, a handy good fellow. "Oh!" cried I, to the first that I saw, "oh! for Heaven's sake send us Robt, Black Robt." Robt approached our state room, with all the dignity of a slow-stalking Indian Chief. "Dear Robt," exclaimed I, "cou'd you be so good as to get us a dish of Tea?" "To be certain, my Lady," replied he, "but Miss is very badly, and Tea is not good for her; I will get her a little good Chicken broth." "Do, dear Robt," cried poor Fanny, in a voice of the utmost thankfulness. Robt stalked off, and it was not long before he made his appearance with a Mess of the most charming chicken broth that ever comforted a sick stomach. . . . Robt dealt out his benefits in Tea cup-fulls, every one had a little, and every one had a desire for more, so that his broth went thro' many Editions. . . .

I must now go and prepare for bed, which, I assure you, is no easy task, the toilet engages much more of my time at Sea than ever it did on land; we sit in bed till we dress, and get into it, when ever we begin to undress.

> [Schaw had thought that only members of her family and friends, in addition to the crew, were on the ship, until she discovered a great number of "emigrants," who had been smuggled on board on orders of the unscrupulous owner and warned to stay under cover until the ship was at sea. Initially horrified by these "wretched human beings," Schaw found her heart melted by their pitiable circumstances and eventually befriended several of them. Bound to the captain of the vessel in return for food and transportation, they would be sold on arrival as indentured servants for a period of years to work off the money expended on them. All the passengers suffered when the weather turned stormy.]

wonderful how her planks stuck together

It Blows harder and harder, the shrouds make a terrible rattling, it is a horrid sound. Oh Lord! here comes the Captain, who tells us the dead lights must be put up. I know the meaning of the word [shutters put up outside the cabin windows to keep out the water in case of a storm] and yet it makes me shudder. . . .

The rains continued, and the winds seemed to gain new strength . . . The sailors's hands were torn to pieces by pulling at the wet ropes. Their stock of Jackets were all wet, nor was there a possibility of getting them dried, as the Steerage was quite full of Emigrants and hard loading; a piece of inhumanity, that I do not believe even Avarice ever equalled in any other owner. . . . But on the fourth evening of the gale (as it was now termed) the whole elements seemed at war: horror, ruin and confusion . . . made the stoutest heart despair of safety.

Just after the midnight watch was set, it began to blow in such a manner, as made all that had gone before seem only a summer breeze. All hands, (a fearful sound) were now called; not only the Crew, but every man who could assist in this dreadful emergency. Every body was on deck, but my young friend and myself, who sat up in bed, patiently waiting that fate, we sincerely believed unavoidable. The waves poured into the state-room, like a deluge, often wetting our bed-cloths, as they burst over the half door. The Vessel which was one moment mounted to the clouds and whirled on the pointed wave, descended with such violence, as made her tremble for half a minute with the shock, and it appears to me wonderful how her planks stuck together, considering how heavy she was loaded, Nine hogsheads of water which were lashed on the deck gave way, and broke from their Moorings, and falling backwards and forwards over our heads, at last went over board with a dreadful noise. Our hen-coops with all our poultry soon followed, as did the Cab-house or kitchen, and with it all our cooking-utensils, together with a barrel of fine pickled tongues and above a dozen hams. We heard our sails fluttering into rags. The helm no longer was able to command the Vessel, tho' four men were lash'd to it, to steer her. We were therefore resigned to the mercy of the winds and waves. At last we heard our fore main mast split from top to bottom. . . .

Poor Billie, who is scarcely ten years old, had been sadly frighted, and could not refrain from crying, "Why, you little fool," said my brother to him, "what the duce do you cry for; you are a good boy, if you are drowned, you will go to heaven, which is a much finer place than Carolina." "Yes, uncle," returned he sobbing, "Yes, Uncle, I know if I had died at land, I would have gone to Heaven, but the thing that vexes me is, if I go to the bottom of this terrible sea, God will never be able to get me up; the fishes will eat me and I am done for ever"; at this thought he cried bitterly, it was annihilation the poor little fellow dreaded, for as soon as he was convinced that God could get him up, he became quite calm and resigned. . . .

one of the most fatal accidents that can happen to a ship

The weather was still very squally, and tho' the wind at times intermitted its violence, yet the sea ran so high, that the motion of the Vessel was intolerable, nor could any fire be made, as the waves came on board and drowned it out as soon as lighted. . . .

We had not yet ventured on deck, nor were our dead lights taken down, when an unforseen accident, had nearly completed what the storm had not been able to effect . . . Were you a sailor, I need only tell you our ship broached to, to inform you of the danger we were in, but as you are not one, I may suppose you unacquainted with sea terms, and will therefore inform you, that it is one of the most fatal accidents that can happen to a ship . . . the meaning of broached to, is, that the Vessel fairly lies down on one side, but you will understand it better by being informed of what we suffered from it.

We were sitting by our melancholy Taper, in no very chearful mood ourselves; my brother . . . was within the companion ladder. The Captain had come down to the Cabin to overhaul his Log-book and Journal, which he had scarcely begun to do, when the Ship gave such a sudden and violent heel over, as broke every thing from their moorings, and in a moment the great Sea-chests, the boys' bed, my brother's cott, Miss Rutherfurd's Harpsicord, with tables, chairs, jointstools, pewter plates etc, etc., together with Fanny, Jack and myself, were tumbling heels over head to the side the Vessel had laid down on. It is impossible to describe the horror of our situation. The candle was instantly extinguished, and all this going on in the dark, without the least idea of what produced it, or what was to be its end. The Capt sprung on deck the moment he felt the first motion, for he knew well enough its consequence; to complete the horror of the scene, the sea poured in on us, over my brother's head, who held fast the ladder tho' almost drowned, while we were floated by a perfect deluge . . . a favourite cat of Billie's. . . . happening to be busily engaged with a cheese, just behind me, she stuck fast by it, and sadly frighted with what she as little understood as we did, mewed in so wild a manner, that if we had thought at all, we would certainly have thought it was Davy Jones the terror of all sailors, come to fetch us away.

Busy as this scene appears in description, it did not last half the time it takes in telling. Nothing can save a ship in this situation, but cutting away her masts, and the time necessary for this generally proves fatal to her, but our masts were so shattered by the late storm, that they went over by the Board of themselves, and the Vessel instantly recovered. This second motion, however, was as severely felt in the Cabin as the first, and as unaccountable, for we were shoved with equal Violence to the other side, and were overwhelmed by a second deluge of Sea water. At last however it in some degree settled, and, thank God, no further mischief has happened, than my forehead cut, Jack's leg a little bruised, and the last of our poultry, a poor duck, squeezed as flat as a pancake.

When the light was rekindled, a most ridiculous scene was exhibited, vizt the sight of the Cabin with us in it, amidst a most uncommon set of articles. For besides the furniture formerly mentioned, the two state rooms had sent forth their contents, and the one occupied by the Captain, being a sort of store room, amongst many other things a barrel of Molasses pitched directly on me, as did also a box of small candles, so I appeared as if tarred and feathered, stuck all over with farthing candles.

[With calm restored, the Schaws contemplated their plight. Almost all of the provisions they had brought on board for their use had been washed overboard and they were forced to rely on the ship's stores.]

What shall we eat?

I . . . had the mortification to find that the whole ship's provision for a voyage cross the Tropick, consisted of a few barrels of what is called neck-beef, or cast beef, a few more of New England pork (on a third voyage cross the Atlantick, and the hot Climates), Oat meal, stinking herrings, and, to own the truth, most excellent Potatoes. . . .

We now called a general council on this truly interesting and important question, What shall we eat? By the returns made by Robert and Mary, we found we had still a cag of excellent butter, a barrel of flower, a barrell of onions, and half a Cheese, besides a few eggs. . . . Of these materials Mary and Robert make us something wonderfully good every day. For example, Lobscourse is one of the most savoury dishes I ever eat. It is composed of Salt beef hung by a string over the side of the ship, till rendered tolerably fresh, then cut in nice little pieces, and with potatoes, onions and pepper, is stewed for some time, with the addition of a proportion of water. This is my favourite dish; but scratch-platter, chouder, stirabout, and some others have all their own merit.

[At this point, the ship was, as Janet Schaw so plainly put it, "a complete wreck," its masts, sails and rigging lying in a heap on the deck. Temporary repairs enabled the vessel to sail on, but the sighting of "an Algerine corsair" was the cause of much consternation as the *Jamaica Packet* had no "Mediterranean pass," a document issued by the British Admiralty as a protection against seizure by Barbary pirates. Luckily the threat was short-lived, the corsair having sailed away. Enduring yet another storm, the vessel was damaged further: "we have not a stick standing, nor a rag of sail to put up, and we lie tumbling amongst the waves." Repairs were immediately undertaken, and Schaw marveled at the skill of the sailors.]

I never saw any thing so neat and handy as our Johns

We have been all this morning on deck, hard at work with the new sails. I never saw any thing so neat and handy as our Johns. Every man appeared with his clew of thread, his sail needle, and his thimble, which he properly terms his palm, as it is worn in the palm of the hand, fastened over the back with a strap of leather. With this he works as cleverly as any semptress with her needle. We will soon look very clean and neat, but you cannot think how much we are ashamed to enter the Islands with our humble masts.

[Luckily the wind picked up, and as the ship sped westward Schaw's spirits rose: "as we are now approaching a new World, we have also reason to look for new objects."]

Every moment gives us something to amuse our fancy

And indeed the Sea, the Sky, and every thing seem to change their appearance. The moon is ten times more bright than in your Northern hemisphere, and attended by a number of Stars, each of whom may claim a superior title, and pass for sparkling suns. The beauty of the evenings is past all description, and tho' the days are rather warm, yet we feel less inconveniency than one could believe. By the help of an awning we are able to sit on the deck, where I now write. Every moment gives us something to amuse our fancy or excite our curiosity; the colour of the water is now a bright azure blue, and at night all round the Ship seems on fire. This fire is like globules, that tho' larger, bear a resemblance to those produced by Electricity, and I dare say is an effect of the same kind from the strong salts of this vast Ocean.

The inhabitants of this wat'ry world seem to bid us welcome; the Sea appears quite populous, droves of porpuses, like flocks of Sheep, pass close by us. They have a droll gait and keep a tumbling, as if they proposed playing tricks for our diversion. The dolphin is a most beautiful fish . . . when he rises out of the water, he appears all over green and like burnished gold. His prey is the flying fish, which, when pursued, rise out of the water, and keep flying while the fins, which answer for their wings, are wet, but the instant that they dry, they drop down, by which means they often fall down on the deck. We have eat some, and I have preserved some for your inspection. We have another fish called pilot fish . . . These greedily take the bait, and we would get them in plenty, had they not such friendships as make them almost superior to the Arts of men; for the moment one is hooked, others come round him, and if you are not very quick they bite and nibble the line, till they break it thro' and let their friend go free. . . .

We have had an unwieldy companion all this day by the Ship, a Grampus, or small whale. He tumbles about, and when we throw him any thing overboard, he turns on his back, and catches it in a very small mouth.

The effect of this fine weather appears in every creature . . . and if we had any thing to eat, I really think our present situation is most delightful. We play at cards and backgammon on deck; the sailors dance horn pipes and Jigs from morning to night. . . .

We have now thrown off our ship-dress and wear muslin Jackets and chip hats [made of thin strips of wood, woody fiber, or straw]: that however is not so wonderful, as our lying under a single Holland sheet, and even that too much. We have got a window cut into our state room from the Companion stair. This is shaded with nothing but a thin lawn curtain, yet is too warm. The people from the Steerage ly on deck, the boys will no longer go into bed, but sleep on the Sea-chests, yet this is the month of December.

We find ourselves greatly the better of bathing which we do every morning in a large cask prepared for the purpose. Tis a very solemn ceremony; when we are to leave the cabin in our bathing dress, all the people quit the deck, and remain below till we return.

the very cat is frisking about for joy

Every thing flatters us with the hope of Land, yet if you saw our state room, you would suppose we designed to continue in it for years. It is decked out with a toilet, pictures and mirror; so calm is the Sea, that the things never move. How soon are our sorrows forgot. . . . The sun is too bright and too warm for me, and as for the earth, I have seen none of it since I left Scotland; I only smelt it off the African Islands. Land, Land, joyful sound, we are in sight of land, the infants are clapping their little hands, and the very cat is frisking about for joy.

[The *Jamaica Packet* reached Antigua on December 12 after a passage of seven weeks. Briefly visiting several islands in the West Indies, the Schaws continued their journey to North Carolina on board the *Rebecca.* Janet Schaw was pleased to note that this ship had adequate provisions, and these were properly stored.]

a Scotch dinner under the Tropick

As we had not been suffered to provide or put on board any thing for ourselves, I was curious to know what our Sea Store consisted of, and begged the Capt to let me look thro' the Ship. . . . Miss Rutherfurd and I were surprised at the neatness of every thing we saw. . . . care . . . was taken to secure the livestock in such a way as to keep them safe even in the worst weather. . . . This is a place paled in between decks in which were geese, pigs, Turkeys, and sheep.

The water too was placed as cool as possible. . . .

We had a sheep killed yesterday, and have had a Scotch dinner under the Tropick in the middle of the Atlantick. We eat haggis, sheep-head, barley-broth and blood puddings. . . . We have never yet had a breeze sufficient to curl the Sea, and I really wonder how we move along. Our sails hang like a Lady's loose gown in the most languishing manner, and our poor Capt sighs ready to break his heart at the slow advance he makes to the port that contains his wishes. . . .

At last America is in my view

Last night the air changed, and tho' the wind did not in the least increase, yet it became very chilly on deck, and this morning is so cold, that we are not able to leave the Cabin. . . . We are now actually on the American coast, and it is so cold that I am not able to go on deck, tho' the Capt invites me to view the woods, as he assures me, they are in sight. I can hardly hold the pen, I left June and found December.

At last America is in my view; a dreary Waste of white barren sand, and melancholy, nodding pines. In the course of many miles, no cheerful cottage has blest my eyes. All seems dreary, savage and desert; and was it for this that such sums of money, such streams of British blood have been lavished away? Oh, thou dear land, how dearly hast thou purchased this habitation for bears and wolves. Dearly has it been purchased, and at a price far dearer still will it be kept.

[Entering the Cape Fear River, the *Rebecca* approached the town of Brunswick where Janet Schaw noted: "We got safe on shore"—twenty-four days after leaving the West Indies.[2]]

LOUISA SUSANNAH WELLS was the daughter of a newspaper publisher in South Carolina, whose loyalist sympathies caused him to leave the colony. Louisa produced the newspaper until 1778 when she decided it would be best to join her father in London. In the company of her uncle, his son, her maid, and a female friend named Miss Thorney, Wells departed from Charleston on July 1 on the *Providence.* In the year following, Wells wrote an account of the voyage from memory for herself and a friend.

"casting up their accounts"

The wind proving fair, we weighed Anchor having a Black Pilot on Board, to whom we promised a hundred dollars, Congress, if he would carry us safely over the Bar. . . . Every Person on board the "Providence" were banished except Captain Stevens. Never did any of us experience joy, so truly, as when we found ourselves in the wide Ocean, out of the dominion of Congress. You know the many difficulties the poor Tories had to encounter in procuring ships, getting Men &c. The poor Pilot by whose skill we were indebted for safety, seemed to enjoy our happiness, independent of our contribution, above his Master's fee. The Pilot boat sailed ahead and tracked our way, notwithstanding which we struck twice on this dangerous Bar. . . . Never shall I forget poor Bluff's (the name of the Pilot) anxiety when our Hay-Stack of a ship missed Stays on the

Bar! He said he was a true friend to British Manufactures and that was as much Loyalty as he durst own, but these Revolution times was not so good as before for poor Negroes. . . .

A finer breeze, or rather gale, could not blow out of the heavens, for us. . . . Every thing went on extremely well, and every one seemed desirous of pleasing each other. Some of us were Sea sick to be sure, but, I escaped pretty well, till the third night, when every Man, Woman and Child were "casting up their accounts". . . .

The Wind still increased, and several squalls ensued; the ship too, was excessively leaky, occasioned by taking in a part of her cargo, six months before. This left two planks of her hold above Water, which when our Indigo and Tobacco were put on board, sunk them below the edge of the water at the Wharf. Guess then how much we gained in our Pumps by the straining of the Ship in the Gales?

[When another ship was sighted, the *Providence* fled to avoid capture.]

Our little moveables . . . began both to walk and talk

Carrying so much more sail, our little movables in the cabin and State rooms began both to *walk* and *talk*. The first thing which awakened me was my work basket and a parcel of books tumbling off a shelf upon my head. I got up, asked for a light, but this was denied me, as we were running from an Enemy, who was then in chase of us. I slipped on a wrapping gown, groped about for some letters which had been delivered to me, by the Wives of several Loyalists, to their husbands, in England, with a charge "not to part with them while art, strength or life remained." I put them into my bed and sat down on the side of it.

[The *Providence* was boarded by an English vessel whose captain, suspecting that its cargo was valuable, claimed it as a prize. Refusing to believe that the passengers were loyalists and the cargo their lawful property, he insisted on having the matter adjudicated by the Admiralty Court in New York City, which was occupied by the British, and toward which they sailed.

Wells continued with her "history of a captive Maid," describing the ship's arrival in New York City on July 13th. Having been ill, she remained on board and used the opportunity to comment on the sights.]

New York . . . makes no figure from the water

I was now able to go upon deck. Our vessel lay just off the King's Brew-House, on Long Island. . . . The East River here makes a bend . . . The Houses on each side of its banks, The Town of Brooklyn, York Island and the adjacent country forms a delightful Landscape.

New York, I must confess makes no figure from the water: nothing to equal the order and regularity of the once beautiful Bay Street of Charlestown! Every house for a mile, three stories high! You see there are few travellers who are not attached to their native place and are ever making comparisons with it.

Poor little Governors-Island is now a perfect waste and ruin. The Rebels had made it an *entire* Fortification, which the British have so completely demolished, as scarcely to leave "a wreck behind." You must recollect, however, that American Forts are not built of stone.

Staten-Island produces nothing now, having Encampments constantly on it; the Inhabitants have almost all deserted it. It has one Fort, from which Signals of vessels appearing, are made to the town. . . . but of all the sights, to me, the most extraordinary was the great concourse of Shipping! All the British Navy to the Northward of the West Indies, were assembled in this Port.

[A stroke of good fortune, Louisa Wells was able to find lodging with friends named Lowther until the admiralty suit should be decided. In the meantime she was called to court to attest to the truth of the *Providence*'s manifest and bills of lading, which included cargo belonging to her.]

Gentlemen went up to the Table to look at my name

It was now high time to lay in our claims on the 'Providence' the twenty one days allowed, being nearly expired. Accompanied by many friends of both sexes, Miss Thorney and I set out for the Court of Admiralty in order to prove our property, or rather to swear to the truth of our Manifest, Bills of Lading, &c. and to sign a paper, which I think our Attorney at Law, called a Charges. . . . Mrs Lowther told me all the Gentlemen went up to the Table to look at my name. It surely was no matter of wonder to see a native of Charlestown write well, for there bad writing was seldom seen and good writing seldomer praised. . . . The Court is held in a room up two pairs of Stairs in the City Hall, and is the same in which General [Charles] Lee was so long a Prisoner.

[Wells accepted an invitation to spend some time on Long Island where she enjoyed splendid views of New York City, took walks and remarked on features of the countryside. She was especially intrigued by "look-outs" on the roofs of houses and by the ubiquitous stone fences so unlike those of "Pitch Pine Rails," with which she was familiar.

Upon learning that Sir Henry Clinton had issued a proclamation allowing ships bound for Europe to leave, Wells hurriedly returned to New York to find that the judge of the Admiralty Court had finally resolved the case regarding the cargo of the *Providence*, ruling that it be restored to its original owners. Louisa Wells got her "poor little Fortune, of two or three casks of Indigo," and she and her companions booked passage on a merchant ship about to sail. Waiting for it to depart, she recalled: "I once expressed a desire of living in New York? I am now totally off that Scheme. . . . I do not like the place nor its climate. What it *was* I know not, but what it *is* gave me a surfeit of every thing on the Continent of America to the Northward of Charlestown."

Wells and her party boarded the *Mary & Charlotte* on October 17, 1778, her birthday. Louisa complained that she kept the day "sorrowfully enough—viz:—'in settling my accounts at the ship's side.' Sea sickness is a great drawback to travelling by water." Stormy weather prevailed for the most part of the voyage across the Atlantic.]

for fear of having my bones broken

How do you think I made shift to pass my time? I can assure you that I was obliged to exert all my Philosophy; which, together with the Guitar, made 'the heavy Hours' supportable. . . . we had no conversation and I detested cards. Frequently, for two or three days together, I have been obliged to keep my State-room, merely for fear of having my bones broken. I was unable to sit up, without being lashed to the bed or trunk on which I sat. I kept the deck until the waves would come dashing over the Quarters.

[Approaching the English Channel on November 21st, between the fog and strong currents, the vessel came near to being dashed on the rocks.]

we were actually wound ashore

We beat about, day and night, at the Chops of the Channel until the 25th at noon, when we, once more, saw the cheerful light of the sun. The quadrants were all in readiness and we blessed the memory of the Inventors of those valuable Instruments. We again saw Scilly and then bore away for the Channel. . . . In the afternoon we saw the lofty Coast of Cornwall. . . . We drove up the Channel at an amazing rate under close reefed courses. . . . We soon made Dover, and, at 4 o'clock in the afternoon of the 27th of November anchored in the Downs. . . .

It is really curious to get on shore here [at Deal]. . . . As soon as the Partners on shore espy the little Frigate, they get the Windlass and poles ready—not less than three men go in the Boat . . . They have with them a large rope . . . this they throw upon the Beach. It is immediately caught up and put into the Windlass, and they turn it round so that we were actually wound ashore, in the same manner as an Anchor is heaved. In this business the people are obliged to be very expeditious, as the dashing of the surge is so great and the waves come so fast, that the boat is in imminent danger of being overwhelmed, but should the rope break! We got a sample. Our backs were well sprinkled with one wave breaking on the stern of the boat: but o! how shall I describe what I felt, when I first set my foot on British ground? I could have kissed the gravel on the salt Beach! It was my home: the Country which I had so long and so earnestly wished to see. The Isle of Liberty and Peace. . . . I did not get the motion of the Ship out of my head for a week.

[This "tolerable Sailor in Petticoats," as Louisa Wells called herself, arrived safely in London where she was reunited with her father.[3]]

SARAH LIVINGSTON JAY, the young wife of John Jay, having been apart from him so much since their marriage, chose to accompany him when he was posted to Spain in 1779 as American minister plenipotentiary, leaving their three-year-old son with his grandparents in New Jersey. Their journey was a near disaster. Weighing anchor in late October, the *Confederacy* soon encountered gale-force winds and rough seas. Sarah made an attempt, in a letter to her mother, to make light of what she called their "awkward situation," the vessel having lost its "bow sprit, foremast, main mast, & missen mast." The loss, the next morning, of the ship's rudder completed Sarah's list of "misfortunes." As it was clearly impossible to reach Europe given the condition of the vessel, the officers decided that "the southern direction was the only one that offered a prospect of safety" and made for Martinique. Even though the *Confederacy* was badly disabled, Sarah recollected some amusing interludes. Crossing the Tropic of Cancer, she described what happened to John Jay's young nephew Peter.

I could not for-bear smiling at Peter's fate

The day happened to be a merry one to the sailors . . . for crossing the Tropick they insisted upon an ancient custom of shaving & ducking every person that had not cross'd it before, excepting only those who paid their fine. I could not for-bear smiling at Peter's fate, who had been diverting himself with observing the operation perform'd on many of them, 'till they exclaim'd at the injustice of exempting him, & insisted upon his being tar'd at least, which by the by was their method of shaving. Peter, sobbing, declared that had not his new coat been spoilt, he would not have regretted so much the difficulty of getting rid of the tar.[4]

[At Martinique, the Jays abandoned the heavily damaged *Confederacy* and resumed their journey in the French *Aurora* that carried them safely to Europe.]

ABIGAIL ADAMS was being pressed by her husband John, in 1783, to join him in Europe as he had to remain there longer than anticipated. His pain at their continued separation is palpable: "What Shall I do for Want of my Family. . . . Will you come to me this fall and go home with me in the Spring? If you will, come with my dear Nabby. . . . This is my sincere Wish, although the Expence will be considerable, the Trouble to you great. . . . I am So unhappy without you that I wish you would come at all Events."[5]

Abigail was reluctant to go: "the ocean so formidable, the quitting my habitation and my Country, leaving my Children, my Friends, with the Idea that prehaps I may never see them again . . . there are hours when I feel unequal to the trial."[6] In the end she succumbed, unable to resist her husband's entreaties, especially since it had been nearly six years since he "first crost the Atlantick." Nevertheless, she worried about how she would be received and how she ought to behave.

mere American as I am

I think if you were abroad in a private Character, and necessitated to continue there; I should not hesitate so much at comeing to you. But a mere American as I am, unacquainted with the Etiquette of courts, taught to say the thing I mean, and to wear my Heart in my countanance, I am sure I should make an awkward figure, and then it would mortify my pride if I should be thought to disgrace you. . . . I have refused every publick invitation to figure in the Gay World, and sequestered myself in this Humble cottage, content with rural Life & my domestick employments in the midst of which I have sometimes Smiled, upon recollecting that I had the Honour of being allied to an Ambassador. . . . But avaunt ye Idle Specters, the desires and requests of my Friend are a Law to me. I will sacrifice my present feelings and hope for a blessing in persuit of my duty.[7]

[Abigail made all the preparations necessary for her departure in the spring of 1784. The two boys were left with her sister Elizabeth Shaw and her husband, the Reverend John Shaw, to be prepared for Harvard. She asked another sister, Mary Cranch, to look in on John's mother. The care of her house and furniture she entrusted to Pheby, a slave whom her father had freed in his will, and who had recently married William Abdee. Abigail expressed confidence in the pair: "I have no doubt of their care and faithfulness, & prefer them to any other family."[8] She let the farm to a tenant and enlisted two servants—a man and a woman—to accompany her. Informing John of her travel arrangements, Abigail expressed apprehension at being on her own.]

embarking . . . without any Male Friend, connection or acquaintance

I am embarking on Board a vessel without any Male Friend, connection or acquaintance, my Servants excepted, a stranger to the capt & every person on Board, a situation which I once thought nothing would tempt me to undertake, but let no person say what they would or would not do, since we are not judges for ourselves untill circumstances call for us to act. I am assured that I shall have a state room to myself and every accommodation and attention that I can wish for, it is said to be a good vessel, copper Bottom & an able captain.[9]

[Satisfied that she had done what she could to ensure that all was in the best possible order, Abigail departed on the ship *Active* that sailed on June 20, 1784, for England, taking Nabby with her. In a diary she kept during the voyage for her sister Mary Cranch, Abigail described her first encounter with sea travel.]

that most . . . disspiriting malady

Tis said of Cato the Roman censor, that one of the 3 things which he regreted during his Life, was going once by sea when he might have made his journey by land; I fancy the philosopher was not proof against that most disheartning, disspiriting malady. Sea Sickness—of this I am very sure, that no Lady None ever wish; or a second time by the Sea, were the objects of her pursuit within the reach of a land journey. . . .

And this was truly the case of your poor sister. & all her female companions when not one of us could make our own Beds, put or take off our shoes, or even lift a finger, as to our other cloathing we wore the greater part of it, untill we were able to help ourselves; added this missfortune Miller my Man Servant was as bad as any of us . . . .

Our Sickness continued for ten days . . . the confinement of the Air below, the constant rolling of the vessel & the Nausea of the Ship which was much too tight, contributed to keep up our disease—the vessel is very deep loaded with oil & potash. the oil leaks the potash smoaks & ferments, all add to the *flavour*. when you add to all this the horrid dirtiness of the Ship, the Slovenness of the

Steward, & the unavoidable sloping spilling occasiond by the tossing of the Ship—I am sure you will be thankful that the pen is not in the hands of Swift, or Smollett, and still more so that you are far removed from the Scene.[10]

[Turning her attention to the realities of life on board ship, Abigail provided her sister with a description of her physical surroundings.]

Necessity has no law

Our accommodations on Board are not what I could wish or hoped for, we cannot be alone, only when the Gentlemen are thoughtfull enough to retire upon deck, which they do for about an hour in the course of the Day; our *state* rooms are about half as large as cousin Betsy's little Chamber, with two Cabbins in each mine had 3, but I could not live so; upon which mrs. [Love] Adams's Brother [Abel Lawrence] gave up his to Nabby, & we are now stowed, two & two, this place has a small grated window, which opens into the Companion, and is the only air admitted, the door opens into the cabbin where the Gentlemen all Sleep, & where we sit dine & we can only live with our door Shut, whilst we dress & undress; Necessity has no law but what should I have thought on shore; to have layed myself down to sleep, in common with half a dozen Gentlemen? we have curtains it is true, & we only in part undress, about as much as the yankee bundlers—but we have the satisfaction of falling in, with a Set of well behaved, decent Gentlemen.[11]

[After the effects of seasickness had abated, it did not take long for Abigail to set to rights what she found unacceptable on board.]

soon exerted my Authority

No sooner was I able to move, then I found it necessary to make a bustle amongst the waiters, & demand a cleaner abode; by this time Miller was upon his feet, and as I found I might reign mistress on Board without any offence soon exerted my Authority with scrapers mops Brushes, infusions of viniger; &c and in a few hours you would have thought yourself in a different Ship—Since which our abode is much more tolerable & the gentlemen all thank me for my care.[12]

[Three weeks into the voyage Abigail wrote to her sister Elizabeth Shaw telling the familiar tale of being at sea in a storm—merely "a Breize" the sailors called it—"everything wet, dirty and cold, ourselves Sick."[13] But "returning sone [sun], a smooth sea and a mild Sky" prompted this paean.]

a blaizing ocean

I went last evening upon deck, at the invitation of Mr. Foster to view that phenomenon of Nature, a blaizing ocean a light flame Spreads over the ocean on appearance, with thousand of thousands Sparkling Gems, resembling our fire flies on a dark Night, it has a most Beautiful appearance, I never view the ocean without being filled with Ideas of the Sublime. & am ready to break forth with the psalmist, "Great and marvilous are thy works, Lord God Almighty; in wisdom hast thou made them all."[14]

[The *Active*, in thirty days, made a safe passage across the Atlantic and up the English Channel, anchoring in the Downs before the small town of Deal. There had been little improvement in the method of getting ashore there since Susannah Wells's experience ten years earlier. Safe but thoroughly soaked, Abigail remarked that the passengers in the small boat ferrying them ashore looked "like a parcel of Naiads just rising from the sea."[15] Friends procured her lodging in London where she penned a note to John, giving an account (and expenses) of the trip, extolling the skill of the captain and the courtesy of the gentlemen passengers. She added: "I think no inducement less than that of comeing to the tenderest of Friends could ever prevail with me to cross the ocean nor do I ever wish to try it but once more."[16]]

Travel on inland waterways was also difficult: often dangerous, and not to be undertaken lightly. Some women accompanied husbands or relatives on official business; others were wives intent on joining their spouses and settling in frontier areas. Their journals and letters record experiences and encounters with friends, officials, and Indians; they enable readers to envision, through their eyes, the land to the north and west as well as the wonders of nature.

HANNAH LAWRENCE, an intelligent and strong-willed young woman with patriot sympathies, had met Jacob Schieffelin, a British officer, during the British occupation of New York and succumbed to his charms. Despite her father's objections, her general dislike of the "unwelcome invaders," and the disapproval of her Quaker Meeting, Hannah secretly married Schieffelin in 1780. Shortly after their wedding, the pair sailed for Quebec, then journeyed to Detroit where Schieffelin served as a government secretary in the Indian Department. As Hannah was a writer and poet, it is no surprise that the diary she kept on her journey (1780-1781) is a richly detailed narrative of her experiences and impressions.

the undulating motion of the never-resting waves

On the fifteenth of september, in the year seventeen hundred and eighty, I embarked on board a small Vessel bound to Quebec. . . . When the first emotions of grief, on a painful seperation from all whom I had been hitherto habituated to regard as essential to my happiness, had subsided I enjoyed . . . the undulating motion of the never-resting waves. . . .

Two fleeting weeks brought to our veiw a new coast. . . . an incident . . . occurred on approaching the vicinity of land; a sudden shock gave me to know that our Vessel had run aground, or struck upon a rock; the alarm was instantaneous throughout our small crew, the creaking of the timbers, and the outcries of the seamen, who all ran forward in confusion were sufficient to intimidate a mind more enured to danger than mine; a few civil persons resident on this barren and uninviting coast, came off in a small boat, on discovering our embarrassment, and lent us their assistance to so good effect that we were soon afloat, without any apparent damage, and proceeded on our course.

[Entering the Gulf of St. Lawrence, the ship sailed up what Hannah called "this noble River, whose width and extent are exceeded by few on the habitable globe." Becalmed at one point, the vessel was obliged to anchor, allowing the Schieffelins to walk on shore and observe the dwelling of some inhabitants.]

endulge ourselves in . . . visiting the land

We endulge ourselves in a felicity we had long been strangers to, in visiting the land. . . . amusing ourselves with picking cranberries and a small well-flavoured black-berry, that still hung on the bushes, till observing something like a road, we followed its course till it led us to an Indian hut on the other side of the Island, but its inhabitants alarmed at the appearance of a vessel in the harbour had passed over to the main-land in their Canoes. We entered their hut, and examined with much curiosity the frail tenement, it is constructed of thin bark in a conical form, with an aperture in the top to afford a passage for the smoke, and poorly calculated to exclude the cold in this severe latitude. The door is small and low, the remains of a fire were visible, and the ground around was strewed with dried leaves, affording a seat or a bed to these comfortless children of Nature. A Canoe lay near formed of the same materials, the seams were neatly sewed and daubed with gum. They are a tribe of Eskimaux.

[Reaching Quebec on October 17, 1780, Hannah could not help but be impressed by its situation. Invited to dine with General Frederick Haldimand, at that time the colonial governor of Quebec, the Schieffelins crossed the famous Plains of Abraham on the way to the general's house. After dinner they were shown an apartment that General Richard Montgomery had occupied before the battle in which he was killed in December of 1775. Hannah was so moved at seeing the site of his death that a short time later she wrote a poem entitled "The Shade of Montgomery." She was not impressed by General Haldimand.]

an irreconciliable enemy to the female sex

[He is] a German veteran, whose sole merits I believe . . . consists in some skill in military tactics . . . I am not disposed to accord him more than common fame, as he is an irreconciliable enemy to the female sex, and consequently enjoys in solitary grandeur the state of his Chateau. He treated my Friend [her husband] with a distinction rather unusual from him, but upon discovering that he had been guilty of the unpardonable error of taking a Wife, expressed much displeasure that an officer should ever marry, and I make no doubt that this circumstance induced him to expedite the orders for our departure to the upper country, as they call the remote frontiers of this extensive Province.

[The Schieffelins shortly did depart for the "upper country." The ascent of the rapids of the St. Lawrence was difficult, involving travel by boat, horse-drawn calèche when there was a passable road, or trudging along the river bank. At night they slept on shore.]

Batteaux. . . . drawn by cords

We embarked on board one of the Batteaux . . . these are flat-bottomed boats which are alone capable of performing this voyage, in which there are frequent interruptions by shoals and ledges of rock over which they are drawn by cords, and sometimes even lifted by men in the water. . . . we continued our course till night, when we landed. . . .

The fatigue of the day gave a relish to the only comfortable meal it afforded, and our bed was spread in our Tent, with the skins of a Buffaloe beneath to intercept the damps exhaling from the moist and shaded soil, where we enjoyed a profound repose, untill the returning dawn roused us to the refreshment of a hasty dish of tea, and the renewal of our journey.

[A chance encounter with Captain John Butler gave Hannah the opportunity to meet a woman traveling with him—an Indian named Molly Brant, "Koñwatsi-tsiaiéñni," who had been the common-law wife of the British colonial leader, Sir William Johnson.]

a degree of respect nearly equal to that of a legal Relict

We were invited to sup in [Butler's] Tent, and complied with pleasure from a curiosity to see this female Indian, whose wealth and influence, as well as the decent propreity of her conduct, procure her a degree of respect nearly equal to that of a legal Relict [widow]. A house has been lately built for her at Carleton Island, at the expense of the Government, where she mostly resides, with several daughters, who bear his name, and are, I am informed, well educated and agreeable young women. Miss Molly, as she is called, is sister to the famous Captain [Joseph] Brandt, whose courage and influence have rendered him a distinguished character during the present war [on the side of the British]. She is below the middle size, as the Indian women generally are, her countenance not displeasing, though grave, and her manner sedate, her complection is fairer than most of her Nation, which is the Mohawk, and which language she speaks with the softest tone imaginable; indeed there is something inconceivably pleasing in the voices of the women of that tribe, and the expression of their countenance is extremely mild and modest, but could we suppose from appearance, that those gentle pleasing creatures, become the fiercest of furies, when the chance of war subjects an ill-fated captive to their mercy. But to return to our tawny companion. She was attended by a female friend, whom she sometimes addressed in her own language, though she understood english, she would not venture to express herself in it, but her behaviour was conformable to our modes of politeness. Our supper was suitable to the scene, and consisted of the wild inhabitants of the forest. Our social companions departed in the morning before we arose.

[The Schieffelins resumed their journey, crossing by boat in three days, "the mighty mass of waters that composes the Lake Ontario." Within sight of their destination, they met with near disaster.]

prayers and strong liquor

Suddenly the wind blew with such violence in a contrary direction, that, our Captain, who was a Frenchman of small knowledge in maritime affairs, left the Vessel to the mercy of the winds and waves, and descended with his Men into the Cabin, where they united the efficacy of alternate prayers and strong liquor to support their spirits, having first lashed fast the helm, and closed up the hatches. . . . I awaited with composure the fate which I conceived to be inevitable . . . The tumultuous waves rolled over the vessel, and dashed through the crevices of the Cabin into the bed where I lay. The return of day revived the hopes of our terrified Commander, and brought some abatement of the storm.

[Hannah and her husband spent the winter in Niagara and in April, 1781 set out to see the "wonderful Fall which has so long been pronounced by those who have beheld it, the greatest effort of Nature in the terrible sublime. I am conscious that every pen must fail in the attempt to convey any Idea of it."]

I grew giddy at the veiw

I proceeded . . . by slow and intricate windings up that rugged mountain, and contemplated the native wilderness of the scene through which we passed, till my ears were struck with the approaching sound of the falling torrent, and a sudden shower gave us to know that it could not be far distant, while innumberable isicles shook from the trees, on our heads, at every breath of wind, and were as quickly replaced by the constant succession of vapours condensing on the branches. A considerable River first appeared, rolling down a gradual descent, and forming with the rapidity of its motion over the broken rocks, as we approached nearer the bank which had been worn away to an amazing depth, we were struck with motionless astonishment at the stupendous object that met our veiw, neither our surprize nor the deafening noise we heard, would admit of exclamation, we therefore stood gazing in silent awe and admiration. The whole River rushing abruptly down a terrific precipice, and rebounding in shattered particles, from the violence of its fall on said rocks, to nearly the height from whence it had precipitated itself. The earth seemed to tremble at the shock, and our sinking hearts corresponded with the idea. . . .

We prepared to descend [the path] to a level with the River . . . this with great difficulty, caution and the assistance of poles to prevent slipping we effected. . . . one of the gentlemen. . . . then led me to a point of the rock that projected out in front of the Fall, from whence I could see the River descend as it were from the clouds, and with my eye follow its course, from its first rushing over the top, till it reached the margin of the stream below. . . . I grew giddy at the veiw.

[At Fort Erie, a further eighteen miles, the Schieffelins received a visit from Joseph Brant. Indians clearly fascinated Hannah and, although she saw merit in individuals like Brant and his sister, she held the view of many of her generation: that Native Americans were for the most part savages, that they were cruel and bloodthirsty, and that what she considered the miserable conditions in which they lived were the result of "Ignorance and indolence."]

a servicable partizan to the British

Soon after our arrival we received a visit from the famous Captain Brandt, who was encamped without the Fort, with a deputation of warriors, from the Six Nations to the Ottawas, Hurons, and other Indians, residing in the district of Detroit. . . . Captain Brandt . . . had acquired habits of neatness, his dress is made in the fashion of his Country, but fine, and ornamented with considerable taste; his linnen is of the best quality, while the shirts of other Indians are made of coarse calico, and worn till they drop off with filth and age; his mantle is black broad-cloth, instead of a paint blanket, which is covered from the shoulders to the waist with wide pink ribbon, neatly stitched on, and edged round the border with silver fringe . . . [He] has been a servicable partizan to the British, during the contest [Revolutionary War]. . . .

Captain Brandt is in person of the middle size, and as the Indians usually are active and well-formed, his manners are easy and polite, gentle and unassuming, his language slow, and tolerably correct; nothing of that fire is discoverable in his countenance, which animates his soul in the hour of battle, for his greatest enemies allow his bravery to be incontestable. . . . He has left a Wife at Niagara, whom I went to see out of curiosity, before I left that place. She is tall and strait, two advantages very uncommon in Indian woman, has good features, and is I think a very handsome brunette, for her complection is little browner than many European women, and fairer than many Canadians can boast. This is accounted for by her being the daughter of an Englishman of rank, and bred with more care than usual with the women of her Nation, but her dress was in the same fashion as that of other female Indians, and unfavourable to her appearance, consisting of a cloth petticoat without plaits, and scarcely reaching to her legs, which were covered with cloth, of a clumsy form, but neatly worked at the edges where they join. Her linnen was fine and adorned with lace, and a chintz short Gown completed her dress; her head was without ornament, or other covering, than her long black hair, parted on the forehead, those who wear it cut are slightly esteemed, as women of a loose character.

[Upon arrival in Detroit on April 21, 1781, Hannah Schieffelin visited a Huron village nearby and remarked on the dwellings, which were different from those she had seen earlier.]

a considerable degree of comfort

The Tribe that settled at the Village . . . live with a considerable degree of comfort, their huts are constructed of small saplings, bent to an arch, and interwoven closely with Bark, which form is capable of a larger size than those that are conical. They are disposed in parallel lines, and surrounded by Peach-Orchards and Corn-Fields, which are cultivated by the women while the Men are mostly engaged in War or Hunting.[17]

[The Schieffelins returned to New York City when the War was over and became respected members of the community.]

ANNE POWELL was a Bostonian by birth. Her older brother William had been educated abroad and was a loyalist during the Revolution. In 1789 he was appointed superior court judge in Detroit. Anne made the journey from Montreal to Detroit with him and his family. She had thought that keeping a diary would be "a pleasant employment" but soon found that the trip posed difficulties that prevented her from writing regularly; she was obliged to record her adventures from memory at a later date. The Powells left Montreal on May 11, 1789.

This mode of traveling is very tedious

We . . . went to our Boats; one was fitted up with an awning to protect us from the weather and held the family and bedding. It was well filled, eighteen persons in all, so you may suppose we had not much room; as it happened that was of no consequence, it was cold on the Water and were glad to sit close.

This mode of traveling is very tedious for we are obliged to keep close along shore and go on very slowly. . . . The next day we reach'd a part of the River where the boats were obliged to be unloaded and taken through a Lock, the rapids being too strong to pass. . . .This part of the Country has been settled since the Peace; it was granted to the Troops raised in America, during the War: we went from a Col. to a Captn., and from a Captn. to a Major. They have most of them built good houses, and with the assistance of their half pay, live very comfortably.

[One evening, walking along the river bank with her brother, Anne saw a style of fishing unfamiliar to her.]

The bank of the River was very high and woody, and Moon shone bright through the trees; some Indians were on the river taking Fish with Harpoons . . . They make large fires in their Canoes, which attract the fish to the surface of the water, when they can see . . . to strike them. The number of fires moving on the water had a pretty and singular effect.

[At the house where her party was staying, Anne surveyed the sleeping arrangements.]

[I] found the whole floor cover'd with Beds. . . . A Blanket was hung before my mattress, which I drew aside to see how the rest were accommodated. My Brother and Sister, myself, five children, and two Maid-servants, made up the groupe. . . . I was in a humour to be easily diverted, and found a thousand things to laugh at; it struck me as very like a party of strolling Players. . . .

the pleasantest vagabond life you can imagine

The weather was now so fine that we ventured to sleep out, and I liked it so
well that I regretted that we had ever gone into a house—it is the pleasantest
vagabond life you can imagine. We stopt before sunset, when a large fire was
instantly made, and tea &c prepared. While we were taking it the Men erected a
tent; the sails of the Boats served for the Top, with Blankets fastened round the
sides; in a few minutes they made a place large enough to spread all our Beds in,
where we slept with as much comfort as I ever did in any chamber in my life.

[Crossing Lake Ontario in four days, the Powells reached Niagara.
Like Hannah Schieffelin, Anne Powell marveled at the Falls: "I was never before sensible of the full power of scenery, nor did I suppose the eye
could carry to the mind such strong emotions of pleasure, wonder and
solemnity." Reaching Fort Erie, Anne had an opportunity to meet Indians
who were gathered for a council. One particularly impressed her.]

the finest appearance I ever saw in my life!

I was very much struck with the figures of these Indians as they approach'd
us. They are remarkably tall and finely made and walk with a degree of grace and
dignity that you can have no idea of. I declare our Beaus look'd quite insignificant
by them. One man call'd to mind some of Homer's finest heroes. One of the gentlemen told me that he was a chief of great distinction, but he spoke English, and if
I pleased he should be introduced to me. I had some curiosity to see how a Chief
of the Six Nations would pay his Compliments, but little expected the elegance
with which he address'd me. The Prince of Wales does not bow with more grace
than Captain David; he spoke English with propriety and return'd all the compliments that were paid him with ease and politeness. As he was not only the hand-
somest but best drest man I saw, I will endeavor to describe him.

His person is tall and fine as it is possible to imagine, his features regular
and handsome, with a countenance of much softness, his complexion not dis-
agreeably dark, and I really believe he washes his face, as it appear'd perfectly
clean without paint. His hair was all shaved off except a little on the top of his
head to fasten his ornaments to; the head and ears painted a glowing red; round
his features was fastened a fillet of highly polished and ornamented silver, from
the left Temple hung two long straps of black velvet, covered with silver, beads
and broches; on the top of his head was fixed a Fox-tail feather, which bow'd to
the wind as did a black one in each ear; a pair of immense ear-rings that hung
below his shoulders completed his headdress which I assure you was not unbe-
coming, tho' I must confess, somewhat fantastical.

His dress was a shirt of color'd calico, the neck and shoulders cover'd with
silver broches, placed so thick as to have the appearance of a very rich net; his
sleeves much like those the Ladies wore when I left England, fastened about the
Arm, with a broad bracelet of silver, highly polish'd and engraved with the
Arms of England; four smaller bracelets of the same kind about his wrists and
arms; round his waist was a large Scarf of a very dark colored stuff lined with
scarlet, which fell almost to his knees, One part of it he generally drew over his

left arm, which had a very graceful effect when he moved; his legs were covered with blue cloth made to fit neatly with an ornamental garter bound below the knee. I know not what kind of a Being your imagination will represent to you, but I sincerely declare that all together Captn. David made the finest appearance I ever saw in my life!

[The Powells crossed Lake Erie and sailed up the Detroit River to a fort, which was technically in possession of the Americans according to the terms of the peace treaty, although the British maintained *de facto* control. Anne noted: "A new Town is now to be built on the other side of the river, where the Courts are held and where my brother must of course reside." Anne found the weather "boiling hot" and could not understand why the ladies who greeted them were in full dress. "What do you think of walking about when the Thermometer is above 90? It was as high as 96 the morning we were returning our visits." Several parties were organized to amuse the Powells. One was held on an island where they were entertained by a band while enjoying a festive dinner.]

nurseries of Thunder storms

We were hurried home in the evening by the appearance of a Thunder Storm. It was the most beautiful I ever remember to have seen. The Clouds were collected about the setting sun and the forked Lightning was darting in a thousand directions from it. You can form no Idea from anything you have seen of what the Lightning is in this Country; these Lakes, I believe, are the nurseries of Thunder Storms, what you see are only stragglers that lose their strength before they reach you.[18]

[Anne Powell married and took up residence in Montreal, where she died in childbirth.]

Hessian prisoners of war, fleeing loyalists, runaway slaves, patriots leaving loyalist-occupied areas, Americans seeking a better life in the West: all were on the move both during the Revolutionary War and afterward.

BARONESS FREDERIKA VON RIEDESEL and her family, along with the Convention Army, were marched to the Massachusetts coast after General Burgoyne's surrender at Saratoga in 1777. She noted in her journal how they fared.

my own field bed

At last we arrived at Boston, and our troops were quartered in barracks not far from Winter hill. We were billeted at the house of a countryman, where we had only one room under the roof. My woman servants slept on the floor, and our men servants in the entry. Some straw, which I placed under the beds, served us for a long time, as I had with me nothing more than my own field bed. . . .

We remained three weeks at this place, until they transferred us to Cambridge, where they lodged us in one of the most beautiful houses of the place, which had formerly been built by the wealth of the royalists.[19]

[The Baroness would have liked to remain in Cambridge, but Congress decided that the prisoners should be moved to Virginia where their maintenance would be less costly. The Baroness and her children traveled by carriage, while her husband made the journey with his troops. But before setting out, the Baroness attended to an important matter.]

Now I was forced to consider how I should safely carry the colors of our German regiments still further, as we had made the Americans at Saratoga believe that they were burnt up. . . . But it was only the staves that had been burned, the colors having been thus far concealed. . . . I, therefore, shut myself in with a right honorable tailor, who helped me make a mattress in which we sewed every one of them. . . . I transferred it into my cabin, and slept, during the whole of the remaining voyage to Canada, upon these honorable badges.[20]

[The journey south was not easy. The Baroness recounted what the family had to contend with and how they lived when they arrived at their destination.]

we suffered from cold and . . . a lack of provisions

Before we passed the so-called Blue mountains, we were forced to make a still further halt of eight days, that our troops might have time to collect together again. In the mean time such a great quantity of snow fell, that four of our servants were obliged to go before my wagon on horseback, in order to make a path for it. We passed through a picturesque portion of the country, which, however, by reason of its wilderness, inspired us with terror. Often we were in danger of our lives while going along these break-neck roads; and more than all this we suffered from cold, and what was still worse, from a lack of provisions. When we arrived in Virginia, and were only a day's journey from the place of our destination, we had actually nothing more remaining but our tea, and none of us could obtain any thing but bread and butter. A countryman, whom we met on the way, gave me only a hand full of acrid fruits. At noon we came to a dwelling where I begged for something to eat. They refused me with hard words, saying that there was nothing for dogs of Royalists. Seeing some Turkish [Indian] meal lying around, I begged for a couple of hands full, that I might mix it with water, and make bread. The woman answered me "No, that is for our negroes, who work for us, but you have wished to kill us."

traveled . . . six hundred and seventy-eight English miles

The place of our destination was Colle in Virginia, where my husband, who had gone ahead with our troops, awaited us with impatient longing. We arrived here about the middle of February, 1779, having, on our journey, passed through the provinces of Connecticut, New York, New Jersey, Pennsylvania and Maryland, and having traveled in twelve weeks, six hundred and seventy-eight English miles. . . .

The troops were stationed in Charlottesville, two hours from us. . . . At first they endured many privations, They occupied block houses, which, however, were without plaster, and destitute of doors and windows, so that they were very cold inside. They worked, however, with great industry to build themselves better dwellings, and, in a short time, I saw a pretty little town spring up. Behind each barrack, they laid out gardens and constructed pretty little inclosures for poultry. . . . We had built for us a large house, with a great drawing room in the centre, and upon each side two rooms which cost my husband one hundred guineas. It was exceeding pretty. Many of the negroes brought us every thing that we needed, in the shape of poultry and vegetables. . . . But the heat bothered us very much in summer; and we lived in constant terror of rattlesnakes. The fruits also were eaten into, by three kinds of ticks. We had, moreover, very heavy thunder-storms, lasting for five or six days at a time, and accompanied by tempests which tore up by the roots more than one hundred trees in our vicinity. . . . We had no chairs to sit on, only round blocks, which we also used for a table, laying boards upon them. . . . My husband . . . was always sad, and could not at all endure the heat, which stood at one hundred and three degrees, and was exceedingly oppressive. . . .

The Virginians are generally inert, a fate which they attribute to their hot climate; but on the slightest inducement, in a twinkling, they leap up and dance about. . . .

The landed proprietors . . . own many negro slaves

The landed proprietors in Virginia own many negro slaves, and treat them badly. Many of them are allowed by their masters to run naked until they are fifteen and sixteen years old, and the dress which is then given them, is scarcely worth wearing. The slaves have an overseer who leads them out at day break into the fields, where they are obliged to work like beasts or receive beatings; and when thoroughly exhausted and burned by the sun, they come into the house. They are given Indian meal called hominy, which they make into pastry. But often they are tired and had rather sleep for a couple of hours, when they are again obliged to go to work. . . . Still, there are also good masters.[21]

[In the autumn of 1780, General von Riedesel was finally exchanged and returned to active duty, General Henry Clinton giving him a command in the English army. Von Riedesel served first on Long Island and then returned to Canada to command that part of his troops left there prior to Saratoga. The vessel on which passage had been arranged for the family proved to be, in the words of the Baroness, "one of the smallest and most miserable ships of the whole fleet." In her journal she recorded the troubles encountered on their voyage. To prevent the ship from being left behind by the convoy, it had to be taken in tow.]

a ship . . . tore away our little necessary

For this purpose, one end of a great cable was attached to the towed ship, and the other was made fast to the man-of-war which drew us along. This, however, was very unpleasant and often, indeed, dangerous; for if there was a calm, one ship would strike against the other, and if we had been so unlucky as to meet a ship of the enemy, we would have been obliged to receive the shock of battle. Besides, our ship had too few sailors, which would have been the cause of additional danger if we had been overtaken by a hurricane; in which case we should probably have been upset, as on account of the small number of men. . . . And to crown all, our ship was badly loaded, and lay so much upon one side, that we were obliged, while on the passage, to fill empty casks with sea-water in order to give the ship the necessary equilibrium. . . .

We had all kinds of mishaps on our passage. Among other things, a ship . . . . with its stern, tore away our little necessary*, and it was very fortunate that no one was in it at the time.

*a lavatory found in the "head", or fore part of the ship

[Before their ship sailed, however, the von Riedesels had to deal with a difficult situation.]

She threw herself at my feet

Just as we were on the eve of embarking, we met with still another great vexation. Our faithful negroes, a man, his wife and a young kinswoman of theirs, were reclaimed by their first owner (from whom they had been taken on the ground that he was a rebel), under the pretense that he had again become a royalist; and he brought an order, that they should be delivered up to him, actually at the very moment in which the signal had been given for our departure. As they had served us faithfully, and the man was a bad master who treated them shockingly, the shrieks and lamentations of these poor people were very great. The young maiden (Phillis by name), fainted, and when she again came to herself, would hear nothing whatever about leaving us. She threw herself at my feet and embraced them with clasped hands so strongly, that they were obliged to tear her away by force. My husband offered their master money for her; but the latter . . . demanded for this girl thirty guineas, a sum which my husband did not wish to give. . . . We gave them a present of their clothing, and also the mattresses, which, in view of the voyage, we had made for them. . . . We afterwards, however, repented that we did not make the sacrifice.[22]

[On reaching Canada, the von Riedesels proceeded up the St. Lawrence River to Sorel, where the General was stationed. The family lived just outside the town; the Baroness provided details of their lives.]

winter provisions . . . ottocas . . . pickles

The Canadian winter is very healthy, although severe; for as the weather is steady, one can take proper precautions against the cold. Thus is it, that the people here do not suffer from cold near as much as with us. In the beginning of

November, each household lays in all their stores for the winter. I was very much astonished when they asked me how many fowls, and particularly how many fish I wished to have for the winter; I asked where I should keep the latter as I had no fishpond? "In the loft," they replied, "where they will keep better than in the cellar." I accordingly laid way, between three and four hundred, which kept fresh and sweet the entire winter. All that was necessary to do, when we wanted something for our table, such as meat, fish, eggs, apples and lemons, was to put them in cold water the day previous. By this means, all the frost was taken out, and the meat and fish became as juicy and tender as they are with us. The fowls, moreover, are packed in the snow, which forms around them such a crust of ice, that they have to be chopped out with a hatchet.

They have a fruit in Canada, which is called ottocas [cranberry]. It grows in the water, is red, and as large as a small cherry, but without a stone. It is carefully gathered, particularly by the Indians, and sold without the stalk. It makes a very good preserve, especially if picked after a hard frost. . . . My husband had a large patch of ground behind our house, converted into a productive garden, in which he planted twelve hundred fruit trees. . . . we raised in it a few vegetables. Every thing grew splendidly; and each evening, we went into the garden and picked between one hundred and fifty and two hundred cucumbers, which I made into pickles. This manner of preparing these vegetables was not known to the Canadians; and I accordingly made them all presents of pickles.[23]

[The Mohawk Indian Chief, Joseph Brant, dined with the von Riedesels. The Baroness was impressed and called him "a very good man, kind and courteous." She did not regard other Indians as highly.]

His character was very gentle

My husband had also Indians under his command who loved him very much. . . . It was at this time that I saw the renowned chief of the Indians, Captain Brant . . . At the time we were in Canada, he was the leader of the Indians. He conversed well, possessed polished manners, and was highly esteemed by General Haldimand. I have dined with him at the general's. He was dressed partly as a military man, and partly as an Indian. He had a manly and intelligent cast of countenance. His character was very gentle. My husband was once invited to a gathering of Indians, where they first made him a speech, and then begged him to take a meal among them. They then offered him a pipe of tobacco, which with them if the highest compliment they can pay. . . He, in turn, invited them to visit him. They came, and he entertained them, after the fashion of their race, with tobacco and rum. One of these Indians especially, was decorated with medals which are marks of personal prowess. We invited him to dinner and forced him to drink. He drank, however, very little, and said to us in broken French, "Bon enfant le sauvage, lorsque sobre, mais trop bû, animal féroce!". . . ["Good child the savage when sober, but when drunk, a wild animal!"]

The Indians behave bravely in battle as long as victory is upon their side. But on retreats, as for example, previous to our being taken prisoner at Saratoga,

I saw them first run and then hide themselves. But it is very likely that this may have been caused by their fear of being captured and then killed.[24]

[The Baroness and her husband, the parents of Augusta, Frederika, Caroline, and America, who was born in New York, had another daughter in 1782. Sadly, "dear little Canada (for so we named her)" died when she was but a few months old. Finally, the time came for the family to return to Europe. A ship was specially fitted out for them, General Haldimand taking great pains to assure his friends a comfortable passage home. The Baroness recalled:]

[He] sent on board a cow and her calf, that we might be supplied constantly with fresh milk. He had also caused a place upon the upper-deck to be covered with earth, and salad-plants set out, which was not only very agreeable but exceedingly healthy on a sea-voyage. We bought also many fowls, sheep, and house vegetables, so careful was I . . . that our table at which twenty-two people sat down daily—should be well supplied.

[Pronouncing herself satisfied with the accommodations, the Baroness remarked with a touch of irony: "In short, everything was as good as could be had in such a floating prison." As a parting gift, her husband gave General Haldimand his favorite horse and a foal; in return the General presented the Baroness with "a magnificent muff and tippet of sable, to remind us of the land where we had so long resided."[25]
The von Riedesels reached Portsmouth in the fall of 1783. After a short stay in England, the family returned to the Continent, and the Baroness went to their home in Wolfenbüttel. A short time later she noted:]

I had the great satisfaction of seeing my husband, with his own troops, pass through the city. Yes! Those very streets, in which, seven and a half years before, I had lost my joy and happiness, were the ones where I now saw this beautiful and soul-stirring spectacle.[26]

It is estimated that between 30,000 and 35,000 loyalist refugees left the United States for destinations in Canada between 1782 and 1783. Most were ordinary people, the well-to-do having already returned to England or gone to the West Indies. The British had intended to provide land as well as food, temporary shelter, clothing, and tools to assist the new settlers until they were established and could take care of their own needs. Unfortunately, many promises were not kept. The land was more rugged and wild than the refugees had been led to expect and the climate more severe, described by one writer as "nine months winter, and three months cold weather." Perhaps most difficult of all, the thinly inhabited existing settlements were ill prepared to deal with the influx of large numbers of people. Hopes were dashed and great hardships endured.

SARAH SCOFIELD FROST and her husband William made their home in Stamford, Connecticut. During the Revolution, as loyalists at odds with Sarah's parents as well as their rebel neighbors, they moved to Lloyd's Neck on British-held Long Island. From there, William Frost led raids into Connecticut, which did not endear him to his former neighbors. When peace was concluded and the British prepared to leave New York City, the Frosts decided to relocate in Canada. In 1783, three convoys transported evacuees: civilian loyalists, slaves who had defected to the British lured by the promise of freedom, and Americans who had fought for the British, all with their families. In May, the second convoy, comprising fourteen vessels, carried upwards of 2,000 evacuees—among whom were the Frosts—most to the village at the mouth of the St. John River (then in Nova Scotia but which later became New Brunswick) that was a distribution point. Sarah kept a diary in which she described the voyage and her impression of what would be her new home.

came on board . . . with the rest of the Loyalist sufferers

May 25, 1783.—I left Lloyd's Neck with my family and came on board the *Two Sisters,* commanded by Capt. Brown, for a voyage to Nova Scotia with the rest of the Loyalist sufferers. . . . We expect to sail as soon as the wind shall favour. We have very fair accommodation in the cabin, although it contains six families, besides our own. There are two hundred and fifty passengers on board.

[On May 27, the ship weighed anchor and made for New York City where it waited for the convoy to assemble. Sarah "went out amongst the shops to trade" and was pleased to receive a visit from her father who brought news of the rest of the family.]

I think sometimes I shall be crazy

Monday, June 9.—Our women all came on board with their children and there is great confusion in the Cabin. We bear with it pretty well through the day, but as it grows towards night, one child cries in one place and one in another, whilst we are getting them to bed. I think sometimes I shall be crazy. . . . I stay on deck tonight till nigh eleven o'clock, and now I think I will go down and get to bed if I can find a place for myself. . . .

Sunday, June 15.—Our people seem cross and quarrelsome today, but I will not differ with any one, if I can help it. . . . About six o'clock this evening we had a terrible squall, and hail stones fell as big as ounce balls. About sunset there was another squall, and it hailed faster than before. Billy [her husband] went out and gathered up a mug full of hail stones, and in the evening we had a glass of punch made out of it, and the ice was in it till we drank the whole of it. . . .

Monday, June 16.—Off at last! We weighed anchor about half after five in the morning. . . . We have now got all our fleet together: we have thirteen ships, two brigs, one frigate. The frigate is our commodore's. . . .

Saturday, June 21.—I rose at eight o'clock, and it was so foggy we could not see one ship belonging to our fleet. They rang their bells and fired guns all the morning to keep company with one another. . . .

Monday, June 23.—The wind becomes more favorable, the fog seems to leave us and the sun looks very pleasant. Mr. Whitney and his wife, Billy and I have been diverting ourselves with a few games of crib. . . .

Wednesday, June 25.—We have *measles* very bad on board our ship.

the roughest land I ever saw

Thursday, June 26.—This morning the sun appears very pleasant. . . . At nine o'clock we begin to see land, at which we all rejoice. . . . Oh, how I long to see that place, though a strange land. I am tired of being on board ship. . . .

Saturday, June 28.—Got up in the morning and found ourselves nigh to land on each side. It was up the river St. John's. At half after nine our captain fired a gun for a pilot; an hour later a pilot came on board, and at a quarter after one our ship anchored off against Fort Howe in St. John's River. Our people went on shore and brought on board spruce and gooseberries, and grass and pea vines with the blossoms on them, all of which grow wild here. They say this is to be our city. Our land is to be five and twenty miles up the river. We are to have here only a building place 40 feet wide and a hundred feet back. Billy has now gone on shore in his whale boat to see how it looks, and he says he will soon come back and take me on shore. I long to set my feet once more on land. He soon came on board again and brought a fine salmon.

Sunday, June 29.—This morning it is very pleasant. I am just going on shore with my children to see how I like it. Later—It is now afternoon and I have been ashore. It is, I think, the roughest land I ever saw. . . . We are to settle here, but are to have our land sixty miles farther up the river. We are all ordered to land to-morrow, and not a shelter to go under.[27]

> [What Sarah went through is all the more impressive given the fact that she was more than eight months pregnant when she arrived in Canada. Her diary contains not a word about her condition.]

HANNAH INGRAHAM was the daughter of a farmer who, during the Revolution, had served for seven years in the loyalist militia. Patriots confiscated his farm near Albany, although they allowed the family to remain on a rental basis. Hannah was eleven when her father returned home and informed the family that they were to make ready for an immediate move to Nova Scotia. As an adult, Hannah recounted her remembrances of the journey and the family's reception in Canada to Mrs. Henry Tippet, wife of the rector of Queensbury, who recorded them.

a sad sick time

September-November, 1783. [Father] said we were to go to Nova Scotia, that a ship was ready to take us there, so we made all haste to get ready, killed the cow, sold the beef and a neighbour took home the tallow and made us a good parcel of candles and put plenty of beeswax in them to make them good and hard. Uncle came down and threshed our wheat, twenty bushels, and grandmother came and made bags for the wheat, and we packed up a tub of butter, a tub of pickles, and a good store of potatoes.

Then on Tuesday, suddenly the house was surrounded by rebels and father was taken prisoner and carried away. . . . I cried and cried that night. When morning came, they said he was free to go.

We had five wagon loads carried down the Hudson in a sloop and then we went on board the transport that was to bring us to Saint John. I was just eleven years old when we left our farm to come here. It was the last transport of the season and had on board all those who could not come sooner. The first transports had come in May so the people had all the summer before them to get settled. This was the last of September. We had a bad storm in the Bay of Fundy but some Frenchmen came off in a canoe and helped us (piloted us I suppose).

There were no deaths on board, but several babies were born. It was a sad sick time after we landed in Saint John. We had to live in tents. The government gave them to us and rations too. It was just at the first snow then and the melting snow and the rain would soak up into our beds as we lay. Mother got so chilled and developed rheumatism and was never well afterwards. We came up the river at last in a schooner and were nine days getting to St. Annes. . . . We were brought as far as Maugerville [New Brunswick] in a schooner but we had to get the rest of the way, twelve miles, walking or any way we could because the schooner could not get past the Oromocto shoals. . . .

We lived in a tent at St. Annes until father got a house ready. He went up through our lot till he found a nice fresh spring of water. He stooped down and pulled away the fallen leaves that were thick over it and tasted it. It was very good so there he built his house. We all had rations given us by the government, flour, butter, and pork. Tools were given to the men also.

One morning when we awoke we found the snow lying deep on the round all round us and then father came wading through it and told us the house was ready and not to stop to light a fire and not to mind the weather, but follow his tracks through the trees, for the trees were so many we soon lost sight of him going up the hill. It was snowing fast and oh, so cold. Father carried a chest and we all took something and followed him up the hill through the trees to see our gable end.

There was no floor laid, no windows, no chimney, no door, but wehad a roof at least. A good fire was blazing and mother had a big loaf of bread and she boiled a kettle of tea and put a good piece of butter in a pewter bowl. We toasted the bread and all sat around the bowl and ate our breakfast that morning and mother said: "Thank God we are no longer in dread of having shots fired through our house. This is the sweetest meal I have tasted for many a day."

It was not long before father got a good floor down of split logs, a floor overhead to make a bedroom and a chimney built. . . . Our chimney was made of stones for the back and a kind of mud mortar. The front and sides were just sticks and mud. They took care to plaster mud all up the inside of the chimney.

1784/1785

We soon got things planted the first spring. They would grow so easy. One bushel of wheat yielded thirty, the ground was all so new, you see. We had brought wheat and beans and seeds with us and we could sell anything we had for money down. Many people wanted the things we had and father was always getting jobs of work to do. . . .

I went to school the first winter up at St. Annes on snowshoes. The next winter I hauled my brother on a hand sled. . . . My brother John had chopped his toe off when cutting wood with father. He was a big boy then. . . . Father said if I would haul John to school he would give me another quarters schooling and I did it, but it was hard work through the deep snow and once it was so cold that the poor boy got his toe frozen before he reached school and that put back the healing. Mother had to poultice it and it was a bad piece of work for him.

1786

"Have you had the smallpox"

There were plenty of Indians coming to sell furs in those days. I've counted forty canoes going up the river all at one time. They used to come ashore to sell their furs. . . . One day when I was all alone in the house except the baby, I saw a big Indian coming up the hill to the door. I was terribly afraid at first for I knew he would perhaps stay all day and eat up everything in the house, so I ran to the cradle and catched up the baby and wrapped him in a quilt and went to the door just as the Indian got there. So I said: "Have you had the smallpox," hushing the baby all the while. And he darted away as if he had been shot and we had no Indians all that summer.[28]

NANCY JEAN CAMERON and her family decided to leave their home in the Mohawk Valley and head for Canada in 1785. Although John Cameron had not served with the British, he nevertheless scouted for them and provided useful information. His neighbors did not look kindly upon his collaboration and made life difficult for the family after the War. Nancy Jean described why they felt compelled to move in a letter to a cousin in Scotland.

a new land of promise

My dear Margaret:—   Broadalbin, New York, May 15, 1785

At last we are preparing to leave forever this land of my birth. The long weary years of war, followed by the peace years, that have been to us worse than the time of fighting, are over.

As soon as it is possible we shall set foot on our travels for a new land of promise. A settlement is to be made on the Northern Shore of the St. Lawrence River, some fifty miles from the town of Montreal.

Our lands are confiscated and it is hard to raise money at forced sales.

We expect the journey to be long and hard and cannot tell how many weeks we will be on the road. We have four horses and John has made our big wagon as comfortable as he can. Through the forests we must trust to Indian guides.

Many of Scotch origin will form the band of travellers. The children little realize the days of hardship before them and long to start off.

I love friendship and neighborly kindness, and I am so glad that there will be no more taunting among the elders, no more bickering among the children.

Bitter feelings are gone forever. Patriot or rebel we are what we see is right to each of us, conscience may make cowards.

When I leave this beautiful Mohawk Valley and the lands that I had hoped we would always hold, I shall hear no more the words "Tory" and "Parricide". . . .

Our grandparents little thought when they sought this new land . . . that a flitting [moving about] would be our fate, but, we must follow the old flag wherever it takes us. . . .

We all send our love to you and Kenneth and when I know where we are to live you shall hear from us.   Your affectionate cousin[29]

People moved for other reasons after the War. Many Americans were attracted to the western frontier where it seemed possible to acquire land easily and make a new start. Women bravely undertook the difficult journey, leaving dear relatives behind, and struggled to establish a home in what was still mostly wilderness, and where Indians posed a threat.

ELIZABETH HOUSE TRIST helped her mother run a well-regarded boarding house in Philadelphia during the Revolution. She had stayed behind with her young son while her husband Nicholas, a former British officer, established himself on land he had purchased in Louisiana. The prolonged separation was hard on them both. Although Elizabeth claimed "resolution enough to undertake the Journey," it was not until peace had been declared that she felt travel was safe.

The clientele at the boarding house included many prominent Americans, among them Thomas Jefferson who became Elizabeth's close friend. Knowing of Jefferson's fascination with geography and natural history, and his eagerness to learn about the lands to the west, she determined to keep a diary recording not only personal details of her trip but also whatever she observed along the way that would be of interest to him.

After months of preparations and planning, which included arranging for the care of her eight-year-old son in her absence, Elizabeth Trist set out in December of 1783 in the company of a woman named Polly and her husband's friend, Alexander Fowler. Their destination was Pittsburgh where Trist intended to stay the winter with Fowler and his family. Although the route through southern Pennsylvania was an established one, the journey was far from easy, especially at that time of year, and decent lodging was hard to find. On the 23rd her party arrived at Lancaster, Pennsylvania, and put up at a tavern.

roads beyond description

24th Arose very early with an intention to set off before Breakfast, but it set in to snow very fast which detained us till 10 O' clock; we rode some distance before we baited [fed] our Horses, the roads beyond description bad: we cou'd get no further that day than Elizabeth Town, which is 18 miles from Lancaster. . . .

On the 25th left . . . before Breakfast. The weather's moderated a little but very ruff roades. . . . We scarse go out of a walk, which makes our journey tedious.

We arrived at Chambers' ferry on the Susquehanna at 3 O Clock PM but found it impassable, such quantity of Ice running. None wou'd attempt to put us over. We were under necessity of staying at the ferry House all night. . . . Were obliged to Sleep in the same room with Mr. Fowler and another man. Not being accustom'd to such inconveniences, I slept but little.

On the 26th Mr. Chambers got several more hands and with great exertions put us over. The boat being full of Horses and the rapidity of the current, together with the Ice, made it very difficult to attain the other shore. My heart almost sunk within me.

[The travelers pushed on, contending with continued cold weather—"Snow up to the Horses bellies"—and dirty lodgings—"I kept my cloaths on, to keep my self from the dirt off the bed cloaths." Trist nevertheless pronounced herself "much pleased with the prospect of the country." But she sorely felt the lack of privacy and was much gratified by efforts to provide it.]

customary for the Men and Women to sleep in the same room

[On the 3rd of January, 1784] Stop'd at a little Hut Kept by one Ryan. The neatness of the place and the attention of the man made us as happy as if we had been in a palace. . . . We had a little particion run along the side of our bed, and we hung our great coats up at the foot, which made our birth very private. Mr. Fowler and Mr. Hamilton retired to the Kitchen for us to go to bed; and I made it a rule to get up before day light that I might not see anybody nor they [see] me dress. It is so customary for the Men and Women to sleep in the same room that some of the Women look upon a Woman as affected that makes any objection to it. One told me that I talk'd to upon the subject that she thought a Woman must be very inecure in her self that was afraid to sleep in the room with a strange man. For her part, she saw nothing indelicate in the matter, and no man wou'd take a liberty with a woman unless he saw a disposition in her to encourage him.

4th After Breakfast, we set out on our journey. . . .

[Trist and her party made their way across the Allegheny Mountains. When "a great fall of rain" melted the snow, they were obliged to proceed on foot through mud "without sinking higher than our knees." When it turned cold, "the whole earth appeared like Glass."[30]]

my Spirits forsook me

In the Morng of the 8th. . . . Our Horses scarse able to keep their feet. . . . for the first time since I left home, my Spirits forsook me. I began to prepare my self for the other world, for I expected every moment when my neck wou'd be broke. I cou'd not help crying. Mr. Fowler kept before me and, it being dark, I did not expose my weakness. Some times I wish'd he wou'd ride on and leave me [so] that I might get down and *die.*

[Reaching Pittsburgh on January 9th, Trist stayed with the Fowlers until May. She provided a detailed description of the settlement for Jefferson's benefit.]

cole Hill

Fort Pitt is situated upon a point of land form'd by the junction of . . . two rivers [the Monongahela and the Allegheny] with the Ohio. . . . On the Monongahala, where the town is chiefly built, there are about a Hundred buildings; all . . . in a very ruinous state. . . . The land is exceeding rich and abounds with an abundance of maple trees, from which they make quantitys of sugar. . . . The low land, lying between the river and the high lands or hills, is call'd bottoms, and nothing can exceed the quallity of those grounds. In the month of May they look like a garden, such a number of beautifull flowers and shrubs. There are several wild vegetables that I wou'd give the preference to those that are cultivated: Wild Asparagus, Indian hemp, shepherd sprouts, lambs quarters, &cc—besides great abundance of Ginsang, Gentian and many other aromatick.

On the other side of the Monongahala, the land is amaizing lofty. Tis supposed that the whole body of it is cole [coal] and goes by the name of the cole Hill. At one side it has been open'd to supply the inhabitants with fuel. . . . The Hill is seven Hundred feet perpendicular, and on the top is a settlement. The land is fertile and capable of raising all kinds of grain. . . . In the spring of the year, the rivers abound with very fine fish, some of them exceeding good—particularly the Pike, which greatly exceed those that are caught below the Mountains in flavor and size, some of them weighing thirty pounds. The cat fish are enormous; some of them are obliged to be carried by 2 Men. The perch are commonly about the size of Sheep heads, but they have been caught that weigh'd 20 pound. There are several other kind—such as herring, &c—but different from ours. The bass look more like our Sea perch, only much larger, and I give them the preference to all the rest for their delicacy of flavor.[31]

[At first Elizabeth liked Pittsburgh: "Was there good Society, I shou'd be contented to end my days in the Western country. . . ." But when she left on May 20 it was "with as little regret as I ever did any place that I had lived so long in." Even though the Fowlers were most hospitable and there were dances and entertainments to help pass the time she was eager to move on. She boarded the flatboat that was to carry passengers down the Ohio and pronounced the accommodations "all things consider'd, not to be complain'd of." At Wheeling, a hundred miles from Pittsburgh, Elizabeth raved about the scenery: "I am allmost in extacy at the Magnificence of the display of nature. The trees are deck'd all in their gay attire, and the earth in its richest verdure. So much for blooming May."]

22d . . . . Passd the little Kanhawa at noon. . . . Along the banks of the river . . . is a great quantity of very large stone supposed to be of an excellent quality for mills stones, equal to the french Burrs.

23d 9 O clock in the Morng came to great Kanahawa or new river, a beautiful situation for a town. The point is clear'd, and the banks are high. There was a very pretty fort at this place, till about 4 years ago. It was destroy'd by the savages. The land is the property of General Washington.* We came a 100 miles in 21 hours and drifted all the way.[32]

*George Washington, like many others, had speculated in western lands. William Loughton Smith, when he was visiting Mount Vernon in 1791, noted in his journal entry for April 23: "The General has lately sold his transmountainous lands, 130,000 acres for 65,000 crowns."[33]

[Soon, however, the travelers encountered many difficulties. The boat ran aground on rocks, and it took eight days for the cargo to be unloaded, allowing the boat to clear the rocks, and then be reloaded. Early in June the river was so low that in order to avoid sand bars the boat had to tie up on shore at night, lengthening the voyage considerably.]

About nine [on the morning of the 7th of June] . . . our people went on shore to hunt and kill'd a tame cow which they mistook for a Buffaloe. However, it turned out very good Beef. They employ'd all the rest of the day jerkin it to preserve it, which is done by cutting it into small thin pieces and running them on sticks, lay them on a scaffold; underneath they make a small fire and a great smoke, which in a few hours drys [the beef strips] so as to keep a long time.

it is good to have friends at court

10th Just before sun rise we passed the Wabash [River]. . . . About 8 oClock we observed two canoes with Indians making towards us. We were prepared for their reception if their intentions had been hostile. The boat in company hail'd them and invited them to come on board. One of the canoes accepted the invitation. Two Indians and a very handsome squaw with a young child. They had formerly been of the Delaware tribe, but a number of them had left that Nation about fourteen years ago and went to live up the Wabash. They have been our very great enemies this War. One of the fellows calls himself James Dickison. He is one of their chiefs, and a sensible fierce looking fellow, but his character is very bad. They say he has plunderd several boats and murderd many people that have been going down this river. My curiossity led me to visit them, as they had all the appearance of friendship. They eat and drank and smoked the calmut [calumet—a pipe with a clay bowl and reed stem, an Indian symbol of peace]. As it is good to have friends at court, I carried the Squaw some bread; and as her Infant was exposed to the sun, I gave her my Hankerchief to shade it, for which she seem'd very thankfull. Mr. McFarlane gave them some flour and meat and a bottle of Whisky. . . . After honoring us with their company for about an hour they wish'd us well and left us in great good humour.

the greatest curiossity I ever beheld

We arrived at the Big Cave [Illinois] early in the evening and went on shore to see it. I lament that we had not a little more day light that I might examine it more minutely. When the river is high, it stands directly on the waters edge. But that happens not to be the case [now], which embellishes the Prospect much, by presenting us with a fine flight of steps of white stone that has the appearance of marble, clean and elegant, directly in front of the Cave which appears to be about forty feet high and sixty in width and resembles an old castle. The entrance is as large as a common door to house. A grape vine runs up on each side, and a tree juts over the top, which adds to its beauty. It was so dark that we were obliged to set fire to some light wood to see our way into the cave. The upper part of the passage is about four feet wide, but near the earth the rocks jut out so as to make the path only a foot and a half. I was disappointed not finding more room, as the passage indicated something capacious; but the widest part does not exceed seven foot. The driping of the water form'd some petrefactions [stalactites or stalagmites] that resembled columns. . . . Upon the whole, I think it one of the most grand and beautifull natural structures and the greatest curiossity I ever beheld. . . .

11th The wind lull'd, but the weather very warm. About 10 oClock was alarm'd by a canoe making for our boat, which we supposed to be Indians. The blunderbuss was mounted, the Muskets loaded, and every matter properly arrainged for fighting. My self disposed of between the flour barrels. But to my great satisfaction they turn'd out to be some french men going to the Cumberland river to trade. Their appearance was perfectly savage, having little or no cloaths on and their hides quite as dark as the Indians. . . .

call'd after Governor Jefferson

13th . . . I arose in expectation of seeing the Grand Riviere [Mississippi] but had not that satisfaction till four Oclock in the afternoon. . . . the Water of the Mississippi uncommonly low so as to discover a large sand bar near the junction of the two rivers—but the current is much stronger than the Ohio. About 3 miles below the mouth of the Ohio, there is a fort or, rather, the remains of one which was erected by the Americans this War and call'd after Governor Jefferson. I was inform'd it at present was occupied by a Nation of Indians call'd the Taumas who have been nutaral [neutral], notwithstanding the English took great pains to make them take up the hatchet against us. To avoid their snares, they abandon'd their grounds on the Miami, about 6o mile from Detroit, and came down to this part of the country. . . . I wish'd to see the fort because it bore the name of my friend, but I was dissuaided from making the attempt as it was not certain what Indians might be there. . . .

I dont like this river

14th At dawn of day we left the shore and soon came in sight of the Iron bank: a great quantity of ore may be picked up on the surface of the earth. . . . In the afternoon we got among the Canadian Islands. . . . so call'd from a number of poeple on their way from Canada down this river having stop'd there for some time. . . . I dont like this river. The passage is attended with much more danger that I had any Idea of. We are obliged to make fast every night; and the banks are so high, the current so rapid, and the river close to the shore so fill'd with fallen timber and brush, that it is attended with great difficulty to accomplish.

the fag end of the world

18th The wind still against us. We came to the first of the Chickasaw Bluffs about Seven o clock in the morng, which is 201 miles from the Ohio. My patience is allmost exausted. What with the Musquitos and head winds, I am allmost sick. The passage early in the Spring wou'd be pleasant, but at present there is nothing but trouble. I have various Ideas about this river:—[I] some times conceit [imagine]—I am got to the fag end of the world; or rather that it is the last of Gods creation and the Seventh day came before it was quite finnish'd. At other times, I fancy there has been some great revolution in nature, and this great body of water has forced a passage where it was not intended and tore up all before it. . . . The water is as muddy as a pond that has been frequently visited by the Hogs. Alltogether its appearance is awfull and Melancholy and some times terrific. . . .[34]

19th. . . . We went about 30 miles when we were obliged to lay by an hour sooner than we woud have done—some heavy clouds appearing that indicated a storm. . . . This is a Passionate sort of climate, quickly raised but soon blows over. However this [storm] was not so easily appeased. . . . a most uncomfortable night. I am so stung with Musquitos that I look as if I was in the hight of the small pox. . . .

20th. . . . A week this day since we enterd the Mississippi and have not got 300 mile.

allmost coddled

25th. . . . There are a great many Pelican about here, the first we have seen. They are a fine Majestick looking bird and at a distance resemble the swan. One of our people kill'd one and brought it on board the boat. They are all white, except the wings which are tinged with black. It measured ten feet from the tip end of one wing to the other. The Bill is about an inch wide and a foot in length. The under jaw or bottom of the bill resembles white leather and expands in an extraordanary manner. I saw 14 quarts of water put into its mouth, and it wou'd have held more. I can not comprehand what use they make of this amaizing pouch, unless to scoop up the little fish, They are very harmless and so tame that they swim almost in reach of our oars. The most curious bird I ever saw. . . . An extremely warm day and night, allmost coddled [parboiled].

28th The wind in our favor, very reviveing to me for I am every day more anxious to be at the end of my journey . . . In the afternoon, our boat—by the violence of the current—was drove against a large tree that was about 20 yds from the shore. It held us by the roof, notwithstanding the water run so rapid as to carry every thing before it. If the boat had not been very strong, we shou'd certainly been cast away. They were obliged to cut away part of the roof before we cou'd get disengaged. . . .

29th. We stoped at an Island for the night, and I lost my poor little Dog, Fawnis. Tis supposed the Allegator got him as one was seen swimming about the boat in the evening—poor little fellow.

1st of July [1784]. . . . My heart sinks within me, and I feel so weak that I can hardly keep my self alive. What can cause these sensations? My journey is most compleated. Three days more I shall be happy in sight of the Natchez. Will write to Mr Trist. Perhaps a boat may be just seting off, and he will be glad to see me, I know. . . .[35] [This last page of Trist's diary breaks off, in mid-sentence.]

> [As fate would have it, Elizabeth was not to meet her husband at the end of her journey. He had died in February while she was wintering over in Pittsburgh, although news of his death did not reach her until July 1, when the boat she was on docked just above Natchez. It remained to the young widow to settle her husband's affairs. In 1785, she decided to return to Philadelphia by water, but that was easier said than done, given the political uncertainties surrounding the navigation of the Mississippi at that time. In the spring, she was finally able to arrange passage to Philadelphia via Jamaica.]

MARY COBURN DEWEES, in 1788, embarked on a journey, which would take her, her husband and children, from Philadelphia to Kentucky, where they had decided to settle. Her journal was probably compiled from notes she made along the way and was intended for family and friends back home. Her story, in contrast to Elizabeth Trist's, had a happy ending.

Obliged to foot it up

September 27th Left Philada. about 5 OClock in the Afternoon and tore our selves from a number of dear friends that assembled to take a last farewell before we set off for Kentucky. Made our first stage 6 Miles from the City, being very sick the greatest part of the way. . . .

October 1st Crost the Conostogo, a good deal uneasie for fear my sickness should return. . . . After refreshing ourselves we took a walk up the Creek and I think I never saw a more beautifull prospect. . . . As the sun was setting we rode through Lancaster a Beautifull inland town, with some Elegant Houses in it. . . .

2d 'Tho but a few days since my friends Concluded I Could not reach Kentucky, will you believe me when I tell you I am setting on the Bank of the Susquehanah, and can take my bit of ham and Biscuit with any of them. . . .

7th Set off for the north mountain which we find so bad we are Obliged to foot it up, and could compair ourselves to nothing but a parcel of Goats climbing up some of the Welch Mountains that I have read of. . . . find this the most fatiguing days Journey we have had, the roads so very bad and so very steep that the horses seem ready to fall backwards. . . . Beleve me my dear friends the sight of a log house on these Mountains after a fatiguing days Journey affords more real pleasure that all the Magnificent buildings your city contains. . . .

she is a Kent.y Lady

Octr. 8th Left the foot of the mountain and crosd Scrub hill which is very bad indeed. . . . The Children are very hearty and bear fatigue much better than we do, 'tho I think we all do wonder full. . . . Rachel Mostly passes half the day in Spelling and Sally in Singing every house we stop at she enquires if it is not a Kent.y. house and seldom leaves it 'till she informs them she is a Kent.y Lady.

9th Crost sidling hill. . . . we were obliged to walk the greatest part of the way up 'tho not without company there was five Waggons with us all the morning to different parts, this night our difficulties began we were Obliged to put up at a Cabin at the foot of the hill. . . . there was between twenty & thirty of us, all lay on the floor, Except Mrs. Rees the Children and your Maria [me], who by our dress or adress or perhaps boath were favoured with a bed and I assure you we that thought ourselves to escape being fleaed Alive. . . .

Octr 13 Proceeded to Larel Creek and Ascended the hill. . . . by reason of the Badness of the roads could not reach a stage the hill being 20 miles across and our horses a good deal tired, we, in Company with a nother waggon were ob-liged to Encamp in the woods, after a Suitable place at a Convenient distance from a run of water was found and a level piece of ground was pitched upon for our encampment our men went to give refreshment to the Horses, we Females having had a good fire made up set about preparing Supper which consisted of an Excellent dish of Coffe having milk with us, those who chose had a dish of cold ham and pickled beats with the addition of Bread, Butter Biscuit, & Cheese made up our repast after supper, Sister, the Children, and myself took up our lodging in the waggon the men with thier Blankets laid down at the fire side. . . .

On the 14 Set out for Chesnut ridge, horrid roads and the Stony's [Stoniest] land in the world I believe, every few hundred Yards, rocks big enough to build a small house upon. . . . I think by this time we may call our selves Mountain proof. . . .

our Boat resembling Noahs Ark not a little

18th Our boat being ready we set off for the river and arrived thier at 12 OClock and went on board immediately. . . . at 2 OClock we push down the river very slowly, intend Stopping at Fort Pitt, where we expect to meet the Waggon with the rest of our Goods. our Boat resembling Noahs Ark not a little. . . .

19th . . . .The water very low, I am much afraid we shall have a tedious passage our boat is 40 foot long our room 16 by 12 with a Comfortable fire place our Bed room partioned off with blankets . . . We are clear of fleas. . . . We are now longing for rain as much as we dreaded on the Land for it is impossible to get down untill the water raises. . . .

the most tedious part of our Journey

Oct. 20th . . . . As the Sun was Setting hove in sight the Coal Hill & ferry house opposite Pittsburgh, this hill is of Amazing height and affords a vast deal more coal than can be Consumed in that place, what a valuable Aquisition would it be near your City.

21st We are now laying about a mile from Pittsburgh, and have receiv'd sev-eral Invitations to come on shore we have declined all, as the trunks with our cloaths is not come up, and we in our travelling dress, not fit to make our appearance in that Gay place. . . .

24 The Town all in arms, a report prevailed that a party of Indians within twenty miles coming to Attack . . . The drums beating to Arms with the Militia collecting from every part of the Town. . . .

26 & 27th Staid at McKees island waiting for water, which is too low to go down. . . . Saw three boats full of troops going up to Pittsburgh we suppose they are going up for Provision for the Garison below. . . .

30 The weather much in our favour it rained all day. sewing & reading, and when the weather is fine walking are the amusements we enjoy, The Gentlemen pass thier time in hunting of deer, Turkeys, ducks, and every other Kind of wild fowl, with which this Country abounds. A Beatifull Doe had the Assurence the other day to come half way down the hill and give a peep at us, but our hunters being out escaped being taken fishing makes up part of thier Amusement.

31st Still in hopes of the waters raising as we had snow again this Morning and a prospect of rain, this the most tedious part of our Journey as we still continue in one place. . . .

[November] 7 Dined on an Excellent pike had the Company of 3 French Gentlemen . . . who came to invite us to a Ball held at Col. Butlers where 30 Ladys & Gentlemen were to Assemble for that purpose it is hardly worth while to say we declined going as it was out of our power to dress fit at this time, to Attend such an Entertainment or else (you know) should be happy to do ourselves the honour. . . .

10th From the 10th to the 18 of November we passed our time in visiting, and receiving Visits on board our boat. When we bid Adieu to the Island friends and pushed down the Ohio saw a small Kentucky Boat go down yesterday which induced us to set off as the water has risen but very little But still continues to rise slowly. . . .

Nov. 20 Just as the day broke, got a ground on a Sandbar, at the beach Bottom. . . . At sun rise we passed by Norris Town on the Indian Shore [the north bank of the Ohio; the southern bank was called the Virginia shore] a Clever little Situation with ten Cabbins plasently Situated saw another Kentucky Boat and passed by Wheeling a place where a Fort was kept and attack'd last war. . . .

full expectations of seeing better days

On the first of Decembr arrived at Lexington, [Kentucky] . . . we were politely recev'd and. . . . staid at my Brothers. . . .

Jany. 1 1789 We Still continue at my Brothers and . . . mean to go down to south elk horn as soon as the place is ready—Since I have been here I have been visited by the genteele people in the place and receivd several Invitations both in town & Country, the Society in this place is very Agreeable and I flatter myself I shall see many happy days in this Country. Lexington is a Clever little Town with a court house and Jail and some pretty good buildings in it, Chiefly Log my abode I have not seen yet a discription of which you shall have by and by.

29th I have this day reached South Elk horn, and am much pleased with it tis a snug little Cabbin about 9 Mile from Lexington on a pretty Asscent surrounded

by Sugar trees, a Beatifull pond a little distance from the house, with an excellent Spring not far from the Door—I can assure you I have enjoyed more happiness the few days I have been here than I have experienced these four or five
years past. I have my little family together And am in full expectations of seeing
better days.   Yours &c MD[36]

Women who went west with their husbands and families had to contend
with the difficulties attendant on such a drastic relocation, particularly to areas
where physical safety was still a concern. Not surprisingly, those who were left
behind often felt bereft being parted from those they loved.

JANE PRINCE ROBBINS and her husband sorely missed their children who were
located at some distance from their parents in Massachusetts. They were especially concerned about their daughter, Hannah Robbins Gilman, who with her
husband and children had settled in the Ohio valley. Robbins's letters to Hannah
reveal how deeply affected she was by their absence.

Oct. 5. [1792]—I love to open my desk, and take a sheet of paper, and fold it up
in this way, if I only say my dear Hannah. . . .

she says, tis Hannah yet

22—Your Par and I went to Boston, He had a great inclination to hear the Tri-
centary sermon that is to be preach'd by Dr Belknap, on the discovery of America by Columbius. . . . went wensday morning and breakfasted at Mrs Mackpeac-
es. She was very glad to see me, "how do you do, Mrs Robbins, I am glad to see
you look so well, I expected when your Children left you, you would be as dead
as a Bat in winter. I have all most worred to death about Hannah, myself, but by
all I can learn she is quite happy." I took your last letter out of my pocket and
read to her, she was very much gratify'd. she says, tis Hannah yet. . . . you are a
good child, to write all oppertunitys, it is a great releif to our minds, as we can't
help feeling anxious for your safty. . . . when you say anything about your dear
little Children, I feel as if I long for wings, to fly to them. . . .

[Nov.] 22—Your Par, and I, at a wedding, at Mrs Cottons. . . . I thought while I
was their, if any persons are to be envied tis those parents, that have their Children settel'd, where their is a possability of seeing them. . . .

talked of our dear absent Children

29—Annual Thanksgiving. aunt and Robbins here. a very fine day, after dinner
aunt, and I, went up in the back Chamber, and talked of our dear absent Children. . . . let us said I fancy that Mr Gilman and Hannah are below the bank [in
the garden], He leading little Jane up the steps, and Hannah behind him, with her
Babby in her armes, Jenny & Isaac coming out of the gate, and Francis taking hold
of her apron, saying I want to go to Mar Robbins, she is up at the window. . . . Par
call'd us to tea, and the pleasing scene vanish'd.[37]

Part III
Women in the Emerging Nation

Figure 6. *Laedy Waschington.* The Sussel-Washington Artist. Berks County, Pennsylvania, ca. 1780. Watercolor and ink on paper. 7 3 /4" x 6 1/4." American Folk Art Museum, New York. Gift of Ralph Esmerian. 2005.8.41

Chapter 10

willing to re-sheathe the sword

The American Revolution officially came to a close on September 3, 1783, with the formal signing of the definitive Treaty of Paris. Britain had acknowledged the independence of the United States as a pre-condition for negotiations and agreed to terms that were extraordinarily favorable to the new nation. Foremost was the acknowledgement of the Mississippi as the western boundary of the United States. Fishing rights in waters off Canada were guaranteed to the Americans, and the British agreed to evacuate posts on American soil. Creditors on both sides would be allowed to recover pre-war debts, and Congress was to "earnestly recommend" to the states that loyalist property be returned. While vague language in some of the Articles and the unwillingness or inability to carry out some of the terms would shortly cause friction, there was great rejoicing in the new nation at the end of the War, though not everyone had cause to celebrate.[1]

SARAH JAY wrote her father from Paris late in 1782, after the Preliminary Articles had been agreed to: "The dawn of peace seems to approach," and she solemnly congratulated him on the prospect. She expressed her personal joy to her sister Kitty in Philadelphia anticipating, at long last, a reunion with her family. "Let us my dr. Kitty rejoice together & bless God! . . . I already begin to enjoy in imagination some delightful scenes. Oh! Kitty perhaps the time draws near when we shall fold each other to our bosoms, and when our Domestic felicity shall again be compleat."[2]

SARAH WINSLOW, the sister of loyalist Edward Winslow, wrote to her cousin Benjamin Marston in Canada of the family's bitterness at their treatment by the Americans and what they considered betrayal by the British government.

This peace brings none to my heart

April 10—1783, New York

What is to become of us, God only can tel, in all our former sufferings we had hope to support us, being depriv'd of that, is too much, my mind, and strength, are unequal to my present, unexpected tryals—was their ever an instance my dear Cousin, can any history produce one where such a number of the best of human beings were deserted by the Government they have sacrific'd there all for.

The open enemys of Great Britain have gaind there point. . . . This peace brings none to my heart, my Brother . . . is now hasting away—may he meet you upon his arrival in Halifax. . . . You my Cousin I hope will be much with him. . . . Let compassion and friendship induce you to inform me always when you can, of his situation, and health, and do my friend as you value the peace of this family caution him to take care of himself. . . .

Here it thought best for us to continue for some months or until it is known what better we can do. Severe are the struggles I must now dayly have with myself. . . . I wish to retire entirely to my own family, and endeavour to remain unmolested, if possible, for which purpose my Brother is now seecking a house for us out of the City. . . .

This servant will make you a partaker of our sufferings . . . you are a Christian and Phylosopher, teach me so to be . . .   your affectionate Cousin S[3]

PHEBE FOWLER WARD found herself in the same position as many wives whose spouses had joined or supported the British. Her husband Edmund had been imprisoned in August 1776 by a group of Americans (including his own brother Stephen); transferred to Massachusetts, Edmund made his way to New York City by March 1777: "His Family he left to shift for themselves on the farm." Being in possession was of no use, as Phebe found out.

our farme is sold

Kind Husband   East Chester [New York] June 6th 1783
    I am sorry to aquant you that our farme is sold also that Land and salt medow in East chester town and that ajoyning to Stephen wards [her brother-in-law] Land is all sold. Major Dilevan bought it he told me that one [David] williams that took major andrew [Major André] is to have five hundred pounds woort out of it and he the Remainder. I told them thay had no Right to servey It nor sell it. He said he was ordered to do it and shood sell it. Thay accordingly survaed it and there was foure men to vallue it—there high sheruv, one of there Judges of there cort and two more men to say what it was acre for at [and] what it was to be sold for & dilevan told me they said £7.10.0 an acre for the whool the number of acres bing not cast [added] up.

    thay said if I did not quitt posesion that they had aright to take any thing on the farme or in the house to pay the Cost of a law sute and imprisen me. I have sufered all most Every thing but death it self to keep posesion all most sevin years in your long absens. Pray Grant me spedy Releaf or God only knows what will be com of me and my frends les Children.

    thay said my posession was nothing. youre husband has forfeted his astate by Joining the British Enemy with a free and vollentery will and thereby was for feted to the Stat and sold.

all at present from your cind and Loveing Wife   phebe Ward

pray send me spedeay anser

[Upon receiving his wife's letter, Edmund submitted a petition to Sir Guy Carleton in which he described his situation and asked for relief. What happened to his family is unclear. Four months later, Edmund sailed for Nova Scotia, having been appointed by Carleton to head troops bound for that destination.[4]]

MERCY OTIS WARREN attempted, in her *History,* to give as objective an account of events as was possible for someone who supported and lived through the War. She explained her motivation, asserting that political matters did not "lay out of the road of female life." Warren and America welcomed peace in 1783.[5]

every prospect of tranquility appeared

The discordant sounds of war that had long grated the ears of the children of America, were now suspended, and the benign and heavenly voice of harmony soothed their wounded feelings, and they flattered themselves the dread summons to slaughter and death would not again resound on their shores. The independence of America acknowledged by the first powers in Europe, and even Great Britain willing to re-sheathe the sword on the same honorable terms for the United States, every prospect of tranquility appeared.

[That there were difficulties facing the victorious nation Warren realized all too well.]

such a state of infancy

Though the connexion was now dissolved, and the gordian knot of union between Great Britain and America cut in sunder; though the independence of the United States was, by the treaty, clearly established on the broad basis of liberty; yet the Americans felt themselves in such a state of infancy, that as a child just learning to walk, they were afraid of their own movements. Their debts were unpaid, their governments unsettled, and the people out of breath by their long struggle for the freedom and independence of their country. They were become poor from the loss of trade, the neglect of their usual occupations, and the drains from every quarter for the support of a long and expensive war. . . .

The operation and consequences of the restoration of peace were now the subject of contemplation. . . . the public mind was now agitated like a forest shaken in a tempest, and stood trembling at the magnitude of opening prospects, and the retrospect of past events.[6]

ABIGAIL ADAMS reported to her husband working in Europe "what passes in the political world."

Domestick jars and confusions

June 20, 1783

Perhaps there has been no juncture in the publick affairs of our country; not even in the hours, of our deepest distress, when able statesmen and wise Counsellors were more wanted than at the present day. Peace abroad leaves us at leisure to look into our own domestick affairs. Altho upon an Estimate of our national debt, it appears but as the Small Dust of the balance, when compared to the object we have obtained, & the benifits we have secured, yet . . . we have reason to fear that Domestick jars and confusions, will take place, of foreign contentions and devastations. Congress have commuted with the Army by engageing to them 5 years pay, in lieu of half pay for Life, with Security for this they will disband contented. But our wise Legislators are about disputing the power of Congress to do either. . . .

We have in this state an impost [tax on imports] of 5 per cent, and an excise act, whilst the Neighbouring states have neither. Foreigners finding this the case, cary their Cargoes to other States, at this the Merchant grumbles, the Farmer groans with his taxes and the Mechanick for want of employ. Heaven Avert that . . . we should by civil discension weaken our power, and crush our rising greatness. . . . We want a Soloman in wisdom, to guide and conduct this great people . . . the counsels which are taken, and the measures which are persued; will mark our future Character either with honour, and Fame, or disgrace, and infamy; in adversity, we have conducted with prudence and magninimity. Heaven forbid, that we should grow giddy with prosperity, or the height to which we have soared, render a fall conspicuously fatal.

[Later in the year, Abigail provided specific details for her husband, relating to her own situation.]

tho the War is ceased, taxes have not

Braintree, November 11, 1783

We are anxious to receive official accounts of the Signing the definitive Treaty. . . . Bills are now sold at par. If you continue abroad, I shall be under a necessity of drawing upon you, for tho the War is ceased, taxes have not. Since I took my pen, & within this hour, I have been visited by the collector with 3 tax Bills; the amount of which is 29 pounds 6 & 8 pence, the continental tax state tax & town tax beside which, I have just paid a parish tax. I live with all the frugality in my power. I have but two domesticks, yet I find it as much as I can do to muster cash enough to pay our sons Quarter Bills & Cloath them decently.[7]

In December 1783, after the British evacuation of New York had been completed, General Washington entered the city. Bidding his officers an emotional farewell at a dinner in Fraunces Tavern, Washington set out for Mount Vernon, stopping at Annapolis, where Congress was meeting, to submit his resignation personally on December 23.

Problems in the post-war period loomed large. Britain refused to negotiate a commercial treaty, and states vied with each other for a share of trade with other nations. Economic recovery depended on the United States making good on its debts, and the states on theirs.

The unity that had prevailed in the face of a common enemy faded rapidly once the War was over, and the drawbacks of the Articles of Confederation, the first constitution of the United States, soon manifested themselves. Congress, as a creature of the states, could exert little authority over them; it could not control commerce, nor could it tax, both powers essential to a viable government. Attempts to strengthen the Confederation came to naught, the amendment process being too difficult. Congress met irregularly and, when it did, rarely was there a quorum necessary to transact business. George Washington feared that the new nation would become "the sport of European politics," treated with derision and scorn.[8]

An incident in Massachusetts in 1786, Shays's Rebellion, tended to support the view that steps had to be taken to create a genuinely national government with powers adequate to the country's needs—or face dissolution. Unhappy farmers in the western part of the state, threatened with mortgage foreclosures, joined by disaffected veterans of the Continental Army, appealed to the state legislature for relief but met with no success. Armed citizens then tried to force the adjournment of the state supreme court to prevent further foreclosures. When some 700 men led by Daniel Shays, who had served honorably in the Revolutionary War, raided the federal arsenal at Springfield to secure arms, they were repulsed by an army hastily organized by Governor James Bowdoin. Four participants were killed and 350 were captured; the rest scattered but were hunted down and forced to surrender. Daniel Shays sought refuge in Vermont and was eventually pardoned.[9]

ELIZABETH PORTER PHELPS in her diary provided details about the Rebellion from her perspective as a resident of western Massachusetts.

a very great Army is coming from toward Boston

[January 18, 1787]—Thursday Morn my Husband set out with sleighs to help the men to Springfield which are raised in this town for the support of Government. David Johnson our Boy is gone and a great number of others, it Looks as Dark as Night, a very great Army is coming from toward Boston and some are Collecting upon the other side. It appears as if nothing but the imediate interposition of providence could prevent Blood and there I think I can say I desire to leave it. . . . My Husband got home that Eve but he proposes to go soon. . . .

Jan. 21. Sun. Mr. Hop[kins] . . . Spoke very well upon the present dark Day. Monday morn Mr. Phelps set out for Springfield. Tuesday Eve he came back. Wednesday Killed two oxen set out with the meat—could not get to Springfield came back. Thursday set out again got back. Fryday morn one [Joseph] Locke (that has Lived here ever since last April) set out with Mr. Phelps for Springfield—I hear they got in safe. . . . Last Thursday the mob attempted to march into Springfield the Government fired the cannon Killed four.

Jan. 28. Sun, Mr. Hop[kins] pr[eached] Proverbs 19, 21. . . . This has been a confused day, the Mob in a large Body at Northampton—another party at Amherst—Just as the last meeting was done the Northampton body came into the Lower end of Hadley street marched thro to Amherst—what will be the event none can tell—we hope in Gods mercy. Just at Dusk my Husband got home. Monday Gen. [Benjamin] Lyncoln came into Hadley with about three Thousand men. Tuesday Mr. Phelps carred the children into town to see 'em. . . . Satt. Eve. Joseph Lock and David Johnson came home from the Army.

Feb. 4. Sun. . . . a confused time—the Troops Marched last Eve; the stores and Baggage this day. Monday Mr. Phelps set out with some Loading belonging to the Army, went to Petersham. Fryday home. . . .

[Feb. 21] Wednesday went to Hatfield to the Funeral of one [Jacob] Walker Killed by the Insurgents. . . . he was buried with the Honours of War. . . .

[March 22] Thursday Fast day called; but not one word of fast in the Proclamation only Humiliation and prayer. I view it and kept it as fast. . . . Satt. Mr. Phelps set out for Boston to do Business for a great number of the inhabitants of this Town respecting pay for Quartering the soldiers here etc.[10]

MERCY OTIS WARREN agreed that Shays's Rebellion had to be dealt with by military force and that a stronger government was necessary to preserve peace and unity.

awakened all to . . . the necessity of concert and union

By well-timed lenity, and decided energy, as the exigencies of the moment required, was terminated an insurrection, that, by its dangerous example, threatened the United States with a general rupture, that might have been more fatal than foreign war, to their freedom, virtue, and prosperity. But though the late disturbances were quelled, and the turbulent spirit, which had been so alarming was subdued by a small military force, yet it awakened all to a full view of the necessity of concert and union in measures that might preserve their internal peace. This required the regulation of commerce on some stable principles, and some steps for the liquidation of both public and private debts. They also saw it necessary to invest congress with sufficient powers for the execution of their own laws, for all general purposes relative to the union.[11]

A convention called for the specific purpose of constitutional revision took place in May 1787. In general, the delegates believed that a more powerful national government was needed and that it should be a republic based on popular sovereignty, answerable not to the states but to the collective population of the Union. An atmosphere of urgency made possible compromises that accommodated competing views. A document was finally approved and sent to the states for ratification by conventions elected for the purpose, a minimum of nine necessary for adoption. Opinion in the nation and in the conventions was divided between Federalists, who supported the new Constitution, and Anti-Federalists, who believed that the Constitution had serious flaws, chiefly the absence of a bill of rights.

MERCY OTIS WARREN, an Anti-Federalist, expressed her thoughts on the proposed constitution in letters to Catharine Macaulay.

the Dignity of Government

Our situation is truly delicate & critical. on the one hand, we stand in need of a strong Federal government founded on principles that will support the prosperity & union of the Colonies. on the other we have struggled for liberty & made costly sacrifices at her Shrine and there are still many among us who revere her name too much to relinquish (beyond a certain medium) the rights of man for the Dignity of Government.[12]

[Battles in the conventions were heated, but eventually all the states except for Rhode Island ratified the new Constitution, with the understanding that a bill of rights would be among the first issues considered by the new Congress. (Faced with isolation, Rhode Island ratified in 1790.) The next step was to choose members of the new government, the most important office being president. "It is time we have a Government established & a Washington at its head."[13] In her *History* Warren discussed what prompted George Washington to respond to this call to duty.]

the call was strong and impressive

The new system of government was ushered into existence under peculiar advantages; and no circumstance tended more rapidly to dissipate every unfavorable impression, than the unanimous choice of a gentleman to the presidential chair, at once meritorious, popular, and beloved, beyond any man. Washington, the favorite of every class of people, was placed at the head of a government of experiment and expectation. Had any character of less popularity and celebrity been designated to this high trust, it might at this period have endangered, if not have proved fatal to the peace of the union. Though some thought the executive vested with too great powers to be entrusted to the hand of any individual, Washington was an individual in whom they had the most unlimited confidence.

After the dissolution of the American army, and the retirement of the commander in chief from the conspicuous station in which he had been placed, the celebrity of his life and manners, associated with the circumstances of a remarkable revolution, in which he always stood on the fore ground, naturally turned the eyes of all toward him. The hearts of the whole continent were united, to give him their approbatory voice, as the most suitable character in the United States to preside at the head of civil government.

The splendid *insignia* of military command laid aside, the voluntary retirement of general Washington had raised his reputation to the zenith of human glory. Had he persevered in his resolution never again to engage in the thorny path of public life, his repose might have been forever insured, in the delightful walks of rural occupation. . . . but man, after long habits of activity, in the meridian of applause, is generally restless in retirement. The difficulty of entirely quitting the luminous scenes on the great stage of public action, is often exemplified in the most exalted characters; thus, even the dignified Washington could not, amid the bustle of the world, become a calm, disinterested spectator of the transactions of statesmen and politicians. . . . urged by the strong voice of his native state, and looked up to by every state in the union, the call was strong and impressive, and he again came forward in public life.[14]

> [George Washington was the unanimous choice for president; John Adams became vice president. New York City, designated as the capital of the new government, planned a splendid welcome for Washington on the occasion of his inauguration.]

ELIZA SUSAN MORTON, the daughter of a New York merchant, recalled in her memoirs what she witnessed that day.

The whole city was one scene of triumphal rejoicing

I remember seeing General Washington land on the 23d of April, 1789, and make his entrance into New York, when he came to take the office of President of the United States. I was at a window in a store on the wharf where he was received. Carpets were spread to the carriage prepared for him; but he preferred walking through the crowded streets, and was attended by Governor Clinton and many officers and gentlemen. He frequently bowed to the multitude, and took off his hat to the ladies at the windows, who waved their handkerchiefs, threw flowers before him, and shed tears of joy and congratulation. The whole city was one scene of triumphal rejoicing. His name, in every form of decoration, appeared on the fronts of the houses; and the streets through which he passed to the Governor's mansion were ornamented with flags, silk banners of various colors, wreaths of flowers, and branches of evergreen. Never did any one enjoy such triumph as Washington, who, indeed, "read his history in a nation's eyes."[15]

SARAH FRANKLIN ROBINSON, in a long letter, furnished her cousin Catharine Wistar with a description of the festivities.

there was a general illumination took place

New York 30th of the 4th Month [1789]

Great rejoicing in New York on the arrival of general Washington, an elegant Barge decorated with an awning of Sattin 12 Oarsmen dressed in white frocks and blue ribbons—went Down to E[lizabeth]. Town last fourth day to bring him up—a Stage was erected at the Coffee house wharf covered with a carpet for him to step on—where a company of light-horse or of Artillery & most of the Inhabitants were waiting to recieve him they paraded through Queen Street in great form—while the music of the Drums and the ringing of bells— were enough to stun one with the noise.

Previous to his coming Uncle Walter's house on cherry Street was taken for him and every room furnishd in the most elegant manner—Aunt [Mary] Osgood & *Lady Kitty Duer* had the whole management of it—I went the morning before the General's arrival to take a look at it—the best of furniture in every room— and the greatest Quantity of plate and China that I ever saw before—the whole of the first and secondary Story is paperd and the floors Coverd with the richest

Kind of Turkey and Wilton Carpets—the house realy did honour to my Aunt and Lady Kitty; they spared no pains nor expense on it—thou must Know that Uncle [Samuel] Osgood and [William] Duer were appointed to procure a house and furnish it—accordingly they pitchd [settled] on their wives as being likely to do it better—

After his excellencys arrival a general Illumination took place except among friends [Quakers] and those styled Anti Federalists—the latters windows sufferd some thou may Imagine—as soon as the General has sworn in—a grand exhibition of firworks is to be displayed—which it is expected will be to morrow—their is scarcly any thing talked of now but General Washington & the Palace—and of little else have I told thee yet tho have spun my miserable scrawl already to great length—but thou requested to Know all that was going forward.[16]

MARTHA WASHINGTON followed her husband to New York City in June. Accompanied by her grandchildren, she described her journey and the welcome she received to Fanny Bassett Washington.

I have not had one half hour to my self since the day of my arrival

My dear Fanny   June the 8th 1789
   I have the pleasure to tell you, that we had a very agreable journey, I arrived in philadelphia on fryday after I left you without the least accident to distress, were met by the president of the state, (Gel Mifflin) with the city troop of Horse and conducted safe to Grays ferry, where a number of Ladies and Gentlemen came to meet me, and after a cold colation we proceed to Town—I went to mr Morrises—the children was very well and chearful all the way. . . .
   I set out on munday with mrs morriss and her two Daughters and was met on Wednesday morning by the president mr morris and Colo H[amilton] at Elizabeth town point with the fine Barge you have seen so much said of in the papers with the same oars men that carried the P- to New York. Dear little Washington seemed to be lost in a mase at the great parad that was made for us all the way we come. . . . The Governor of the state meet me as soon as we landed, and led me up to the House, the papers will tell you how I was complemented on my landing. I thank god the Prdt is very well, and the Gentle men with him are all very well. The House he is in is a very good one and is handsomly furnished all new for the General. . . .
   I have not had one half hour to my self since the day of my arrival,—my first care was to get the children to a good school,—which they are boath very much pleased at,—nelly shall begin Musick next week. She has made two or three attempts to write to you; but has never finished a letter. She is a little wild creature and spends her time at the windows looking at carriages &c passing by which is new to her and very common for children to do. . . .
   My Hair is cut and dressed every day—and I have put on white muslin Habits for the summer—you would I fear think me a good deal in the fashon if you could but see me.[17]

[In response to a letter of congratulation from Mercy Otis Warren, Martha Washington wrote of mixed feelings about her husband's reentry into public life.]

we should have been left to grow old in solitude and tranquility to gather

My Dear Madam   New York December the 26th 1789

Your very friendly letter of the 27th of last month has afforded me much more satisfaction than all the formal compliments, and emty ceremonies of meer Etiquette could possably have done.—I am not apt to forget the feelings that have been inspired by my former society with good acquaintances, nor to be insensible to thair expressions of gratitude to the President of the United States; for you know me well enough to do me the justice to beleive that I am only fond of what comes from the heart.—Under a conviction that the demonstrations of respect and affection which have been made to the President originate from that source I cannot deny that I have taken some interest and pleasure in them. The difficulties which presented them selves to view upon his first entering upon the Presidency, seem thus to be in some measure surmounted: it is owing to this kindness of our numerous friends in all quarters that my new and unwished for situation is not indeed a burden to me. When I was much younger I should, probably, have enjoyed the innocent gayeties of life as much as most of my age; but I had long since placed all the prospects of my future worldly happyness in the still enjoyments of the fire side at mount vernon.

I little thought when the war was finished, that any circumstances could possible have happend which would call the General into public life again. I had anticipated, that from this moment we should have been left to grow old in solitude and tranquility to gather: that was, my Dear madam, the first and dearest wish of my heart;—but in *that* I have been disapointed. I will not, however, contemplate with too much regret disapointments that were enevitable, though the Generals feelings and my own were perfectly in unison with respect to our prediliction for privet life, yet I cannot blame him for having acted according to his ideas of duty in obaying the voice of his country. The consciousness of having attempted to do all the good in his power, and the pleasure of finding his fellow citizens so well sattisfied with the disintrestedness of his conduct, will, doubtless, be some compensation for the great sacrifices which I know he has made; indeed in his journeys from mount vernon to this place; in his late Tour through the eastern states, by every public and by every privet information which has come to him, I am perswaded that he has experienced nothing to make him repent his having acted from what he conceived to be alone a sense of indispensable duty: on the contrary, all his sensibility has been awakened in receiving such repeated and unaquivocal proofs of sincear regards from all his country men.—

With respect to myself, I sometimes think the arrangement is not quite as it ought to have been, that I, who had much rather be at home should occupy a place with which a great many younger and gayer women would be prodigiously pleased.—As my Grand children and domestic connections made up a great portion of the felicity which I looked for in this world, I shall hardly be able to find any substitute that would indemnify me for the Loss of a part of such endearing society. I do not say this because I feel dissatisfied with my present station—no, God forbid!—for every body and every thing conspire to make me as contented as possable in it; yet I have too much of the vanity of human affairs to expect felicity from the splendid scenes of public life.—I am still determind to be cheerful and to be happy in whatever situation I may be, for I have also learnt from experianence that the greater part of our happyness or misary depends upon our dispositions, and not upon our circumstances; we carry the seeds of the one, or the other about with us, in our minds, wherever we go.

I have two of my grand children with me who enjoy advantages in point of Education, and who, I trust by the goodness of providence, will continue to be a great blessing to me, my other two Grand children are with thair mother in virginia.

The Presidents health is quite reestablished by his late journey; mine is much better than it used to be—I am sorry to hear that General Warren has been ill: hope before this time that he may be entirely recovered. We should rejoice to see you both. . . .   M. Washington[18]

ABIGAIL ADAMS described to her sister Mary Cranch her first days in New York as the vice president's wife at the house they rented called Richmond Hill.

an account of my first appearence

My dear Sister: Richmond Hill, June 28th, 1789
I took the earliest opportunity (the morning after my arrival) to go & pay my respects to Mrs. Washington. . . . She received me with great ease & politeness. She is plain in her dress, but that plainness is the best of every article. . . . Her Hair is white, her Teeth beautifull, her person rather short than otherways, hardly so large as my Ladyship, and if I was to speak sincerly, I think she is a much better figure, her manners are modest and unassuming, dignified and femenine, not the Tincture of ha'ture [hauteur] about her. *His Majesty* was ill & confined to his Room. I had not the pleasure of a presentation to him, but the satisfaction of hearing that he regreted it equally with myself. . . . Thus you have an account of my first appearence. The Principal Ladies who have visited me are the Lady & daughter of the Governour [of New York], Lady Temple, the Countess de Brehim [Brehan], Mrs. Knox & 25 other Ladies many of the Senators, all their Ladies, all the Foreign ministers & some of the Representatives.[19]

[Soon after, Abigail requested her sister to let all her friends know that they were to notify her immediately if she should show signs of an inflated ego because of her new station.]

watch over my conduct

My dear Sister: Richmond Hill, July 12th, 1789
I have a favour to request of all my near and intimate Friends. It is to desire them to watch over my conduct and if at any time they perceive any alteration in me with respect to them, arising as they may suppose from my situation in Life, I beg they would with the utmost freedom acquaint me with it. I do not feel within myself the least disposition of the kind, but I know mankind are prone to

decieve themselves, and some are disposed to misconstrue the conduct of those whom they conceive placed above them.

Our August Pressident is a singular example of modesty and diffidence. He has a dignity which forbids Familiarity mixed with an easy affibility which creates Love and reverence. The Fever which he had terminated in an absess, so that he cannot sit up. Upon my second visit to Mrs. Washington he sent for me into his Chamber, he was laying upon a settee and half raising himself up, beggd me to excuse his receiving me in that posture, congratulated me upon my arrival in N York and asked me how I could Relish the Simple manners of America after having been accustomed to those of Europe. I replied to him that where I found simple manners I esteemed them. . . . The Pressident has a Bed put into his Carriage and rides out in that way, allways with six Horses . . . & four attendants. Mrs. Washington accompanies him. . . . I found myself much more deeply impressd than I ever did before their Majesties of Britain.[20]

[Social matters took up much of Abigail's time, to her dismay.]

fully employd in entertaining company

Richmond Hill, August 9, 1789

I propose to fix a Levey day soon. I have waited for Mrs. Washington to begin and she has fixd on every fryday 8 oclock. I attended upon the last . . . I found it quite a crowded Room. The form of Reception is this, the Servants announce & Col. [David] Humphries or Mr. [Tobias] Lear, receives every Lady at the door, & Hands her up to Mrs. Washington to whom she makes a most Respectfull courtsey and then is seated without noticeing any of the rest of the company. The President then comes up and speaks to the Lady, which he does with a grace dignity & ease, that leaves Royal George far behind him. The company are entertaind with Ice creems & Lemonade, and retire at their pleasure performing the same ceremony when they quit the room. . . .

Indeed I have been fully employd in entertaining company, in the first place all the Senators who had Ladies & families, then the remaining Senators, and this week we have begun with the House, and tho we have a room in which we dine 24 persons at a Time, I shall not get through them all, together with the publick Ministers for a month to come.[21]

[Complaining about the quality of the servants necessary to a household where a great deal of entertaining was expected, Abigail wrote in November 1789: "The hire of servants is an other very heavy article. . . . I have a pretty good Housekeeper, a tolerable footman, a midling cook, an indifferent steward and a vixen of a House maid."[22]

While the social niceties were being tended to, President Washington was nominating members of his cabinet; Alexander Hamilton, Secretary of the Treasury, was formulating a plan to establish the country on a firm financial footing; Congress was drawing up the promised bill of rights, passing legislation to establish the federal judiciary, and considering revenue-raising measures. Abigail Adams kept a close eye on what was happening, especially in matters that involved her husband;

she sometimes attended Congressional sessions when important bills were being considered.]

I am going for the first Time to the House

Richmond Hill, Febry. 20, 1790

I presume . . . that some one or other of the plans proposed by the Secretary of the Treasury will be adopted. It is thought that tomorrow will be the desisive day with respect to the question, as the vote will be calld for. On this occasion I am going for the first Time to the House with Mrs. [Tristram] Dalton, Mrs. Jay & Mrs. [Justice William] Cushing to hear the debate. . . . I hope some method will be adopted speedily for the relief of those who have so long been the sufferers by the instability of Government. The next question I presume that will occupy Congress will be the Assumption of the State debts, and here I apprehend warm work, and much opposition, but I firmly believe it will terminate for the General Good.[23]

[Ever solicitous of her husband—Adams presided over the Senate and could cast a vote in case of a tie—Abigail thought he was working too hard. Concerned about perceived slights to him, she was especially sensitive to criticisms by the press.]

no easy task

N York, july 4th, 1790

Mr. Adams wants some exercise. Ever since the 4th of Janry he has not mist one hour from attendance at Congress. He goes from Home at ten and seldom gets back till four, and 5 hours constant sitting in a day for six months together, (for He cannot leave his Chair) is pretty tight service. Reading long Bills, hearing debates, and not always those the most consonant to his mind and opinions, putting questions, stating them, constant attention to them that in putting questions they may not be misled, is no easy task whatever Grumblers may think, but Grumblers there always was & always will be.   Adieu my dear sister[24]

[Abigail, wanting to know how things were faring in Braintree, often peppered her sister with requests, asking her to oversee the property and do a multitude of favors for her. Sometimes she made important decisions on her own or, as in this letter, wished she could undo some made by her husband.]

so unfortunate as to differ from my partner

N York, October l0th, 1790

With Regard to our House, I should have no objection to a carefull person living in the kitchin to take care of it, but as to letting it I cannot consent unless any person offers to take House and furniture all together. . . . In short I do not know of any persons property so unproductive as ours is. I do not believe that it yealds us one pr cent pr Annum. I have the vanity however to think that if Dr. [Cotton] Tufts and my Lady Ship had been left to the sole management of our affairs, they would have been upon a more profitable footing. In the first place I

never desired so much Land unless we could have lived upon it. The money paid
for useless land I would have purchased publick securities with. The interest of
which, poorly as it is funded, would have been less troublesome to take charge
of then Land and much more productive. But in these Ideas I have always been
so unfortunate as to differ from my partner, who thinks he never saved any thing
but what he vested in Land.[25]

[In December 1790, the government moved to Philadelphia. "Politicks, they begin to grow pretty warm," Abigail related to her sister in
March 1792, as opposition to the new government's policies developed.
She was also alarmed by the "Rage of speculation," which had reared
its head the previous summer. The situation had become considerably
worse by the next month with many bank failures.[26]]

a devision of the Southern & Northern States

Philadelphia, April 20th, 1792

Terrible is the distress in N York, from the failure of many of the richest
people there, and from the Spirit of Speculation which has prevaild & brought to
Ruin many industerous Families who lent their Money in hopes of Gain. . . . In
the House of Representatives of the U. States matters are not going better. The
Southern members are determined if possible to Ruin the Secretary of the Treasury [Alexander Hamilton], distroy all his well built systems, if possible and give
a Fatal Stab to the funding system. In Senate they have harmonized well, no
unbecomeing heats or animosity. The Members are however weary & long for a
recess one after an other are droping off, which gives weight to the opposite
side. Many of the Southern Members have written long speaches & had them
printed, which has had more influence than our Northern Friends are aware of
who, depending upon the goodness of their cause, have been inattentive to such
Methods to influence the populace. The V President, they have permitted to
sleep in peace this winter, whilst the minister at War [Henry Knox], & the Secretary of the Treasury have been their Game. The Secretary of State [Thomas
Jefferson] & even the President has not escaped. I firmly believe if I live Ten
Years longer, I shall see a devision of the Southern & Northern States, unless
more candour & less intrigue, of which I have no hopes, should prevail.[27]

Among the many problems demanding President Washington's attention
was the necessity of dealing with the Indians. The area in the Northwest—which
included state claims given over to the Confederation government as well as
land ceded to the United States by the Treaty of Paris—lured land-hungry Americans, both settlers and speculators. The Indian Nations, organized into a loose
confederacy, resisted incursions on what they considered their homeland. Repeated clashes aroused public ire, not only against the Indians but also against
the British, who retained military posts in American territory along the northern
frontier and aided and abetted the Indians to protect their fur trade. While Washington theoretically believed that Indian nations had a prior right to certain terri-

tories, which meant respecting treaty terms and pursuing just settlements with them, he would not tolerate attacks on Americans.

In 1791, to stop the violence, he ordered General Arthur St. Clair to raise an American army and establish and maintain a series of forts in northern Ohio to ward off Indian raids. On November 4, in a surprise attack near present-day Ft. Wayne, St. Clair's troops suffered a devastating defeat. Of 1400 men, nearly 700 were killed and hundreds wounded. General St. Clair resigned his commission, was subsequently brought before a congressional investigating committee on charges of incompetence, but was cleared of any wrongdoing.[28]

MERCY OTIS WARREN was dismayed by the treatment of the Indians. Although she considered them "an unhappy race of men hunted throughout the vast wilderness of America . . . original proprietors of the soil,"[29] she had a personal reason to be distressed about developments in Ohio: her son Winslow had been killed in the Indian attack.

JANE PRINCE ROBBINS worried so about her daughter Hannah Robbins Gilman and her family, who had moved to Ohio, that she and her husband begged them to come back to Massachusetts until the tension subsided.

remove from thence to us

My dear, very dear Children,   Plimouth Decr 19 1791

Our principal concern & Anxiety at present is on your Acct who live on the Ohio, at this alarming Period.

Imagine the distress of the friends of those poor Soldiers, who went from us into your country, since last Fryday Evening, which was the first we heard of the surprizing & awful acct from our Army—We have, as yet, had no official Accts—expect them daily—but a Letter from a Gent[lema]n in NYork to his friend in Boston, says, that the Indians have gained a shocking Victory—killd 700 privates & 27 Officers—among whom is poor Winslow Warren &c probably some if not all the young Soldrs from Plimo[uth] are slain, Torry &c &c whose friends are filld with grief in anxs Expectn of the Event—But poor Mrs Warren seems inconsolable. But what shall we say of our dear Children & their connections there? Tis natural to think & forbode the worst—We cant but fear greatly for you. The savage foe, flushd at the Victory they have obtaind, will in all probability pursue the Advantage, & is there not reason to fear will fall upon the new Settlements—at least greatly distress & put them in perpetual fear! May a merciful God restrain their rage & prevent the dreadful effects of their barbarous Spirit.

We have a proposition to make to you, my children, to which must intreat you to attend—We cannot but think, & most earnestly advise you, as a rational & prudent measure, that considering the present gloomy situation of affairs with you & the uncertainty when things will be in a quiet state & above all, considering your (Mr G) ill State of health and the increase of that distress & disorder upon you [probably kidney stones], you had better (with your dear ones) remove from thence to us, at least for a season. What are all earthly possessions, where health is wanting? especially if in addition to this, one lives in fear, on Acct of the most inhuman of all Enemies! You dont conceive the Joy & Satisfaction you wd hereby give us. Our house arms & heart are open to receive you. Do think of it, my dear Children.[30]

ABIGAIL ADAMS commented on the conflict in Ohio to Mary Cranch.

a distressing subject

Philadelphia, Febry. 5th, 1792

The Indian War has been a distressing subject. Who . . . have been in fault is not for me to say. Where a commander is to be found fit for the Buisness I believe will puzzel more wise Heads than one. The War is an unpopular one. If it is a necessary War as I presume it is, it is to be hoped that measures will be pressed to render it more successfull than it has yet been, but I believe those whose judgments are good have little expectation that it will be so.[31]

MERCY OTIS WARREN, while she tended to idealize the Indians and their way of life, foresaw their extinction. In addition, she also feared that warring white settlers in frontier areas could become a liability for the United States.

the lust of domination

The American claims to a vast, uncultivated tract of wilderness, which neither Great Britain, France, or America had any right to invade may ultimately prove a most unfortunate circumstance to the Atlantic states, unless the primary object of the American government should be, to civilize and soften the habits of savage life. But if the lust of domination, which takes hold of the ambitious and the powerful in all ages and nations, should be indulged by the authority of the United States, and those simple tribes of men, contented with the gifts of nature that had filled their forests with game sufficient for their subsistence, should be invaded, it will probably be a source of most cruel warfare and bloodshed, until the extermination of the original possessors. In such a result, the mountains and the plains will perhaps be filled with a fierce, independent race of European and American emigrants, too hostile to the borderers on the seas to submit willingly to their laws and government, and perhaps too distant, numerous, and powerful to subdue by arms.[32]

In the South, Georgians had been moving west even before the Revolution ended, encroaching on lands claimed by the Creek nation. After the war, Georgia presumed to negotiate treaties with the Indians on its own. When violence between Creek war parties and settlers continued to escalate, President Washington sent a commission to assess the situation and attempt to negotiate a treaty with the powerful Creek leader Alexander McGillivray. The mission failed, but Washington was able to persuade McGillivray to come to New York to confer personally. The meeting resulted in a treaty that temporarily suspended attacks and mollified the Creeks by acknowledging the sovereignty of their nation. It was Washington's hope that the Indians would eventually be "civilized," that is converted into farmers with lifestyles similar to those of Americans, and assimilated: "We should be greatly gratified with the opportunity of imparting to you all the blessings of civilized life, of teaching you to cultivate the earth, and raise corn, to raise . . . domestic animals; to build comfortable houses, and to educate your children, so as ever to dwell upon the land."[33]

ABIGAIL ADAMS entertained, and was entertained, by the Creek Indians on the occasion of the ratification of the treaty. Her sister was undoubtedly diverted by her description.

the first savages I ever saw

New York 8 August, 1790

I have nothing new to entertain you with unless it is my Neighbours the Creek Savages who visit us daily. They are lodgd at an Inn at a little distance from us. They are very fond of visiting us as we entertain them kindly, and they behave with much civility. Yesterday they signd the Treaty, and last Night they had a great Bondfire dancing round it like so many spirits hooping, singing, yelling, and expressing their pleasure and satisfaction in the true savage stile. These are the first Savages I ever saw. Mico Maco, one of their kings dinned here yesterday and after dinner he confered a Name upon me, the meaning of which I do not know, Mammea. He took me by the Hand, bowd his Head and bent his knee, calling me Mammea, Mammea. They are very fine looking Men, placid countenances & fine shape. Mr. Trumble [the artist John Trumbull] says, they are many of them perfect models. MacGillvery dresses in our own fashion speaks English like a Native, & I should never suspect him to be of that Nation, as he is not very dark. He is grave and solid, intelligent and much of a Gentleman, but in very bad Health. They return in a few days.[34]

[To many Americans, the Indians were fearsome savages whose ways might be changed by converting them to Christianity.]

SARAH CARY wrote to her son Samuel, who was in Grenada overseeing the family business, regarding missionary work among the Indians. She had quite an unusual attitude for the time.

Why are we arrogantly to presume to dictate

My Dear Sam   Retreat, Chelsea [Massachusetts], July 10, 1792

There was always since my remembrance a Society for Propagating the Gospel among the Indians, with how much success I am not able to tell, but I am rather inclined to believe very little; for I remember, about twenty-two years since, one Indian who was converted, and afterwards brought here by one of our clergy, and really so far civilized as to be introduced into our meeting-houses, where he actually preached several times, but, like poor puss in the fable, he could not disguise his natural propensities, one of which was the immoderate use of strong drink. New England rum, I am told, is a temptation the best of those poor creatures can never withstand, and which baffles all the eloquence of those who wish a reform among them.

As to their religion, there are various accounts about it. Some say they worship the sun, and at break of day every person upward of twelve years old goes to the waterside until sunrise, then offers tobacco to this planet, and does the same again at sunset; that they acknowledge one Supreme God, but do not adore him, believing him to be too far exalted above them, and too happy in himself to be concerned about the trifling affairs of poor mortals. My dear Sam, is not the particular mode of their worship as acceptable to their Maker as ours? Why are we arrogantly to presume to dictate to any sect of people if they have not the advantages of Christianity revealed to them? Neither will the fruits of that holy religion be expected to influence their conduct. For wise purposes, no doubt, have our doctrines been withheld from them. The Judge of all the earth will do right. He is the great Creator of all, and doubtless receives with equal condescension the worship of the Pagan and the Christian. Do these sentiments agree with yours?[35]

In two years' time Alexander McGillivray had renounced the treaty with the Americans and negotiated one with the Spanish to the west, certain to cause unrest in the area. In the Ohio territory, once the English had withdrawn from their outposts, the United States decisively defeated the Indians in 1794. Given the subsequent influx of American settlers that has been called a "demographic avalanche," American policy toward the Indians became one of removal and decimation.[36]

While President Washington had serious domestic issues to deal with, he was obliged to consider how the United States should react to the French Revolution. As it was thought to have been inspired in part by the American experience, the Revolution was at first joyously welcomed by the American public— liberty and individual rights seemed to be in the ascendant.

MERCY OTIS WARREN, writing to her friend Catharine Macaulay in the fall of 1789, had high hopes for France and its Revolution: "Would it not be surprising if that nation should reap Greater advantages from the Spirit of liberty lately diffused through this Continent than the Americans may be able to boast after all their struggle & Sacrifices to become a free people."[37]

CATHARINE MACAULAY was likewise elated and expressed the thought, in a letter to Samuel Adams, that the French Revolution might have more important and lasting effects than the American Revolution.

a little too much of the leaven of their ancestors

Sir   [draft] March 1, 1791
    I cannot . . . forbear to communicate to you those mixed sentiments . . . with which the present state of affaires in Europe have filled the mind of every zealous friend to equal liberty. That wonderful Event the french Revolution fills all our thoughts and occupies the whole mind we desire its permanence and prosperity

with more paternal solicitude for we look upon its firm establishment as an event which will—bring after it the final emancipation of every other society in Europe from those Monarchies and aristocratic chains imposed by the violence of arms and visited on mankind by ignorance credability and—craft and you will pardon me if I tell you that in my opinion notwithstanding the brilliancy of American exertions in the case of independence that the continuation of the freedom of that vast Continent equaly depends on the stability of the french Democracy. The Americans have a little too much of the leaven of their Ancestors in them.[38]

By 1793, events in France had taken a radical turn; news of thousands of executions, including those of the king and queen, alarmed Federalists. While many Americans, especially Anti-Federalists now calling themselves Republicans, still believed that the United States owed its support to the country that had come to its assistance in its war against Britain, they too were disturbed by the bloodshed.

The rash of executions and a climate of fear in France led many French aristocrats to flee the country. Some sought refuge in the United States.

HENRIETTE-LUCIE DE LA TOUR DU PIN DE GOUVERNET had at one time been a lady-in-waiting to Marie Antoinette. She married a French nobleman who, after his father died on the scaffold, became Comte de La Tour du Pin de Gouvernet. Husband and wife—with their children Humbert and Séraphine—fled in 1794 to avoid a similar fate. Boston was their destination. The family managed to make a life in America, though it was quite different from the one they had led in France. During a large part of her adult life, Madame de La Tour du Pin kept a journal upon which she based her memoirs begun in 1820.

Accepting an offer from General Philip Schuyler to come to Albany where, he assured them, they would be able to establish themselves, the de La Tour du Pins sold much of what they had brought with them being of no use in their reduced circumstances: laces, a piano, music, porcelains.[39] In her journal, Henriette-Lucie recorded details of the overland journey to Albany via Lebanon, New York, where the family took dinner, noting the words of their host at the end of the meal.

this act of love for the great Washington

The master of the house rose, removed his cap, and, with a respectful air, pronounced these words: "We will drink the health of our beloved President." You would not then have found a cabin, no matter how buried it was in the depths of the woods, where this act of love for the great Washington did not terminate every meal. Sometimes there was also added a toast to the "Marquis," Monsieur de La Fayette, who had left a well-loved name in the United States.[40]

[Arriving at the home of General Schuyler, the family was warmly received. The French woman was astonished that her host spoke French perfectly. When Madame visited one of the General's daughters, Margarita, who was married to Stephen Van Rensselaer, she found that she too "spoke French very well."]

She had learned the language while accompanying her father to the general headquarters of the American and French armies. . . . By reading the papers she had kept informed as to the state of parties in France, the mistakes which had brought on the Revolution, the vices of the higher class of society, and the folly of the medium classes. With an extraordinary perspicuity she had penetrated the causes and the effects of the troubles of our country better than we ourselves. She was very impatient to make the acquaintance of Monsieur de Talleyrand, who had arrived at Philadelphia having. . . . made up his mind that France had not yet finished the different phases of the Revolution.[41]

[Madame de La Tour du Pin and her husband leased a farm in the area and, until the house was vacated, stayed with another family from which they hoped to learn American manners. There she encountered Charles Maurice de Talleyrand, another French exile.]

a leg of mutton

One day at the end of September, I was in the yard with a hatchet in my hand, occupied with cutting the bone of a leg of mutton which I was preparing to put on the spit for our dinner. All of a sudden, I heard behind me a loud voice which said in French: "On ne peut embrocher un gigot avec plus de majesté." [No one can skewer a leg of mutton with such nobility as you.] Turning quickly, I saw Monsieur de Talleyrand. . . . En route [to General Schuyler's for dinner] we talked a great deal upon all kinds of subjects. . . . The latest news from Europe . . . was more terrible than ever. Blood flowed in floods at Paris. . . . our relatives, and our friends were counted among the victims of the Terror. When we arrived at the house of the good General, he . . . cried: "Come quickly, come quickly! There is great news from France!" We entered the sitting-room and every one of us took a paper. Here we found the news of the Revolution of the 9 Thermidor; the death of Robespierre and his followers, the end of the shedding of blood and the just punishment of the Revolutionary Tribunal.

[Madame's assessment of Talleyrand was not flattering.]

so many reasons for not holding him in esteem

Monsieur de Talleyrand was amiable as he has always been for me, without any variation, with that charm of conversation which no one has ever possessed to a greater degree than himself. He had known me since my childhood, and therefore assumed a sort of paternal and gracious tone which was very charming. I regretted sincerely to find so many reasons for not holding him in esteem, but I could not avoid forgetting my disagreeable recollections when I had passed an hour in listening to him. As he had no moral value himself, by singular contrast, he had a horror of that which was evil in others. To listen to him without knowing him, you would have believed that he was a worthy man.[42]

Colonel Hamilton was expected

Two days later we were to pass the day at Mrs. Van Rensselaer's, with all the Schuylers. Monsieur de Talleyrand had been extremely impressed by . . . Mrs. Van Rensselaer. . . . She had a very clear understanding of American affairs and the Revolution, of which she had gained a profound and extended knowledge through her brother-in-law, Colonel Hamilton, who was the friend and also the most intimate confidant of Washington. Colonel Hamilton was expected at Albany where he intended to pass some time with his father-in-law, General Schuyler. He had just resigned the position of Secretary of the Treasury, which he had held since the peace. It was to him that the country owed the good order which had been established in this branch of the government of the United States. Monsieur de Talleyrand knew him and had the very highest opinion of him. But he found it very remarkable that a man of his value, and endowed with talents so superior, should leave the Ministry to resume the profession of lawyer, giving as his reason for this decision that the position of Minister did not give him the means of bringing up his family of eight children. Such a pretext seemed to Talleyrand very singular and, so to speak, even a little naïf.[43]

[As winter set in, the family took possession of their farm, purchasing tools and animals, as well as several slaves. They had their first encounter with the Indians.]

the last survivors of the Mohawk tribe

We had acquired moccasins, a kind of foot-covering of buffalo-skin, made and sold by the Indians. The price of these articles was sometimes quite high when they were embroidered with dyed bark or with porcupine quills. It was in purchasing these moccasins that I saw the Indians for the first time. They were the last survivors of the Mohawk tribe whose territory had been purchased or taken by the Americans since the peace. The Onondagas, established near Lake Champlain, also were selling their forests and disappearing at this epoch. From time to time some of them came to us.[44]

[Madame de La Tour du Pin proved to be a capable farm manager. She kept cows and sold cream and butter. One slave had talents that she soon discovered.]

kept his accounts with such exactitude

Our slave, Prime, although he did not know how to read or write, nevertheless kept his accounts with such exactitude that there was never the slightest error. He often brought back some fresh meat which he had bought at Albany, and, upon his return, my husband, from his report, wrote out the sum of the receipts and expenditures. Property like ours was generally burdened with a small rent. . . . paid to the patroon, Van Rensselaer, twenty-two pecks of corn, either in kind or in money. All of the farms in his immense estate, which was eighteen miles wide by forty-two miles long, were held under the same conditions.[45]

I adopted the costume worn by the women on the neighboring places

The day that we took possession of our farm, I adopted the costume worn by the women on the neighboring places, that is to say, a skirt of blue and black striped wool, a little camisole of light brown cotton cloth, a handkerchief of the same color, with my hair parted . . . and caught up with a comb. In winter, I wore gray or blue woolen stockings, with moccasins or slippers of buffalo skin; in summer, cotton stockings, and shoes. I never put on a dress or a corset, except to go into the city. Among the effects which I had brought to America were two or three riding-costumes. These I used to transform myself into a dame élégante, when I wished to pay a visit to the Schuylers or Van Rensselaers.[46]

[Life on the farm assumed a routine that was not unpleasant. "We took our déjeuner at eight o'clock, and our dinner at one o'clock. In the evening at nine o'clock we had tea, with slices of bread, our excellent butter and some fine Stilton cheese which Monsieur de Talleyrand sent us." In 1795, with the coming of spring, the Indians reappeared.]

I was very careful not to give my visitors any rum

One of them, at the beginning of the cold weather, had asked my permission to cut some branches of a kind of willow tree which had shoots, large as my thumb and five or six feet long. He promised me to weave some baskets during the winter season. I counted little upon this promise, as I did not believe that Indians would keep their word to this degree, although I had been so informed. I was mistaken. Within a week after the snow had melted, my Indian came back with a load of baskets. He gave me six of them which were nested in one another. The first, which was round and very large, was so well made that, when filled with water, it retained it like an earthen vessel. I wished to pay him for the baskets, but he absolutely refused and would accept only a bowl of buttermilk of which the Indians are very fond. I was very careful not to give my visitors any rum, for which they have a great liking. But I had in an old paste-board box some remnants (artificial flowers, feathers, pieces of ribbons of all colors and glass beads, which were formerly much in vogue) and I distributed these among the squaws, who were delighted with them.

[Henriette-Lucie allowed her son Humbert, who was five, to live with a respectable neighbor lady who promised to teach him to read and write.]

awaiting a favorable moment to take my son

This arrangement relieved me of a great deal of care. On the farm I was always afraid that he would have some accident with the horses of which he was very fond. It was almost impossible to prevent him from accompanying the negroes to the fields, and above all from mingling with the Indians, with whom he always wished to go away. I had been told that the Indians sometimes kidnapped children. Therefore, when I saw them hanging for hours around my door I imagined they were awaiting a favorable moment to take my son.[47]

[The sect called Shakers, living nearby, interested Madame, and she arranged to be taken on a tour of their property. She was quite impressed by their way of life.]

a superb kitchen-garden perfectly cultivated

A nice wagon, loaded with fine vegetables, often passed before our door. It belonged to the Shakers, who were located at a distance of six or seven miles. The driver of the wagon always stopped at our house, and I never failed to talk with him about their manner of life, their customs, and their belief. He urged us to visit their establishment, and we decided to go there some day. It is known that this sect of Quakers belonged to the reformed school of the original Quakers who took refuge in America with Penn.

After the war of 1763, an English woman [Ann Lee] set herself up for a reformer apostle. She made many proselytes in the states of Vermont and Massachusetts. Several families put their property in common and bought land in the then uninhabited parts of the country. . . . Those of whom I speak were then protected on all sides by a forest several miles deep. This establishment was a branch of their headquarters at Lebanon [New York]. . . .

We came out in a vast clearing traversed by a pretty stream and surrounded on all sides by woods. In the midst was erected the establishment, composed of a large number of nice wooden houses, a church, schools, and a community house of brick. The Shakers . . . greeted us with kindness, although with a certain reserve. . . . We had been advised that nobody would offer us anything, and that our guide would be the only one to speak to us. He first led us to a superb kitchen-garden perfectly cultivated. Everything was in a state of the greatest prosperity, but without the least evidence of elegance. Many men and women were working at the cultivation or the weeding of the garden. The sale of vegetables represented the principal source of revenue to the community.

We visited the schools for the boys and girls, the immense community stables, the dairies, and the factories in which they produced the butter and cheese. Everywhere we remarked upon the order and the absolute silence. The children, boys and girls alike, were clothed in a costume of the same form and the same color. The women of all ages wore the same kind of garments of gray wool, well kept and very neat. Through the windows we could see the looms of the weavers, and the pieces of cloth which they were dyeing, also the workshops of the tailors and dress-makers. But not a word or a song was to be heard anywhere.

[Madame and Monsieur de La Tour du Pin stayed to witness a religious ceremony during "the hour of prayer," but found it more puzzling than enlightening. "Having . . . visited all parts of the establishment, we took leave of our kind guide and entered our wagon to return home, very little edified regarding the hospitality of the Shakers."[48]

On a visit to New York the couple renewed their acquaintance with Alexander Hamilton and his family. Monsieur made a short trip to Philadelphia to claim funds due him and met "the great Washington . . . my hero," as Henriette-Lucie put it.]

the conversation . . . lasted until midnight

I found again at New York the whole Hamilton family. . . . Mr. Hamilton at that time was about thirty-eight years of age. Although he had never been in Europe, he nevertheless spoke our language like a Frenchman. His remarkable mind, and the clearness of his thoughts, mingled well with the originality of Monsieur de Talleyrand and the vivacity of Monsieur de La Tour du Pin. Every night these distinguished men, with two or three others, came for tea. Seated upon the terrace, the conversation which was started between them lasted until midnight and sometimes later. . . . Mr. Hamilton would relate the story of the beginnings of the War of Independence, of which the dull memoirs of that imbecile, Lafayette, have since rendered the details so insipid.[49]

[Crushed by the sudden death of her daughter from "infant paralysis," Henriette-Lucie turned to religion for solace. And she kept busy. During the winter there was sewing to be done.]

I lived in the same manner as my neighbors

I bought a large piece of coarse blue and white checked flannel to make two shirts for each of my negroes. A tailor was employed by the day at the farm to make them coats and welllined caps. This man ate with us because he was white. He would certainly have refused if we had asked him to eat with the slaves, although they were incomparably better dressed and had better manners than he. But I was very careful not to express the least remark upon this custom. My neighbors acted in this way, and I followed their example and in our reciprocal relations I was always careful not to make any allusion to the place which I had formerly occupied on the social ladder. I was the proprietor of a farm of 250 acres. I lived in the same manner as my neighbors, neither better nor worse. This simplicity and abnegation gave me more respect and consideration than as if I had wished to play the lady.[50]

[In the spring of 1796, word was received from France that their confiscated property had been restored to the family but required the presence of Monsieur de La Tour du Pin to validate it. One condition that his wife insisted upon before the family's departure: their slaves must be freed.]

"Is it possible? Do you mean that we are free?"

These poor people, on seeing the letters arrive from Europe, had feared some change in our life. They were disturbed and alarmed. Therefore, all four of them were trembling when they entered my room to which I had called them. They found me alone. I said to them with emotion: "My friends, we are going to return to Europe. What shall I do with you?" The poor creatures were overcome. Judith dropped into a chair, in tears, while the three men covered their faces with their hands, and all remained silent. I continued: "We have been so satisfied with you that it is just that you should be recompensed. My husband has charged me to tell you that he will give you your liberty." On hearing this word our good servants were so stupified that they remained for several seconds without speech. Then all four threw themselves at my feet crying: "Is it possible? Do you mean that we are free?" I replied: "Yes, upon my honor, from this moment, as free as I am myself."

Who can describe the poignant emotion of such a moment! Never in my life had I experienced anything so sweet. Those whom I had just promised their liberty surrounded me in tears. . . .

The following day my husband took them to Albany before a judge, for the ceremony of the manumission, an act which had to be public. All the negroes of the city were present. The Justice of the Peace, who was at the same time the steward of Mr. Van Rensselaer, was in very bad humor. He attempted to assert that Prime, being fifty years of age, could not under the terms of the law be given his liberty unless he was assured a pension of a hundred dollars. But Prime had foreseen this case, and he produced his certificate of baptism which attested that he was only forty-nine. They made the slaves kneel before my husband, and he placed his hand upon the head of each to sanction his liberation, exactly in the manner of ancient Rome.[51]

[Madame confessed that she "felt no pleasure in returning to France. On the contrary, the sufferings which I had endured during the last six months of my sojourn had left in my mind a sentiment of terror and horror which I could not overcome." But Henriette-Lucie de La Tour du Pin always looked back on her stay in America with pleasure.[52]]

When Anglo-French hostilities broke out in Europe, Britain blockaded French ports and began stopping American ships in search of contraband goods, or capturing them, often impressing crew members. With anti-British sentiment running high, war with Britain seemed a real possibility. President Washington, however, determined on a diplomatic initiative: in 1794, he called upon John Jay to go to London to try to diffuse the situation. Jay's appointment generated criticism: he was considered an Anglophile, not trusted to press hard for concessions from Britain. He himself was not keen on going, knowing his motives and actions would be questioned, but he felt duty bound.[53]

While Jay was in transit, President Washington also had to contend with a domestic problem. In 1791, Congress had imposed a tax on whiskey in order to raise revenue. That the duty provoked protests among westerners comes as no surprise: people in frontier areas tended to be suspicious of the federal government, which they viewed as remote and in the control of easterners, with little concern for their interests. For the growers of corn in western Pennsylvania there was a strong economic reason for making whiskey, which the federal government failed to appreciate. With no access to a water route—the Spaniards controlled the mouth of the Mississippi—it was much easier and cheaper to transport whiskey overland than the corn from which it was made. Distillers therefore resisted paying what they considered an unfair tax; they organized mass meetings and intimidated tax collectors.

When violence flared in western Pennsylvania in 1794, President Washington decided to take military action against the protesters. He believed that the refusal to obey a federal law represented a challenge to the authority of the federal government, and he wanted to make an example of the case. Having called up the militias of several states, he marched part of the way with 15,000 troops, commanded by Alexander Hamilton, to crush the so-called Whiskey Rebellion. (Washington is the only president to have actually led an army as commander in chief.) Resistance collapsed; three culprits died, and those convicted were later pardoned. While the action proved that the federal government could and would act to quell disorder, it was criticized both by those who defended states rights and feared a powerful federal authority, as well as by those who believed that Washington's action was an ill-considered attempt to suppress dissent.[54]

MARTHA WASHINGTON wrote to Fanny Washington about the President's action.

to go him self . . . to Carlyle to meet the troops

My dear Fanny   Philadelphia September 29th 1794
    The insurgents in the back country has carred matters so high that the President has been obliged to send a larg body of men to settle the matter—and is to go him self to morrow to Carlyle to meet the troops; god knows when he will return again.—I shall be left quite alone with the children. Should you go to Berkley be so good as to send the keys you have of our House to Mr. Pearce; in case the President should take mount vernon in his way back to this place.—My love and good wishes attend you in which the President joins me.[55]

CHRISTIANA YOUNG LEECH of Kinsessing, Pennsylvania, recorded in her diary the departure of a son.

the whiskey rebels as they call them

September 30th [1794]
    My son, Joseph Leech, has gone with the Blockley and Kingsessing Militia under Captain Smith, to the western counties of Pennsylvania, after the whiskey rebels as they call them. God be with him![56]

SUSAN LIVINGSTON SYMMES, recently married, set out for Ohio in 1794 with her husband, John Cleves Symmes. One of three judges in the Northwest Territory, Symmes owned large tracts of land in the North Bend area. On their way, they met troops returning after the defeat of the whiskey rebels. She described their encounter with them to her sister Sarah Jay in New York.

Col. Hamilton . . . looked a little weather-beaten

My dr Sister   22d Novr 1794 2 oClock
    We have just crossed the Junietta, the return of the Army impedes our progress very much, we have been detained on the opposite side of the river since yesterday, owing to the number of Waggons to be ferryed over—we do not proceed above 10 miles a day, & to-day we shall not get about 7—The roads surpass all description, no one can have an idea of any thing half so bad, such a

season as this has not been known these 10 years, while the army was passing it rained a fortnight, the teams cut up the roads most dreadfully—it is one succession of mountains from Straasburgh to Pittsburgh, we have yet 2 very considerable ones to pass, the Allegeny & Lawrel—Col. Hamilton breakfasted at the Inn this morning where we lodged—he looked a little weather-beaten as well as ourselves—We are so happy as to be preserved in Health—expect to winter at Pitts-burgh. It will make the journey less heavy—we shall be sufficiently tired by the time we reach that—An officer that's now here proposes to leave this in the Post-Office at Phila.

[Susan Symmes, two days later, wrote again to Sarah.]

it is an important object to avoid the Army

Bedford Town 100 miles from Pittsburgh
My dr Sister   Monday 24 Novr 1794

We are thus far on our way, have come over dreadful roads & for our comfort what remains is still worse—The House where we now are & expect to remain to-day as the Horses want shoeing & is filled with Officers, they behave to us with the greatest politeness, & are in excessive spirits to be on their return, they have endured amazing hardships this campaign owing to the inclemency of the weather, & the faults in the Quarter masters Department. Gen. [Frederick] Frelinghuysen is to take charge of this [letter] as far as he goes & then to deposit it in the Post-Office—He says this Country looks as if the Deity had thrown all the Rocks & Stones in the whole World here & employed all the Devils to raise them into Mountains—They call them Nobs here, but to be sure the Nobs are such mountains as you never have & I hope never will see—A Gentleman who lately traveled to Pitts. said he had heard that it was hill & dale all the way, but he thought it was hill & hill & no dale. If nature had made a Gap for roads as well as for Rivers it would have been an accommodating circumstance—5 or 6 miles in advance of this we expect to strike into a different road from that which the Army is travelling, it would never do for us to encounter 500 waggons & 17000 troops, it is an important object to avoid the Army.[57]

In November of 1794, John Jay signed a treaty with the British by which some troublesome issues were resolved—the British agreed finally to evacuate forts in American territory and to refer certain other issues to arbitration. They refused, however, to deal with neutral rights or the subject of impressments, and were willing to make only minor concessions regarding trade. Although Washington was disappointed in the Jay Treaty, he believed that its chief purpose—to avert a war with Britain—had been achieved, therefore he submitted it for ratification to the Senate, called into special session for the purpose.[58]

ABIGAIL ADAMS received a letter from her husband in which he predicted "A Battle royal" over ratification of the treaty "and snarling enough afterwards." She agreed.

a sufferer . . . for the good he has done

Boston Febry 21 1795

If it was a Treaty from Heaven pronouncing Peace on Earth & good will to Man, there would not be wanting a sufficient Number of deamons to Nash their teeth & send it to peices if they can. Mr Jays mission was an unpleasent one and I fear he will be a sufferer for a while for the good he has done, and the Service he has renderd.[59]

[When the Senate convened to consider the Treaty, Abigail, writing to her sister Mary Cranch, seemed confident that it would be ratified.]

Party will shew itself, and be bitter

N York, 25 June, 1795

I was in hopes to have been on my way home by this time, but the Senate are not yet up, and Mr Adams does not give me much hopes of its rising till Saturday. The Fate of the Treaty is not yet known. It is however the general opinion that it will be ratified. I say the out door opinion, for the Senate are Secret and Silent. It has been discussed with much calmness, coolness and deliberation, and considerd in all its various lights and opperations. I hope the decision will be wise & judicious, satisfactory & benificial to the Country. The Grumblers will growl however. Party will shew itself, and be bitter.[60]

In fact, the Treaty was ratified on June 24—by the required two-thirds vote: twenty to ten, strictly along party lines. When the terms became known, there was a public outcry. Both Jay and Washington were vilified for accepting a treaty considered humiliating to the nation and injurious to American commercial interests. Debate continued into 1796: in taverns, public forums, and newspapers. Federalists and Republicans pressed citizens to make their views known in petitions to the House of Representatives, whose members had to decide whether to appropriate funds for the Treaty's implementation.

SOPHIA WATERHOUSE BROWN, writing from Perth Amboy to her mother-in-law on April 21, 1796, concluded her letter with these words:

our little village is peacefully inclined

I wish I had some news to write for my dear Papa [in-law], but I declare I have none. All I hear is that the Treaty is very warmly debated on in Congress, that there are meetings in all the different towns, & petitions preparing to be presented to Congress. There was a meeting held in this town a few days ago every one I am told voted for the Treaty being carried into effect so you see our little village is peacefully inclined. Let public affairs go as they may. I hope I shall always remember with the Psalmist that the Lord reigns be the earth ever so unquiet.[61]

REBECCA FAULKNER FOSTER conveyed news about local actions regarding the treaty to her husband Dwight, a member of the House of Representatives.

they voted for the Treaty . . . after public worship

My Dearest Freind   Brookfield [Massachusetts] May 2nd 1796

    I was in hopes to have had a Line from you by the Mail which arrived in Town this afternoon—but Sidney has Just returned from the Post office and says there is no Letters come in the Mail this time—I will wait patiently till the Day after tomorrow when the Mail is to arrive from the southward again—I feel anxious to know how you are and how you are like to succeed in the important question respecting the Treaty—This Town have the subject before them this afternoon. I have no Doubt but what they will be unanimous in favour of the Treaty—the matter was mentioned in each Parish in this Town yesterday after Meeting—It is intended on account of their Doings shall be put into the Mail to Morrow morning—that they may arrive at Congress as quick as possible—I hope they will behave with so much Dignity that you will be pleased to see their Votes of your native Town. . . .

PS I have this Moment heard from Barry [Barre, Massachusetts] at that place they voted for the Treaty yesterday after public worship was over—they were unanimous to a Man—you may be assured the people in the Country are much alarmd.[62]

    With the Jay Treaty ratified, and the necessary funds to implement it appropriated, war with Britain had been forestalled, but the possibility of armed conflict between the United States and France loomed large. While relations with France worsened during George Washington's presidency, it would remain for his successor to deal with the crisis, for Washington had decided to retire at the end of his second term.

Chapter 11

a flattering and a Glorious Reward

HENRIETTA LISTON and her husband Robert, newly appointed as British minister to the United States in 1796, were "harrassd with attentions" on their arrival in New York City, as she put it in a letter to her uncle, James Jackson. She also commented on a "very fortunate circumstance. . . . the Treaty with Great Britain [negotiated by John Jay in 1794] was *ratified* about the time of our coming into Port, after a very warm opposition. . . . disputes, it seems, ran so high the week before our arrival. . . . no warmth on politics have occurr'd in any Company where We have been."[1]

Arriving in Philadelphia, the Listons took a house, Henrietta complaining about the expense and that foreign ministers were taken advantage of, being deemed "lawful Game & there is less real principle in this Country than I expected to find, particularly in the lower orders of the People,—yet, was our Door left open all night we should not, probably, be robbed, *cheating* not *stealing* seems to be the error in America."[2]

On a trip to the South in September, the couple paid a brief visit to President Washington at Mount Vernon, who was intending to retire shortly at the end of his second term.

one of the best Farmers in America

[We] were received with the utmost kindness by the President & Mrs. Washington, his Family consists of the Marquis la Fayettes Son, & his tutor [George Washington de Lafayette and Félix Frestel], the former a gentle, melancholy, interesting youth, the latter clever & accomplished but . . . proud & sullen.—the President's Secretary, a modest young Man, & a Miss Custis, the Grand Daughter of Mrs. Washington by a former Marriage, one of the prettiest Girls I have seen. . . . We departed, after three days stay, in spight of entreaties:—the President was at great pains to show Us every part of his Farm, He is, indeed, one of the best Farmers in America, & it seems to be his favourite occupation.[3]

ABIGAIL ADAMS, knowing that her husband would be a likely candidate for the presidency, but that he was ambivalent about the prospect, wrote him a thoughtful letter.

a flattering and a Glorious Reward

Quincy Feb,ry 20 1796

My Dearest friend

Upon some Subjects I think much more than I write, I think what is Duty to others and what is duty to ourselves. I contemplate unpleasent concequences to our Country if your decision should be the same with the p[resident].s. . . . You write me fully assured that the P. is unalterably determind to retire. This is an event not yet contemplated by the people at large, we must be attentive to their feelings and to their voice, no Successor, can expect such support as the P. has had. The first Ministers have retired, and a man without intrigue, without party Spirit, with an honest mind and a judicious Head, with an unspotted Character may be difficult to find as v. p. This will still render the first Station more diffi-cult, you know what is before you, the Whips and Scorpions, the Thorns without Roses—the dangers, anxieties and weight of Empire. . . .

This tho a hard and arduous Task, would be a flattering and a Glorious Re-ward, and such a reward as all good men will unite in giving to Washington, and such a Reward as I pray his Successor may merrit and obtain. Should Provi-dence allot the task to my Friend, but think not that I am alone anxious for the part he will be calld to act, tho by far the most important, I am anxious for the proper discharge of that share which will devolve upon me. Whether I have pa-tience, prudence, discretion sufficent to fill a station so unexceptionably as the Worthy Lady who now holds it, I fear I have not. As Second I have had the hap-piness of Stearing clear of censure as far as I know. If the contemplation did not make me feel very serious, I should say that I have been so used to a freedom of sentiment that I know not how to place so many gaurds about me, as will be indispensable, to look at every word before I utter it, and to impose a silence upon my self, when I long to talk. Here in this retird village, I live beloved by my Neighbours, and as I assume no State, and practise no pagentry, unenvy'd I sit calm and easy, mixing very little with the World.[4]

HENRIETTA LISTON, attending a dinner given by the retiring President in the fall of 1796, rightly assumed that the election would be a topic of conversation. She tried to explain the complicated process of electing the president to her uncle.

a peculiar Mode of voting for President and Vice President

We had a great deal of conversation—as the conduct of the French Minister during this Election has very much disgusted Washington & his Ministers. . . . the spirits of the Party . . . were a little damped . . . when the Proclamation came that Jeffersons ticket had gained the Election in this state—it is still possible that Ad-ams may ultimately Succeed, & even possible that Pinckney, late Minister in Lon-don may be President—this arises from a peculiar Mode of voting for President & Vice President at the same time without particularizing which is the former &

which the latter, so that in March when the matter is decided the Majority of votes carry it & this Majority may render the Man President who the People intended as vice President yet present appearances are in favor of Jefferson chiefly from the indefatigable pains & unjustifiable means used by his party—[5]

[Congress convened in December to hear President Washington's last annual message. Mrs. Liston was there and reported on the event.]

extreme agitation . . . when He mentioned the French

—the Hall was crowded & a prodigious Mob at the Door, about twelve oClock Washington entered in full dress, as He always is on publick occasions, black velvet, sword &c., followed by three Secretarys,—Secretary of State, of War, & of the Treasury; a group of people with white staffs. He was preceded by the Sergeant at Arms, with His Mace—He bowed on each side as He past to an arm chair upon a plat-form raised some steps from the ground & railed-in; after composing himself He drew a paper from his pocket.—Washington Writes better than He reads, there is even a little hesitation in his common speaking, but He possesses so much natural unaffected dignity, & is so noble a figure as to give always a pleasing impression. I happened to sit very near him, & as every Person stood-up at his entrance & again when He began to read I had an opportunity of seeing the extreme agitation He felt when He mentioned the *French.*[6]

[In a letter of January 15, 1797, Henrietta Liston informed her uncle that John Adams would be the new president and Thomas Jefferson the vice president. "At a publick dinner of the Presidents yester day, I sat between the rising & setting sun, there is a good deal of amusement in the conversation of Adams, a considerable degree of Wit and Humour, & I feel myself perfectly easy & familiar with both the Great Men."[7] The Listons also attended the celebration of Washington's birthday in February which proved to be quite a spectacle.]

The President . . . moved a Monarch

Guns were fired & Bells rung—in the morning the Gentlemen waited on the President, & the Ladies on Mrs. Washington, & were entertained with cake & wine—Ricketts Amphitheater was fitted up & in the Evening a Ball given to about a thousand Persons; the President appeared in the American Uniform, (blue & buff), with the Cross of Cincinatus at his breast in diamonds. . . . I went in about seven o Clock to the Presidents Box, from which we had a very compleat view of the Company; the Country dances & Cottillions were danced. . . . The American Ladies dance better than any set of People I ever saw. . . . the appearance was very beautiful, many pretty Women & all showing in their dress, cheerfull, happy, & gay . . . the President . . . moved a Monarch. . . . at eleven o Clock supper was announced, The President walked alone, his March playing, He was followed by Mrs. Washington handed by the Vice President, I went next handed by the Portugueze Minister, then his Lady handed by Mr. Liston . . . the supper tables were very splendid, the President & his Party sat at the centre one. . . . a trumpet sounded, & the Company huzzaed, the President rose drank their healths, & thanked them for the last honor done him. . . . Mr. Liston & I stole away soon after our return to the Ball-room, We extremely entertained, & *I* tolerably tired, tho' pleased.[8]

[John Adams was sworn in on March 4, 1797. The Listons attended a farewell dinner given by Washington prior to his successor's inauguration. Henrietta reflected on her hero's character in her journal.]

a majestic figure

Yesterday General Washington voluntarily resigned his office of Chief Magistrate of the United States of America; Mr: Adams was sworn in President as his successor, carrying the Election by a majority of three votes over his opponent Mr. Jefferson—who, at the same time, took the oath as Vice President.

On the third of March,—it being the last day of General Washington's power as President,—he gave a publick dinner to the officers of State, Foreign Ministers, principal Senators, & to their respective Ladies.

I had, as usual, the gratification of being handed to Table & of sitting by the President.—Had I never before considered the character of Washington, I should certainly have joined the general voice, & pronounced him greater in this voluntary retreat, & in the resignation of power over an immense country,—than when, having by his conduct as a Soldier, been the principal means of rendering his Country independent, he became, by the universal suffrage of the people, its ruler & director. I should have repeated with others—Washington is the first of Men,— wise, great, & good,—whereas as I now view him, he is in truth & reality,— honest, prudent & fortunate, &, wonderful to say, almost without ambition. . . .

Naturally grave & silent, his mode of life had rendered him frugal & temperate.—Vanity in him was a very limited passion, & prudence his striking trait. Most people say & do too much,—Washington, partly from constitutional taciturnity,—but still more from natural sagacity & careful observation, never fell into this common error.—Nature had been liberal to him, to a majestic figure was added a native unaffected gracefulness of deportment, & dignity of manner, which was rather improved by a liking—I will not say a fondness—for dress. . . .

Naturally hot:tempered, coldhearted, & guarded, he acquired a uniform command over his passions on publick occasions,—but in private & particularly with his Servants, its violence sometimes broke out. His countenance was peculiarly pleasant when he laughed. . . . His first & last pleasure appeared to be *farming*; on that theme he always talked freely. . . .

About ten days before his quitting his situation, I congratulated him on his approaching happiness.—Yes, said he, like a Child within view of the Holydays, I have counted the months, then the weeks, & I now reckon the days previous to my release. I observed that his countenance indicated the pleasure to which he looked forward.—you are wrong, replied he;—my countenance never yet betrayed my feelings. . . .

The World gives General Washington more credit for his retirement from publick life than I am disposed to do. . . . he was become tired of his situation, fretted by the opposition often made to his measures; & his pride revolted against the ingratitude he experienced,—and he was also disgusted by the scurrilous abuse lavished upon him by his political enemies.[9]

ELEANOR PARKE CUSTIS described the journey from Philadelphia to Mount Vernon, after George Washington retired as president, to her friend Elizabeth Bordley.

the Inhabitants . . . came out to . . . Welcome My Dear Grandpapa

My Dearest Elizabeth,   Mount Vernon March 18th 1797

We arrived here last Wednesday after a tedious & fatiguing journey of seven days. The roads from Philadelphia to the Head of Elk were very good, from thence to this place they are very bad. But as they have been much worse than they are at present, we were very well satisfied to make the best of them.

We encountered no adventures of any kind, & saw nothing uncommon, except the light Horse of Delaware, & Maryland, who insisted upon attending us through their states, all the Inhabitants of Baltimore who came out to *see*, & *be seen* & to Welcome My Dear Grandpapa—some in carriages, some on Horseback, the others on foot. The gentlemen of George Town also attended us to the River, & four of them rowed us over in a barge. . . . We left the City on Wednesday, & arrived here without accident at four o'clock.

The weather untill today has been very damp and disagreeable, but this has been a charming morning—& every thing appears to be revived. The grass begins to look green. Some trees are in blossom, others budding. The flowers are coming out—& the numerous different Birds keep up a constant serenading. Next month every thing will look charmingly. When I look at this noble river, & all the beautifull prospects around—I pity all those who are in Cities, for surely a country life, is the most rational & the most happy of any—& all the refinements of art & luxury are nothing in comparison to the Beauties of Nature.

Since I left Philadelphia every thing has appeared to be a dream, I can hardly realise my being *here*, & that Grandpapa is no longer in office. If it is a dream I hope never to awaken from it—for although I shall ever remember my friends with regret yet I am delighted to be once more settled here, & surrounded by my Dearest relatives. I passed last winter very happily in Philadelphia but I do not regret its amusements, & shall be much happier *here* without them. . . .

My Beloved Grandmama has a very bad cold & cough—but I trust that she will be soon entirely recovered. Grandpapa is very well, & has already turned Farmer again. I am on Monday to begin gardening. I hope to make some proficiency in it.

I am also deputy Housekeeper, in which employment I expect to improve much, as I am very partial to it. When my Harpsichord comes, I shall practice a great deal, & make my Sister sing your parts of our Duetts. I think you had better come here to sing them with me. I do not despair of seeing you, & I shall be very much disappointed if you do not visit us.

My love, & respects to your Papa, & Mama & tell them that the air of Mount Vernon would be of infinite service to them I am sure. . . . My Grandparents join in affectionate regards to your Parents, & yourself. . . .   Eleanor Parke Custis

PS. direct your letters under cover to General Washington—M-t V-n Virginia, & I shall be sure of getting them directly.[10]

ABIGAIL ADAMS and John, now President, moved into the former mansion of Robert Morris in Philadelphia. As usual Abigail provided details about her activities to her sister, Mary Cranch.

splendid misery

My dear Sister: Philadelphia, May 16, 1797

Yesterday being Monday, from 12 to half past two I received visits, 32 Ladies and near as many Gentlemen. I shall have the same ceremony to pass through to day, and the rest part of the week. As I am not prepaird with furniture for a Regular drawing Room, I shall not commence one I believe, as the Summer is to near at hand, and my Health very precarious. At the Winter Sessions I shall begin. Mrs. [Cotton] Tufts once stiled my situation, splendid misery. She was not far from Truth. To day the President meets both Houses at 12 to deliver His speech. I will inclose it to you. I should like to learn the comments upon it, with a veiw to discover the Temper and Sentiments of the publick mind. We are indeed as Milton expresses it, "Thrown on perilous Times". . . .

Evening 8 oclock The day is past, and a fatiguing one it has been. The Ladies of Foreign Ministers and the Ministers, with our own Secretaries & Ladies have visited me to day, and add to them, the whole Levee to day of senate & house. Strangers &c making near one Hundred asked permission to visit me, so that from half past 12 till near 4, 1 was rising up & sitting down. Mr. A[dams] will never be too big to have his Friends.[11]

I begin to feel . . . less anxiety about the ceremonious part of my duty

My dear Sister: Philadelphia, May 24, 1797

I keep up my old Habit of rising at an early hour. If I did not I should have little command of my Time. At 5 I rise. From that time till 8 1 have a few leisure hours. At 8 I breakfast, after which untill Eleven I attend to my Family arrangements. At that hour I dress for the day. From 12 until two I receive company, sometimes untill 3. We dine at that hour unless on company days which are tuesdays & thursdays. After dinner I usually ride out untill seven. I begin to feel a little more at Home, and less anxiety about the ceremonious part of my duty, tho by not having a drawing Room for the summer I am obliged every day, to devote two Hours for the purpose of seeing company. Tomorrow we are to dine the Secretaries of State &c with the whole Senate.[12]

Relations with France were at a low point when John Adams took office. President Washington, enraged by the audacious behavior of the French minister, Edmond Charles Edouard Genêt, in the United States, had demanded his recall. Matters deteriorated further when France, believing the Jay Treaty signified closer ties with Britain, commenced an undeclared naval war against the United States, seizing vessels bound for England and selling them at auction. The diplomatic news from abroad was not encouraging. When Washington's appointee Charles Coatesworth Pinckney arrived in Paris to replace James Monroe as American minister to France, Charles Delacroix, French Minister of Foreign Affairs, refused to accept his credentials.

MARY STEAD PINCKNEY, who accompanied her husband to Paris, kept a letter-book during her stay abroad. On December 13, 1796, she noted:

till the grievances . . . are redressed

the executive of this republic having notified yesterday to Mr. Monroe that they would not receive a minister from ours till the grievances of which they complain are redressed. As this event has been so lately announced I can give you no account of what is to become of ourselves—whether we are immediately to leave Paris, or to finish our winter in it. . . . In two days we shall know whether we are to remain here this winter or wander further in quest of peace.[13]

[While the Pinckneys waited on further developments, Mary admitted to a cousin, Alice DeLancey Izard, sadness at leaving Paris, a city that she found most interesting.]

I go to the opera

Sunday evening, decr 18th

I . . . shall leave Paris with regret. Our little society of the boulevards is very pleasing, and there is so much to engage and amuse a stranger in this vast city! The gallery of the Louvre alone, when it is properly arranged, would furnish pleasure for a month's mornings, and Me. La Tour's acting at the opera and Me. Gardel's dancing, and Madlle. Contat's acting at the théâtre de la rue Feydeau will not easily tire. And then, my dear Cousin, the freedom with regard to dress is agreeable to me. I go to the opera, & sit in the front row of the first boxes, in one of the large caps worn here, and without a perriwig, or having my hair dress'd, or even visible; & in my robe wadée, which is a most comfortable warm dress, made of silk like a close bodied great coat, and large enough to go over the other dress . . . Mine is puce inside and outside, trimmed with black velvet. . . . Me. Tallien . . . dresses her hair or perriwig in tiny little curls all over her head, and very low on the forehead, and passes narrow ribband in various directions over her head. This is called à la grecque. Mrs. Monroe dresses her own hair (for she told me she was tired of wigs) in the same way. The ear is quite uncovered, and the ribband goes under it, and the whole of the hind hair is crêped and curled all over the head, and is hardly lower behind than the top of the shoulder. I think it very pretty. . . . Mr. & Mrs. Monroe have behaved with great politeness to me, and Genl Pinckey thinks the behaviour of the former to him has been very candid. Their house is a little temple. . . . Mr. Monroes furniture is handsome, but as he order'd it with a view to take to America the chairs are not gilt, & do not suit the rooms. . . . He is going to sell his house for whatever it will fetch, which, probably, under the present appearances of things will not be more than he gave for it.[14]

[Monsieur Delacroix not only refused to honor General Pinckney's letters of credence, his representative further insulted Pinckney by ignoring his diplomatic status entirely, suggesting that he apply for a "card of hospitality," which would allow a private foreigner to remain in France. Mrs. Pinckney reported that Talleyrand, returned to France in 1796, had provided the government with this assessment of Americans.]

I am excessively vexed with M. Tallerand

Mr. Tallerand . . . has told those in power that he knows America well—that there are no men of ability in it—that the male part of the community do nothing but drink Madeira wine, and the women are only employed in suckling their children—that America possesses only three millions of inhabitants scattered along an extensive coast, and that—poor conclusion—the french nation may treat America just as it does Genoa and Geneva. . . . I am excessively vexed with M. Tallerand, but I hope his mean endeavours to curry favor will tend to his own abasement.[15]

[On January 6, 1797, Mary informed her sister: "We have begun our new year in this city . . . but I am sure I shall not . . . venture to foretell where we shall finish it. . . ." She complained that "we have no cards of hospitality, and if they are determined to consider us as private americans only are liable to be stopped every time we go out."[16] To her cousin she explained: "even the members of the legislature [are] very cautious how they visit or have any communication with foreign ministers not receiv'd. . . ." She added that relations with the United States had worsened: "by private letters from America we hear that the french government have directed their vessels to seize those of America under the same circumstances as they were taken by the english before America made the treaty with that nation."[17]]

The Pinckneys left France and relocated in Holland to await further instructions. Incensed at the treatment General Pinckney had received, President Adams dispatched John Marshall and Elbridge Gerry to join Pinckney in Amsterdam and proceed to Paris to address the crisis. Three French agents met with the American commissioners and, per instructions from Talleyrand, now French Minister of Foreign Affairs, demanded a $250,000 bribe from the United States as well as a loan before negotiations could even begin. When the news reached Adams, he reported the insulting episode to Congress, at the same time urging preparations for a possible war. To satisfy suspicious Republicans, Adams sent Congress the actual report detailing the incident but substituting the letters X, Y, and Z for the names of the Frenchmen.

The American people, upon learning of the "XYZ affair," were enraged and overcome with nationalistic fervor. President Adams cut off all trade with France, abrogated the treaty of 1778 with that nation, and commissioned privateers to attack their ships. Opposition was muted. Abigail Adams believed that the Republicans "dare not openly countanance the conduct of France, but they want to court and coax her. With . . . Pinckneys dispatches, which fully prove the unbecomeing and indignant conduct of France toward the United States, these degraded Beings would still have their Countrymen 'lick the Hand just raisd to shed their Blood.'"[18]

ELEANOR PARKE CUSTIS confessed to her correspondent Elizabeth Bordley:

I cannot avoid expressing my opinion of the French

My Dearest Eliza,   Mount Vernon November 23rd [1797]

Soon after we came home [from a trip to Washington], our amiable & esteemed friends Messrs La Fayette & Frestel left us for New York, from whence (as they informed us by letters) they sailed for Havre de Grace, the 25th October in the Brig Clio. We regretted very much that they left us, although their prospects were then very favorable, & they left us in the hope of soon meeting their excellent & suffering friends, restored to liberty & happiness. . . . By the bye Dear Eliza excuse me for troubling you with a political opinion, but although I am no politician I can assure you, yet I cannot avoid expressing my opinion of the *French.*

Were I drowning & a *straw* only in sight, I would as soon think of trusting to that *slender support* (which in fact could not save me) as place the smallest dependance upon the stability of the *French republican* government. Neither would I trust the life of a *Cat* in the hands of a sett of people who hardly know religion, humanity or Justice, even *by name.* Do not think me so narrow minded or prejudiced as to judge a whole nation by a few individuals. Some frenchmen I esteem highly—but those barbarous *democratic murderers*, or rather *Demons*, I shall ever abominate. I pity those poor misguided multitudes who follow every phantom with avidity—who whilst they hear the cry of *liberty* forget how they are to smart for it & whilst they follow with eagerness the *shadow*—lose the *substance* beyond recovery.

I am afraid you will think this digression rather malapropos, but when I am writing to a friend whatever thought strikes me must appear on paper immediately, without ever considering whether it will be interesting or entertaining to my readers.[19]

[Flushed with patriotism, Eleanor entertained the notion of organizing a corps of volunteer soldiers and invited her friend Elizabeth to join.]

lend a hand to extirpate the Demons

Hope Park May 14th 1798

I left Mount Vernon with My Sister Law to come here on a visit to My Dearest Mother whom I had not seen for several months. . . . Many thanks My Charming Friend for the song sent, I sing it every day with *strong patriotic feelings*, & think it very fine.

I am full as patriotic as you can be *Bett*, & to speak truth, I am becoming an outrageous politician, perfectly *federal*, & determined even to lend a hand to extirpate the Demons if their unparellel'd impudence, & thirst of conquest should make them attempt an invasion of our peaceable happy Land.

Have you courage enough think you to turn *Soldier* on such an occasion? If you have, let me know it, & I will enroll you in *my* corps of *independent volunteers*, if occasion suits, we may perhaps *dub* ourselves *knights.* You must procure a black dress, the *fashion* of it we will settle hereafter, we shall have black helmets, of morocco leather, ornamented with black bugles, & an immense Plume of black feathers. You have no idea how becoming it will be, "we shall tow'r above the rest"—our arms shall be, Lances, Pistols, Bows & arrows. & I shall take especial care to provide *burnt corks*, or *charcoal* sufficient to furnish amply the whole association of valorous *knights* with immense *whiskers, & mustachios*, of uncommon magnitude, to strike with awe the beholders. "My Ambition fires at the thought", & I feel chok full of fight. Think child how glorious, to be celebrated as the preservers of our *Friends & Country*, "In such a cause a Womans vengeance tow'rs above her Sex!" We shall perform wonders I am sure, & our fame will be transmitted to latest posterity. I have already engaged several of the sisterhood to be ready at a moments warning, I am *Commander in Chief* of the corps. I am at present quietly seated in this still retreat, free from noise & bustle, enjoying the present, & keeping myself in readiness for, & prepared to meet anything that may come round in the course of events. I do not wish to dance again until next Winter. I allmost lamed myself last Winter. I am not at all surprised that you wish for retirement, I would not exchange mine, for all the pomp & Vanity of this wicked world. . . .

Be assured My Dearest Eliza of the firm & lasting attachment of your

Eleanor Parke Custis[20]

HENRIETTA LISTON declared in a letter to her uncle in May 1798 that she was amazed at how markedly the mood in the country had changed. "With respect to politics I scarcely know what to say."

apparent Unanimity of the Americans against them

The tide is turned, & I look with astonishment at the violence with which it flows,—the President went to the Play last night for the first time, He . . . goes seldomer into publick than Washington did.—Mr. Listons Box was oposite to him, the Portugueze Minister & his Lady went with Us,—nothing could equal the noise & uproar, the President's March was play'd, & called for over & over again, it was sung to, & danced to. . . . when I tell you that five years ago the *Mania* was as strongly in favor of the French you will say, that a cold national character is no security against madness, the Democrates [Jeffersonians] are silent, some indeed have seemed to recant, whether convinced, or waiting a fit moment to Rally I know not, but at this moment the British are extolled as the first People (next to themselves I mean) for having so long resisted the Tyrants of France; an alien-bill is to be brought in to the Senate immediately, a Secretary of the Navy is appointed, Frigates are fitting out, Men & Money voted & every Man speaking with a degree of violence on which I often stare with astonishment; surely if any thing can surprise the General Directory, it must be, the present apparent Unanimity of the Americans against them.[21]

[Liston remarked in a subsequent letter: "in truth the insolence of the French has done the Work." And she passed along more information.]

The Congress have carried every measure against the French except the declaration of *War*. . . . Washington has been named Commander in chief & agrees to accept . . . every thing here is Military & the Americans are actually carrying on War against France without the open declaration. Last Week one of the new American Brigs took a French Privateer Vessel near the Coast with twenty Men, who were treated as Prisoners of War.[22]

ELEANOR PARKE CUSTIS continued to express her anger toward the French to Elizabeth Bordley.

> *I hope . . . that the Americans may humble them compleatly*

Mount Vernon July 1st 1798

Were you not pleased at General [John] Marshall's reception [upon his return from France]? *I* was delighted at it—he has richly deserved every attention. I hope General Pinkney will soon return, his family are very amiable & his character is very respectable indeed. His friends in Charleston must be very uneasy on his account. . . .

What think you *Bett*, of the delectable Apostate Bishop of Autun [Talleyrand] what an intolerable wretch he is, I could positively hang *him*, the five Directors, & *Monsieur* le *Philosophe* Chasseboeuf de Volney—without the smallest remorse, I should rather glory in ridding this earth of such *fiends.* Does not your wrath often kindle at the recollection of Talleyrand, & Volney, when with their smooth tongues & woe begone faces, they excited the sympathy of the Americans, & were treated with so much kindness—that they were both Spy's, and are doing all in their power to injure those who befriended them.* However I hope if the insolent french should dare to come here, that the Americans may humble them compleatly, I would not care a pin for any relation of mine, who could do it, if he would hesitate one moment to fight with all his Heart & strength, and lay down his life & fortune for the service of his country.[23]

*Talleyrand had been appointed Bishop of Autun before the Revolution. He and Volney spent some time in exile in the United States.

President Adams resisted open warfare, choosing instead to use rising American indignation at French conduct and preparations for war to exert pressure on the French in the hope of achieving reconciliation through diplomacy. Meanwhile, extreme Federalists in Congress, against the background of increasingly acrimonious public exchanges between factions, crafted legislation to suppress criticism of the government, which they deemed to be dangerous during this time of crisis. The Alien Act would allow the president to deport any foreigner whose presence was considered risky, and the Sedition Act would punish those who spoke, wrote, or published anti-government material, i.e., Republicans.

ABIGAIL ADAMS, protective of her husband and more enraged at criticism of him than ever, believed that the Alien and Sedition Acts were necessary and argued in their favor.

to punish the stirrer up of Sedition

Yet dairingly do the vile incendaries keep up in Baches* paper the most wicked and base, voilent & caluminiating abuse. It was formerly considerd as leveld against the Government, but now it is contrary to their declared sentiments daily manifested, so that it insults the Majesty of the Sovereign People. But nothing will have an Effect untill congress pass a Sedition Bill, which I presume they will do before they rise.[24]

*Benjamin Franklin Bache, grandson of Benjamin Franklin, who founded the Republican paper *Aurora* in Philadelphia in 1790.

[She vented her anger in another letter to her sister.]

I wish the Laws of our Country were competant to punish the stirer up of Sedition, the writer and printer of base and unfounded calumny. This would contribute as much to the Peace and harmony of our Country as any measure, and in times like the present, a more carefull and attentive watch ought to be kept over foreigners. This will be done in future if the Alien Bill passes, without being curtaild & clipt untill it is made nearly useless. The Volunteer Corps which are forming not only of young Men, but others will keep in check these people, I trust.[25]

Even George Washington, alarmed by the activities of the Republicans, supported restrictions on civil liberties. Having agreed to take charge of troops being raised in light of the French threat, he feared that partisans "would endeavor to divide, & contaminate the army, by artful & seditious discourses, and perhaps at a critical moment, bring on confusion. . . . a profest Democrat . . . will leave nothing unattempted to overturn the Government of this Country."[26]

Another matter, however, would divert the nation from its preoccupation with France: the untimely death of George Washington.

Chapter 12

a favored nation

The Revolution had given birth to a new and independent nation, and the Constitution had provided a structure for its survival. Blessed with a president who had broad public support, the government had enacted a Bill of Rights and it had steered a course through perilous times, slowly gaining confidence in its ability to govern. On the international scene, it had been acknowledged (if grudgingly) as a force to be reckoned with, managing to avoid war with both Great Britain and France. Its principles, based on individual rights, had attracted the attention of the world. After George Washington declined to run for a third term, John Adams had been elected president. A peaceful transfer of power took place when Adams, unable to win the next election, turned over the reins of government to Thomas Jefferson, the leader of the new Republican party. But before this took place at the turn of the century, the nation mourned the death of its first president.

HENRIETTA LISTON and her husband, Robert, visited Mount Vernon frequently and observed that George Washington seemed "improved by retirement. He now converses with more ease & less guardedly than when in publick life. His hospitality is in no way diminished, though the Splendor of his table is considerably lessened."[1] Mrs. Liston had this to say about their last visit in early November 1799.

still devoted to his farm

The General & his amiable Wife received us with much kindness. The pleasing change we had on former occasions remarked in Washington's manners continued; but I was sorry to observe a late fit of illness seemed to have somewhat altered his looks, his figure appeared less & an approaching deafness, had a little affected his spirits.—We found him still devoted to his Farm,—& saw with regret that he was also occupied in repairing the *family* vault. . . . At our departure he kissed me, & kindly shaking hands with Mr. Liston, ordered his Horse & escorted us to his own boundaries.[2]

ELIZA AMBLER BRENT CARRINGTON, the wife of General Edward Carrington, a comrade in arms and friend of George Washington, stopped at Mount Vernon. She conveyed her observations to her sister, Anne Fisher.

the tranquil happiness that reigns throughout the house

Mount Vernon, November 22nd, 1799

We arrived here on the 20th just in time enough for dinner. . . . Yes, we arrived at this venerable mansion in perfect safety, where we are experiencing every mark of hospitality & kindness that the good old General's continued friendship to Col. C[arrington] could lead us to expect; his reception of my husband was that of a Brother; he took us each by the hand & with a warmth of expression not to be described, pressed mine, & told me that I had conferred a favour, never to be forgotten, in bringing his old friend to see him; then bidding a servant to call the ladies, entertained us most facetiously [wittily] till they appeared. . . .

In vain does the General insist upon our stay, promising to take him [her husband] over the grounds and farm, & showing him the mill &c &c which will occupy him till 3—but no—the world could not tempt him to stay, at a time, when he said, everyone should leave the family entirely undisturbed, ["Nelly" Custis Lewis was about to give birth] but that after a few days, when we should have finished our visit to our friends in Maryland, we would again see them and prolong our visit—is it not vexatious to have so scrupulous a husband; nothing could distress me more than to leave that charming family at such a moment but I am bound to obey & at 2 we are to leave this place for Washington. . . .

27th November . . . we returned to finish our visit to this revered mansion. . . . It is really an enjoyment to be here, to witness the tranquil happiness that reigns throughout the house (except now & then a little hustle, occasioned by the young squire Custis when he returns from hunting, bringing in a "*Valiant Deer*" as he terms it, "that Grand Pa & the Col. will devour")—nice venison I assure you it is, & my taste in seasoning the stew is not passed unnoticed while the whole party, I won't say devour it, but do it ample Justice.

My mornings are spent charmingly alternately in the different chambers; first an hour after breakfast with the lady in the straw*—dressing the pretty little stranger, who is the delight of the Grand-Ma, then we repair to the old lady's room, which is precisely on the style of our good old aunt's, that is to say nicely fixed for all sorts of work—on one side sits the chambermaid with her knitting on the other a little colored pet, learning to sew, an old, decent woman with her table and shears cutting out the negroes winter clothes, while the good old lady directs them all, incessantly knitting herself, & pointing out to me several pair of nice coloured stockings & gloves she had just finished, & presenting me with a pair half done, begs me to finish, & wear for her sake—

Her netting too is a great source of amusement, & is so neatly done, that all the younger part of the family are proud of trimming their dresses with it and have furnished me with a whole suit, so that I shall appear "A la domestique" at the first party we have when we get home.

It is wonderful after a life spent as these good people have necessarily spent theirs to see them in retirement assume domestic manners that prevail in our country, when but a year since they were forced to forego all the innocent delights which are so congenial to their years and tastes, to sacrifice to the parade of the drawing room & the Levee.

The recollection of these last days as Mrs. W—calls them, seem to fill her with regret, but the extensive knowledge she has gained in this general intercourse with persons from all parts of the world has made her a most interesting companion, & having a vastly retentive memory, she presents an entire history of half a century.

The weather is too wintry to enjoy outdoor scenes . . . everything within doors is neat & elegant, but nothing remarkable, except the paintings of different artists which have been sent as specimens of their talents—I think there are five portraits of the General, some done in Europe, some in America that do honour to the painter—There are other specimens of the fine arts from various parts of the world, that are admirably executed, & furnish pleasant conversation. Besides these there is a complete Green-house which at this season is a vast, a great source of pleasure. . . .

We have met with no company here, but are told that scarcely a week passes without some and often more than is comfortable or agreeable—

When transient persons, who call from curiosity, they are treated with civility, but never interfere with the order of the house, or the General's disposition of time, which is as regular as when at the head of the Army or in the President's chair. Even friends who make a point of visiting him are left much to themselves, indeed scarcely see him from breakfast to dinner, unless he engages them in a ride, which is very agreeable to him—But from dinner till tea our time is most charmingly spent, indeed one evening the General was so fascinating & drew my husband out into so many old stories, relating to several campaigns where they had been much together, & had so many inquiries to make respecting their mutual friends, particularly Kosiusko & Pulaski who had always corresponded with Col. C— whose characters afford great interest that it was long after twelve when we separated.[3]

*Eleanor "Nelly" Custis Lewis was confined to bed after giving birth to her first child.

HENRIETTA LISTON, on December 18, 1799, received the news of Washington's death.

the magic attached to his name

An express arrived this day from MountVernon with the melancholy accounts of the death of Washington.—An inflammatory sore throat carried him off in 24 hours. He had complained some days of a cold; rose on Friday morning, the 13th, but becoming worse, returned to bed, & although every assistance was immediately called—He died betwixt Saturday & Sunday, at the age of sixtyseven Perfectly sensible & resigned.—

At no time could the Death of Washington have been a matter of indifference to the people of America, but at this moment,—when a rupture with France is apprehended,—it is critical & unfortunate—He was appointed Commander in Chief of the Army (by President Adams & with much difficulty was prevailed upon to accept on condition of chusing his General officers) & the magic attached to his name—a magic greater perhaps than can ever be attached to any other in this Country, was deemed necessary to keep the parties united.[4]

[A few days later, she described the service for Washington held at the German Lutheran Church in Philadelphia on December 26.]

the most sombre of which we had ever partaken

The President, Vice President, Senators & House of Representatives—Foreign Ministers—the Military, & all the different trades &c—paraded in proper order—A Bier was placed near the Pulpit—decorated with Military Ensigns—Bishop [William] White read the Prayers (Washington was an Episcopal) & General [Henry] Lee delivered his oration—pleasing rather than brilliant. . . . A Band of Singers from the Theatre accompanied the Organ, & all was conducted with decency & decorum—A general mourning had been ordered, & commenced that day. The President afterwards gave a publick dinner & certainly the most sombre of which we had ever partaken.

Notice has been given that the 22d of February, The Birth day of Washington—will be held as a solemn Fast,—with Sermons, Orations &c.[5]

MARY WHITE MORRIS was one of many who wrote letters of condolence to Mrs. Washington.

you have lost the friend of your heart

Philadelphia, Decr 27th 1799

Permit me my dear Madam to pour into your afflicted Bosom the sympathetic feelings of sincere affection and friendship as some small consolation in the hour of distress, few very among the numerous admirers of our deceased friend had opportunities of contemplating his virtues,—and I believe there is not one on whom they have made stronger impressions—they are such as can never be effaced whilst memory exists reverencing and esteeming Him as you know I did you will admit me to mingle tears and share your sorrow, you have lost the friend of your heart the sharer of former bliss the dispenser of happy hours, I feel the loss of one who in paying me respectful attentions gratified the sensibilities of a mind strongly attached by having witnessed the frequent exhibition of most excellent qualities in a systematic conduct that commanded respect and esteem from all—But what are the sacrifices of friendship as compared with the deprivation which our Country sustains the Public sentiment receives such an universal and lively expression that even grief like yours must subside at times in the contemplation of it,—my attachment to you my dear Mrs Washington being founded upon Intamacy that has led to the knowledge of your merits,—is most sincere and my present wishes is that I could be with you to manifest the truth there—of by such attentions as might assist in leading your mind to the possession of such peace and comfort as is left. Mr. Morris to whom I have shown what I have writen sayd He most sincerely unites with me in every word and request, that you will accept at my hand these as his as well as my senti-ments—He intended writing to you also but as you will probably have too many calls upon your feelings he hopes that the expression of his affectionate regard through my Pen will be accepted and he joins me in assuring you that if any circumstance should occur in the course of our lives which we or either of us can manifest our regard it will be seized with avidity—should future events draw either of us to the southeard we will not fail to pay you our Personal re-spects. Accept dear Madam the best wishes of your truly affectionate

Mary Morris[6]

ABIGAIL ADAMS summed up her feelings—and the nation's—about Washington in a letter to her sister.

History will not produce to us a Parrallel

Philadelphia, Sunday Eve'ng, Decbr. 22, 1799

This Event so important to our Country at this period, will be universally deplored. No Man ever lived, more deservedly beloved and Respected. The praise and I may say addulation which followed his administration for several years, never made him forget that he was a Man, subject to the weakness and frailty attached to humane Nature. He never grew giddy, but ever mantaind a modest diffidence of his own talents; and if that was an error, it was of the ami-able and engageing kind, tho it might lead sometimes to a want of decisions in some great Emergencys. Possesst of power, posest of an extensive influence, he never used it but for the benifit of his Country. Witness his retirement to private Life when Peace closed the Scenes of War; When call'd by the unanimous Suffrages of the People to the chief Majestracy of the Nation, he acquitted him-self to the satisfaction and applause of all Good Men. When assailed by faction, when reviled by Party, he sufferd with dignity, and Retired from his exalted sta-tion with a Character which malice could not wound, nor envy tarnish. If we look through the whole tennor of his Life, History will not produce to us a Par-rallel. Heaven has seen fit to take him from us. Our Mourning is sincere, in the midst of which, we ought not to lose sight of the Blessings we have enjoy'd and still partake of, that he was spaired to us, untill he saw a successor filling his place, persueing the same system which he had adopted, and that in times which have been equally dangerous and Critical; It becomes not me to say more upon this Head.[7]

[Abigail Adams looked forward to the "release from public life" for herself and her husband. For the country, she wished "for the pres-ervation of the Government, and a wise administration of it. In the best situation, with the wisest head and firmest Heart, it will be surrounded with perplexities, dangers and troubles, that are little conceived of by those into whose Hands it is like to fall."[8]]

MERCY OTIS WARREN paid tribute in her *History* to "the worthy band of patriots who first supported an opposition to the tyrannic measures of Great Britain" and urged that America bear them always "in grateful remembrance," including those who "have long since been consigned to the tomb." She believed the future of the United States was bright if pitfalls could be avoided. Envisioning what the nation might become if it remained true to the principles it espoused in the Revolution, she continued:

The sword now sheathed

The United States of America have now a fair experiment of a republican system to make for themselves. . . . [an] excellent constitution; a strict adherence to which . . . is the best security of the rights and liberties of a country that has bled at every vein, to purchase and transmit them to posterity. The sword now sheathed, the army dismissed, a wise, energetic government established and organized, it is to be hoped many generations will pass away in the lapse of time, before America again becomes a theatre of war.

[But Warren cautioned that care should be taken to "prevent the vesting any individual or body of men with too much power," especially since "the confederation is recent, and their experience immatured." While priding themselves on a government "established on the broad basis of the elective voice of the people," its success "now depends on their own virtue, to continue the United States of America an example of the respectability and dignity of this mode of government."]

The senators of the United States should be wise, her representatives uncorrupt, the judiciary firm, equitable and humane, and the bench of justice ever adorned by men uninfluenced by little passions, and adhering only to the principles of law and equity! The people should be economical and sober; and the clergy should keep within their own line. . . .

America exhibits the happiest prospects

From the accumulated blessings which are showered down on the United States, there is reason to indulge the benign hope, that America may long stand a favored nation. . . .

The hand of nature has displayed its magnificence on this quarter of the globe, in the astonishing rivers, lakes, and mountains, replete with the richest minerals and the most useful materials for manufactures. At the same time, the indigenous produce of its fertile lands yields medicine, food, and clothing, and every thing needful for man in his present condition. America may with propriety be styled land of promise; a happy climate, though remarkably variegated; fruitful and populous, independent and free, both necessity and pleasure invite the hand of the industrious to cherish and cultivate the prolific soil, which is ready to yield all that nature requires to satisfy the reasonable wishes of man, as well as to contribute to the wealth, pleasure, and luxury of the inhabitants. It is a portion of the globe that appears as a fair and fertile vineyard, which requires only the industrious care of the laborers to render it for a long time productive of the finest clusters in the full harvest of prosperity and freedom. Instead of yielding thorns, thistles, and sour grapes, which must be the certain fruits of animosity, disunion, venality, or vice.

Though in her infantile state, the young republic of America exhibits the happiest prospects. Her extensive population, commerce, and wealth, the progress of agriculture, arts, sciences, and manufactures, have increased with a rapidity beyond example. Colleges and academies have been reared, multiplied, and endowed with the best advantages for public instruction, on the broad scale of liberality and truth. The effects of industry and enterprise appear in the numerous canals, turnpikes, elegant buildings, and well constructed bridges, over lengths and depths of water that open, and render the communication easy and agreeable, throughout a country almost without bounds. . . . The wisdom and justice of the American governments, and the virtue of the inhabitants, may, if they are not deficient in the improvement of their own advantages, render the United States of America an enviable example to all the world, of peace, liberty, righteousness, and truth.[9]

Figure 7. Prudence Punderson, *The First, Second, and Last Scene of Mortality*, ca. 1773. Silk on silk needlework, 13" x 17.5"; The Connecticut Historical Society, Hartford, Connecticut. Gift of Newtown Brainard.

Notes

Abbreviations of Oft-cited Public Collections

AAS   American Antiquarian Society
AFP   [electronic edition] *Adams Family Papers: Electronic Archive* MHi, www.masshist.org/digitaladams/
CSmH   Henry E. Huntington Library and Art Gallery
CtHi   Connecticut Historical Society, Hartford, Connecticut
CtY   Yale University Library
DLC   Library of Congress
DNA   National Archives
MHi   Massachusetts Historical Society
NHi   New-York Historical Society
NLS   National Library of Scotland
NN   New York Public Library
NNC   Columbia University Rare Book & Manuscript Library
NNGL   Gilder Lehrman Collection, New York
PHi   Pennsylvania Historical Society
PPAmP   American Philosophical Society
RIHi   Rhode Island Historical Society
ViMtV   Mount Vernon Ladies Association, George Washington's Mount Vernon Estate & Gardens, Mount Vernon, Virgina
ViU   University of Virginia

Editorial Guidelines

1. *Jemima Condict Her Book Being a Transcript of the Diary of An Essex County Maid During the Revolutionary War* (Newark, New Jersey: The Carteret Book Club, 1930), 41.

2. Re Helen E. Smith's stories, our acknowledgments to Elizabeth Shapiro at the Sharon (Connecticut) Historical Society, and Laurel Thatcher Ulrich for their insightful comments (emails 11/08-12/08). Love Lawrence was really Lovey Lawrence Adams and had been married for ten years to the loyalist Joseph Adams, who had fled in 1777 to England where he was named Master Sur-

geon of His Majesty's Royal Navy. Lovey Adams just happened to sail on the same ship as Abigail Smith Adams.

Setting the Scene

1. Elias Boudinot, *Journal or Historical recollections of American Events During the Revolutionary War* (Philadelphia, 1894), 50.

2. Carol Berkin, "The Historian's Perspective: Teaching the Revolution," *History Now,* 21 (Sept. 2009), online at The Gilder Lehrman Institute of American History website.

3. William R. Polk, *Violent Politics: A History of Insurgency, Terrorism, & Guerilla War, From the American Revolution to Iraq* (New York: Harper Collins, 2007) 1-19.

4. In fact, Pennsylvania was contesting its territories with Virginia and Connecticut, while New York and New Hampshire both claimed the area that would become Vermont.

5. Susan Dion, "Women in the *Boston Gazette* 1755-1775," *Historical Journal of Massachusetts* 14, no. 2 (June 1986): 87-97.

6. Elaine Forman Crane, ed. and abridger, *The Diary of Elizabeth Drinker* (Boston: Northeastern University Press, 1994), 304.

7. William Livingston essay, published posthumously March 1791; see Claire McCurdy, "Domestic Politics and Inheritance Patterns—The Family Papers of William Livingston," *The Livingston Legacy—Three Centuries of American History,* Richard C. Wiles, ed. (Bard College Office of Publications, 1987), 162-86.

8. Lorena S. Walsh points out in "Slavery and Agriculture at Mount Vernon" in *Slavery at the Home of George Washington*, Philip J. Schwarz, ed. (The Mount Vernon Ladies' Association, 2009), that black slave women there had to build fences, cleaned stables, loaded or spread manure, among other undesirable work.

9. 10 November 1776, Silliman Family Papers, Manuscripts and Archives, Yale University Library, hereafter CtY; Abigail Adams to John Adams, 17 June 1782 [electronic edition], *Adams Family Papers: An Electronic Archive.* Massachusetts Historical Society. www.masshist.org/digitaladams/, hereafter AFP.

10. GLC1800.01, Letter, M.O. Warren to C. Macaulay, 29 Dec. 1774, The Gilder Lehrman Collection, The Gilder Lehrman Institute of American History, hereafter NNGL.

11. John Jay Smith, ed., *Letters of Dr. Richard Hill and His Children or The History of a Family As Told by Themselves* (Philadelphia: Privately Printed for the Descendants, 1854), 239.

12. "Extracts from the Journal of Mrs. Ann Ashby Manigault," *South Carolina Historical & Genealogical Magazine* 20 (1919-1920): 117.

13. "Sally Cary Fairfax Diary," *Virginia Magazine of History and Biography* 11 (1903-1904), 212-14.

14. William Kelby, compiler, *Centennial Notes New York City One Hundred years Ago From the Newspapers of the Day* (Philadelphia: Altemus & Co., 1874) 5, at The New-York Historical Society, hereafter NHi.

15. Michael P. Kinch, "The Meteoric Career of William Young Jr. (1742-1785) Pennsylvania Botanist to the Queen," *The Pennsylvania Magazine of History and Biography* 110 (July 1986): 386.

16. Petition of 21 May 1774 as quoted in Kerby A. Miller et al., eds., *Irish Immigrants in the Land of Canaan: Letters and Memoirs from Colonial and Revolutionary America, 1675-1815* (New York: Oxford University Press, 2003), 257.

17. National Archives; as quoted in John C. Dann, ed., *The Revolution Remembered: Eyewitness Accounts of the War for Independence* (Chicago: University Press, 1980), 242, 243, 245. See also www.footnotes.com.

18. Mercy Otis Warren, *History of the Rise, Progress and Termination of the American Revolution* (Boston: Printed by Manning & Long for E. Larkin, no. 27, Cornhill, 1805), 1: 130.

19. Rev. Joseph B. Code, *Letters of Mother Seton to Mrs. Julianna Scott* (New York: The Father Salvator M. Burgio Memorial Foundation in Honor of Mother Seton, 1960), 294; Letter, Elizabeth Murray Inman to John Murray, 10 September, 1783, James Murray Robbins Family Papers, Massachusetts Historical Society, hereafter MHi.

For excellent discussions on how, or whether, the lives of women changed, see Elaine Forman Crane, *Ebb Tide in New England: Women, Seaports, and Social Change 1630-1800.* (Boston: Northeastern University Press, 1998); Mary Beth Norton, *Liberty's Daughters: The Revolutionary Experience of American Women, 1750-1800.* (New York: HarperCollins, 1980); Rosemary Zagarri, *Revolutionary Backlash: Women and Politics in the Early American Republic* (Philadelphia: University of Pennsylvania Press, 2007).

advancing toward a State of Independancy

1. Samuel E. Morison, *History of the American People* (New York: Oxford University Press, 1965); Frank W. Brecher, *Losing a Continent: France's North American Policy, 1753-1763* (Westport, Connecticut: Greenwood Press, 1998); Fred Anderson, *The War That Made America: A Short History of the French and Indian War* (New York: Viking, 2005).

2. *The Papers of Benjamin Franklin*, Leonard W. Labaree, et al., eds., (New Haven and London: Yale University Press, 1968), vol. 12: 43-46, 270-74, 301-04; hereafter *Franklin Papers*; see also www.BenjaminFranklinHouse.org.

3. "Patriotic Poesy," *William & Mary Quarterly*, Third Series, 34, no. 2, 1977 (April): 307-08; Catherine Le Courrege Blecki and Karin E. Wulf, eds., *Milcah Martha Moore's Book—A Commonplace Book from Revolutionary America* (University Park: Pennsylvania State University Press, 1977), 172-73.

4. Moore Family Papers, Columbiana Ms. 2, Rare Book & Manuscript Library, Columbia University, New York, hereafter NNC. At the end of the letter 31 March 1769, Charity drew a doodle of a face.

5. *Letters of a Loyalist Lady Being the Letters of Anne Hulton, sister of Henry Hulton, Commissioner of Customs in Boston, 1767-1776* (Cambridge: Harvard University Press, 1927), 11-13, 22-24, 33-38; see also Wallace Brown, "An Englishman Views the American Revolution—The Letters of Henry

Hulton, 1769-1776," *Huntington Library Quarterly* 36, no. 1 (Nov. 1972): 1-26; 36, no. 2 (Feb. 1973): 139-51.

6. Papers of Mrs. Christian Barnes, DM16, 157, Library of Congress, DLC.

7. GLC1797.01A (25 April 1769), GLC1797.02 (8 Dec. 1769), GLC 1797.03 (24 March 1770). Letters, Sarah Prince Gill "Sophronia" to Catharine Sawbridge Macaulay, NNGL.

8. Phillis Wheatley, *Poems on various subjects, religious and moral* (London: Printed for A. Bell, 1773), 73-75.

9. Alice Morse Earle, ed., *Diary of Anna Green Winslow A Boston School Girl of 1771* (Boston: Houghton Mifflin, 1894), 5-7, 9, 13, 15-17, 20- 22, 31-34, 36-37, 40, 65.

10. Mercy Otis Warren, *History*, 1: 130.

11. *Condict*, 36-37.

12. Blecki and Wulf, *Milcah Martha Moore's Book*, 247, 250.

13. Library of Congress print; www.edenton.com/history/miscfact.htm. (7/18/2006).

14. Moore Family Papers, NNC.

15. Mercy O. Warren to Abigail Adams, 9 August 1774, Adams Papers, 1639-1899, microfilm edition, reel 344, MHi. See also *Founding Families: Digital Editions of the Papers of the Winthrops and the Adamses*, ed. C. James Taylor. Boston: Massachusets Historical Society, 2007, at www.masshist.org/ff/ and L. H. Butterfield, et al., eds., *Adams Family Correspondence* (Cambridge: The Belknap Press of Harvard University Press, 1963-).

16. Carl van Doren, ed., *The Letters of Benjamin Franklin and Jane Mecom* (Published for The American Philosophical Society by Princeton University Press, 1950), 149-51.

17. 1774 edition at Honnold/Mudd Library, Claremont, California. See also Norman Philbrick, ed., *Trumpets Sounding: Propaganda Plays of the American Revolution* (New York: Benjamin Blom, 1972), 35-38. If "Mary V. V." was a man, the play reflects the attitude of many American women at this time.

18. *Condict*, 51-52.

19. Hannah Fayerweather Winthrop to Mercy Otis Warren, April 1775, N-28 1752-1789, Correspondence with Mercy O. Warren, MHi. Winthrop cites John Milton's *Paradise Lost*, 11, lines 268-70.

20. *American Monthly Magazine*, 1894 (Jan.), 4: 45-49.

21. *Letters of Anne Hulton*, 77-79.

22. van Doren, 153-54.

23. Collections of the Clements Library, Michigan, Gold Star Collection: www.si.umich.edu/spies/people. (1/19/2008).

24. William D. McCrackan, ed., *The Huntington Letters in the Possession of Julia Chester Wells* (New York: Appleton-Century-Crofts, 1897), 174; www.berlinvt.org/DEWEY-WRIGHT. (1/19/2008) Glastonbury, Connecticut website.

25. Abigail Adams to John Adams, 18-20 June 1775, 25 June 1775, 5 July 1775, AFP; see also Butterfield.

26. Hannah F. Winthrop to Mercy O. Warren, June 1775, Correspondence with Mercy O. Warren, MHi.

27. Nina M. Tiffany, ed., *Letters of James Murray Loyalist* (1901. Reprint. Boston: Gregg Press, 1972), 184-85, 215-18; see also Carol R. Berkin and Mary Beth Norton, *Women of America: A History* (Boston: Houghton Mifflin, 1979),48-67; Patricia Cleary, *Elizabeth Murray* (Amherst: University of Massachusetts Press, 2000).

28. *Abigail and Elizabeth Foote Diaries,1775*, Ms. 54425, Connecticut Historical Society, Hartford, Connecticut, hereafter CtHi.

29. Pierpont Morgan Library, Dept. of Literary and Historical Manuscripts, MA 0999. See also Joseph E. Fields, comp., *"Worthy Partner": The Papers of Martha Washington* (Westport, Connecticut: Greenwood Press, 1994), 164.

30. Ann Hollingsworth Wharton, *Women of Colonial and Revolutionary Times: Martha Washington*, New York (C. Scribner's Sons, 1897), 102-04, which states that the letter is in possession of the "Washington Association of N.J. in the old headquarters at Morristown. . . . the address to Mrs. Bassett of Eltham is in General Washington's familiar handwriting." See also *The Historical Magazine and Notes and Queries Concerning the Antiquities, History and Biography of America,* 1858 (May), 2, no. 5, 134-35, submission from Charles Campbell, whose papers are held by the Special Collections Research Center at the College of William and Mary. There are minor variations of spelling and punctuation in these two versions. Fields, *"Worthy Partner,"* 166-67, follows Wharton and states incorrectly that the letter is at the Washington Headquarters Library, Morristown, New Jersey.

31. Abigail Adams to John Adams, 17-18 March 1776, AFP.

32. Abigail Adams to John Adams, 31 July 1777, AFP.

33. "A New Touch on the Times" Broadside, Mass., 1779, NHi.

34. Abigail Adams to John Adams, 27 November 1775, 7-9 May 1776, 31 March 1776, 27 May 1776, AFP. Abigail Adams to Mercy O. Warren, 27 April, 1776, Warren-Adams Papers P-164, MHi. Adams quotes Alexander Pope's *Epistle: To a Lady/Of the Characters of Women*, lines 263-64. For Abigail Adams's use of literature for her own purposes, see Elaine Forman Crane, "Political Dialogue and the Spring of Abigail's Discontent," *William & Mary Quarterly*, Third Series, 56, no. 4 (Oct. 1999): 745-74, and "Abigail Adams, Gender Politics, and *The History of Emily Montague*: A Postscript," *William & Mary Quarterly*, Third Series, 64, no. 4 (Oct. 2007): 839, in which Prof. Crane cites Frances Brooke's 1769 novel as a source for Abigail Adams's thoughts. The unhappy Nancy Shippen Livingston quotes the same passage in her journal (15 May 1783). But see also the writings of Françoise Aubigné, Madame de Maintenon, particularly *On the Drawbacks of Marriage*.

35. Frank C. Mevers, ed., *The Papers of Josiah Bartlett* (Hanover: Published for the New Hampshire Historical Society by the University Press of New England,1979), 80, 93, 97, 117-18.

Things indeed look dark

1. Kelby, comp., Scrapbook, NHi.

2. Richard Maass Collection of Westchester and New York State 1645-1910; Mss 055-001-a-0096, Fales Library and Special Collections, New York

University, New York City, http://maass.nyu.edu. (7/18/2007). See also letter from Rev. Charles Inglis to Col. Thomas Ellison, 28 Sept. 1775, at Knox's Headquarters State Historic Site, with thanks to site manager Nina Pierro.

3. Silliman Family Papers, CtY.

4. Silliman Family Papers, Correspondence, No. 450, Series No. 1, CtY.

5. Herbert T. Wade and Robert A. Lively, *this Glorious Cause . . . The Adventures of Two Company Officers in Washington's Army* (Princeton: Princeton University Press, 1958), 189-90, 203-04, 224-25.

6. "A Claim for Damages in 1776," *The Westchester County Historical Bulletin*, 28, no. 1 (Jan. 1952): 11-15.

7. Lewis Morris Jr. to his father, 6 Sept. 1776, www.colonialhall. com/morris/morrisMary.php. (2/04/2004).

8. Otto Hufeland, *Westchester County During the American Revolution* (White Plains, New York: Westchester County Historical Society, 1926), 161-63; Westchester County Archives/Westchester Historical Society, *McDonald Papers*, 308, 660, 1055; the burning of Adams's house and barns may also have been due to local animosities.

9. *Prudence Punderson Diary: Punderson Family Papers, 1751-1889*. CtHi.

10. Thomas Jefferson Wertenbaker, *Father Knickerbocker Rebels: New York City During the Revolution* (New York: Charles Scribner's Sons, 1948), 104.

11. Henry Steele Commager and Richard B. Morris eds., *The Spirit of 'Seventy-Six'* (New York: Harper & Row, 1958), 496.

12. GLC 02437.00638, Letter, Lucy Knox to Henry Knox, 23 August 1777, NNGL.

13. John Jay Letter Book II, 51, hereafter Jay Papers, NNC.

14. Jay Papers, NNC, www.columbia.edu/cu/lweb/digital/jay #10424; National Archives. Captain Conyngham, under the direction of Benjamin Franklin and Silas Deane, had led raids (1777-1779) on British shipping in the North Sea and the Atlantic Ocean. Nicknamed "The Dunkirk Pirate," he was captured in the spring of 1779 and sent to New York City. Congress, on July 17, 1779, wrote Sir George Collier, the commanding officer of the British fleet in New York, requesting Conyngham's release from "ignominious confinement" or similar treatment would be given British prisoners. Conyngham was sent to Plymouth, England; in November 1779, he escaped with fifty "unfortunate countrymen" and made his way to Holland; on the return voyage to America, his ship was captured by the British. Conyngham was eventually exchanged in 1781, his wife having traveled to L'Orient in the hopes of joining him. See Robert Wilden Neeser, *Letters & Papers Relating to the Cruises of Gustavus Conynghm, A Captain in the Continental Navy*, 1779-1779 (Printed for the Naval Historical Society by the DeVinne Press, 1915) www.books.Google.com (4/28/2008).

15. Silliman Family Papers, No. 450, Series I, Box 2, Folder 16, CtY. After hearing that Mary had invited the Judge to breakfast, Mrs. Jones wrote her a polite note: "P.S. . . . Mrs. Jones sent me a Billet as follows. 'Mrs Jones Compliments to Mrs. Silliman and as she understands that she has been very civil to Mr. Jones She begs she would accept as a Token of her gratitude a Pound of

green Tea.' A very genteel present indeed, and very acceptable at this time. I wish my dear Mother had some of it."

16. Silliman Family Papers, No. 450, Series 2, Box 35, Folder 62: Diaries, Journals, Reminiscences & Manuscripts, 62-75, CtY. Captain David Hawley saw much action during the War. He acquired gunpowder in the West Indies for the Bridgeport-Fairfield, Connecticut, area. Later, he was taken prisoner by the British, but escaped. He also captured four enemy vessels as bounty. With such an adventurous spirit as well as being a friend of the Sillimans, it is perhaps not surprising that he volunteered to participate in the kidnapping of Judge Jones.

every one of them . . . could shoot very well

1. Abigail Adams to John Adams, 25 July 1775, AFP; see also Butterfield.

2. Kenneth Lewis Roberts, comp. and annotator, *March to Quebec: Journals of the Members of Arnold's Expedition,* "John Joseph Henry's Journal" (New York: Doubleday Doran, 1938), 337-38, "Caleb Haskell's Journal," 495.

3. Quoted in Marvin L. Brown, Jr. trans., *Baroness von Riedesel and the American Revolution* (Chapel Hill: Published for the Institute of Early American History and Culture at Williamsburg, Virginia by the University of North Carolina Press, 1965), xxii, from Max von Elking, *The German Allied Troops in the North American War of Independence, 1776-1783,* trans. J. G. Rosengarten (Albany, 1893), 238; quoted in Brown, xxii from Walter Hart Blumenthal, *Women Camp Followers of the American Revolution* (Philadelphia, 1952), 34.

4. Mrs. General Riedesel, *Letters and Journals Relating to the War for the American Revolution and the Capture of the German Troops at Saratoga,* William L. Stone, trans. (Albany: Joel Munsel, 1867), 38-39.

5. Riedesel, *Letters and Journals,* 68-72, 74-76.

6. *Memoirs of Mrs. Elizabeth Fisher, of the City of New York, Daughter of the Rev. Harry Munro, who was a Chaplain in the British Army, during the American Revolution—Giving a particular account of a variety of domestic Misfortunes, and also of her trial, and cruel condemnation to the State's prison for six years, at the instance of her brother, Peter Jay Munro. Written by herself.* (New York: Printed for the Author, ca. 1810).

7. *Their Own Voices: Oral accounts of Early Settlers in Washington County, New York, collected by Dr. Asa Fitch,* Winston Adler, ed., (Interlaken, New York: Heart of the Lakes Publishing, 1983), 44-45.

8. Sharon M. Harris, *Executing Race: Early American Women's Narratives of Race, Society, and the Law* (Columbus: Ohio State University Press, 2005), 90.

9. Margaretta V. Faugères, ed., *The Posthumous Works of Ann Eliza Bleecker* (New York: Printed by T. and J. Swords, 1793), 215-17.

10. Riedesel, *Letters and Journals,* 92-93.

11. Joseph T. Glatthaar and James Kirgy Martin, *Forgotten Allies: the Oneida Indians and the American Revolution* (New York: Hill and Wang, 2006), 180. Quotation in Richard M. Ketchum, *Saratoga* (New York: Henry Holt, 1997), 267-68, from Lt. Colonel George F. G. Stanley, ed., *For Want of a Horse: Being a Journal of the Campaign Against the Americans in 1776 and*

1777 conducted from Canada by an Officer Who Served with Lt. Gen. Burgoyne (Sackville, New Brunswick: Tribune Press, 1961), 119fn, 26.

12. Fitch, *Their Own Voices*, 48-49.

13. Ketchum, *Saratoga*, 274-76.

14. Riedesel, *Letters and Journals*, 115-16, 119-22, 124-33.

15. Fisher, *Memoirs*.

16. Quoted in Catherine S. Crary, *The Price of Loyalty* (New York: McGraw-Hill, 1973), 249-50, from Loyalist Transcripts, *Transcript of the Manuscript Books and Papers of the Commissions of Enquiry into the Losses and Services of the American Loyalists Held under Acts of Parliament of 23, 25, 26, 28, and 29 of George III*, 21, 399-401.

17. Riedesel, *Letters and Journals*, 134, 137-38.

18. Hannah Winthrop to Mercy Otis Warren, 11 November 1777, Correspondence with Mercy O. Warren N-28 1752-1789, MHi.

19. Jay Papers, NNC, www.columbia.edu/cu/lweb/digital/jay #8083.

branded by the names of rebellion and treason

1. Arthur Mekeel, *The Quakers and the American Revolution* (York, UK: Sessions Book Trust, 1996), 89; see also his *The Relation of the Quakers to the American Revolution* (Washington, D.C.: University Press of America, 1979).

2. Charles Wetherell, *History of The Religious Society of Friends Called by Some The Free Quakers, in the City of Philadelphia* (Philadelphia: 1894), www.qhpress.org/quakerpages/qwhp/freequakers04.htm (4/25/2007).

3. Thomas B. Taylor, "The Philadelphia Counterpart of the Boston Tea Party, as shown in the Letters of James & Drinker, Part I," *Bulletin of Friends' Historical Society of Philadelphia* 2, no. 3 (Nov. 1908): 102.

4. Elaine Forman Crane, ed., *The Diary of Elizabeth Drinker* (Boston: Northeastern Press, 1991), vol. 1, 196-97.

5. Charles C. Sellers, *Patience Wright American Artist and Spy in George III's London* (Middletown, Connecticut: Wesleyan University Press, 1976), 81-84, 250-51.

6. *Eliza Farmar Letterbook (1774-1789)*, Pennsylvania Historical Society (PHi) AM.063. See also Lewis D. Cook. "Farmar of Ardevalaine, County Tipperary, Ireland and of Whitemarsh, Philadelphia County, Pennsylvania," *The Pennsylvania Genealogical Magazine* 21, no. 2 (1959): 89-124.

7. William B. Reed, *The Life of Esther De Berdt, afterwards Esther Reed, of Pennsylvania* (Philadelphia: 1853), 206.

8. Joseph Reed Papers (BV Reed, Joseph), Microfilm #1, NHi.

9. William B. Reed, 235-36.

10. Joseph Reed Papers (BV Reed, Joseph), Microfilm #4, NHi; William B. Reed, 246.

11. John W. Jackson, ed., *Margaret Morris: Her Journal* (Philadelphia: George S. MacManus Company, 1949), 39-40, 46-50, 52-55, 58-59, 60-62, 63-64. Sergeant William Young, serving in the 3rd Battalion Pennsylvania Militia, wrote in his journal on 28, 29 December 1776: "got in the Colonel Cox house before dark. As soon as we got our Baggage housed set about foraging for wood,

got some pretty Readily made a good fire. Got supper, went to sleep. Sunday morning got up pretty Early . . . I Expect to set out this morning to join our company; the good woman [Margaret Hill Morris] next Door Sent us 2 Mince pies Last Night, which I took very kind." in *The Pennsylvania Magazine of History and Biography* 8 (1884): 259.

12. Charles Lee (1731-1782), born in Cheshire, England, first came to America during the French and Indian War. Served under Burgoyne in Portugal (1762) and in Poland. In 1773 he moved to Virginia and supported independence. Repeatedly disregarding Washington's command to cross the Hudson River after the battle of White Plains, Lee was captured at Basking Ridge (13 December 1776) and gave General William Howe a plan to defeat the Americans. His treason was not discovered, and he was later exchanged and joined Washington at Valley Forge (1778). At the battle of Monmouth, he ordered a retreat, was court-martialed, and subsequently dismissed from the service.

13. Mary W. Morris to Robert Morris, 20 December 1776, 30 December 1776, HM 9942-9943; Mary W. Morris to E.H. White, 25 March 1777, 1 April 1777, 8 April 1777, 14 April 1777, HM 9924, 9931-32, 9957, reproduced by permission of The Huntington Library, San Marino, California, hereafter CSmH. Microfilm courtesy of Dr. Elizabeth Nuxoll.

14. Edwin Anderson Alderman, Joel Chandler Harris, Charles William Kent, eds., *Library of Southern Literature*, vol. 13 (Atlanta: Martin & Hoyt, 1909-1923).

15. J. Lawrence Boggs, ed., "The Cornelia (Bell) Paterson Letters," *Proceedings of the New Jersey Historical Society*, New Series, 15 (1930): 508-17; 16 (1931): 56-67, 186-201.

16. William H. Guthman, ed., *The Correspondence of Captain Nathan and Lois Peters, April 25, 1775-February 5, 1777* (Connecticut Historical Society, 1980), 50-51.

17. *Proceedings of the New Jersey Historical Society* 51, no. 3 (July 1933): 250-53 (misprinted as 150-53). Joseph Reed was no longer part of the General's "family": he had resigned his post after Washington accidentally discovered that Reed did not fully support his military tactics. See also *Margaret Hill Morris' Journal*, 14 June 1777.

18. GLC05895, Letter, Lucy Flucker Knox to Henry Knox, Boston May 1777; GLC02437.00638, Letter, Boston 23 August 1777, NNGL. Lucy Knox also provided her husband (19 June 1777) with casks of Madeira, port and Lisbon wine; sugar, green tea, chocolate, coffee, pepper, brandy sweet meats, "a very elegant black Silk coat lined with white," breeches, handkerchiefs, and "three pounds of powder, in a bag."

19. Frank Moore, comp., John Anthony Scott, ed., *Diary of the American Revolution* [abridged] (New York: Washington Square Press, 1967), 249, quoting the *Pennsylvania Ledger*, 6 December.

20. As quoted in Esmond Wright, comp., *The Fire of Liberty* (New York: St. Martin's Press, 1983), 116-17.

21. Joseph Plumb Martin, *Private Yankee Doodle*, George E. Scheer, ed. (Eastern National, 2000), 74, 102-03.

22. Jay Papers, NNC, www.columbia.edu/cu/lweb/eresources/archives/jay.

23. Crane, *Elizabeth Drinker* (1991), vol. 1: 226-7, 229, 235, 240-41, 243, 245-46, 265-66, 271, 276, 280-82, 296, 297-300, 302-04. General Washington wrote on 6 April 1778: "Mrs. Jones Mrs. Pleasant and two other Ladies connected with the Quaker's confined at Winchester in Virginia waited upon me this day for permission to pass to York Town [Pennsylvania] to endeavour to obtain the release of their Friends," as quoted in William S. Baker, *Itinerary of General Washington.* (1892; Reprint. Lambertville, New Jersey: Hunterdon House 1970), 124. Sally Logan Fisher's husband Thomas was among those exiled; for her poignant account of her life and delivery of a daughter in his absence, see Nicholas B. Wainwright, "A Diary of Trifling Occurences: Philadelphia, 1776-1777," *The Pennsylvania Magazine of History and Biography* 82 (Oct. 1958): 411-65.

24. Albert C. Myers, ed., *Sally Wister's Journal: A True Narrative, Being a Quaker Maiden's Account of her Experiences with Officers of the Continental Army 1777-1778* (Philadelphia: Ferris & Leach Publishers, 1902), 65, 69-70, 76, 77, 81, 91-92, 94, 95-96, 108-09, 119-20, 138; also www.books.google.com. See also Kathryn Zabelle Derounian, ed., *The Journal and Occasional Writings of Sarah Wister* (Rutherford, New Jersey: Fairleigh Dickinson University Press, 1987).

25. Ethel Armes, comp., *Nancy Shippen, Her Journal Book—The International Romance of a Young Lady of Fashion of Colonial Philadelphia* (Philadelphia: J.B. Lippincott, 1935), 40-41, 60-61.

26. "Letter of Miss Rebecca Franks to Anne Harrison Paca," *The Pennsylvania Magazine of History and Biography* 16 (1892): 216-18. The Loyalist merchant David Franks, the father of Rebecca Franks, is often confused with David Salisbury Franks, the American diplomat, and aide-de-camp to General Benedict Arnold at West Point in 1780, but exonerated from any complicity in the General's treason. He died in the yellow fever epidemic of 1793 in Philadelphia. The Loyalist Franks was named an agent to provide food for British prisoners. Unable to collect payment, he was financially ruined, imprisoned, then exiled with Rebecca to New York by the Americans and moved to England.

27. Thomas Fleming, *Washington's Secret War: The Hidden History of Valley Forge* (New York: HarperCollins, 2005), 263, 213, 214.

28. Noel F. Busch, *Winter Quarters: George Washington and the Continental Army at Valley Forge* (New York: Liveright, 1974), 114.

29. Martin, *Private Yankee Doodle*, 118.

30. Moore, *Diary*, 295, 300-304.

31. Martha Washington to Mercy O. Warren, 7 March 1778, Warren-Adams Papers, 1767-1822, microfilm edition, reel 1, MHi. See also Fields, *"Worthy Partner,"* 177.

32. Armes, *Nancy Shippen*, 63. Also Thomas Fleming. *Washington's Secret War*, 265-70.

33. Myers, *Sally Wister*, 184-85.

34. Crane, *Elizabeth Drinker* (1991), vol. 1: 308, 310-11, 313-14, 318-19, 321, 328-29, 333.

35. Raymond C. Werner, "Diary of Grace Growden Galloway," *The Pennsylvania Magazine of History and Biography* 55, no. 1 (Jan. 1931): 36, 40-41, 51-72; http://dpubs.libraries.psu.edu (03/04/08).

36. Carol Berkin and Leslie Horowitz, *Women's Voices, Women's Lives—Documents in Early American History* (Boston: Northeastern University Press, 1998), 48-53; Mary Beth Norton, *Liberty's Daughters*, 41-51.

37. Werner, "Diary of Grace Growden Galloway," 55, no. 1 (Jan. 1931): 75-76; 58, no. 2 (April 1934): 177; http://dpubs.libraries.psu.edu (03/04/08). For a different outcome, see Wayne Bodle, "Jane Bartram's 'Application': Her Struggle for Survival, Stability, and Self-Determination in Revolutionary Pennsylvania," *The Pennsylvania Magazine of History and Biography* 115, no. 2 (1991): 185-220. Jane Martin Bartram, when her loyalist husband, a shopkeeper and property owner, fled to New York in 1778, petitioned the state for aid (23 May 1782), maintaining that she was being punished "merely from a fault of her Husbands", that she had always been attached to the "Liberties and rights of the United States of America." Over the next decade, Bartram took the initiative and, with the help of friends, lawyers, and even the British consul general, Sir John Temple, petitioned again and again to be allowed to run the family business as well as to receive a share of her estranged husband's compensation.

38. Simon Gratz, "Some Materiel for a Biography of Mrs. Elizabeth Fergusson, née Graeme," *The Pennsylvania Magazine of History and Biography* 39, no. 4 (1915): 398-400; 41, no. 4 (1917): 397.

39. *Franklin Papers* (1988), vol. 27, 602-05.

40. Mary W. Morris to E.H. White, 10 November 1778, HM 13505, CSmH.

41. Mary W. Morris to Catharine Livingston, 10 June 1780, CSmH. In fact, Liberty Hall, the home of the Livingstons, was raided by the British in June 1780; the soldiers were frightened off, according to family legend, by Catharine Livingston's ghostly appearance.

42. "The Sentiments of an American Woman" was published in a Philadelphia newspaper in June 1780. See Hezekiah Niles, *Principles and Acts of the Revolution in America* (Baltimore: William O. Niles, 1822), 389-90.

43. William B. Reed, 318-19, 322-24. Tory Anna Rawle in Philadelphia wrote to her mother Rebecca Shoemaker in New York on 30 June 1780: "But of all the absurdities the Ladies going about for money exceeded everything: they were extremely importunate that people were obliged to give them something to get rid of them. . . . H. Thompson, Mrs. [Mary] Morris, Mrs. Wilson, and a number of very genteel women, paraded about the streets in this manner, some carrying ink stands, nor did they let the meanest ale house escape." Quoted in William B. Rawle, "Laurel Hill and Some Colonial Dames Who Once Lived There," *The Pennsylvania Magazine of History and Biography* 35 (Oct. 1911): 398; http://dpubs.libraries.psu.edu.

The heavy Cloud that hangs over us

1. Evangeline W. Andrews and Charles M. Andrews, eds., *Journal of a Lady of Quality: Being the Narrative of a Journey from Scotland to the West Indies, North Carolina, and Portugal, in the years 1774 to 1776* (New Haven:

Yale University Press, 1922), 20, 148-54, 171, 175-77, 189-91, 210-12.

2. Harriott Horry Ravenel, *Eliza Pinckney* (New York: Charles Scribner's Sons, 1896), 267-68.

3. Elizabeth Gray Vining, *Flora: A Biography* (Philadelphia: Lippincott, 1966), 168, 194.

4. Henry Lee, *Memoirs of the War in the Southern Department of the United States* (1869. Reprint. New York: University Publishing Co., 1969), quoted in Richard Wheeler, *Voices of 1776* (Thomas Crowell Co., 1973), 426-28.

5. "Extracts from the Journal of Mrs. Ann Manigault": 117-18.

6. "Historical Notes. A Woman's Letters in 1779 and 1782," *South Carolina Historical and Genealogical Magazine* 10, no. 2 (April 1919): 125-28.

7. Ravenel, *Eliza Pinckney*, 275-77.

8. Ravenel, *Eliza Pinckney*, 278.

9. Caroline Gilman, ed., *Letters of Eliza Wilkinson* (New York: S. Coleman, 1839. Reprint. New York: Arno Press, Inc., 1969), 9-10, 17, 24-30, 76-77; General Benjamin Lincoln was wounded at the Battle of Saratoga.

10. Catharine W. Livingston to Sarah Livingston Jay, 13 February 1780, Jay Papers, NNC, www.columbia.edu/cu/ lweb/digital/jay #8093.

11. Walter Clark, ed., *The State Records of North Carolina* (Goldsboro: Nash Bros. Book and Job Printers, 1898), vol. 15, 187-88.

12. Gilman, *Letters of Eliza Wilkinson*, 88.

13. Jacob R. Marcus, comp., *The American Jewish Woman—A Documentary History* (New York: Ktav Publishing House, 1981), 30-31; see also www.jewishworldreview.com/jewish/sheftall.asp (7/12/2006).

14. Mary W. Morris to Sarah Livingston Jay, 29 July 1781, HM 13507, CSmH.

15. Ravenel, *Eliza Pinckney*, 301-03; Eliza Pinckney's son-in-law, Daniel Horry, had bought "protection" for his rice plantation "Hampton" from the British, thus, though plundered, it was not burnt to the ground. This would cause him problems at the end of the War.

16. *Total of rebel forces . . . at the surrender of Charles town, May 12, 1780, now prisoners of war*, www.southcarolinahistoricalsociety.org/wire/RevWar/archives-online/Tarleton (5/8/08).

17. Dr. Peter Fayssoux to Dr. David Ramsay, Charleston, 26 March 1785, www.southcarolinahistoricalsociety.org/wire/RevWar/archives-online/Gibbes (6/21/06).

18. William S. Baker, *Itinerary of General Washington for June 15, 1775, to December 23, 1783* (1892. Reprint. Lambertville, New Jersey: Hunterdon House, 1970), 193.

19. Susan Livingston to Sarah Livingston Jay, 18 July 1781, Jay Papers, NNC, www.columbia.edu/cu/lweb/digital/jay #8299; *Monody on Major André*, written by the English author, Anna Seward (Lichfield, England, 1781), who was a friend of the Major, harshly censured his execution: "Oh Washington! I

thought thee great and good,/Nor I knew thy Nero thirst for guiltless blood;/Severe to use the power that fortune gave,/Thou cool determined murderer of the grave./Remorseless Washington! the day shall come/Of deep repentance for this barbarous doom."

20. National Archives; as quoted in Dann, *The Revolution Remembered,* 242-43, 244-45.

21. Baker, *Itinerary of General Washington,* 245; for Cornwallis's letter, see www.southcarolinahistorical society. org.

22. Catharine Livingston to Sarah Jay, 18 October 1781, Jay Papers, NNC, www. columbia.edu/cu/lweb/digital/ jay #8102.

23. "Loyalist's Account of Certain Occurrences in Philadelphia after Cornwallis's Surrender at Yorktown," *The Pennsylvania Magazine of History and Biography* 16 (1892): 104-05.

24. William Moultrie, *Memoirs of the American Revolution, So Far As It Related To The States of North and South Carolina and Georgia* (New York: Printed by David Longworth for the Author, 1802), vol. 2, 336.

25. Allan L. Damon, "A Melancholy Case," www.americanheritage.com/ articles/magazine/ah/1970/2/1970_2_18.shtml (11/19/2007).

26. Letter, Sarah Burd Yeates to Jasper Yeates, Lancaster (Pennsylvania) County Historical Society, MG-207, Box 1, Folder 25, #7.

27. Hezekiah Niles, ed., *Principles and Acts of the Revolution,* 318.

28. For a full discussion of the peace negotiations, see Walter Stahr, *John Jay Founding Father* (New York: Hambledon and London, 2005), 145-74; also Frank W. Brecher, *Securing American Independence: John Jay and the French Alliance* (Westport, Connecticut: Praeger, 2003), 169-218.

29. Edgar J. McManus, *A History of Negro Slavery in New York* (Syracuse: Syracuse University Press, 2001), 155-57; Sidney Kaplan, *The Black Presence in the Era of the American Revolution* (New York: New York Graphic Society Ltd., 1973), 32. Margareta Powell's petition is in the Maryland State Archives and is printed in Sylvia R. Frey and Marian J. Morton, *New World, New Roles: A Documentary History of Women in Pre-Industrial America* (Westport, Connecticut: Greenwood Press, 1986), 138. Johnson was Maryland's first elected governor and was later an associate justice of the United States Supreme Court. Ray Raphael, *A People's History of the American Revolution* (New York: Perennial, 2002), 309-79.

30. www.blackloyalist.com/canadadigitalcollection, Black Loyalist Directory, Book One (May 2008). An excellent website.

This week . . . my Family are all sick

1. Laurel T. Ulrich, *A Midwife's Tale, The Life of Martha Ballard, Based on Her Diary, 1785–1812* (New York: Vintage Books, 1990), 11.

2. Abigail Adams to Mary Smith Cranch, 9 Aug. 1789, 30 May 1790, American Antiquarian Society, hereafter AAS; see also Stewart Mitchell, ed., *New Letters of Abigail Adams 1788-1801* (Boston: Houghton Mifflin, 1947).

3. Reprinted from *The Family Letters of Thomas Jefferson,* edited by Edwin M. Betts and James A. Bear, Jr. by permission of the University of

Missouri Press. Copyrighted © 1966 by the Curators of the University of Missouri, 153.

4. Rebecca J. Tannenbaum, *The Housewife as Healer: Medicine as Women's Work in Colonial New England*, The Dublin Seminar, Boston University, 2001. William Buchan, *Domestic Medicine: or the Family Physician. Being an Attempt to render the Medical Art more generally useful, by shewing people what is in their own power both with respect to the Prevention and Cure of Diseases, Chiefly Calculated to recommend a proper attention to Regimen and Simple Medicines* (Philadelphia: 1772).

5. Sarah Anna Emery, ed., *Reminiscences of a Nonagenarian* (Newburyport, Massachusetts: W.H. Huse, 1879), 24.

6. Haverford College Library, Box 7, Folder 1, www.haverford.edu/library/special.

7. John Jay Smith, ed., *Letters of Dr. Richard Hill*, 414-16.

8. John W. Jackson, ed., *Margaret Morris*, 72-74.

9. John Duffy, *Epidemics in Colonial America* (Baton Rouge: Louisiana State University Press, 1953), 229.

10. Elizabeth A. Fenn, *Pox Americana* (New York: Hill and Wang, 2001), 102.

11. Quoted in Linda K. Kerber, *Women of the Republic: Intellect and Ideology in Revolutionary America* (Chapel Hill: University of North Carolina Press, 1980), 59.

12. A. Redman, *Maryland Historical Magazine* 17 (1922): 379; Maryland State Archives, www.msa.md.gov, has records indicating that Redman was reimbursed 28 March 1781.

13. Duffy, *Epidemics*, 7, 9. In caring for sick troops during the Revolutionary War, one doctor's medical chest included: "elixir of camphor, hiero pera (a powder of aloes and carella) used as a tonic and stomachic, powdered rhei (rhubarb) for diarrhea, and jalap, a cathartic that was a remedy of the Indians in Mexico. He also had a supply of powdered ipecacuanha and tartar emetic, pills of cathartic salts, and Artemisia." Oscar Reiss, *Medicine and the American Revolution* (Jefferson, North Carolina: McFarland, 1998), 96.

14. Emily H.G. Noyes, ed., *A Family History in Letters and Documents 1667-1837* (St. Paul, Minnesota: Privately printed, 1919), 179-80.

15. Joanna Bethune, ed., *The Unpublished Letters and Correspondence of Mrs. Isabella Graham, From the Year 1767 to 1814: Exhibiting Her Religious Character in the Different Relations of Life* (New York: John S. Taylor, 1838), 51.

16. Code, *Letters of Mother Seton,* 32.

17. *Journal of Prudence Punderson*, Punderson Papers, CtH.

18. Duffy, *Epidemics*, 113-14.

19. Mevers, ed., *Papers of Josiah Bartlett*, 59.

20. John Brown Papers, 1761-1835. NHi.

21. Van Doren, ed., *Letters of Benjamin Franklin and Jane Mecom*, 223.

22. Dale Taylor, *The Writer's Guide to Everyday Life in Colonial America: 1607-1783* (Cincinnati: Writer's Digest Books, 1997), 140.

23. Sarah Stone, *A Complete Practice of Midwifery* (London: printed for T. Cooper, 1737), xiv, as quoted in Ulrich, 12.

24. Papers of Mrs. Christian Barnes, DM16, 157, DLC.

25. Abigail Adams to John Adams, 9-10 July, 1777, AFP.

26. Silliman Family Papers, CtY.

27. Code, *Letters of Mother Seton,* 29-30.

28. Crane (1991), *Diary of Elizabeth Drinker*, vol. 2, 1226-29.

29. Linda Grant DePauw and Conover Hunt, *"Remember the Ladies": Women in America 1750-1815* (New York: Viking, 1976), 22.

30. William K. Bottorff and Roy C. Flannagan, eds., "The Diary of Frances Baylor Hill of 'Hillsborough' King and Queen County, Virginia, (1797)," *Early American Literature Newsletter* 2, no. 3, Special Issue (Winter 1967): 42, 43.

31 Jay Papers, NNC; see also Landa M. Freeman, Louise V. North, Janet M. Wedge, *Selected Letters of John Jay and Sarah Livingston Jay.* (Jefferson, North Carolina: McFarland & Company, Inc., 2005), 91.

32. Reiss, *Medicine*, 27; Fenn, *Pox Americana*, 23.

33. Gilman, ed., *Letters of Eliza Wilkinson,* 93.

34. Noyes, *Family History*, 185-86. Marcus Rediker, The Slave Ship: A Human History (New York: Viking, 2007), 343: relates that Capt. James D'Wolf of Newport, Rhode Island, had taken 142 Coromantee captives and delivered 121 alive in Havana, Cuba. In 1791, one of the sailors testified to a federal grand jury that the captain had thrown a middle-aged "Negro Woman," gagged and tied to a chair, overboard; whether she had smallpox was unclear as there was no doctor on board. D'Wolf was indicted for murder but fled Newport and did not return for three years. D'Wolf was later elected to the United States Senate.

35. Reiss, *Medicine*, 48. Robert H. Hinckley, "Selections from the Diary of Christiana Young Leach of Kingsessing, 1765-1796*," The Pennsylvania Magazine of History and Biography* 35, no. 3 (July 1911), 344. wwwdpubs.libraries.psu.edu. See also William Brooke Fetters, *Six Columbiana County, Ohio, Pioneer Families* (©William Brooke Fetters, 1991), 1:43-89, and Supplement (©William Brooke Fetters, 2003).

36. Abigail Adams to Mercy Otis Warren, ca. January 26, 1777, Doc# AFC02d109, and Mercy Otis Warren to Abigail Adams, 1 March 1777, Doc#AFC02d123, *Founding Families: Digital Editions of the Papers of the Winthrops and the Adamses*, ed. C. James Taylor. Boston: Massachusetts Historical Society, 2007; at http://www.masshist.org/ff/; Nancy Rubin Stuart, *The Muse of the Revolution: The Secret Pen of Mercy Otis Warren and the Founding of a Nation* (Boston: Beacon, 2008), 116, 124, 126.

37. GLC02437.00573, GLC02437.00582, Letters, Lucy F. Knox to Henry Knox. 13 April 1777, 31 April 1777, NNGL.

38. Mrs. Gordon B. Ambler, "Diary of M. Ambler, 1770," *Virginia Historical Magazine* 45, no. 2 (April 1937): 152-70.

39. Mevers, ed., *Papers of Josiah Bartlett*, 93.

40. Fenn, *Pox Americana*, 230.

41. Silliman Family Papers, CtY.

42. Duffy, *Epidemics*, 138, 139; J. H. Powell, *Bring Out Your Dead: The Great Plague of Yellow Fever in Philadelphia in 1793* (Philadelphia: University of Pennsylvania, reprint 1993), xvii.

43. Hinckley, "Diary of Christiana Young Leach," *The Pennsylvania Magazine of History and Biography* 35, no. 3 (July 1911), 349. wwwdpubs. libraries. psu.edu. See also Fetters, *Six Columbiana County, Ohio, Pioneer Families*, vol. 1, Appendix B. "Family 1. William Fetters (1794-1851) and Mary B. Leech, Ancestors and Descendants," ©William Brooke Fetters, 1991.

44. Bethune, *Unpublished Letters*, 176-77.

45. Ulrich, *A Midwife's Tale*, 4.

safely arrived at the Haven of Matrimony

1. Elizabeth Smith Shaw to Abigail Adams Smith, 27 Nov. 1786, Shaw Family Papers, DLC. See also L.H. Butterfield, et al., eds., *Adams Family Correspondence* (Cambridge: The Belknap Press of Harvard University Press, 2005) 7: 402-03.

2. David Ramsay, M.D., *Memoirs of The Life of Martha Laurens Ramsay* (Boston: Printed by Samuel T. Armstrong, 1812), 3rd edition, 25; Kenneth Roberts and Anna M. Roberts, trans. and eds., *Moreau de St. Méry's American Journey [1793-1798]*, (Garden City, New York: Doubleday, 1947), 286.

3. See Norton, *Liberty's Daughters*, 40-70; Carol R. Berkin and Mary Beth Norton. *Women of America, A History* (Boston: Houghton Mifflin, 1979).

4. *Dear Papa, Dear Charley, The Peregrinations of a Revolutionary Aristocrat, as told by Charles Carroll of Carrolton and his Father Charles Carroll of Annapolis* (Williamsburg, Virginia: Omohundo Institute of Early American History and Culture, 2001) 1: 175; *Diary of Mary Cooper: Life on a Long Island Farm 1768-1773*, Field Horne, ed. (Oyster Bay, Long Island Historical Society, 1981), 15; Armes, *Nancy Shippen*. Susan Livingston wrote her sister Sarah Jay from Rhinebeck, New York [1 Oct. 1781]: "We have the oddest couple in the world in the neighbourhood, Col. Harry & his wife (Miss Nancy Shippen) they are very ingenious in the art of tormenting, they say Cats love one another, & they fight & scratch, so perhaps they have cats love." Jay Papers, NNC.

5. "Randolph and Tucker Letters," Mrs. George P. Coleman. ed., *The Virginia Magazine of History and Biography* 42, no. 1 (Jan. 1934). Despite Anne Randolph's caution, the marriage took place the following year. In 1792, Richard and his eighteen-year-old sister-in-law Ann "Nancy" Randolph were accused of infanticide. Though Richard was acquitted, slander swirled around the family for years afterwards. He died in 1796. Nancy married Gouverneur Morris of New York in 1809. Judith's and Nancy's brother, Thomas Mann Randolph Jr., was married to Martha "Patsy" Jefferson.

6. J. Hall Pleasants, ed., "Letters of Molly and Hetty Tilghman, Eighteenth Century Gossip of Two Maryland Girls," *Maryland Historical Magazine* 21, no. 1 (March 1926): 20-39; no. 2 (June 1926): 123-49; (Sept. 1926): 219-41.

7. John A. H. Sweeney, ed., "The Norris-Fisher Correspondence: A Circle of Friends, 1779-1782," *Delaware History* VI, no. 3 (March 1955): 208, 203. Neither girl remained single: Deborah Norris married Dr. George Logan, a

cousin of John Dickinson, in 1781; Sally Fisher (1758-1789) married William Corbit in 1784 in Delaware.

8. Holly C. Shulman, ed., *The Dolley Madison Digital Edition* (Charlottesville: University of Virginia Press, 2004), at http://rotunda.upress.virginia.edu/ dmde/DPM0566 (6/25/2006). Elizabeth Brooke married George Ellicott in 1790. See also David B. Mattern and Holly C. Shulman, eds., *The Selected Letters of Dolley Payne Madison* (Charlottesville: University of Virginia Press, 2003).

9. Marcus, *American Jewish Woman*, 56-58.

10. Patricia Brady, ed., *George Washington's Beautiful Nelly: The Letters of Eleanor Parke Custis Lewis to Elizabeth Bordley Gibson, 1794-1851* (Columbia: University of South Carolina Press, 1991, expanded ed., 2006), 25, 38-39, 58-59.

11. Giles Family Papers 1750-1851, Box 1, Folder 2, NHi. A portrait of Aquila Giles by Gilbert Stuart is at the Wadsworth Atheneum Museum of Art, Hartford, Connecticut.

12. Genêt Papers, NHi. The historian Samuel E. Morison called Genêt the "quaintest of many curious diplomats sent by European governments to the United States," *The Oxford History of the American People* (New York: Oxford University Press, 1965), 337.

13. Marcus, *American Jewish Woman*, 48.

14. Caroline G. C. Curtis, ed., *The Cary Letters Edited at the Request of the Family* (Cambridge: Riverside Press, 1891), 89-90. Harriet Horsford did marry George Rose. See also for the Governor Bellingham Cary House in Chelsea, Massachusetts, www.olgp.net/ohs/d1/caryhouse/htm (8/31/2008).

15. Shulman. http://rotunda.upress.virginia.edu/dmde/DPM0012, DPM0015 (6/25/06); also Mattern and Shulman, eds., 27-28, 31. Quaker Ann Head Warder of Philadelphia commented on Dolley Payne's remarriage: "Her conduct has certainly been very indecent. If she had no sincere regard for her husband, the attachment he ever demonstrated for her, demanded at least the shew of more respect to his memory"; June 1794, The Historical Society of Pennsylvania, Collection 2175. See Catherine Allgor, *A Perfect Union Dolley Madison and the Creation of the American Nation* (New York: Henry Holt and Company, 2006), 27-31.

16. Quoted in J. Brett Langstaff, *Dr. Bard of Hyde Park* (New York: E. P. Dutton, 1942), 135.

17. George F. Dow, ed., *The Holyoke Diaries 1709-1865* (Salem, Massachusetts: The Essex Institute, 1911), xvii, 137, 175-76. See also J. P. Brissot de Warville, *New Travels in the United States of America 1788*, Mara S. Vamos, trans., Durand Echeverria, ed. (Cambridge: The Belknap Press of Harvard University Press, 1964), 290.

18. Catherine Kerrison, "By the Book Eliza Ambler Brent Carrington and Conduct Literature in Late Eighteenth-Century Virginia," *Virginia Magazine of History and Biography* 105, no. 1 (Winter 1997): 27-52. Lewis Warrington (1782-1851) received a Congressional medal of honor in 1814.

19. Abigail Adams to Mary Cranch, 20 Jan. 1787, AAS.

20. Shulman. http://rotunda.upress.virginia.edu/ dmde/DPM0024 (6/25/06).

21. James Iredell Letters, PC67.1-1779, North Carolina Department of Archives and History at Raleigh.

22. Barbara E Lacey, ed., *The World of Hannah Heaton: The Diary of an Eighteenth-Century New England Farm Woman* (DeKalb: N. Illinois University Press, 2003), 181-83. See also Barbara E. Lacey, "The World of Hannah Heaton: The Autobiography of an Eighteenth-Century Connecticut Farm Woman," *William & Mary Quarterly* 45 (April 1988).

23. Abigail A Bailey, *Memoirs of Mrs. Abigail Bailey who had been the wife of Major Asa Bailey formerly of Landaff, Written by herself . . . ed. by Ethan Smith, A.M. minister of the Gospel in Hopkinton, N.H.* (Boston: Published by Samuel T. Armstrong, 1815), 11-14, 31-32, 41, 113, 195.

24. Fisher; *Memoirs.* New York State Archives at Albany: *State Prison Register of Prisoners Received*, AO 775:VI32/4, 56, 55 (for John N. Smith). In 1801, twenty-three white women and thirteen black women were incarcerated at Newgate Prison in New York City; Criminal Case Document 1797-1801 (J2011-82; A52/6); Executive Pardons 1799-1931, B0042-78, signed by Morgan Lewis 23 May, 1806; John Chambers Papers, Box 2, P 9885 #93-198; John Williams Papers, HY 12382 in Legal Papers SC12382. See also Munro Papers at the Museum of the City of New York Archives as well as the Jay Papers, NNC; also *Longworth's American Almanac New-York Register and City Directories 1806-1813*. It is possible that Fisher's daughter Eliza lived near her mother after her release.

25. James E. Seaver, *Life of Mary Jemison De-he-wä-mis* (New York: Miller, Orton & Mulligan, 1856), 4th ed., 150; Susannah French Livingston to William Livingston, 18 Nov. 1786, *William Livingston Family Papers II, 1698-1822*, microfilm edition, reel 9, MHi; Robert Morris to Mary W. Morris, 15 November 1787, CSmH; Matthew L. Davis, *Memoirs of Aaron Burr* (New York: Harper & Brothers, 1836. Reprint. New York: Da Capo Press, 1971), 279.

26. "Journal of Elizabeth Foote Washington, 1779-1796," *Washington Family Papers*, DLC, Ms. Division LC-MS-56408-3, www.lcweb2 loc.gov.

27 GLC02437.00575, Letter, Lucy Flucker Knox to Henry Knox, 16 April 1777, NNGL.

28. Rev. Samuel S. Smith, *A Funeral Sermon, on the Death of the Hon. Richard Stockton, Esq, Princeton, March 2, 1781* (Trenton: Printed by Isaac Collins, 1781), 47-48. See also Carla Mulford, ed., *Only for the Eye of a Friend: The Poems of Annis Boudinot Stockton* (Charlottesville: University Press of Virginia, 1995), 50 (note 75), 100-101.

29. Letter, Janet L. Montgomery to Martha Washington, March 10, 1800, R-10, MS-272, Martha Washington Collection, Mount Vernon Ladies' Association, George Washington's Mount Vernon Estate & Gardens, Mount Vernon, Virginia, hereafter ViMtV; Martha Washington to Janet L. Montgomery, 5 April 1800, Courtesy of the Trustees of the Boston Public Library/Rare Books.

in her own sphere

1. Jacob Judd, comp., *Correspondence of the Van Cortlandt Family of Cortlandt Manor 1748-1800* (Tarrytown, New York: Sleepy Hollow Restora-

tions, 1977), 513, Letter #289 (in the Archival Collection, Historic Hudson Valley, Tarrytown, New York); Ruth Belknap's verse of 1782 as quoted in Carol Berkin and Leslie Horowitz, eds., *Women's Voices, Women's Lives: Documents in Early American History* (Boston: Northeastern University Press, 1998), 112.

2. Re raising money, see Martha Jefferson's letter to Elizabeth Gates, 8 Aug. 1780 in Gates Papers (Reel 11:193), NHi; re slaves, see Jack McLaughlin, *Jefferson and Monticello: The Biography of a Building* (New York: Henry Holt & Co, 1988); also Annette Gordon-Reed, *Thomas Jefferson and Sally Hemings: An American Controversy* (Charlottesville: University Press of Virginia, 1999), 245-49; also *The Hemingses of Monticello: An American Family* (New York: W.W. Norton & Co., 2008).

3. Page from Martha Jefferson's Account Book is in the Library of Congress, reproduced in McLaughlin, 189.

4. *Zerviah Sanger Chapman Diary*, 1775, Miscellaneous Manuscript Collection, MSS 9001-C, Rhode Island Historical Society, hereafter RIHi. The 'B' is a dominical letter used to denote the Sundays in a particular year (OED).

5. *The Diary of Mary Cooper*, 16-18, 30, 33, 46-47.

6. Beekman Family Papers: William Beekman and Cornelia Beekman Walton, box 22, folder 5, NHi.

7. Seaver, 60, 62-63, 69-70, 72-74, 124-25. See also *A Narrative of the Life of Mrs. Mary Jemison*, Introduction by June Namias (Norman: Oklahoma University Press, 1992). Mary Lewis Kinnan (1763-1848), in her account of her captivity with the Delaware Indians, was much more critical of their women. "Here the female sex, instead of polishing and improving the rough manners of the men, are equally ferocious, cruel, and obdurate." *A True Narrative of the Sufferings of Mary Kinnan* (Elizabethtown, New Jersey: Kollock, 1795).

8. Nancy Woloch, *Early American Women: A Documentary History, 1600-1900* (Belmont, California: Wadsworth Publishing Co., 1992), 79.

9. Frederick Tupper and Helen Tyler Brown, *Grandmother Tyler's Book: The Recollections of Mary Palmer Tyler, 1775-1868* (New York: G. P. Putnam's Sons, 1925), 112-15.

10. Miller et al. eds., *Irish Immigrants*, 257.

11. Crane, *The Diary of Elizabeth Drinker* (1994), 131, 132, 138, 139, 140, 141, 145, 148, 151-52, 162-63, 255.

12. Mary White Morris to Catharine W. Livingston, Matthew Ridley Papers II (1783-1784), box 2, ms. N-797, MHi.

13. Russell G. Handsman, "Indentured Servitude in Indian New England," *RACE Matters in Indian New England,* Mashantucket Pequot Museum and Research Center (2008). Dr. Henry Channing preached a sermon on the execution. See also Frances Manwaring Caulkins, *History of New London, Connecticut* (New London: H.D. Utley, 1895), 576.

14. Carl Bridenbaugh, "Patrick M'Roberts Tour through Parts of the North Provinces of America," *The Pennsylvania Magazine of History & Biography* 59 (1935): 142. Thomas L. Purvis. *Revolutionary America 1763 to 1800* (New York: Facts on File, Inc. 1995) states that between 1763 and 1775, African laborers made up twelve percent of New York's population (page 122) and that,

when the Revolutionary War began, approximately twenty percent of American workers were slaves and two or three percent indentured servants (page 120).

15. Arthur Zilversmit, *The First Emancipation of the Abolition of Slavery in the North* (Chicago: University of Chicago Press, 1967), 4-5.

16. Papers of Mrs. Christian Barnes, DLC, DM16, 157. Correspondence with the Boston Museum of Fine Arts failed to discover any possible work by Prince. For a fascinating study of portraiture at this time, see Margaretta M. Lovell, *Art in a Season of Revolution: Painters, Artisans, and Patrons in Early America* (Philadelphia: University of Pennsylvania Press, 2005).

17. Graham R. Hodges and Alan E. Brown, eds., *"Pretends to be Free" Runaway Slave Advertisements from Colonial and Revolutionary New York and New Jersey* (New York: Garland Publishing, Inc., 1994), Table 1: "Gender of Fugitive Slaves, 1776-1783." See also Cassandra Pybus, "Jefferson's Faulty Math: the Question of Slave Defections in the American Revolution," *William & Mary Quarterly*, Third Series, 62, no. 2 (April 2005), 243-64.

18. Advertisement of 17 October 1785 in *Virginia Gazette or American Advertiser*, Richmond, Virginia: www.vcdh.virginia.edu/saxon/servlet (2/8/08). The Stratford (Connecticut) Historical Society owns a unique profile portrait of a slave named Flora, which accompanied her bill of sale as identification; her owner, Margaret Dwight of Milford, Connecticut, sold her for £25 in 1796.

19. www.colonialwilliamsburg.com/Almanack/people/bios/bioeve.cfm (1/17/2008)

20. Judd, *Van Cortlandt Family*, 185-86.

21. John Brown Papers (1761-1835), NHi.

22. Stephen Decatur, Jr., *Private Affairs of George Washington From the Records and Accounts of Tobias Lear, His Secretary* (Boston: Houghton Mifflin Co., 1933), 147, 160, 201, 268. Hercules also ran away after Oney Judge did, but was never found. His supposed portrait, attributed to Gilbert Stuart, is at the Museo Thyssen-Bornemisza in Madrid.

23. Interview with the Rev. Benjamin Chase in a "Letter to the Editor," *The Liberator*, January 1, 1847, as quoted in John W. Blassingame, ed., *Slave Testimony: Two Centuries of Letters, Speeches, Interviews, and Autobiographies* (Baton Rouge: Louisiana State University Press, 1977), 248-49. For different tactics to gain freedom employed by five slaves belonging to James and Margaret Caldwell McHenry of Baltimore in 1796, see Karen Robbins, "Power among the Powerless: Domestic Resistance by Free and Slave Women in the McHenry Family in the New Republic," *Journal of the Early Republic* 23, no. 1 (Spring 2003): 47-68.

24. www.ushistory.org/presidentshouse/slaves/oney.htm (3/12/2007); see also www.seacoastnh.com/blackhistory/ona.html (12/11/2006).

25. Theodore Sedgwick Jr., Address given in 1831, in William C. Nell, *The Colored Patriots of the American Revolution* (Boston: Robert F. Wallcut, 1855. Reprint. New York: Arno Press, 1968), 54-55.

26. Catharine Maria Sedgwick, *Life and Letters of Catharine M. Sedgwick*, Mary E. Dewey, ed. (New York: Harper & Brothers, 1871), 41-43.

27. See also Sidney Kaplan, *The Black Presence in the Era of the American Revolution, 1770-1800* (Washington, D.C.: Smithsonian Institution, National Portrait Gallery, 1973), 216-17; color plate 7, portrait of Elizabeth Freeman (1811), watercolor on ivory by Susan L. Ridley Sedgwick, wife of Theodore Jr., and daughter of Catharine Livingston Ridley, Massachusetts Historical Society. For text of tombstone, photograph in possession of authors. See also www.mumbet.com. John Ashley's house in Sheffield, Massachusetts is now a museum. David L. Lewis in *W.E.B. Du Bois: Biography of a Race 1868-1919* (New York: Henry Holt and Co., 1991, p. 14) states that Freeman married the much younger Jack Burghardt, Du Bois's great-grandfather, in 1790; this is echoed by Douglas R. Egerton in *Death or Liberty: African Americans and Revolutionary America* (Oxford University Press, 2009, p. 170). Barbara Allen, curator, Stockbridge (Massachusetts) Library Historical Collection, stated this was "misinformation" (email 5/22/09). Moreover, there is no mention of the Burghardt family in the Sedgwick recollections of Freeman nor is that connection mentioned in her will.

28. Gary B. Mills, "Coincoin: An Eighteenth-Century 'Liberated' Woman," *The Journal of Southern History* 42, no. 2 (May 1976): 205-22.

29. *Journal of Elizabeth Foote*, CtHi.

30. Van Doren, ed., *Letters of Benjamin Franklin and Jane Mecom*, 305-06.

31. *Diary of Elizabeth Porter Phelps*, Porter-Phelps-Huntington Family Papers, on deposit at Amherst College Archives and Special Collections, Amherst, Massachusetts. See also Thomas E. Andrews, ed., "The Diary of Elizabeth Porter Phelps," *The New England Historical and Genealogical Register* 119, no. 474 (April 1965): 128, 129. The Porter-Phelps-Huntington House in Hadley, Massachusetts, is now a museum.

32. "Extracts from the Journal of Miss Sarah Eve," *The Pennsylvania Magazine of History and Biography* 5, no. 1 (1881): 26, 27; for wearing apparel of the eighteenth century, see www.thestaymaker.co.uk/gallery-dressing.php (6/23/08).

33. "The Bartons in Lancaster in 1776," Papers of the Lancaster County Historical Society, 1, 2, no. 8 (1948): 215, reproduced in Stuart E. Brown, Jr., *Reverend Thomas Barton (1728-1780) and Some of His Descendants and Some of Their In-Laws* (Berryville: Virginia Book Co., 1988), 199-201. The choral tradition continues to this day in Lancaster. For the Bards, see J. Brett Langstaff, *Dr. Bard of Hyde Park: The Famous Physician of Revolutionary Times, the Man Who Saved Washington's Life* (New York: E. P. Dutton, 1942).

34. Harriet Wadsworth letter: Wadsworth-Terry Family Papers, 1753-1866, CtHi; the balloon hat was a wide-brimmed straw hat with a puffed crown made of fabric; the Lavinia bonnet was a variety of wide-brimmed straw hat with a scarf over the top that tied under the chin; see also Janet Wedge, "Detach'd From Earth," *The Westchester Historian* 81, no. 1 (Summer 2005): 78-85.

35. Mary W. Morris to Catharine W. Livingston, 3 April 1781, Matthew Ridley Papers II, MHi. Perhaps this same musician was still performing in Philadelphia on 9 Dec. 1783, when the young Dutch nobleman Carel de Vos van

Steenwijk attended "a concert, at which were many ladies, although the music wasn't very good. There seems to be little taste for music here. There was a German flutist named Brown who was the best. The harpsichord was passable but the violin very bad, the other instruments in proportion." from *Een Grand Tour naar de Nieuwe Republiek: Journaal van een reis door Amerika, 1783-1784*, Wayne te Brake, Jeroen Blaak, and Katherine M. Grant, eds. (Hilversum, the Netherlands: Uitgeverij Verloren, 1999), 95, (excerpt translated by Louise V. North).

36. "Randolph and Tucker Letters," (Jan. 1935): 41-46. Martha Bland refers to Anne-César, Chevalier de la Luzerne, French minister to the U.S.; François Barbé-Marbois, French chargé d'affaires in the U.S.; Louis-Guillaume Otto, also with the French delegation (who was courting Nancy Shippen), and Don Francisco Rendón, Spanish agent.

37. "Letter of Mrs. Willett to General Kosciusko," *The Pennsylvania Magazine of History and Biography* 23 (1899): 122.

38. "Letters of Hannah Thomson, 1785-1788," *The Pennsylvania Magazine of History and Biography* 14, no. 1 (1890): 35-37; note that the publication has misdated some of the letters, i.e., the letter of 12 Dec. 1786 is printed as being from 17 Sept. 1786. There would not have been piles of snow at that time of year. Similarly, the letter of 28 Dec. 1786 is dated 12 Dec. 1786, but it was clearly written after Christmas Day. For an article on Hannah Harrison Thomson, see "Curator's Report," *Bulletin of the Harriton Association* (Spring 2003), 500 Harriton Rd., Bryn Mawr, Pennsylvania. Hannah Thomson's Household Memorandum Book 1792-1793 is at the Historical Society of Pennsylvania.

39. The *Invitations to Supper & Dinner 1787 & 1788* is at the John Jay Homestead State Historic Site, Katonah, New York. See also Louise V. North, "Sarah Jay's Invitations to Dinner/Supper, 1787-1788," *The Hudson River Valley Review* 21, no. 2 (Spring 2005): 68-79. This dinner party was to welcome the new French minister, the Marquis Eléonore-François-Elie de Moustier, accompanied by his sister-in-law (and mistress), Anne Flore Millet, Marquise de Bréhan. Other guests were Louis-Guillaume Otto; J. Hector St. Jean de Crèvecoeur and his daughter, América-Francès; the British consul Sir John Temple and his wife, Elizabeth Bowdoin; the Dutch minister Pieter van Berckel and his daughter, Jacoba; the Spanish minister Don Diego de Gardoqui; the President of Congress Cyrus Griffin, and Jeremiah Wadsworth, member of Congress.

40. *A Colonial Plantation Cookbook: The Receipt Book of Harriott Pinckney Horry, 1770*, Richard J. Hooker, ed. (Columbia: University of South Carolina Press, 1984), 6, 52, 96.

41. Freeman, North, Wedge, *Selected Letters*, 247, 291-93.

42. Osborn Papers, AAS; as quoted in Woloch, *Early American Women*, 156, 157, 158; Mary Beth Norton, "My Resting Reaping Times: Sarah Osborn's Defense of her 'Unfeminine' Activities, 1767," *Signs: Journal of Women and Culture in Society* 2, no. 2 (1976), 515-529.

43. Emery, *Reminiscences*, 20-21.

44. C. M. Sedgwick, *Life*, 43-45.

45. Letter, American Historical Manuscript Collection–Akerly, Margaretta, NHi; see also William C. Reichel and William H. Bigler, *A History of the Rise, Progress and Present Condition of the Moravian Seminary for Young Ladies at Bethlehem, Pa. with a catalogue of its pupils 1785-1858*, 2nd edition (Philadelphia: J.B. Lippincott, 1870), 333, 338; Catherine Akerly had attended the school in 1791.

46. *Elizabeth "Betsy" Metcalf Baker's Diary*, 1798, Miscellaneous Manuscript Collection, MSS 9001-B, RIHi. The entries of the Journal are dated 1798 to 1804 but were written ca. 1810.

47. Ramsay, *Memoirs*, 12, 56.

48. *Family Letters of Thomas Jefferson* , 31; for Abigail Adams's letter, see The Thomas Jefferson Papers Series 1, General Correspondence, 1651-1829; images 611-13 at http://memory.loc.gov/cgi-bin/am (8/10/2008); Abigail Adams had written Jefferson earlier that his daughter had arrived June 26, but had been unwilling to part from Captain Ramsay, the captain of the ship. She also felt that "the Girl who is with her is quite a child . . . she seems fond of the child and appears goodnatured."

49. *Family Letters of Thomas Jefferson*, 68-69. Martha had her first child on 23 January 1791, named Anne Cary by her father.

50. Marcus, *American Jewish Woman*, 44-46.

51. Colin G. Calloway, ed., *The World Turned Upside Down: Indian Voices from Early America* (Boston: Bedford Books of St. Martin's Press, 1994), 64-65; "Nancy Ward ca. 1738-1782, Cherokee Tribal Leader," at www.gale/com/ free_resources/whm/bio/ward (4/23/06); Nancy Ward's comments are cited in Samuel C. Williams, *Tennessee During the Revolutionary War* (Nashville: Tennessee Historical Commission, 1944), 201. The white Army officer's reply included the following: "We will not meddle with your people if they will be still and quiet at home and let us live in peace." "Ainse (Hands), Sarah Montour; Maxwell; Willson" at www.biographi.ca/EN (2/8/2008); Lois M. Huey and Bonnie Pulis, *Molly Brant: A Legacy of Her Own* (Youngstown, New York: Old Fort Niagara Association, Inc., 1997); Katherine Kish and Thomas Dublin, eds., *Women and Power in American History* (Englewood Cliffs, New Jersey: Prentice-Hall, 1991), 1: 12.

52. William R. Riddell, *The Life of William Dummer Powell: First Judge of Detroit and Fifth Chief Justice of Upper Canada* (Lansing: Michigan Historical Commission, 1924), "Journey to Detroit," 69.

53. *Susanna Lear (Duncan) Diary May 6 to August 26, 1788* [typed annotated transcription], 31 July 1788, Miscellaneous Manuscript Collection, MSS 9001-B, RIHi; a news item in the *Boston Advertiser*, 6 Aug. 1788 noted the visit of "Peter Otsiquette . . . whom the Marquis de La Fayette sometime since sent to France to be educated. He speaks the French and English languages with accuracy, and is acquainted with most branches of polite education—musical, etc., and is on his way to the Indian Country," as quoted in George Morgan, *The True Lafayette* (Philadelphia: J. B. Lippincott, 1919), fn. 224. John Trumbull's portrait of Good Peter is at the Yale University Art Gallery.

54. American Historical Manuscripts Collection - Flagg, Mary Magdalene, *Account of an Indian visit to Moravian Seminary, Bethlehem, Pennsylvania, 1792,* NHi; also Reichel and Bigler, *A History,* 97, 100-104; on page 123 is a verse written by Maria M. Flagg; Peter Otsiquette died soon after, aged twenty-six.

55. Freeman, North, Wedge, *Selected Letters,* 170; Norton, *Liberty's Daughters,* 283-87.

56. Judith Sargent Stevens Murray, "On the Equality of the Sexes," *The Massachusetts Magazine* (March 1790): 133-34; see also http://www. hurd smith.com/judith/equality.htm.

57. Mulford, *Only for the Eye,* 304-07.

58. Norton, *Liberty's Daughters,* 256-94; Letter, Abigail Smith Adams to Elizabeth Smith Shaw Peabody, 19 July 1799, Shaw Family Papers, box 1, 1636-1829, microfilm 16,453-4P, DLC.

we set out on our journey

1. Abigail Adams to Isaac Smith Jr., 20 April 1771, Smith-Townsend Papers, 1767-1822, microfilm edition, reel 1, MHi. Also L. H. Butterfield, et al., eds, *The Book of Abigail and John: Selected Letters of the Adams Family, 1762-1784* (Cambridge: Harvard University Press, 1975), 49-50.

2. Andrews and Andrews, *Journal of a Lady of Quality,* 20, 19, 22-25, 31, 37, 28, 42-43, 47- 54, 62, 64, 66-69, 73, 138-41, 144.

3. Louisa Susannah Wells, *The Journal of a Voyage from Charlestown, S. C. to London undertaken during the American Revolution* (New York: Printed for the New-York Historical Society, 1906. Reprint. New York: Arno Press, 1968), 2, 4-5, 6, 28, 34, 43, 47-49, 51-52, 58-63.

4. Freeman, North, Wedge, *Selected Letters,* 65-67.

5. John Adams to Abigail Adams, 7 Sept. 1783, AFP.

6. Abigail Adams to John Adams, 11 Feb. 1784, AFP.

7. Abigail Adams to John Adams, 15 Dec. 1783, 11 Feb. 1784, AFP.

8. Abigail Adams to John Adams, 11 Feb. 1784, AFP.

9. Abigail Adams to John Adams, 25 May 1784, AFP.

10. Abigail Adams to Mary Smith Cranch, "Voyage to America," 6-20 June 1784, p. 1-2, AAS.

11. Abigail Adams to Mary Smith Cranch, "Voyage," p. 4, AAS.

12. Abigail Adams to Mary Smith Cranch, "Voyage," p. 2, AAS.

13. Butterfield, *Adams Family Correspondence,* Abigail Adams to Elizabeth Smith Shaw, 10 July 1784, 382, 383.

14. Abigail Adams to Mary Smith Cranch, "Voyage," p. 8, AAS.

15. Abigail Adams to Mary Smith Cranch, "Voyage," p. 13, AAS.

16. Abigail Adams to John Adams, 23 July 1784, AFP.

17. Schieffelin Family Papers, Box 7. Manuscripts and Archives Division. The New York Public Library. Astor, Lenox and Tilden Foundations, NN.

18. Riddell, *The Life of William Dummer Powell,* 61-62, 64-65, 67-70, 72.

19. Mrs. General Riedesel, *Letters and Journals,* 138-40.

20. Riedesel, 143-44.

21. Riedesel, 152-57, 159-60.

22. Riedesel, 187, 189, 188.

23. Riedesel, 197-98.

24. Riedesel, 199-203.

25. Riedesel, 210, 209, 211.

26. Riedesel, 227.

27. The original of Sarah Scofield Frost's Diary seems to have been lost. There are, however, extant transcriptions; though these differ in some respects, the narrative overall has the ring of authenticity. The first published version of the diary, edited by W. O. Raymond, was appended to the narrative of Walter Bates, *Kingston and The Loyalists of the "Spring Fleet" of 1783* (St. John, New Brunswick: Barnes & Company, 1889. Reprint. Woodstock, New Brunswick: Non-Entity Press, 1990), 29-32, www.ourroots.ca/e/page.aspx?id=1054486 (10/25/08). Raymond's notes (at the New Brunswick Museum) as well as his transcription in the above work for the version available at www.atlanticportal.hil.unb.ca/acva/loyalistwomen/fr/documents/frost/sarahfrost.pdf on which Frost's diary in this book is largely based. In "The Diaries of Sarah Frost, 1783: The Sounds and Silences of a Woman's Exile," *Papers of the Bibliographical Society of Canada*, 42, 2 (2004): 57-69, Gwendolyn Davies compared various transcriptions of Frost's diaries (at least four) and suggested possible reasons for differences, i.e., the drinking of rum punch may have been omitted by editors who were believers in temperance.

28. R. P. Gorham, trans. and ed., "The Narrative of Hannah Ingraham, Loyalist Colonist at St. Anne's Point, 1783," from the manuscript for publication in Saint John *Telegraph*, 23, December 1933: 26-29. http://atlanticportal.hil.unb.ca /acva/loyalistwomen/en/documents/ingraham.

29. Nancy Jean Cameron, quoted in Catherine S. Crary, narr. and ed., *The Price of Loyalty: Tory Writings from the Revolutionary Era* (New York: McGraw-Hill, 1973), 413-14 from Nancy Jean (Mrs. John) Cameron, Private papers of Mrs. D. J. Macpherson, Wales, Ontario, (now in Public Archives of Canada), Loyalist Transcripts 24, 148.

30. Annette Kolodny, "The Travel Diary of Elizabeth House Trist: Philadelphia to Natchez, 1783-84," *Journeys in New Worlds: Early American Women's Narratives*, Wm. F. Andrews, ed. (Madison: University of Wisconsin Press, 1990), 201-02, 204, 205, 206-07, 208, 209.

31. Kolodny, 209, 210, 211-12, 213.

32. Kolodny, 213, 214, 215-16.

33. Albert Matthews, ed., "Journal of William Loughton Smith, 1790–1791," *Massachusetts Historical Society Proceedings* 51 (1918): 64.

34. Kolodny, 221, 222-25, 226, 227.

35. Kolodny, 228, 229, 230, 232. Original at University of Virginia Library.

36. "Mrs. Mary Dewees's Journal from Philadelphia to Kentucky, 178[8]-178[9]," Reuben T. Durrett Collection on Kentucky and the Ohio River Valley, Durrett Codex Collection, Special Collections Research Center, University of Chicago Library; digital ID: icufaw cmc0024; see also "Mrs. Mary Dewees's Journal from Philadelphia to Kentucky 1787-1788," Samuel P. Cochran, ed., *Pennsylvania Magazine of History and Biography* 28, no. 2 (1904), 182-198.

37. Noyes, *Family History*, 182, 184, 188.

willing to re-sheathe the sword

1. Robert Middlekauff, *The Glorious Cause: The American Revolution, 1763-1789* (New York: Oxford University Press, 1982), 571-75; Samuel Eliot Morison and Henry Steele Commager, *The Growth of the American Republic*, vol. 1 (New York: Oxford University Press), 1958, 224-28.

2. Freeman, North, Wedge, *Selected Letters*, 126.

3. Winslow Family Papers, University of New Brunswick, Atlantic Canada Virtual Archives, "The Winslow Family's Hardship" in "An Introduction to the Trails," vol. 2, 67, http://atlanticportal.hil.unb.ca/acva/loyalistwomen/en; see also Maud Maxwell Vesey, "Benjamin Marston, loyalist," *The New England Quarterly* 15 (Dec. 1942): 622-52.

4. New York Public Library, Manuscripts Division, *Transcript of various Papers relating to the Losses, Services, and Support of the American Loyalists and to His Majesty's Provincial Forces during the War of Independence, preserved amongst the American Manuscripts in the <u>Royal</u> <u>Institution</u> of Great Britain, London, 1777-1783*. Mss Col 83, vol. 71, microfilm reel 24, pages 49-50 (Phebe Ward's letter), 115-16 (Edmund Ward's petition to Sir Guy Carlton, 10 June 1783); see also John V. Hinshaw, "The WARDS of Eastchester," *The Westchester Historian* 52, no. 3 (Summer 1976): 53-57. The property was sold ten days after Phebe sent her letter. By mid-October, seventy-seven acres of Edmund's land were deeded to his brother Stephen. In July 1786, Edmund presented another memorial to the British government detailing his property in Eastchester; though his claim was for £2812, his award was £1235.

5. Mercy Otis Warren, *History*, Introduction: "An Address to the Inhabitants of the United States of America."

6. Warren, *History*, vol. 3, 323-24, 249, 296.

7. Letters, Abigail Adams to John Adams, 20 June 1783, 11 November 1783, and 12 April 1784, AFP. Two sons were attending Harvard.

8. John Ferling, *A Leap in the Dark: The Struggle to Create the American Republic* (New York: Oxford University Press, 2003), 253-59.

9. Morison and Commager, *Growth of the American Republic*, 272-76.

10. *Diary of Elizabeth Porter Phelps*, Porter-Phelps-Huntington Family Papers. See also *The New England Historical and Genealogical Register* 119, no. 476 (Oct. 1965): 289-90.

11. Warren, *History*, vol. 3, 355-56.

12. GLC 1800.03, Letter, Mercy O. Warren to Catharine S. Macaulay, 28 September 1787, NNGL.

13. GLC 1800.04, Letter, Mercy O. Warren to Catharine S. Macaulay, 20 September 1789, NNGL.

14. Warren, *History*, vol. 3, 366-68.

15. Eliza S. M. Quincy, *Memoir of the Life of Eliza S. M. Quincy* (Boston: Printed by John Wilson and Son, 1861), Part I, 50-51.

16. Sarah Franklin Robinson, 30 April 1789, AAS; photocopy at New York Public Library, Manuscripts Dept., *Miscellaneous Personal Name Files*, Box 89.

17. GLC 7908, Letter, Martha Washington to Frances B. Washington, 8 June 1789, NNGL.

18. Letter, Martha Washington to Mercy O. Warren, 26 December 1789, Fogg Autograph Collection, Coll. 420, vol. 46, Collections of the Maine Historical Society, Portland, Maine. See also Fields, 223-24.

19. Abigail Adams to Mary Smith Cranch, 28 June 1789, AAS; see also Mitchell, *New Letters.*

20. Abigail Adams to Mary Cranch, 12 July 1789, AAS.

21. Abigail Adams to Mary Cranch, 9 Aug. 1789, AAS.

22. Abigail Adams to Mary Cranch, 3 Nov. 1789, AAS.

23. Abigail Adams to Mary Cranch, 20 Feb. 1790, AAS.

24. Abigail Adams to Mary Cranch, 4 July 1790, AAS.

25. Abigail Adams to Mary Cranch, 10 Oct. 1790, AAS.

26. Abigail Adams to Mary Cranch, March 1792, AAS.

27. Abigail Adams to Mary Cranch, 20 April 1792, AAS.

28. George W. Knepper, *Ohio and Its People* (Kent, Ohio: Kent State University Press, 2003), Chapter 4, "From Territory to State."

29. Warren, *History,* vol. 1, 121-22.

30. Noyes, *Family History*, 178-79.

31. Abigail Adams to Mary Cranch, 5 Feb. 1792, AAS.

32. Warren, *History*, vol. 3, 206.

33. Joseph J. Ellis, *American Creation: Triumphs and Tragedies of the Founding of the Republic* (New York: Alfred A. Knopf, 2007), 127-64. Lee Miller, ed. and narr., *From the Heart: Voices of the American Indian* (New York: Vintage Books, 1995), 179.

34. Abigail Adams to Mary Cranch, 8 Aug. 1790, AAS.

35. Curtis, *Cary Letters,* 98-99.

36. Ellis, *American Creation*, 155; Knepper, Chapter 4.

37. GLC 1800.04, Letter, Mercy Otis Warren to Catharine Macaulay, 20 September 1789, NNGL.

38. GLC 11794.03, Letter, Catharine Macaulay to Samuel Adams, [draft], 1 March 1791, NNGL.

39. Henriette-Lucie Dillon de la Tour du Pin de Gouvernet, *Recollections of the Revolution and the Empire: From the French of the "Journal D'Une Femme de Cinquante Ans,"* Walter Geer, ed. and trans. (New York: Brentano's, 1920), 189, also http://www.questia.com/PM.qst?a=o&d=1452500.

40. de la Tour du Pin, 191.

41. de la Tour du Pin, 194-95.

42. de la Tour du Pin, 200-201, 203.

43. de la Tour du Pin, 204-05.

44. de la Tour du Pin, 207.

45. de la Tour du Pin, 210-11.

46. de la Tour du Pin, 219.

47. de la Tour du Pin, 211-14.

48. de la Tour du Pin, 214-18.

49. de la Tour du Pin, 226-27.

50. de la Tour du Pin, 229, 234.

51. de la Tour du Pin, 239-40.

52. de la Tour du Pin, 261.

53. Freeman, North, Wedge, *Selected Letters,* 220-21; Stahr, *John Jay,* 315.

54. Ferling, *Leap in the Dark,* 370-75.

55. GLC 01055, Letter, Martha Washington to Frances B. Washington, 29 September 1794, NNGL.

56. Hinckley, "Diary of Christiana Young Leach," *The Pennsylvania Magazine of History and Biography* 35, no. 3 (July 1911): 349. On 29 November he returned "from the western counties well and hearty."

57. Jay Papers, NNC, www.columbia.edu/cu/lweb/digital/jay, #12988, #12989.

58. Ferling, *Leap in the Dark,* 379-80; see also Stahr's discussion.

59. John Adams to Abigail Adams, 9 February 1795; Abigail Adams to John Adams, 21 February 1795, AFP.

60. Abigail Adams to Mary Cranch, 25 June 1795, AAS.

61. John Brown Papers, NHi.

62. Rebecca Faulkner Foster, 2 May 1796, Foster Family Papers, AAS.

a flattering and a Glorious Reward

1. Henrietta Marchant Liston to James Jackson, 8 May 1796, with permission of the Trustees of the National Library of Scotland, hereafter NLS. Microfilms Sir Robert and Henrietta Marchant Liston Papers, 1795-1803, DLC. See also Bradford Perkins, "A Diplomat's Wife in Philadelphia: Letters of Henrietta Liston," *William and Mary Quarterly,* 3d series, 11, no. 4 (October 1954).

2. Henrietta Liston to James Jackson, 21 July 1796, NLS.

3. Henrietta Liston to James Jackson, 6 September 1796, NLS.

4. Abigail Adams to John Adams, 20 February 1796, AFP.

5. Henrietta Liston to James Jackson, after 31 October 1796, NLS.

6. Henrietta Liston to James Jackson, 9 December 1796, NLS.

7. Henrietta Liston to James Jackson, 15 January 1797, NLS.

8. Henrietta Liston to.James Jackson, 24 February 1797, NLS.

9. Journal of Henrietta Liston, 5 March 1797, with permission of the Trustees of the National Library of Scotland. Microfilm ms5698-5704, DLC. See also James C. Nicholls, "Lady Henrietta Liston's Journal of Washington's 'Resignation,' Retirement, and Death," *The Pennsylvania Magazine of History and Biography* 95, no. 4 (Oct. 1971).

10. Brady, *George Washington's Beautiful Nelly,* 30-33.

11. Abigail Adams to Mary Cranch, 16 May 1797, AAS.

12. Abigail Adams to Mary Cranch, 24 May 1797, AAS.

13. Charles F. McCombs, ed., *Letter-book of Mary Stead Pinckney* (New York: Grolier Club, 1946), 28-30. Permission of The Grolier Club of New York.

14. McCombs, 33-35.

15. McCombs, 40-41.

16. McCombs, 42-43.

17. McCombs, 47, 48.

18. Abigail Adams to Mary Cranch, 24 May 1797, AAS.

19. Brady, *Beautiful Nelly*, 40-41.

20. Brady, 51-53.

21. Henrietta Liston to James Jackson, 3 May 1798, NLS.

22. Henrietta Liston to James Jackson, 11 June 1798, and 2 July 1798, NLS.

23. Brady, *Beautiful Nelly*, 56, 57.

24. Abigail Adams to Mary Cranch, 26 April 1798, AAS.

25. Abigail Adams to Mary Cranch, 26 May 1798, AAS.

26. GLC 581, Letter, George Washington to Secretary of War James McHenry, 30 September 1798, NNGL.

a favored nation

1. Journal of Henrietta Liston, 29 November 1799, describing events of "A week or two ago," NLS.

2. Journal of Henrietta Liston, 29 November 1799, NLS.

3. "A Visit to Mount Vernon—A Letter of Mrs. Edward Carrington to her Sister, Mrs. George Fisher," *William & Mary Quarterly*, 2nd series, 18, no. 2 (April 1938): 198-202. Incomplete letter: copy in the Marshall Papers, location of original unknown.

4. Journal of Henrietta Liston, 18 December 1799, NLS.

5. Journal of Henrietta Liston, after 26 December 1799, NLS.

6. Mary White Morris to Martha Washington, 27 December 1799, R-10, MS-259, ViMtV; see also Fields, "*Worthy Partner*," 326-27.

7. Abigail Adams to Mary Cranch, 22 December 1799, AAS.

8. Abigail Adams to Mary Cranch, 22 December 1799, AAS.

9. Warren, *History*, 418, 400, 417, 418, 420, 424, 425, 431, 434-35; see also http://books.google.com.

BIBLIOGRAPHY

Works Consulted but not Cited in Endnotes

Adams, Charles F. *Letters of Mrs. Adams, the wife of John Adams.* Boston: Charles C. Little & James Brown, 1840.

Bailey, Thomas A. *The American Pageant: A History of the Republic.* Boston: D. C. Heath and Company, Third Edition, 1966.

Bailyn, Bernard. *The Ideological Origins of the American Revolution.* Cambridge: The Belknap Press of Harvard University Press, 1967.

Bakeless, John. *Turncoats, Traitors, and Heroes.* Philadelphia: J. B. Lippincott Co., 1959.

Bales, Richard. *The American Revolution: A Cantata Based on the Music of the American Colonies During the Years 1775-1800.* The Columbia Records LEGACY Collection, 1960. Produced by Goddard Lieberson, R60-1191.

Barbour, Hugh, et al., eds. *Quaker Crosscurrents: Three Hundred Years of Friends in the New York Yearly Meetings.* Syracuse: Syracuse University Press, 1995.

Baumgarten, Linda. *What Clothes Reveal: The Language of Clothing in Colonial and Federal America.* Williamsburg, VA: The Colonial Williamsburg Foundation in association with Yale University Press, New Haven, Connecticut, 2002.

Bayard, Ferdinand-Marie. *Travels of a Frenchman in Maryland and Virginia with a description of Philadelphia and Baltimore in 1791.* Trans. and ed. by Ben C. McCary. Williamsburg, Virginia, 1950.

Billias, George Athan, ed. *George Washington's Generals and Opponents: Their Exploits and Leadership.* New York: Da Capo Press, 1994.

Bolton, Robert, Jr. *A History of the County of Westchester, from its First Settlement to the Present Time.* New York: Printed by Alexander S. Gould, 1848.

Bond, Beverley W. Jr., ed. *The Intimate Letters of John Cleves Symmes and his Family.* Cincinnati: Historical and Philosophical Society of Ohio, 1956.

Bowne, Eliza S. *A Girl's Life Eighty Years Ago: Selections from the Letters of Eliza Southgate Bowne.* New York: Charles Scribner's Sons, 1887. Reprint. New York: Arno Press, 1974.

Branson, Susan. "Women and the Family Economy in the Early Republic: the Case of Elizabeth Meredith." *Journal of the Early Republic* 16, no. 1 (Spring 1996).

Brinton, Howard H. *Quaker Journals: Varieties of Religious Experiences Among Friends*. Wallingford, Pennsylvania: Pendle Hill Publications, 1972.

Brooke, Frances. *The History of Emily Montague*. Filiquarian Publishing LLC, n. d.

Buckman, Peter. *Lafayette: A Biography*. New York: Paddington Press Ltd., 1977.

Buel, Joy Day, and Richard Buel, Jr. *The Way of Duty, A Woman and Her Family in Revolutionary America*. New York: W. W. Norton & Co., 1984.

Cadbury, Henry J. "Negro Membership in the Society of Friends." *Journal of Negro History* 21, no. 2 (April 1936).

Calhoon, Robert M. *The Loyalists in Revolutionary America 1760-1781*. New York: Harcourt Brace Jovanovich, 1973.

Calhoon, Robert M., Timothy M. Barnes, and George A. Rawlyle. *Loyalists and Community in North America*. Westport, CT: Greenwood Press, 1994.

Carlisle, Elizabeth Pendergast. *Earthbound and Heavenbent: Elizabeth Porter Phelps and Life at Forty Acres [1747-1817]*. New York: Scribner, 2004.

Carretta, Vincent ed. *Unchained Voices: An Anthology of Black Authors in the English-Speaking World of the 18th Century*. Lexington: University Press of Kentucky, 1996.

Clary, David A. *Adopted Son: Washington, Lafayette, and the Friendship That Saved the Revolution*. New York: Bantam Dell, 2007.

Clinton, Catherine. *The Plantation Mistress: Woman's World in the Old South*. New York: Pantheon Books, 1982.

Coghlan, Margaret. *Memoirs of Mrs. Coghlan Daughter of the late Major Moncrieffe: Written By Herself*. New York: T. H. Morrell, 1864. Reprint. New York: Arno Press Inc., 1971.

Coldham, Peter Wilson. *American Loyalist Claims, Abstract from Public Record Office*. Washington, DC: National Genealogical Society, 1980.

Collins, Varnum Lansing, ed. *A Brief Narrative of the Ravages of the British and Hessians at Princeton 1776-1777*. Princeton: Princeton Historical Association, Number One, 1906.

Corner, George W., ed. *The Autobiography of Benjamin Rush: His "Thoughts Through Life" together with his Commonplace Book for 1789-1813*. Princeton: The American Philosophical Society, Princeton University Press, 1948.

Cott, Nancy F. "Divorce and the Changing Status of Women in Eighteenth-Century Massachusetts." *William & Mary Quarterly*, Third Series, 33, no. 4 (Oct. 1976).

Countryman, Edward. *A People in Revolution: The American Revolution and Political Society in New York 1760-1790*. Baltimore: Johns Hopkins University Press, 1981.

Crowe, Jeffrey J., and Larry E. Tise. *The Southern Experience in the American Revolution*. Chapel Hill: University of North Carolina Press, 1978.

Darrach, Henry. "Lydia Darragh, of the Revolution." *The Pennsylvania Magazine of History and Biography* 23, no. 1 (1899).

Deák, Gloria. *Picturing New York: The City from its Beginnings to the Present*. New York: Columbia University Press, 2000.

Degler, Carl N. *Out of Our Past: The Forces That Shaped Modern America.* New York: Harper & Row, Revised Edition, 1970.

DePauw, Linda G. *Battle Cries and Lullabies: Women in War from Prehistory to the Present.* Norman: University of Oklahoma Press, 1998.

Earle, Alice Morse, and Emily Ellsworth Ford, eds. *Early Prose and Verse "The Distaff Series."* New York: Harper & Brothers Publishers, 1898.

Edgar, Walter. *Partisans and Redcoats: The Southern Conflict That Turned the Tide of the American Revolution.* New York: William Morrow, 2001.

Evans, Elizabeth. *Weathering the Storm: Women of the American Revolution.* New York: Charles Scribner's Sons, 1975.

Finkenbine, Roy E. "Belinda's Petition: Reparations for Slavery in Revolutionary Massachusetts." *William & Mary Quarterly* 64, no. 1.

Fischer, David Hackett. *Liberty and Freedom: A Visual History of America's Founding Ideas.* New York: Oxford University Press, 2005.

———. *Washington's Crossing.* New York: Oxford University Press, 2004.

Fowler, William M. Jr. *The Baron of Beacon Hill: A Biography of John Hancock.* Boston: Houghton Mifflin, 1980.

Freeman, Landa M. "Mr. Jay Rides Circuit." *Journal of Supreme Court History* 31, no. 1 (2006).

Frey, Sylvia R. *The British Soldier in America: A Social History of Military Life in the Revolutionary Period.* Austin: University of Texas Press, 1981.

———. *Water from the Rock: Black Resistance in a Revolutionary Age.* Princeton: Princeton University Press, 1991.

Frey, Sylvia R., and Marian J. Morton. *New World, New Roles: A Documentary History of Women in Pre-Industrial America.* Westport, CT: Greenwood Press, 1986.

Gelles, Edith B. *Abigail Adams: A Writing Life.* New York: Routledge, 2002.

———. *Portia: The World of Abigail Adams.* Bloomington: Indiana University Press, 1992.

Gerzina, Gretchen Holbrook. *Mr. and Mrs. Prince: How an Extraordinary Eighteenth-Century Family Moved Out of Slavery and into Legend.* New York: Amistad, 2008.

Gillespie, Joanna Bowen. *Life and Times of Martha Laurens Ramsay 1759-1811.* Columbia: University of South Carolina Press, 2001.

Glatthaar, Joseph T., and James K. Martin. *Forgotten Allies: The Oneida Indians and the American Revolution.* New York: Hill and Wang, 2006.

Golway, Terry. *Washington's General Nathanael Green and the Triumph of the American Revolution.* New York: Henry Holt and Co., 2005.

Goodfriend, Joyce D. and Claudia M. Christie. *Lives of American Women: A History with Documents.* Boston: Little, Brown and Co., 1981.

Gottesman, Rita S. *The Arts and Crafts in New York 1726-1776.* Reprint. New York: DaCapo Press, 1970.

Grant, Anne MacVicar. *Memoirs of an American Lady.* Boston: Wells, 1809.

Green, Henry C., and Mary W. Green. *The Pioneer Mothers of America.* New York: G. P. Putnam's Sons, 1912.

Griffin, Patrick. *American Leviathan: Empire, Nation, and Revolutionary Frontier*. New York: Hill and Wang, 2007.

Grunwald, Lisa and Stephen J. Adler, eds. *Women's Letters: America from the Revolutionary War to the Present*. New York: The Dial Press, 2005.

Gunderson, Joan R. *To Be Useful to the World: Women in Revolutionary America, 1740-1790*. Chapel Hill: University of North Carolina Press, Revised Edition, 2006.

Hoffman, Renoda. *It Happened in Old White Plains*. White Plains, NY: © Renoda Williams, 1981.

Hoffman, Ronald and Peter J. Albert, eds. *Women in the Age of the American Revolution*. Charlottesville, published for the United States Capitol Historical Society by the University Press of Virginia, 1992.

———, Thad W. Tate, and Peter J. Albert, eds. *An Uncivil War: The Southern Backcountry during the American Revolution*. Charlottesville: University Press of Virginia, 1985.

Hopkins, Samuel, DD. *Memoirs of the Life of Mrs. Sarah Osborn*. Printed at Worcester, Massachusetts, by Leonard Worcester, 1799.

Horsman, Reginald. "The British Indian Department and the Resistance to Anthony Wayne, 1793-1795." *Mississippi Valley Historical Review* 49, no. 2 (Sept. 1962).

Hudak, Leona M. *Early American Women Printers and Publishers 1639-1820*. Metuchen, NJ: The Scarecrow Press, Inc., 1978.

Imbarrato, Susan Clair. *Declarations of Independency in Eighteenth-Century American Autobiography*. Knoxville: University of Tennessee Press, 1998.

Isenberg, Nancy. *Fallen Founder: The Life of Aaron Burr*. New York: Viking, 2007.

Jones, Michael Wynn. *The Cartoon History of the American Revolution*. New York: G. P. Putnam's Sons, 1975.

Jordan, John W. "Bethlehem during the Revolution: Extracts from the Diaries in the Moravian Archives at Bethlehem, Pennsylvania." *The Pennsylvania Magazine of History and Biography* 12, no. 4 (1888).

Katz, William L. *Black Indians: A Hidden Heritage*. New York: Athenaeum, 1986.

Kerber, Linda K. *No Constitutional Right to Be Ladies: Women and the Obligations of Citizenship*. New York: Hill and Wang, 1998.

———. *Toward an Intellectual History of Women*. Chapel Hill: University of North Carolina Press, 1997.

Ketchum, Richard M. *Divided Loyalties: How the American Revolution Came to New York*. New York: Henry Holt and Company, 2002.

Kish, Katherine, and Thomas Dublin, eds. *Women and Power in American History*. Englewood Cliffs, NJ: Prentice-Hall, 1991.

Klinghoffer, Judith Apter, and Lois Elkis. "'The Petticoat Electors': Women's Suffrage in New Jersey, 1776-1807." *Journal of the Early Republic* 12, no. 2 (Spring 1992).

Koger, Larry. *Black Slaveowners: Free Black Slave Masters in South Carolina, 1790-1860*. Jefferson, NC: McFarland & Co., 1985.

Lancaster, Jane. "By the Pens of Females: Girls' Diaries from Rhode Island, 1788-1821." *Rhode Island History* 57, no. 3 (1999).

La Tour du Pin, Marquise de. *Journal d'une Femme de Cinquante Ans 1778-1815 Publié par son arrière-petit-fils.* 2 vols. Paris: Berger-Levrault, Éditeurs, 1924.

Lebsock, Suzanne. *The Free Women of Petersburg: Status and Culture in a Southern Town, 1784-1860.* New York: W. W. Norton & Company, 1984.

Lewis, Jan. "'of every age sex & condition': The Representation of Women in the Constitution." *Journal of the Early Republic* 15, no. 3 (Fall 1995).

Lucey, Donna M. *I Dwell in Possibility: Women Build a Nation 1600-1920.* Washington, DC: National Geographic, 2001.

Maier, Pauline. *From Resistance to Revolution: Colonial Radicals and the Development of American Opposition to Britain, 1765-1776.* New York: A. Knopf, 1974.

Maintenon, Madame de (Françoise d'Aubigné). *Dialogues and Addresses*, John J. Conley, ed. and trans. Chicago: University of Chicago Press, 2004.

Mason, Lizzie Norton, and James Duncan Phillips. "The Journal of Elizabeth Cranch." *The Essex Institute Historical Collections* 80, no. 1 (Jan. 1944).

Maurois, André. *Adrienne The Life of the Marquise de La Fayette.* Trans. by Gerard Hopkins. New York: McGraw-Hill Book Co., Inc., 1961.

May, Robin. *The British Army in North America 1775-83.* Oxford, UK: Osprey Publishing, 1997.

Mayer, Holly A. *Belonging to the Army: Camp Followers and Community during the American Revolution.* Columbia: University of South Carolina Press, 1996.

Mayer, Lance, and Gay Myers, eds. *The Devotion Family: The Lives and Possessions of Three Generations in Eighteenth-Century Connecticut.* New London, CT: The Lyman Allyn Art Museum, 1991.

McCullough, David. *1776.* New York: Simon & Schuster, 2005.

Morrissey, Brendan. *Saratoga 1777: Turning Point of a Revolution.* Oxford, UK: Osprey Publishing, 2005.

———. *Yorktown 1781: The world turned upside down.* Oxford, UK: Osprey Publishing, 1997.

Morton, Susan Wentworth. *Ouâbi: Or the Virtues of Nature. An Indian Tale In four Cantos By Philenia, a Lady of Boston.* Printed at Boston, 1790.

Nash, Gary B. *Forging Freedom: the Formation of Philadelphia's Black Community 1720-1840.* Cambridge: Harvard University Press, 1988.

———. *The Unknown American Revolution.* New York: Viking, 2005.

National Maritime Museum, Greenwich, UK, *1776: The British Story of the American Revolution.* London, UK: Times Newspapers Ltd., 1976.

Nelson, Paul David. *William Alexander, Lord Stirling.* Tuscaloosa: University of Alabama Press, 1977.

Newman, Debra L. "Black Women in the Era of the American Revolution in Pennsylvania." in *"We Specialize in the Wholly Impossible": A Reader in Black Women's History*, Darlene Clarke Hine, et al., eds. Brooklyn, NY: Carlson Publishing, Inc., 1995.

Norton, Mary Beth. "Eighteenth-Century American Women in Peace and War: The Case of the Loyalists." *William & Mary Quarterly*, Third Series, 33, no. 3 (July 1976).

―――. "Letter to the Editor." *William & Mary Quarterly*, Third Series, 48, no. 4 (Oct. 1991).

Premo, Terri L. *Winter Friends: Women Growing Old in the New Republic, 1785-1835*. Chicago: University of Illinois Press, 1990.

Ring, Betty. *Girlhood Embroidery: American Samplers & Pictorial Needlework 1650-1850*. New York: Alfred A. Knopf, 1993.

Rogers, Katharine M., ed. *The Meridian Anthology of Early American Women Writers From Anne Bradstreet to Louisa May Alcott, 1650-1865*. New York: Meridian, 1991.

Royster, Charles. *A Revolutionary People at War . . . 1775-1783*. Chapel Hill: University of North Carolina Press, 1979.

Sabine, Lorenzo. *Biographical Sketches of Loyalists of the American Revolution with an historical essay*. Baltimore: Genealogical Publishing Co., Inc. 1864. Reprint. 1979.

Sabine, William H.W. *Historical Memoirs from 16 March 1763 to 25 July 1778 of William Smith*. 2 vols. Hollis, NY: Colburn & Tegg, 1956.

Scholten, Catherine M. "'On the Importance of the Obstetrick Art': Changing Customs of Childbirth in America, 1760-1825." *William & Mary Quarterly*, Third Series, 34, no. 3 (July 1977).

Scott, Kenneth, comp. *Rivington's New York Newspaper: Excerpts from a Loyalist Press, 1773-1783*. New York: The New-York Historical Society, 1973.

Sheridan, Eugene R., and John M. Murrin. *Congress at Princeton Being the Letters of Charles Thomson to Hannah Thomson June-October 1783*. Princeton: Princeton University Library, 1985.

Siebert, Wilbur H. "Colony of Massachusetts Loyalists in Bristol, England." *Massachusetts Historical Society Proceedings* 45 (1912).

Smith, Jewel A. *Music, Women, and Pianos in Antebellum Bethlehem, Pennsylvania*. Lehigh, PA: Lehigh University Press, 2008.

Smith, Helen Everston. *Colonial Days and Ways, as Gathered from Family Papers*. New York: The Century Co., 1900.

Smith, Sidonie, and Julia Watson. *Reading Autobiography: A Guide for Interpreting Life Narratives*. Minneapolis: University of Minnesota Press, 2001.

Stark, James H. *The Loyalists of Massachusetts and the Other Side of the American Revolution*. Boston: W. B. Clarke Co., 1907.

Stedman, Margaret. "Excitement in Philadelphia on Hearing of the Defeat at Brandywine." *The Pennsylvania Magazine of History and Biography* 14, no. 1 (1890).

Stegeman, John. *Caty: a Biography of Catherine Littlefield Greene*. Athens, GA: Harry Crews, 1985.

Steinmetz, Rollin C. *Loyalists, Pacifists, and Prisoners*. Lancaster, PA: Lancaster County Historical Society, A Bicentennial Book, 1976.

Stephenson, Michael. *Patriot Battles: How the War of Independence Was Fought*. New York: HarperCollins, 2007.

Tharp, Louise Hall. *The Baroness and the General*. Boston: Little, Brown and Company, 1962.

Tillotson, Harry S. *The Exquisite Exile: the Life and Fortune of Mrs. Benedict Arnold*. Boston: Lothrop, Lee & Shephard Co., 1932.

Tise, Larry E. *Benjamin Franklin and Women*. University Park: Penn State University Press, 2000.

Tuchman, Barbara W. *The First Salute*. New York: Alfred A. Knopf, 1988.

Tuckerman, Bayard. *A Sketch of the Cotton Mather Smith Family of Sharon, Connecticut*. Boston: Privately Printed [the Plimpton Press], 1915.

Willard, Margaret Wheeler, ed. *Letters on the American Revolution 1774-1776*. Boston: Houghton Mifflin, 1925.

Williams, Selma R. *Demeter's Daughters: The Women who Founded America 1587-1787*. New York: Athenaeum, 1976.

Wilson, Robert H. *Philadelphia Quakers 1681-1981*. Philadelphia: Philadelphia Yearly Meeting, The Religious Society of Friends, 1981.

Wood, Peter H. *Black Majority: Negroes in Colonial South Carolina From 1670 through the Stono Rebellion*. New York: W.W. Norton & Co, 1996.

Wulf, Karin. *Not All Wives: Women of Colonial Philadelphia*. Ithaca: Cornell University Press, 2000.

Zagarri, Rosemarie. *Revolutionary Backlash: Women and Politics in the Early American Republic*. Philadelphia: University of Pennsylvania Press, 2007.

———. "The Rights of Man and Woman in Post-Revolutionary America." *William and Mary Quarterly* 55, no. 2 (April 1998).

———. *A Woman's Dilemma: Mercy Otis Warren and the American Revolution*. Wheeling, IL: Harlan Davidson, Inc., 1995.

Zimmerman, John J. "Charles Thomson The Sam Adams of Philadelphia." *Mississippi Valley History Review* 45, no. 3 (Dec. 1958).

WEBSITES:

www.blackloyalist.com.canadadigitalcollection

www.boston1775.net

www.dpubs.libraries.psu.edu

www.jewishworldreview.com/jewish/sheftall.asp

www.lancasterhistory.org/collections

www.memory.loc/gov

www.Nova Scotia Archives, collections.ic.gc.ca/blackloyalist/documents

www.rotunda.upress.virginia.edu/dmde/DPM

www.royalprovincial.com

www.si.umich.edu/spies/people

www.thestaymaker.co.uk/gallery-dressing.php

www.ushistory.org/presidentshouse/slaves

Index

Illustrations are in italics and listed as "Figures"

About the Authors

The authors' first book was *Selected Letters of John Jay and Sarah Livingston Jay*, published by McFarland & Company in hardcover in 2005, and in soft cover in 2010. Particularly drawn to circumstances surrounding the birth of our nation and gratified by the experience of dealing with primary sources, especially those written by women, the authors committed themselves wholeheartedly to the project that resulted in the present book.

Louise V. North received a B.A. from Barnard College and an M.A. in Art History from Columbia University. In addition to her work as an independent scholar, she is a docent at the Neuberger Museum in Purchase, New York. In December 2004, she presented a paper titled "The 'Amiable' Children of John and Sarah Livingston Jay" at the New-York Historical Society (available on line at Columbia University's *The Jay Papers* website). Ms. North is also the author of an article "Sarah Jay's Invitations to Dinner/Supper, 1787-1788" that appeared in *The Hudson River Valley Review* (Spring, 2005).

Janet M. Wedge, also a graduate of Barnard College, earned an M.A. at Teachers College, Columbia University, and another in Political Science from The New School in New York City. She taught high-school American Studies for 23 years and for several years was an adjunct professor at Manhattanville College where she taught a required course on research and writing. She has extensive writing and editorial experience. "Detach'd from Earth," an article she authored about the first flight of the Montgolfier balloon in Paris in 1783, observed by Sarah Jay and described in letters to her husband, appeared in the magazine *The Westchester Historian* (Summer, 2005).

Landa M. Freeman is a graduate of Mount Holyoke College, where she was a Frances Perkins Scholar. In connection with the Jay book Ms. Freeman developed a lecture with slides titled "Sarah Livingston Jay, the Extraordinary Wife of John Jay," which she delivered at the New York State History Conference in June 2002 and has since presented to numerous historical societies and university groups. She is the author of "Mr. Jay Rides Circuit," that appeared in the *Journal of Supreme Court History* (March, 2006) based on the Chief Justice's letters to his family while he was away on court business.